center-draft Kerosene Lamps 1884–1940

identification and value guide

J. W. Courter

COLLECTOR BOOKS
A Division of Schroeder Publishing Co., Inc.

On the front cover, left to right: Miller New Vestal, $125.00; Rochester, $225.00; Bristol Improved banquet, $185.00; Little Royal, $150.00; B & H 1905, $50.00; Little Royal, $175.00; B & H No. 1, $175.00; Miller Home Lamp, $50.00; Hipwell Victor, $225.00

On the back cover, left to right, top: Wrigley Premium, $350.00; bottom: Eureka, American Lamp & Brass, $1,250.00 (courtesy Kent Stratton); P & A Colonial, $125.00; Holmes, Booth & Haydens Keystone, $150.00; P & A parlor lamp, $250.00, Handel shade, $750.00 (shade courtesy Doug & Judy Myers); P & A Improved Royal, $250.00; P & A Royal, $175.00

J. W. "Bill" and Treva Courter live in western Kentucky where they enjoy gardening, grandkids, and great felines. They write and publish books about antique lighting: *Aladdin — The Magic Name in Lamps, Aladdin Electric Lamps, The Aladdin Collectors Manuals*, and *Angle Lamps Collectors Manual & Price Guide*. Their newsletter for Aladdin collectors, *The Mystic Light of the Aladdin Knights*, is now in its 35th year. Bill is known to collectors as the Bright Knight, and you may contact him at: brtknight@aol.com.

Treva died in a tragic automobile wreck on April 23, 2007.

The worth of collectibles and artifacts, such as old lamps, is not only in their monetary value but also in what they can tell us about the past.
– J. W. "Bill" Courter

Cover design: Beth Summers
Book design: Lisa Henderson
Cover photography: Charles R. Lynch

COLLECTOR BOOKS
P.O. Box 3009
Paducah, Kentucky 42002–3009

www.collectorbooks.com

The current values in this book should be used only as a guide. They are not intended to set prices, which vary from one section of the country to another. Auction prices, as well as dealer prices, vary greatly and are affected by condition as well as demand. Neither the author nor the publisher assumes responsibility for any losses that might be incurred as a result of consulting this guide.

Preface

I have admired the quality and craftsmanship of embossed brass center-draft lamps for many years. This book grew out of curiosity about my collection of lamps and an effort to learn who made them.

Most of the lamps in this book provided light for everyday chores — they were practical and were improvements over many older lamps. This book is about lamps that burned a bright flame for light. These center-draft lamps were sold as home lamps, study lamps, store lamps, hotel lamps, and factory and mill lamps. Fires starting from lamps were troublesome, and safety standards were developed to improve fuel, wicks, and glass chimneys. Brass lamps did not break easily and rarely exploded.

I paint a picture of the 1890s when the brass industry flourished; colorful vase lamps became popular and cities were being wired for gas and electricity. Catalogs of the 1890s offered center-draft lamps priced about one dollar more than standard flat wick lamps. Fancy decorative and silver-plated lamps were made for affluent buyers.

The number and variety of center-draft lamps sold during the late nineteenth century is overwhelming. My goal is to present a synopsis of companies that manufactured the principal brands of center-draft lamps lighting America's homes. I present my research with humble acknowledgment as I create snapshots of this time period in our history — over one century ago.

It is possible to show only a few examples of lamps made by different companies. My study of lamps and burners, patterns and designs, names, trademarks, patents, and other characteristics will help you identify and appreciate your lamps. I cannot help but mention achievements made by the inventors and their companies, and I include information which adds to the romance of the era.

I believe a book could be written about nearly every one of the companies in this book. The mysteries and histories of the companies, the inventors, and the entrepreneurs are stories waiting to be told. Many of the companies manufactured flat-wick lamps, bicycle lamps, lanterns, and heating stoves, not to mention many other products. I include lists of trade names for lighting products made by each company.

This book focuses on center-draft lamps made in the United States. However, certain foreign lamps were imported very early and sold in our market. The German Student Lamp and the Belgian Lamp, in particular, are included because they were adapted to kerosene fuel and found ready sales in this country.

After kerosene light was no longer needed, many embossed lamps, student lamps, and colorful decorated lamps were wired for conversion to electricity. These were the first to be saved rather than thrown in the trash.

Lamps still "in oil" may be cleaned and prepared for lighting to enjoy nostalgic evenings with the ambience of years past.

As a retired professor I have a penchant for order and organizing information. Likewise, it seems I am working up the alphabet in my selection of subjects — Aladdin, Angle, and now "Argand" type (center-draft) lamps.

The lamps illustrated in this book are from my collection unless other provenance is given. None of my lamps have been professionally restored. Some of the lamps and parts illustrated have survived a century of use and neglect and are not in perfect condition. The emphasis is on table or stand lamps because parts were less likely to be substituted or interchanged. Large hardware stores and catalog sellers sometimes offered hanging and vase lamps with a choice of manufacturers' oil pots or founts.

When few examples of lamps were available, I included copy of illustrations from trade magazines, catalogs, and advertising.

I invite readers to share information to enhance and improve our knowledge. There is much more to learn and your suggestions are welcome. I have included some unidentified lamps in the appendix.

As hard as one tries to avoid errors, some may creep into this book. Readers' comments and corrections are welcome.

This book is a beginning in study and documentation of center-draft lighting of 100+ years ago.

Old kerosene lamps were thrown away in creeks and down into outdoor privys. Lamps kept for emergency light are the ones we find in the best condition today. Someone placed this banquet lamp in the crotch of a tree, for whatever reason, only for it to be found "ingrown" many years later.

Contents

Acknowledgments

To my wife, Treva Courter, for her love, patience, and understanding during this long project. Treva typed the manuscipt and offered many improvements. Thanks also to Kelley Garcia for library research, and MaryAnn Black for editorial review. Thanks to my granddaughter Mary Beth Riley for all of her help on this book.

I am deeply obligated to Allen Weathers, who provided substantial information by sending files for my review; to Catherine Thuro for her friendship and warm hospitality, opening her private office files to me; David Broughton, who shared his ephemera collection; and Dan Edminster for generous sharing of catalog and research files. Thanks to Heinz and Ursula Baumann, who helped in many ways, such as providing photographs from personal collections, and to Heinz especially, for his vast knowledge and helping me to focus on the target. Fil Graff and Doug Myers reviewed draft manuscripts with many suggestions, and allowed me to photograph many of their lamps as well. Thanks to the Guild of Lamp Researchers and Leon McCormack for their online websites that greatly aided study of utility and design patents; Fil Graff and Aladdin Knights for presenting helpful seminars on flame spreaders; and Kent Stratton for his keen observation to bring many lamps and parts "to light." And, as I write these words, I deeply miss Bill Schreiber and our many discussions about the lamps in this book.

The Corning Rakow Library deserves special kudos and mention for assistance in researching lamps. The librarians were most cooperative, and one can literally spend days studying glass and lamps there. (I send all my writings to the the library for future students.) Besides, the Corning Museum of Glass is an education in itself!

Bill Schroeder, founder of Collector Books, has marketed my books since 1972. His son Billy Schroeder carries on the business and agreed to publish this book. Thanks to Gail Ashburn, Amy Sullivan, Charley Lynch, Lisa Henderson, and Beth Summers for improving my tome.

I especially thank many dedicated people and fine libraries, lighting clubs, museums and historical societies, and others. Without your valuable assistance this book would not be possible: Andover Historical Society, Andover, MA; Pat Armstrong, Bellaire Public Library, Bellaire, OH; Chris Bailey, American Clock & Watch Museum, Bristol, CT; Gail Bardhan, Rakow Library, Corning Museum of Glass, Corning, NY; Anna Bennett and Mary Arrojo, Fostoria Glass Museum, Moundsville, WV; Hyman Brenner, Genealogy Research, Lynn, MA; Amanda Burrows, Carnegie Library, Pittsburgh, PA; Bridgeport Public Library, Bridgeport, CT; R. Jeanne Cobb, T.W. Phillips Library, Bethany College, WV; Cait Dallas, Kenosha County Historical Society and Museum, Kenosha, WI; ExxonMobil Corporation, Irving, TX; Margaret J. Gibbs, Municipal Historian, City of Ansonia, CT; Susan Hengel, Hagley Museum and Library, Wilmington, DE; Historical Society of Berks County, Reading, PA; Glenn Humphreys, Chicago Public Library, Chicago, IL; Illinois State Archives, Illinois Secretary of State, Springfield, IL; Jean E. Meeh Gosebrink, St. Louis Public Library, St. Louis, MO; Susan Hengel, Hagley Museum and Library, New Castle, DE; Louis Horacek, Ohio County Public Library, Wheeling, WV; Lisa F. Leibfacher, Ohio Historical Society, Columbus, OH; Marian K. O'Keefe, The Derby Historical Society, Derby, CT; Leatrice M. Kemp, Rochester Museum Library, Rochester, NY; Bill King and Melvin Murray, The Glass Heritage Gallery and Museum, Fostoria, OH; Beverley Mamion, Louisville Free Public Library, Louisville, KY; Robert Miller, New Brunswick Free Public Library, New Brunswick, NJ; Allan Raney, New York State Library, Albany, NY; John Reinhardt, Illinois State Archives, Springfield, IL; Carol Sandler, Research Library Strong Museum, Rochester, NY; Amy Schuman, Bristol Public Library, Bristol, CT; Martha H. Smart, The Connecticut Historical Society, Hartford, CT; Laura K. Smith, University of Connecticut, Thomas J. Dodd Research Center, Storrs, CT; Mel E. Smith, Connecticut State Library, Hartford, CT; Jason D. Stratman, Missouri Historical Society, St. Louis, MO; John B. Straw, Bracken Library, Ball State University, Muncie, IN; Allen Weathers, Meriden Historical Society, Meriden, CT; Charles D. Webster IV, Trenton Public Library, Trenton, NJ; Kelly A. Wolfe, University of Wisconsin-Parkside, Kenosha, WI; Dianne J. Wood, Wheaton Village Museum of Glass, Millville, NJ.

My appreciation to colleagues, collectors, authors, and lighting researchers. I trust this book will honor the gifts of knowledge you have shared with me: Mary Arrojo, Gale Belliveau, Paul Benkover, Linda L. Black, George and Kathy Bock, David Boysel, Mike Bradley (England), Tim and Debbie Breen, Hyman Brenner, Monte Calhoun, Jim Christner, George Christy, John Claypole (England), George Collins, Dave Corbissero, David Denny (England), Tom Diehl, Thomas Diosy, Richard and Barbara Dudley, Bob Duffield, Howard Eastland, Jeff Ebersole, Ralph Fierro, John Florian, Alan Freeman, Ron Gibson, Steve Gnan, Leonard Gutekunst, James Hargis, Ted Hinsdale, Harry H. Hipwell, Jr., Lou Hopf, M. J. Howell, Anton Kaim (Holland), Richard Kastner, Ara Kebapcioglu (France), Tim and Sue Kruger, Rod L'Italien, Herb Leflet, Alex Marrack (England), Dan Mattausch, Walter Matthews, Joe McDonald, Jack K. McNearney, Don Meily, Mark Mitchell, Don Moore, Richard O'Connell, Dave Ostblom, George C. Parks, C. Roger Paul, Paul Rausch, John Remackel, Nigel Reynolds (England), Brent Rowell, Bob Sanford, William E. Schreiber, Alvin Sellens, George Sherwood, John and Patricia Smith, Mel Soderholm, Glen Southard, Robert and Donna Sperow, Patricia St. John, Jon Stratton, Bo Sullivan, Rick Valentine, Jim Van Es, Jack Washka, Jeanne Weinrich, Eileen White, Frank Wiedlocher, Bruce Wood, Cliff Youngstrom, and Gale Zelnick.

Advertisement, *Crockery and Glass Journal*, July 20, 1905.

Introduction

This book is about lamps with a central-draft tube fitted with a flame spreader to supply air (oxygen) to the flame of a round wick. The central-draft tube was a significant improvement in lighting, evident in Argand lamps, Sinumbra lamps, Astral lamps, and Solar lamps. Most patentees used the term "central-draft." I use "central-draft" and "center-draft" as synonymous terms.

The flame spreader is a critical part of burners for lamps in this book and, with a few exceptions, is a perforated thimble design.

I wanted to subtitle this book "Rochester to Rayo" because those lamps bracket the time period for my research.

The starting date is 1884 because that year Leonard Henkle received U.S. patent No. 292,114 for a thimble flame spreader. His patent specified a burner with a wick tube (draft tube) and a thimble perforated to "turn the air in jets against the flame." Charles Upton bought rights to the patent and named Rochester brand lamps that were sold worldwide. Many competitors entered the market during the next 20 years.

An end point is 1940, because that is when Bradley and Hubbard, maker of the famous Rayo lamp, ceased doing business as an independent company. Most cities and large towns had electric lighting by then, even though kerosene lamps were still necessary in some rural areas.

I identify center-draft lamps and their manufacturers, concentrating on American lamps. I primarily illustrate stand lamps with their original burners, because many banquet lamps, vase lamps, and hanging lamps may not have their original oil pots and burners today.

I introduce the reader to a glimpse of America during the 1890s and the variety of lamps that manufacturers promised to be brighter, safer, and more economical. The homeowners' choices of kerosene lamps were many.

I would be remiss to imply that center-draft lamps were new inventions in 1884. They were not. The center-draft lamp dates back more than 100 years. The Argand "air lamp" was patented by Ami Argand in 1784 in England and in 1787 in France. Development and improvement of center-draft lamps progressed steadily as improved and safer fuels were perfected.

The first American burner designed for kerosene was in the mid-1850s. When kerosene became generally available during the 1860s, solar lamps were still in widespread use burning fuels such as vegetable oils, tallow, and coarser grades of whale oil, lard, or lard oil. Some Solar lamps were modified to burn kerosene, also called coal oil.

Kerosene, the lamp fuel of choice by the 1880s, was also used for cooking and heating in rural America. The export of kerosene was a significant market for the American petroleum industry.

Center-draft lamps burning kerosene were developed simultaneously in Europe. There are many European lamps, but I include only the Belgian Lamp and a brief mention of German student lamps since both were sold extensively in America. American center-draft lamps were exported in great numbers to countries around the world.

German student lamps were among the first center-drafts to burn kerosene. Student lamps, commonly imported during the 1870s, were proclaimed safe and practical for home and office. Note that many student lamps did not require flame spreaders. Flame spreaders became necessary as the size of burners (i.e., larger central-draft tubes) was increased in order to produce more light.

Also during the 1870s, American inventors Combs, Hoyt, and Leighton, among others, were adapting glass fonts with draft tubes to improve combustion and light output from their lamps.

The source of light for lighthouse beacons is mentioned, albeit briefly. Kerosene "mineral oils" changed the burners and lamps used in lighthouses in the 1880s.

Lamps for lighting railcars, engine headlights, and mailcars were unique developments in the railroad industry. Ninety percent of all railcars were fitted with kerosene lamps by 1890. The better lamps were center-draft.

By the late 1880s, brass manufacturers were able to spin and press brass into unbreakable lamps that were produced by the millions. The lamps in this book were made under patents of inventors and companies during the high point in the art of producing brass center-draft lamps. Connecticut was home of the brass industry, where the majority of lamps and burners were manufactured.

Metal designs, decorative embossing, and colorful glass vase lamps became accepted standards for lamps in the home. This industry prospered until the early 1900s, when companies consolidated or changed to manufacture gas and electric lighting fixtures.

Meanwhile, improvements in kerosene lighting continued. The gas mantle perfected by Auer von Welsbach in Europe during the late 1880s was well adapted for gas lighting in cities. German inventors applied the mantle to kerosene burners that burned blue flames to produce heat, not large bright flames for light. The blue flame caused the mantle to incandesce with an intense white light. Mantle lamps, developed around 1900, introduced a new generation of kerosene lamps. Mantle lamps, such as Aladdin (see my book *Aladdin — The Magic Name in Lamps*), are not included in this book.

How to Identify Your Lamp

This book is organized alphabetically by manufacturers and major sellers of center-draft lamps. Some companies conspicuously marked their lamps with brand names or trade names. Names helped the consumer reorder wicks and chimneys. Lamps of unknown makers are found in the appendix.

Names and marks. All names and marks may not be easily seen, especially on old dirty and dusty lamps. Look for names, initials, trademarks, and patent dates embossed or stamped in various places — the flame spreaders, burners, or lamp bodies. The most obvious places are on top of the flame spreaders and on the wick knobs. But search carefully around and on the sides of all parts. I have found patent dates around the burner bases, or collars, on the wick raiser mechanisms, or pull rods, on the outer wick tubes, around the tops of the galleries, and in the casting of the iron bases, or feet.

Your lamp burner, fount, or oil pot may have been manufactured by one company but assembled into a vase lamp, a banquet lamp, a hanging frame, or a piano lamp by another company such as a large department store or distributor. The second company may also have patent dates or other marks on their parts.

Patent dates are relatively easy to research today and give much information about the inventor and to which company, if any, a patent was assigned.

Trade names are listed for lamps, burners, and lanterns manufactured by each company. These trade names are found in trade catalogs and advertising and are embossed on lamps and burners. The names may not be registered trademarks. The names may or may not be proprietary, as the company may have manufactured items under license while they held the trademarks for other lamps and parts. My lists generally do not include driving lamps, marine lamps, and other transportation lamps.

Selected patents. My lists of selected patents are primarily utility improvements dealing with center-draft principle and design patents that illustrate the lamps under study. I have included few patents that improve form or function, such as hanging frames and shade supports. Individuals who pursue all patents for the companies will fill more books this size.

Dating your lamp. Lamps in this book generally can be dated according to production dates of the manufacturer. Some lamps were sold over a long period of years while others were made for a short time and replaced with an improved model. Lamps marked with patent dates were generally sold after the last patent date. This is not always a fact, as I have documented lamps advertised and sold as much as a full year before the patent was granted. Lamps are often dated on parts such as galleries and flame spreaders. In these cases the parts may have been used on "new" lamps for many years.

Trade magazines were used extensively to document and date lamps through press notices, advertisements, and other business references. I used these abbreviations: *PGR — Pottery and Glassware Reporter, CGL — China, Glass and Lamps*, and *CGJ — Crockery and Glass Journal.*

The quality of artwork and drawings in 100-year-old trade magazines and catalogs varies widely. I have elected to include important images and advertisements to document their content rather than for their artistic beauty. Many images are drawings that show characteristics to help identify the manufacturer. The images, however, are often the last year's model and may or may not illustrate the lamp currently offered for sale. In some cases, catalog images were incorrectly named, and caution is advised in relying on catalog descriptions and artwork images.

Shades and appurtenances are not included on lamps in this book. Collectors certainly seek these items to complete their lamps; however, original and authentic shades, chimneys, prisms, etc., are difficult to date and ascertain. I have opted to show as many catalog images as possible.

Abbreviations used to conserve space: AAFLGM — American Assoc. Flint & Lime Glass Mfrs.; B & H — Bradley & Hubbard; GWTW — Gone with the Wind lamp, more correctly a decorated vase lamp; HBH — Holmes, Booth & Haydens; HLSC — Historic Lighting Club of Canada; KYSO — Standard Oil of Kentucky; M & W — Matthews & Willard Mfg. Co.; MMI — Meriden Malleable Iron; P & A — Plume & Atwood Mfg. Co.; S & W — Swann & Whitehead; SO — Standard Oil; UK — United Kingdom; USPTO — United States Patent & Trademark Office; W & S — Wallace & Sons; and Ward — Montgomery Ward.

A word about values. The values in this book are not a price list. The values are a guide of prices for average, complete, unrestored lamps in the collectible marketplace. The prices for 100-year-old lamps vary widely depending on condition and availability. The values given are for lamps with original parts — complete burners, flame spreaders, wick raisers, and oil fill caps (please note that a few lamps pictured are not complete). Damaged or incomplete lamps may only be valued at a fraction, for parts. The values given do not include chimneys, trimmings, shades, and shade holders. A lamp in pristine original finish with an original chimney and unburned wick will be priced much higher. Embossed lamps are usually valued higher than plain lamps. A lamp in original condition, or restored, with old trimmings will often double the value. Note that values vary from region to region, influenced by demand in those areas.

Learn More

I have included a list of references to help students pursue further research. Citations in the text have been kept to a minimum; however, where cited I give the author and year, e.g., Welker (1980) or (Welker, 1980), which you can find in the list of references.

The Kerosene Center-draft Stand Lamp

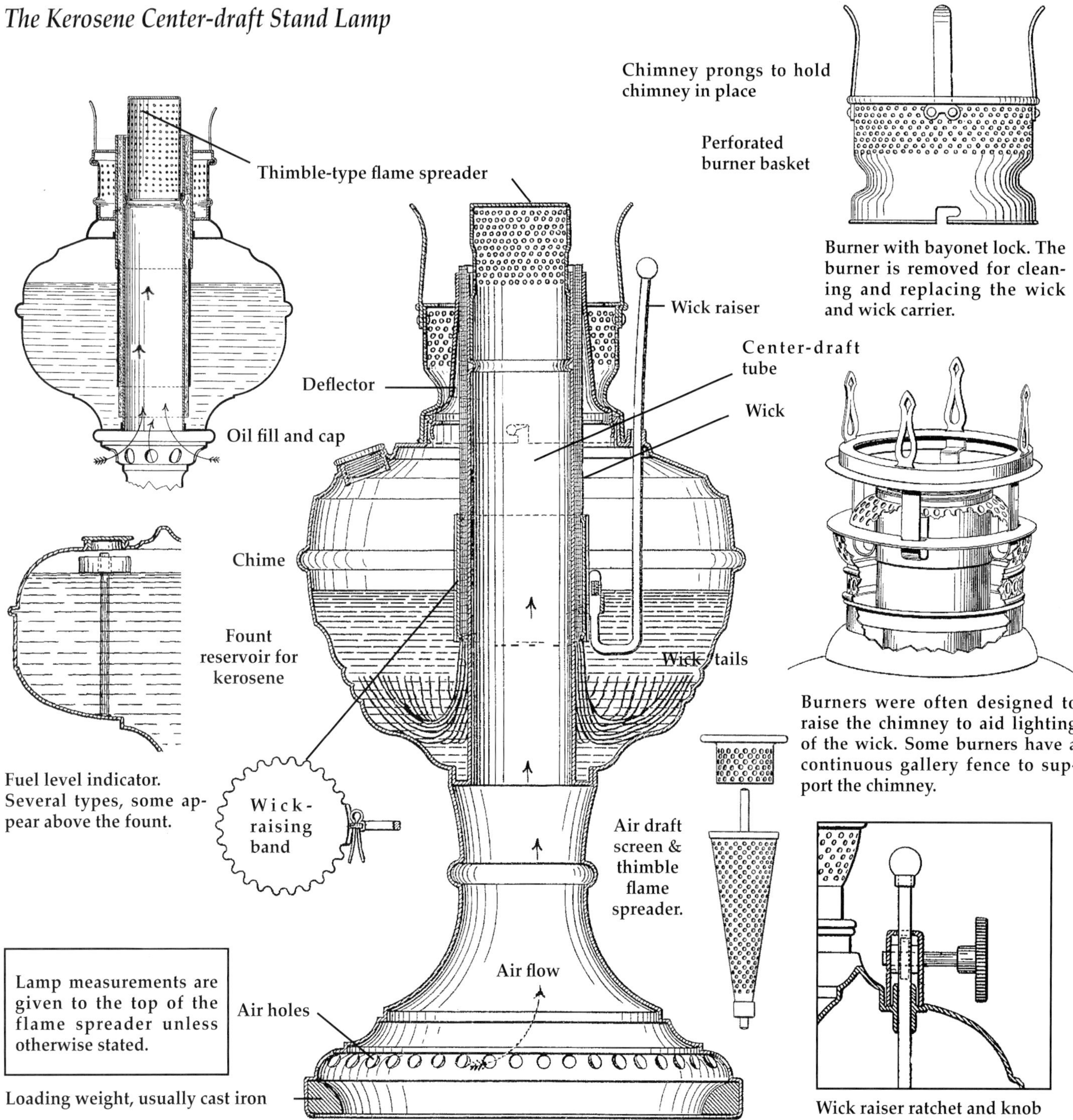

Burner with bayonet lock. The burner is removed for cleaning and replacing the wick and wick carrier.

Burners were often designed to raise the chimney to aid lighting of the wick. Some burners have a continuous gallery fence to support the chimney.

Fuel level indicator. Several types, some appear above the fount.

Lamp measurements are given to the top of the flame spreader unless otherwise stated.

Wick raiser ratchet and knob

This is a typical stand lamp made of brass and commonly nickel plated for easy cleaning. Air to the center of the round wick flows into the base through the openings and up into the wick tube (also called central draft tube). The perforated flame spreader distributes air to the flame. Some lamps have air intake openings in the stem under the oil reservoir (see above left); others are made with a decorative cast-iron foot with many openings through the foot. The loading weight provides support, gives strength to thin brass, and provides weight to stabilize the lamp. This view of a center-draft lamp is adapted from J. H. White patent 444,867, assigned to Manhattan Brass Co. in 1891. The small inset (upper left) is G. W. Woodard patent 386,681, assigned to Ansonia Brass & Clock Co. in 1888. The fuel level insert (left) is from Frank Rhind patent 356,962 assigned to Bridgeport Brass Co. in 1887. The lift gallery insert (right center) is Frank Rhind patent 499,273 assigned to Edward Miller Co. in 1893. There are many kinds of wick raisers (see right, which is Atwood's 1895 patent 538,476), ranging from simple rods or bars to smooth gear devices. The wick raiser may appear above or below the oil reservoir. Air draft moderator devices such as the screens above (Atwood patent 370,516, 1887) may be found in the draft tube, in the flame spreader, or incorporated into the burner (also see deflector above left). A drip cup may be found under the foot. Flame extinguishing mechanisms are beneficial devices in some burners.

Forms of Center-draft Lamps

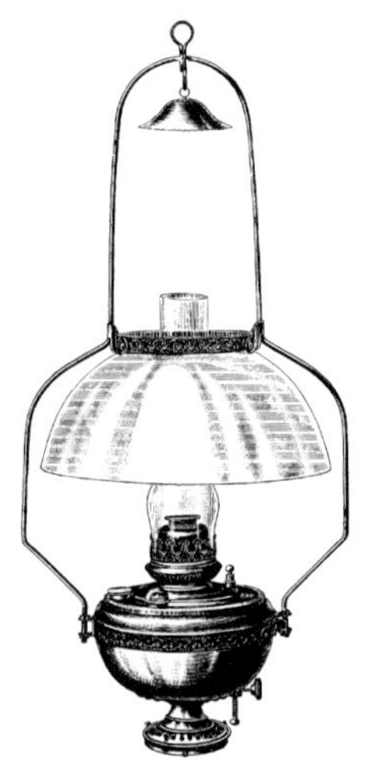
Store Lamp
Pendant Lamp
Mammoth Lamp No. 3

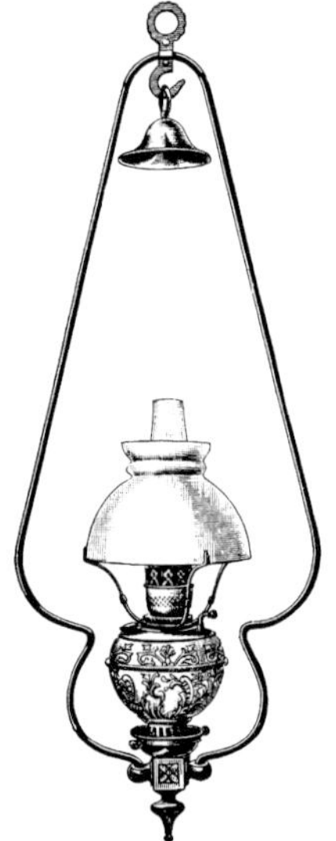
Harp Lamp

Library Lamp
(often with prisms)

Chandelier

Wall Lamp
Side Lamp

Stand Lamp
Table Lamp No. 2

Vase Lamp
Parlor Lamp
Reception Lamp

Decorated Table Lamp
Parlor Lamp
Vase Lamp
GWTW Lamp

Banquet Lamp
Tall Stand Lamp

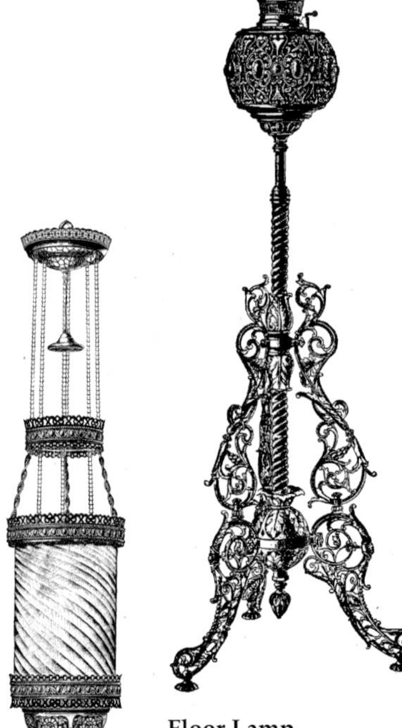
Hall Lamp

Floor Lamp
Piano Lamp
Extension Lamp
(sometimes with table)

Wall Lamp
Bracket Lamp
(with No. 1
Table Lamp)

Hand Lamp
Night Lamp

Station Lamp
Porch Lamp
Barn Lamp

Student Lamp
Reading Lamp
Study Lamp

Newel Post Lamp
Figural Lamp

History

The discovery of petroleum in Pennsylvania in 1859 opened the way for new industries to refine kerosene for use in lamps and stoves. Peterson (1973) surveyed the sharp increase in U.S. lamp patents corresponding with the refinement of kerosene for lamp fuel — improvements in burners, wicks, chimneys, glass lamps, and illuminating oils (kerosene). Improvements in use of kerosene fuels developed rapidly in side-draft burners with flat wicks fitted into glass or metal founts. The fuel itself was of variable content and quality, causing concern about its safety.

Library lamp, stand lamp, and chandelier with flat-wick burners, early 1880s.

A survey of 1880s lamp catalogs reveals many colorful and decorative lamps designed for the Victorian home, such as those illustrated above. Fancy vase lamps and shades, cast figural stand lamps, and elaborate hanging fixtures were signatures of the times. Gas lighting dominated better homes in the cities. Other forms of lighting coming on the scene included electric generating systems, the incandescent mantle, and other fuel systems.

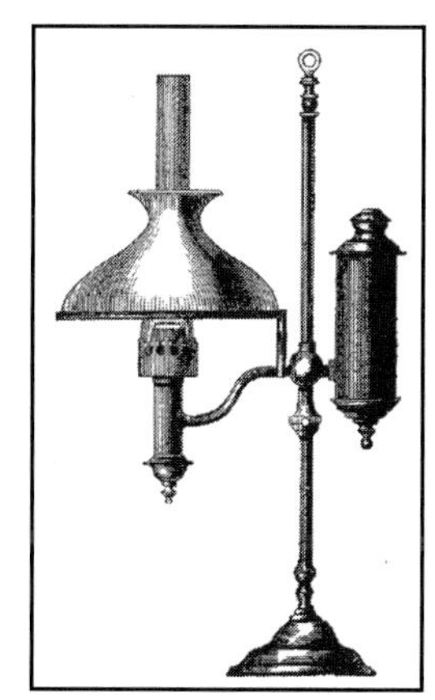

Center-draft student lamps, such as Perfection, Kleemann (see right), and the "non-explosive" lamps were developed during the 1870s. Glass center-draft founts developed by Hoyt and Combs were unique in the 1870s. At the same time, expensive mechanical lamps such as DeKeravenan, Jones, Dyott, Hitchcock, and others were meeting with considerable success. Brass center-draft lamps were widely offered in catalogs by the early 1890s. Many were embossed, fancy, or decorated to enhance their appeal.

Patents and Improvements

Inventors patented their ideas to improve every aspect of the center-draft lamp. Many ideas probably never saw the light of day; however, the study of patents and old lamps is interesting as a hobby/pastime. I have provided a list of patents that apply to center-draft lamps made by the various companies. These lists are not complete.

Edward Miller & Co. collection of patents relating to Argand lamps, 1886 – 1893. A companion collection of patents 1893 – 1900 is in the Rakow Library, Corning, New York.

The period from 1870 through the early 1900s is a productive period for research in kerosene lighting and development.

Study of patents, as well as the lamps, reveals changes and improvements in the development of center-draft lamps. Changes may be made for patent advantage or simply to be more cost effective. Following is a broad summary of improvements designed to give manufacturers or patent owners an advantage in the market place. These improvements might be grouped into these categories:

- Air distribution to the flame:
  - — thimble vs. Liverpool button with all sorts of modifications,
  - — many variations in flame spreaders
- Source of air through the central-draft tube:
  - — through the bottom, from ports, etc.
  - — air deflectors, screens, flanges, etc.
- The art of wick adjustment:
  - — many, many ideas to raise and lower the wick — screw, rack, bar, slide, ratchet, crank, tongs, chain, combinations, and more.
- Lighting aids and extinguishers:
  - — gallery lifts and locking devices
- Size and special features including:
  - — burner attachment, siphon control, drip cups, fuel level indicators
- Design patents

Many lamps are marked with patent dates or the words "Patented" or "Patent Pending." These marks usually refer to utility patents for inventions granted by the U.S. Patent and Trademark Office (USPTO). A patent is the grant of a property right to an inventor. Beginning in 1861, utility patents were granted for 17 years. Today the term is 20 years.

The Patent Act of 1842 required the owner to mark the invention with the patent date. This requirement was cancelled in 1861; however, marking was continued by many patentees. Today the patentee who makes or sells patented articles (or another person or company who does so for the patentee) is required to mark the article with the word "Patent" and the number of the patent. It is illegal to so mark an article that is not patented. The terms "Patent Pending" or "Patent Applied For" have no legal effect.

Design patents were established in 1842 and only apply to the appearance of an object, not its function or usefulness. Terms were 3½ , 7, or 14 years.

The patentee may assign a patent to another person or company or may license rights to another person or a manufacturer.

Brief descriptions of patents are published each week in the *Official Gazette* of the United States Patent and Trademark Office. The full patent is available from the USPTO. Each patent records the name of the patentee(s), the date of application, the date of patent granted, and the assignee(s), if any.

Research and study of patents provides valuable information about the invention and may give data about previous work and sometimes history relating to the object.

Caution is required when deciding which patent applies to your lamp when you discover several patents granted on a given date. They may be similar in nature and only one may be correct. Your interpretation requires some knowledge and study of the lamp in question.

Trademarks

Many companies obtained trademarks to identify the company and its lamps.

A trademark is a name, word, or symbol used in trade to identify the source of goods and distinguish them from goods of others. Trademarks may be used to prevent others from using similar marks but not to prevent others from selling (or using their own marks to sell) the same types of goods.

The USPTO has registered trademarks since 1870. Protection rights of trademarks are acquired by use in the marketplace. For more information regarding patents and trademarks and lamps, contact the USPTO or see Peterson (1973) and Thuro (2001).

The Brass Industry

The development of brass rolling, stamping, and spinning gave the impetus to manufacturing the lamps illustrated in this book. Progress came rapidly. Prior to 1900, 80 – 85 percent of all U.S. output in rolled brass and brass products was manufactured in Connecticut.

The brass industry flourished in Connecticut because: 1) household industries such as buttons, pins, and tinwares were established there, 2) wood was available for annealing and water for power and washing, 3) the early start in brass manufacturing set the stage for peddlers to establish markets throughout Canada and west to the Mississippi River, 4) the skills of America's "brass-maker's art" developed there, and 5) of the foresight, inventiveness, and business acumen of industry leaders.

In 1898 Connecticut was called the "Land of Steady Habits" by the Orange Judd publishing company, with further description saying that "to sum up the manufactures of Connecticut is like quoting a list of the material needs of civilization."

Israel Holmes, along with many other prominent men such as Anson G. Phelps, H. W. Hayden, and Lewis J. Atwood, to name a few, were leaders who created the industry that produced 85 percent or more of all brass burners (including flat wick burners) and brass lamps sold in the U.S. during the late nineteenth century.

***The Brass Industry* by William G. Lathrop, 1926, with embossed brass covers. This special presentation book is signed "Compliments of Scovill Manufacturing Company" on a brass plate inside the book.**

The "Genealogy of the Naugatuck Brass Industry" in Connecticut is presented by Lathrop (1936) in chart form to illustrate the relationships of men and their companies from 1790 to 1914.

The American Brass Association was formed during the 1850s by brass companies in the Naugatuck Valley. Marketing agreements and (monetary) pools were formed to control production and price, and to stabilize markets (see Lathrop, 1926). The American Burner Association formed similar agreements for kerosene lamp burners (Scheips and Weathers, 1995, and appendix).

By 1909 the American Brass Company was the largest user of copper in the world, producing more than two-thirds of all brass manufactured in the United States. American Brass was created through consolidation of several brass companies, including Coe Brass; Waterbury Brass; Ansonia Brass; Holmes, Booth & Haydens; and others (see appendix).

Brass — The Metal

Brass is an alloy of copper and zinc, commonly two parts copper to one part zinc; however, proportions vary according to special purposes. Brass alloys vary in color from red to yellow to nearly white.

Other alloys made with copper include bronze (copper, zinc, and tin) and German silver (copper, zinc, and nickel). Each has characteristics of the proportions and additives to the alloy. German silver, for example, is white in color and takes on a good polish, making it useful to make household utensils and spoons.

These definitions are over-simplifications — brass men carefully guarded their formulas and procedures in manufacturing. Read Hopkins (1913) to learn more about brass and its alloys during the early twentieth century.

Brass can be rolled into sheets, extruded, and cast into many shapes and forms. Brass objects are durable, easily machined, and will not rust. Brass resists corrosion from most chemicals in the air and those ordinarily encountered in the home or workplace. Brass has permanent beauty and can be plated with nickel, silver, or gold. Brass objects have strength and toughness.

Brass workers were craftsmen with reputations for toughness too. They were hard-working, hard-swearing, and came up the hard way through apprenticeship and tough experience. Like glass workers, many brass men were heavy drinkers of whiskey and other liquor.

A brass man was said to have "copper and spelter in his veins with just a wee touch of lead." And maybe he did, from inhaling fumes from boiling zinc in making brass. Read *Bristol Fashion* (1950) for an account of the brass industry written in interesting storytelling fashion.

Meriden, Connecticut, was a major manufacturing center for metal table lamps until the 1920s. The town was described as "the heart of the metal lamp industry."

Prof. W. H. WELLS, Late Supt. of Public Schools, Chicago, says:— "This Lamp is an embodiment of applied Science. It is perfectly non-explosive, and gives a better light and is more economical than any other Lamp in use."

THE DANGER FROM GLASS LAMPS.

Glass Lamps will explode, as they are doing every-where daily, destroying life and property.

Glass Lamps will break, spill oil, and start a fire which is almost inextinguishable.

Glass Lamps use more oil and give less light than this. They give a bad kerosene odor, especially when turned down low, and are very unwholesome for night lamps or sick rooms.

Glass Lamps easily get out of repair. Children are never safe where glass lamps are used. But you can safely leave this lamp with your children or careless servants.

No man has a moral right to endanger the safety of his family and property by using glass lamps, since there is no longer any necessity for it.

Perkins and House's Non-Explosive Lamps are made of Metal.

Save your lives by using this Lamp

Save your houses from burning.

Save your family from burning and death.

Save your money by getting a durable, oil-saving Lamp.

Save your eyes by having a better light.

Fatal Burning Accident.—Mrs. Margaret Greenleaf, an estimable lady, was so badly burned by the explosion of a kerosene lamp, that death ensued Wednesday, A. M. The explosion occurred while the lady was on her way up stairs for the purpose of retiring; her eyes almost burned out, hands so badly burned that the skin and nails pealed off, the hair burned completely from the head.—*Middlesex Co. Democrat.*

The Glass Industry

During the gas boom of the 1880s, the glass industry expanded westward from Pittsburgh and Wheeling into Ohio and Indiana, enticed by cheap fuel. Glass founts were not well suited for center-draft lamps. Even so, Rochester and Plume & Atwood developed center-draft glass lamps, as Combs and Hoyt did earlier.

Colorful pattern glass lamps (mostly flat wicks) were inexpensive and popular in rural homes. The glassmaker's art was challenged to produce a better lamp, a prettier lamp, and a less expensive lamp as technology and sand and gas resources allowed. Glass lamps, however, were said to be unsafe because they might break or explode.

The brass oil pot, which came into widespread use during the 1890s, allowed glass companies to design and create their own vase lamps with matching globes and shades. These colorful lamps are commonly called "Gone with the Wind" or parlor lamps today, even though the former term is incorrect. These lamps are better called vase lamps, parlor lamps, or decorated table lamps.

The glass industry, however, was undergoing changes of its own. Business owners formed two national groups to protect their interests, mainly due to competitive pricing, imports, and cost of labor. The American Association of Flint & Lime Glass Manufacturers and the Glass Manufacturers Protective Association were both active during the 1890s as strikes by union workers and cheaper imports affected the industry. In addition, glass factories were combined for efficiency and other business reasons. The United States Glass Company (1891 – 1894) was formed through consolidation of 18 factories. The National Glass Company combined 19 factories in 1899 (disbanded in 1904).

For more information on the individual companies and the glassmakers' strikes of 1893 – 1896, see Revi (1973) and read "The Glass Pool — The End of an Era" by Innes (1976) in his excellent book *Pittsburgh Glass, 1797 – 1891.*

The Age of Electricity

The age of electricity began during the 1870s with arc-lighting systems on city streets and in large theatres in New York, Boston,

This early theory of electricity persisted into the 1860s:

"I cannot tell," says Dr. Faraday, "whether there are two fluids of electricity, or any fluid at all; such is our profound uncertainty in relation to this mysterious agent. Yet it is commonly assumed to be a subtle fluid, distributed through all substances, and lying buried beneath their surfaces in a condition of equilibrium, or rest. Various causes may disturb this state, producing electrical excitement, when the fluid is supposed to accumulate in some substances to excess, which are then said to be positively electrified, — while in others it is deficient, and these are negatively electrified....

"The friction of unlike bodies against each other creates electrical excitement....The friction of masses of air, of different temperatures, or containing different degrees of moisture, by rubbing against each other, or grinding against the earth, develops electricity. So, also does evaporation....Combustion produces electricity; the escaping carbonic acid being positive, while the burning body is negative....

"It has become fashionable, latterly, to offer electricity in explanation of all obscurities, material and spiritual. Beyond doubt it is profoundly involved in the phenomena of our being, but we as yet understand but little about it."

Youmans, 1858

and Chicago. Displays of electric lighting were designed to be impressive as well as a mark of status. William Wallace, of Wallace & Sons, developed arc lamps and lighted the town of Ansonia by 1878. Thomas Edison visited Wallace to study his inventions.

Arc lamps were among the very first electric lights to be used commercially in factories, theatres, and lighthouses, and on streets.

During the early 1880s, electrical systems employed direct current (DC); direct current was also used in Thomas Edison's laboratory. The means to economically transmit alternating current (AC) for consumer use had not yet been invented. The Edison Electric Illuminating Company sold direct current lighting systems in 1882.

Edison proposed AC as lethal electricity best used for electrocution. His employee, Harold P. Brown, invented the first practical electric chair, tested at Edison's laboratory. Edison thought consumers would not want the same electricity in their homes as was used to kill criminals.

The word *electric* first appeared in English during the mid-1600s. According to Webster's 1913 Dictionary the word originated because "electricity" was produced by friction rubbing amber (L. electrum, derived from the Greek word *elektron).*

> According to the theory of Siemens (Royal Society of Great Britain), flame is the result of an infinite number of exceedingly minute electrical flashes, which are caused by the swift motion of gaseous particles.
>
> *American Potter and Illuminator*, 1885
>
> This quote may refer to "Ernst Werner von" Siemens (or his famous brother, Carl Wilhelm), for his work in electric conductance.

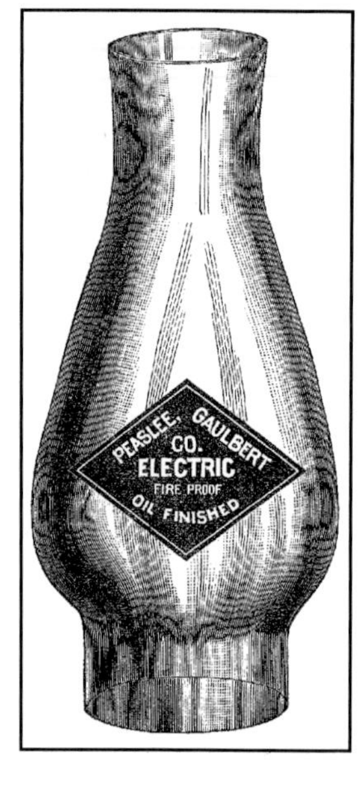

"Electric" and "Incandescent"

The development of affordable brass center-draft lamps improved lighting in millions of homes. The new lamps were promoted as safe or as "safety lamps," and as "incandescent" and "electric," providing the advantages of "perfect combustion and as easy to light as gas."

Even kerosene suppliers were attuned to the promise of better light — The Electric Light Oil Company operated in Philadelphia and New York during the 1880s.

Medicines named "Eclectric Oil" promised to cure every malady. Were such promises, attested to with endorsements, a misleading play on words?

It is impossible to peer into the minds of inventors and admen of the 1880s who advertised oil lamps as "electric." Companies that described their lamps as electric during the mid-1880s included Ansonia; Geiss & Co.; F. Meyrose & Co.; Holmes, Booth & Haydens; Manhattan Brass Co.; and Plume and Atwood.

Electric lighting, exhibited more or less as a novelty in 1893, was exploited at the St. Louis World's Fair in 1904. The Court of Electricity, with lighting exhibits, stayed open until 11 pm. Electric

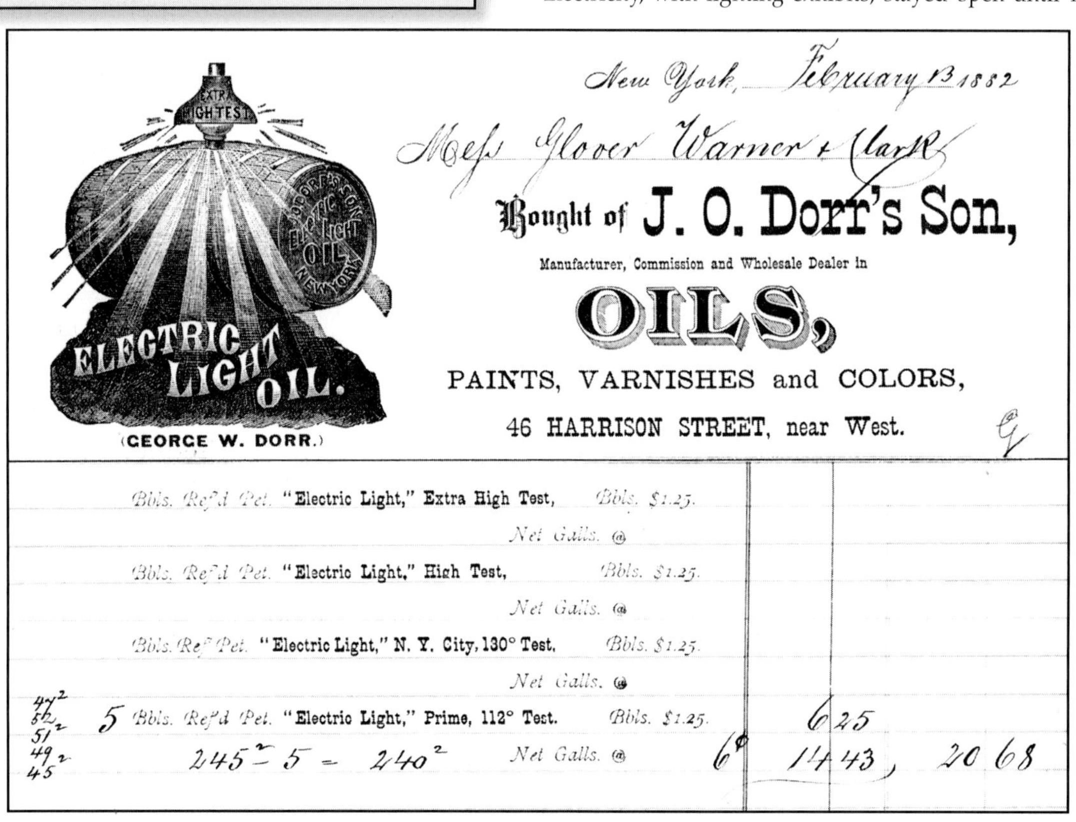

New York, February 13 1882

Mess Glover Warner & Clark

Bought of J. O. Dorr's Son,

Manufacturer, Commission and Wholesale Dealer in

OILS,

PAINTS, VARNISHES and COLORS,

46 HARRISON STREET, near West.

Bbls. Ref'd Pet. "Electric Light," Extra High Test, Bbls. $1.25.
Net Galls. @

Bbls. Ref'd Pet. "Electric Light," High Test, Bbls. $1.25.
Net Galls. @

Bbls. Ref'd Pet. "Electric Light," N. Y. City, 130° Test, Bbls. $1.25.
Net Galls. @

5 Bbls. Ref'd Pet. "Electric Light," Prime, 112° Test. Bbls. $1.25. 6 25
245 - 5 = 240 Net Galls. @ 6 14 43 20 68

Billhead listing four grades of "Electric Light" oil — Extra High Test, High Test, N.Y. City 130° Test, Prime 112° Test. J. O. Dorr's Son trademarked "Electric Light" for refined petroleum grades from 112° to 300° flash point.

lighting in early theatre was said to serve "as a metaphor for life force and sexual desire" (*Light!* 2000).

The work electric suggested superior light, better than that from previous lamps, or implied excitement from using this new "breath-taking" lamp invention to lengthen the day, or both.

Certainly, promotion of trendy center-draft lamps with the "electric" implied they functioned as good or better than those electric lights in the city. The term "incandescent" also implied light as good as Edison's light bulb.

Thus, central-draft kerosene lamps were described as "electric" or "incandescent" before electric lighting, as we know it today, became commonplace.

Age of Kerosene

The kerosene lamp was a primary source of light for Americans during the latter part of the nineteenth century. The period from 1882 to 1911 was called the "Age of Kerosene" by Standard Oil historians when the company produced kerosene "for the lamps of the world." Russell (1968) described the times as the "Swan Song of the Kerosene Lamp." Perhaps rightly so, as Thomas Edison patented his bulb in 1879 and began selling electricity in New York City in 1882.

This time was an age of invention and mass production of household tools and appliances. The bicycle became immensely popular, only to be followed by the automobile soon after the turn of the century. Such were the Victorian days when the lamps in this book lighted millions of homes, not only in America, but around the world.

Kerosene

During the late nineteenth century, kerosene was refined petroleum used in lamps and heaters. Kerosene was the primary product of the distiller until well after 1900. At the time, kerosene was a mixture of closely related petroleum fractions determined by the source of petroleum and the quality of operation procedures of the distiller.

Samuel Kier distilled petroleum to yield a lamp oil as early as 1854 in Pittsburgh.

Characteristics of kerosene that are important for lamp oil include low viscosity, high flash point, light and stable color, free of substances that smell or burn with a smoky flame, low sulphur content, good wick capillarity, and the ability to remain clear to 0°F and liquid to –20°F.

I am sure that inventors of lamp burners in the leading companies of the time were aware of differences in sources of petroleum and kerosenes distilled from them. The inventors' goals were to improve burning characteristics and light output. Companies that paid no attention to fuels likely ran into poor performance, smoky flame when the lamp was turned up, and dissatisfied customers.

According to Gruse and Stevens, publishing in 1942, the typical Pennsylvania kerosene was lighter in gravity and higher in paraffin fraction than other kerosenes (distilled from western or California petroleum, for example), which contained a greater proportion of naphthenic hydrocarbons.

Burning a large flame without smoking was extremely important to increase "candle power." The paraffinic rich kerosenes were reported to give a flame four-to-eight times larger than aromatic kerosenes.

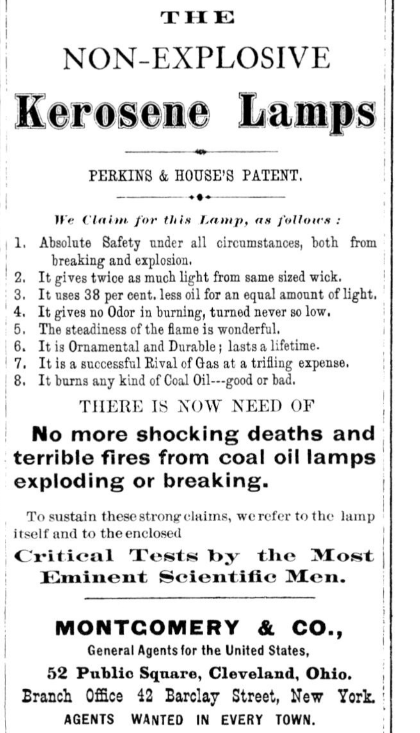

Cover from Montgomery & Co. ca. 1870 catalog for Perkins & House's non-explosive lamps. This concern for safety was written one year before the Great Chicago Fire. For more information, see "Cleveland Non-Explosive Lamp Company."

Rarely were separate grades of kerosene distilled for specific purposes, such as for use in heaters or mantle lamps. In these instances, the goal was burning for heat (blue flame) rather than for a large luminous flame. For these uses, a fuel with high calorific value, such as an aromatic kerosene, has been shown to be more efficient. Gruse and Stevens (1942) used the term "power kerosene" for such a special use fuel.

Safety of Kerosene

Kerosene has not always been the safe fuel that it is today. The term *kerosene* (also spelled *kerosine*) was coined by Dr. Abraham Gesner, a Canadian, after inventing a process (U.S. Patent 11,203, 1854) to distill lighting fuel popularly called "coal oil." In 1854 he formed the North American Kerosene Gas Light Company in New York City. Englishman James Young patented his process to distill "paraffine oil" in 1850 (U.S. patent 8,833, granted in 1852). Kerosene has been known as paraffin in England ever since.

Soon after "Colonel" Drake drilled a successful oil well (35 barrels per day) in Titusville, Pennsylvania, kerosene became the primary fuel for home lighting. Edwin L. Drake, an ex-railroad conductor, was dubbed "Colonel" to impress the local people. Overkill of whales (for whale oil) in the late 1840s plus the lower price of kerosene created huge demand for this "new" fuel.

Early refining in "teakettle stills" was relatively simple compared with modern methods. Distillation was not sophisticated nor was it conducted by chemical engineers. John D. Rockefeller financed his first refinery in 1862 and established Standard Oil in 1870. Colonel Drake died broke and Rockefeller became the richest man in the world.

Literally hundreds of inventions were patented from the 1860s through the early 1900s for improvements in lamps to burn kerosene. Even so, there was fear of kerosene lamps and the new fuel.

Kerosene lamps were considered dangerous because fires and explosions were blamed on oil lamps. Charles Marvin published *The Moloch of Paraffin* in London in 1887 extolling the dangers (Moloch is a deity to which parents would offer their children as burnt offerings). Marvin (1887) presented the dangers of lamps illustrating his points from the Great Chicago Fire and the Duplex burner, and advocating a law to suppress dangerous lamps.

Kerosene for home lighting was the largest product of petroleum distillation through 1910.

Morse (1914) listed the causes of explosions to be these: upsetting a burning lamp, filling a burning lamp (this is why many old lamps do not have oil fills), low flash point of kerosene, and blowing out a lamp in full flame.

The *American Messenger* reported 5,250 people killed and nearly 20,000 maimed by explosions and fires caused by lamps burning illuminating oils in 1872, one year after the Chicago fire.

The German student lamp, with its oil reservoir separated from the burner, was touted as a safe lamp. Likewise, burners with extinguisher mechanisms were considered safe. Ordinary lamps were declared unsafe to turn low and burn for night light. Consequently, small size lamps (miniatures) became popular after dark. Smaller lamps and burners were more economical to use as well.

The unsafe fuel problem was largely solved with improved distillation (and thermal cracking) and raising the flash point. Early kerosene that contained naphtha fractions was dangerous. A simple procedure for the home owner to test the flash point of kerosene was described in *Household Discoveries* in 1914. Raising flash point standards to 110°F and higher made kerosene much safer to handle, store, and use. Fuel products today have flash points ranging from 145°F to 200°F.

Problems of safety were still evident when center-draft lamps became popular in America. The inadvertent filling of a lamp with gasoline, or a contaminated fuel, resulted in disaster. Mistakes, for sure, perhaps aided by consumer misunderstanding of the related fuels.

Gasoline gravity lamps and gasolene pressure lamps and lanterns were sold as competitors in the marketplace. The safety of brass lamps as "non-explosive" was promoted by several manufacturers.

The traveling Aladdin lamp salesman demonstrated the safety of kerosene by extinguishing a lighted match by quickly dipping it into kerosene.

A Test of Oil

The head of every family should at least make the following simple test of each parcel of oil that he buys. Pour a few drops into a saucer and apply a match; if the material burns it is unsafe. The following, however, is given by the *Petroleum Reporter* as a simple, but infallible test to ascertain exactly the quality and explosive point of any sample of kerosene oil — no matter by what fancy or attractive name it may be designated in specious advertisements: Take a common tin pan of water, or an ordinary tin pail, say seven inches in diameter and five inches deep; fill the vessel with water and place it on the stove or over a lamp, so as to heat very gradually; put an ordinary thermometer upright in the water, to indicate the gradual rise of temperature. Take a little pan such as is used to bake small patties, sold for a cent each. Into the patty pan put a tablespoonful of kerosene and let it float upon the surface of the gradually heating water. When you see the thermometer begin to indicate 70°, 75° or 80°, apply a blazing match to the kerosene in the little pan. If the oil is safe no flash will ensue, but if it is impure, and therefore dangerous, a flash like the ignition of gas will appear. In case a flash occurs while the thermometer indicates a temperature below 100° it is safe to assume that the oil is highly dangerous and utterly unfit for use.

Crockery & Glass Journal, Dec. 21, 1876

Manufacture and Testing Kerosene (Gruse & Stevens, 1942)

Consumption of all kerosene products was estimated at 6 billion gallons per year in the early 1940s. The predominant uses were for burning in tractors and for lighting plants, lamps, and stoves. Other uses included as solvents, deodorized carriers for cosmetics and pharmaceutical preparations, insecticides, and herbicides.

Crude oil of paraffinic types, low in sulfur, was preferred for making lamp oil. Such crude was found in Pennsylvania and Mid-Continent wells. Other crude such as found in California required additional refining to remove unstable compounds that produced odors and blooming of chimneys, or deposited ash in wicks and burners. Kerosene made from such crude usually discolored in storage.

Conventional tests for lamp oils looked at specific gravity, distillation range, sulfur content, color, and flash point.

Flash point tests measured volatile components likely to cause lamp explosions. Flash point is the temperature at which oil will flash when flame is passed over its surface. Raising the flash point, coupled with removal of impurities, significantly improved kerosene lamp oils.

The Flame Spreader

The flame spreader is a critically important part of most American kerosene center-draft lamps. Many patents for center-draft lamps involve improvements in design or function of this part, found in the very center of the burner. Some flame spreaders were designed to perform also as extinguishers. Flame spreaders represent a significant advancement that improved operation and function of oil lamps dating back many years.

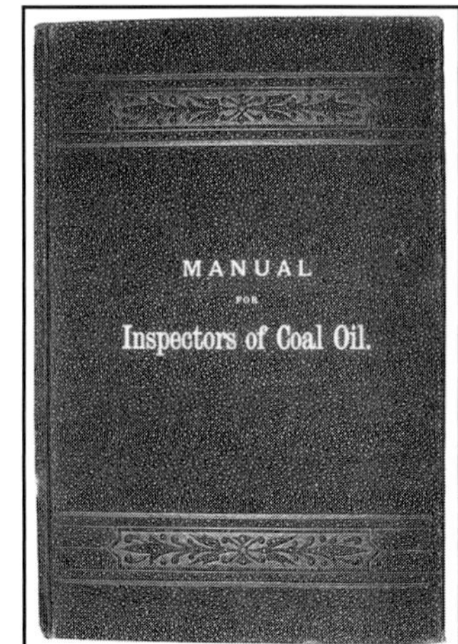

However, not all center-draft lamps were fitted with a flame spreader. Many of the early student

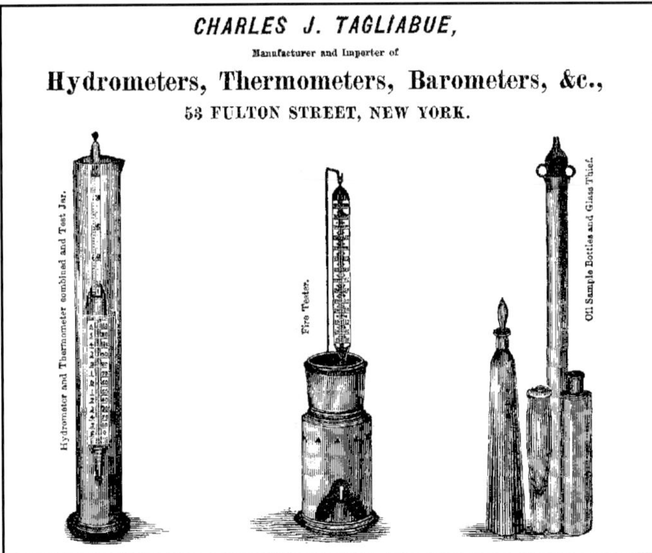

Charles J. Tagliabue, New York, sold testing equipment and the *Manual for Inspectors of Coal Oil.*

lamps burned a bright flame from a round wick without benefit of "air distribution" to the flame. The flame spreader is essential for proper combustion of lamps with large center-draft burners (Baumann and Wolfe, 1994 – 1996).

Flame spreaders are found in sizes ranging from small ones that fit in night lights to large ones found in kerosene heaters. Flame spreaders are generally not interchangeable among lamps, although some will fit another brand and cause improper lamp identification.

The Liverpool Button

The flame spreader called a "Liverpool Button" dates to the early 1800s. This button, installed in the center of the draft tube, forced the flame to spread out and around the disc of the button. The result was a larger and brighter flame.

Russell (1958) credits Edwin E. Cassell as the inventor of the Liverpool Button in 1838, British Patent No. 7908. Cuffley (1982) cites early lamps using the principle of the Liverpool Button as Young's Spirit Lamp, 1843; Robert's Lamp, 1845; and King's Lamp, 1859. James Young's Vesta Lamp used a Liverpool Button in 1840. Edwin B. Horn illustrated a button or cone flame spreader in his patent of 1842.

Calvin (1983), however, reported that the Liverpool Button was well known and widely used in America by 1832, and in England at least since 1811.

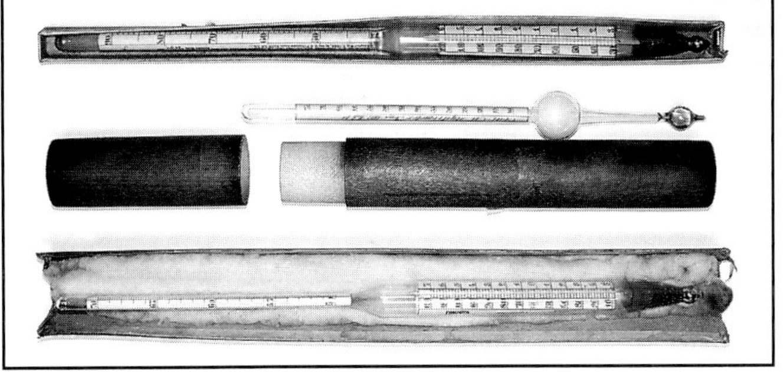

Tagliabue Coal Oil Hydrometers found today have little use other than to remind collectors of the past.

OILS.

Kerosene Oils.

We do not sell less than a barrel of kerosene oil, except our Perfect Oil, AA 4431. No charge for barrels. Barrels contain about 52 gals.

All oil is shipped at purchaser's risk. In all cases when inspection of oils is necessary by state inspector, the charges for inspection must be paid by party purchasing the oil.

The only oil suitable for use in incubators is our Perfect Oil, which is a double refined oil; other grades will not work satisfactorily.

We make the lowest wholesale price the day your order is received.

Per gal.

AA 4425—M. W. & Co.'s White Swan Brand, 150 degrees test. A fine white oil.. $0.13

AA 4427—Legal test Prime White, 150 degrees test.............................. .11

AA 4429—Legal test Water White, 150 degrees test.............................. .11

AA 4431—M. W. & Co.'s Perfect Kerosene 150 degrees, absolutely the best carbon oil at any price. Doubly refined and fully guaranteed.................... .16¼

AA 4433—M. W. & Co.'s Perfect Oil, in cases containing two 5-gal. cans put up in this style for shipment to distant points; the case is very substantial. Per case, $2.55.

AA 4434—M. W. & Co.'s Perfect Oil, 10 gals. in jacket can, per can, $2.10; 5 gals., in jacket can, $1.10.

AA 4438—Gasoline, 88 degrees. To be used for the manufacture of illuminating gas in gas machine, barrels only.... .20

AA 4440—Stove Gasoline, deodorized, barrels only................................ .16

AA 4442—Penn 76 Gasoline for gas engines and automobiles, barrels only.... 16½

AA 4445—Naphtha, or Benzine, 63 degrees, barrels only........................ .13

Montgomery Ward & Co., Chicago, catalog 74, 1905 – 1906.

The Belgian, Success, and Liberty lamps used button flame spreaders well into the twentieth century.

Terminology for Flame Spreaders

The common terms found in patents and adopted by collectors are *flame spreader* and *air distributor.* The terms are descriptive and imply important functions to improve combustion. Air distributors do more than simply deflect the flow of air through the center draft tube — they are constructed in such a way as to actually distribute tiny jets of air to improve burning the fuel.

Other terms for flame spreaders include *perforated thimble, air deflector, spreading device, cap* or *perforated cap, sun disc, air conductor, cone* or *over-cone, air distributing cap, flame minder, generator* (a term mostly used for vapor and gasoline pressure lamps), and *flame thrower,* a term found today in eBay auction descriptions.

X-RAY BURNING OIL.

We do not make a business of selling burning oil, but if some of our customers want it, we will furnish them with a bright 150° Water White Pennsylvania Oil, 49° gravity. Guaranteed not to smoke or char the wick and not to give out the disagreeable odor so common to most of burning oils. This oil, while it retails for a few cents more than the ordinary grades, is nevertheless much more economical in actual use, as one lamp filled with it will give as much illumination as two similar lamps will give, filled with the cheap article. Besides, the light is whiter and softer, and does not injure the eyes. The wick never becomes clogged, and the lamp remains clean and free from gum or grease. A lamp filled with the ordinary oil will frequently go out when only half empty. Every drop of this oil will be consumed without affecting the quality of the light. To those wanting a high grade perfect illuminant, we especially recommend this oil.

The Commercial Oil Co., Cleveland, Ohio, early 1900s, undated.

Flame spreaders may involve design patents for form rather than function. Flame spreaders may also involve more than a single function, such as combination of air distribution plus an extinguishing safety feature.

Researching Flame Spreaders

The following tips may help you find the identity of a flame spreader or seek the proper one for an unknown lamp:

- Search patent numbers marked on them.
- Search data bases, such as the Lamp Guild website (www.lampguild.org), using descriptive terms listed previously.
- Compare shapes of flame spreaders.
- Search and identify trademarks found on them.
- Study illustrations in this book and in *The Lamp Collector's Guide* (Graff, 2004).

Identifying Your Lamp

Flame spreaders of center-draft lamps were often marked with names, patent dates or company logos that identified the lamp for which they were made. As a result flame spreaders have been removed and collected over the years as center-draft lamps have been electrified (electrocuted, say some purists).

Some lamps are unmarked, and identification as to manufacturer is unknown. The flame spreader found in the lamp may, or may not, be helpful. Be aware that some flame spreaders will fit into different lamps and may be branded for a specific lamp and only appear correct when misplaced.

The Rochester Thimble

Leonard Henkle's patent granted in 1884 introduced the perforated thimble flame spreader for improvement of the large center-draft burner. Charles S. Upton obtained rights to Henkle's work and further obtained patents for his own improvements. Upton, however, was not a manufacturer but instead a keen marketer.

Thanks to Charles Upton, the Rochester lamp became one of the first major brands of center-draft lamps to become known world-wide. Rochester lamps were widely marketed: they were affordable, offered fancy workmanship, and gave dependable light. The 1891/1892 catalog of the Rochester Lamp Company states, "The number of Rochester Lamps now sold is over half a million a year; many of them most artistic, and some single ones costing $1,000."

In the United States, the name Rochester became synonymous with any brasscenter-draft lamp for many years, just as "Aladdin" and "Rayo" are commonly used to describe many brass oil lamps today.

Along with the Rochester Lamp Company, Edward Miller & Co., Plume & Atwood, and Bradley & Hubbard (which made the Rayo) dominated the national market, judging by their extensive advertising and the numbers of lamps extant. Many other companies produced lamps for national and regional markets — such as Bristol Brass and Clock Co.; Clark Bros.; Holmes, Booth & Haydens; Manhattan Brass; Parker; and Pittsburgh Lamp & Brass, to name a few. These companies developed their own competing brands, each proclaiming unique or superior qualities. Many of these companies were already well established in kerosene lighting when Rochester center-draft lamps came into the market.

The Aladdin mantle lamp is often attributed to the 1880 – 1890s; however, it was not produced until 1908.

Companies competed with bold statements to convince consumers their product was best — the "largest lamp store in the world," the "best lamp in America," or the "safest lamp for your home" were some examples. The claims make interesting reading as we contemplate the importance of the people, patents, and companies during this brief history of lighting.

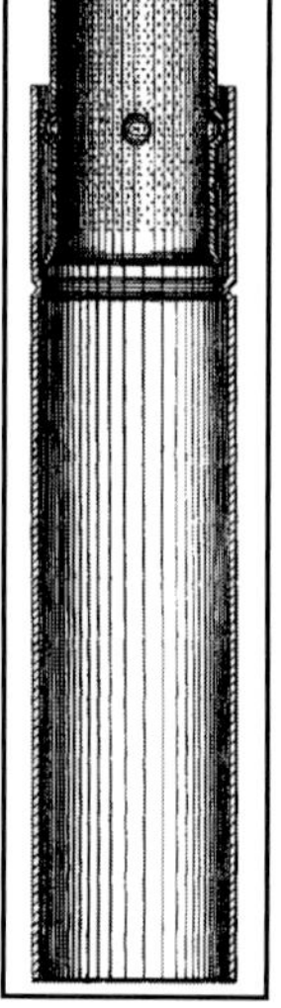

Leonard Henkle's Lamp Patent 365,996 clearly illustrated the wick tube for central draft and the thimble flame spreader.

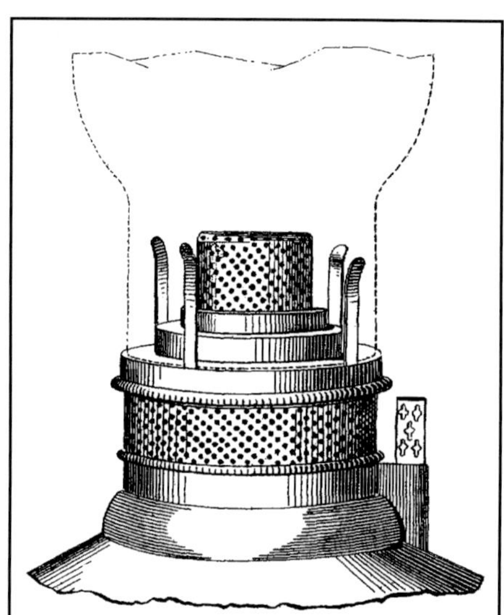

Leonard Henkle's Lamp Burner, Patent D17,090. This burner design became the standard form for many companies.

Claim.—1. In a burner for Argand lamps, a wick-tube provided at its upper end with a thimble, forming, with the wick-tube, a passage for the inner upward-moving current of air, said thimble being vertically adjustable in the wick-tube and made conical at its upper end, with perforations through its straight and conical parts, so that some of the jets of air flowing outward through the perforations shall impinge horizontally and others obliquely against the inner surface of the flame, substantially as set forth.

2. In a burner for Argand lamps, the inner wick-tube provided internally at its upper end with a circular part or thimble, forming, with said wick-tube, a passage for the central upward-moving air for the flame, said thimble being reduced in diameter at its upper end, or made conical thereat, and perforated in such a manner that some of the jets of air flowing outward through the perforations move horizontally and others obliquely against the flame, substantially as set forth.

3. In a burner for Argand lamps, a wick-tube provided at its upper end with an internal thimble, forming, with said wick-tube, a passage for the inner upward-moving current of air for the flame, said thimble being perforated to turn the air in jets against the flame and made adjustable within the tube, substantially as described.

Text of Leonard Henkle's Lamp Patent 292,114 as it appeared in the *Official Gazette*. This patent, filed June 16, 1883, was granted on Jan. 15, 1884.

Panic of 1893

The 1880s was a time of major economic growth in America. Railroads expanded rapidly across the country, and manufacturing brought new products to market. Farmers produced record crops but suffered low prices. Companies and farmers increased their debt.

The 1890s became difficult times for American business. Commodity prices declined at the rate of 3.6 percent per year from 1880 to 1896. The failure of the Reading Railroad was a major blow, followed by the failure of other railroads. Labor unions and cheap imported goods complicated the picture for businessmen.

The financial panic of 1893 has been written into the history books of every sector in America.

Gold and silver coins circulated as money, and the United States dollar was worldwide currency because it was backed by gold. Treasury notes could be exchanged for gold or silver; however, silver prices were unstable and declining. The Sherman Silver Purchase Act of 1890 obligated the government to pay out gold in exchange for newly mined silver, which was pegged at artificial prices.

Gold was the monetary choice of exchange of European investors who cashed in American investments.

To avoid depletion of the nation's gold reserve, the Treasury redeemed currency with silver instead of gold — to the dismay of many investors. At the same time, spending by the "Billion Dollar Congress" of 1889 to 1891 further decreased confidence and public trust. The stock market plunged. More than 15,000 businesses and 500 banks failed when farmers and businesses could not pay their mortgages. Widespread unemployment resulted.

The worldwide panic of 1893 ended the prosperous "Gilded Age" (1878 to 1889) when great fortunes were amassed. Many businesses and farms were adversely affected until 1896 or 1897.

Many manufacturers in this book struggled as they developed center-draft lamps during the 1890s. Those with strong leadership and innovative new products competed best. Even so, not all of them survived.

Lamp Men Dine — 1890

A most enjoyable dinner was partaken of at Delmonico's on Friday evening last by the American Lamp Burner Association. The following firms and manufacturing companies were represented: Holmes, Booth & Haydens, by C. N. Wayland, Thos. B. Kent, and Thos. L. Scovill; Edwin [sic] Miller & Co., by Chas. Holbrook and C. A. Ashmead; Plume & Atwood Mfg. Co., by D. S. Plume, R. H. Swayze and Mortimer McRoberts; The Rochester Lamp Co., by Chas. S. Upton and J. H. Brigham; Bristol Brass & Clock Co., by George S. Brown and Oliver S. Brown; Bradley & Hubbard Mfg. Co., by Frank W. Goodwin; Benedict & Burnham Mfg. Co., by E. L. Frisbie, Arthur Dickinson, W. A. Hungerford; Manhattan Brass Co., by J. H. Crane and H. S. White; Ansonia Brass & Copper Co., by George W. Woodward; Wallace & Sons, by Thos. Wallace; and the Bridgeport Brass Co., by Chas. A. Hamilton and Charles X. Cordier.

The banquet was held in the large dining parlors up stairs. An orchestra enlivened the occasion by pleasant music, and the viands and service were such as only Delmonico can furnish. When the cigars were passed around, Mr. D. S. Plume, the chairman, arose and made a few remarks pertinent to the occasion. He alluded to his many years' connection with the trade, to the old faces which he now missed, and which had been so familiar on such occasions, and congratulated the younger members of the trade who were coming to the front. Mr. Plume closed by inviting W. A. Hungerford to act as toast master.

Mr. Hungerford, in a happy vein called upon different members of the association and their guests to enlighten the company on various subjects connected with the trade.

Responses were made by most of the company. Mr. C. A. Hollbrook alluded to the satisfactory condition of trade, and referred in commendatory terms to the finer quality of goods of the present day compared with former times; Mr. Thos. B. Kent, Mr. R. H. Swayze, Mr. J. H. Brigham and Mr. J. H. Crane all followed with brief and appropriate speeches; while Mr. Mortimer McRoberts told a story as to his experience in [the] booming horse-car railroad [sic], which was relished with gusto; and Mr. C. N. Wayland enlarged upon the ancient and historical status of the central draft lamp, which in view of the many intricate claims of priority brought down the house. Mr. C. S. Upton expressed his gratification at meeting so many good fellows in the trade, and referred feelingly to the absent ones, and proposed the health of the American Jobber. Mr. Thos. Wallace alluded with much feeling to the few old members present, and to his hearty co-operation in the cordial feeling existing among the different representatives of the great houses engaged in the trade; while Mr. E. L. Frisbie spoke with much earnestness on the condition of the burner business, the great advance in the goods placed on the market, etc.; and Mr. G. S. Brown referred in a witty manner to his entrance into the charmed circle which surrounded him. Messrs. Frank Goodwin, C. A. Hamilton, and others, also made short and appropriate speeches.

The American Lamp Burner Association is composed of the leading manufacturers in that line. D. S. Plume is president of the Association, and W. A. Hungerford secretary. The Central Draft Lamp Association is made up of the largest lamp manufacturers in America. C. F. Lindsey is president, Thos. B. Kent vice-president, and Frank W. Goodwin secretary.

Such social gatherings as the above can but be productive of a good feeling among the representatives of rival houses in the trade.

Crockery and Glass Journal, Nov. 20, 1890

Kerosene Center-draft Lamps, 1870 – 1880s

Kerosene became widely available and lamp manufacturers worked to improve safety and light output of burners and lamps. Flat-wick burners were increased in size and number of wicks. Many Solar lamps in popular use (not included here) were converted to burn kerosene. Round wicks fitted to small draft tubes were adapted to glass founts as "improvements" over lamps in popular use.

The center-draft wick tubes and wicks were increased in size during the mid-1880s. Those lamps required a flame spreader — the heart of this book. Folded wick burners replaced flat wick lamps during this time.

German student lamps were imported because of their perceived safety when burning kerosene and producing more light. The large elegant student lamps are highly valued by collectors today.

Kerosene lamps replaced many lamps that burned lard oil in lighthouses where light beacons were critical.

The German Student Lamp

The student lamp, burning by center-draft principle, was popular for several decades. Student lamps appeared in the 1860s and were widely sold in America during the 1870s through the 1890s. These lamps were also called study lamps, reading lamps, library lamps, and office lamps.

Popularity was due to direct lighting of the tabletop or work surface, adjustable height, sturdy brass construction, and concept of safety with the fuel reservoir separated from the burner and flame. In addition, most student lamps have a removable fuel tank for easy filling.

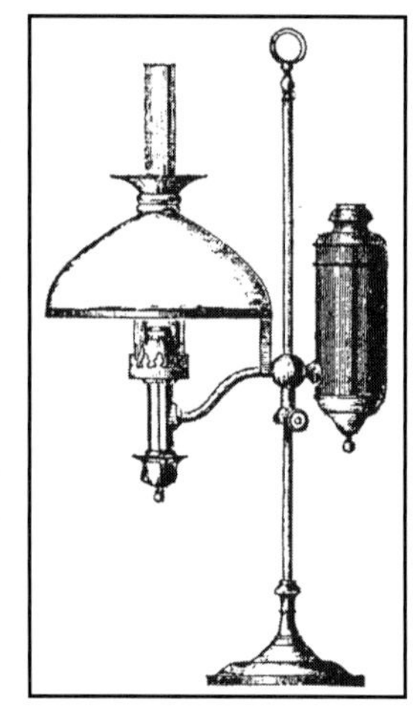

Most, but not all, student lamps supply continuous flow of fuel to the wick at a constant level by the Cardan principle (see Thuro 1987 and 2001 and Baumann and Wolfe, 1994, for more information and illustration).

Baumann and Wolfe (1994, 1996) document and illustrate the development of student lamps in four excellent articles, pointing out that European student lamps, with their burner construction, were immediately adaptable to burn the new kerosene fuels in the 1860s.

Several companies claimed to be sole importers or agents for German study lamps as they attempted to capture the market in the U.S.A. These included Douglas, Hinrichs, and Schneider, all of New York City. Companies such as Bradley and Hubbard sold Kleemann student lamps, while Miller and other companies developed their own models and styles.

Charles F. A. Hinrichs, New York City, recognized market potential and imported German Kleemann student lamps for many years. Hinrichs imported colorful nouveau art glass and table glassware in the 1870s. He called his building at 29 – 33 Park Place the "Palace of Art."

Hinrichs was awarded and assigned patents for Kleemann student lamps. Hinrichs & Co. trademarked "KLEEMANN" in 1894, stating that the word was used for lamps since 1871. Hinrichs & Co. trademarked "The German-American" and "C. A. Kleemann" in 1894, stating their use for lamps since 1893.

Bennett B. Schneider, also of New York City, sold "The Improved German Study Lamp (Kleemann's Patent) — The Perfection of Safety Lamps!" Schneider was successor to Richard Douglas & Co. (*CGJ*, Apr. 19, 1883). Schneider also was awarded and assigned patents for improvement in student lamps, including a design for a metal center-draft tube inside a glass fount (Pat. 379,610, 1888). W. R. Noe bought Schneider's business upon his retirement in 1894.

Scovill and Manhattan Brass Company may have manufactured the "Improved German Student Lamps" for one or more of the above agents. (I wonder if there was a connection between Schneider and Manhattan Brass?)

The Cleveland Non-Explosive Lamp Company sold House's Patent Library (student) Lamp in the 1870s. Manhattan Brass Company was one of the dominant American manufacturers of student lamps with its Perfection brand. Many other companies in this book made student lamps, and I make no claim to include all of them.

Read Baumann and Wolfe (1994, 1996), who review historical development of the student lamp over 200 years, noting that many predate center-draft student lamps that burn kerosene. Baumann (2006) has pointed out that large bore (diameter) center-draft lamps burning kerosene were not introduced until the 1880s, and then with flame spreaders.

The Celebrated C. A. Kleemann's St. Germain German Student Lamps

Best, safest, handsomest, most economical, no odor, no smoke, pure, brilliant, unwavering light, very agreeable to the eye. None genuine without my name on chimney holder. This lamp is all metal and easily managed.

This cut represents the original and only Genuine St. Germain or German Student Lamp, invented by Mr. C. A. Kleemann, in Erfurt, Germany, patented in 1863, and still the manufacturer, although I have acquired the ownership of patent.

Imitations in shape, also in the well-known name of the German Student Lamp have been again and again put in the market, but without success, although people may have often been misled through such misrepresentation.

The German Student Lamp received the prize medal at the American Institute Exhibition, October 1867, the diploma of the Pennsylvania State Fair, in 1868, and the testimonials for its excellence and superiority in regard to perfect safety and brilliant light from the most prominent business, scientific and literary men throughout the country. The acknowledged merits of the German Student Lamp have caused a steadily increasing demand since its first appearance.

Besides the standard pattern in brass as well as nickel plated, I also have lamps with two burners or double lamps; also brackets or side lamps, and all with the German Student patent burners.

The improvement of the lamp for chandeliers has given an increased popularity in another field. The German Student Lamp attached to one of my various extension fixtures, which may be lowered and raised to any desired height, makes it the handsomest and cheapest chandelier that has ever been offered for sale.

Kerosene at the present price makes the cost of burning less than half a cent per hour. It gives more satisfactory light than gas, in fact it is the only pure, brilliant and unwavering light agreeable to the eye, giving no odor nor smoke.

These lamps are safe against explosion, since the vapor of the Petroleum is entirely cut off from the flame, the reservoir being at a distance from the burning point, and the supply tube constantly filled with the liquid.

The German Student Lamp burner has also been adapted to the burning of lard oil; and lamps for Postal and Railway cars, as well as binnacle lamps for steamers, ships, or yachts, are now manufactured by me, and already extensively in use, and giving the greatest satisfaction.

C. F. A. Hinrichs, 30, 31 and 33 Park Place, New York.

CGJ, Dec. 7, 1876

Miller and Solverson (1992) illustrate and identify many companies and varieties of student lamps in *Student Lamps of the Victorian Era*.

Trade Names

The following trade names for German student lamps are found in the literature: Empress, Erfurt, Franklin, German-American, Improved Kaiser, Isabella, Kaiser, Kleemann, and Saint Germain.

Selected Patents, German Student Lamps

Carl A. Kleemann

1863 37,867
1868 .... RE3068 (Kleemann 37,867)
1870 .... RE3900 (Kleemann, 1863 – 1837,867)

R. S. Merrill

1870 ..104,481, assigned self, Wm. B. Merrill, Joshua Merrill
1870 .... D4089

C. F. A. Hinrichs

1870 110,464
1872 134,281
1873 .... RE5708, (reissue of RE3900)
1874 157,330
1876 182,825
1877 198,300
1879 214,134
1881 .... 247,580, with Charles Reistle
1881 .... 247,824, with Charles Reistle

Albert Angell[1] assigned to C.F.A. Hinrichs

1883 270,719

Bennett B. Schneider

1870 102,163
1875 167,128
1875 167,792

J. Horton assigned to Schneider

1869 98,264
1874 .... RE6094

J. W. Carter assigned to Schneider

1875 170,522
1875 170,523

Wilhelm Dette assigned to Schneider

1877 198,085

1883 290,001
Adolph Kleemann assigned to Hinrichs & Co.
1889 405,740

[1]Also patents on mineral wicks and burner.

The Improved German Study Lamp,

[KLEEMANN'S PATENT.]

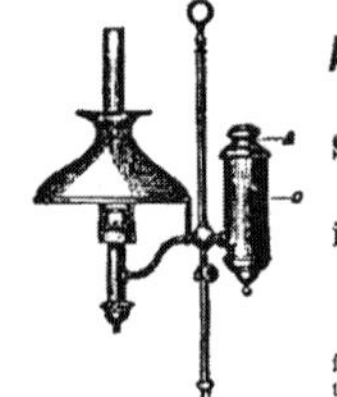

ALL DANGER OF ACCIDENTS REMOVED.

Can be Filled at any time Without Spilling the Oil.

The Capacity of the Oil Reservoir is Increased One-third.

The Perfection of Safety Lamps!

Has been Thoroughly Tested, and has given Universal Satisfaction. These Lamps are also arranged with Patent Drip Cup to attach to Chandeliers or Brackets, and can be Lighted and Extinguished without handling the Shade or Chimney.

Richard Douglas & Co.
Sole Agents,
97 CHAMBERS STREET,
NEW YORK.

Advertisement in *Crockery & Glass Journal,* Aug. 3, 1876.

Latest Improvement in Kleemann's Student Lamps!

"ISABELLA" STUDENT LAMP.

PATENTED JANUARY 16, 1883.

To Light the Lamp without removing Shade or Chimney.

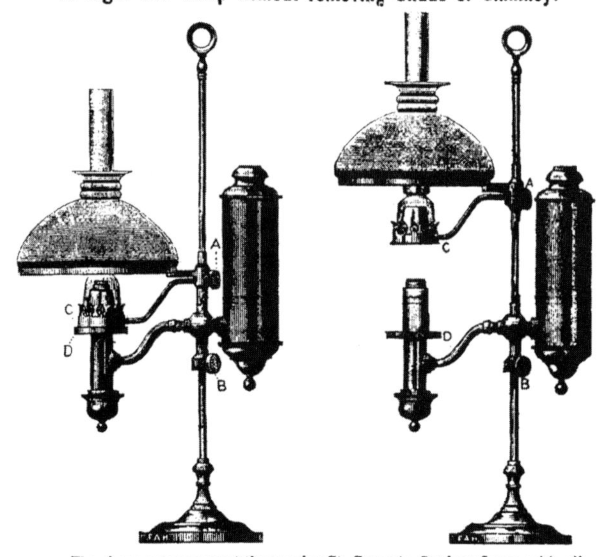

The above cuts represent the regular St. Germain Student Lamp with all improvements, including the new patent attachment for lighting the lamp without removing the shade or chimney.

I guarantee these lamps, which are made of highly polished brass or nickel-plated, will give perfect satisfaction in every respect as heretofore. *My Non-Combustible Wick can be used in these lamps.*

C. F. A. HINRICHS,

Manufacturer and Patentee, **31 Park Place, N. Y.**

Advertisement in *Crockery and Glass Journal,* March 29, 1883.

Perfection Study Lamps.

Recommended by the U. S. Government, who have over 10,000 in use in their various offices.

	Each.
Perfection Standard complete nickle plated [see cut]	**$ 3 25**
Perfection double, two burners, nickle plated complete	**7 00**

Warranted not to leak or get out of order.

Advertisement in *The American Potter and Illuminator,* 1885. Perfection Student Lamps were made by the Manhattan Brass Company.

German Student Lamp.

Adapted for Round or Square Burners.

We beg leave to call the attention of the Trade to the celebrated **ST. GERMAIN LAMP**, which we are now manufacturing, and of which we keep a stock constantly on hand, and from our long experience in the manufacture of these Lamps in Europe, we feel justified in saying that we will furnish a Lamp, that for Durability, Elegance and Safety, has not its superior.

J. G. Knapp M'f'g Co.,

Nos. 26, 28 & 30 Frankfort Street, NEW YORK.

☞ For Sale by all Dealers in Lamps and Glassware.

Send for Price List.

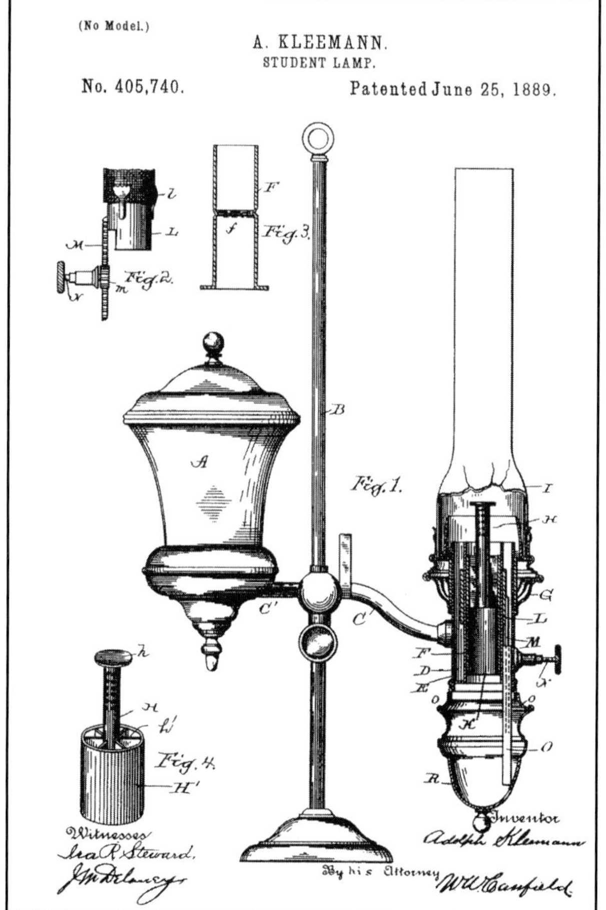

Glass Center-draft Lamps

Glass lamps and composite lamps made with glass founts on metal stands were the predominant stand lamps made for home use during the 1870s and 1880s. Multitudes of cast figures were popular during this time.

Various methods of installing a tube inside a glass fount for a center-draft burner were invented. Some tubes were glass, others metal.

Rufus Spaulding Merrill, of Hyde Park, New York, was an early and prolific inventor of center-draft lamps, including a student lamp (Patents 104,481 and 111,072).

The Merrill, Hoyt, Combs, and Leighton lamps were among the earliest glass, round-wick center-draft lamps. They are well endowed with patents; however, they were overlooked in *Early Lighting, A Pictorial Guide* by the Rushlight Club (1972). The round wick was formed by folding flat wicks into round form. All have small-diameter draft tubes. Note that Combs also made brass center-draft lamps.

John M. Perkins and Mark W. House, of Cleveland, Ohio, obtained patent 60,416 in 1866. Their lamp provided air passage between the burning chamber and the fuel reservoir to supply air for the burner, with the purpose to keep the fuel cool. This is a flat-wick lamp but certainly center-draft in concept. The Cleveland lamps were sold as metal non-explosive lamps. The patent, however, does not specify whether the "reservoir for holding oil" be made of glass or metal. I suspect that omission was intentional.

Other companies that later made or sold glass center-draft stand or fount lamps include:

George F. Bassett & Co.	Nail City Stamping Co.
Downer Kerosene Oil Co.	Plume & Atwood
Edward Miller & Co.	Rochester Lamp Co.
W. J. Gordon	Wallace & Sons

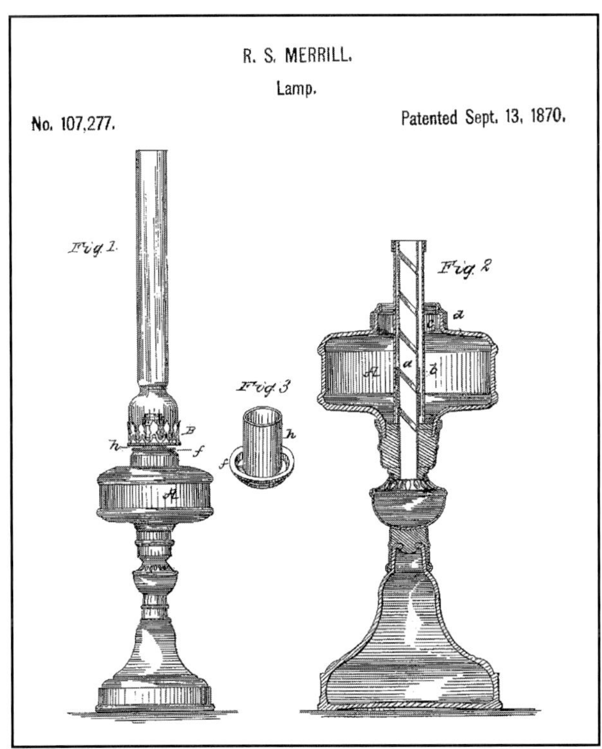

Selected Patents, Glass Center-draft Lamps

Andrew B. Howland

1869 94,961

Hezekiah M. Clark

1870 101,584

Rufus Spaulding Merrill

1870 .... 100,653 assigned self, Wm. B.

Merrill, Joshua Merrill

1870 104,623
1870 107,277
1870 111,074

Jonathan J. Hoyt

1871 w/ J. E. Crane 112,598 assigned J.J. Hoyt & Lowell Oil Cup Co.
1872 129,828
1875 ...... 164,374 assigned Standard Lamp & Glass Pipe Co.

Abel Combs

1872 126,025
1874 150,939
1885 324,087

James E. Leighton

1873 138,509

William Boekel

1878 202,693

Frank Rhind

1886 .... 342,463 assigned self & Charles Upton

George S. Schuchman

1887 361,723

Bennett B. Schneider

1888 379,610

Lewis J. Atwood

1888 .... 386,953 assigned P & A
1888 .... 388,105 assigned P & A

Archibald W. Paull

1889 409,863

William A. Young and Asa G. Neville

1892 .... 484,277 mfg. process

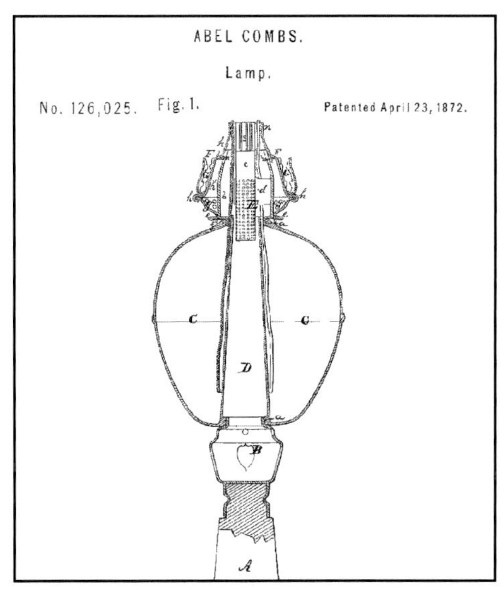

Combs Lamp

Combs lamps were most likely made by Benedict & Burnham Mfg. Co. This company was a leader in the manufacture of brass burners. (I wonder if the company made other center-draft lamps unknown to us at this time?)

The bottom of the brass fitting that supports the fount is marked "Patented April 23, 1872, B & B Mfg. Co." The unique oil fill is marked "Pat. Feb. 3, 1874," for W. N. Weeden's patent 147,211 assigned to Benedict & Burnham.

The burner is marked "Combs B & B Co." The wick adjusts by turning the burner. The burner has fine threads.

Combs lamps with brass founts have been seen.

Combs stand lamp. $1,200.00.
Courtesy Gale Zelnick.

Hoyt Lamp

Most Hoyt lamps have clear glass founts, although white opal glass founts are known. The founts are dated inside with patent dates, e.g., "Pat'd March 14, 1871, July 23, 1872." The same dates are sometimes embossed in the brass connectors fitting above the air intake holes.

The Hoyt burners, made specifically for Hoyt lamps, are often missing.

Hoyt lamps are usually stand lamps, but have been found mounted in hanging fixtures and in other configurations.

Hoyt stand lamp. $1,000.00.
Courtesy Catherine Thuro.

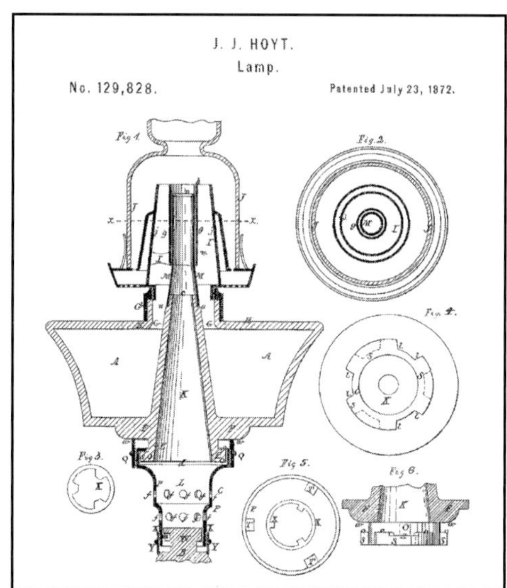

Combs lamp fount.
Courtesy M. J. Howell.

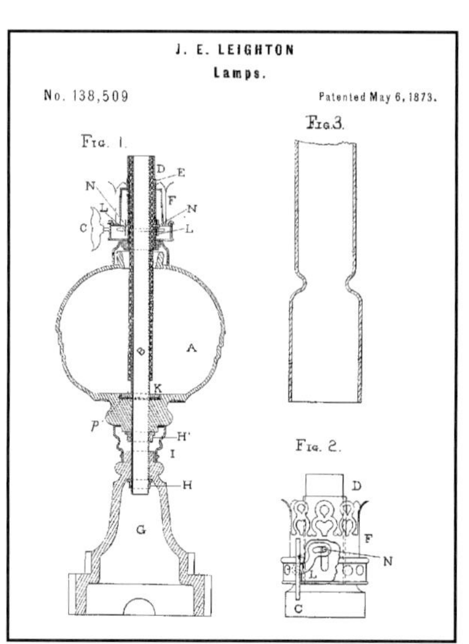

Lighthouse Lamps

Lamps that provided the beacon of light for lighthouses ranged from very large and sophisticated machines to small lamps that collectors today associate with oil lamps of the time period. I believe most "lighthouse lamps" were made by the Light House Service; exceptions were Belgian and Aladdin lamps.

Lamps employing Argand's center-draft principle have been used in lighthouses since the early 1800s. Lighthouse lamps developed by Captain Winslow Lewis (1812 – 1840) burned whale oil in Argand-style lamps.

Early lighthouse lamps burned sperm oil, colza oil, and lard oil; later ones used acetylene or kerosene. Lard oil was primarily burned in the large First Order lamps and kerosene in the smaller lamps.

In the 1870s lighthouse lamps were devised with three, four, or more concentric wicks to increase illumination. Henry Harrison Doty, of Norfolk, Virginia, and Joseph Funck, of Tomkinsville, New York, held several patents for multiple-wick burners. Funck later improved lamps that became standard in Fourth Order lighthouses. Read Tag (2002) for excellent review, history, and illustrations of lighthouse illumination, from coal brazier to the electric bulb.

Kerosene was the universal oil used in lighthouses by 1892. *Scientific American* (1892) reported that virtually all lighthouses used kerosene illuminating oil at this time. Kerosene oil was required to be "140° flash test, 154° fire test, free from acid, and, burnt in an Argand burner of the Funck-Heap style, light must show 18 candles illuminating power on a consumption of 10/16 of a gill per hour." The Funck-Heap lamp, rated 50 CP, was said to have a "flame so white and intense that it is almost painful to look at." Major D. P. Heap was an engineer in charge of the Third District Lighthouse Department and helped write the *Scientific American* article.

The period from 1850 to 1939 has been described as the "Golden Age of American Lighthouses." No ship was to be without sight of a lighthouse along America's coasts. Lighthouses provided a warning beacon by light, and many were equipped with steam-powered foghorns. Some 331 lighthouses (and 42 lightships) were in operation by 1852.

Lighthouses were often built in isolated and remote locations to provide their beacons. Lighthouse families lived in or near the lighthouses, and some lighthouses were operated by women after the deaths of their husbands. Today, there are an estimated 400 active lighthouses, many using automatic electric rotating beacons, administered by the U. S. Coast Guard. Some are still equiped with their original Fresnel lenses.

The Fresnel lens was invented in 1822 by Frenchman Augustin Fresnel. His lens became the standard means by which light rays were focused to increase intensity and then be transmitted out to sea. Fresnel lenses were made in six Orders (sizes) for lighthouse illumination — each Order of different size and intensity. First Order was the largest and most powerful, for coastal lighthouses, which transmitted their light beam the greatest distance out to sea, up to 20 miles or more. Fourth, Fifth, and Sixth Orders marked prominent headlands, points and shoals in large bays, and warned of obstructions, piers, and wharves.

Likewise, lamps were designated as sizes third, fourth, fifth Order, etc. Virtually all lighthouse lamps were custom made. The smaller center-draft lamps were dependable, practical, and produced bright light. Mantle lamps, such as the Aladdin kerosene lamps, were used in some lighthouses. Although conversion to electricity began in 1900, many lighthouses used kerosene lamps until the late 1940s.

Left to Right: Fourth, Fifth and Sixth Order Lighthouse lamps reprinted from *Instructions to Light-Keepers and Masters of Light-House Vessels by Authority of the Light-House Board.* Government Printing Office. 1902. Courtesy of the Great Lakes Lighthouse Keepers Association.

The electric-arc lamp was very powerful but proved unsatisfactory in fog. The electric incandescent bulb was used in special applications such as channel buoys. A major problem was the source of electricity in remote locations.

Selected Patents, Lighthouse Lamps

H. H. Doty[1]

1870	109,303
1876	RE 7165
1877	RE 7867

Joseph Funck[2]

1876	177,825
1876	184,855
1882	266,457

John R. Wigham[3] multiple wicks

1888	387,939

Charles M. Lungren[4]

1895	532,077

[1]Also patents for single-cone, triple-wick burners and railroad signal lamp.

[2]The Funck First Order Lamp (circa 1870 – 1890) burned lard oil and had four concentric wicks producing 400 candlepower. Also patents for student lamp, and "shadowless" table lamp.

[3]Dublin, Ireland.

[4]Also patents for gas mantle lamps.

There are many books about lighthouses — an excellent source of books is Kenrick A. Claflin & Son, 1227 Pleasant St., Worcester, MA 01602. Numerous groups and societies preserve the history and heritage of America's lighthouses. Nonprofit associations include the Great Lakes Lighthouse Keepers Assoc., P.O. Box 219, Mackinaw City, MI 49701; Michigan Lighthouse Conservancy (www.michiganlights.com), P.O. Box 973, Fenton, MI 48430, and the American Lighthouse Foundation (wwwlighthousefoundation.org), P.O. Box 889, Wells, ME 04090.

Funck-Heap Fourth Order lighthouse lamp. The tag is marked "4th Order." $250.00. Courtesy Paul Rausch.

Lanterns

Beginning in 1898, the U.S. Lighthouse Service issued kerosene tubular lanterns to all lighthouses. The Blizzard lanterns were issued as a set of No. 1 (⅝" wick) and No. 2 (⅞" wick), made by Dietz.

Lighthouse table lamp used in the living quarters. The lamp burner is made of heavy brass machined or cast construction. $175.00. Courtesy Jack Washka.

Report of Lighthouse Board, 1888 and 1889

"Three hours after lighting, the Belgian exceeded in brilliancy the improved fourth order lighthouse lamp, and was the only commercial lamp which had yet done so; another great advantage was that its chimney remained clear, while that of improved fourth order became whitened by the heat...the chimney from its shape is easily cleaned."

Kind of Lamp	*Wick Diameter* (inches)	*Oil Temperature* (3 Hours after Lighting)	*Candle Power* (3 Hours after Lighting)
Niagara	1⅜"	102	28.93
Rochester	1⅞"	118	37.20
Belgian No. 1	1 1/16"	104	43.50
Waterbury Electric	1 5/16"	106	27.15
Imperial, large	1 7/16"	107	31.39
Imperial, small	1"	104	29.19
Royal Argand	1⅜"	93	20.82

Advertisement by the American Belgian Lamp Co., ***Crockery & Glass Journal,*** **Dec. 11, 1890.**

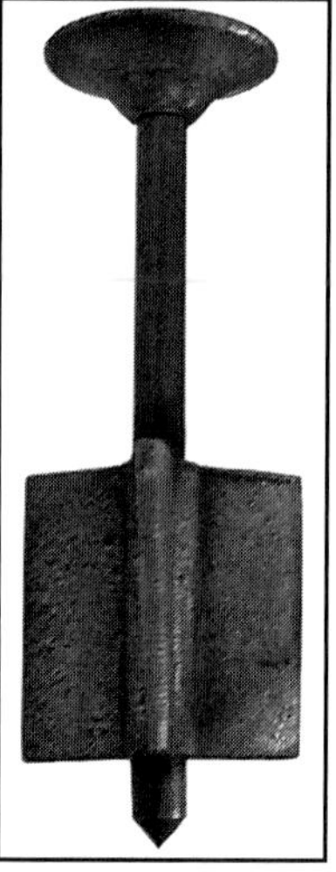

Burner and flame spreader for the lighthouse keeper's table lamp. The flame spreader is cast brass. Courtesy Fil Graff.

Lighting the Yaquina Head Light Station First Order Lighthouse Oregon Coast

Courtesy of George M. Collins (1999)

Lighthouse tower — 93 feet high, 162 feet above sea level.
Construction Engineer — Major Henry M. Robert, also known for *Robert's Rules of Order*. The lighthouse was first "exhibited" in 1873.
Fresnel lens — 7' 10" tall.
Lamps and fuel — see below. These are large lamps.
Light beam transmitted — about 18 nautical miles, 21 statute miles.

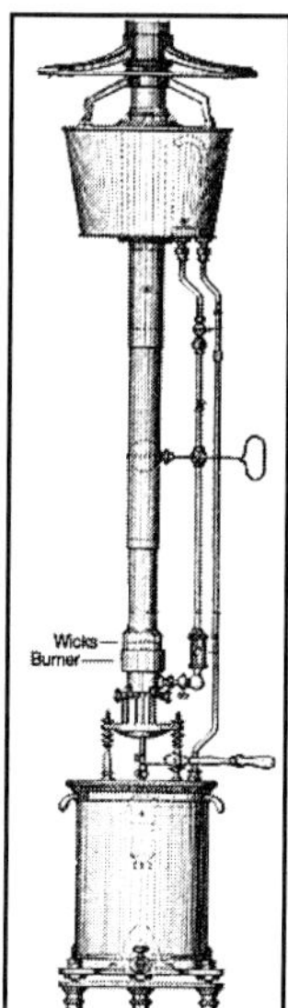

Fuel — lard oil, 1873 – 1887.

Lamp — Funck's First Order Hydraulic Float Lamp (constant level); four concentric wicks burned an average of two gallons per night.

Table stand lamp used in the lighthouse keeper's living quarters. The flame spreader is missing. The tripod is part of the burner, which differs from the Washka lamp. The lamp is marked "Table Lamp" on a brass tag. Height 13". The underside is marked "U. S. Light•House Service." Courtesy of Monte Calhoun. $175.00.

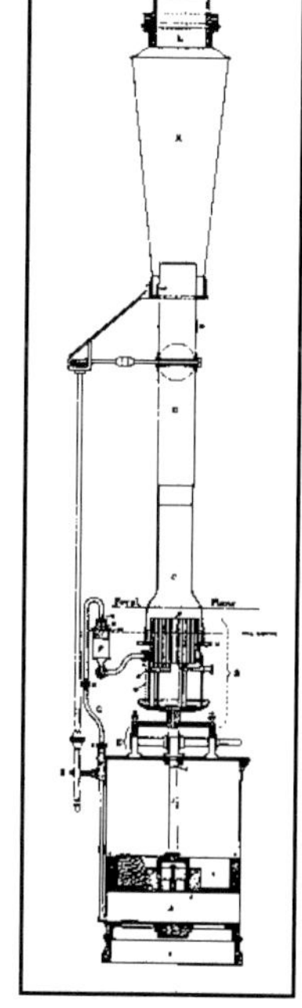

Fuel — kerosene, called mineral oil or "earth oil," 1887 - 1911.

Lamp — Mechanical moderator lamp, five concentric wicks burned about six+ gallons per night.

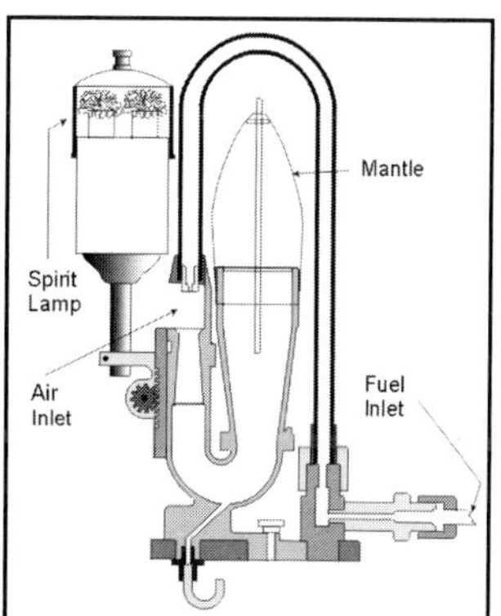

Fuel — kerosene vaporized under pressure, 1911 – 1933.

Lamp — Incandescent oil vapor lamp (Luchaire I.O.V. burner). The lamp burned about three+ gallons per night.

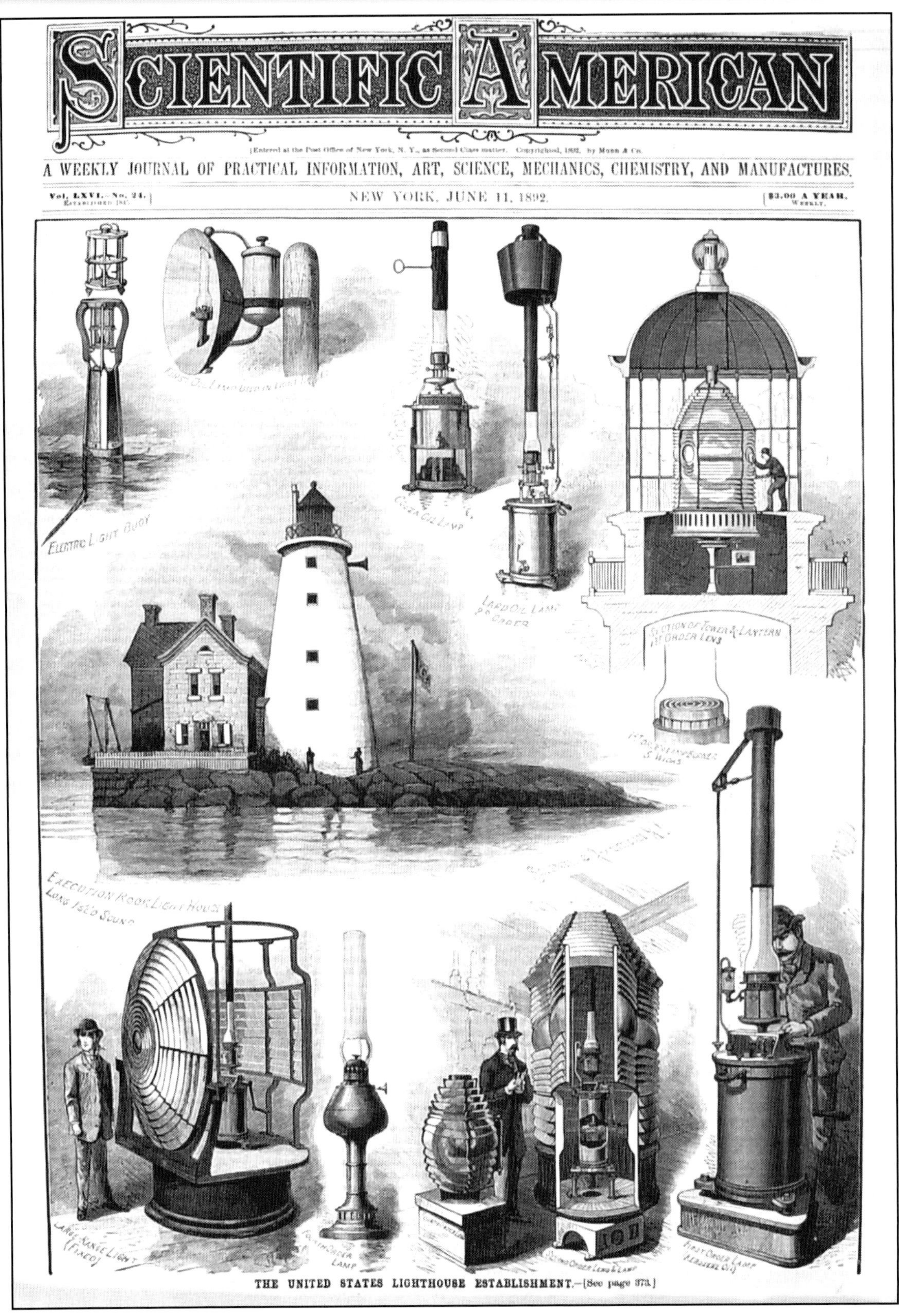

SCIENTIFIC AMERICAN

[Entered at the Post Office of New York, N. Y., as Second Class matter. Copyrighted, 1892, by Munn & Co.

A WEEKLY JOURNAL OF PRACTICAL INFORMATION, ART, SCIENCE, MECHANICS, CHEMISTRY, AND MANUFACTURES.

Vol. LXVI.—No. 24.] NEW YORK, JUNE 11, 1892. [$3.00 A YEAR. WEEKLY.

THE UNITED STATES LIGHTHOUSE ESTABLISHMENT.—[See page 373.]

Illustrations on the cover of *Scientific American*, June 11, 1892. Top left to right: "Electric Light Buoy"; "First Oil Lamp Used in Light Houses"; "Colza Oil Lamp"; "Lard Oil Lamp, 2nd Order"; "Section of Tower & Lantern, 1st Order Lens." Center: "Execution Rock Light House," "Long Isl'd Sound." Bottom left to right: "Large Range Light (Fixed)"; "Fourth Order Lamp (Funck-Heap lamp)"; "Second Order Lens & Lamp"; "First Order Lamp (Kerosene Oil)," showing the First Order lamp burner with five concentric wicks, above.

Kerosene Center-draft Lamps, 1890

The market for kerosene lamps continued to grow through the 1890s, although city dwellers changed to gas and electric lighting. Even so, Rochester kerosene lamps continued to be offered in the Waldorf-Astoria Hotel, New York City, as late as 1893 because many guests were more familiar with oil lamps than gas or electricity (O'Brien, 1937).

Lifestyle in America was portrayed in manuals of etiquette and by material wealth in the home. The family's parlor became the focal point for evening entertainment and display of prized possessions, portraits, fine furniture, the library, and elegant lamps. Opulence was certainly evident by decorated parlor lamps, silver-plated lamps, art glass library lamps, and the lighting fixtures in railcars.

The removable oil pot played a significant role in expanding lamp production in the 1890s. Oil pots, complete with burner, were made to standard size and sold to glass companies and metal fabrication companies. These new "lamp" manufacturers were able to design their own lamps, independent of the traditional brass and lamp companies.

The Removable Oil Pot

Oil pots were used extensively in vase lamps, banquet lamps, piano lamps, and hanging lamps. The oil pot was a simple idea and a huge step to increase popularity and practical use of decorated vase lamps. The pot may be removed and taken outside for filling to avoid spills on the table or on the doily in Mother's clean parlor.

The standard or universal oil pot is just under 5" in diameter and usually 3¼" deep below the rim. However, all pots are not interchangeable. The design of ribs and top lip may prevent placement into the vase. Different sizes of oil pots were made by some companies. The pot was intended to fit vase lamps and hanging fixtures made for center-draft burners. A draft tube through the center of the pot supplies air to the burner.

The removable fount, or detachable tank, was not a new idea. Removable tanks were a feature of most student lamps. The oil fount is removable for Hitchcock, Wanzer, and similar lamps. Some hanging lamps were designed with easily removed founts. Other examples found in patent records include tanks for lanterns and similar devices. The Iden Gothic lamps were made in two parts and, albeit quite heavy, the top founts can be carried outside for filling. Removable brass founts are found in many Sandwich lamps, cica 1870s – 1880s. Most, but not all, of these founts, or oil pots, required removing the burners to fill the lamps.

James H. White was granted patent 283,177 on August 14, 1883, for a glass container (oil fount) supported in a vase lamp. The patent was assigned to the Manhattan Brass Company. These founts were used primarily for flat wick lamps and burners. Charles Upton's patent No. 379,836 in 1888 was essentially a vase lamp for center-draft.

Most brass oil pots were designed with oil fills and caps to facilitate filling with kerosene oil. Many of the caps are dated or signed, which helps identify the manufacturer.

Oil pots were sold to a wide variety of lamp manufacturers, assemblers, and resellers. The oil pots could be exchanged, substituted, and replaced. Some dealers advertised that they would gladly insert the oil pot and burner of choice!

A collector today cannot verify the manufacturer of a vase lamp, banquet lamp, or a hanging lamp solely by the manufacturer of an oil pot and burner.

> The lamp trade of the United States has developed to such an extent that it has become one of the wonders of commercial activity in the nineteenth century of wonders. Inventive skill and mechanical ingenuity have so increased the illuminating qualities of light-giving oils that there is little left to be desired in the way of a perfect lamp. It is extremely doubtful, therefore, if the future will bring greater improvement in lamps than we have at the present time, and it is evident that whatever is done to improve upon existing forms must come in the form of an entirely radical departure from known methods of burning mineral oils. The centre draft burner in the many forms now on the market is about as near perfection as it is possible to get a burner, producing absolute certainty of results; and it may be safely said that the bright genius who will improve on the centre draft by anything entirely different in its operation is not yet born. We pay our respects to the centre draft and its many makers, and prophesy a long continuance of popularity for the best burner that has ever been made. All of the makes are good; possibly not equally so; but in view of the doubt that exists in the minds of those who buy them we can say, May the best man win!
>
> *CGJ*, Sept. 11, 1890

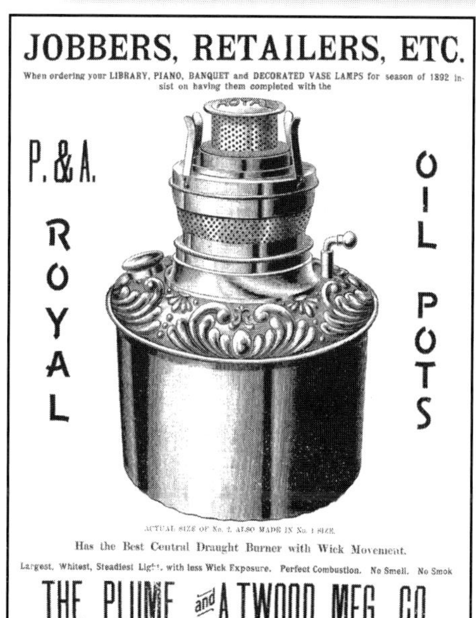

Royal oil pots were advertised for retailers and manufacturers to complete their library, piano, banquet, and vase lamps. Advertisement is from *China, Glass and Lamps*, July 6, 1892.

Meteor oil pot sold by Edward Miller Co. Standard pots for No. 2 burners have a 4¾" bottom diameter. $125.00.

Oil pot made by Edward Miller Co. and fitted with the Hornberger burner found in better lamps. $175.00.

Decorated Parlor Lamps

The oil pot allowed glass companies to produce a variety of decorated parlor lamps or vase lamps. These lamps are sometimes called Gone with the Wind lamps (GWTW), a description that came about after release of the movie *Gone with the Wind* in 1939. Lamps in the movie inspired the name, which became widely accepted by antique dealers and collectors.

Loris Russell (1968), in *A Heritage of Light,* said it clearly: "Part of this modern popularity resulted from a preposterous anachronism...from...the motion picture 'Gone With The Wind'...where...lavish use was made of vase lamps to convey the impression of the opulent 'before-the-war' southern mansion."

Decorated vase lamps were created some 20 or more years after the Civil War and were not available during the time portrayed by the famous movie. The lamps were originally called decorated table lamps, parlor lamps, vase lamps, or reception lamps. Hanging lamps in the GWTW form are not common.

Center-draft parlor lamps were popular from the 1890s through the 1920s. Colorful electric versions continued to find prominence in living rooms and in picture windows for many years after the classic movie.

Collectors consider decorated parlor lamps as having a more-or-less round shade to complement the base (see Pitkins and Brooks illustration, above). The glass was decorated with highly colored flowers or scenes. The heavy, flamboyant painted decoration reduced light output but created Victorian ambience. The shade (sometimes called globe) may be formed as a round ball or shaped in form to match the base. Vase lamps have half shades, or Tam-o-shanter shades, and these lamps emit better tabletop light for working or reading.

The early parlor lamps were often fitted with Duplex burners with two wicks, which gave more light than single wicks. Decorated parlor lamps became popular when center-draft burners and removeable oil pots were developed.

Pitkins and Brooks offered to replace any lamp manufacturer's oil pot with the Belgian oil pot and burner in its 1904 lamp catalog.

Companies[1] That Made or Sold Decorated Vase Lamps:

American Glass Company
American Lamp & Brass Company
Bradley & Hubbard
Bristol Brass and Clock Company
Buckeye Glass Company
Byesville Glass and Lamp Company
Clark Brothers Lamp, Brass and Glass Company
Consolidated Lamp and Glass Company
Dithridge & Company
Eagle Glass & Mfg. Company
Ellwood City Glass Co.
Empire Glass Co.
Fostoria Glass Company
Fostoria Shade and Lamp Company
Gill & Co.
Jefferson Glass Co.
Judd Mfg. Co.
M. E. Moore Plating Co.
Mount Washington Glass Company
Nail City Stamping Co.
National Glass Company
Pittsburgh Brass, Lamp and Glass Company
Smith-Brunewold Glass Company
Swann, Whitehead & Clark
Washington Glass Mfg. Company

[1]This is an incomplete list and not all of these companies made center-draft lamps.

Tiny Miller oil pot made by Edward Miller Co. This pot and the one to the right each have a bottom diameter of 3¾". $125.00.

Little Jewel oil pot made by Ansonia. $125.00.

Washington Glass Mfg. Co. flame spreader most likely from an oil pot made by Hipwell Mfg. Co., Pittsburgh. This flame spreader will fit into several brands of burners.

Parlor lamps may be brass, cast iron, or white metal in decorative form. These lamps were called table lamps in some catalogs. The shade may be a round globe or a half shade. This brass table lamp made, and signed, by Plume and Atwood is fitted with a Royal oil pot. The burner has a shade holder to support a large round ball shade. These shades were usually decorated in colorful flowers, scenes, or designs. $250.00.

Decorated vase or parlor lamps were popular during the 1890s. These are fitted with Success and Royal oil pots and burners.

Premium Offers

Inexpensive lamps were popular premiums offered by Wrigley to sell chewing gum, J. D. Larkin to sell soap, and F. M. Lupton to sell subscriptions to the *People's Home Journal*. These attractive colorful decorated premiums were popular during the turn of the century. Many of these lamps were converted to electricity and survive today. They were often placed on a table in front of a window in the parlor or sitting room.

The shade or globe of glass lamps was usually painted or decorated to match the base.

See *The Illuminator*, 2(1), pages 12 – 13, for more information about Larkin and premium parlor lamps 1898 – 1905. Read Broughton (2005) for more information about lamps offered as premiums in general.

A premium "give-away" lamp offered by Wm. Wrigley Co. to sell chewing gum. Royal oil pot and burner. $350.00.

Wm. Wrigley Jr. & Co. premium offer for 1896. This lamp was "free with 8 boxes of Wrigley's Chewing Gum worth $8.00." The gum and lamp were sold for $5.50; "The Lamp alone is well worth price asked..." I suspect this lamp was made by Consolidated Lamp and Glass Co.

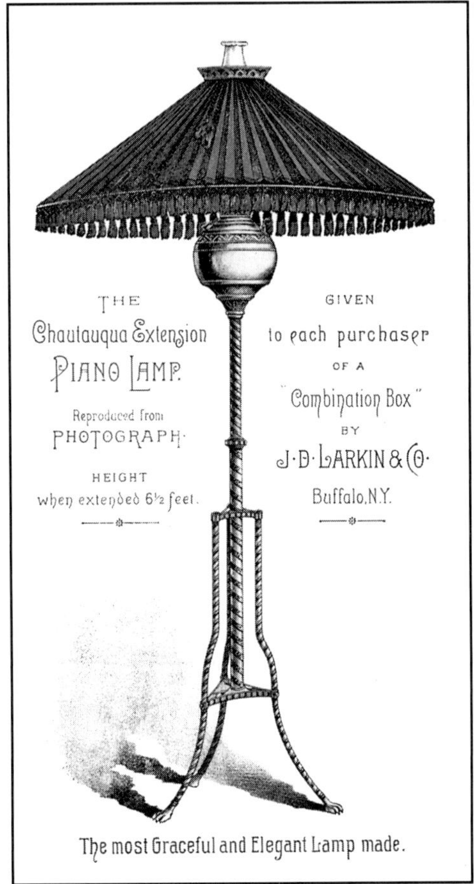

Handbill advertisement by J. D. Larkin & Co. offering the Chautauqua center-draft piano lamp. The Chautauqua was also offered as a decorated vase lamp.

Silver-plated Kerosene Lamps

Victorian elegance was perhaps best exhibited in the wares of Meriden Britannia Company and similar manufacturers. Vase lamps, table lamps, hand lamps, and extension piano lamps were made in silver and gold plate for "the carriage trade" (see more in *The Illuminator* 2(1):3-5, 1988). Oil pots were commonly used in the large lamps.

Meriden, Connecticut, was called "the Silver City" in the 1870s due to production of silver-plated wares and lamps. Decorative housewares ranging from flatware and food service were produced in styles symbolized by the Victorian era.

Catalogs of the 1880s illustrated fancy lamps with choices of double flat-wick burners or newly developed center-draft burners. Many silver-plated vase lamps were fitted with center-draft oil pots. Elegant art glass and hand-painted shades adorned the lamps. Silver-plate companies did not manufacture lamp burners and oil pots but obtained them from Edward Miller, Bradley and Hubbard, Parker, Meriden Bronze, or other sources found in this book. There was considerable cross fertilization of people and investment among companies. For example, Edward Miller owned stock in Simpson, Hall and Miller (a different Miller) and sat on its board for many years, and Simpson sat on the board of Meriden Britannia (Weathers, 2003).

Some companies that manufactured elegant silver-plated Victorian wares and oil lamps: Bristol Brass and Copper Company, Bristol, CT; Derby Silver Company, Derby, CT; Meriden Britannia Company, Meriden, CT; The Meriden Silver Plate Company, Meriden, CT; Pairpoint Manufacturing Company, New Bedford, MA; Reed & Barton, Taunton, MA; C. Rogers & Brothers, Meriden, CT; Rogers Silver Plate Co., Danbury, CT; Simpson, Hall & Miller Company, Wallingford, CT; R. Wallace & Sons, Wallingford, CT; Wilcox Silver Plate Company, Meriden, CT.

Silver-plated lamps were expensive, ranging from $12 to $15 for hand lamps, $18 to $30 for table and vase lamps, and $85 and higher for piano lamps. Shades and globes were extra. See Shuman (1988) for a comprehensive list of companies, with their trademarks, that manufactured silver-plated Victorian wares.

Daylight silver-plate vase lamp, Craighead & Kintz. Courtesy Allen Weathers.

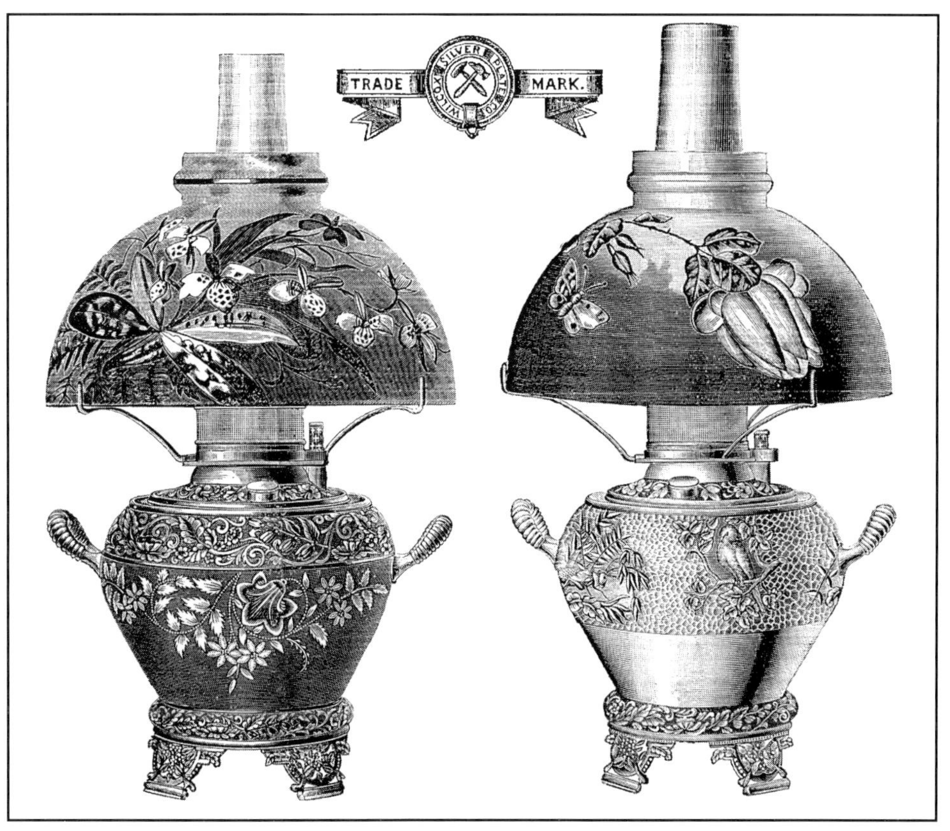

Fine silver-plate vase lamps, Wilcox Silver Plate Company, 1886. The lamps appear to be fitted with Rochester oil pots and burners. Courtesy Allen Weathers.

Kerosene Center-draft Lamps, 1890

Silver-plated Oil Lamps, 1886 – 1896

Silver-plate vase lamps, Wilcox Silver Plate Company, 1886. The lamps are fitted with Rochester oil pots and burners. Courtesy Allen Weathers.

Flame spreader marked "Rogers Silver Plate Co., Danbury, Conn., U.S. A," made by Bristol Brass & Clock Co.

Repoussé silver-plate table and banquet lamps, Simpson, Hall, Miller & Co. The burners appear to be Pittsburgh Brass Company, ca. 1896. Courtesy Allen Weathers.

Library Lamps

Library lamps are among the most elegant and colorful hanging lamps for any home décor. That was a selling point in the 1880s and 1890s and remains true today. Few books adequately illustrate these lamps, and I show examples from catalog illustrations of those with center-draft burners. Library lamps were introduced with single or double flat-wick burners before center-draft burners and oil pots became prominent.

Library lamps with ornamental brass frames and counterweight pull-downs, or tension motors, became popular following the heavy cast-iron frames of the late 1870s and early 1880s.

Library lamps ranged from rather common and plain to very fancy and exquisite, always aimed for specific use in the home.

The better library lamps, in terms of today's values, were expensive during the nineteenth century. I suspect they were primarily sold in retail stores operated by the manufacturers in New York (see list in appendix) and other cities, although library lamps of various sorts were offered in catalogs. Companies that created highly collectible library lamps include Charles Parker, Bradley and Hubbard, Edward Miller, Rochester Lamp Co., Ansonia, Meriden Bronze, and Wallace and Sons. I am sure other companies made them as well, but collectors have much to learn and yet to identify them with all of their correct components. Charles Parker made some unusual and unique library lamps.

Library lamps are striking because of their ornate brass frames adorned with jewels, prisms, and ornamental trappings. The lamps are especially colorful when fitted with art-glass shades and matching fount holders (see right). The glass was provided from sources such as the New England and Mt. Washington Glass companies. Other shades were decorated in hand-painted scenes and flowers. Library lamps were also sold with large umbrella silk shades.

Some library lamps were fitted with colorful prisms rather than clear crystals, and with colored chimneys in place of clear ones. Such appurtenances certainly were colorful, but reduced the light for reading. Undershades and bisque figure swingers adorned the lamps as well. Fancy match holders could be added, of course.

Library lamps were made to impress guests who came to visit. I suspect library lamps were lighted to show the beauty of the lamp and its glass as well as to illuminate the parlour or library. Catherine Thuro (2001) appropriately described library lamps as "Jewels of the Night."

For collectors wanting to learn more about library lamps, Jeffery Ebersole's *Hanging Victorian Lamps of the Nineteenth Century* (Collector Books, Paducah, KY) is recommended. This book is in full color and describes and identifies elegant library lamps of the 1890s. The manufacturers of many library lamps are identified for the first time in Ebersole's book.

Rochester brand library lamp sold by Hibbard, Spencer, and Bartlett & Company in 1891. The jewelled frame, made by Edward Miller & Co., was finished in antique brass. The matching art-glass shade and vase (for removeable oil pot) was offered in a choice of blue, pink, or ruby glass. The specific kind of glass and its manufacturer were not identified. The price was $21.67. These black and white catalog images simply do not reveal the vibrant colors and workmanship that attract collectors to these lamps today.

A Note about Victorian Opulence:

Many companies in this book designed kerosene lamps, such as library lamps, with embellishments and art-glass shades beyond the need or affordability of the average family. Manhattan Brass, as an example, furnished student lamps sold by Tiffany. Such lamps, sold in upscale stores to the wealthy, provided no better light than standard models. These "better" lamps are highly prized by collectors today.

Railcar Lighting

Lighting for railroad passenger cars and stations was largely provided by companies such as Adams & Westlake, Dayton Mfg. Co., Dietz, C. T. Ham, Handlan, and others. Collectors immediately think of railroad lanterns and unique heavy, ornate brass railcar fixtures, which are not primary topics in this book. Center-draft kerosene lamps, however, were designed and manufactured specifically for railcars. Some of these lamps were unique and ornate fixtures that reflected the opulence of the Victorian Age.

Dayton chandelier #164 with Acme center-draft burners. This frame appears to be identical with Willits's 1890 patent 427,491.

Station lighting was more or less done with conventional lamps similar to those used in offices and homes. Student lamps were popular for station offices. Station lamps were often purchased from Edward Miller, Rochester, or other manufacturers for resale to railroad customers.

The book *The Comparative Merits of Various Systems of Car Lighting* (Wellington, 1892) gives an excellent picture of railcar lighting in America during the 1890s. At that time, 90 percent of all passenger cars were using kerosene lamps. Round-wick center-draft lamps were stated to give superior light compared to lamps with flat wick burners; however, no estimate of their proportion was given. The rest used Pintsch gas, or "light gasoline," carburetor systems. "Pintsch" was a registered trademark (#20,678) of the Safety Car Heating and Lighting Co., New York, Dec. 21, 1891.

An 1892 study compared kerosene lamps with Pintsch compressed gas, Frost gasoline carburetors, and electric lighting. Candles were said to be too expensive and poor illumination. Electric lighting was favored, "yet too expensive." Safety, cost, and practical use were factors considered.

In foreign countries rapeseed oil, colza oil, and kerosene were railway fuels. Rapeseed oil and vegetable oils were popular largely because of high cost for imported kerosene.

Concerns for safety were reflected by two grades of kerosene specified by most states and railroads. The two grades were 150 °F fire test, for general use, and 300 °F fire test, for passenger cars. The 300 °F fire test kerosene must not flash below 250 °F and must not fire below 300 °F. Read more details and specifications by the Pennsylvania Railroad Company in the appendix.

Railway car lamps that provided ample light were desired in passenger cars and also in mail cars, where mail was sorted as the train moved to its next destination. Important characteristics of car lamps were these:

- The lamp must have been securely held in place.
- Passenger car lamps should not have given off disagreeable odor. Combustion fumes were largely controlled by a ventilating flue through the roof over the lamp.
- A removable oil reservoir for easy filling (preferably of the student lamp principle).
- Removable drip cup to prevent drip on carpets with glass preferred.
- The wick must not "jar down with motion of the car."
- Lght should not have flared with drafts or motion of the car.
- The lamp and its supports "designed with good taste" and easily kept clean and bright.

Manufacturers in this book who developed center-draft railroad lamps include Adams & Westlake, Dayton Mfg. Co., Handlan-Buck, F. H. Lovell, F. Meyrose Co., and Post & Co. Others, such as Plume & Atwood, provided center-draft burners for the above manufacturers. These companies and others, such as Peter Gray in Boston, sold center-draft mammoth hanging lamps for use in depots and offices.

Headlights

Impressive were center-draft headlights for horsecars, trolleys, and locomotives (see below). These large specialty lamps or lanterns were sold by C. T. Ham, Dietz, Rochester Headlight Co., and others (see Wenrich, 1988).

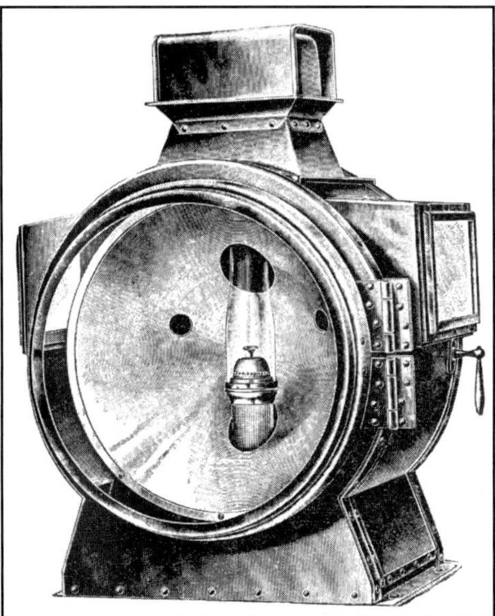

Wabash headlight, made in sizes 16", 18", and 20". Others were made 23" in diameter. Patent improvements for railroad headlights included Edmund Meredith, 416,116, 1889 and H. C. Crowley, 422,503, 1890.

America in the 1890s

America recovered after the Civil War, rebuilding the South, stretching railroads West, developing the petroleum industry, mechanizing industry, manufacturing consumer goods, moving into the city, and inventing, inventing.

Lamps to lengthen the day gained importance as families read magazines and newspapers, listened to the phonograph, or simply worked longer during the evening.

Mark Twain wrote, "In Hannibal, Missouri, when I was a boy, everybody was poor, but didn't know it; and everybody was comfortable and did know it."

The transcontinental railroad carried citizens West and cattle East. Railroads consumed 60 percent of all steel produced. People were migrating West, settling Indian lands and farming and mining.

Life expectancy was 47 years. One in 10 could not read or write. One in 15 graduated from high school.

Populations of cities in the East and Midwest were increasing rapidly. New York was the largest city in 1900 with 3.4 million; however, 45 million Americans lived on farms and in villages of 5000 or less. Alabama, Mississippi, Iowa, and Tennessee each had more people than California.

Victorian extravagance was evident in the city.

The financial panic of 1893 drained U.S. gold reserves and led to a four-year depression.

The average wage was 22¢ per hour — the average worker earned $200 – 500 per year. An accountant earned $2,000, a dentist $2,500, and an engineer $5,000 per year.

Standard Oil dominated the petroleum industry. Crude petroleum production was 30 million barrels in 1892. The average wholesale price of kerosene was 7¢ per gallon.

Bicycle pedal power transported millions of people.

The Duryea brothers built a horseless carriage in 1893.

Leading causes of death were pneumonia, influenza, tuberculosis, diarrhea, heart disease, and stroke.

Patent medicines — pills, pellets, extracts, tonics, syrups, salves, plasters, and more, even electricity — and nostrums "cured" every ill — asthma, catarrh, neuralgia, rheumatism, sciatica, dyspepsia, and consumption. The newfangled electricity led to the ingenuity of the "electric toothbrush" and even an "electric belt" for ladies, meant to benefit most any condition imaginable.

Marijuana, heroin, and opium were bought in medicines over the counter — and promoted for questionable health benefits.

Lamps were favored wedding presents. Penmanship was important. McGuffey's Readers were read and recited. *Huckleberry Finn* was published. Beards were popular.

Wrigley's Chewing Gum appeared. Cigarettes made American Tobacco Company rich. There was no income tax.

The Statue of Liberty was dedicated in 1886.

The flag had 45 stars — Arizona, Oklahoma, New Mexico, Hawaii (annexed in 1898), and Alaska were not yet admitted to the Union.

President McKinley, re-elected in 1900 (on a gold standard), was assassinated in Buffalo, NY, in 1901. He was visiting the Pan-American Exposition.

PATENTS!

MESSRS. MUNN & CO., in connection with the publication of the SCIENTIFIC AMERICAN, continue to examine improvements, and to act as Solicitors of Patents for Inventors.

In this line of business they have had *forty-five years' experience*, and now have *unequaled facilities* for the preparation of Patent Drawings, Specifications, and the prosecution of Applications for Patents in the United States, Canada, and Foreign Countries. Messrs. Munn & Co. also attend to the preparation of Caveats, Copyrights for Books, Labels, Reissues, Assignments, and Reports on Infringements of Patents. All business intrusted to them is done with special care and promptness, on very reasonable terms.

A pamphlet sent free of charge, on application, containing full information about Patents and how to procure them; directions concerning Labels, Copyrights, Designs, Patents, Appeals, Reissues, Infringements, Assignments, Rejected Cases. Hints on the sale of Patents, etc.

We also send, *free of charge*, a Synopsis of Foreign Patent Laws, showing the cost and method of securing Patents in all the principal countries of the world.

MUNN & CO., Solicitors of Patents,
361 Broadway, New York.

BRANCH OFFICES.—No. 622 and 624 F Street, Pacific Building, near 7th Street, Washington, D. C.

Advertisement, *Scientific American*, Jan. 1892.

CALIFORNIA.

If you are going to California, and want to make the journey cheaply, quickly, and comfortably, purchase your tickets *via* the Chicago and North-Western, Union Pacific, and Southern Pacific Railways. Pullman drawing room sleeping cars are run on fast trains from Chicago to San Francisco without change, and dining cars serve all meals *en route*. Completely furnished Pullman tourist sleeping cars are also run, in which accommodations can be procured by passengers holding either first or second class tickets at a cost of only $4 per berth from Chicago to San Francisco and other California points. The hour of departure of trains from Chicago affords prompt connection with all trains from the East and South. First class one way and excursion tickets good returning six months from date of sale, also second class tickets at low rates, sleeping car reservations, and full information can be procured of any Ticket Agent, or by addressing W. A. Thrall, General Passenger and Ticket Agent, Chicago and North-Western Railway, Chicago, Illinois.

Advertisement, *Scientific American*, Dec. 1891.

BUSINESS

Bicycle Dealer:—A bicycle will be better for you than a horse. It doesn't eat anything.

Frugal Merchant:—(not entirely convinced) — No, it won't eat anything, but I'm afraid it'll give me a thundering big appetite.—*Chicago Tribune*.

The moral is yours — so's a Columbia bicycle — Business men, the Pope Mfg. Co. offer you health and happiness, clear headedness, renovated money-making brains — 221 Columbus Ave., Boston.

Advertisement, *Scientific American*, June 1892.

Advertisement, *Success Magazine*, May 1901.

Mineral Production

The following report and the table below were published in *Scientific American*, January 30, 1892. The data was taken from the *Engineering and Mining Journal*:

There have been no discoveries of great bonanzas, no mining "booms," during the year 1891, but the mining industry never was more prosperous, and its prosperity never before was founded on so substantial a basis.

The immense increase during 1891 in production of most of the metals has been a surprise. Copper in particular will, as usual, astonish the trade. The consumption of metals increases steadily, as might be expected from the growing wealth and prosperity of the country.

Nothing more forcibly demonstrates the absurdity of our barbarous system of weights and measures than the compilation of statistics. We have tons of 2,240 pounds, of 2,000 pounds, and the metric ton of 2,2041/2 pounds, or 1,000 kilos, to say nothing of the other special tons used in certain industries. We have ounces troy and avoirdupois, and grains and grammes, with innumerable other weights. It is indeed high time that all civilized countries adopt the single metric standard of weights and measures...

MINERAL PRODUCTION OF THE UNITED STATES IN 1890 AND 1891.

	1890.	1891.
Gold, ounces	1,588,880	1,620,000
Silver, ounces	54,500,000	58,000,000
Pig Iron, tons of 2,000 lb	10,307,028	8,976,000
Steel Rails, tons of 2,240 lb	2,095,996	1,090,000
Copper, lb	264,920,000	292,620,000
Lead, tons of 2,000 lb	181,494	205,488
Zinc, tons of 2,000 lb	66,342	76,500
Nickel, lb	200,332	144,841
Quicksilver, flasks	22,926	21,022
Aluminum, lb	94,881	163,820
Tin, lb	....	123,366
Antimony Ore, tons of 2,240 lb	....	700
Anthracite Coal, tons of 2,240 lb	38,006,483	42,839,799
Bituminous Coal, tons of 2,240 lb	93,000,000	98,000,000
Phosphate Rock, tons of 2,000 lb	637,000	659,731
Salt, bbls. of 280 lb	9,727,697	10,229,691
Bromine, lb	310,000	415,000
Pyrites, tons of 2,000 lb	109,431	122,438
Sulphur, tons of 2,000 lb	....	1,200

P. T. Barnum Dead.

The greatest showman on earth, as he prided himself on being called, died at his home, in Bridgeport, Conn., on the 7th inst., after a protracted illness.

Mr. Barnum was deservedly popular among all classes, and the city in which he had long lived, and where he died, has lost one of its most public-spirited and useful citizens.

Mr. Barnum's energy was exhaustless, and he took great pride and delight in his own achievements. He was a striking example of what perseverance and assurance can accomplish. Forty years of his life was devoted to the show business, in which he had no peer. He understood the business and enjoyed it, and he has left a large fortune as the result of his active life.

The veteran showman was probably the best known man in the United States. He has made a succession of generations of children happy, and his genial face, with "I am coming," which ornamented part of the gigantic bill announcing the coming show, will be recalled to the mind of multitudes in both hemispheres.

Obituary of P. T. Barnum.

ABSOLUTELY FREE

TRIAL FOR 30 DAYS.

The 1900 Ball Bearing Washer

will be sent **absolutely** free on 30 days' trial. We pay freight both ways. We could not afford to ship on these terms, had experience not demonstrated that no one will part with our Washer once a thorough trial is given. It revolves on ball bearings. Simplest, easiest running washer on the market. It washes **clean** large quantities of clothes in 6 minutes. Impossible to injure the most delicate fabrics. **Sent anywhere free on 30 days' trial. It costs you nothing to try.** For particulars address

THE 1900 WASHER CO.,
171 F, STATE STREET, - BINGHAMPTON, N. Y.

Advertisement, *Success* magazine, May 1901.

KODAKS are always sold loaded ready for immediate use. They can be used for roll films or glass plates. The new

Daylight Kodak

can be loaded in daylight. Registers exposures and locks automatically when a new film is turned into place.

$8.50 to $25.00

Send for Circulars.

THE EASTMAN COMPANY,
ROCHESTER, N. Y.

Advertisement, *Scientific American*, Feb. 1892.

"Rail Fence Bicycle Railway. A system of passenger travel between Mt. Holly and Smithville, N.J. will be known as the Hotchkiss Bicycle Railway. A special form of bicycle is required. Each passenger furnishes his own motive power. The illustration will give a good idea of the construction."

Scientific American, April 1892.

Cost of Lamps Then and Now

Kerosene lamps were made in a variety of price ranges during the 1890s. The following list of prices was given for a large hardware store in 1895.

NS = no shade, S = with shade.

All lamps complete with burners:

Common glass hand lamp .... $2.00 – 3.00/doz.
Common glass stand lamp .... $3.00 – 4.00/doz.
10" dome shade, plain .... $4.00 – 5.00/doz
Decorated stand lamp .... $6.00 – 9.00/doz.
14" shade, decorated .... $10.00 – 15.00/doz.
14" shade, fancy glass .... $10.00 – 25.00/doz.
10" dome shade, cased .... $15.00 – 30.00/doz.
No. 2 brass table lamp, NS .... $.50 – 3.00 ea.
Decorated vase lamp, S .... $4.00 – 6.00 ea.
No. 1 student lamp, S .... $4.50 – 5.00 ea.
Mammoth hanging lamp, S .... $5.00 – 6.00 ea.
No. 2 brass vase lamp, NS .... $5.00 – 10.00 ea.
Fancy cloth shades .... $3.00 – 20.00/ea.
No. 2 fancy vase lamp, NS .... $10.00 – 20.00 ea.
No. 2 library lamp, S .... $10.00 – 20.00 ea.
Mammoth Perfection study lamp, S .... $15.00 ea.
10" dome shade, decorated .... $13.00 – 25.00 ea.
Piano extension lamp, NS .... $20.00 – 30.00 ea.

What Would the Lamp Cost Today[1] Based on Original Price in 1895?

Original Price ($)	Cost Today ($)
1.00	22.47
2.00	44.94
5.00	112.36
10.00	224.72
20.00	449.43
30.00	674.15

[1]Calculated to year 2006 by The Inflation Calculator. (www.westegg.com/inflation/)

AUGUST BELMONT & CO., New York
LEE, HIGGINSON & CO., Boston.

Subscription for

$3,000,000

7 per cent Cumulative Preferred Stock.

SHARES, $50 EACH.

WESTINGHOUSE

Electric & Manufacturing Co

NO. 120 BROADWAY, NEW YORK.

Advertisement, *Scientific American*, October 1891.

Hartford and Vedette Bicycles

$75.00 to $25.00

Combine the Best Results of 22 Years Experience.

Our factories comprise the largest bicycle manufacturing plant in the world. We have unequalled resources for obtaining material, the best devised automatic machinery, the most skilled artisans, the greatest output—a combination of advantages which produces the Standard Bicycles of the World and enables us to offer them at the lowest possible prices.

Entirely New Models for 1899.

Ask any Columbia dealer for Catalog, or write us direct, enclosing 2c. stamp.

POPE MFG. CO., HARTFORD, CONN.

Advertisement, *Delineator Magazine*, 1899.

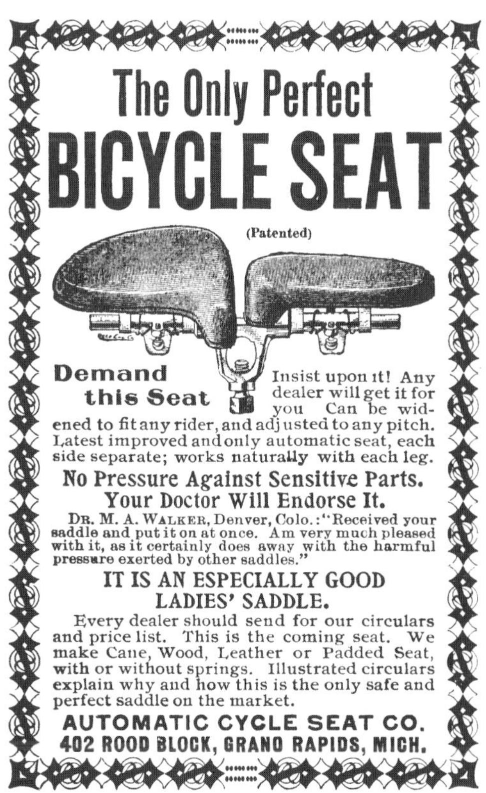

Advertisement, *Muncey's Magazine*, 1896.

Light Output

The Mantle Lamp Company of America, Chicago, commissioned universities and research institutes to measure light output of the Aladdin lamp compared with leading brands of the day. I have summarized one report from the Lewis Institute for some familiar center-draft lamps in the table below. Flat-wick lamps emitted 9 to 12 candle power, to give some idea of the excellent light output from center-draft lamps.

Light Output of Selected Center-draft Lamps, Lewis Institute, Chicago, 1914

Lamp[1]	Horizontal Candle Power (HCP)	Time to Consume One Gallon (hours)
Mammoth (Miller)	34	16.2
New Vestal (Miller)	26	27.3
Radiant No. 4 (B&H)	24	34.3
Rayo (B&H)	25	29.0
Rochester No. 2 (Miller)	30	26.1
Smokeless (Manhattan Brass)	23	29.9
Success (Pittsburgh L,B&G)	29	29.0
Aladdin 101 (MLCA)	62	50.6

[1]All are bright flame lamps except the Aladdin table lamp 101, which is a blue flame incandescent mantle lamp. In other tests, common 1½" flat-wick lamps were rated 9 to 12 HCP.

Fathers of Electrical Science.

At a meeting of the Committee on Electricity, Electrical and Pneumatic Appliances, of the World's Columbian Exposition, the following names were decided upon as those of eminent electricians not now living, to be placed over the Electricity Building at the Exposition, namely:

Franklin,	Page,	Joule,
Galvani,	Weber,	Saussure,
Ampere,	Gilbert,	Cooke,
Faraday,	Davenport,	Varley,
Ohm,	Soemmering,	Steinheil,
Sturgeon,	Don Silva,	Guericke,
Morse,	Arago,	La Place,
Siemens,	Daniell,	Channing,
Davy,	Jacobi,	Priestley,
Volta,	Wheatstone,	Maxwell,
Henry,	Gauss,	Coxe,
Oersted,	Vail,	Thales,
Coulomb,	Bain,	Cavendish.
Ronald,	De la Rive,	

Scientific American, Nov. 1891.

Honors for Mr. Edison.

The Society of Arts, London, has awarded the Albert Medal to Mr. Edison in consideration of his distinguished services in the progress of electric lighting, telegraphy and telephony. The Albert Medal was first awarded in 1864, and has often been given to distinguished electricians, among whom may be mentioned Faraday in 1866, Cooke and Wheatstone in 1867, Sir William Thomson in 1879, J. P. Joule in 1880, and Helmholtz in 1888.

Scientific American, June 1892.

Electricity was the dynamic business of the times. Two famous names preparing for the future were Albert Einstein and Milvea Maric, who met at the University of Zurich, 1896 – 1901.

LIST OF

Books on Electricity.

Alternate Current Machinery. By Gilbert Kapp, Assoc. M.I.C.E. Reprinted from the Minutes of Proceedings of the Inst. of Civil Engineers. London, 1889.. **.50**

Alternate Current Transformer in Theory and Practice. Vol. I. The Induction of Electric Currents. 500 pages, fully illustrated and with copious index. By J. A. Fleming. 8vo, cloth. London, 1889.......... **$3.00**
This book treats both practically and theoretically the subject of Electric Current Induction and the Alternating Current Transformer.

Arithmetic of Electricity. By T. O'Conor Sloane, A.M., E.M., Ph.D. This work gives Electric Calculations in such a simple manner that it can be used by any one having a knowledge of Arithmetic. It treats of calculations for wiring, resistance in general, arrangement of batteries for different work, and is supplemented by the most practical series of tables ever published. It is absolutely indispensable to the practical electrician, as well as to the amateur. Fully illustrated. 1891.... **$1.00**

Art of Electrolytic Separation of Metals. By G. Gore. Theoretical and practical. Fully illustrated. 8vo, cloth. London, 1890.......................... **$3.50**

Dynamo. How to make a Dynamo. A Practical Treatise for Amateurs. Containing numerous illustrations, and detailed instructions for constructing a small dynamo to produce the electric light. By Alfred Crofts. 12mo, cl. London. Second edition. 1889.......... **.80**

Edison and his Inventions. Including the many incidents, anecdotes, and interesting particulars connected with the early and later life of the great inventor. Also full explanations of the newly perfected phonograph, telephone, tasimeter, electric light, and all his principal discoveries, with copious illustrations. Edited by J. B. McClure, M.A. Chicago, 1889.............. **$1.00**

Electric Batteries. Elementary Treatise on. From the French of Alfred Niaudet, translated by L. M. Fishback. Fifth edition. N. Y., 1888................... **$2.50**

Electric Lighting. The Elements of Electric Lighting, including Electric Generation, Measurement, Storage, and Distribution. By Philip Atkinson, A.M., Ph.D., author of "Elements of Static Electricity." Contents: Electricity a Mode of Molecular Motion; Alternate Current Dynamos; Direct Current Dynamos; Electric Terms and Units; Electric Measurement; The Arc Lamp; The Incandescent Lamp; The Storage Battery; Electric Distribution, etc. Fourth edition. 260 pages. 104 illustrations. 1889................................ **$1.50**
This is a very complete work, and should be in the hands of all who have to do with electric lighting apparatus of any kind whatever.

Electricity. In Theory and Practice; or, the Elements of Electrical Engineering. By Lieut. Bradley A. Fiske. U.S.N. 258 pages, and many illustrations. 1888.... **$2.50**

Electricity. The A B C of. An elementary manual giving in simple language a general outline of the science. 108 pages, with 36 illustrations. Wm. H. Meadowcroft.. 12mo, cloth, 1889............................ **.50**

Electricity in our Homes and Workshops. A practical Treatise on Auxiliary Electrical Apparatus. With numerous illustrations. Sydney F. Walker. 12mo, cloth. London, 1889....................................... **$1.50**
The author aims to explain in simple terms the ordinary every day working of some of the forms of electrical apparatus that are in use by outsiders, and not under the supervision of electrical engineers. He appreciates that a connecting link is wanting between the electricity of the schools and the electrical engineering of practical life.

Advertisement, *Scientific American*, February 1891.

Advertisement, *Success Magazine*, May 1901.

Uses of Kerosene — 1909 - 1914

The book *Health and Longevity* by Joseph G. Richardson, 1909, is a massive work (almost 1,400 pages) of interesting reading. The following is from the 1914 edition, published by the Home Health Society, Philadelphia:

Gas Lighting. This common mode of lighting in cities and towns has its conveniences and dangers. Its greatest merit is convenience. It does not rank as an economic light. It can never be classed as a safe light.

Petroleum. Petroleum, or kerosene, ranks next to gas as an illuminant. It was at first dangerous, but since the "flashing point" of kerosene has been ascertained, and laws have been enacted as to refining processes, the danger has been greatly reduced. Moreover, there has been a great improvement in lamps, so that now kerosene ranks as the favorite rural light.

Kerosene oil was a handy home remedy in addition to being a fuel and household cleaning agent. We certainly do not suggest or recommend any of these treatments today:

Appendicitis — Since the theory that this disease is curable by absorption has gained prominence, the use of kerosene oil in connection with the cure has been found useful.

Consumption — A cloth saturated with kerosene oil, bound around the chest at night and frequently repeated, will remove lung soreness, and it may be taken inwardly with advantage. Eight to ten drops three or four times a day in sarsaparilla. It has been tried efficaciously as a cure for consumption.

Colds — Ten to twelve drops of kerosene oil on cut loaf sugar, taken every two or three hours, has been found effective in curing colds, also rub neck and chest.

Toothache — Cotton saturated with kerosene and placed in the tooth, often affords immediate relief.

Croup — Kerosene has been used in croup with success. It may be taken internally and applied externally.

Burns — Cloths saturated with kerosene, and applied to burns, exclude the air and bring desired relief from pain.

Bunions and corns — A continuous application to corns and bunions for a few days will reduce inflammation and pain, and removal of the corn may be brought about.

Diphtheria — Swabbing of the throat, at intervals of two to three hours has been found effective in destroying the membrane of diphtheria and reducing inflammation.

Vegetable poisons — Kerosene is an excellent lotion for the external inflammation resulting from vegetable poisons. It should be applied frequently until relief is had.

Quinsy — External and internal use of kerosene has a remedial effect in this obstinate disease.

Rheumatism — Petroleum was a favorite Indian remedy for rheumatism. In the purer form of kerosene it is still regarded as a favorite remedy for this painful disease. It may be applied by frequent rubbing.

Cleansing the scalp — A little kerosene in glycerin, constitutes an ointment that will speedily remove dandruff and contribute to a clean and healthy scalp.

The Standard Oil Company of Indiana published a 16-page booklet about 1920 entitled *32 Tested Uses of Perfection Kerosene for the Home, Farm, Garage.*

OILS.

The following are barrel prices, in small quantities ; an advance of 2 cents per gallon will be charged on all oils except Benzine, Gasoline and Cylinder Oils, which will be 5 cents over barrel price and containers charged extra.

Burning Oils.

	PER GAL.		PER GAL.
Coal Oil 130°	6½	150° Water White	8
" 150°	6½	Elaine	15
" 160°	8	Fire Proof	9½
" 175° Headlight	9	150 Indiana,	6½
Crude Petroleum	8	Benzine Deordorized 63°	8
White Miners Lewis	42	Gasoline 74°	9

Prices of burning oils available from Bridges-McDowell Co., Louisville, Kentucky, Oct. 1891.

Illumination.

PYRONAPHTHA.

According to the *Organ fur Oelhandle*, an interesting trial was lately made in St Petersburg with a new illuminating material, which is destined, it is considered, to take the place of kerosene. This is a new illuminating oil, absolutely free from danger of fire. An experiment was made as to the power which pyronaphtha has of extinguishing fire; and it was found that burning kerosene was easily put out by it. Pyronaphtha can, however, itself be extinguished by water. It is a product of the distillation of naphtha residue, of which large quantities remain from the Baku distillation of petroleum. From these illuminating gas is produced, and likewise pyronaphtha. The idea would seem to have hitherto been carried out only by the firm of Ragosin & Co, of Baku. The celebrated Russian chemist, Prof. Beilstein, has examined pyronaphtha, and has expressed his conviction that it has a briliant future before it, and that it must eventually replace American and Russian kerosene. Tne specific gravity of pyronaphtha is 0.864, and it ignites only at 230° Fah. It burns without smoke and vapor at 257°; gives a better light than keresene; is consumed less rapidly; while its prime cost is less. At St. Petersburg it is being adopted for domestic use; and a special burner has been constructed for the purpose

American Potter and Illuminator, **March 1885.**

Paraffine in Diphtheria.

Mr. A. M. Sydney-Turner, Surgeon to the Gloucester County Infirmary, informs the *Lancet*, in reply to inquiries, that he has treated thirty cases of diphtheria (children and adults) with paraffine, and has had the satisfaction of seeing every one recover. His plan is to ask for the ordinary paraffine used in lamps, and, having scraped off the diphtheritic patch, to apply the paraffine every hour to the throat (internally) with a large camel's hair brush. As a rule, the throat gets well in from twenty-four to forty-eight hours, and with improvement in the throat the paraffine is applied less frequently, but he continues its use for two or three days after the complete disappearance of the patches. He speaks definitely as to the therapeutic effects, but is unable to state what the chemical action of paraffine on the diphtheritic membrane is; probably the hydrocarbons in the liquid exert some powerful influence on the membrane.

Scientific American, **Oct. 1891.**

Adams & Westlake Mfg. Co.

1874 – 1887

Adams & Westlake Company, 1887 – 1982; Center-draft Lamp Manufacture 1885 – 1900

Adams & Westlake was one of the most successful manufacturers of railroad lanterns in American history. The company began in Chicago in 1874 when William Westlake (patent holder for the removable globe lantern in 1864) merged with John McGregor Adams to form the new company.

The company changed its name from Adams & Westlake Manufacturing Company to Adams & Westlake Company in 1887 (remaining under this name until 1982).

Adams & Westlake was a leader in development of center-draft lighting for railway cars. The company introduced the glass drip cup and improved the Acme burner developed by Post & Company (Wellington, 1892).

William Westlake and William S. Hamm, among others, held many patents for railroad headlights, car lamps, bicycle lamps, and lanterns. William S. Hamm assigned patents 564,882 (1896) and 588,904 (1897) to Adams & Westlake for bicycle lamps. The X-Rays bicycle lamp is a complex, well-made lamp.

Adams & Westlake Mfg. Co. sold student lamps in 1886. Its ad in the *American Potter and Illuminator* suggests the company manufactured one student lamp — the "A. & W., the Burners have our Central Draft Tube."

The Brilliant burner, made by Holmes, Booth & Haydens, was used in the A. & W. No. 30 student lamp.

The Adams & Westlake Co. advertised the "New Arc Safety Lamp in 1890. This lamp featured a patented harp to support a mammouth fount. The company claimed the Arc was the only lamp made with air space around the wick tube, "making explosion impossible."

Ward W. Willits held patents for hanging railroad car lamps (395,937 and 427,491) and lanterns assigned to Adams & Westlake.

Adams & Westlake purchased the Lovell-Dressel Co. in 1968.

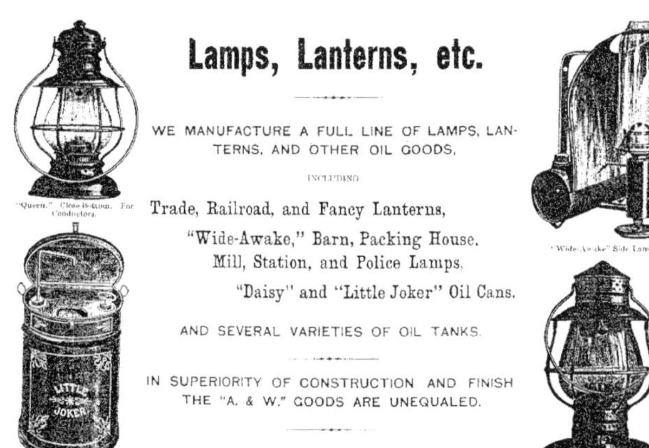

Advertisement, *Crockery and Glass Journal*, Sept. 20, 1883.

Trade Names

Center-draft lamps — A. & W., Arc Safety Lamp.

Center-draft burners — Acme, Postal (mail car). The Westlake Improved Ventilating Car Lamp used Belgian burners (White, 1978).

Lanterns — Adlake, Pullman, Queen.

Bicycle lamps — X-Rays.

A. & W. Student Lamps.

This shows our new No. 30 Lamp. Has "Brilliant" Central Draught Burner, and reservoir with spring valve which cannot be removed from the Lamp without shutting off the oil.

The Reservoir is locked when Lamp is in use.

Burns about six hours. The wick is the regular circular woven wick.

This Lamp is equal in every respect to any of the ordinary class of Student Lamps, and we will take back any of them that do not give satisfaction.

No. 30.

PRICES.

No. 30 Student Lamp, Nickel-plated, complete...... each, $3 80

"A. & W." Student Lamps.

SINGLE AND DOUBLE BURNER.

This Lamp supplies a want which the cheap Student Lamp cannot. The fittings are made of heavy brass, and are not so cheap and frail as to render the Lamps useless from being continually out of order.

The Burners have our Central Draft Tube, over which a *solid circular woven wick* is placed,

These Lamps give a brilliant and steady light, and are not equalled for household or office use,

PRICES.

No. 3, Single Burner, Brass, complete............. each, $5 25
No. 3, Single Burner, Nickel-plated, complete........each, 6 00
No. 4, Double Burner, Brass, complete...............each, 9 50
No. 4, Double Burner, Nickel, complete..............each, 11 00

Advertisement, *The American Potter and Illuminator*, April 1886.

Top of the Adams & Westlake Company "X-Rays" Bicycle Lamp. Patented July 29, 1896. The X-Rays trademark was approved June 9, 1896.

Adams & Westlake Center-Draft Railroad Lamp, ca. 1885 – 1900

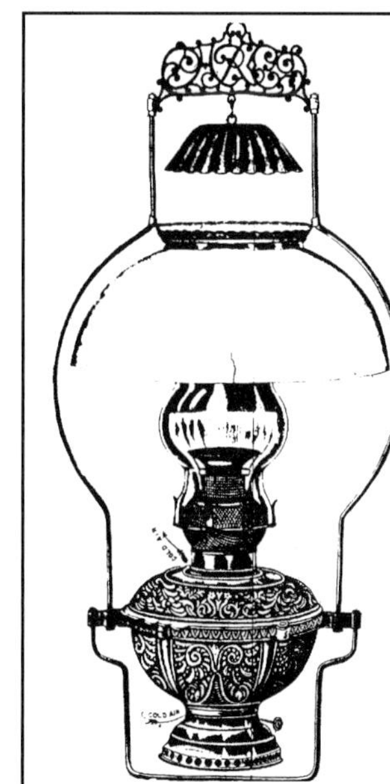

3 NEW

"Arc" Safety Lamps

All with Embossed Founts.

No. 10 "Arc" Oxidized Embossed Fount.
No. 10 Patent Hinged Harp Ring.
No. 20 "Arc" Brass Embossed Fount.
No. 20 Open Harp Ring.
No. 30 "Arc" Brass Embossed Fount.
Without air space around wick-tube.
No. 20 Open Harp Ring.

The "Arc" is the only lamp made with air space around the wick-tube, keeping the air cold, making explosion impossible.

The "Arc" is the only lamp provided with the Babcock Patent Hinged Harp Ring, the safest and most convenient device for securing and handling a mammoth fount lamp.

The "Arc" has some selling points, and more valuable features for safety and convenience in handling than any lamp made.

Send for full illustrated circular and price list.

THE ADAMS & WESTLAKE CO.,

Franklin, Ontario, Ohio and Market Sts.

CHICAGO, ILL.

Advertisement, *Crockery and Glass Journal,* Nov. 6, 1890. This lamp suggests Pittsburgh Brass as the frame manufacturer. I have not located the Babcock patent.

Wick knob.

Adams & Westlake center-draft railroad lamp made for the Rock Island Lines. The lamp fount fit in a wall bracket with a chimney support and smoke bell. The lamp is 8" long. The burner appears similar to Moehring. The knob is marked "The Plume & Atwood Mfg. Co., USA." The top of the fount is stamped "The Adams & Wes[...], Maker, Chicago." The bottom drip cup screws off. See Dayton Mfg. for illustration of P & A Railroad lamp burners. **$75.00.** Courtesy Tim and Sue Krueger.

Adams & Westlake car-side lamp with improved Acme burner. The drip cup is glass. Flame spreader and white glass shade are missing. The brass label is marked "The Adams & Westlake Company, Makers, Chicago." Overall height 16". This identical lamp was illustrated as car-side lamp No. 74 in Dayton Catalog No. 166. **$1,000.00.** Courtesy William Schreiber.

American-Belgian Lamp Co.

La Lampe Belge ("The Belgian Lamp"), 1884 – 1930s

The Belgian center-draft lamp was developed in Europe during the mid-1880s. The American-Belgian Lamp Company, New York City, claimed to be both importer and manufacturer. Belgian lamps were heavily promoted and sold well into the 1930s by many stores and in several catalogs, such as Pitkin and Brooks, Sears & Roebuck, and Montgomery Ward for many years. Sales exceeded 600,000 lamps per year, according to *CGJ*, Aug. 20, 1891.

The original Belgian lamp was made by the Lempereur & Bernard Company in Liege, Belgium, founded by Joseph Lempereur and Lambert Bernard in 1868. They developed the center-draft lamp that became known as "La Lampe Belge." The logos "Lampe Belge Brevete and L & B" and "Lempereur & Bernard, Brevette" were trademarked in Belgium in 1904.

The Belgian lamp was awarded the gold medal in the 1889 Paris Exposition; Hinks and Rochester lamps were awarded silver medals.

Patents were obtained in 1884 and 1886 in the UK, and Belgian lamps were made there by Midland Lighting Co., LTD, Belge Lamp Works, Birmingham, England. These lamps are marked "La Lampe Belge" and with a Smiley Sun logo. The Smiley Sun with"L & B" was trademarked in Belgium in 1895, stating use since June 1887.

The Belgian lamp was patented in Germany in 1885 and made there by Albert Riegermann. These lamps are marked with "L & B" and "AR," 1899 trademarks.

Pitkin & Brooks published a 24-page Belgian catalog in 1898 touting the Belgian lamp as superior to all other oil lamps. The catalog includes American lamps of all types, offering to replace the American oil pot with the "superior Belgian burner." Belgian chimneys and wicks were also sold at higher prices than American replacements. The chimneys and wicks were marked "AR."

(Pitkins & Brooks)

BELGIAN STORE and HOUSE LAMPS

ARE THE

BEST KEROSENE OIL LAMPS IN THE WORLD

SEE OUR SEPARATE CATALOGUE

Belgian lamps were made in all forms, ranging from plain style and heavy brass construction to ornate and elegant cast banquet lamps. Pitkin & Brooks said they were of "metal so heavy, [you] can almost drive nails with one of these founts." Some of the glass shades illustrated in the American-Belgian catalog of 1908 – 1909 were among the finest of the day.

Baumann & Wolfe (1994) suggest that one Manhattan student lamp and the Belgian student lamp are identical, except for the burners. The Dressel Railway Lamp & Signal Company sold Belgian lamps in its 1926 catalog, including "one- and two light centre lamps" (ceiling lamps) for Pullman cars.

Trade Names

The Belgian Lamp — Marked on fill cap: "Brevete L & B," "Brevete L & B 1883," "La Lampe Belge L & B."

The Belgian Lamp — Marked on flame spreader: "'Thermidor' Belge Patent 50 CP," "L & B Lampe Belge Brevete," "Lempereur" and "Bernard Brevete."

Lamps are marked on the knob, on the fill cap, and some founts are dated 1883 on the bottom. Lamps were finished in nickel, dark brown japan finish, polished brass, gold finish, and gold plated.

The fill cap has a vent plus a spring loaded valve.

Selected Patents, Center-draft Lamps

Henry Harris Lake (agent for Lempereur & Bernard)

UK	1884	11,285
	1886	11,296
Albert Riegermann		
Germany	1885	33,906
J. Lempereur & L. Bernard[1]		
USA	1885	333,237
Louis Sepulchre[1]		
USA	1887	356,507
Howard Walker (agent for Midland Lighting Co., Ltd.)		
UK	1892	19,331

[1]Ara Kebapcioglu has an excellent and informative website (http://members.aol.com/Lumiara/) showing L&B and Sepulchre lamps.

Trademarks

The Belgian center-draft lamp was developed by Joseph Lempereur and Lambert Bernard in Liege, Belgium. The famous La Lampe Belge (The Belgian Lamp) was sold in countries around the world for over 50 years.

Advertisement, *Crockery and Glass Journal*, Dec. 11, 1890.

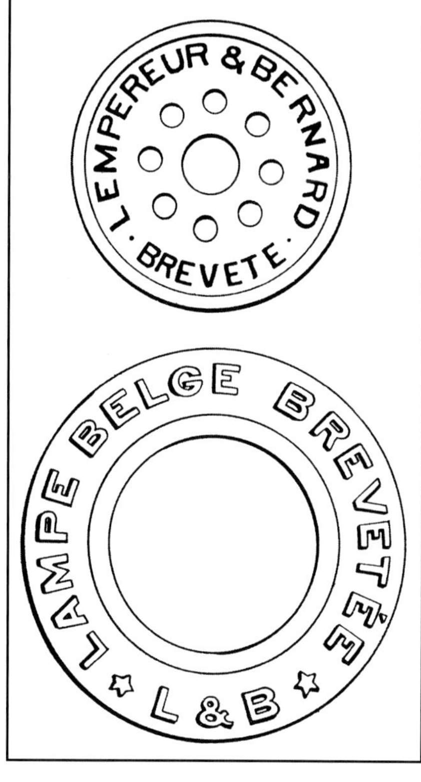

Lempereur & Bernard trademark, registered 1904 in Belgium. Courtesy Anton Kaim.

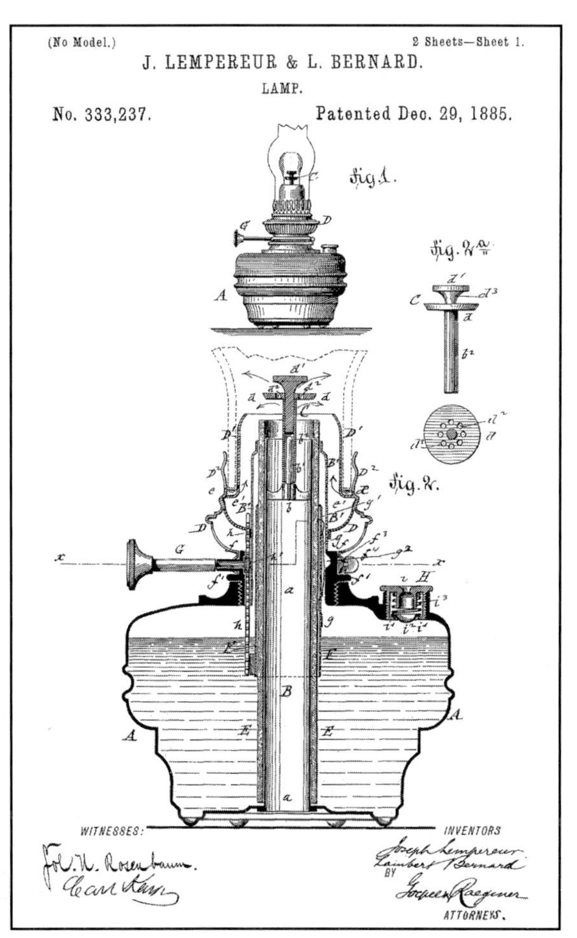

Nr. 35339. R. 2639. Alb. Riegermann, Elberfeld. Anmeldung vom 12. 9. 98/21. 12. 93. Eintragung am 11. 1. 99.
Geschäftsbetrieb: Herstellung und Vertrieb nachgenannter Waaren.
Waarenverzeichniß: Lampengläser aller Art.

Albert Riegermann trademark, 1899.
Courtesy Anton Kaim.

Lempereur & Bernard trademark, registered 1915.
Courtesy Anton Kaim.

Improvements in Petroleum Lamps, August 14, 1884

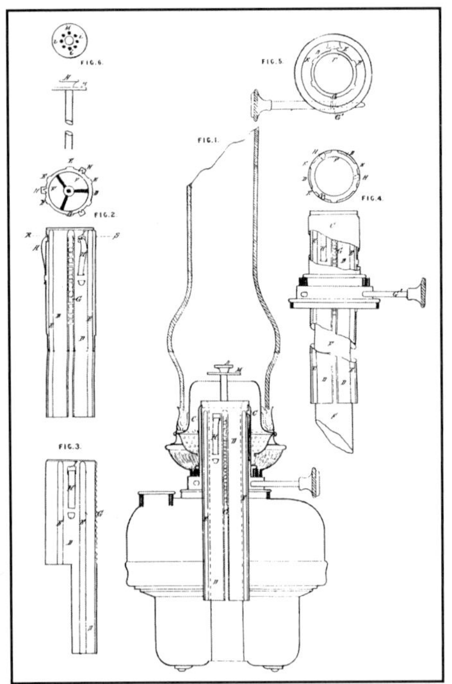

Lempereur and Bernard UK Patent 11,285.
Courtesy Anton Kaim.

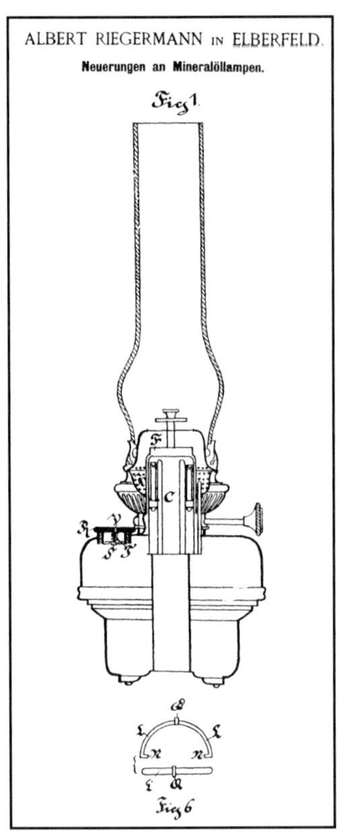

Albert Riegermann 1885 Patent 33,906, Germany. Courtesy Anton Kaim.

Improvements in Lamp for Burning Mineral Oil, Jan. 7, 1886

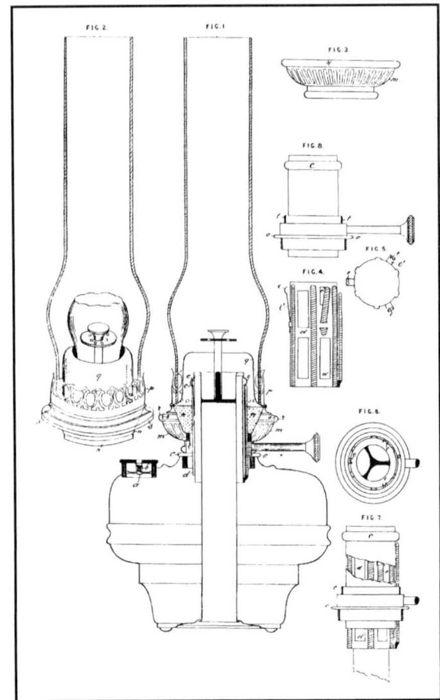

Lempereur and Bernard UK Patent 11,296.
Courtesy Anton Kaim.

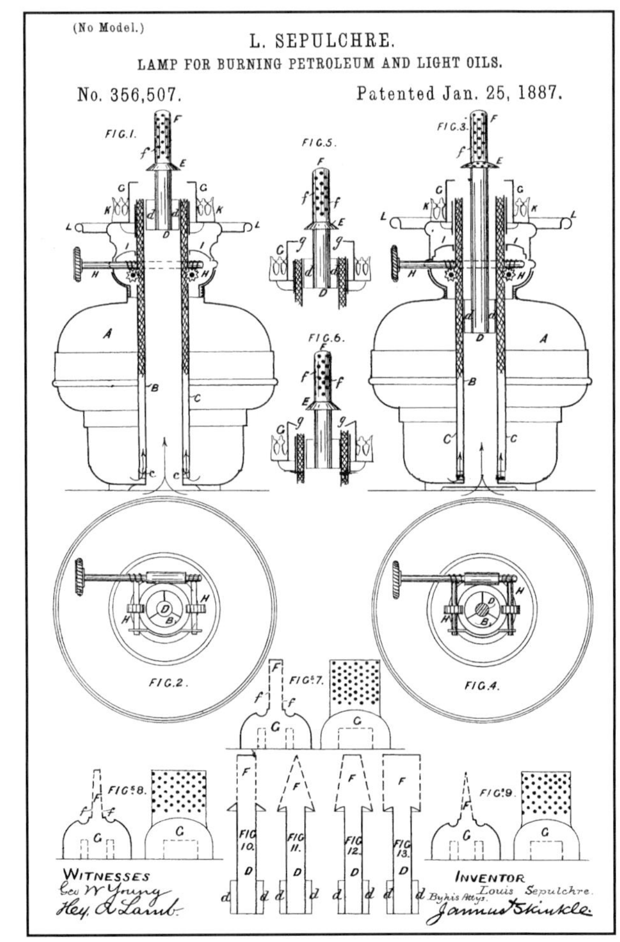

The Belgian Lamp

Cylinder Burners are especially used in altering Lamps of other makes; also in Student Lamps, Railroad Car Lamps, Express Messenger Lamps, etc.

Flame spreader.

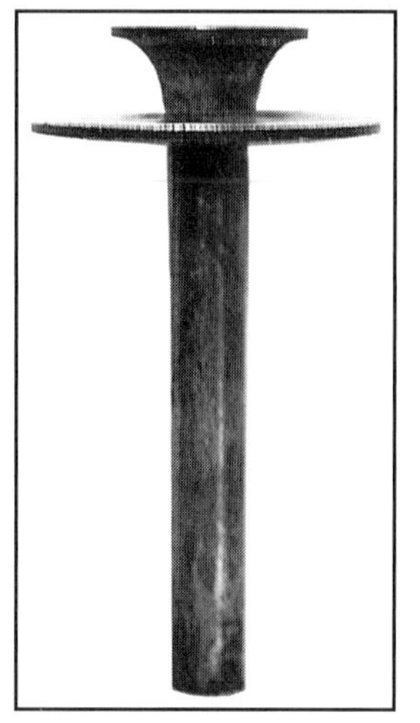

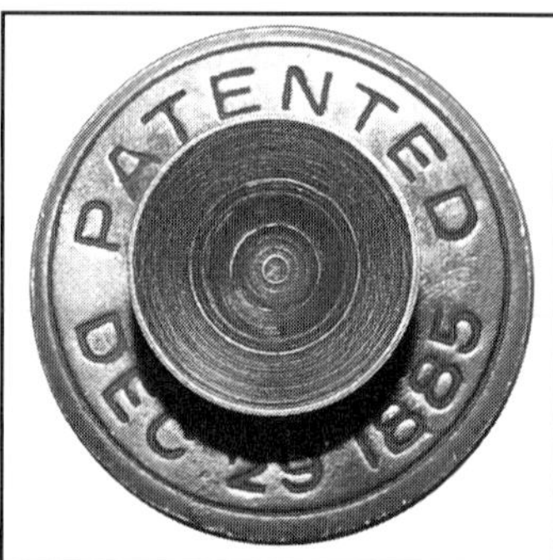

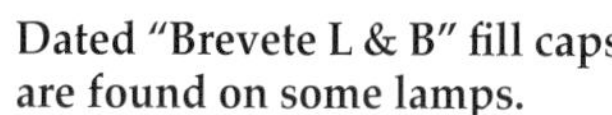

Dated "Brevete L & B" fill caps are found on some lamps.

Smiley Sun on wick knob (left) and oil fill cap (right) found on Belgian lamps.

Belgian oil pot, 8" tall with original shade ring. Other shapes were also made to fit most 5" vase lamps. Missing the flame spreader illustrated above. $50.00.

Belgian table lamp, 12½" tall. This is a common table lamp. These were finished in brass, nickel, and dark Old English. Capacity 2½ pints, 43 candlepower. $75.00.

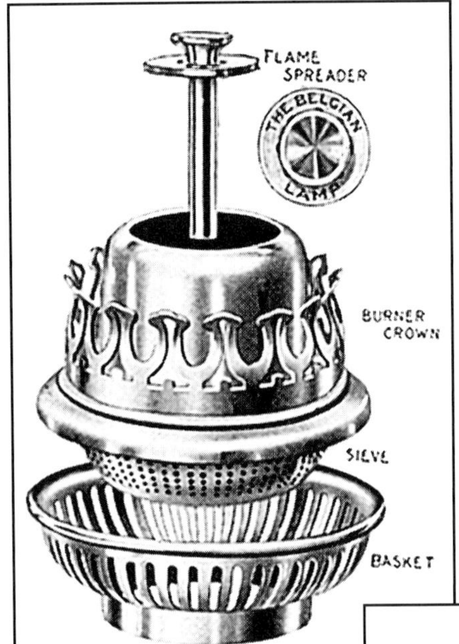

Courtesy Alex Marrack.

Some Belgian lamps are found with unmarked wick knobs.

Flame spreader.

Oil fill cap.

Belgian mammoth fount for hanging lamp. Height 10¼". Capacity 6 pints, 100 CP (candle power). Brass or nickel finish. Some founts are marked and dated in the bottom. $100.00.

Belgian hanging lamp fount, 9" tall. Capacity 2½ pints, 43 CP. Missing bottom drip plate. $75.00.

The Celebrated Belgian Lamps

The American-Belgian Lamp Company was formed about 1889, with offices and factory at 31 Barclay St. and later at 3860 – 3878 Park Avenue, New York City. Officers were F. W. Dressel, president; R. Black, vice-president; S. W. Parker, treasurer; and J. Dawans, secretary-manager. According to catalog No. 3, 1908/1909, "The Belgian Lamp was introduced into the United States twenty years ago. Imitations of the BELGIAN have been many, but all have lost prestige. The Belgian Lamp positively gives the greatest light with the least consumption of oil. United States Government tests have fully demonstrated its high candle power. The U. S. Lighthouse Board adopted various valuable features exclusive to the Belgian burner."

These lamps are from catalog No. 3, 1908/1909.

No. 650 cast brass parlor lamp.

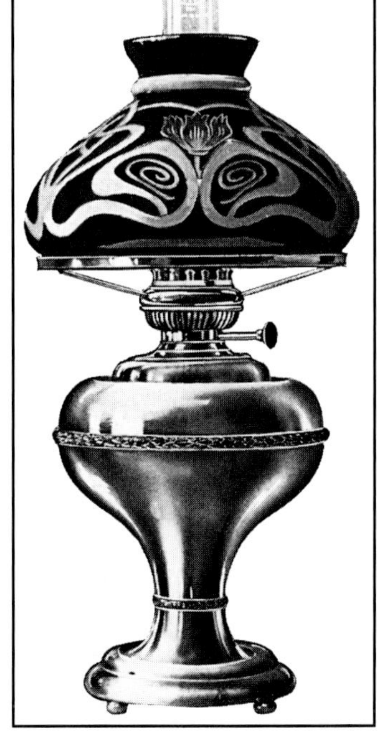

No. 351 parlor lamp.

No. 216 table lamp.

No. 18A station lamp.

No. 701 piano or desk lamp.

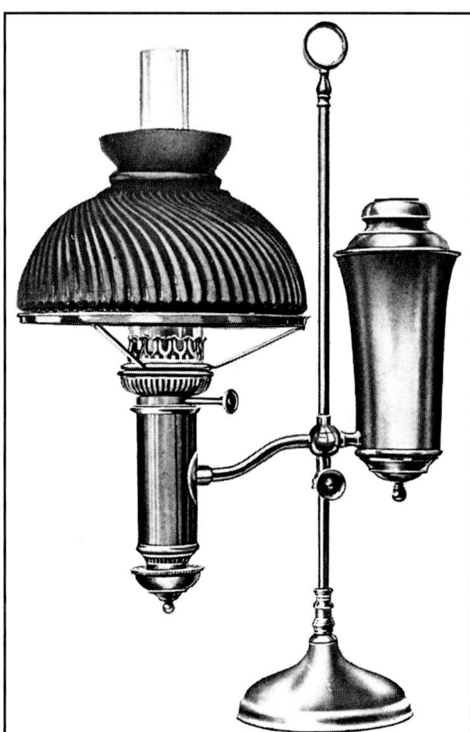

No. 339 student lamp.

No. 58 globe canopy lamp.

No. 56 post lamp.

Vase lamp.
Courtesy Dave Broughton.

No. 499 brass hanging lamp with 20" corrugated tin shade. The lamp was also offered in nickel (No. 492).

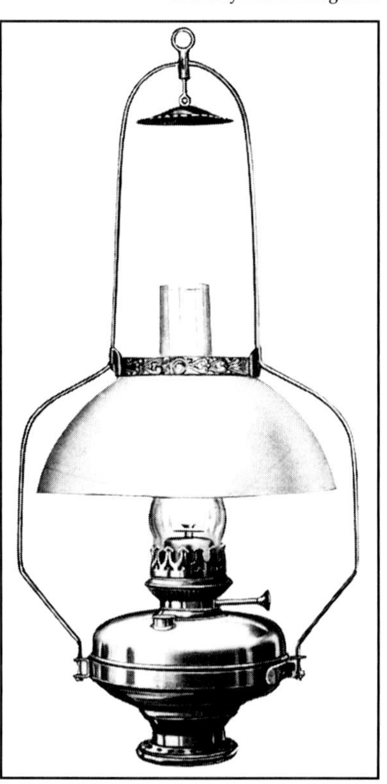

No. 403 brass hanging mammoth lamp with opal dome shade, 14" diameter. The lamp was also offered in nickel (No. 483).

American Brass Company

1899 – 1960

Lamp Manufacture 1899 – early 1900s

The period of 1895 – 1901 was a time of consolidation by the brass companies in Waterbury, Connecticut — the "Brass City." Originally Plume & Atwood and Scovill Manufacturing intended to participate, but they declined by the time the special charter was accepted by other brass fabricators.

American Brass Company was finally formed as a holding company in 1899, with the consolidation of Ansonia Brass & Copper Company, Waterbury Brass Company, and Coe Brass Company.

Coe Brass had taken over Wallace and Sons in 1896. In 1901 Coe Brass bought Chicago Brass Co., of Kenosha, Wisconsin.

In 1900 Benedict & Burnham Manufacturing Company joined the consolidation, and in 1901 Holmes, Booth & Haydens became a member. In 1905 Holmes, Booth & Haydens merged with Benedict & Burnham Mfg. Company.

I believe the member companies continued to produce kerosene lamps and burners for a short time after consolidation in American Brass. Manufacture of kerosene lamps diminished as the companies merged to concentrate on their primary business of copper and brass fabrication.

I suspect that kerosene lamps were no longer made by 1912, when American Brass reorganized as an operating company. At that time Charles F. Brooker, leader of the original consolidation, was elected president.

I have not found advertisements by American Brass for lamps found in this book, although such ads may well exist.

I include lamps made by Ansonia; Holmes, Booth & Haydens; Matthews & Willard Mfg. Co.; and Wallace & Sons in their respective chapters.

The Genealogy of the Naugatuck Brass Industry is illustrated in chart form by Lathrop (1936) in *The Development of the Brass Industry in Connecticut*.

The American Brass Company was acquired in 1922 by the Anaconda Mining Company (of Montana), though it kept its name until it was changed to Anaconda American Brass in 1960. The Anaconda Company merged with Atlantic Richfield in 1977, and then became ARCO Metals.

A Group of Pioneer Brass Manufacturers

Additional history of American Brass and division companies may be found at the Thomas J. Dodd Research Center, University of Connecticut Libraries.

American Lamp & Brass Co.

1892 – 1904

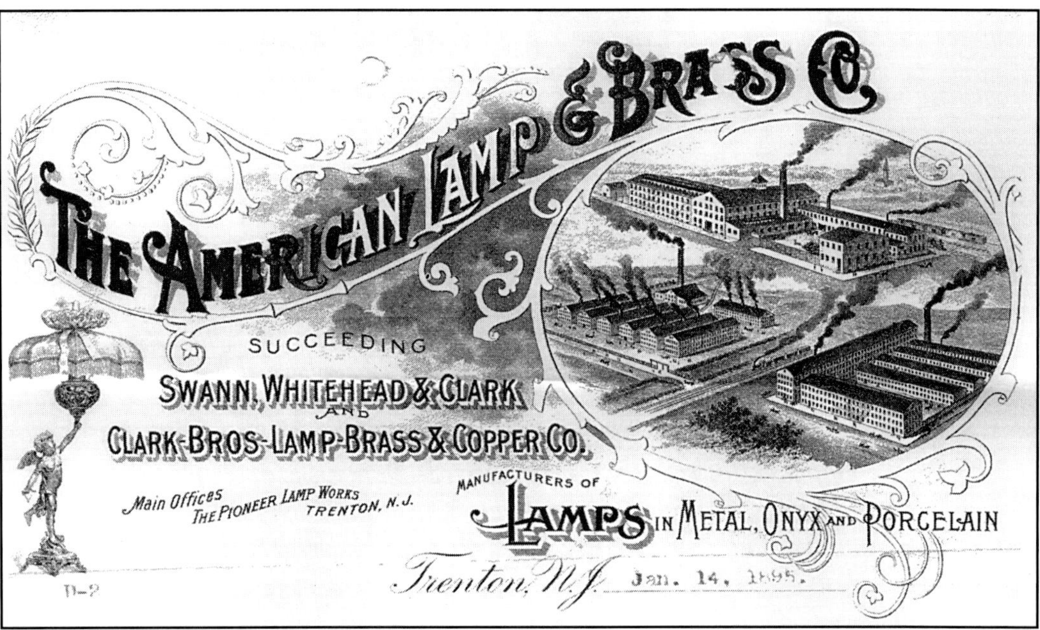

1895 letterhead.
Courtesy Wheaton Village Museum of American Glass.

American Lamp & Brass Company was formed by the consolidation of Swann, Whitehead & Clark of Trenton, New Jersey, McLewee Brass Manufacturing Company of New York, and Clark Brothers Lamp, Brass & Copper Company of Trenton. A story published in the Trenton *Daily State Gazette*, July 31, 1897, stated that the "American Lamp & Brass Company was incorporated in 1891 with capital of $1,000,000." The merger, however, was not officially registered until Nov. 19, 1892, and the merged companies continued to operate as divisions until 1893. The new company advertised, "In union there is strength."

I assume McLewee Brass Co. was owned or operated by William S. McLewee, who was also involved with the Hektograph Manufacturing Company. McLewee held several design patents for lamp shades. Swann and McLewee operated a lamp store in New York in 1896.

Officers of American Lamp & Brass Co. were William R. Whitehead, president; P. K. Clark, vice president and sales manager; Charles Clark, treasurer; and F. B. Clark, secretary. William S. Clark was general manager.

The factory was located at Mulberry and Delaware streets, Trenton, NJ, in seven large buildings where employment ranged from 250 to 500. Complete brass and spelter foundries were on this site. The company manufactured lamps in metal, onyx, and decorated opal glass. Opal glass, purchased from glasshouses near Pittsburgh, was decorated by hand as well as by designs printed on globes and lamp bases. The decorations included floral designs and special styles named Delft, Copenhagen, and Teck. Some cast-iron feet on lamps were marked "ALBC."

In 1893 the company made an impressive presentation at the Columbian Exposition, extensively advertising its "American" lamp.

Retail outlets were operated in New York, Chicago, San Francisco, Philadelphia, Baltimore, and Boston.

The Banner lamp, made by Plume & Atwood, was advertised and sold by American Lamp & Brass Co. I believe P & A also provided oil pots and burners for lamps sold by this company. Matthews & Willard may also have provided brass fittings. M & W sued American Lamp & Brass in late 1894 for patent infringement.

Trade journals reported metal fabrication in Trenton; however, I believe the company assembled most of the lamps from components made by other manufacturers.

I believe the American Lamp is identical to the U.S. Trenton Lamp sold by Clark Brothers'. Likewise, the same small-size oil pot seems to have been sold by both companies.

American Lamp & Brass was converting its lamps to electricity by 1900 when the president was granted patent 661,332 for wiring through the central-draft air tube. Gas and electrical fixtures were being manufactured in 1901 in an effort to develop new products. *China, Glass & Lamps* (February 1901) reported that the glass decorating department would move to Ellwood City, near Pittsburgh, to save shipping costs of glass and reduce breakage since most lamps were shipped West. One hundred employees in Trenton were put out of work.

The company went out of business in 1904 due to "general depression and strong competition in the lamp business" (*CGL*, March 5, 1904).

Trade Names

Center-draft lamps — American, American Lamp 95, Banner Lamp, Eureka.

Selected Patents

William R. Whitehead assigned to American Lamp & Brass Co.
1900 661,332

IN UNION THERE IS STRENGTH.
AMERICAN LAMP & BRASS CO.
CAPITAL STOCK - - - ONE MILLION DOLLARS.

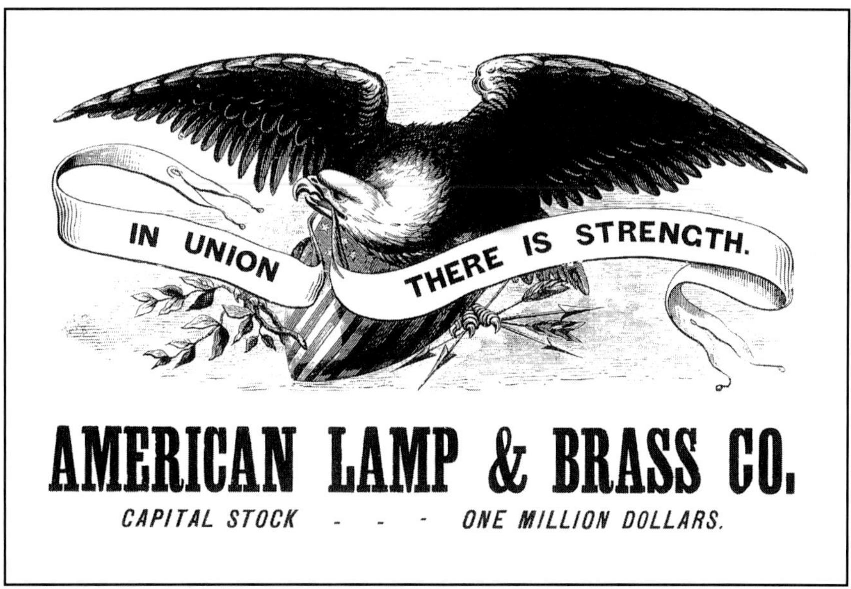

Advertisement, *CGJ*, January 12, 1893.

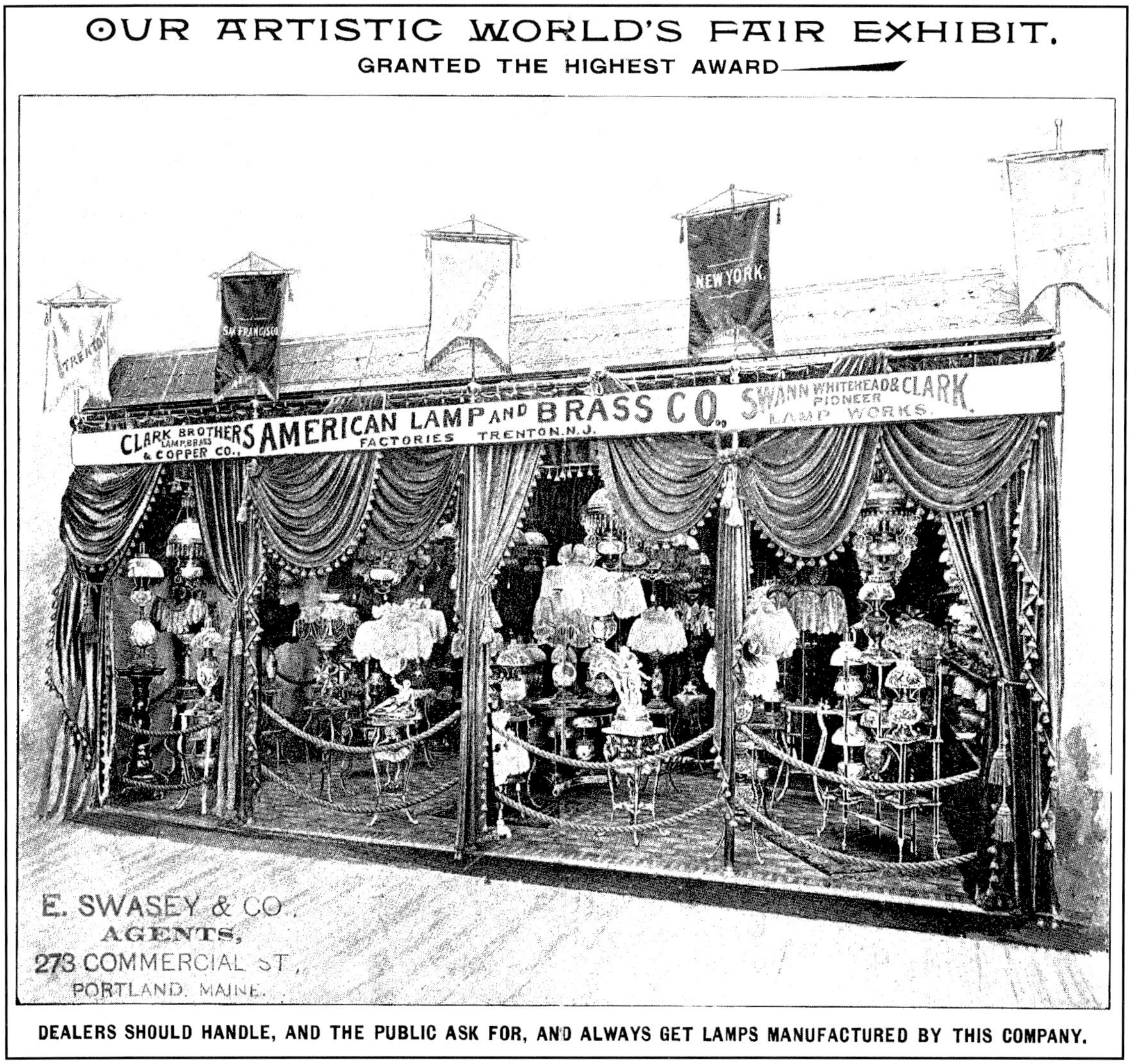
OUR ARTISTIC WORLD'S FAIR EXHIBIT.
GRANTED THE HIGHEST AWARD
TRENTON
SAN FRANCISCO
NEW YORK
CLARK BROTHERS LAMP, BRASS & COPPER CO.
AMERICAN LAMP AND BRASS CO.
FACTORIES TRENTON, N.J.
SWANN WHITEHEAD & CLARK PIONEER LAMP WORKS.
E. SWASEY & CO.
AGENTS,
273 COMMERCIAL ST.,
PORTLAND, MAINE.
DEALERS SHOULD HANDLE, AND THE PUBLIC ASK FOR, AND ALWAYS GET LAMPS MANUFACTURED BY THIS COMPANY.

Trade Card. American Lamp & Brass Company, 1893 Columbian Exposition, Chicago.

American Lamp

AMERICAN LAMP & BRASS CO.

CAPITAL STOCK - - - ONE MILLION DOLLARS.

CONSOLIDATING

AMERICA'S GREATEST LAMP ENTERPRISES

The Pioneer Factory of Swann & Whitehead,

The Empire Factory of Swann, Whitehead & Clark,

And the Factories of

The Clark Bros. Lamp, Brass and Copper Co.

Our Aim: The Illumination of the World.

Advertisement, *Crockery and Glass Journal*, 1893.

Flame spreader for the American lamp.

Do You Want A Lamp?

If so, buy the best on earth, the

AMERICAN

which was the prize winner at the World's Fair, and the ONLY centre draft lamp receiving the HIGHEST AWARD. There are ELEVEN REASONS why it is the best, which will be mailed upon application; or, take our word and that of the World's Fair judges for it, mail us $3.00, and we will send to you, charges prepaid, a lamp like that shown in the cut, handsomely finished in nickel silver, and fitted with a beautiful decorated shade.

This Lamp is full parlor size. Gives a light equal to four gas jets. Is easy to wick, easy to extinguish, easy to keep clean. Can be lighted without removing chimney or shade, and is absolutely safe.

Over three million of our lamps in use.

We guarantee every lamp. If not satisfactory will refund money.

Remit by check, postal note or money order to

The American Lamp and Brass Co., Manfrs.

TRENTON, NEW JERSEY

The World Greatest Centre Draft-Lamp

Advertisement, *Ladies' Home Journal*, January 1894.

Oil fill cap for American lamp.

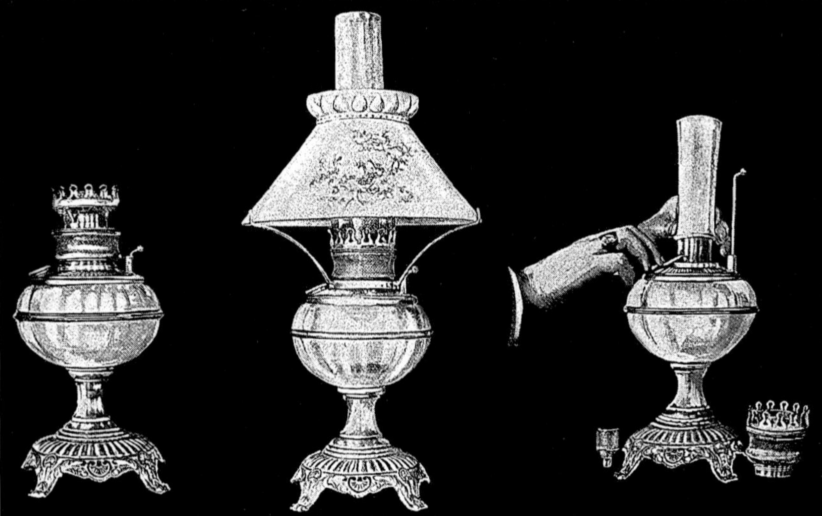

"The Great 'American' Centre-Draft Lamp. Having all desirable improvements and a wicking device so simple that its workings are self-demonstrating."

American stand lamp with cast-iron foot. Lift gallery as illustrated left. The lamp is 12½" tall. $85.00.

American Lamp, Promoting the World's Fair Medal, Columbian Exposition in 1893.

Flame spreader. Many, but not all, of these and the Eureka flame spreaders are interchangeable. Note the "ring," or "rib," that sets the correct level in the wick tube.

No. 1 flame spreader, "Highest Award, The American Lamp, World's Fair."

Fill cap.

Wick knob.

No. 1 American oil pot.

Fill cap.

American stand lamp made during or shortly after the 1893 Columbian Exposition. Note curved burner basket. Height 12½". Burner with lift gallery. $75.00.

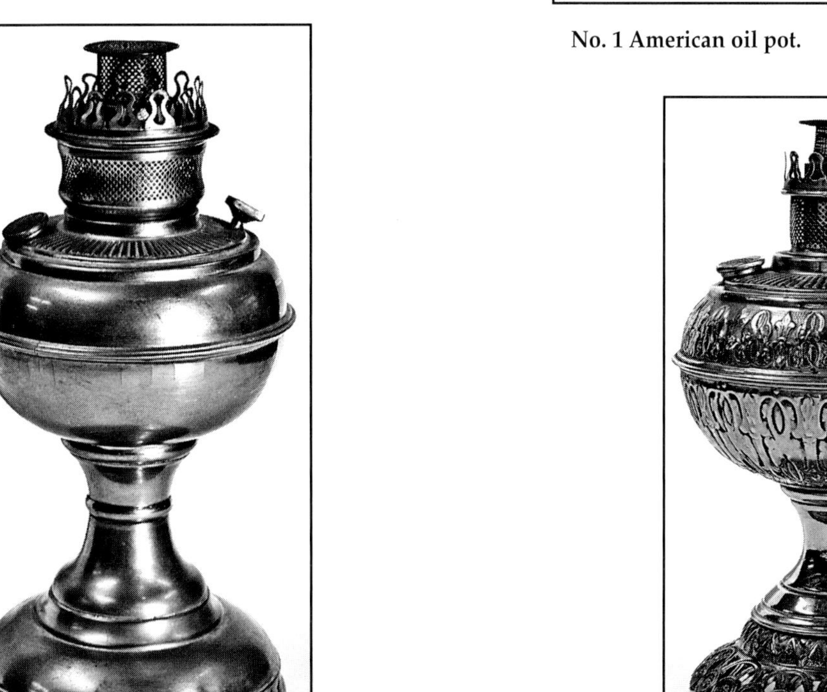

Junior-size American stand lamp with cast-iron foot, believed made for the 1893 Columbian Exposition. Height 11". The same small burner is found in oil pots used in decorated vase lamps. $200.00.

This lamp is also found plain, not embossed. The burner was also used in oil pots and is found with the American-Eureka flame spreader.

Flame spreader.

Wick knob.

Fill cap.

American Lamp 95, Plume & Atwood Oil Pot

American 95 flame spreader with patent dates: "Aug. 14, 88," "Aug. 26, 90," "Sept. 9, 90," "March 24, 91," and "Jan. 5, 92." None of the patents for these dates were assigned to American Lamp & Brass. The burner and flame spreader in this lamp were bought from Plume & Atwood.

American stand lamp, World's Fair. Height 13". The wick knob is marked "Made in U.S. of America, Pat. App'd For," also dated "Pat. Aug. 3, 1897." The flame spreader is marked "The American Lamp, Highest Award, World's Fair," or "The American Lamp." Embossed, $175.00; plain, $75.00.

American 95 vase lamp with P & A oil pot. I do not know who cast the metal vase; possibly, it was made in Trenton. $200.00. Courtesy of Glen Southard.

Eureka

Eureka oil pots and burners were used in a wide variety of lamps and are found in some of the better kerosene lamps collected today.

The Eureka flame spreader is found in two shapes that seem to be interchangeable. See tops of both on right.

Some Eureka flame spreaders contain a screen inside for draft control.

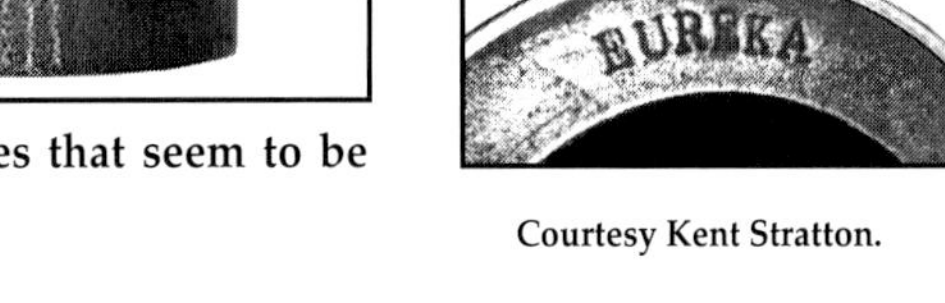

Courtesy Kent Stratton.

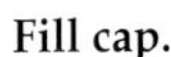

Fill cap.

Wick knob.

Base variations found on Eureka stand lamps. These contain a heavy cast loading weight, some of which are stamped "Eureka" (see above). Some burners have non–lift gallery.

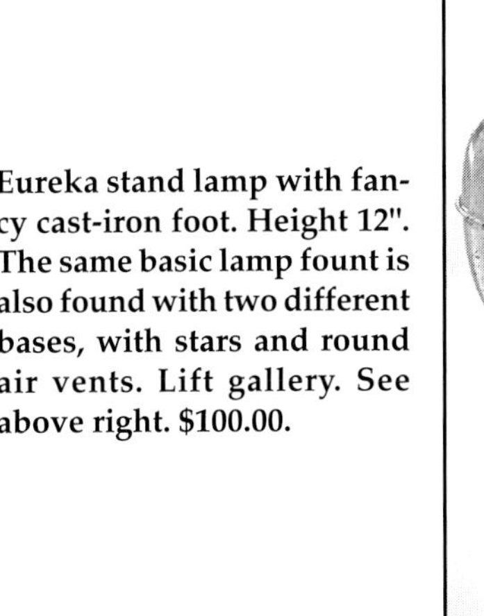

Eureka stand lamp with fancy cast-iron foot. Height 12". The same basic lamp fount is also found with two different bases, with stars and round air vents. Lift gallery. See above right. $100.00.

Advertisement promoting the American lamp after the World's Fair, *Crockery and Glass Journal*, Dec. 1893.

Eureka vase lamp, Marshall Field & Co., Fall 1901 catalog. Courtesy Heinz and Ursula Baumann.

Eureka vase lamp with angels. $1,250.00. Courtesy Kent Stratton.

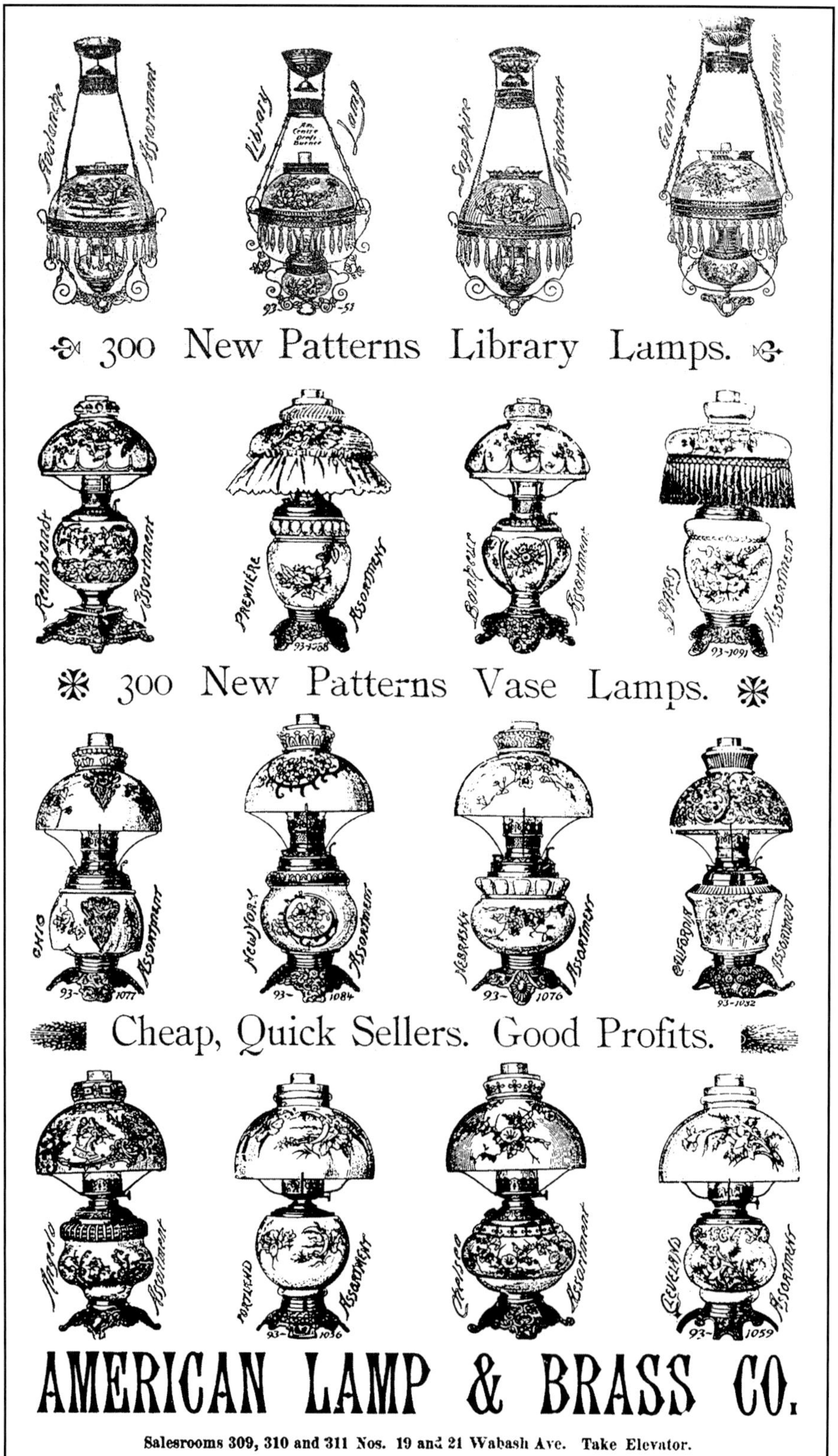

300 New Patterns Library Lamps.

300 New Patterns Vase Lamps.

Cheap, Quick Sellers. Good Profits.

AMERICAN LAMP & BRASS CO.

Salesrooms 309, 310 and 311 Nos. 19 and 21 Wabash Ave. Take Elevator.

Advertisement, *Pottery and Glassware Reporter,* September 1895. At this time the company was selling an inexpensive line that included both center-draft and flat-wick decorated vase lamps.

Ansonia Brass & Copper Co.

1845 – 1899

Lamp Manufacture Early 1880s – 1899

Anson G. Phelps was an importer of tin, brass, and copper in New York City, with an overseas office in Liverpool, England. In 1836 he started manufacturing sheet copper and brass in a settlement he called Birmingham, after the famous town in England, near Derby, Connecticut. The factory also manufactured brass pins from wire. In 1844, he built a rolling mill two miles up the river from Derby. The new location became Ansonia, named in 1845 for Phelps — and the Ansonia Brass & Copper Co. was thereby born. Officially, however, the company was incorporated in 1854, after Phelps died.

The Ansonia Brass & Copper Company was headed by George P. Cowles until 1887. In 1889, the town of Ansonia separated officially from Derby, which then became Connecticut's smallest city.

Ansonia Brass manufactured brass pins, copper sheets, and brass kettles, which it exhibited in 1876 at the Centennial Exposition. The company offered an assortment of flat-wick lamps before entering the center-draft market in 1885. Ansonia sold lamps to the Dominion Tubular Lamp Company in Montreal, Quebec, and to other companies.

Phelps established the Ansonia Clock Company in 1850. Ansonia Clock, which became one of the world's large clock factories, was moved from Ansonia to Brooklyn, where clocks were made from 1880 to 1930. The company was the world leader in statuary clocks adorned with figures from Greco-Roman and Renaissance literature.

The Ansonia Brass & Copper Co. became part of American Brass Company in 1899. Subsequently, the Ansonia Brass division was sold several times, eventually becoming a privately owned company in 1986. Today, the "new" Ansonia Copper & Brass Co. (note the name change) makes wire products, seamless tubing, and specialty alloys of brass and copper.

Trade Names

Center-draft lamps — Ansonia Electric, The Bassett, The Improved, The Apex, Little Jewel, The New Universal Mammoth, The Improved Mammoth, Wilson. Ansonia advertised "The Apex Safety Lamp and The New Universal Mammoth" hanging lamps in 1891 and 1892.

Folded-wick burner — Advance.

Ansonia Brass and Copper Company,
ANSONIA, - - - CONN.
MANUFACTURERS OF
ROLLED BRASS,
Sheet and Bolt Copper,
Brass Kettles, Brass and Copper Wire, Brass and Copper Tubing, Iron Wire, Copper Bottoms, Lamp Burners,
BRONZE, WOOD AND MARINE
EIGHT-DAY and THIRTY-HOUR CLOCKS.
JAMES STOKES, Pres't. J. H. BARTHOLOMEW, Agt. G. P. COWLES, Treas.
Warehouse, 21 Cliff Street, - - - NEW YORK.

Advertisement 1875, *Connecticut Business Directory*. Courtesy Allen Weathers.

Selected Patents, Center-draft Lamps

George W. Woodward assigned to Ansonia Brass & Copper

Year	Patent
1887	366,805 (½ w. W.A. Hull)
1888	386,861
1889	406,016
1889	417,620 & 621
1890	429,181
1890	440,683
1895	539,467

Charles H. Lyman[1] assigned to Ansonia Brass & Copper

Year	Patent
1889	399,912

Wolcott A. Hull[2] assigned to Ansonia Brass & Copper

Year	Patent
1886	345,233
1887	D17,848
1892	467,975

Joseph E. Bohner[3] unassigned

Year	Patent
1895	538,862

[1]Also patents for hanging lamps.
[2]Joseph E. Bohner held unassigned design patents, 1895.
[3]Also patents for hanging lamps.

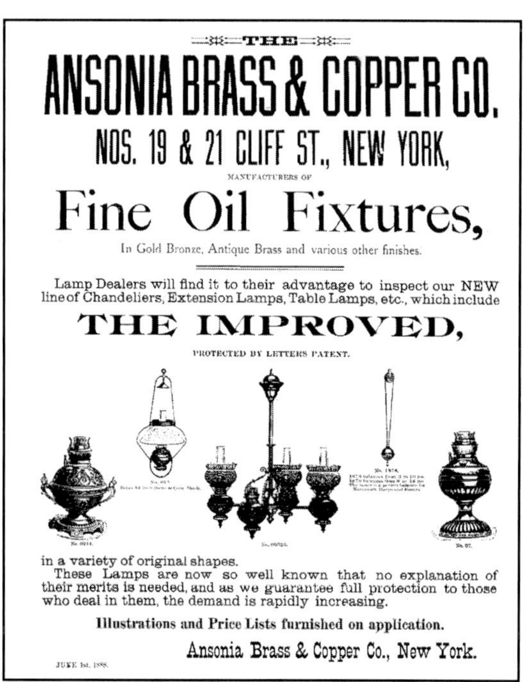

Advertisement, *Pottery and Glassware Reporter*, Aug. 23, 1888.

Ansonia Electric, The Bassett

George F. Bassett Co. sold this lamp as the Bassett in 1885/1886. Henry and Nathan Russell advertised the same lamp as the Ansonia Electric in 1885, with "rich gold finish, $60.00/doz." The Dec. 12, 1882, patent date is a mystery.

The Improved

Ansonia Brass apparently considered changes in its earlier lamps and stamped the 1887 models "The Improved." I suspect there are other early Ansonia lamps to be discovered.

Wick knob on lamp below.

Improved tripod is marked "This side up" and "Pat. Appl For." The arms are square and fit tightly.

Lift tab for lamp below is marked "A," for Ansonia.

"The Bassett" stamped on the wick knob. Height 12" to top of chimney prongs. Flame spreader missing. This lamp appears identical to the Ansonia lamp advertised by Henry & Nathan Russell in its 1885 catalog (see above). The wick tube is a slightly larger diameter than that on the "Improved" lamp. $175.00.

Wick raiser for the Improved lamps. Courtesy Kent Stratton.

"The Improved, Pat'd July 19, '87" stamped in collar where the burner locks. Height 12½". Flame spreader marked "Top." Non–lift gallery. $175.00.

Ansonia Brass introduced the "The Improved" center-draft lamp in 1887, apparently to the alarm of Charles Upton and the Rochester Lamp Company. Upton announced a court injunction against Ansonia in 1888 and published notice in the trade journals (see next page). I do not know the outcome but trade journal advertising is clear that Ansonia continued marketing its center-draft lamps.

Virtually all Ansonia stand lamps with pull-rod wick raisers are found with plain ("TOP") undated flame spreaders (see below). Lamps with more complicated wick-raiser mechanisms are found with dated flame spreaders.

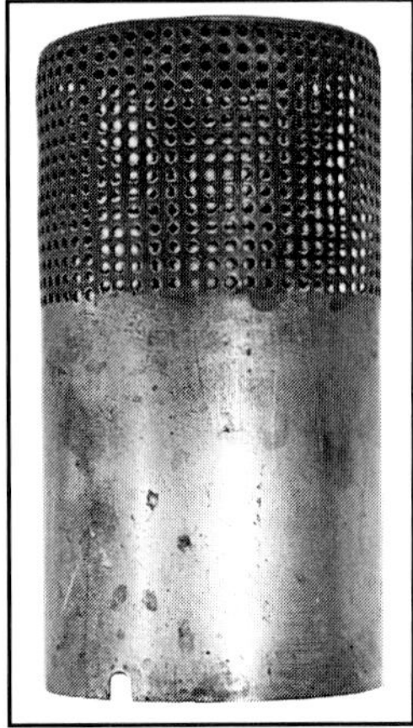

Ansonia flame spreaders for "The Improved" lamps may or may not be marked "Pat'd. Dec. 17, 1889."

"The Improved" is stamped in the fount (below) or around the collar (above).

"The Improved, Pat'd July 19, '87" stamped in collar where the burner locks. Height 11". Non-lift gallery. $125.00.

Oil fill cap.

"The Improved, Pat'd July 19, '87" stamped into top of fount. Height 11". Lift gallery. Wick knob on side of fount marked "Manufactured in the U. S. A." $175.00.

CAUTION TO THE TRADE!!

The Rochester Lamp Co. ask these questions:

Which pays the best? To sell the Rochester Lamp and please your customers, or deceive them by pawning off upon them some infringement or imitation of the Rochester Lamp, and get caught at it, and be obliged to produce your books and clerks before the U. S. Courts? Who do you say will protect you and make your expenses good, Gentlemen. They are getting desperate or they would not consign you these infringing Lamps. Look at the jobbers who have already returned the consigned imitation Lamps. They say "Get the lowest figures from the Rochester Lamp Co. and we will give you the same thing (counterfeit Lamps) at ten and even twenty per cent. better, if you will push them." Why do they say this? Because they feel the danger they are in and wish your aid, some of them have already had the law at their door and have made advances for a settlement. Can you afford to take chances of this sort? Can you afford to approach your customers and find these same desperate pirates there ahead of you, selling the dry goods stores, saloons or any who will buy? Even your expected customer has bought as cheap and if needs be cheaper than they sold you.

Before the October sun shines in your store windows you will say, the Rochester Lamp Co. have advised us, protected their prices, placed us in a way to make a fair percentage, and we in return for this must give them our patronage that we may have a clear conscience, having followed the Golden Rule of "Doing unto others as you would have others do unto you." You will notice they stamp "Patent applied for." Then they must know there is a Patent Law. We enjoy for the Rochester Lamp more than a dozen patents and have the best talent money can procure to protect them, and should all prove to be worthless can any concern make Rochester Lamps cheaper? Has any one one-fourth of the designs? All Europe as well as this great country answers, No!

We invite you all to call and see our new designs, our new patented Hangers, Piano Lamps and fixtures. See for yourself and use your own judgment. Respectfully, yours,

ROCHESTER LAMP COMPANY,

CHAS. S. UPTON, Manager.

Pottery and Glassware Reporter, May 17, 1888.

Read Judge Andrews' Opinion and Be Convinced.

Do Not Be Deceived, the "ROCHESTER" is Still Ahead.

The statements made by the Ansonia Brass and Copper Company, that the injunction granted by Judge Andrews of the New York Supreme Court on behalf of the Rochester Lamp Company had been vacated, are incorrect. The injunction was made permanent, to continue during the pendency of the action, February 8th, 1888.

The following is an extract from the opinion of Judge Andrews, upon the decision of the motion to continue the injunction: "What the plaintiff does contend, however, is that the „defendant has FRAUDULENTLY attempted to sell and has „sold its lamps as and for the lamps of the plaintiff, by means "of the simulative indicia set forth in the complaint, and en-"title the plaintiff to an injunction restraining the continu-"ance thereof, wholly irrespective of any question of patents "or technical trade-marks. This contention of the plaintiff "is in my opinion sustained by the facts proved, and by many "decisions of the Courts in similar cases."

The injunction order restrains the Ansonia Brass and Copper Company and its confederates from preparing their goods for market in a manner in imitation of that employed by the Rochester Lamp Company. A large number of the lamps manufactured by the Ansonia Brass and Copper Company are already in the hands of jobbers and dealers. All of these lamps bear the stamp "The Improved" in the manner restrained by the permanent injunction, and all persons offering or exposing the same for sale will be called to account by the Rochester Lamp Company.

Suit has also been brought in the United States Court against the Ansonia Brass and Copper Company to restrain it from infringing the numerous patents on the Rochester lamp and for damages. All jobbers and dealers handling the so-called improved lamp are personally responsible to the Rochester Lamp Company for damages, under the United States Patent Laws, and will be duly prosecuted.

Dated February 24th, 1888.

Attorneys: Hon. ROSCOE CONKLING, B. F. THURSTON, Esq., CHARLES E. MITCHELL, Esq.

ROCHESTER LAMP COMPANY,

Per CHARLES S. UPTON, President and Manager.

Pottery and Glassware Reporter, June 28, 1888.

"The Improved, Pat'd July 19, '87" stamped in collar where the burner locks. Height 12". Non–lift gallery. "TOP" flame spreader without date. $200.00.

"The Improved, Pat'd July 19, '87" stamped in collar where the burner locks. Height 12". Non–lift gallery. "TOP" flame spreader without date. $200.00.

Sea Horse pattern with handles. "The Improved, Pat'd July 19, '87" stamped in collar where the burner locks. Height 11". Non–lift gallery. Dated "TOP" flame spreader. $250.00.

The Improved — Lift Gallery

I believe Ansonia changed from the single pull-rod (see left) to the more complicated wick raisers (below) after Upton's court challenge in 1888. Undated flame spreaders marked "McK & W" are identical in size and shape (below) suggesting that Ansonia manufactured lamps for this company.

Ansonia stand lamp. Courtesy Kent Stratton.

Flame spreader marked "Pat'd Dec. 17, 1889." Burners with lift galleries usually are found with this dated flame spreader.

"The Improved, Pat'd July 19, 87" marked on burner collar. Height 10½". $250.00.
Courtesy Doug and Judy Myers.

Ansonia "sugar bowl" lamp stamped "The Improved, Pat'd July 19, '87" in collar where the burner locks. Height 12". Same basic lamp as right with Bohner's patent wick raiser. Flame spreader is dated "Pat'd Dec. 17, 1889." Lift gallery. $250.00.

Oil fill cap.

Wick knob (right).

Ansonia "sugar bowl" lamp stamped "The Improved, Pat'd July 19, '87" in collar where the burner locks. Height 12". The wick knob on the side of the fount is marked "Manufactured in the U. S. A." Flame spreader is dated "Pat'd Dec. 17, 1889." Lift gallery. $275.00.

Ansonia Hanging Lamps

Advertisement, *Pottery and Glassware Reporter*, July 18, 1889.

Advertisement, *Pottery and Glassware Reporter*, July 7, 1892.

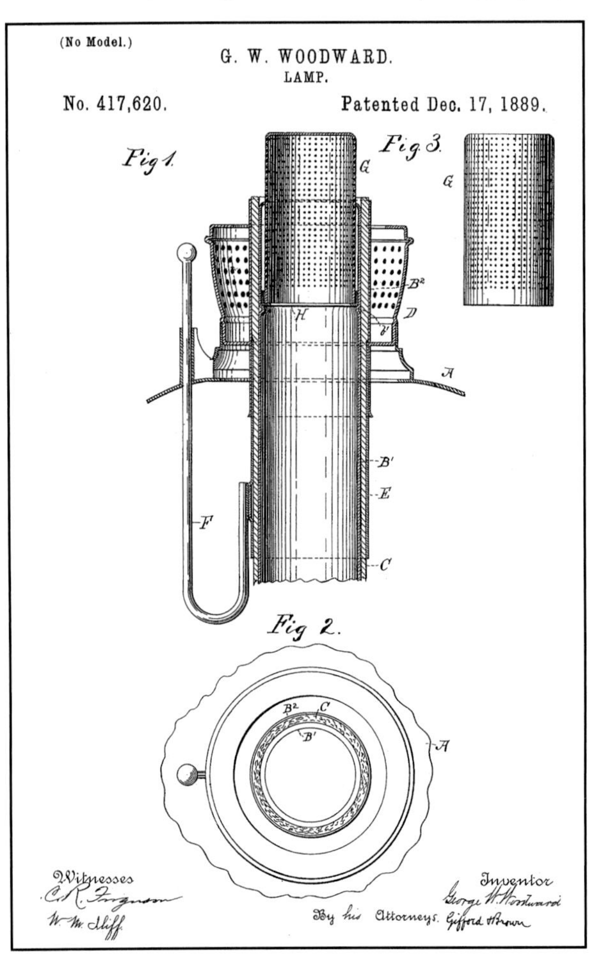

Wick knob.

Oil fill cap.

The Improved Ansonia hanging lamp fount. Also marked "Pat July 19, 1887" on the burner collar. Height 11". Fount possibly used for heater as well. The flame spreader is unmarked. $100.00.

Little Jewel — Improved Little Jewel

Little Jewel lamps, made by Ansonia, were widely sold by several companies. The burner is the same as that found in Apex lamps. Some lamps were marked "Improved Little Jewel." Ansonia sold 8,000 dozen Little Jewel lamps in five months in 1890 (*PGR*, Nov. 19, 1891).

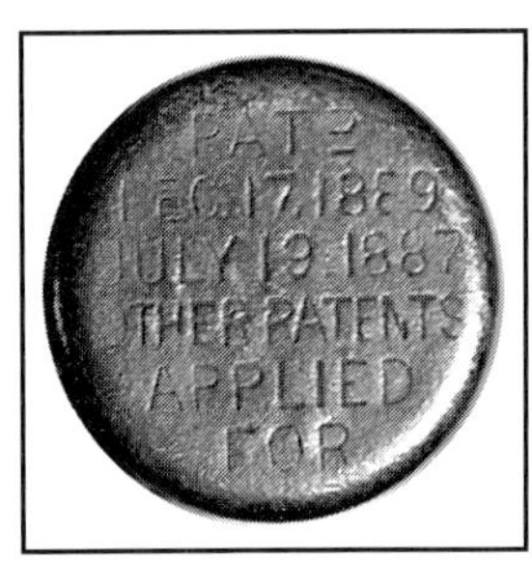

The flame spreader is marked "Pat'd Dec. 17, 1889, July 19, 1887. Other Patents Applied For."

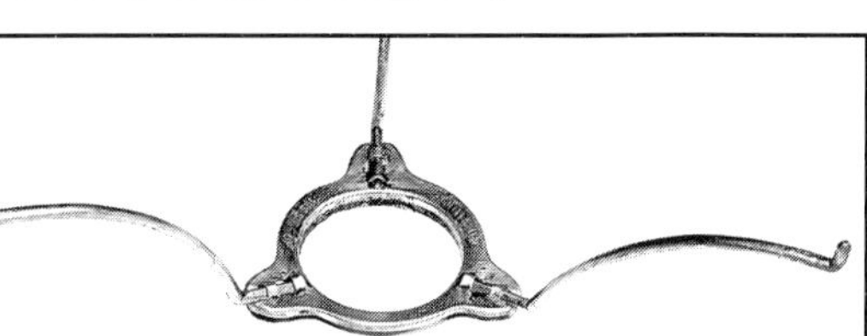

Oil fill cap. Little Jewel tripod is marked "This side up" and "Pat Appl For."

The Little Jewel oil pot is 5¼" tall and 3¾" pot diameter. These pots were sold to Fostoria Shade and Lamp Company, which offered an assortment of Little Jewel vase lamps. Little Jewel was sold by F. H. Lovell Co., Swann and Whitehead, and others. $125.00.

"Little Jewel" stamped in top of the fount. (below).

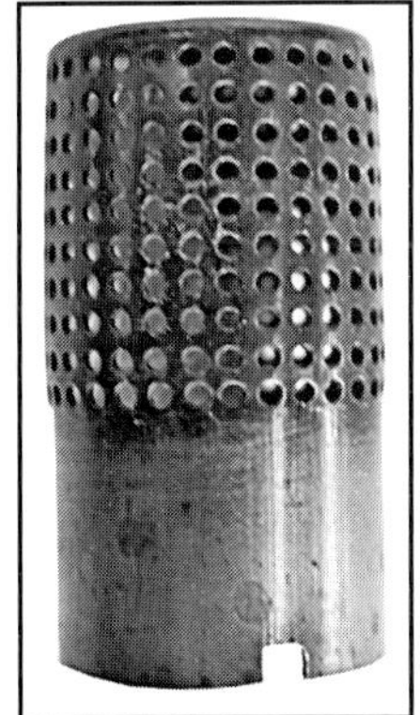

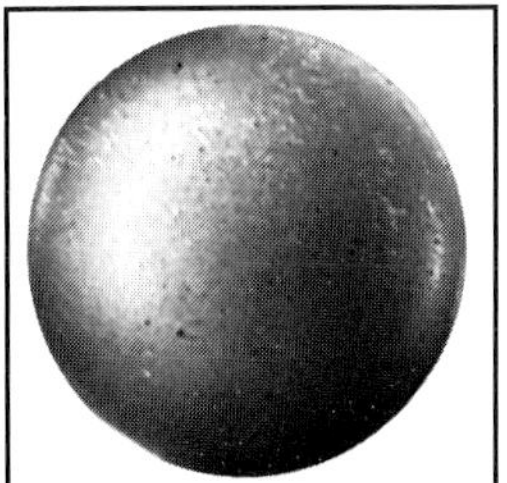

Oil fill cap.

Little Jewel is 8" tall. This lamp is found plain as well as embossed. The plain lamp is stamped "Little Jewel" in top of the fount. $150.00.

Little Jewel variant is 8" tall. Same flame spreader and oil fill cap on left. This lamp appears similar to the Young Canadian sold by Dominion Tubular Lamp Co. $125.00.

The Apex

The Apex is a unique lamp with a large fount and the small Little Jewel burner. The Apex was touted as "the latest and best safety lamp," burning 12 hours. It was offered with a 7" white shade, advertised in *CGL*, June 17, 1891.

The Apex lamp, original finish. Height 7¼", missing flame spreader. Fount unmarked. $225.00. Courtesy Eileen White.

Advertisement, *Pottery and Glassware Reporter,* Oct. 30, 1890.

The name is stamped into the upper portion of the fount.

The Apex lamp. Height 9½". The burner and flame spreader are the same as found in the Little Jewel. Apex was made in styles for wall lamps, banquet lamps, and floor lamps. $200.00.

Advertisement, *Crockery and Glass Journal,* Nov. 6, 1890.

Bellaire Stamping Co.

1871 – Early 1900s

Lamp Manufacture 1888 – 1891

The Bellaire Stamping Company was established in 1871 by the Baron Manufacturing Co. to produce railroad lanterns and pressed tinware. Management in 1880 was John T. Mercer, president; C. H. Tallman, secretary-treasurer; and C. S. S. Baron, superintendent. Charles S. S. and Alfred L. Baron held several patents for lanterns 1870 – 1891. A. L. Baron helped form the Ohio Lantern Co. in 1881, which moved to Tiffin, Ohio, in 1889. I have found no patents for Bellaire center-draft lamps.

According to Welker (1985), the Bellaire Stamping Company expanded in 1888 and took over the Bellaire Goblet Works buildings (1876 – 1888) in Bellaire, Ohio, after Bellaire Goblet moved to Findlay, Ohio. The glassworks had one furnace making 600 dozen goblets per day. At this time Bellaire was the largest city in Belmont County.

In 1880, Bellaire Stamping produced a full line of pressed enameled tinware sold under the Columbian trade name with a factory or sales offices in Harvey, Illinois.

The company employed 100, and by 1888 it added fruit jars, Crank Tubular lanterns, Mascot oil cans, and center-draft lamps to its goods. The center-draft lamps are not commonly found by collectors.

The production of lamps and lanterns in Bellaire was short lived, as two factory buildings were destroyed by fire in late November 1890. At that time employment was 400. Officers were John T. Mercer, president, and W. C. Steward, secretary. They planned to rebuild the factory; however, advertising of Bellaire lamps in *Pottery and Glassware Reporter* ceased after 1891.

Courtesy Bellaire Public Library.

CRANK TUBULAR.

Without exception the Best Lantern on the market.

Convenience, Strength, Durability, Beauty, Good Combustion.

Mascot Oil Can.

In use for years. Gives complete satisfaction.

Above is a cut of our latest improvement in Centre Draft Lamps. We guarantee our entire line in every respect; they are up with the times. Don't buy until you see them.

Bellaire Stamping Co.,

BELLAIRE, OHIO.

Crockery and Glass Journal, Dec. 11, 1890.

White enamel Bellaire table lamp. Height $9\frac{1}{4}$" to top of chimney prongs. Cast-iron foot, tin fount. The wick tube is $1\frac{3}{8}$" diameter. A thimble flame spreader missing. $175.00. Courtesy Kent Stratton.

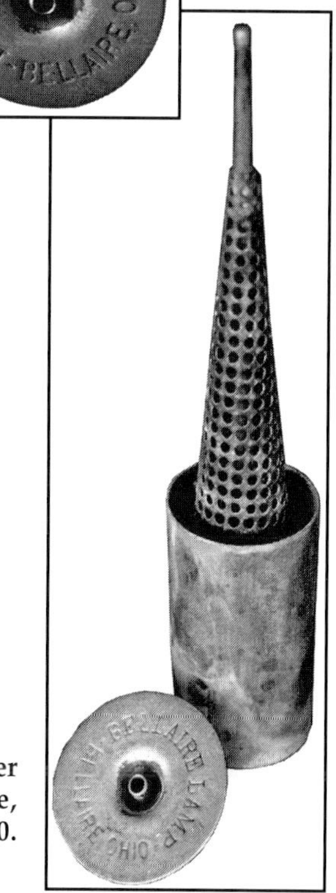

Bellaire stand lamp. The flame spreader is marked "Bellaire Lamp, Bellaire, Ohio." See ad on next page. $225.00. Courtesy David Boysel.

The Bellaire Lamp!

Takes Precedence With Discerning Buyers Because of

Its Fine Finish,
Simple Wicking Device,
Perfect Centre Draft,

Elegant Designs and Decorations

It Is Not Complicated,

But is at once so simple and yet so perfect in all the principal features that recommend CENTRE DRAFT Lamps that an examination of it will convince any one that it is the most desirable lamp in the market. It is made in all styles, and in such few parts as to make it popular with the trade.

Compare it with any other lamp in the market, and send us sample order.

THE BELLAIRE STAMPING CO.
BELLAIRE, OHIO.

No. 200 STAND LAMP

Crockery and Glass Journal, July 9, 1891.

THE

BELLAIRE LAMP

Recommends Itself to the Trade

BECAUSE OF

The Simplicity of Its Wicking Device,
The Perfectness of the Centre Draft,
The Elegance of Its Decorations,
The Fineness of Its Finish.

NO CARD OF EXPLANATION NEED ACCOMPANY IT.

It is at once so simple and yet so perfect in all the principal features that recommend CENTRE DRAFT Lamps that an examination of it dispels all doubt or question as to it being the most desirable lamp in the market. It is made in all styles: LACQUERED BRASS, JAPANESE BRONZE and NICKEL PLATED. Compare it with any other lamp in the market and send us sample order.

THE BELLAIRE STAMPING CO.
BELLAIRE, OHIO.

No 100 VASE LAMP EMBOSSED

Crockery and Glass Journal, May 14, 1891.

Bradley & Hubbard Mfg. Co.

1852 – 1940

Lamp Manufacture 1868 – 1940

Bradley & Hubbard Manufacturing Company (B & H) was one of the largest producers of kerosene lamps and other household items such as andirons, match safes, desk sets, and clocks during the late nineteenth to early twentieth century. The company became widely known for its famous B & H brand of consumer goods, manufacturing consumer products rather than operating a brass mill.

The company began in 1852 as a partnership of Nathaniel and William Bradley, Orson and Chitten Hatch, and Walter Hubbard, in Meriden, Connecticut. Bradley, Hatch & Company manufactured clocks as its sole product. In 1854 the Hatch brothers sold their interests in the company, which then became Bradley & Hubbard. Clocks were the main product throughout the 1850s and 1860s. B & H patented Blinking Eye clocks in 1856. The company manufactured fancy cast-iron clock cases.

In 1875, a joint-stock company was formed under the name of the Bradley & Hubbard Manufacturing Company. The officers were Walter Hubbard, president; Nathaniel Bradley, treasurer; and Charles Lindsley, secretary.

After the Civil War, markets expanded west of the Mississippi River for many domestic products. Bradley and Hubbard added new items to their line, such as hoop skirts, spring measuring tapes, and match safes. Nathaniel Bradley encouraged production of kerosene lamps. He patented several figurine pedestals for lamps, including the Liberty Bell in 1876 (patent D8,890, Design for Stand Lamps).

From 1868 to 1875, Bradley & Hubbard was assigned 33 patents for lamp and chandelier designs and improvements in flat-wick oil burners as the company expanded lamp manufacturing. The company exhibited at the Centennial Exposition in 1876 and grew rapidly throughout the 1880s. Bradley & Hubbard employed over 1,000 workers in 1888.

Patents for student lamps were assigned to Bradley & Hubbard by Edmund Parker in 1880 and Augustus Jones in 1881. The No. 8 study lamp appears in an 1883/1884 catalog, suggesting that Bradley & Hubbard began producing center-draft lamps before introduction of the B & H Central Draught Burner featured in catalog No. 46, 1888. The new burner became the heart of the B & H signature lamps.

Many marks were used to identify company products; however, no official registered trademarks have been found.

A gas fixture department was established by 1897 and the company became a major supplier of gas and electric light fixtures.

Bradley & Hubbard products were considered of highest quality and artistic merit. The company made chandeliers, piano lamps, brackets of all kinds, banquet lamps, table lamps, and hanging lamps in countless varieties of brass, bronze, and wrought iron. Other products included oil stoves, gas portable lamps, electric light fixtures, statuary, Newel lights, tables, stationers' art goods, clocks, andirons and fire sets, and other elegant wares. The company owned showrooms in New York, Boston, Chicago, and Philadelphia.

Bradley & Hubbard advertised B & H goods widely, especially B & H lamps, judged by the numbers of ads found in magazines during the 1890s.

After the deaths of Walter Hubbard in 1911 and Nathaniel Bradley in 1915, the company continued to manufacture time-proven products such as the nickel-plated Rayo lamp made for the Standard Oil Company.

In 1940 Bradley & Hubbard was purchased by the Charles Parker Company, also of Meriden, known for the manufacture of the Springfield rifle and the development of one of the early repeating rifles in the mid-nineteenth century. Operations continued throughout the 1940s as the Parker Company's "Bradley and Hubbard Division." Products included machinist's vises, bathroom accessories, lighting fixtures, architectural bronze and brass work, ornamental cast iron, and the famous Rayo lamp. Electric versions of the Rayo table and student lamps were produced during the 1940s and early 1950s. B & H factory buildings were demolished in 1973.

Advertisement, *McClure's Magazine*, 1895.

Trade Names

Center-draft lamps — B & H, The B & H, B & H No. 89 Mammoth, B & H No. 96 Mammoth, Empire, The Little B & H, Radiant No. 4, Radiant No. 5, Perfection, Rayo (sold by Standard Oil).

Flat-wick burners — B & H, B & H Regulator, B & H Duplex.

Heaters — Radiant No. 6, No. 95 Mammoth.

Mantle lamps — San Diego made for the San Diego Kerosene Mantle Lamp Company, and a converted Rayo for Montomery Ward in 1937.

Bradley & Hubbard embossed "The B & H," "B & H," or "Radiant" on its founts. Other trade names or model designations for center-draft lamps have not been discovered. Some lamps were unmarked, only identified by the names on the flame spreader and oil fill cap. Later lamps were sold as Perfection, Rayo, and Socony Rayo.

Bradley and Hubbard was not a major supplier of burners and accessories as separate product lines. Instead, the company relied on its skills in metallic arts to sell complete lamps to retailers such as department stores, catalog sellers, and distributors. Extensive advertising marketed lamps directly to the consumer.

B & H burners were made in four sizes (Little O size, No. 1, No. 2, and Mammoth), according to information in an early catalog. Most stand and banquet lamps found today are No. 2 burner size.

Bradley & Hubbard marked its lamps well. Many are signed "B & H" on the founts and embossed in cast-iron bases.

Advertisement, *Delineator Magazine*, April 1894.

Selected Patents, Center-draft Lamps

Edmund A. Parker assigned to B & H

1880 231,353

Augustus H. Jones[1]

1881 .... 246,316 (assigned to B & H)
1882 .... 258,427 (unassigned)

Albert Patitz assigned to B & H

1888 .... D18,262

Charles A. Evarts[1] **assigned to B & H**

1888 387,156
1888 389,371
1888 392,547
1888 .... D18,202
1889 404,186
1890 430,380
1890 432,264

Joseph Jauch[2] **assigned to B & H**

1889 409,466
1889 412,958
1890 421,171
1890 427,870
1890 431,359
1892 473,667
1892 474,171
1892 479,598
1893 508,572
1894 529,496
1896 554,491
1896 561,321
1897 590,415
1898 603,105

Waldo L. Upson assigned to B & H

1892 473,681
1892 481,741

William A. Penfield[3] **assigned to B & H**

1893 492,585
1895 537,849
1895 552,327
1898 605,186
1901 672,178
1901 678,126
1901 692,701
1902 691,710
1905 783,799
1913 1,082,284

Charles F. Linsley and Reuben F. Crooke assigned to B & H

1898 .... D29,223

[1]Also patents on hanging lamps.
[2]Also patent on an incandescent mantle burner.
[3]Also patents on organ lamps.

B & H No. 2 Burners and Wick Raisers

Collectors can use information below in conjunction with flame spreaders and lamps illustrated on following pages to identify B & H lamps. The time frames are estimates based on advertising, patents, and obvious changes in the burner basket, gallery, wick mechanism, wick tube, and flame spreader.

Evarts Patent

1888 – 1889. The first B & H center-draft burner. Gallery marked "Pat'd July 31, 1888, Mar 27, 1888." The wick rod has angular support fitted into the burner collar.

Evarts Patent

1889 – 1896. B & H burner designed for "double air" draught. Gallery marked "Pat Apl'd For, Pat'd July 31, 1888, Mar 27, 1888." The wick rod has parallel support.

Jauch Patent

1896 – 1898. Gallery dated "Patent Applied For, Pat'd Aug. 30, 1892, Apl. 23, 1896." Wick knobs marked "Pat. Applied For" were used for many years before and after the Jauch patent (590,415) for this was granted.

Penfield Patent

1898 – 1904. Lamps with this wick mechanism use the spring grip wick raiser, Penfield patent 605,186. Gallery dated "Pat'd Aug. 30, 1892, Pat'd Dec. 31, 1895, Pat'd Apl. 23, 1896."

Penfield Patent

1898 – early 1900s. The Radiant No. 4 burners are threaded, and the knobs are marked "Pat. Applied For."

Penfield Patent

ca. 1900 – 1905 or later. Radiant No. 4, embossed.

Wick-carrier Burner

1904, possibly earlier. This B & H wick-carrier burner sold for many years. Gallery dated "Pat'd Aug. 30, 1892, Pat'd Dec. 31, 1895, Pat'd Apl. 23, 1896." Burners threaded. Penfield Patent 783,799.

Wick-carrier Burner

ca. 1904 – 1910. The wick-carrier burner destined to become the Rayo. First sold with 1904 flame spreader and possibly as Perfection by Standard Oil Co.

Wick-carrier Burner

1910 – 1940. The wick-carrier burner sold as Rayo by Standard Oil for many years. The earliest burners have a narrow gallery that fits into the burner base.

B & H "Kohinoor" Center-Draft Lamps and Burners, 1888 – 1889

Bradley & Hubbard introduced "The B & H Central Draught Burner" on the first two pages of catalog No. 46 in June 1888. Burners were fitted in oil pots for vase and banquet lamps. Until that time, the company had offered student lamps or lamps and chandeliers with flat-wick burners. The first B & H flame spreaders were large thimbles similar to those used in Rochester brand lamps. Read the response to Charles Upton's allegations of patent infringement below.

Burley & Tyrell, of Chicago, sold early single draft B & H lamps as "Kohinoor Electric Lamps" in 1889. The term *Kohinoor* translates to "Mountain of Light" is taken from the famous 105-carat Koh-i-noor diamond from India.

B & H stand lamp No. 2 with single draft burner and large thimble flame spreader. Also found with embossed fount. $75.00.

B & H flame spreaders marked "Pat. Applied For, The B. & H., Top" and "Pat'd Sept. 11, 1888, The B. & H. Lamp." These flame spreaders are Evarts patent 389,371.

B & H vase lamp with single draft burner and large thimble flame spreader. Image from B & H catalog No. 46, dated 1888. Many of the vase lamps were floral decorations without matching shades. Most lamps in catalog No. 46 used flat-wick burners. Courtesy Dave Broughton.

INFORMATION FOR THE TRADE.

Referring to the "Caution to the Trade," signed by Chas. S. Upton, in this journal June 5, 1890, we take this opportunity to say that it refers only to an old style straight thimble, which WE patented September 11, 1888, but discontinued using more than a year ago, having invented and patented a flame spreader or cone which is superior in every respect. The notice has no special reference whatever to the "B. & H. Lamp" as we are now and have been for a long time making it.

It has been our endeavor to make the "B. & H." the BEST of the many central draught lamps that are on the market, and the very great and constantly increasing demand from all parts of the world proves the success of our efforts.

We say MOST EMPHATICALLY THAT we guarantee to the trade protection against any legal damages by reason of any alleged infringements of patents on any goods manufactured by us.

An invitation is extended to all the trade to visit our salesrooms and see the finest and largest assortment of new goods ever shown.

We invite the most severe test of the "B. & H." with the Rochester, confident that the result will prove the truth of our assertion that the "B. & H." is by far the superior lamp.

BRADLEY & HUBBARD MFG. CO.

Advertisement, *Crockery and Glass Journal,* June 19, 1890.

B & H Burners, Short "Mushroom Cone" Flame Spreaders, ca. 1889 – 1896

These flame spreaders fit on an air supply tube installed inside the wick tube.

Flame spreader marked "Pat Applied For, The B & H Lamp."

Flame spreader marked "Pat'd Aug. 20, 1889, The B & H Lamp."

Flame spreader marked "Pat'd Aug. 20 & Oct. 15, 1889, The B & H Lamp."

Single draft burner. Burner with non–lift gallery marked "Pat'd July 31, 1888, Mar 27, 1888." Bayonet connection.

Double draught burner featured for 1891. Burner with non–lift gallery marked "Pat Apl'd For, Pat'd July 31, 1888, Mar 27, 1888." Other burners without the top row of vent holes are marked "Mar 27, 1888, Feb 11, 1890," and may have the Aug. 20 and Oct. 15, 1889 flame spreader. Bayonet connection.

Double draught burner with lift gallery marked "Pat'd Mar 27, 1888, July 26, 1892, Aug 30, 1892." Bayonet connection. The flame spreader above may also be marked "Pat'd Aug. 20, 1889, Empire."

The B & H — "Patitz" Stand Lamps

Lamps in this pattern, patented by Patitz in 1888 (D18,262), are found in several forms. The B & H stand lamps with mushroom flame spreader are found with both single and double draft burners. The early wick tubes and flame spreader tubes are seamed. This pattern was sold as Kohinoor with thimble flame spreader in 1889.

The "double draught" burner was highly promoted to improve combustion and better light. The double draught was created by inserting a second baffle around the wick tube to direct air coming through sides of the burner basket.

The lamps below were found with "mushroom cone" flame spreaders illustrated on the previous page.

"The B & H" is stamped above the chime on both lamps.

Advertisement, *Century Magazine*, 1892.

"Single draft."

The B & H stand lamp No. 2. Burner with early non–lift gallery, bayonet connection. Top of fount marked "Pat'd Apr 17, 1888." Height 12". $150.00.

Oil fill cap.

"Double draft."

The B & H stand lamp No. 2. Double draught burner with early non–lift gallery, bayonet connection. Top of fount marked "Pat'd Apr 17, 1888." Height 12". $150.00.

THE B & H — "Sunflower," ca. 1890 – 1896

Collectors call this embossed pattern "Sunflower." This pattern is found in many forms of lamps with Evarts's push-pull rod wick raiser.

The lamps are stamped "The B & H" in one of two places — above the chime or on top of the fount. Usually lamps marked on top of the fount (see below) have burners with lift galleries.

The mushroom cone flame spreaders dated Aug. 20, 1889, or Aug. 20 and Oct. 15, 1889, were found in these lamps.

The B & H logo stamped on top of the fount.

The B & H No. 2 table lamp with handles. Double draught burner with early non–lift gallery, bayonet connection. Fount marked "The B & H" above the chime. Height 12". $250.00.

Oil fill cap.

The B & H No. 2 stand lamp. Double draught burner with early non–lift gallery, bayonet connection. Fount marked "The B & H" above the chime. Height 12". $175.00. Courtesy Kent Stratton.

The B & H fount lamp No. 2. Double draught burner with lift gallery, bayonet connection. Original 4" shade holder. Height 9". $150.00.

"Sunflower," ca. 1898 – 1904, Probably Later

"Sunflower" banquet lamp with early thimble flame spreader. The flame spreader is marked "Pat'd Nov. 20 '94, Mar. 24 '88, Apr. 28 '95, B & H." I believe the flame spreader is original in this lamp. A similar flame spreader simply marked "B & H" also fits this lamp. These flame spreaders are 1⅜" long, ¼" shorter than most common B & H flame spreaders.

These flame spreaders are 1⅜" in length. Other lamps likely used this flame spreader in later years.

"Sunflower" banquet lamp No. 2. Height 19". This lamp has burner with lift gallery and dated thimble flame spreader. $250.00.

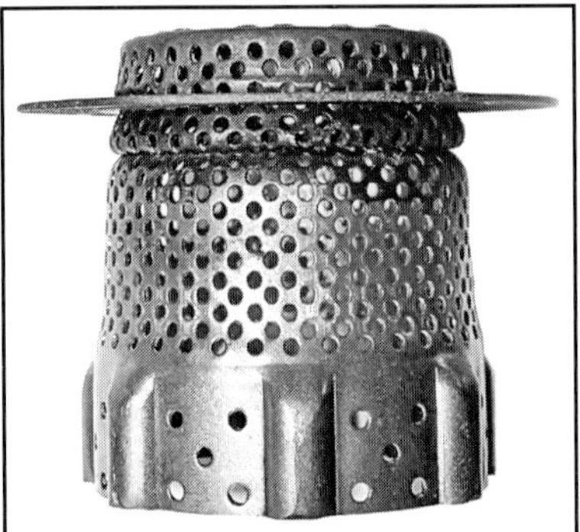

This flame spreader has been stamped over a Mehlen flame spreader. The Mehlen may have had two discs. Length 1⅜".

Bradley & Hubbard usually marked the bottom of its cast-iron pieces.

B & H Lamps — Long Flame Spreader Tubes, ca. 1890 – 1896

The air supply tubes slide into the wick tube where they are secured in position by indentations in the wick tube. The tubes normally are not removed. The wick raiser is an Evarts patent (392,547; 404,186; or 430,380).

This mushroom cone top, marked "The B & H Lamp, Pat'd Aug. 20, 1889," was found in both of the lamps illustrated here. The mushroom top is removeable from the tube.

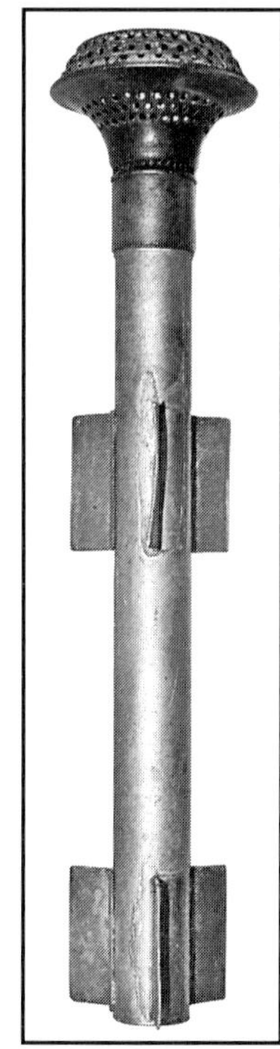

The B & H Lamp flame spreader, "Pat'd Aug. 20, 1889." Length 7".

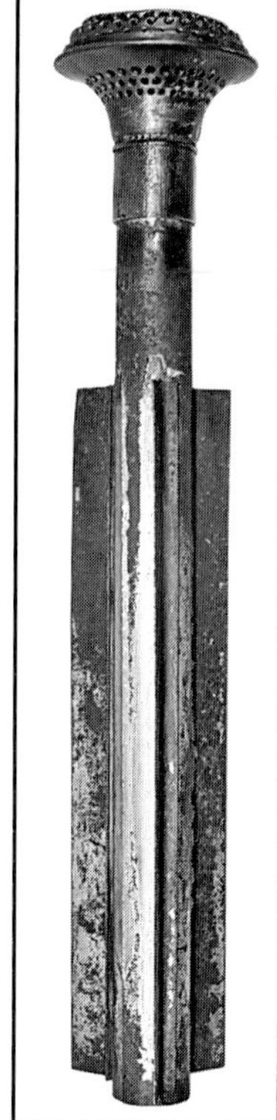

The B & H Lamp flame spreader, "Pat'd Aug. 20, 1889." Length 8". This flame spreader was also found 7" in length.

B & H embossed, onyx-stem banquet lamp No. 2, white metal foot. Height 19". This lamp has burner with non–lift gallery dated "Pat. Apl'd For, March 27, 1888, Pat'd July 31, 1888." $225.00.

B & H embossed banquet lamp No. 2. Height 14". This lamp has burner with non–lift gallery dated "Pat. Apl'd For, March 27, 1888, Pat'd July 31, 1888." Very long flame spreader. $200.00.

B & H Lamps — Jauch Patent, ca. 1896 – 1898

Lamps with the Jauch patent (590,415) wick-raising mechanism introduced new flame spreaders that only fit these lamps. I use "B & H Lamps — Jauch Patent" to identify lamps with the U-shape Jauch patent wick raiser.

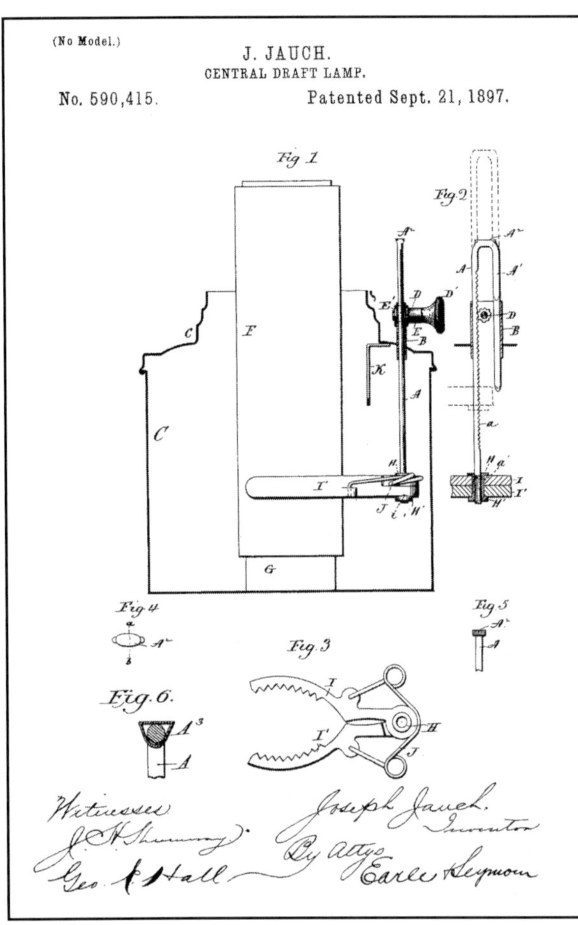

Jauch flame spreader found in both lamps illustrated. Marked "The B & H Lamp, Pat'd Aug. 20, 1889, July 1, 1890." Length 3¾".

Wick knobs were marked "Pat. Applied For."

B & H plain stand lamp No. 2, same as right but with transition burner screen. Lift gallery dated "Pat. Applied For, Pat'd Aug. 30, 1892, Pat'd Ap'l 23, 1895" (an error). Height 12".

B & H embossed stand lamp No. 2. Bayonet connection. Height 12". Lift gallery dated "Pat. Applied For, Pat'd Aug. 30, 1892, Pat'd Ap'l 23, 1896." $175.00.

Jauch flame spreader above marked "Pat'd July 1, 90, June 2, 96, B & H." Right — "Patented July 1, 1890, B & H."

Oil pot for vase lamp below. Flame spreader marked "Patented, B & H, July 1, 1890," otherwise same size as flame spreader found in lamp below. $75.00.

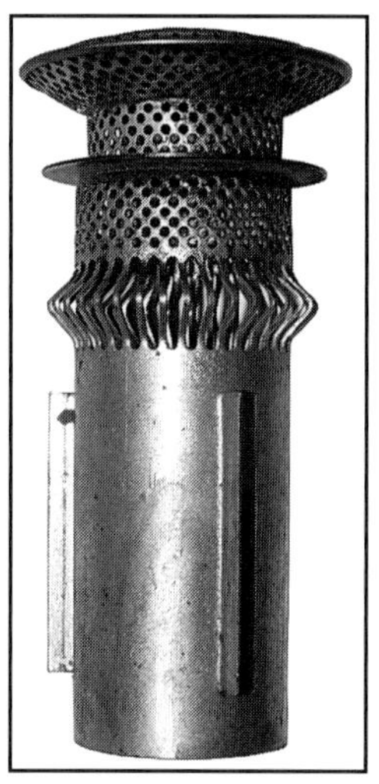

Jauch flame spreader, 3½" long.

Wick knob.

B & H stand lamp No. 2, with cast-iron foot marked "B & H." Bayonet connection. Lift gallery dated "Aug. 30, 1892, Pat'd Ap'l 23, 1895, Dec. 31, 1895." Height 12½". Long flame spreader. $200.00.

B & H vase lamp No. 2 with cast-iron foot. Bayonet connection. Lift gallery dated "Patent Applied For, Pat'd Aug. 30, 1892, Pat'd Ap'l 23, 1896." Height 12½". Long flame spreader. $175.00.

B & H No. 1 Junior Lamps, ca. 1896 – 1898

Chandelier Fount

Jauch flame spreader marked "Pat'd July 1, 90, June 2, 96, B & H." Length 3½". See patent below left.

Both lamps marked on top of fount.

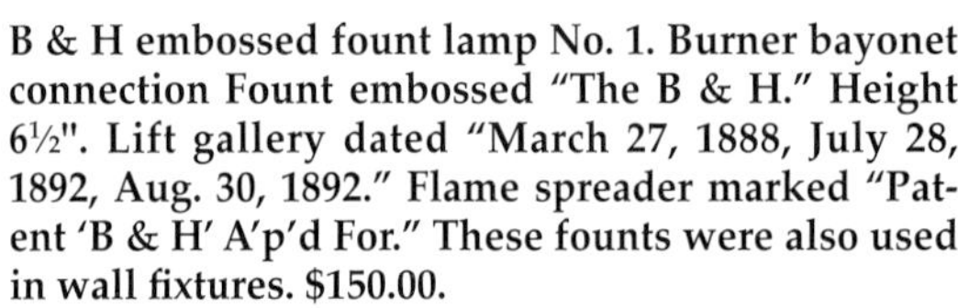

B & H embossed fount lamp No. 1. Burner bayonet connection Fount embossed "The B & H." Height 6½". Lift gallery dated "March 27, 1888, July 28, 1892, Aug. 30, 1892." Flame spreader marked "Patent 'B & H' A'p'd For." These founts were also used in wall fixtures. $150.00.

Jauch Patent

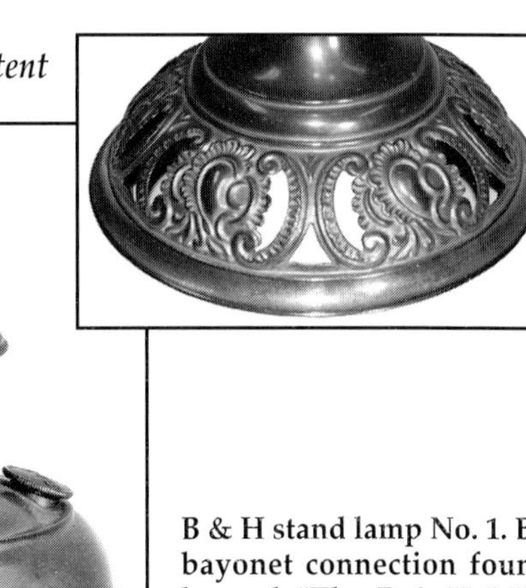

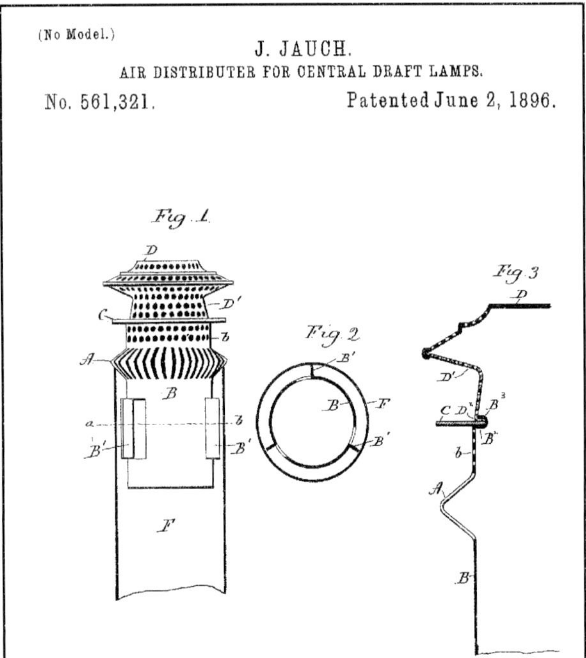

B & H stand lamp No. 1. Burner bayonet connection fount embossed "The B & H." Height 11". Lift gallery dated "Aug. 30, 1892, Pat'd Ap'l 23, 1896, Dec. 31, 1895." Wick knob marked "Pat. Applied For." The design in the foot has extra cutouts compared with Penfield lamps. $125.00. Courtesy Kent Stratton.

B & H Lamps — Penfield Patent, 1898 – 1905 or later

Lamps with the Penfield patent (605,186) wick-raising mechanism continue the trend of flame spreaders which only fit these lamps. Some lamp founts were continued from earlier years. All lamps are embossed "The B & H" on top of the founts. The wick knob, marked "Pat. Applied For," is slightly smaller than that found on the Jauch patent lamps. The lamps illustrated all have B & H oil fill caps and are found with one of four flame spreaders illustrated on the next page.

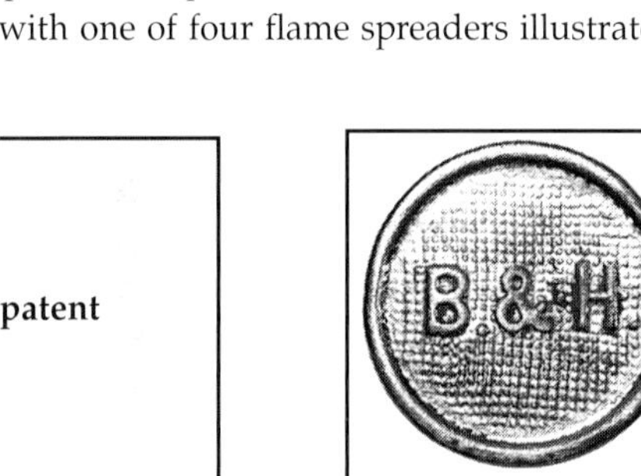

The vent holes in the burner basket are not round but six sided. Several of the Jauch-patent lamps have similar burner baskets.

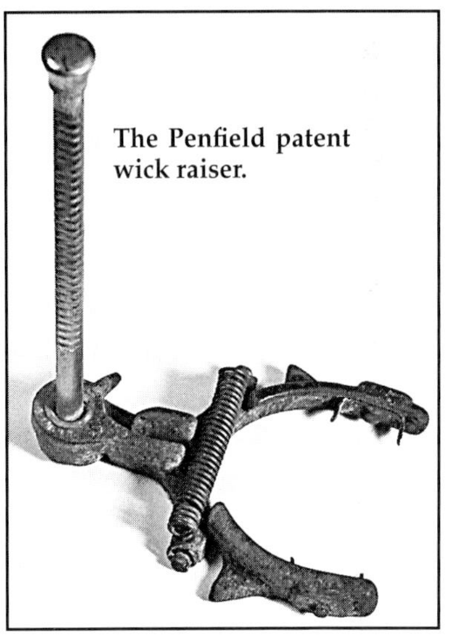

The Penfield patent wick raiser.

Oil fill cap.

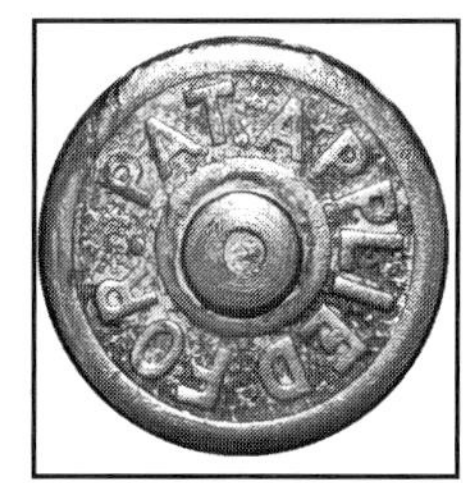

Wick knob.

B & H embossed stand lamp No. 2, cast-iron foot marked "B & H 1998." Bayonet connection. Height 12½". Lift gallery dated "Pat'd Aug. 30, 1892, Pat'd Dec. 31, 1895, Pat'd Ap'l 23, 1896." $200.00.

B & H embossed stand lamp No. 2. Bayonet connection. Height 12". Lift gallery dated "Pat'd Aug. 30, 1892, Pat'd Dec. 31, 1895, Pat'd Ap'l 23, 1896." $175.00.

Flame spreaders, 2¼" long, found in these B & H Penfield lamps. These flame spreaders are interchangeable. The center flame spreader without disc is common in this group of lamps. The flame spreader, top lower right, carries B & H patents but is not marked "B & H." It may have been sold on a special lamp or to another retailer.

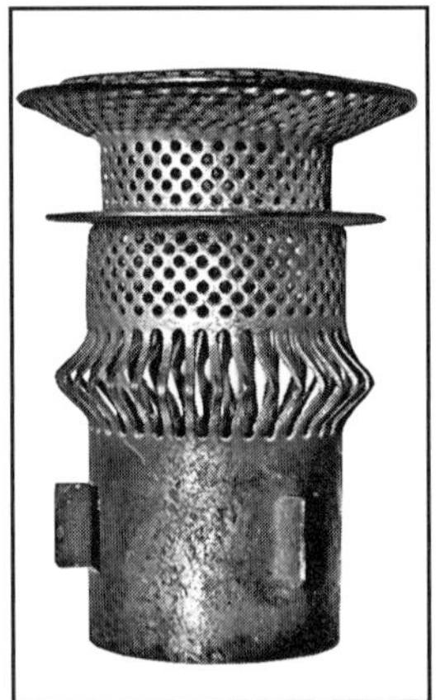

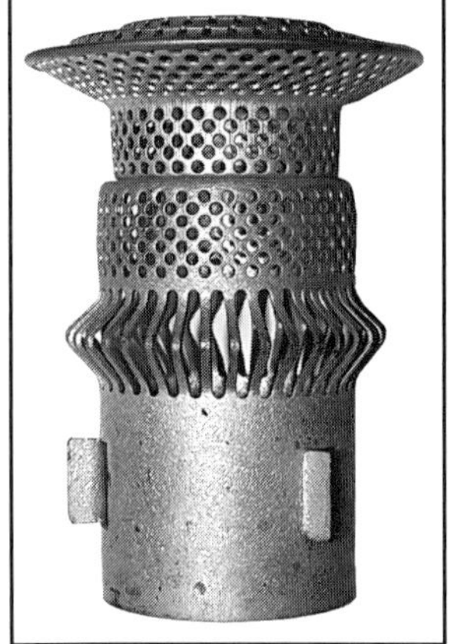

Dates are July 1, 1890, and Nov. 20, 1894.

B & H embossed stand lamp No. 2. Height 12". Bayonet connection. Lift gallery dated "Pat'd Aug. 30, 1892, Pat'd Dec. 31, 1895, Pat'd Ap'l 23, 1896." Also found with threaded burner. $175.00.

B & H embossed stand lamp No. 2. Height 12". Bayonet connection. Lift gallery dated "Pat'd Aug. 30, 1892, Pat'd Dec. 31, 1895, Pat'd Ap'l 23, 1896." This lamp has air vents under the fount. $175.00.

B & H Lamps — Penfield Patent, Short Flame Spreaders, 1905 and Later

These lamps, with the Penfield patent (605,186) wick-raising mechanism, have wick knobs and flame spreaders commonly found on later lamps. Some lamp founts were continued from earlier years with burners using thread connection. The lamps were no longer embossed "The B & H" on top of the fount.

Flame spreaders found on B & H Penfield-patent lamps with 1905 wick knob.

The lamp below (and inset, left, commonly found with plain bowl and embossed foot) was sold by Montgomery Ward beginning in 1910 and for many years. The lift gallery was no longer dated.

$50.00.

B & H embossed stand lamp No. 2. Height 12". Burner is thread connection. Lift gallery dated "Pat'd Dec. 31, 1895, Pat'd Feb. 28, 1905." $175.00.

Oil fill cap, both lamps.

B & H embossed stand lamp No. 2. Height 12". Burner is thread connection. Lift gallery dated "Pat'd Dec. 31, 1895, Pat'd Feb. 28, 1905." Later galleries not dated. $175.00.

Radiant — Penfield Patent, ca. 1898 – 1905 and Later

The Radiant No. 4 wick tube is 1" diameter, a change from most earlier stand lamps with 1½" wick tubes. First appearance of this gallery fence. This lamp was sold as No. 7324 Brilliant by Pitkins and Brooks beginning in 1898; it was described as follows: "...best Central Draft made in America. Imported Belgian, best in the World, is closely copied in this lamp. We heartily recommend the 7324 if the Belgian has been found too high in cost for your trade." Radiant burners are found in oil pots, vase lamps, fancy table lamps, and hanging lamps. Radiant lamps No. 4 and No. 5 were sold by Montgomery Ward from 1904 and 1905 to 1921 and 1922.

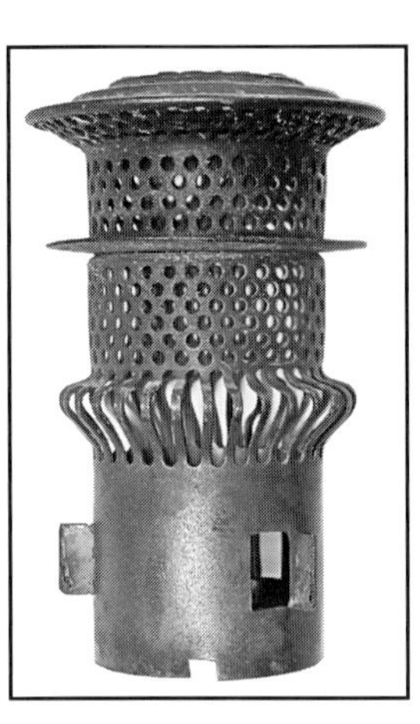

Radiant No. 4 flame spreader dated "Pat'd July 1, 90, June 2, 96." This flame spreader is 2" long.

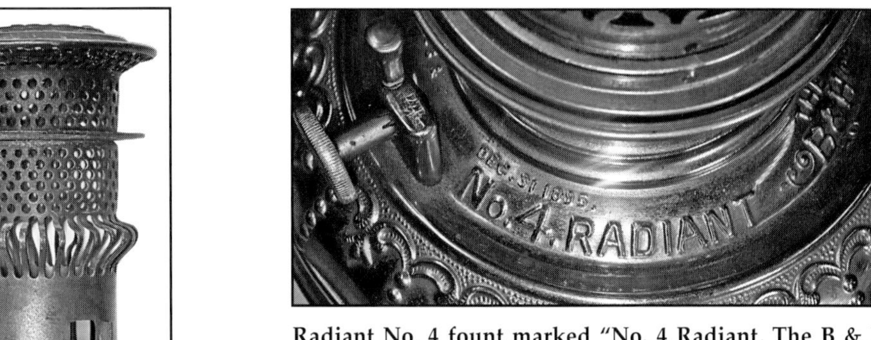

Radiant No. 4 fount marked "No. 4 Radiant, The B & H, Pat'd Aug. 16, 1898." Some lamps possibly marked "Brilliant."

Radiant No. 4 stand lamp, lift gallery. The fount is dated "Pat'd. Aug. 16, 1898." The wick knob is marked "Pat. Applied For." Height 13". Polished brass, nickel, or gilt finish. $150.00.

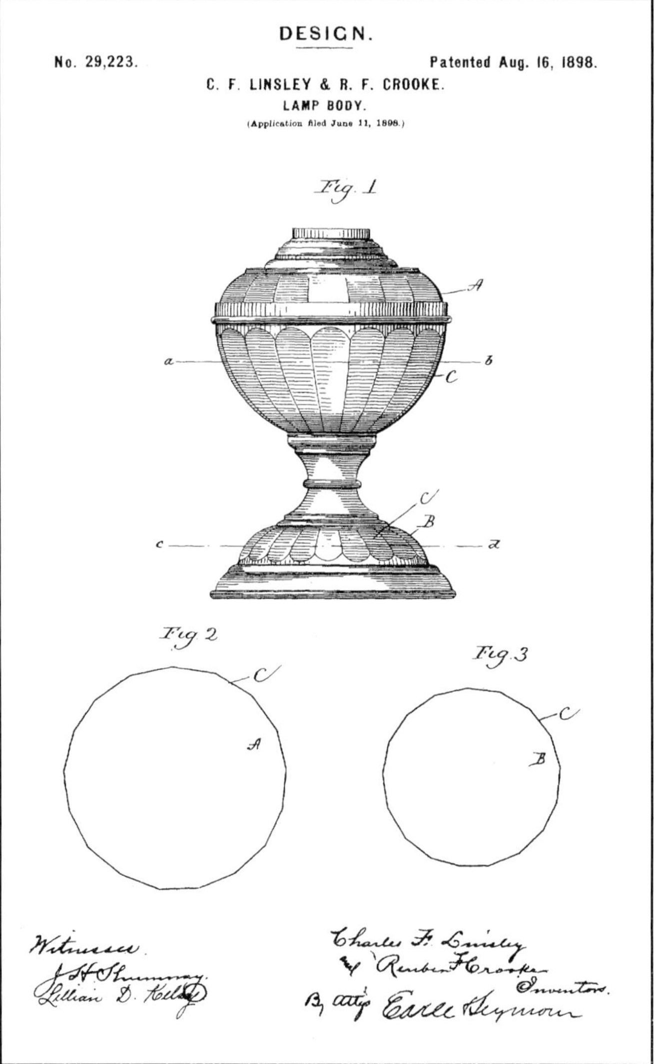

Radiant Lamps — Penfield Patent B & H Answer to Belgian and Miller's Liberty Lamps, 1905 and Later

Radiant No. 4 flame spreader dated "Pat'd July 1, 90, June 2, 96, Feb. 28, 05." Wick tube 1" diameter.

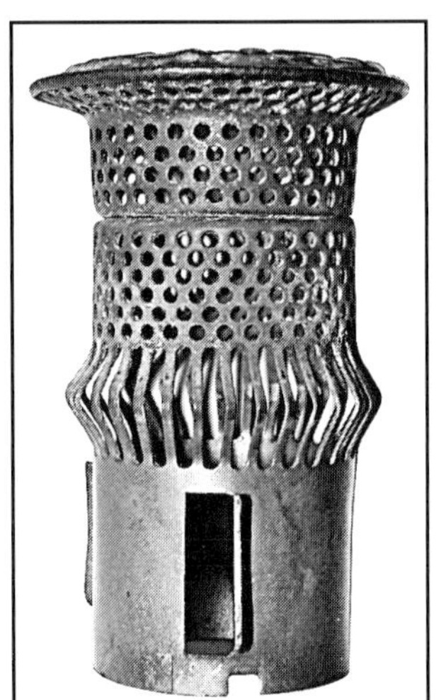

Radiant No. 5 flame spreader dated "Pat'd July 1, 90, June 2, 96, Feb. 28, 05." Length 2".

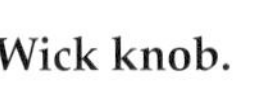

Wick knob.

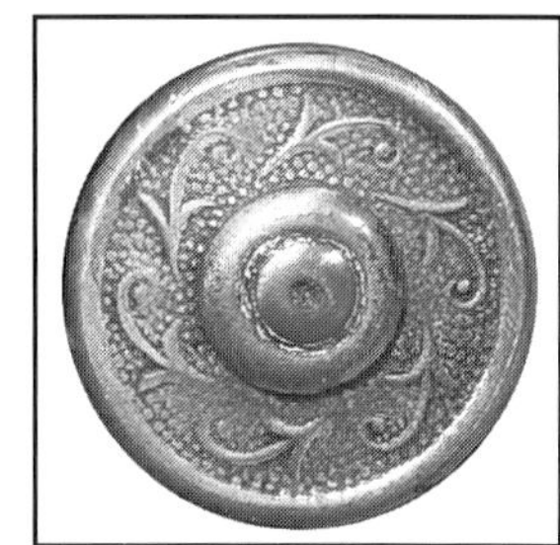

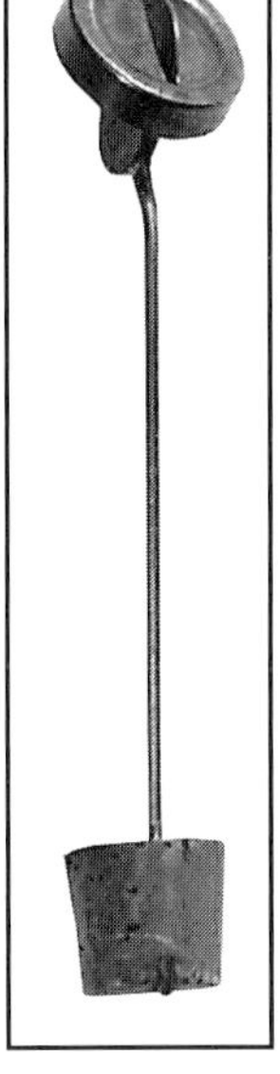

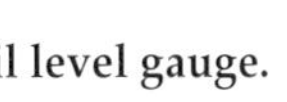

Oil level gauge.

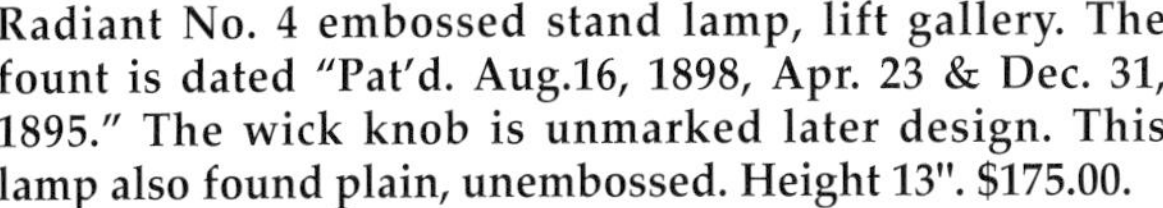

Radiant No. 4 embossed stand lamp, lift gallery. The fount is dated "Pat'd. Aug.16, 1898, Apr. 23 & Dec. 31, 1895." The wick knob is unmarked later design. This lamp also found plain, unembossed. Height 13". $175.00.

Radiant No. 5 hanging lamp fount marked "No. 5 Radiant, The B & H, Pat'd Aug. 16, 1898." Height 11". Wick 1½" diameter. Oil fill gauge dated "Pat'd Apr. 16, 1901." This example finished in brass. Oil fill marked "B & H." $100.00.

B & H No. 1 Junior Lamps — Penfield Patent Wick Raiser, ca. 1898 – 1905 or Later

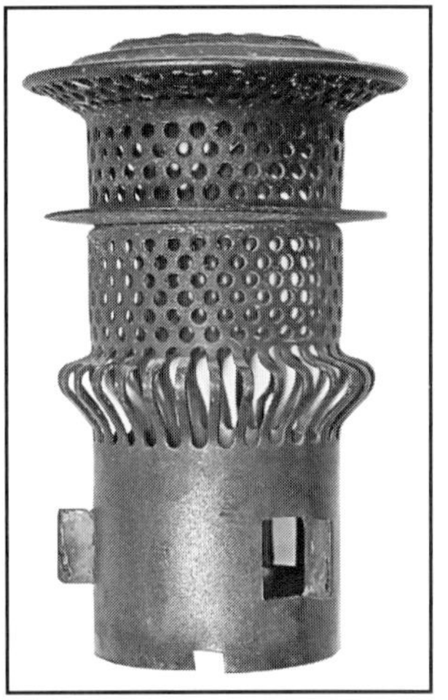

Flame spreader dated Pat'd. July 1, 90, June 2, 96, B & H." Length 1⅞". Also found without the disc.

Flame spreader marked " B&H Pat'd. March 24, 1896." Length 1¾". Also found marked "Pat. Applied For."

Oil fill cap.

Wick knob.

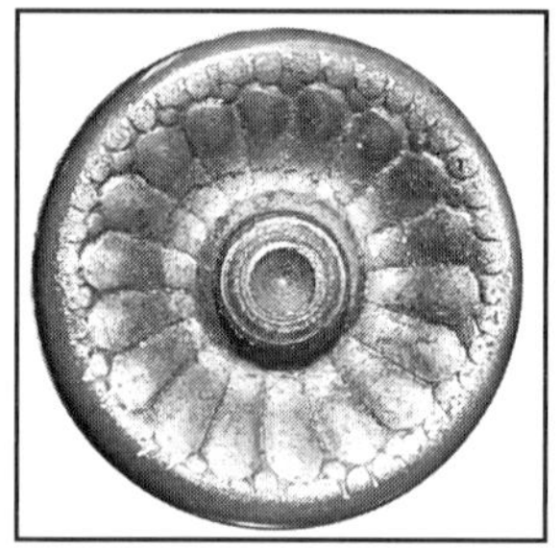

Wick knob.

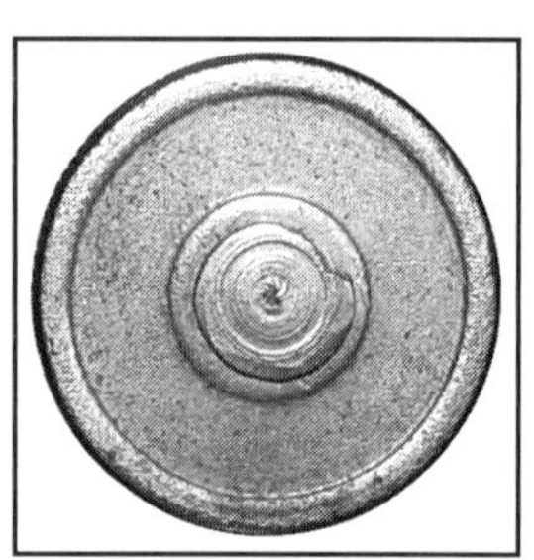

Wick knob is unmarked on some lamps.

B & H embossed stand lamp No. 1. Burner bayonet connection Fount embossed "The B & H." Height 10". Lift gallery dated "Aug. 30, 1892, Pat'd Ap'l 23, 1895, Dec. 31, 1895." Wick knob "Pat. Applied For." Also found with unmarked wick knob. $175.00.

B & H stand lamp No. 1. Burner thread connection and late wick knob. Fount embossed "The B & H." Height 10". Lift gallery dated "Pat'd. Nov. 20, 1894, Pat'd. Feb. 28, 1895, Pat'd Ap'l 23, 1895, Dec. 31, 1895." $125.00.

Little B & H, No. 0 Size

Homan's patent 556,980, March 24, 1896, for an air distributor, was assigned to Edward Miller & Co. The patent for Nov. 20, 1894, cited on the Rex lamp (next page), is Jauch patent 529,496 assigned to B & H for the "familiar" disc of many B & H flame spreaders.

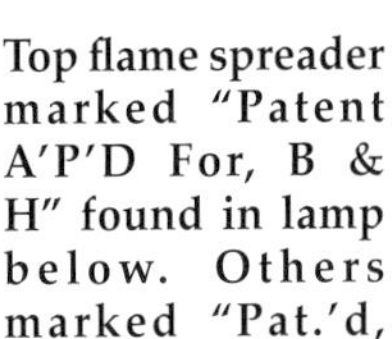

Top flame spreader marked "Patent A'P'D For, B & H" found in lamp below. Others marked "Pat.'d, March 24, 1896, B & H." Length 1¼".

Little B & H oil pots. Left: diameter 4". Right: diameter 3". Height of both is 5¾". The handle and feet were added by the company to sell as hotel lamps or home night lights. Flame spreaders same as left. $150.00 each.

Flame spreader dated "Pat.'d, March 24, 1896, B & H." Length 1⅞".

Oil fill cap.

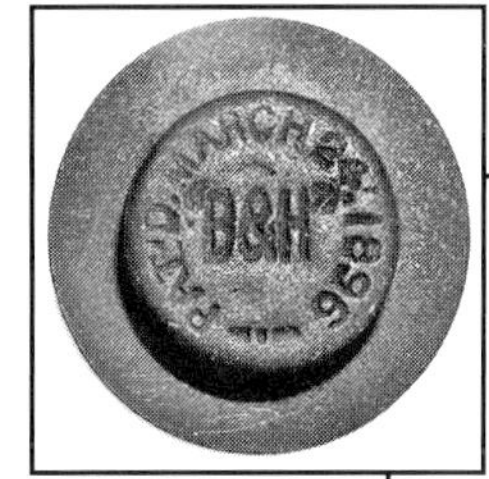

Also found without flat ring.

Little B & H stand lamp. Some founts marked "The B & H, Pat.'d May 3, 1892." Burner bayonet connection. The shade rest thought to be original. Height 8¼". $175.00. Courtesy Glenn Southard.

Little B & H No. 0 with early burner and small thimble flame spreader. Height 8¼". $175.00. Courtesy Heinz and Ursula Baumann.

Little B & H hand lamp. Height 6¾". The burner is thread connection. The disc flame spreader is uncommon. This lamp also found with burner and bayonet connection, shown right. $175.00.

Little B & H and Rex, No. 0 Size

The Rex lamp is almost identical with the Little B & H. I believe Rex lamps were rebranded by Bradley and Hubbard, possibly for the P. M. & H. Rex Lamp Co. (see appendix). The Rex flame spreader is possibly missing the disc specified in patent 529,496 (Nov. 20, 1894).

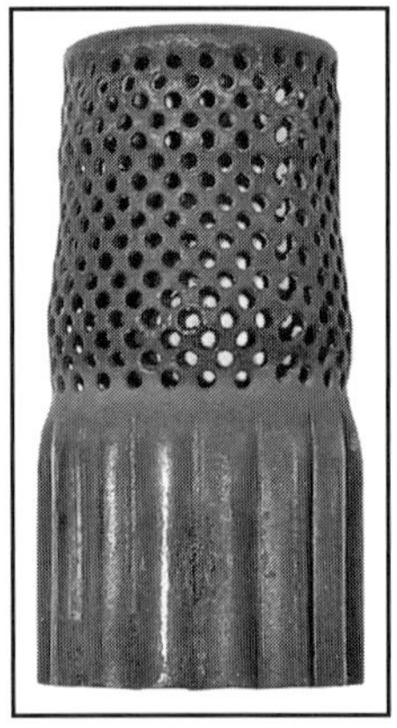

Flame spreader marked "Rex, Pat., Nov. 20, 94, March 24, 96." Missing a disc? Length $^{13}/_{16}$".

Flame spreader marked "B & H, Pat.'d, March 24, 1896." Length $^{13}/_{16}$". The "disc" is formed in the mesh.

Rex (left) and B & H (right). Height 8½". The B & H is slightly shorter. Rex base is 4⅛" diameter; B & H is 3$^{13}/_{16}$" diameter.

Oil fill cap.

Logo for Rex No. 2 chimney. Courtesy Kent Stratton.

Rex No. 0 stand lamp. Height 8½". Burner thread connection. The shade tripod is thought to be original. $175.00. These photographs courtesy Dave Corbissero.

Oil fill cap.

Little B & H stand lamp. Lamp approximately ⅛" shorter than Rex. Burner thread connection. $150.00. Courtesy Dave Corbissero.

B & H Early Wick Carrier Lamps, ca. 1904, Possibly Earlier

I think Bradley & Hubbard sold these lamps one or two years before patent 783,799 for the wick raiser was granted.

I bought the lamp below in 1986 from Vera Eger, of Fostoria, Ohio. She related that the lamp was used to study school lessons by three small children in Pleasant Bend, Ohio. The oldest girl cleaned the chimney and white shade, the boy filled the lamp, and the youngest "bothered the other two." In 1906 they moved to Fostoria and the lamp lighted their high school lessons. The lamp remained in Eger's attic for 70 years, until I rescued it for my collection.

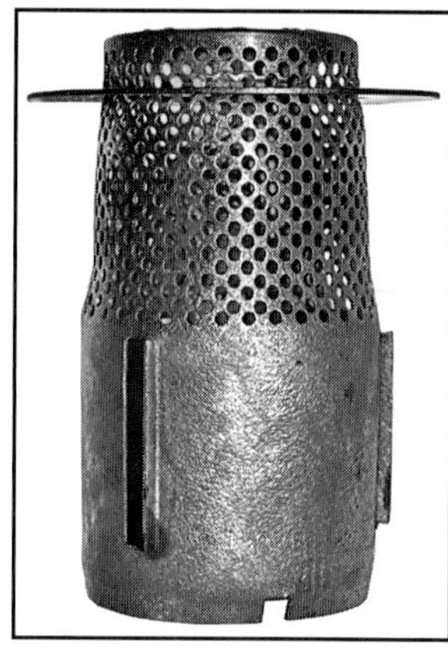

Flame spreader found in both of these lamps is 2¼" long. Marked "Patented July 1, 90, Nov. 20, 94, B & H."

Tripods may be cast or stamped. Some arms are round, others square. Tripods also dated "Pat'd. Feb. 16, 97" and "Patent Pending."

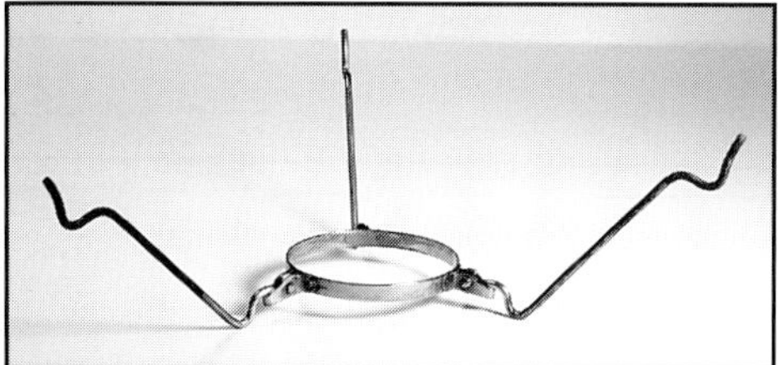

B & H under burner tripod found with this lamp marked "Patent Pending."

The Change in Body Style

Oil fill cap.

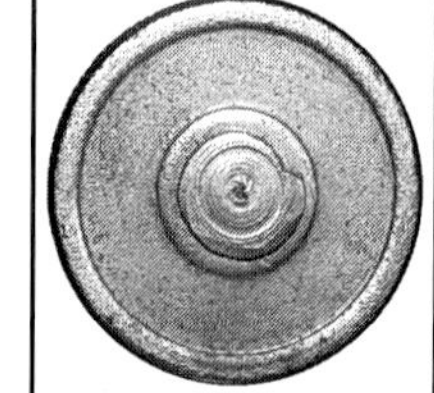

Wick knob.

Oil fill cap.

Wick knob.

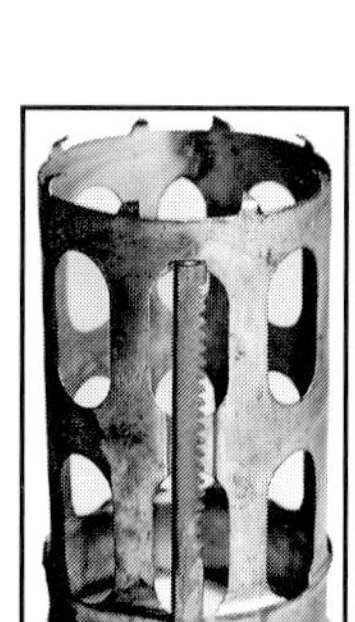

Penfield patent 783,799 wick carrier.

B & H stand lamp No. 2 with wick carrier. Height 12". Burner is thread connection. Lift gallery dated "Pat'd Aug. 30, 1892, Pat'd Dec. 31, 1895, Pat'd Ap'l 23, 1895." The holes in the burner basket are round. $75.00.

B & H stand lamp No. 2 with wick carrier. Height 12". Burner has unmarked knob (also found with "Pat Applied For" knob) and thread connection. Lift gallery dated " Pat'd Ap'l 23, 1895, Pat'd Dec. 31, 1895." Round holes in the burner basket. $50.00.

B & H Wick-Carrier Lamps, 1904 – 1910 and Later

These lamps were made for many years. The B & H always has four chimney prongs. The chimney gallery and wick knob were obvious changes for the 1904 and 1905 lamps. The lamps below are often found with replacement Rayo flame spreaders or replacement Rayo oil fill caps.

Flame spreaders found in B & H lamps marked "Pat'd Nov. 20, 94, Mar. 24, 96, Apr. 23, 96, B & H" or "Pat'd. Nov. 20, 94, Mar. 24, 96, Feb. 28, 05, 1904 [or 1905]." Length 1½".

1904 & 1905

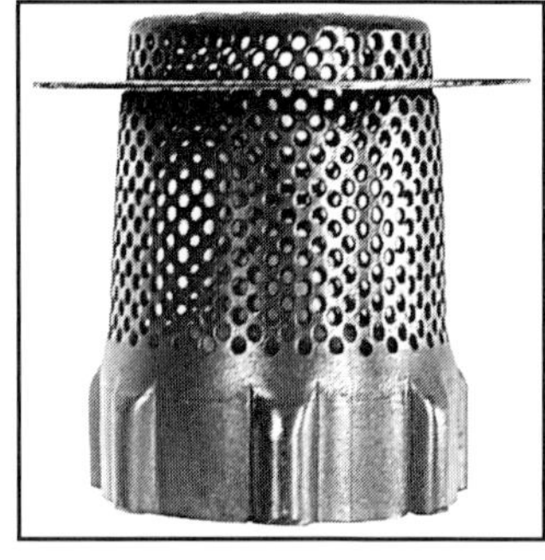

Wick knob.

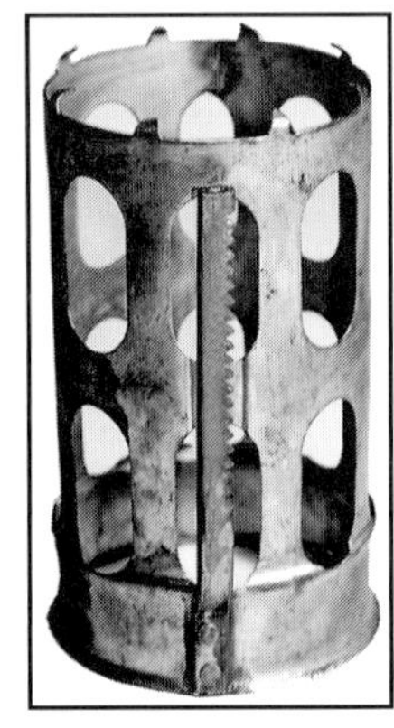

Wick carrier used for many years in B & H, Perfection, and Rayo lamps.

B & H stand lamp No. 2 with wick carrier. Height 12". Burner is thread connection. Lift gallery marked "Pat'd Aug. 30, 1892, Pat'd Dec. 31, 1895, Pat'd Ap'l 23, 1896." The holes in the burner basket are round. $50.00.

This burner and fount design was sold by Bradley & Hubbard as lamps 1904 and 1905 (virtually the same as Perfection 1904 and 1905) for some time, before the Rayo became a major brand (see Standard Oil). Lamp 1905 has lift gallery, lamp 1904 does not. $50.00.

1904 or 1905 Lamp?

The "Reading Lamp" below was offered without brand name in 1906. The tag (right) identified the 1904 lamp, without brand, clearly with the gallery fence burner. I believe B & H sold 1904 and 1905 lamps before the Rayo became established.

PRESERVE THIS TAG.

In ordering Burners or Burner Parts for this lamp specify 1904.

DIRECTIONS FOR CARE.

For Best Results use Good Oil and "American" Wicks.

FILL EVERY DAY, being careful not to run the oil over.

KEEP ALL PARTS CLEAN. Empty Fount at least once a month.

TO LIGHT—Raise wick just above top of tube, remove chimney, apply the match, then replace chimney.

TO EXTINGUISH—Turn Wick down as far as it will go and light will flicker out.

KEEP WICK BELOW TOP OF TUBE when not lighted to prevent overflow of oil.

(over)

Nickel
READING LAMP

Given for Six (6) Subscriptions

The modern advantages of this lamp may be easily recognized by merely examining the illustration. It possesses all the latest improvements and is in every respect a first-class article. Its appearance is greatly enhanced by its heavily nickel-plated base and oil tank; burner is the improved central draft model with patented chimney holder; fitted with a large 10-inch shade of opalescent glass; entire lamp is 20 inches high and weighs about 12 pounds when packed, ready for shipment. Sent by express or freight at receiver's expense

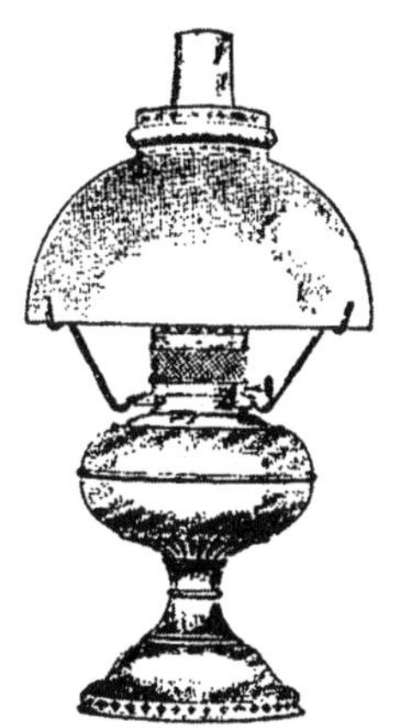

OFFER No. 565. This Reading Lamp sent as a premium for sending us Six Subscriptions (new or old) at 35 cents each.

Or, we will send Farm and Home one year, postpaid, and this Lamp, both to any address for only $1.75.

Reading Lamp premium offered by *Farm and Home Magazine* in 1906 and the tag found with a B & H 1904 lamp by Doug and Judy Myers.

B & H No. 2 wall lamp and support missing the wall bracket. Fount also used in chandeliers. $150.00.

Cast-iron holder for lamp fount designed by Albert Patitz, assigned to Bradley & Hubbard. Patitz designed several similar ornamental stands in 1895. These are often signed and/or dated in the casting under the foot. The holder accepts standard 5" oil pot. Height 11". $100.00.

B & H banquet lamps, Pitkin & Brooks catalog 1892. Courtesy Dave Broughton.

B & H Lamps, 1890s

Little B & H lamps, Marshall Field, 1894.

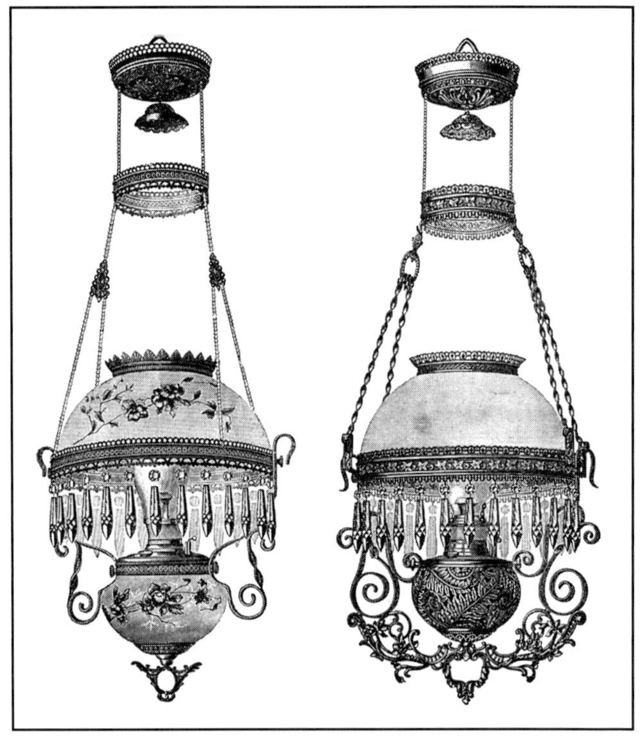

B & H library lamps, Marshall Field, 1894.

Little B & H oil pots. Height 5¼". Flame spreader marked "Pat. App'd For." Oil fill cap and fount marked "B & H." Feet and handle factory added for inexpensive night light. Left: $125.00; right: $150.00.

Little B & H banquet or vase lamp; same oil pot as above. Height 11½". $275.00. Courtesy Jon Stratton.

B & H banquet lamps, Marshall Field, 1894. Left to right: No. 2, Little B & H (No. 0), No. 1, No. 2. Note: The Little Gem lamps are not a B & H product.

B & H Lamps, 1890 – 1905

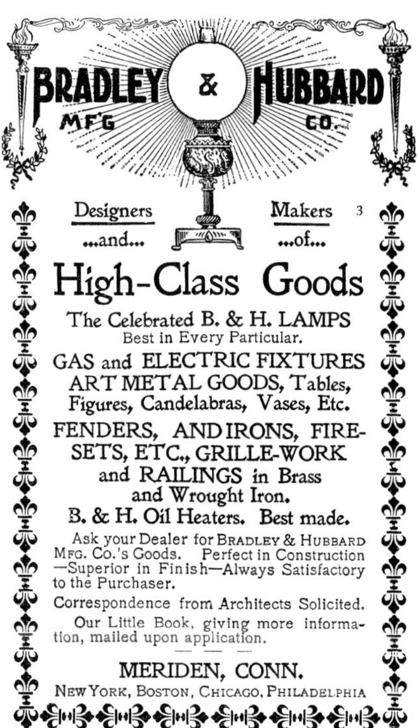

Advertisement, *McClure's Magazine,* 1897.

Bridgeport Brass Company
1865 – Today

Lamp Manufacture 1870 – ca. 1920s

Bridgeport Brass Company was incorporated in 1865 in Bridgeport, Connecticut, by three Brooklyn manufacturers — D. W. Kissam, S. R. Wilmot, and John Davol, president. The company made brass strip preferred by dressmakers to replace whale bone for hoop skirts, and by 1870, the company was making lamp burners, lamp parts, and Fowler's Patented Fly-Fans. The company also manufactured clocks, kerosene bicycle lamps, student lamps, and acetylene lamps.

The company sold its clock-making machinery to the Ansonia Brass and Copper Company in 1875 and focused on lamps — both kerosene and electric. Bridgeport Brass developed a brass electric light socket following Edison's invention of the incandescent lamp in 1880. The company made the first hard drawn copper telephone wire which connected New York and Boston, and wire specialties also became company products.

An October 23, 1879, advertisement in the *Crockery and Glass Journal* listed oil lamp products from the Bridgeport Company that included: Leader burners, Leader shade rings, Leader chimneys, Leader student lamps, Excelsior Sun burners, solid Sun burners, Eagle No-Chimney burners, tin reflectors, globe and shade rings, reducers, collars, and lamps. By 1880 the company was producing a product line of fine parlour lamps.

Frank Rhind assigned important patents to Bridgeport Brass, Edward Miller, and Charles Upton. During his productive career, Rhind lived in both Bridgeport and Meriden, dying in Bridgeport in 1903. He left the employment of Edward Miller & Company in 1892 to work for the Bridgeport Brass Company during his final 10 years. Charles Upton licensed Bridgeport Brass to manufacture The New Rochester lamps which were sold by the Rochester Lamp Company (and Bridgeport Brass) beginning in 1895. Upton may have licensed his Rochester brand to other companies as well.

Products made in the 1930s included engravers' copper, Ledrite High Speed brass rod, Plumrite brass and copper pipe, trolley wire, tubing, and automobile tire valves. The company employed approximately 3,250 workers. Bridgeport Brass was an important supplier of brass shell casings, wire, and tube during World War II.

Company Trademark

Bridgeport Brass registered "M — Boss — D" on March 21, 1893, for lamps and lamp burners.

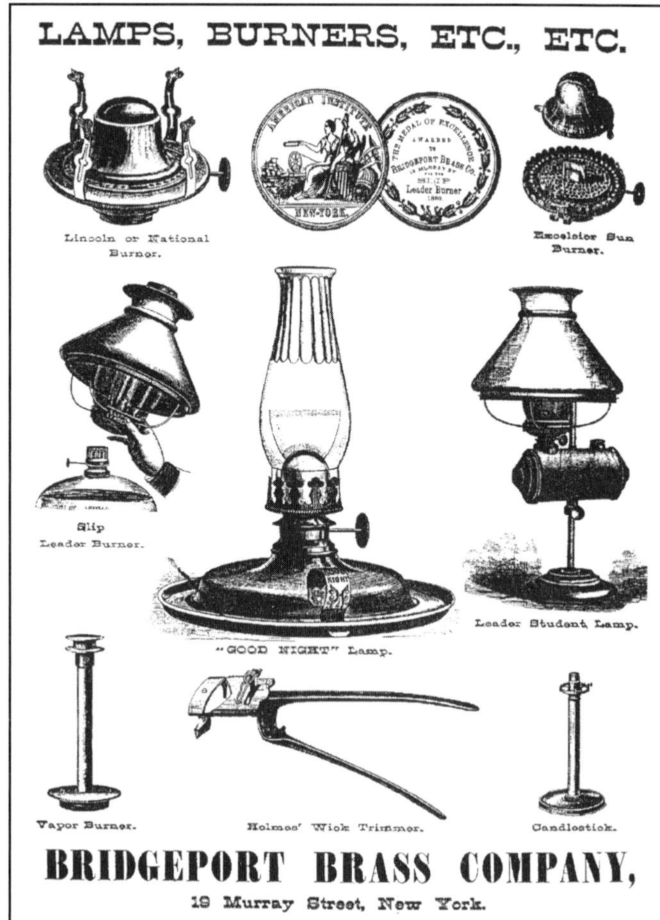

Advertisement, *Crockery and Glass Journal*, 1883, The Lincoln and National flat wick burner were identical — The National sold in the South and the Lincoln sold in the North after the Civil War. Note the Vapor burner for camphene fuel still advertised in 1883.

Trade Names

Center-draft lamps — Bridgeport Lamp, New Rochester Lamp (under license from The Rochester Lamp Company).
Folded wick burners — Leader Argand.
Flat wick lamps[1] — Leader Student Lamp, Leader Parlour lamps (some ornate bronze), Good Night, All Night.
Flat wick burners[1] — Bridgeport, Leader, Lincoln, National, New York Slip, Excelsior Sun, Solid Sun, Eagle (no chimney), Sun Hinge, Wilmot.
Bicycle Lamps — Searchlight (sold for nearly 20 years).
Lanterns — Farmer's, Marcy (tin & brass).
Heaters — New Rochester.

[1]A complete price list of kerosene burners and lamp trimmings was published in *Crockery and Glass Journal*, Feb. 8, 1883, page 19.

Selected Patents, Center-draft Lamps

Frank Rhind[1] assigned to Bridgeport Brass

Year	Patent
1887	356,962
1887	356,968
1893	501,025
1894	RE11436 (Reissue of 501,025 one-half BBCo.)
1894	531,219
1895	532,335
1897	577,583

Frank Rhind[2] unassigned

Year	Patent
1885	312,762
1885	322,321
1887	361,545
1892	478,639½ Edward Miller
1892	480,373
1892	481,674½ Edward Miller
1892	483,167½ Edward Miller

Samuel G. Stoddard assigned to Bridgeport Brass

Year	Patent
1887	356,968 sidedraft burner
1891	451,140

Charles H. Broad unassigned

Year	Patent
1892	467,571

[1]Also patents for signal bicycle lantern.

[2]Also many patents for all aspects of lamps and lighting, including bicycle lamps and glass founts. In 1875, Frank Rhind awarded patent 165,755 for a railroad car lamp. Rhind assigned many patents to Edward Miller Company.

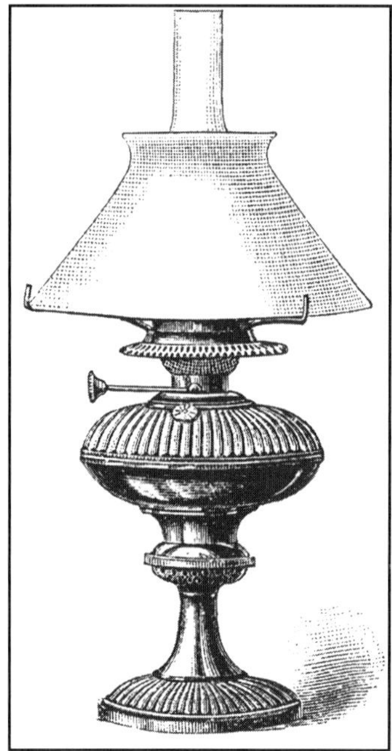

The Bridgeport lamp.
Courtesy Dave Broughton.

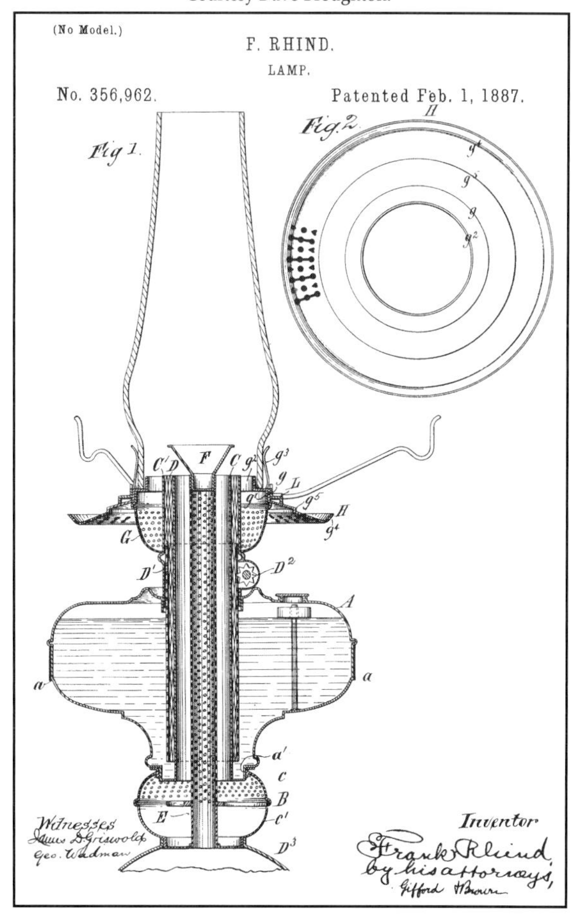

Patent 356,962 is actually for the globe holder; however, the Bridgeport lamp is clearly illustrated.

Death of Frank Rhind

Was Experimenter Inventor at Bridgeport Brass Co.

Among the death notices in this issue will be found the name of Frank Rhind of this city. Born in England, he came to this country at the age of twelve, residing in Brooklyn, N. Y., until 1886, when he removed to Meriden, Conn. During the past ten years he has lived in Bridgeport, being employed for a large part of that time by the Bridgeport Brass Co., as experimenter and inventor. For more than a year past Mr. Rhind has been practically retired from business, devoting his time to the perfecting of some valuable inventions.

His name stands near the head of the list of "prolific inventors" in the United States Patent Office, he having taken out many scores of patents, both in this country and abroad.

During his residence here, Mr. Rhind has, by his sterling honesty, unfailing generosity and abounding good-nature, endeared himself to a host of friends. His loss will be most deeply mourned by his widow, no children surviving to perpetuate his name.

The funeral will take place at 10:30 a. m. on Tuesday next and will doubtless be largely attended. The body will be taken to Brooklyn for interment.

Bridgeport Evening Post, Dec. 20, 1902

Obituary of Frank Rhind. Courtesy Allen Weathers.

The New Rochester Lamp

Bridgeport Brass Co. claimed to make 70 or more styles of New Rochester lamps in 1895. The company obviously produced and sold lamps in a big way, aided by extensive advertising of the Rochester Lamp Company. The sewing lamp below was advertised as "the desideratum [a desideratum is, in the words of *Merriam-Webster's Collegiate Dictionary*, 11th ed., "something desired as essential."] for a Summer Lamp."

New Rochester lamps were made in at least three sizes — No. 2, No. 3 (for heaters) and No. 0, (for the sewing lamp). Perhaps someone will find a catalog to verify New Rochester hanging lamps.

Large banquet and vase lamps with cast-iron loading weights may be marked "R. L. Co., N. Y. City, Made in U. S. A."

See Rochester Lamp Company for more information and history.

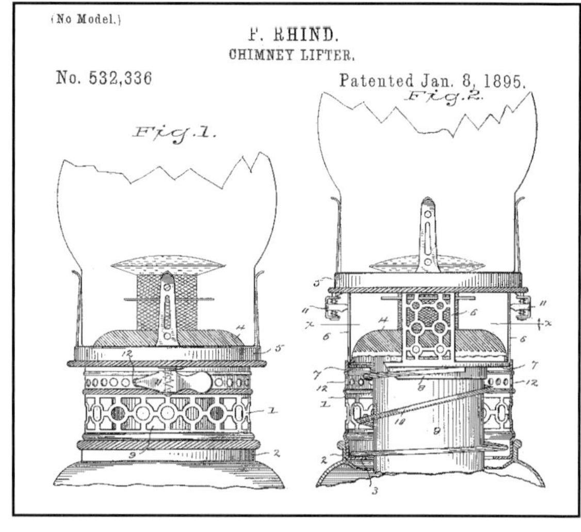

To give you some idea how entirely different the

Bridgeport 'New' Rochester

is from all other lamps, we give the No. 2 burner photographed exact size; are these draft holes likely to get filled up to endanger **your life?**

We cannot tell you here *why* there is **no climbing** of the flame, **no soiling** table covers, **no breaking** of chimney springs, no **running over** in filling, etc.; but our new Catalogue will — and give other important information which every lamp user *ought to know* — free for the asking — but mention this publication.

Don't jeopardize the life of your family as we can supply new fonts to fit your old unsatisfactory and unsafe lamps.

Don't mistake and think we are advertising a burner; this illustration shows that part only of the central draft **Bridgeport "New" Rochester Lamps**—*the Catalogue explains everything you want to know; send for it now, please.*

Bridgeport Brass Co., Bridgeport, Conn., or 19 Murray St., N. Y.

Muncey's Magazine, November 1895.

McClure's Magazine, November 1895.

Advertisement, *Muncey's Magazine*, November 1895.

The New Rochester, 1895

The New Rochester lamps are found with two different burners — the first introduced about 1894 and the second in 1897. The latter burner has a twist gallery lift (Rhind patent 577,583). Lamps may be found with either burner, depending on when they were made. Some loading weights are marked — "DP," "DB," "P," or "HN."

Flame spreaders for New Rochester burners fit over the wick tube. The smooth base flame spreaders are marked with these patent dates: June 7, 1887 (Rhind 364,438 assigned to Miller); Oct. 1, 1889 (Henkle 412,181 assigned to Upton); July 12, 1892 (Rhind 478,639 assigned one-half to Miller); Aug. 30, 1892 (Rhind 481,674 assigned one-half to Miller); Sept. 27, 1892 (Rhind 483,167 assigned one-half to Miller). Both of the lamps below used the tall, smooth base flame spreader.

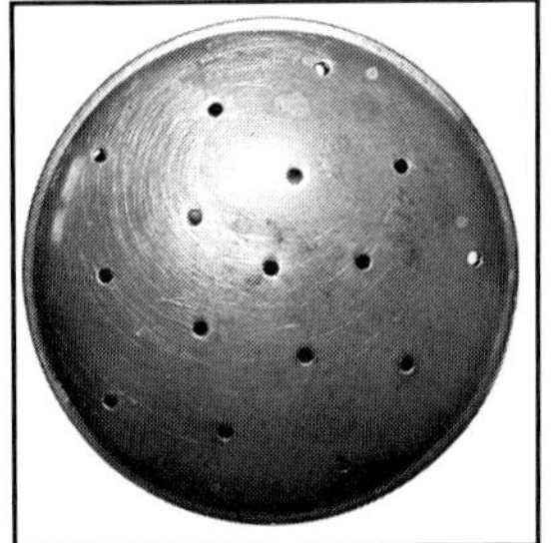

The ribbed base flame spreader is found with two sizes of top discs — $1\frac{5}{8}$" or $1\frac{6}{8}$" in diameter. The wider disc has a flatter contour.

Oil fill cap on New Rochester and New Rochester Jr. lamps.

Wick raiser found in early New Rochester stand lamps. The raiser is marked "Jan'y 26, 92" on the pull rod, with more dates on both sides. One side: "Pat'd Sept. 14 86, Oct. 1 89, Aug. 26 90, Other Pats Pending." Other side: "Patented Sept. 27 92, July 12 92, Aug. 30 92, July 4 93, Aug. 28 94."

The New Rochester (No. 2) stand lamp with push-pull wick raiser and early gallery lift, nickel finish. Height 13". This lamp also found plain without embossing. $175.00.

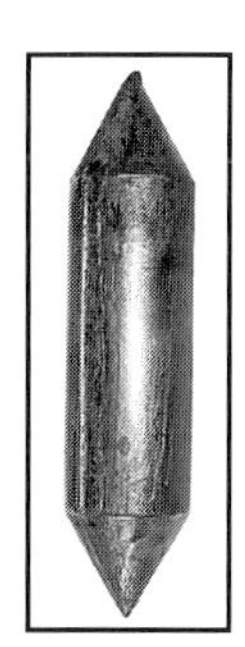

These lamps have floats inside the oil fills.

The New Rochester (No. 2) stand lamp with characteristic wick-raising knob and early gallery lift, brass finish. Height 13". This lamp found plain and with embossing over complete fount. $175.00.

The New Rochester Flame Spreaders

The 1887 – 1889 Rochester patent flame spreader and the 1889 – 1890 Rochester flame spreaders are sometimes found in New Rochester lamps. These are likely replacements or, possibly, an indication the lamps were sold by the Rochester Lamp Company, which replaced the Bridgeport flame spreader.

The lamps are marked "The New Rochester, Made in U. S. A."

Wick carrier, 4¼" x 1⅝".

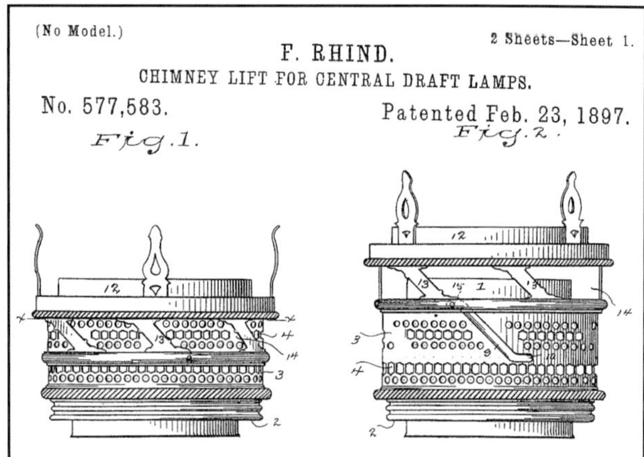

Wick-raising knob on New Rochester and New Rochester Jr. lamps. Some knobs are plain (without spoke-like design).

The New Rochester embossed table lamp with cast-iron foot and cast arms (No. 2). Height 11¼". Tripod marked "Patented Oct. 09, 94" (Rhind patent 527,289 assigned to BBCo.). $300.00.

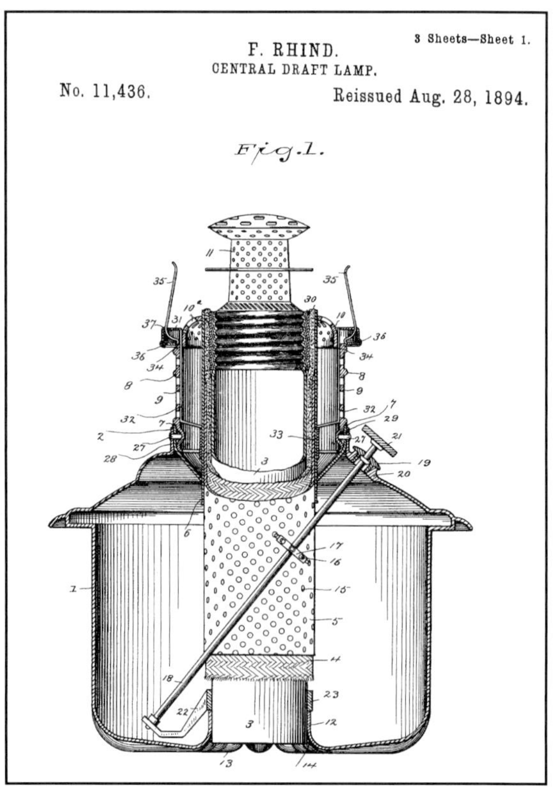

The wick-raising mechanism is well illustrated in Rhind's patents 501,025 and RE 11436.

The New Rochester JR.

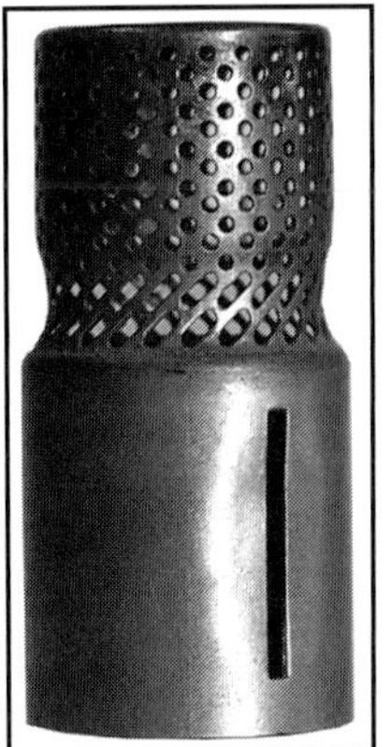

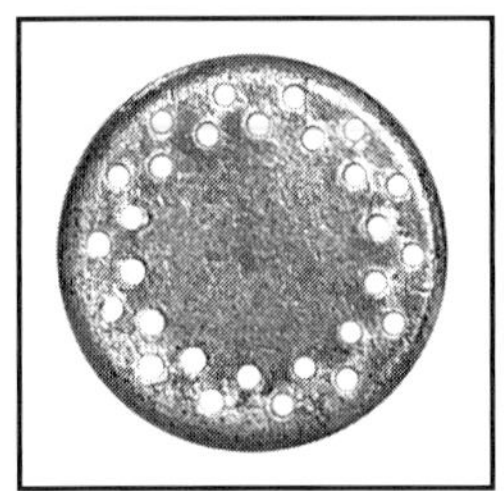

Flame spreader for The New Rochester JR lamps. The single vertical slot and the "curved slots" identify this flame spreader as New Rochester JR.

The JR Rochester chimney logo.

The New Rochester JR (No. 0), brass finish. Height 10½". A ball shade holder installed on this lamp. $275.00. Courtesy Doug and Judy Myers.

The New Rochester JR (No. 0), brass finish, with decorative arms. Height about 9¾". $250.00.

The New Rochester JR (No. 0), brass finish. Height 10". Lamp has been polished. A ball shade holder is installed on this burner. $200.00. Courtesy Kent Stratton.

"THE NEW ROCHESTER JR, HOTEL LAMP, Made in U. S. A." Height 6$^{1}/_{16}$". Tin lamp with brass color plating. Burner, oil fill, flame spreader, and wick knob are brass. $75.00.

The New Rochester, 1897

The New Rochester (No. 2) stand lamp with twist gallery lift, brass finish. Height 11". There is a filter screen under the oil fill. $275.00.

New Rochester vase lamp. This lamp was possibly sold by F. H. Lovell & Co. $250.00.
Courtesy M. J. Howell.

The New Rochester, 1898 – 1899

These lamps and the stove are from a UK catalog.

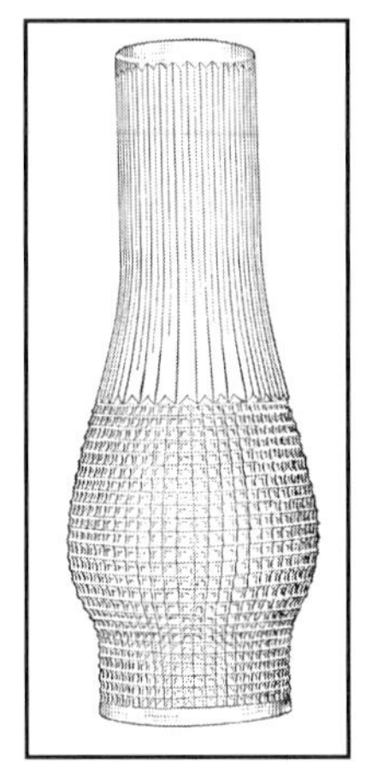

Junior hand lamp.

Mammoth stove fitted with Xrays chimney.

Junior banquet lamp.

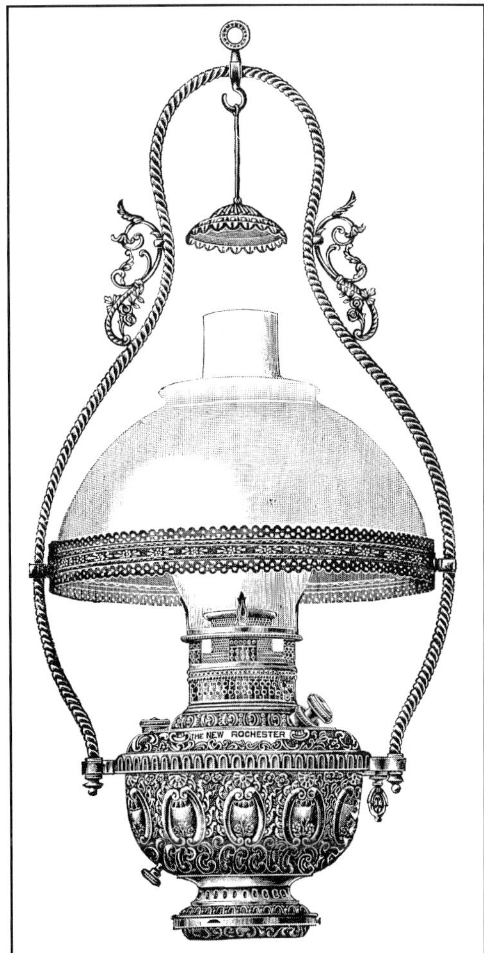

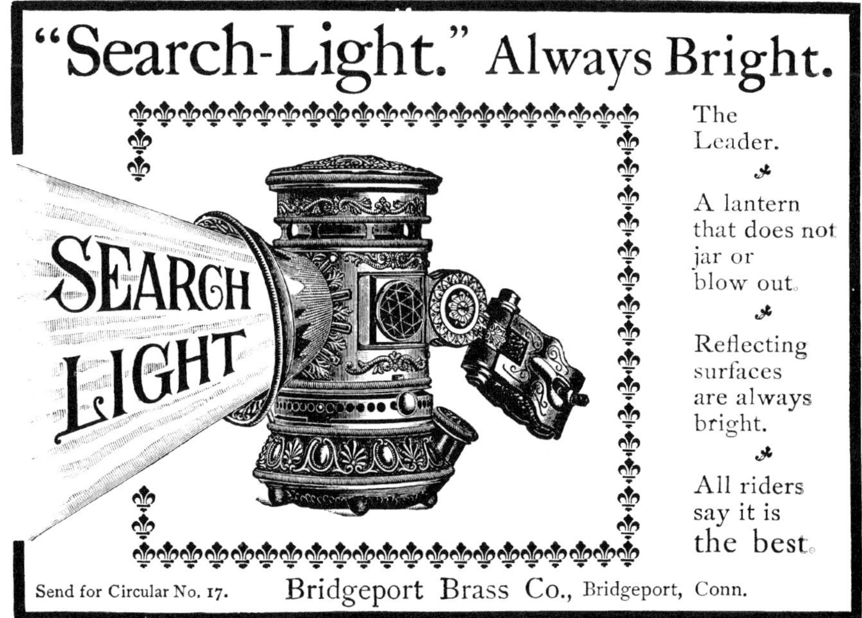

Advertisement, *Muncey's Magazine,* 1897. The Search Light is an acetylene bicycle lamp; Rhind's patents were D23,582; 570,893; and 570,894.

Bristol Brass & Clock Company

1850 – 1903

The Bristol Brass Company, 1903 – 1982; Lamp Manufacture 1868 – 1911

The Bristol Brass and Clock Company, of Bristol, Connecticut, was founded in 1850 by 11 clock makers and 5 brass financier-industrialists. The primary organizers were Israel Holmes of Waterbury, the first president, and Elisha Welch of Bristol. They established the company to make brass for clock makers in Bristol, thereby saving time and transport of brass from Waterbury. Welch became president one year later when Holmes moved on to other ventures. Welch remained president and primary stock holder until his death in 1887.

The company was not a major clock manufacturer, although it made brass clock mechanisms and parts. During hard times, the company resold clocks taken in from customers to pay debts of its accounts.

The company manufactured brass, German silver, souvenir spoons, and silver flatware.

To diversify, Bristol Brass purchased the burner shop from George W. Brown, of Forestville, Connecticut, in 1868. Brown, an American pioneer in early kerosene burners, began lamp manufacture in 1862 (Anon, 1972).

Brass lamp collars most often found on Sandwich lamps were patented by Alvin Taplin (161,912) or G. W. Brown (175,022). See Barlow & Kaiser (1989) for more information. Bristol Brass published a notice of "Caution!" that the company would hold parties who were selling spun or stamped thread collars without appropriate patent markings to strict accountability for patent infringement.

George W. Brown developed early tin clockwork toys — worth their weight in gold to collectors today. Brown continued toy manufacture even while the "new" kerosene burner business was growing rapidly. Brown merged his toy business with the Stevens brothers to form the Stevens and Brown Mfg. Company in Cromwell, Connecticut. Brown died in 1889.

The burner business was reported to be a consistent and dependable profit center through the years as Brown, Taplin, and others developed burners and kerosene lamps and lanterns. The company improved cost-cutting techniques to manufacture brass collars, vase lamps, and stand lamps. They also developed the Security Burner for railroads, and exported Bristol Brass parlor burners to China and India.

The burner shop in Forestville was destroyed by fire in 1881 at considerable loss to the company. The facility was rebuilt within the decade, after which center-draft lamps became new and important products. Burners and lanterns may be marked "B. B. & C. Co." Lamps may be marked "Bristol," "Bristol USA," or "Genuine Bristol" on the fount.

No center-draft lamps were illustrated in a Bristol catalog dated 1884; however, numerous decorated center-draft vase and hanging lamps were shown on 35 pages in its 1889 catalog. Bristol Brass Company was a major producer of lamps for department stores and other retail distributors. The company made an extensive variety of stand, vase, parlor, banquet, and library lamps. F. H. Lovell carried a full line of "Bristol Electric Lamps" in its 1887 – 1888 export catalogs.

In 1903, the company name was changed to the Bristol Brass Company to better reflect itscore business.

The burner shop was sold to National Marine Lamp Company in 1911.

Bristol Brass produced brass cartridge cases, bullet jackets, shells, truck parts, ship fittings, and parts for automobiles. The Bristol Brass Company closed in 1982.

Bristol Brass manufactured lamps for the Haida Lamp & China Company and F. H. Lovell in New York City, as well as many other companies, department stores, and retailers. The names given to the library lamps (see below) suggest extensive marketing by George Brown and Bristol Brass.

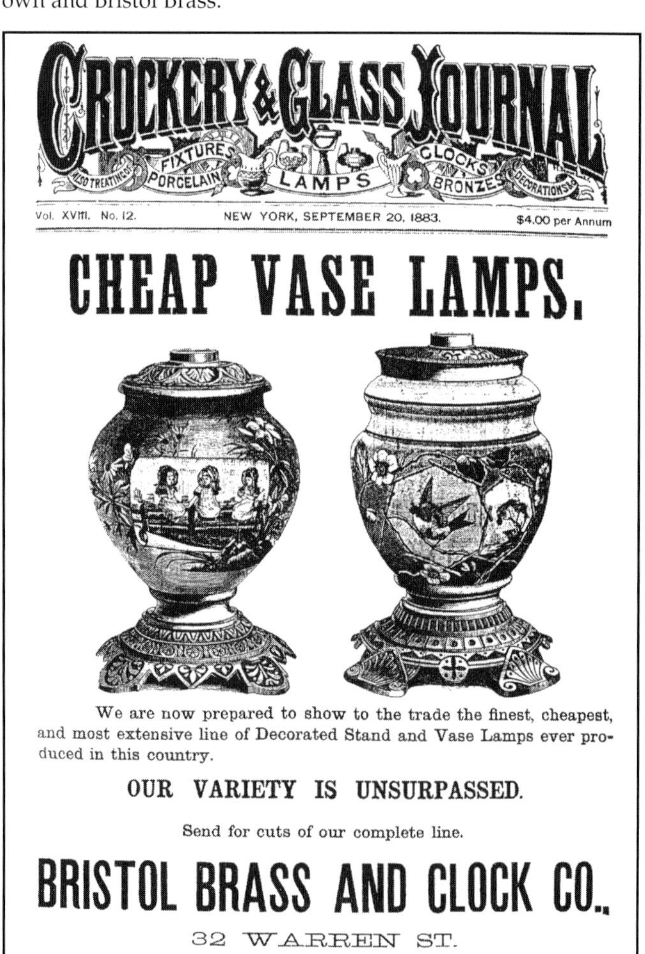

Advertisement, Sept. 20, 1883. Bristol Brass was recovering from a disastrous fire in the burner shop by introducing a new line of decorated vase lamps.

Trade Names

Center-draft lamps — Bristol, Bristol Electric, Drummond Electric, Chief, The Improved, Genuine Bristol, Genuine Mammoth, Improved Bristol, Imperial Bristol, The Empire, Victor, Champion, The French, Victor, New Darling, Drummond Electric.

Folded wick burners — Bristol Argand, Bristol Electric, Crystal Light, Kent Argand.

Flat-wick burners — Parlor Burner, Prize Burner, Collins Sun, Security Burner, Union Burner, Rajah, Ratchet, Improved Duplex, Blaze, Drummond, Slip Drummond, New Drummond, Sun Duplex, Hinge, New Dyott.

Lanterns — Diamond, Racket, Boy, Baby.

Bicycle Lamps — I.C. Lantern.

Night lamps — Student night lamp, Magic Night Lamp, Union Night Lamp, Daisy, Wide-Awake, Fairy, Hammered Brass, Pride of America time indicating night lamp.

Hanging extension library lamps with glass founts named in the 1889 catalog: Baltimore, Cottage, Cleveland, Triumph, Queen, Home, St. Louis, Villa, Venetian, Fern, Syracuse, Eclipse, Bangor, Newport, Philadelphia, Saratoga, Princess, Senator, Clipper, Stella (Hall lamp), Diamond, Windsor, Albany, Palace, Hartford. Hanging center-draft extension lamps with brass founts were named in the 1889 catalog: the Beauty, Genuine Bristol, the Victor, the Favorite, Emperor, Peerless, Henrietta, Boston.

George W. Brown

George W. Brown, brother of Charles W. Brown, died at the Cosmopolitan Hotel, New York on Wednesday (Dec. 18) at 2:30 p.m. from pneumonia. He was 59 years of age. For 15 years or more he has had charge of the New York house of Bristol Brass and Clock Company and has been superintendent during that time of the burner shop. His death is a great blow to the company as well as to his family. He leaves a widow, who resides in Forestville, and 4 children, one son and three daughters and five grand children. His son, George, holds a position in the New York house. The funeral will occur in Forestville Saturdry [sic] when the shops will be closed.

The Bristol Press, page 5, Dec. 19, 1889

Selected Patents, Center-draft Lamps

Alvin Taplin[1] assigned to Bristol Brass & Clock

1889 404,121
1889 415,400
1890 .... 432,339 (unassigned)

Bartlett P. Luce[2] assigned to Bristol Brass & Clock

1890 .... 435,663 (unassigned)
1891 444,598
1891 450,106

Elisha S. Hollister assigned to Bristol Brass & Clock

1891 457,083

George W. Brown[3] assigned to Bristol Brass & Clock

1891 466,029

George S. Brown[4] assigned to Bristol Brass & Clock

1892 483,279

[1]Also patents on hanging lamps and early lamp burners.
[2]Also patents assigned to Wallace & Sons, Ansonia, CT.
[3]Deceased, with Alvin Taplin.
[4]Also patents on bicycle lamps

J. HART WELCH, Pres't. J. R. HOLLEY, Sec'y and Treas.
G. S. BROWN, Ass't Treas.

BRISTOL

Brass and Clock Co.,

MANUFACTURERS OF

Rolled Sheet and Platers' Brass and Brass Castings.

Silver Plated and German Silver Flatware.

MANUFACTURERS OF

BICYCLE LANTERNS,
KEROSENE OIL BURNERS,
BRASS TUBULAR LANTERNS,
LAMPS and LAMP TRIMMINGS.

POST OFFICE ADDRESS,

BRISTOL, - CONN.

Advertisement, *Bristol City Directory*, 1900. Courtesy Amy Schumann.

Bristol Electric Lamps, ca. 1887 – 1890

Bristol Brass became established in the lamp business with manufacture of flat-wick burners and accessories. George W. Brown was the driving force and sales agent after 1875. His son carried on lamp manufacturing after his death in 1889. The company first made an assortment of vase lamps and piano lamps along with night lights and lanterns. I suspect the company manufactured a complete line of brass center-draft lamps for F. H. Lovell beginning in 1886, possibly earlier. I also suspect that Bristol Brass manufactured the Toronto Light King which uses the identical burner gallery. Bristol may also have manufactured lamps or parts for F. Meyrose in St. Louis. I have not found patents for Bristol Electric lamps.

"The Wonder of the World!" proclaimed F. H. Lovell in its 1887 catalog illustrating the stand lamp below. Lovell advertised this embossed lamp as the Drummond Electric Lamp in 1888.

The fount lamp below was illustrated as "Bracket Lamp with Chief Brass Fount" as late as 1892 in the Pitkin and Brooks catalog.

Gallery and flame spreader. The flame spreader fits in a tube inside the wick tube.

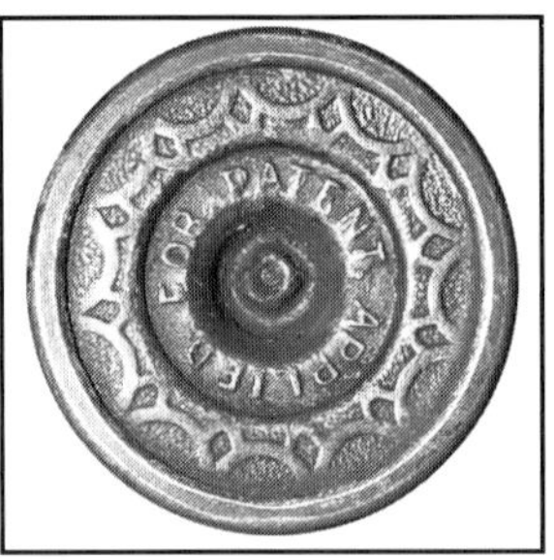

Wick knob marked "Patent Applied For."

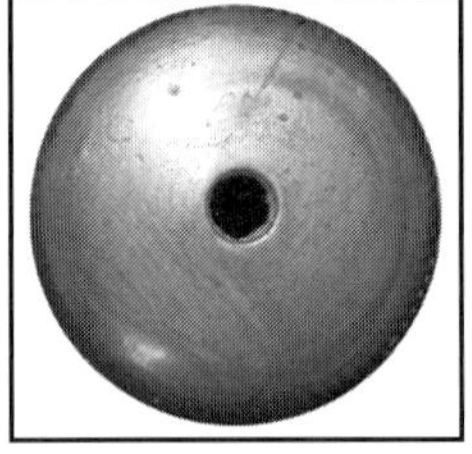

Oil fill cap.

Wick carrier, 5½" long.

Electric Lamp No. 100, F. H. Lovell, 1887. Bristol stand lamp 12½" tall. Unmarked except for wick knob. Wick tube 1⅜" diameter. This lamp was nickel plated and was also found in brass finish. $150.00.

Electric Lamp No. 120, F. H. Lovell, 1887. Bristol fount lamp for wall bracket or hanging frame. Height 8½". This lamp had a brass finish and was seen in other shapes. $125.00.

Champion, ca. 1887 – 1888

The Champion was an early Bristol lamp sold through agents and other distributors. The Champion burner and oil pot was sold by F. H. Lovell simply as "Electric Lamp" in its 1887 export catalog.

Champion mushroom flame spreader, similar to those illustrated in early patents.

"Champion, Patent Applied For" is stamped in top of the fount.

The Champion stand lamp was sold by A. J. Weidener, lamp merchant in Philadelphia. Weidener was assigned one-half of patent #258,281 for center-draft wick raiser by August R. Conrad in 1882. This information and trade card courtesy of Dan Edminster.

CHAMPION

POSITIVELY Non-Explosive

Will not BREAK the CHIMNEY.

No Offensive Odor While BURNING!

Patent Safety EXTINGUISHER

Cleanly.

NO DRIPPING of OIL.

Gives a LIGHT equal in Brilliancy to 50 Candles, or 2½ Gas Burners. This is the most Powerful and Perfect LIGHT ever made FROM OIL.

THE FOUNTS Can be used on your old Gas or Oil Chandeliers or brackets, and will increase your light THREE-FOLD.

AGENTS WANTED

THE CHAMPION is the Best, Cheapest and Safest Lamp for Churches, Halls, or Family Use.

Send for Illustrated Circular.

A. J. WEIDENER, 36 S. 2d St., PHILA. Sole Owner of Patent.

Cast-iron loading weight of Champion lamp.

The Champion is an early lamp in the Bristol line. The fount is stamped "Champion Patent Applied For." The fount tooling seems to be identical to that of the Empire. Height 13½". $150.00. Courtesy Fil Graff.

These Champion library lamps were sold by Dodd, Glaescher & Werner, a lamp merchandiser in Cincinnati.

Bristol and Genuine Bristol Hanging Lamps

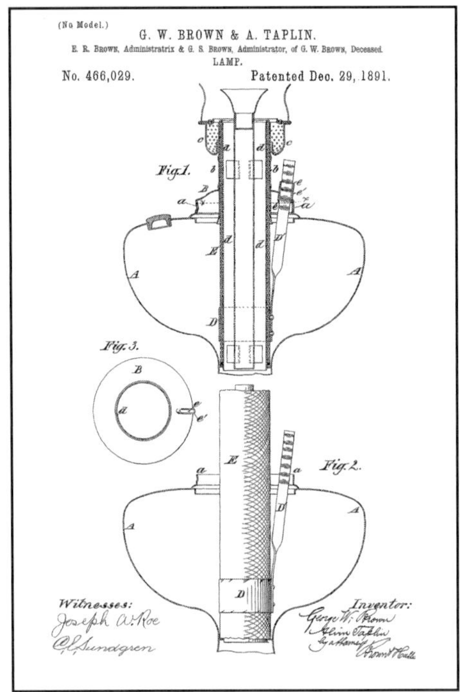
(No Model.)
G. W. BROWN & A. TAPLIN.
E. R. BROWN, Administratrix & G. S. BROWN, Administrator, of G. W. BROWN, Deceased.
LAMP.
No. 466,029. Patented Dec. 29, 1891.

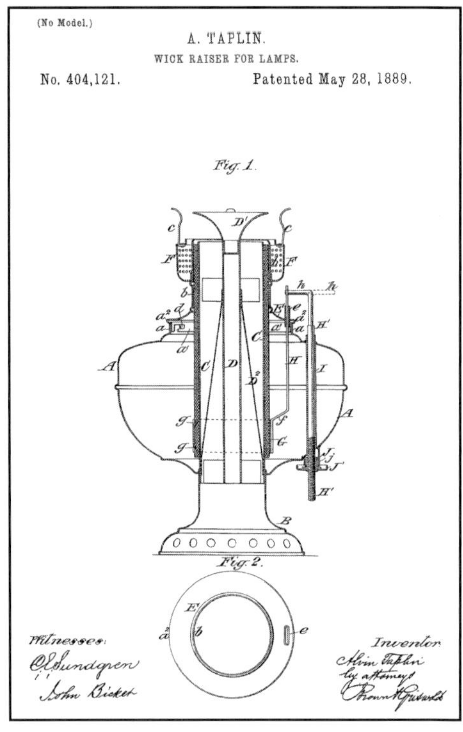
(No Model.)
A. TAPLIN.
WICK RAISER FOR LAMPS.
No. 404,121. Patented May 28, 1889.

"Bristol" is stamped in the burner assembly.

"Genuine Bristol" is stamped in the burner assembly.

Flame spreader for Genuine Bristol. Length 10".

This flame spreader is incorrect.

Bristol mammoth hanging lamp fount, pattern also found as stand lamp. The patent above was applied for in May 1888, but this lamp was clearly sold in F. H. Lovell in 1887 (see next page). $125.00. Courtesy Fil Graff.

Genuine Bristol mammoth hanging lamp fount. Height 11". The lower screen of the flame spreader, above left, is heavily rusted. $125.00. Courtesy Doug and Judy Myers.

"Genuine Bristol" Mammoth Hanging Lamps

GENUINE MAMMOTH LAMP. GENUINE MAMMOTH LAMP.

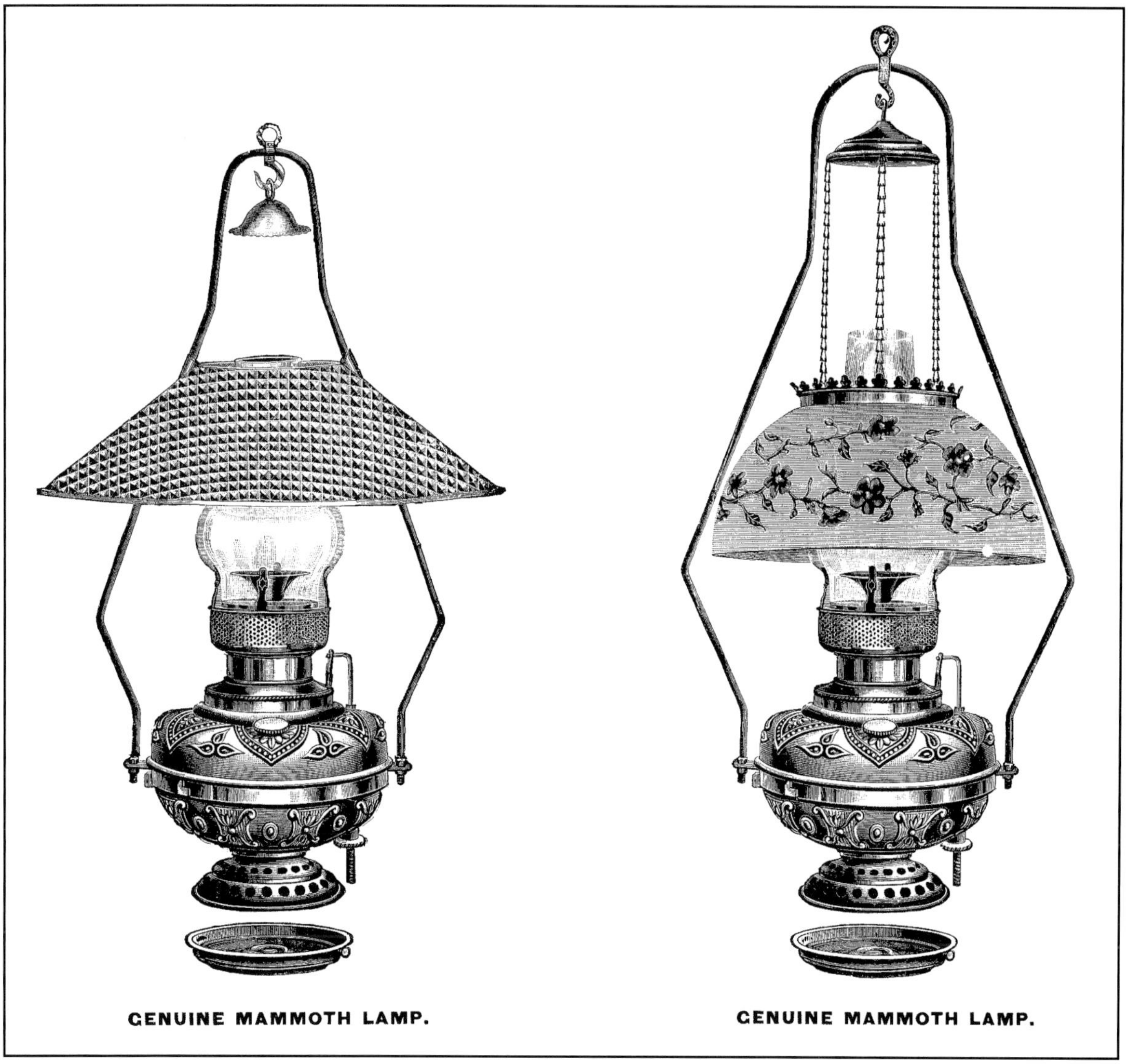

This fount was not embossed and had an extended foot in Bristol's 1889 catalog. These hanging lamps were sold as "Genuine Mammoth" by Pitkin and Brooks in 1892 and as "Mammoth Haida" by Haida Lamp & China Co. in 1893. This is an example of an instance in which old images from 1889 were used in 1892 and 1893. Courtesy David Broughton.

Bristol Mammoth hanging lamp sold by F. H. Lovell as Drummond Electric Lamp No. 620 in 1887.

Bristol "Electric" Lamps

This lamp was called the Bristol Electric in the 1889 catalog. Bristol Brass sold lamps to several retailers, identified by names on their flame spreaders. Some flame spreaders are unmarked on top. The same flame spreaders fit Bristol or Improved Bristol lamps.

Bristol Brass sold lamps to these companies (also see Haida).

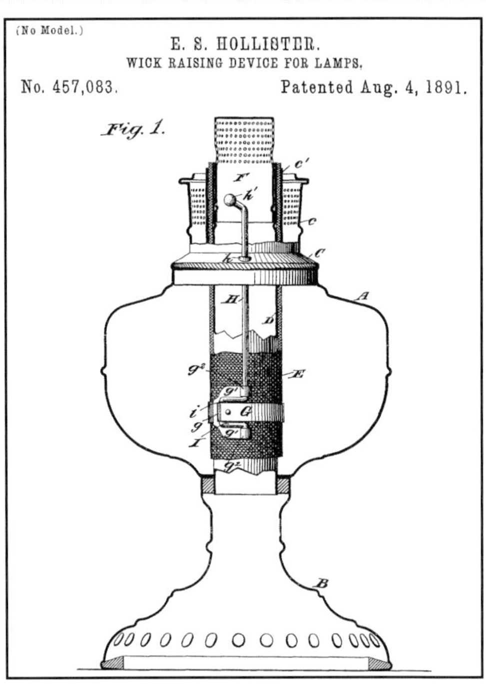

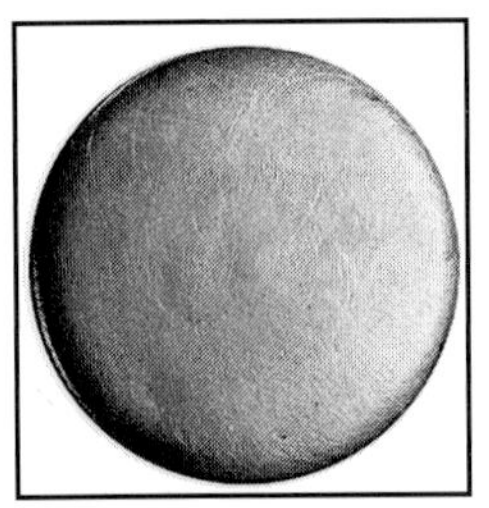

Flame spreaders of identical size and shape as The Improved Bristol are found marked (left to right): unmarked, "M. E. Moore B. & P. Co."; "Rogers Silver Plate Co."; "Geo. F. Bassett & Co."; "M. S. Benedict Mfg. Co."; "American Wringer Co., New York"; and "The National Reading. Also, some are marked "Winchester, Pat. July 15, 90, U.S.A."

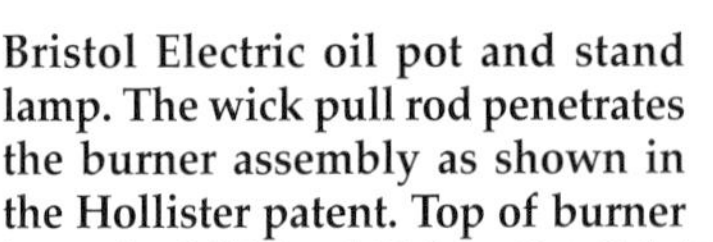

Bristol Electric oil pot and stand lamp. The wick pull rod penetrates the burner assembly as shown in the Hollister patent. Top of burner is marked "Bristol U.S.A., Pat. Jul 15 '90"; however, not all lamps are marked. This lamp was sold as the Chief in Pitkin and Brooks and Ward catalogs. Right: $100.00. Stand lamp courtesy Lou Hopf.

Flame spreaders used in some Bristol center-draft lamps. The top is marked "Bristol Brass & Clock Co., Made in U. S. A." around the form of an elk's head. The form is identical to the Victor flame spreader, which fits an unknown early Bristol lamp or was sold to another retailer. The top of these flame spreaders is easily compressed to make the spreader appear shorter.

"Bassett Electric" Lamps

George F. Bassett & Company had stores in New York, Philadelphia, and Chicago. The 1889 New York catalog, reproduced by David Broughton, illustrates lamps manufactured by Bristol Brass and Clock Co., Edward Miller, Bradley & Hubbard, Wallace & Sons, and several glass companies. Bristol lamps were rebranded as Bassett Electric lamps by George Bassett.

The Bassett Electric Lamp has the same burner as the Bristol Electric, where the wick pull rod penetrates the burner base. These lamps were sold by George F. Bassett & Co. in the 1889 catalog. This fount was fitted with the Bristol Electric burner in the 1887 Lovell Export catalog. Courtesy David Broughton.

Chief

Chief lamps are rebranded lamps with Bristol or Improved Bristol burners. We do not know which flame spreaders were used in these lamps. Hanging library lamps, illustrated in the Pitkin and Brooks 1892 catalog, appear to have Improved Bristol burners.

Chief center-draft lamp in Montgomery Ward 1895 catalog.

Montgomery Ward & Co.'s Chief Central Draft Metal Table and Hand Lamps.

We have selected this burner (after a careful comparison with all others) as being the very best; it will give more light according to the amount of oil consumed than any other lamp made. Try one and you will be more than pleased.

No. 2 Chief 80 Candle Power Central Draft Stand Lamp Complete, with opal dome shade 10-inch, shade holder and chimney; height to top of chimney, 20 inches, ; takes No. 2 Rochester round wick and chimney.

Why use an inferior lamp when one guaranteed by a reputable firm can be purchased at price quoted? Order one and return at our expense if it does not bear out the following description:

1st. Gives a strong, steady white light.
2d. Easiest wicking device invented.
3d. Wick never sticks and can be raised and lowered instantly.
4th. Well made and shapely throughout.

55677 Brass finish Price..........$1.50
55678 Nickel finish. Price..........$1.75

"CHIEF" TABLE LAMP.

Chief stand lamp sold by Pitkin and Brooks in its Chicago catalog No. 63, 1892. The image appears to be the early Bristol lamp burner. However, I believe the image was out-of-date and that Improved Bristol lamps were being sold by that time. Courtesy David Broughton.

Improved Bristol 1890 – 1900

Bristol Brass declared the Improved Bristol Lamp "a marvel of simplicity, the burner part can be removed for cleaning without interfering with the wick attachment." Note that the Taplin patent (right) preceded the Hollister patent (previous page).

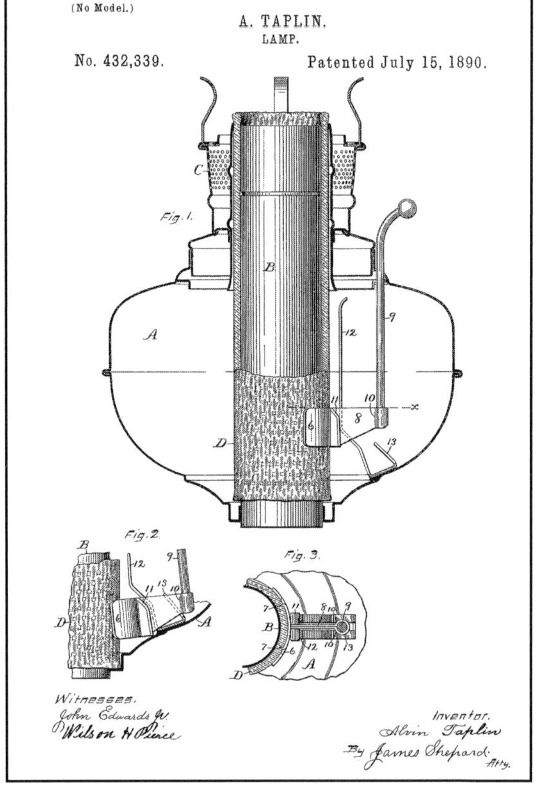

Improved Bristol burner shows the lift gallery "legs," which allow the gallery to be raised for lighting the lamp.

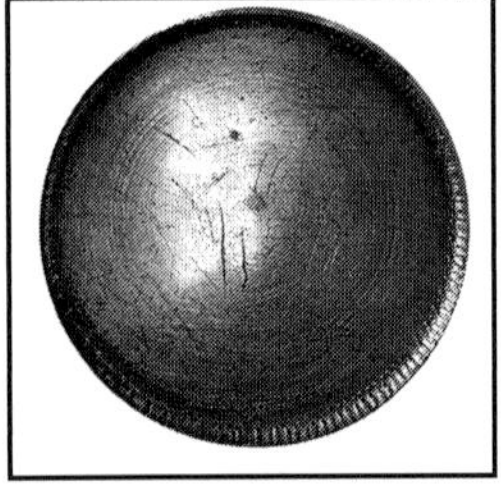

Plain oil fill cap found on Bristol lamps.

Improved Bristol table lamp. Height 11½". Lift gallery and bayonet burner connection. $125.00.

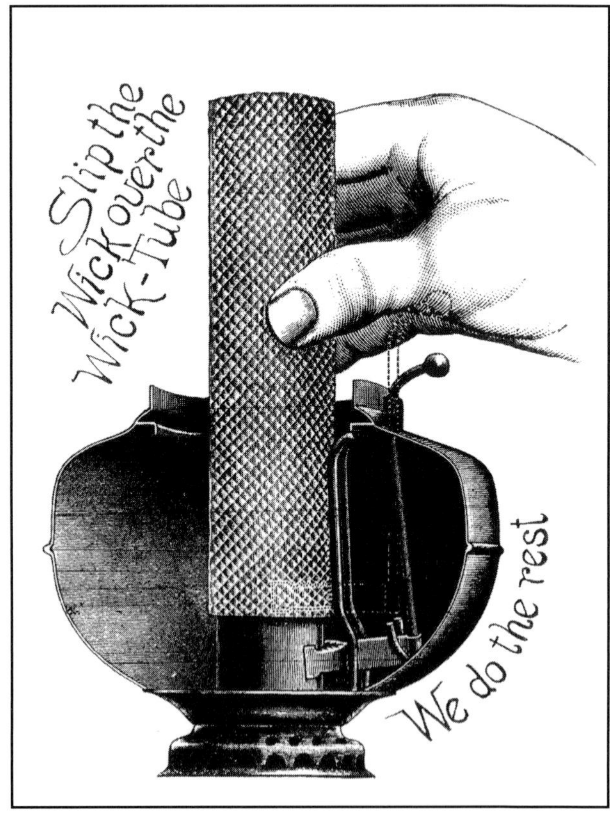

This cut represents a sectional view of the Improved Bristol Oil Fount, showing the marvelous simplicity of the wick-raising device. *China, Glass and Lamps,* May 13, 1891.

Improved Bristol lamps were made in large numbers judged by the number found extant. The burner assembly of Improved Bristol lamps is unmarked.

Flame spreaders found on Improved Bristol lamps. They are marked "Improved Pat. Jul. 15, 90, U. S. A. Bristol" or "Improved Bristol, Made in U. S. A., B. B. & C. Co."

Improved Bristol banquet lamp, lift gallery and air intake under the fount. Height 20". $185.00.

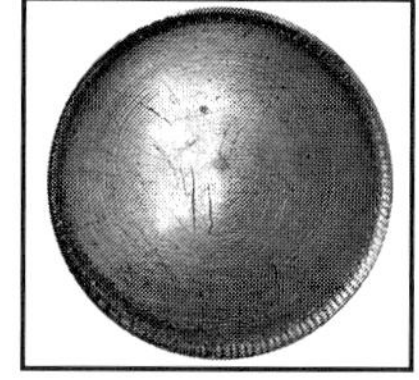

The oil fill cap is plain and small; only ¾" diameter.

Improved Bristol banquet lamp, lift gallery. Height 20". $175.00.

Improved Bristol banquet lamp, lift gallery. Height 18". $175.00.

Junior Bristol

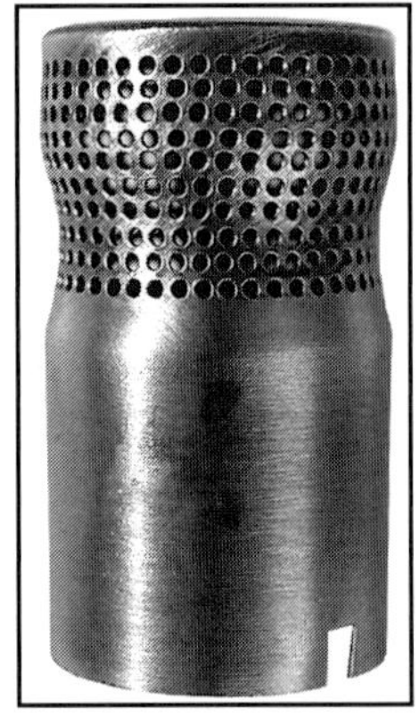

Junior flame spreader, "PAT. JUL 15, 90 U. S. A."

Bristol hand lamp, Junior size. $100.00. Courtesy Heinz and Ursula Baumann.

Bristol Junior oil pot for vase lamp. The tank is 4" in diameter, 3" to rim. $50.00. Courtesy Lou Hopf.

New Darling

I believe the New Darling junior lamp (below) was sold by Haida Lamp and China Co. Haida sold another lamp named Our Darling made by Holmes, Booth and Haydens.

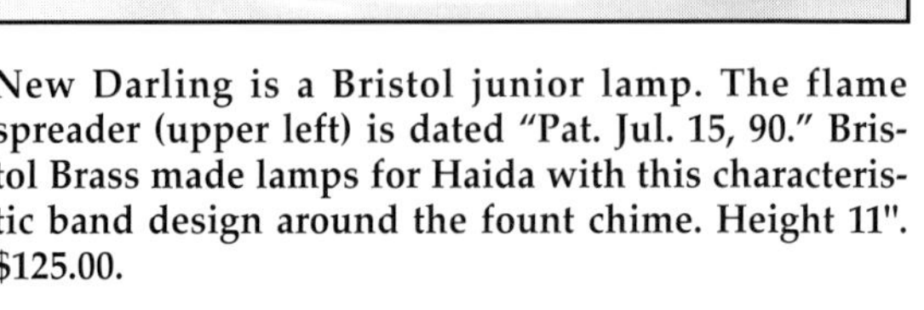

New Darling is a Bristol junior lamp. The flame spreader (upper left) is dated "Pat. Jul. 15, 90." Bristol Brass made lamps for Haida with this characteristic band design around the fount chime. Height 11". $125.00.

The Empire

The Empire and The French lamps were most likely sold to unknown stores or distributors. Both have the Improved Bristol burners.

The Empire stand lamp with the Improved Bristol burner assembly, stamped "The Empire, Pat. July 15, 1890." The flame spreader is unmarked Bristol. Height 12¾". The fount tooling seems identical with the Champion lamp. The chimney prongs are missing. $100.00. Courtesy of Fil Graff.

The French

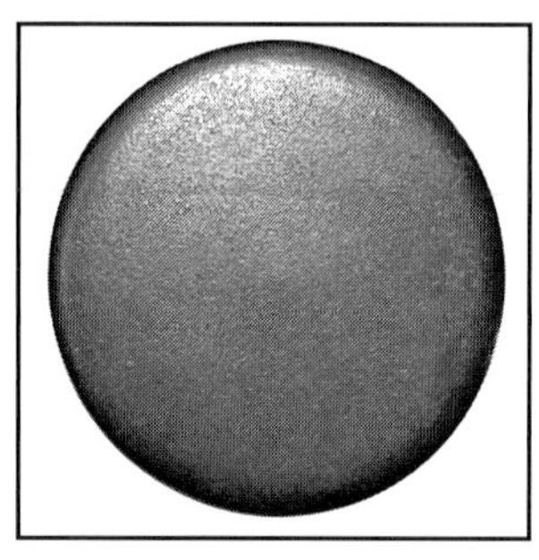

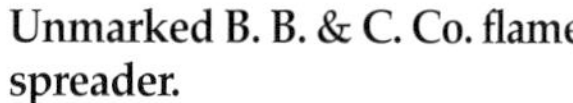

Unmarked B. B. & C. Co. flame spreader.

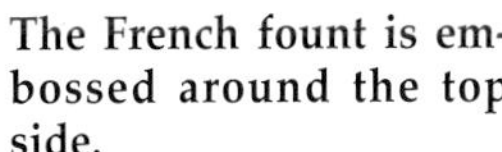

The French fount is embossed around the top side.

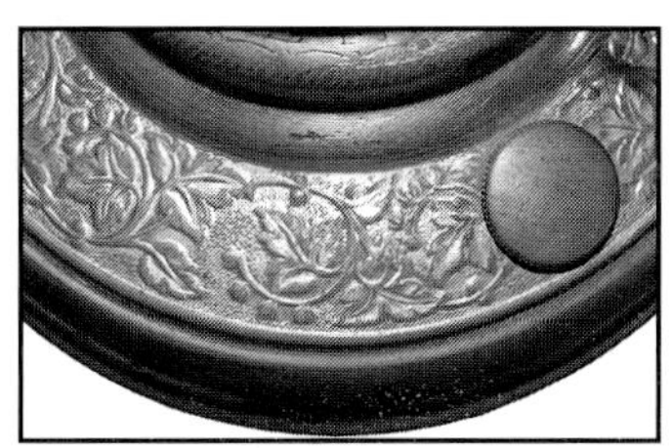

The French lamp has the Improved Bristol burner assembly, which is stamped "The French, Pat. July 15, 1890." This lamp may have been made for an exclusive lamp distributor. The flame spreader is unmarked. Height 12". Air for central draft enters holes in the underside of the fount. $125.00.

The Haida

The Haida Lamp & China Company was an importer and retailer in New York City from 1890 to 1898 (read more in the chapter on Haida). Haida lamps were marked "The Haida" on the burner assembly, which was basically that of the Improved Bristol. Most Haida stand and banquet lamps made by Bristol Brass have a characteristic band around the fount chime. Haida flame spreaders are shown below. Unmarked and Improved Bristol flame spreaders are also found in Haida lamps.

The burner assembly of Haida lamps is stamped "The Haida, Pat'd July 15 '90."

Haida flame spreaders. The "Improved Haida" found in lamp with Improved Bristol burner and lift gallery. The "Screw Lift, U. S. A., Haida." Courtesy Fil Graff.

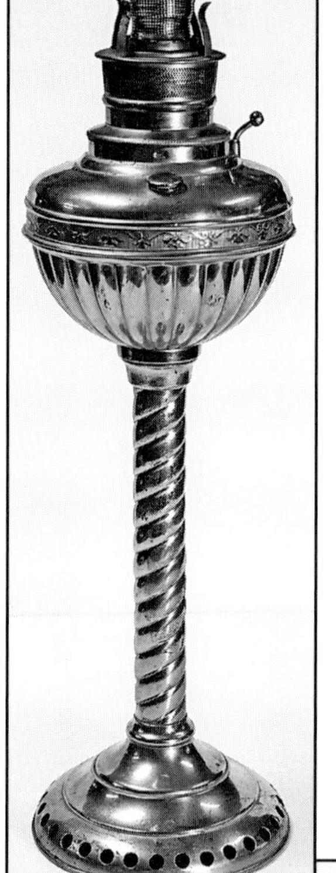

Haida banquet lamp, non-lift gallery. Height 20". $175.00.

Haida stand lamp, height 12". The decorative chime band is characteristic of many Haida lamps. $100.00.

Haida hanging lamp fount, non-lift gallery. This example has an unmarked flame spreader. $75.00.

Haida oil pot, non-lift gallery. The tank is 5" diameter and 3½" to rim. This example has an unmarked flame spreader. $75.00.

Oil Pots

Improved Bristol oil pot, lift gallery. The tank is 5" diameter and 3½" to rim, the same as The Haida oil pot. Found with any one of several flame spreaders. $75.00.

Unmarked Bristol oil pot with redesigned burner with lift gallery, bayonet connection. The tank is 5" diameter and 3½" to rim. This burner with Victor flame spreader. The Victor and Elk flame spreaders fit these wick tubes smoothly and correctly, but they are often too tight to fit the Improved oil pot. $75.00.

Transition Burners

These lamps combine the Improved-style burner basket with the wick knob riser mounted on top of the fount. Redesigned burners are found with this configuration and wick raiser. I have not found the patent for this wick raiser assembly.

Bristol banquet lamp sold as "Hercules" by Pitkin and Brooks, 1898 catalog. Height to top of chimney 27". The burner was described as "No. 2 Chicago Chief" which appears to be the Improved Bristol burner basket combined with wick knob riser mounted on top of the fount. Courtesy Jeff Ebersole.

Unmarked Bristol lamp with Improved-style burner basket, bayonet connection and Improved Bristol flame spreader. Height 10½". $150.00. Courtesy Doug and Judy Myers.

Unmarked Bristol Lamps

These are unmarked lamps made by Bristol Brass and Clock Co. I suspect they were manufactured for other distributors or retailers. I would not be surprised to find oil pots with either one of these burners. The lamps have lift galleries and burner thread connections.

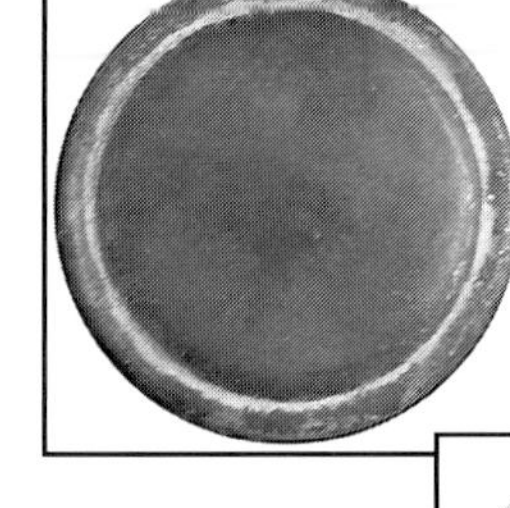

Flame spreader found in unmarked lamps made by B. B. & C. Co. The top is unmarked. Some have a baffle inside. I believe these are original Bristol flame spreaders.

Burner found in two lamps below right. The wick raiser is cylinder, wick carrier, similar to lamps of the early 1900s. No patents found for this assembly.

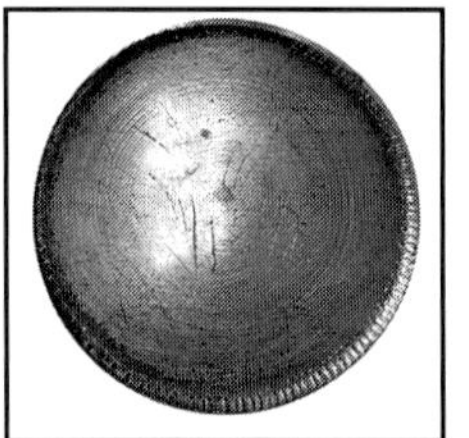

Same oil fill cap as found on Haida and other Bristol lamps.

Wick raising thumbwheel marked "Made in U.S. of America."

Plain stand lamps. I believe the elk flame spreader (left) is possibly correct, as it fits properly. Height 11". Burner threaded connection. $75.00 each. The lamp on left courtesy Lou Hopf.

Plain stand lamp with unusual air vents under fount. Height 12". Flame spreader is illustrated above. The same lamp fount has been found with Daylight flame spreaders. $125.00.

F. H. Lovell & Co. Mogul Lamps

F. H. Lovell & Company was a major distributor and retailer of oil lamps, marine lighting, and railroad lighting in New York City (read more in the chapter on Lovell). Lovell sold many brands of lamps, including those made by Bristol Brass, which it called Electric, and later, these named Mogul, possibly as appeal to foreign or immigrant buyers. Lovell moved its warehouse to Arlington, New Jersey, in 1898, where the company expanded assembly and manufacturing operations.

Improved Mogul

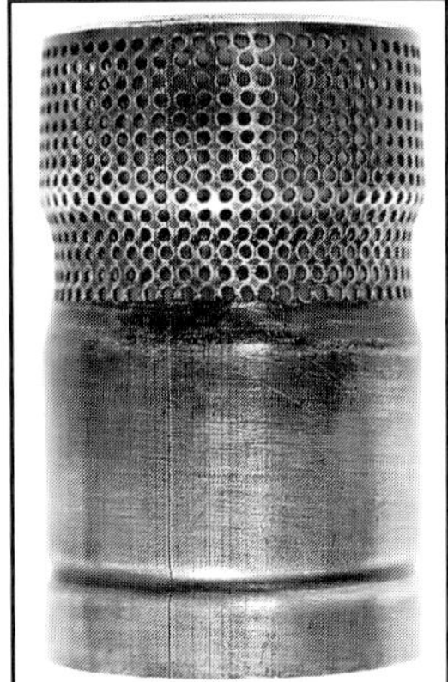

Flame spreader for Improved Mogul stand lamp.

Improved Mogul stand lamp. The shape of the fount is the same as The French lamp, but with no air vents in bottom of the fount. Height 12". $175.00.

The elk flame spreader fits the unmarked lamp below.

Same oil fill cap as found on Improved Bristol, Haida, and other Bristol lamps.

Embossed stand lamp. Height 12". Burner has bayonet connection. I do not know if this lamp was sold by F. H. Lovell or some other company. The flame spreader was missing; however, the elk flame spreader fits perfectly. $175.00.

FANCY MOGUL LAMPS.

This is the celebrated center draft lamp which heretofore has only been supplied either in plain nickel finish or in very expensive ornamental designs. These lamps have been produced in the hope of supplying something extremely attractive at a low figure.

X 195.
As shown, $2.25 each.
Lamp and tripod only $2.10 each.

X 197.
As shown, $3 00 each.
Lamp and tripod only $2.85 each.

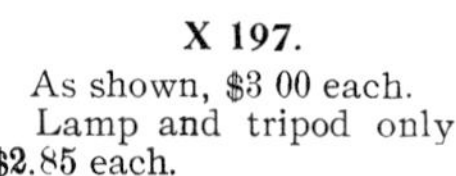

X 196.
As shown, $3 10 each.
Lamp and ring only $2.45 each.

X 198.
As shown, $3.60 each.
Lamp and tripod $2.85 each.

Bristol stand lamps in 1898/1899 Lovell catalog that featured Hitchcock lamps. The burners appear to be same as the unmarked embossed B. B. & C. Co. burners on the previous page.

Bristol hanging lamp, 1895. This burner appears to be the Improved Bristol. Lovell catalog courtesy of Norman Jones.

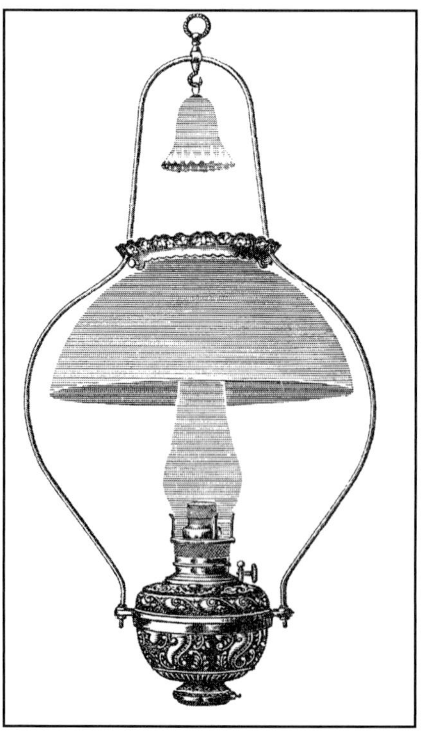

Bristol hanging lamp called No. 2 Mogul in 1916 Lovell catalog. This lamp also offered with a tin shade. We do not know if National Marine supplied the lamps at this time or whether Lovell purchased tooling from Bristol Brass in 1911.

Bristol "Daylight" and "Radio" Lamps

The lamps below are not marked with patent dates; however, the flame spreaders are marked "Daylight." Some identical flame spreaders are unmarked. I believe these lamps were manufactured by Bristol Brass & Clock Co. for Fessenden and Jacobsen, who held the trademark for Daylight lamps (see Craighead and Kintz). The lamp, below left, was illustrated in 1910 Hibbard, Spencer, Bartlett & Co. Catalog; it was sold as "Radio lamp No. 9060," described as follows: "The extra large fount and well proportioned base make this a very attractive lamp." Radio lamps were priced 20 percent cheaper than Miller Juno lamps in the same catalog.

Flame spreaders may be plain or marked "Daylight."

Burners on both lamps are identical with lift galleries. Wick knobs are marked "Made in U. S. of America."

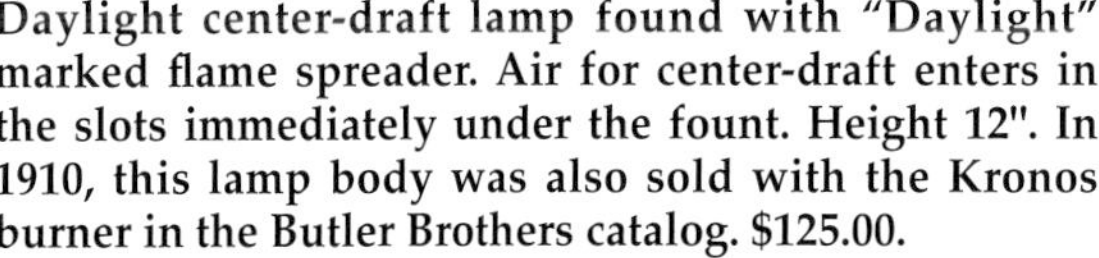

Daylight center-draft lamp found with "Daylight" marked flame spreader. Air for center-draft enters in the slots immediately under the fount. Height 12". In 1910, this lamp body was also sold with the Kronos burner in the Butler Brothers catalog. $125.00.

Daylight center-draft lamp completely unmarked. The flame spreader is identical in size and shape to the one marked "Daylight" without marking on top. Air for center-draft enters in the holes in the foot. Height 12". $125.00. Courtesy Doug & Judy Myers.

Byesville Glass and Lamp Company

Byesville Glass Company, 1904 – ca. 1907

The Byesville Glass and Lamp Company was the successor to the American Art Glass and Lamp Company, of Byesville, Ohio. Charles L. Campbell was president and Charles N. L. Brudewold was general manager. Extensive damage from a cyclone delayed opening the company glasshouse until early 1900.

The factory had 1 furnace, 2 day tanks, and 12 pots. In 1903, *China, Glass and Lamps* reported that the company employed 22 shops making shades, chimneys, and a general line of blown ware (Oct. 24).

The company manufactured lamps and lighting wares in decorated, opal, flint, and colored glass. The main production was "large and elegant" vase lamps. The Byesville Glass & Lamp Company was considered for merger into Pittsburgh Lamp, Brass & Glass Company in 1901 (*CGL*, Nov. 1901). The brass hardware was purchased from unknown sources, although I believe Holmes, Booth & Haydens and possibly Pittsburgh Brass Co. were sources of oil pots and burners.

In 1904 the company was bankrupt, and it was sold to Charles M. Schott, Jr., of New York City. He formed a new company and reopened the factory under the name Byesville Glass Company. The new company advertised lamps, patent globes, electric wares, decorated opal, flint, and colored glass in 1905. The company had a salesroom in New York City.

I do not know how Byesville lamps may be identified. The same is true for lamps produced by Ellwood City Glass Co. and Washington Glass Mfg. Co.

The idle factory was purchased by the Cambridge Glass Company in 1911. Electrical glassware was produced there until Cambridge Glass closed the factory in 1917.

CHAS. L. CAMPBELL, President. CHAS. L. N. BRUDEWOLD, Vice-President and Gen. Mgr.
JNO. C. BECKETT, Treasurer. GEO. A. BECKETT, Secretary.

THE BYESVILLE GLASS & LAMP CO.,
BYESVILLE, OHIO,
MANUFACTURERS OF
DECORATED ART GLASS LAMPS,
DECORATED SHADES, GLOBES, ETC.
BLOWN AND PRESSED ELECTRIC GLASSWARE
OF ALL DESCRIPTIONS.
OPAL. FLINT COLORS.
New York Salesroom, 46 West Broadway, A. H. Hoag, Salesman.

Advertisement, *China, Glass and Lamps*, Jan. 25, 1900.

OUR
Patent Draft Globes
are the only things of their kind on the market and are bound to be sellers.
Before Placing Orders See Them.
We also Manufacture
Lamps, Globes,
Shades,
Electric Ware,
Decorated Opal,
Flint and Colors.
New York Salesroom,
46 WEST BROADWAY
The Byesville Glass Co.
BYESVILLE, OHIO.

Advertisement, *China, Glass and Lamps*, Jan. 14, 1905.

Byesville flame spreader is the same size and shape as those marked "Fort Pitt" and "Tuxedo." These flame spreaders were made by Holmes, Booth and Haydens.

Chicago Lamp Company

1885 – 1906

Chicago Lamp Company advertised lamps at 238 Lake Street, Chicago, Illinois, on billheads and envelope covers. The company appears to be the retail outlet for lamps manufactured by the A. G. Geiss Company, Chicago. Adolph Geiss and Edmond Bigelow held patents for center-draft lamps illustrated on the billheads.

Chicago Lamp Company was incorporated in December 1885 by Solomon L. Bignall, Charles J. Glenn, and Edward B. Bigelow. Bignall was the owner of a hardware company bearing his name at 238 Lake Street. The corporate papers stated purpose was to manufacture and sell lamps and lanterns. There was no mention of Adolph Geiss and the Illinois Secretary of State has no records for the A. G. Geiss Company.

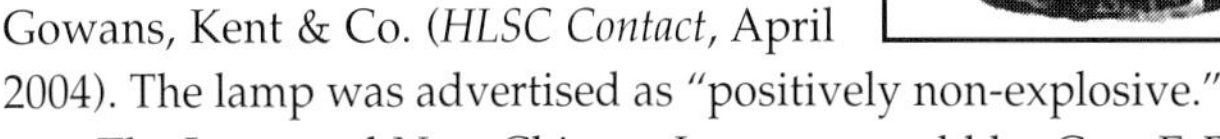

Adolph Geiss was listed from 1885 to 1890 in *The Lakeside Annual Directory of the City of Chicago*. Geiss was "manufacturer of every description of spun, stamped, drawn metal goods" and the "patentee and sole manufacturer of the Chicago Electric Lamp; a pure white light of 52½ candle power, postively non-explosive. Office and factories: Wendell St. near Wells. Tele. 3252."

The Geiss Chicago Font is named and illustrated on a Toronto billhead of Gowans, Kent & Co. (*HLSC Contact*, April 2004). The lamp was advertised as "positively non-explosive."

The Improved New Chicago Lamp was sold by Geo. F. Bassett & Co., New York; it was known also as the Geiss Electric Lamp, and the Geiss Chicago Lamp.

The Geiss and Bigelow patent lamps were also sold by Tilton's Incandescent Lamp Company, Pittsburgh, owned by J. C. Tilton. Joseph K. Andrews, of Antrim, Ohio, assigned patents for vapor and chimneyless burners to Tilton from 1865 to 1867. I have no more information on Tilton or his company.

Both companies sold fount lamps and stand (table) lamps. The fount lamps were fitted to library lamps and adapted to street lights.

Geiss and Bigelow patents (next page) were early developments in center-draft lighting. The Chicago Lamp won awards in several fairs and expositions in 1884.

Geiss Electric 5" wicks were offered in the 1888 H. Leonard & Sons catalog, Grand Rapids. Geiss Chicago lamp wicks were listed by American Wick in 1891 (*CGL*, Oct. 28, 1891).

Company Trade Names

Center-draft lamps — Chicago, Chicago Electric, Geiss, Geiss Electric, Geiss Chicago Lamp, Tilton.

Trademark. The trademark "Chicago Electric" for kerosene lamps was awarded to Adolph Geiss and Leonard L. Kleine on June 30, 1885.

Chicago Electric Lamp

Wick knob is unmarked.

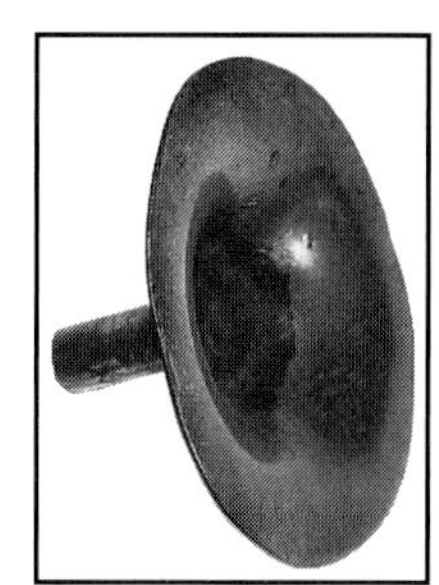

Flame spreader.

Oil fill cap.

Chicago Electric stand lamp, 12¾" in height. The top of the fount is marked "Chicago Lamp Co., Chicago, Ill." $150.00.

Chicago Electric Lamp

Burner and gallery and top of fount of the Chicago Electric stand lamp. The top of the fount is marked "Chicago Lamp Co., Chicago, Ill." The neck of the burner is stamped "Pat. Oct. 28, '84."

Selected Patents, Center-draft Lamps

Edmond B. Bigelow and Adolph Geiss, unassigned

1884 307,262

Adolph Geiss, unassigned

1885 329,897

Edmond B. Bigelow, Solomon L. Bignall, and Charles J. Glenn, assigned

1886 334,558

Adolph Geiss, unassigned

1886 .... 353,674 side-draft round-wick burner

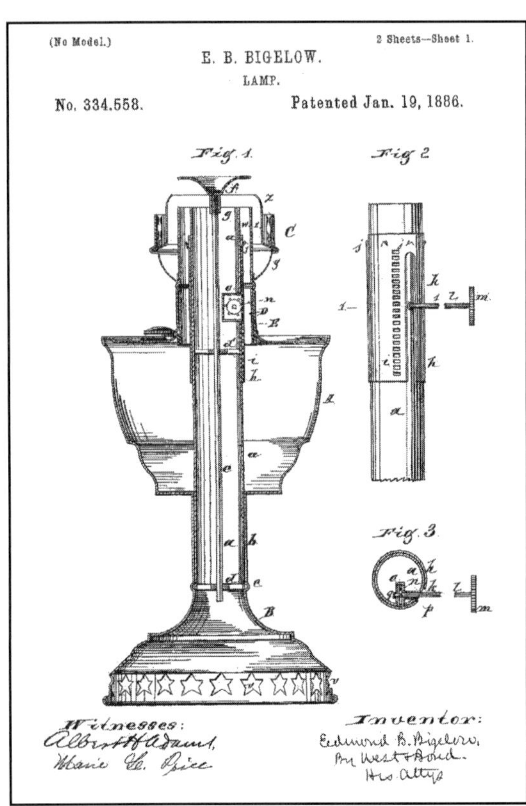

Geiss Electric Lamp

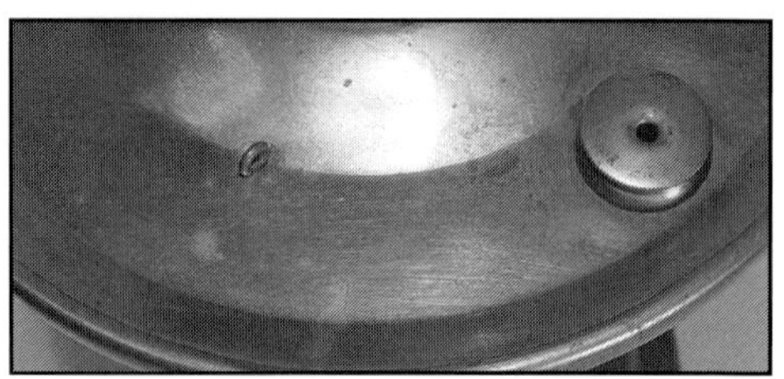

Geiss Electric stand lamp marked "Pat. Apl'd For, A. Geiss & Co., Chicago" on the neck below the burner. Height 13½" to top of flame spreader. Small plain oil fill cap (see above). $150.00.

Geiss Electric Lamp

George F. Bassett & Company, New York, claimed to be sole agents for Chicago Electric Lamps on an advertising flyer, ca. 1885. The Chicago Electric Lamp was also known as the Geiss Electric Lamp or the Geiss Chicago Lamp. The gallery turns and locks in place exactly like that of the Chicago Electric Lamp.

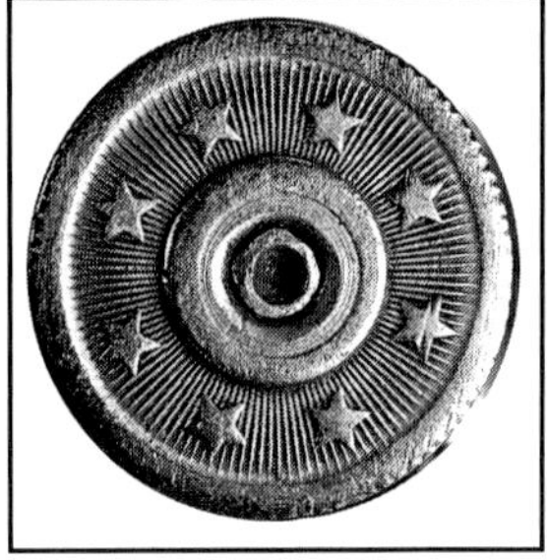

Either of these wick knobs found on these lamps.

Wick knob marked "A. Geiss & Co., Chicago, U. S. A., Pat. Oct. 28th, 1884."

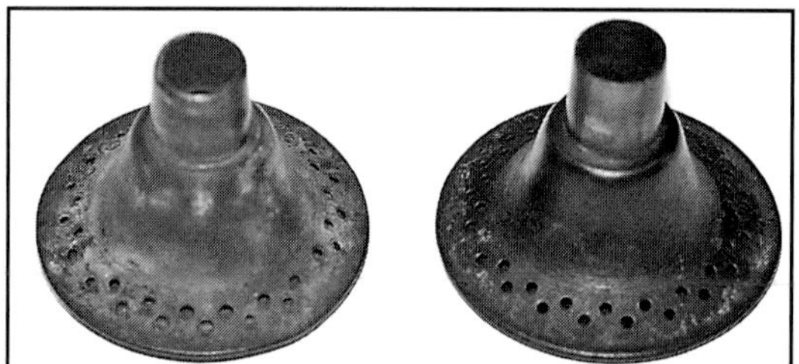

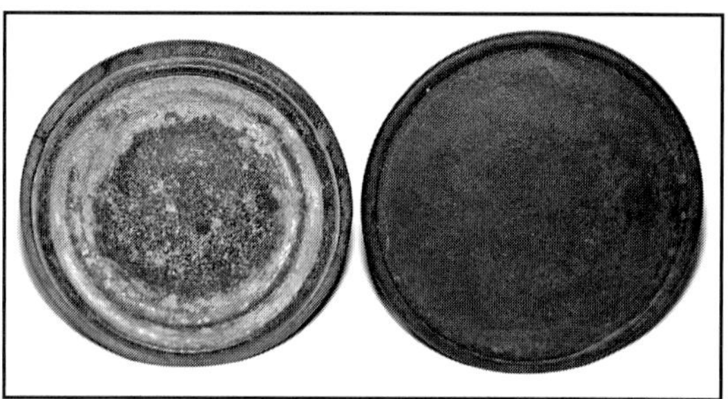

Geiss flame spreaders. Left: 1¾" dia. and dome top; right: 1⅞" dia. and flat top.

Geiss Electric stand lamp marked "A. Geiss & Co., Chicago, Pat. Apl'd For" in the neck below the burner. Height 14" to top of flame spreader. Virtually the same lamp as the Tilton Incandescent. $150.00.

Oil fill cap used on both lamps.

Geiss Electric lamp. Height 8½". The lamp is stamped "A. Geiss & Co. Chicago, Pat. Apl'd For" on the neck below the burner. Three little "feet" support the fount. $100.00.

Tilton's Incandescent Lamp

In 1888/1889 the Incandescent Lamp Company was listed under Lamps and Lamp Goods in the *Pittsburgh and Allegheny Business Directory*. The company advertised Tilton's Incandescent Lamps in 1887, illustrating stand lamps, hanging lamps, and a street lamp (Thuro, 1987).

I believe the Tilton Incandescent lamp is a rebranded Geiss Electric Lamp.

Geo. F. Bassett & Co. sold The Improved New Chicago Lamp as "Postively Non-Explosive."

Courtesy Catherine Thuro.

Geiss Electric lamp wick tube and wick raiser.

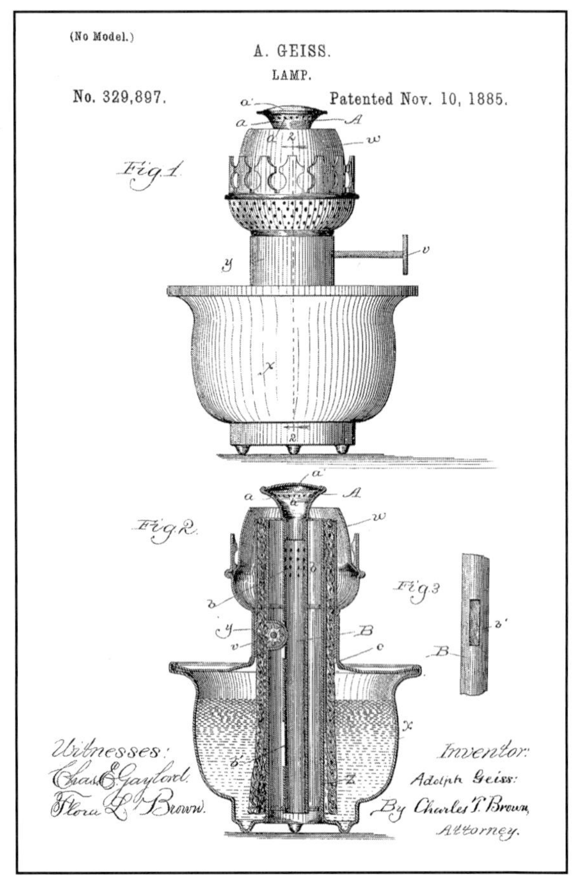

The Improved New Chicago Lamp

POSITIVELY NON-EXPLOSIVE.

THE IMPROVED NEW CHICAGO LAMP

Known also as:
"The Geiss Electric Lamp," "The Chicago Electric Lamp" and "The Geiss Chicago Lamp."

Produces from any test of Kerosene Oil a pure white, steady light of 52½ candle power. It has the brilliancy of 2 gas jets at one-seventh the cost. The light of six ordinary lamps is eclipsed by one "Improved New Chicago Lamp". Hence, we claim that with our lamp the problem of obtaining a brilliant light at a small cost is effectually solved.

AMONG ITS MANY
ADVANTAGES
may be enumerated the following:

1. The lamp, by the laws of nature, **is positively Non-Explosive.**
2. It cannot break or smoke a chimney.
3. An ordinary chimney can be used.
4. The lamps burn at a cost of ½ cent per hour.
5. The wick movement of this lamp is very durable, and cannot get out of order, yet so simple that anybody can wick a lamp in 20 seconds.
6. A wick is furnished free with every lamp. One wick will last 6—8 months.
7. The lamps being made of brass cannot break, but will last a life-time.
8. What you save on chimneys in one year alone will suffice to pay for a lamp.
9. This lamp has the only wick movement that requires no tieing of wick, and also the only movement that brings the wick up perfectly even.
10. The wick trims itself if turned down until the stop work acts, and permitted to go out without being blown, a minute or less being all the time required.
11. The top of the Fount is so constructed as to hold any small quantity of oil that might accidentally run over, thereby preventing damage to furniture, carpets, etc.
12. The Insurance Companies recommend their use, because they are non-explosive.

Etc., Etc., Etc.

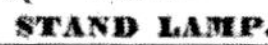

STAND LAMP.

The Brilliant and Steady Light

produced by these lamps is because of their peculiar construction, the main principle being a double draught; the outer air tube giving abundant supply of oxygen, which is necessary to insure perfect combustion (and thereby burning the odorous and poisonous matter, which escapes in other lamps) and the inner or "spreader" air tube draught steadying the flame, and preventing its coming in contact with the chimney.

The Test of Light

made by a prominent authority gives the following result:

Ordinary Lamps, 8—11 candle power
Gas - - 20 " "
Improved New Chicago Lamp, 52½ " "

The Following Styles

are manufactured and can be had in either Brass, Nickel or Gold Bronze:

Fount Lamp. Can be attached to any gas or oil fixture, side bracket, etc., holds 1 quart oil, and burns 7—8 hours.

Stand Lamp. For table or desk use. Holds 1 quart oil, and burns 7—8 hours.

Library Fount. Made expressly for Library Extension Hangers. Holds 1 quart oil, and will burn 7—8 hours.

All Night Fount. Same as Fount Lamp—only has a larger oil reservoir, and consequently will burn longer.

The Improved New Chicago Lamp has received the following Awards over all competitors:

Mass. Charitable Mechanics Ass'c'n, Boston, Mass., 1884, Silver Medal
State Fair, - - - - Sacramento, Cal., 1884, Silver Medal
Denver Exposition, - - - Denver, Col., 1884, Silver Medal
Mech. Institute Fair, San Francisco, Cal., 1884, Silver Medal
State Fair, - - - - Portland, Oregon, 1884, Silver Medal

(And several Diplomas at smaller towns.)

Geo. F. Bassett & Co.

Importers, Exporters and Wholesale Dealers in

China, Crockery and Glassware, Plated Wares, Table Cutlery,

KEROSENE GOODS, ETC.,

49 Barclay St. and 52 & 54 Park Place, - - - NEW YORK.

Sole Agents for Chicago Electric Lamps.

Advertising Flyer from George Bassett & Co., ca. 1885. (Not found with original catalog.)
Courtesy David Broughton.

Clark Brothers' Company

1887 – 1891

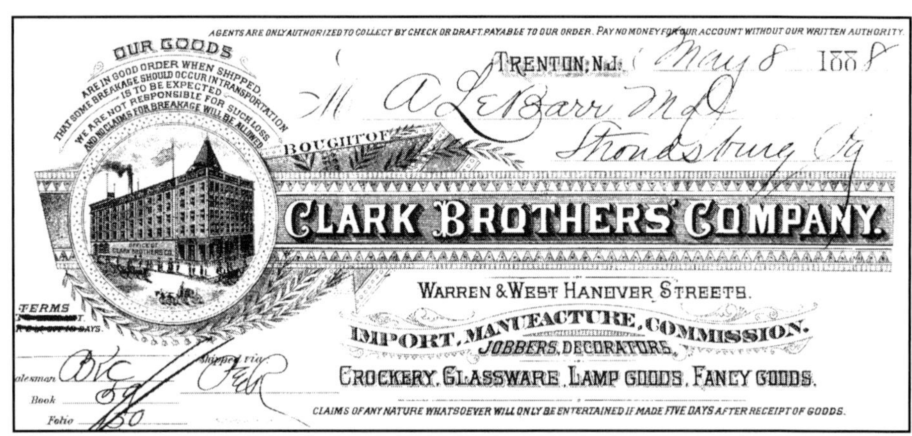

AGENTS ARE ONLY AUTHORIZED TO COLLECT BY CHECK OR DRAFT PAYABLE TO OUR ORDER. PAY NO MONEY FOR OUR ACCOUNT WITHOUT OUR WRITTEN AUTHORITY.

OUR GOODS ARE IN GOOD ORDER WHEN SHIPPED. THAT SOME BREAKAGE SHOULD OCCUR IN TRANSPORTATION IS TO BE EXPECTED. WE ARE NOT RESPONSIBLE FOR SUCH LOSS AND NO CLAIMS FOR BREAKAGE WILL BE ALLOWED.

TRENTON, N.J. May 8 1888

BOUGHT OF

CLARK BROTHERS' COMPANY.

WARREN & WEST HANOVER STREETS.

IMPORT, MANUFACTURE, COMMISSION.

JOBBERS, DECORATORS,

CROCKERY, GLASSWARE, LAMP GOODS, FANCY GOODS.

TERMS

Salesman

Book

Folio

CLAIMS OF ANY NATURE WHATSOEVER WILL ONLY BE ENTERTAINED IF MADE FIVE DAYS AFTER RECEIPT OF GOODS.

Clark Brothers' Lamp, Brass & Copper Company, 1891 – 1892; merged into American Lamp, Brass & Copper Company, 1892 – 1904

Joseph Y., Peter K., and Charles Clark operated Clark Brothers Company, beginning about 1881 in Trenton, New Jersey. They imported and sold crockery dinner, tea, and toilet sets, fancy glass goods, and lamps. Clark Brothers purchased the American Crockery Company in 1887. Due to growing lamp sales, the brothers converted their plant into a factory to manufacture and decorate lamps in January 1891 under the name of Clark Brothers' Lamp, Brass & Copper Company (*CGJ*, Jan. 29, 1891). At that time, the McLewee Brass Mfg. Co. and the Globe Lamp Works also became part of the new company. The Globe Lamp Works, of Trenton, claimed to be "the largest works and most extensive decorators of Opal Glass in America" (*CGJ*, May 1, 1890).

Clark Brothers', however, often advertised simply as "Clark Brothers Company."

By 1890, *China, Glass and Lamps* stated that the company "was gaining celebrity as the principal headquarters of the lamp manufacturing industry of the United States."

In 1891, Clark Brothers' Glass Mfg. Company was incorporated to furnish glass for lamps from a glass factory in Blairsville, Pennsylvania. That factory was abandoned in 1898 with the purchase of the glass factory in Ellwood City, Pennsylvania, formerly operated by Harry Northwood and the Northwood Company. Additional land was purchased in 1901, chimneys were being made in 1901, and a fire destroyed the factory in 1903 (Welkers, 1985).

According to memoirs written by F. B. Clark (1941), lamp hardware was shipped from Trenton to Ellwood for assembly and shipping around the world. The company made numerous hanging lamps fitted with glass founts and flat-wick burners. Glass lamp founts were often marked "Clark Bros" by embossing the name in the glass mold.

Clark Brothers advertised itself as the "Largest Lamp Works in America," which seems questionable in view of our knowledge of so many other well-known manufacturers of oil lamps. The statement originated due to the addition of Swann and Whitehead, which gave total employment to the largest number of workers in "any one (lamp) factory."

Clark Brothers'

Clark Brothers' apparently continued (or established) a separate business identity as Clark Brothers' Company after the merger and formation of American Lamp & Brass. It is unclear whether Clark Brothers' Glass Mfg. Company was merged into American Lamp & Brass company in 1892.

The Clarks acquired Elite Lamp & Novelty Company of Trenton in the early 1920s and formed the New Jersey Lamp & Manufacturing Company. This company produced electric lamps and lighting for about two years before a fire put it out of business.

Trade Names

Center-draft lamps — The Trenton Lamp, U.S. Trenton Lamp, Trenton Improved, Trenton Jr., Trenton College Lamp.

"U-Trenton-S" was trademarked by Clark Brothers Lamp, Brass & Copper Company on Aug. 16, 1892; the company stated that the words were first used June 24, 1891.

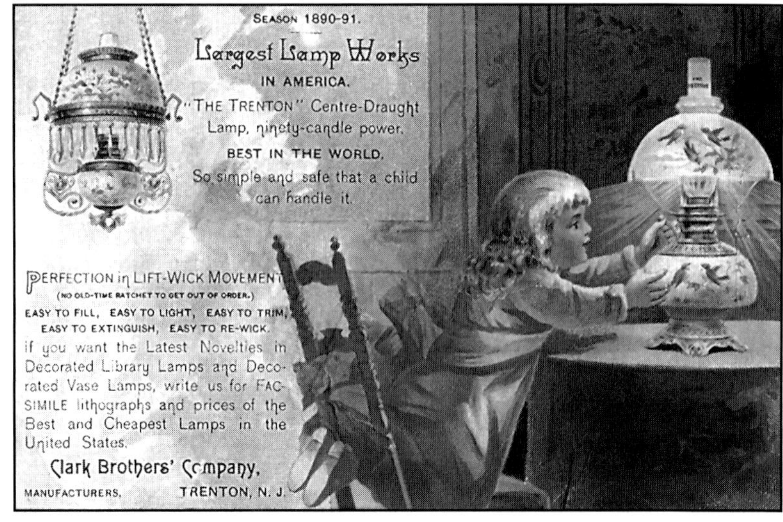

Trade card advertisement, 1890.

Selected Patents, Center-draft Lamps

William S. McLewee unassigned

1892 471,822
1892 471,823

1890 letterhead.
Courtesy Wheaton Village Museum of Glass.

A Big Thing for Trenton
Clark Bros.' to Operate a Great Lamp Works Here
Trenton True American, January 20, 1891

The certificate of incorporation of the Clark Brothers' Lamp, Brass and Copper Company was filed yesterday in the office of the County Clerk. This corporation will acquire the extensive manufacturing machinery, stock and entire property of the Globe Lamp Works of Trenton, the lamp stock, tools, machinery plant and all patent rights of the McLewee Brass and Copper Company of New York City, and the valuable wholesale lamp business, trade marks, machinery, moulds and appliances of the Clark Brother's Company of Trenton. The new company has for its object the manufacture of lamps of all descriptions, lamp burners, lamp fixtures, chandeliers, bronzes, brass castings, and the manufacture and decorating of opal glass shades, lamp vases, globes, etc. The works, which will be the most extensive of their kind in the United States, will be located in East Trenton, on the property formerly owned by the Globe Lamp Works.

In addition to seven spacious brick buildings, containing one hundred and ninety thousand square feet of floor space now on the land, the company will erect a four-story brick structure fifty feet wide by one hundred and sixty feet in length, besides capacious storage sheds four hundred and fifty feet in length. A tramway will also be built to connect the various buildings containing the several departments of manufacture with the storage houses and railroads. The railroad shipping facilities from the company's factories will be of extraordinary value and convenience. Besides the Delaware and Raritan Canal for water transportation east and south, on the west side of the works there is the P & R and B & O Railroad; on the east side the Pennsylvania Company, connecting each and every trunk line in the United States and Canada directly with the works.

Amongst the advantages accruing from the merging of these various plants in one will be that of making all the parts of a lamp at one place and under one roof. Heretofore the various parts constituting a complete decorated lamp have been made in different sections of the Eastern States, no one firm making them all and the expenses incidental to collecting these parts to one point in order to market the complete article has materially increased the cost of this class of goods to the public. It will thus be seen that the economy in the production of lamps by these means will be to reduce the price to the interested trade.

The incorporators and persons interested are the six brothers, Charles Clark, P. K. Clark, J. Y. Clark, F. B. Clark, J. S Clark, W. S. Clark and W. S. McLewee. The place of business and main office will be at the works in Trenton, with branch offices in New York City, Boston, Philadelphia, Chicago and St. Louis. The capital stock of the company is one quarter million dollars, and about four hundred hands will be employed when the company get down to business.

Crockery and Glass Journal, January 29, 1891

Clark Bros.' Lamp,
"THE TRENTON"
CENTRE DRAUGHT PARLOR LAMP.
TRENTON JUNIOR VASE LAMP
No. 1373
TRENTON CENTRE DRAUGHT
PIANO LAMP
"TRENTON JUNIOR VASE LAMP"
"THE TRENTON IMPROVED"
CENTRE DRAUGHT PARLOR LAMP.

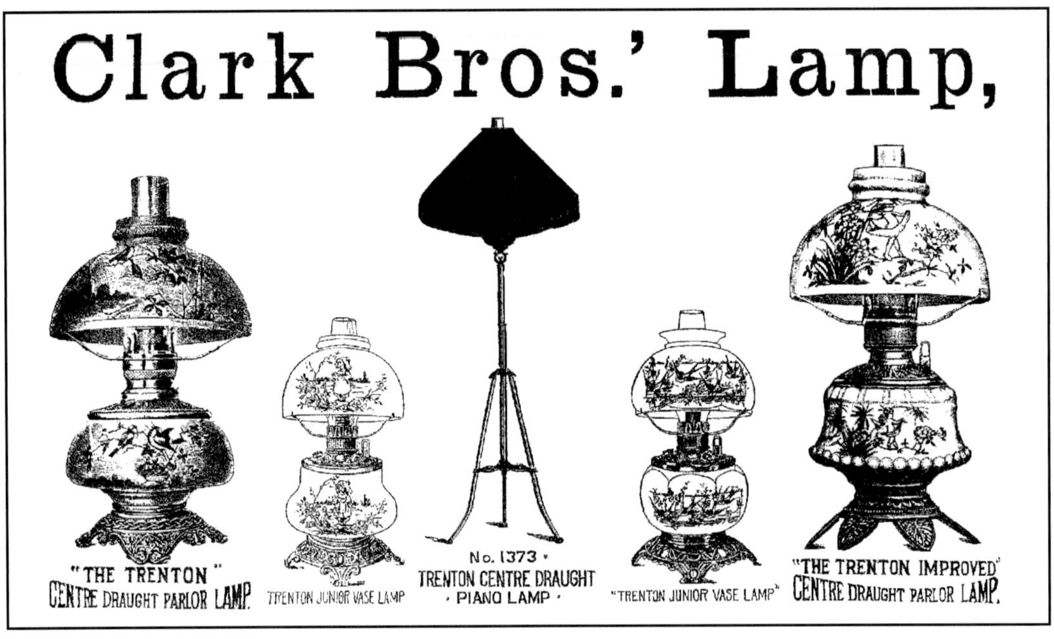

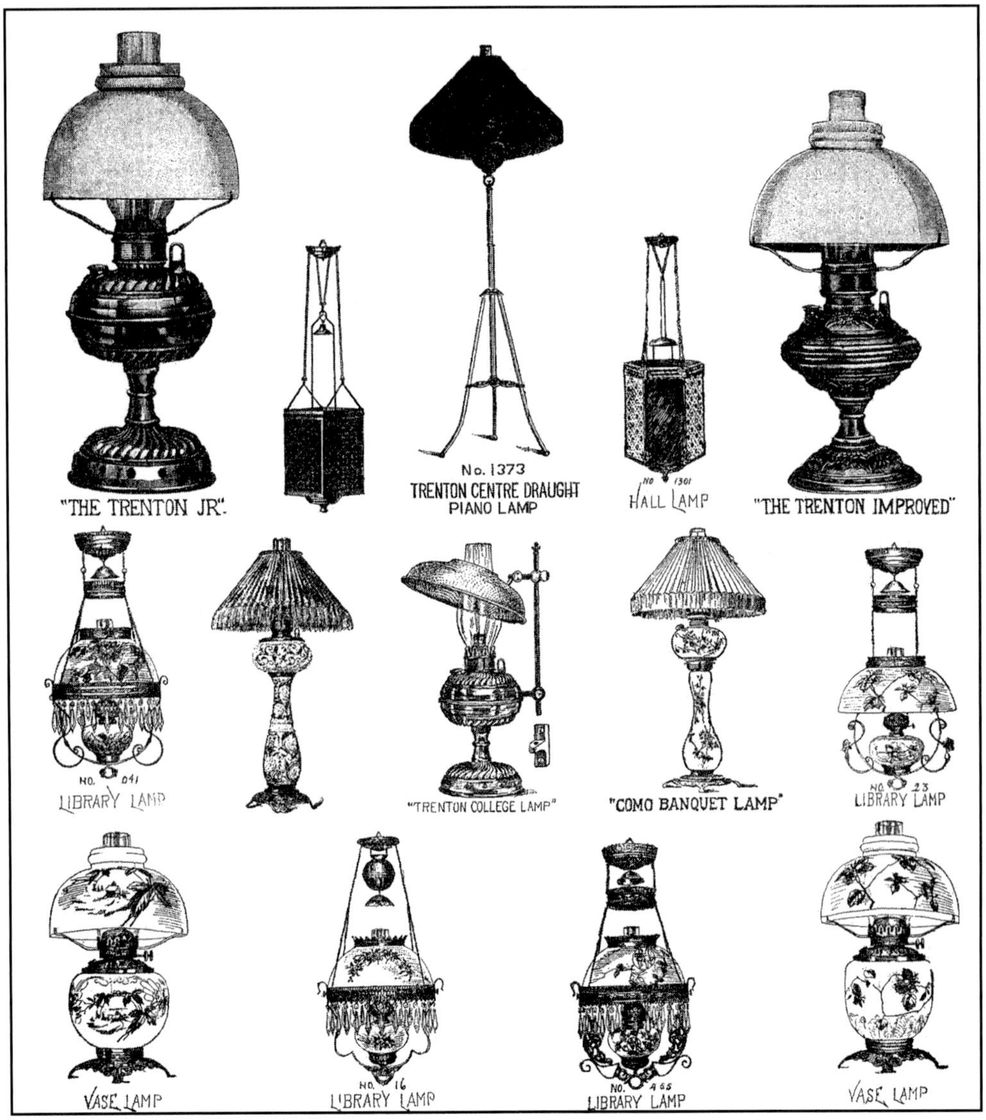
"THE TRENTON JR".
No. 1373
TRENTON CENTRE DRAUGHT
PIANO LAMP
NO. 1301
HALL LAMP
"THE TRENTON IMPROVED"
NO. 041
LIBRARY LAMP
"TRENTON COLLEGE LAMP"
"COMO BANQUET LAMP"
NO. 23
LIBRARY LAMP
VASE LAMP
NO. 16
LIBRARY LAMP
NO. 465
LIBRARY LAMP
VASE LAMP

Portions from two full advertising pages in *China, Glass and Lamps*, August 20, 1891.

The Trenton

Advertisement, December 1890.

Trenton burner and wick-raiser assembly. The burner basket slides over the outer wick tube, which locks in place.

The Trenton No. 2 oil pot and flame spreader. Flame spreader dated "Pat. Aug. 14 '88" (Atwood patent 387,756). Clark Brothers purchased this hardware from Plume and Atwood. Diameter of the tank is 5", height to rim is 3⅛". Note the fatigue stress cracks in the tank. The brass is thin and fragile. $50.00.

The Trenton JR.

The Trenton JR. flame spreader marked "The Trenton Jr., Pat. Ap'd For." The Trenton No. 1 lamp is unusual in construction. The female burner threads are inside the burner basket, the reverse of how most burners attach to the founts. Courtesy Alan Freeman.

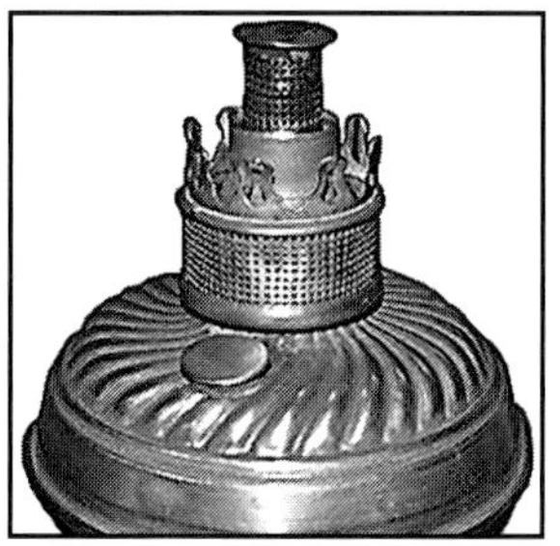

Trenton JR with different burner than below. Same flame spreader as above. Courtesy Ralph Fierro.

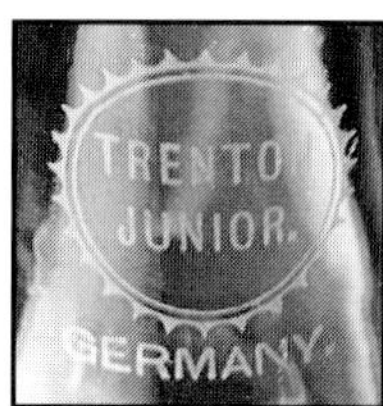

Chimney logo.

The Trenton JR. No. 1 stand lamp. Height 7". This lamp appears to be same as McLewee patent 471,822. $200.00. Courtesy Alan Freeman.

ALEXANDER THE GREAT

Is reported to have said: "If I were not Alexander, I would be Diogenes." But the man who makes the light to shine in dark places and who has lengthened the days of his fellow man by the invention of the

"TRENTON" LAMP

is greater than a heathen King or a Cynic Philosopher.

Advertisement *China, Glass and Lamps*, Oct. 28. 1891.

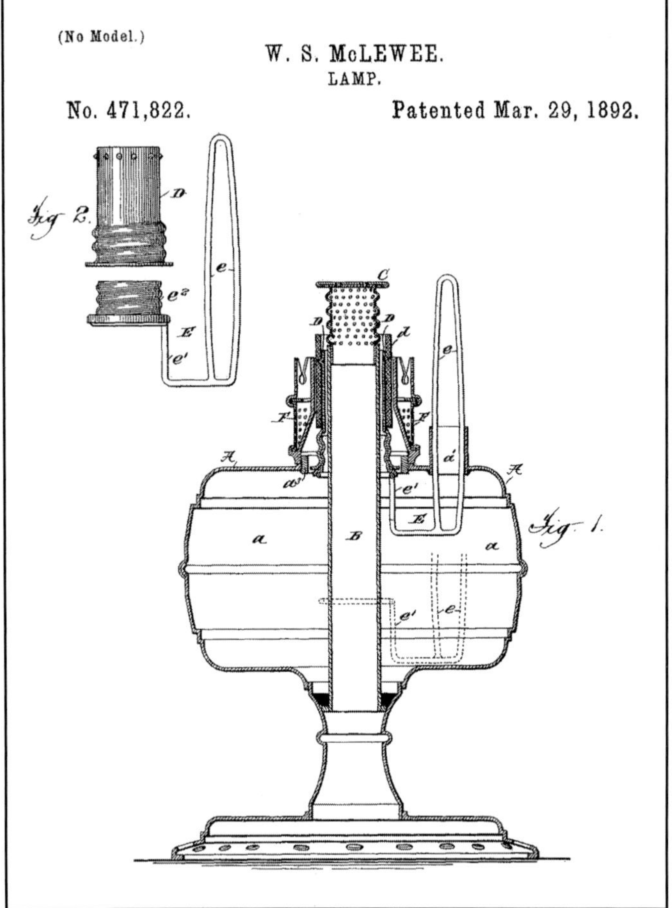

The Trenton Improved

The Trenton Improved flame spreader. The brass is very thin and easily bent. The ridges appear similar to the drawing in McLewee's patent 471,822.

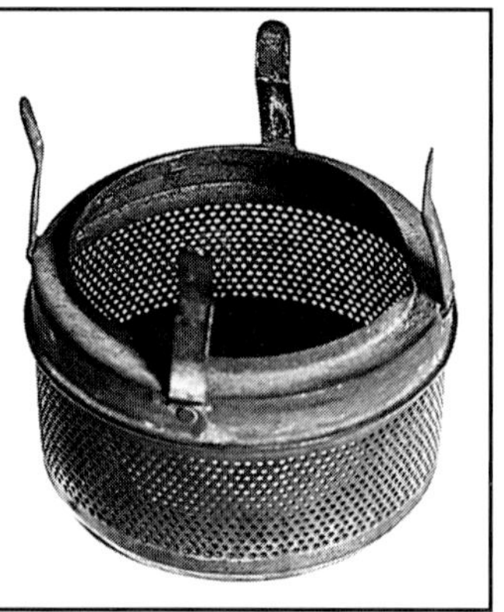

The Trenton Improved burner basket slips off the outer wick tube same as The Trenton.

The Trenton Improved No. 2 oil pot appears to conform to McLewee's unassigned patent 471,822. Diameter of the tank is 5", height to rim is 3⅛". $75.00.

U.S. Trenton

The U.S. Trenton was made in at least two sizes. There seems to be some retooling common with The Trenton lamp and the American Lamp.

U.S. Trenton flame spreader No. 1 junior size. These flame spreaders are made with rings to help position them correctly in the wick tube.

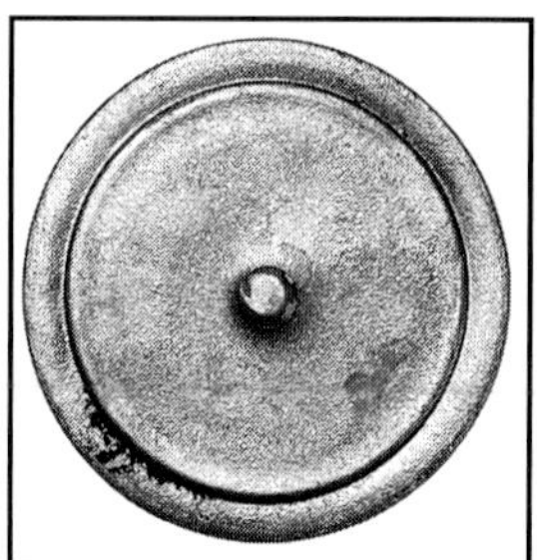

U.S. Trenton flame spreader No. 2 size. An umarked cap or top has been added to the flame spreader on right. Courtesy Kent Stratton.

Junior oil pot fitted with U.S. Trenton flame spreader. This oil pot may also have been used by American Lamp, Brass & Copper Co. Diameter of the tank is 4¼", height to rim is 3¼". The inner wick tube does not have a stop to position the flame spreader (see above). $50.00.

Advertisement, *Pottery and Glass Reporter*, July 21, 1892.

Cleveland Non-Explosive Lamp Co.

1868 – 1884

The company name clearly states the perceived advantage of its interesting lamps — Cleveland Non-Explosive Lamps. Mark W. House patented "House's Argand Safety Lamp," a center-draft fount found in large and small sizes. The company, however, is better known today for its oil fount with flat-wick burner and closed collar for air passage to provide cooling of the fuel reservoir by air intake through the bottom of the oil fount.

John M. Perkins and Mark W. House, of Cleveland, Ohio, set out to solve a major problem of their day — fires and explosions caused by oil lamps and the fuel. They began work to improve burners and lamps soon after oil was discovered in Titusville. Their patent claim of 1866 (patent 60,416) said "our invention consists in making a non-explosive lamp." Other related patents include John M. Perkins (103,334 in 1870) and M. W. House (76,764 in 1868 and 121,521 in 1871).

The Cleveland Non-Explosive Lamp Co. was incorporated in 1868 and listed in the *1869 Cleveland City Directory* as being at 87 Water Street. Montgomery & Company claimed to be "Sole General Agents for the United States" for Perkins and House's patent lamps in a small 16-page catalog, ca. 1870. Later catalogs identified Cleveland Non-Explosive Lamp Company and gave its address in Cleveland.

Officers in 1872 and 1873 were Thomas Walton, president, and M. R. Keith, secretary. Charles Gordon became general manager by 1875, and he held patents for burners and railroad "car lamps," (patents 219,636, 1879; 263,166, 1882; 267,075, 1882; and 275,641, 1883).

More history of the Cleveland Non-Explosive Lamp Company and numerous illustrations of lamps have been published by Nolan and Jones (2000).

A wide variety of lamps were made — No. 1 & 2 stand lamps, hand lamps, chandeliers, street lamps, station and barn lamps, factory lamps, and several sizes of student lamps (library lamps). Early Non-Explosive lamps were offered with a choice of Argand burner or flat-wick Hinge burner. The chandelier founts with House's Argand Burner were highly touted to adapt any gas or kerosene fixture for improved and safe light. The factory had capacity to produce 1500 lamps per day by 1871.

A Patent Safety Filling Can was promoted — "Our Lamp and Can cannot be exploded, either of them, even with boiling benzine, gasoline, naphtha, or the explosive gases of any illuminating oil..."

Company success was aided by W. J. Gordon, a wealthy businessman in Cleveland who provided financial support. However, historical writings about Cleveland and its citizens overlooked the lamp business and Gordon's accomplishments in lighting of the time.

William J. Gordon was recorded in Cleveland city directories as follows: "Proprietor Non-Explosive Lamp Works in 1871 – 1872." He held two unassigned patents with M. W. House (patents 129,728 and 132,655, both dated 1872), and his obituary stated that he was "largely interested in the Cleveland Non-Explosive Lamp Company, which became one of the leading industries in the state."

Burner wick knobs are marked or dated with one or a variety of dates: Dec. 11, 1866; June 19, 1867; Oct. 14, 1862; July 21, 1863; Dec. 10, 1867; and April 7, 1868. The oil fill caps may also be marked with patent dates.

Advertisement, *China and Glass Journal*, 1876. The company exhibited at the Centennial Exposition in 1876.

Edward Miller Company sold Cleveland Non-Explosive lamps in its catalogs, and it seems likely that Miller manufactured burners for the Cleveland company in exchange for license to sell the lamps, which Miller did well into the twentieth century.

A fire destroyed the Cleveland factory in 1878. A new factory was built at 51 Water Street.

The company failed in 1884 followed by years of litigation by creditors (*CGJ*, June 4, 1885, and Oct. 26, 1892). Nolan and Jones (2000) reported that the company books were officially closed in 1914.

An advertisement in 1886 stated that the Lamp and Brass Works of W. J. Gordon was "Successor to the Cleveland Non-Explosion Lamp Company." Gordon's new company developed its own brands of center-draft lamps.

W. J. Gordon continued to sell lamps under his name until he sold the business to Lane Mfg. Co. about 1888. Lane continued to promote non-explosive lamps.

Trade Names

Lamps — Perkins & House Safety Lamp, Perkins & House Non-Explosive Lamp, House's Patent Library Lamp.

Burner — Argand burner, Cleveland Hinge Burner.

Selected Patents, Center-draft Lamps

Year	Patent No.
John M. Perkins and Mark W. House	
1865	46,819
1866	60,416
Mark W. House[1]	
1868	76,764
1870	103,334
1871	121,521
Wm. J. Gordon and Mark W. House unassigned	
1872	129,728
1872	132,655

[1]Also patent on lantern.

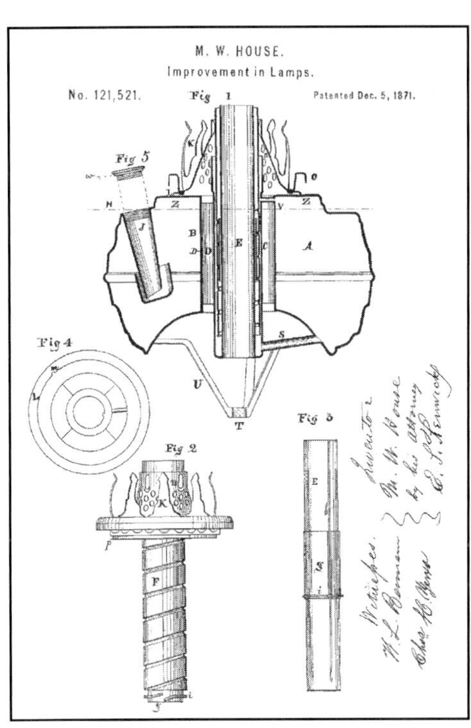

Oil fill cap.

Perkins & House Safety Lamp, 14¼" to top burner. The top of the center-draft fount is well marked (see above). The wick raiser adjusts similar to student lamps (see left). There is no flame spreader. $900.00. Courtesy Heinz and Ursula Baumann.

Courtesy Ohio Historical Society.

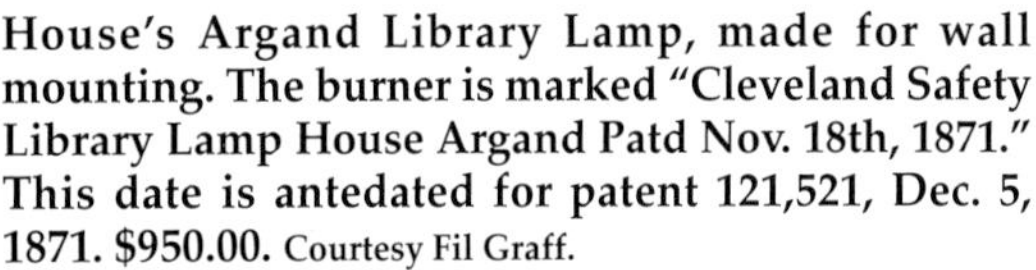

House's Argand Library Lamp, made for wall mounting. The burner is marked "Cleveland Safety Library Lamp House Argand Patd Nov. 18th, 1871." This date is antedated for patent 121,521, Dec. 5, 1871. $950.00. Courtesy Fil Graff.

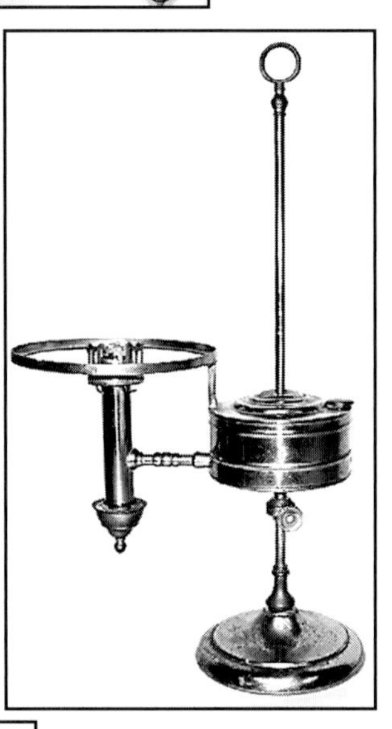

Cleveland student lamp, 7" shade. Height 21". $900.00. Courtesy Rod L' Italien.

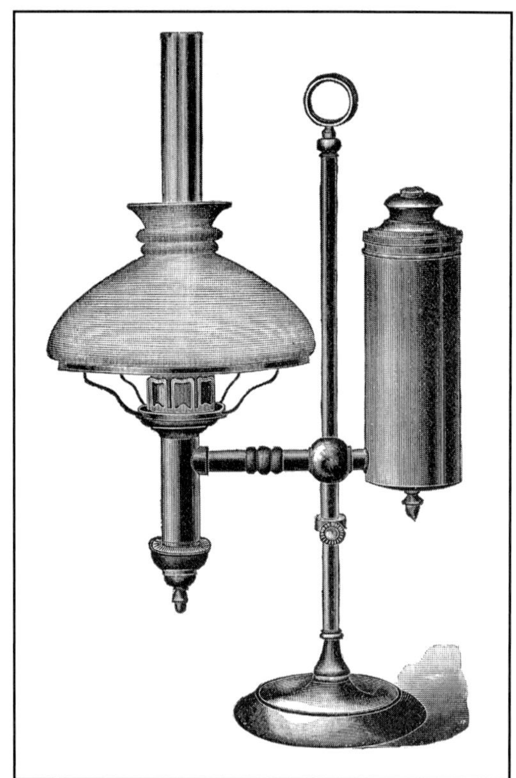

Cleveland student lamp No. 32. "Best Student Lamp in the Market." Marshall Field, 1894. Made by Lane Mfg. Co.

PRICES OF PERKINS & HOUSE'S PATENT LAMPS.

No. 5, Hand Lamp, Hinge Burner,........................$ 1.75
" 6, Argand Hand Lamp........................2.00
" 30, Tripod Stand, Hinge Burner........................2.50
" 10, Square Stand, Hinge Burner........................3.00
" 10, Square Stand Argand Lamp........................3.25
" 40, Tripod Stand, Hinge Burner........................3.00
" 40, Tripod Stand, Argand Burner........................3.25
" 20, Round Stand, Hinge Burner........................3.00
" 20, Round Stand, Argand Lamp........................3.25
" 15, Octagon, Italian Bronze, Hinge Burner........................3.25
" 15, Octagon, Italian Bronze, Argand Lamp........................3.50
" 16, Cone. Italian Bronze, Hinge Burner........................3.25
" 16, Cone, Italian Bronze, Argand Lamp........................3.50
" 41, Flower Girl, Hinge Burner........................3.50
" 41, Flower Girl, Argand Lamp........................3.75
" 35, Tripod, Hinge Burner, No. 2 size........................4.25
" 35, Tripod, Argand Lamp, No. 2 size........................4.50
" 18, Round, Hinge Burner, No. 2 size........................4.50
" 18, Round, Argand Lamp, No. 2 size........................4.75
" 44, Hexagon, Parlor Lamp, No. 2 size........................6.00
" 44, Hexagon, Parlor Argand, No. 2 size........................6.25
" 12, Egyptian Parlor Lamp, No. 2 size........................6.50
" 12, Egyptian Parlor Argand. No. 2 size........................6.75
" 42, Kneeling Woman, Parlor, No. 2 size........................6.50
" 42, Kneeling Woman, Argand, No. 2 size........................6.75
" 45, Hexagon Base with Extension Rod, by which the lamp can be elevated; price of the Base only 3.00

Lamps for Chandeliers, Brackets, or Gas Fixtures.

No. 1 size, Hinge Burner, Brass Basket........................$ 2.60
No. 1 size, Argand Burner, Brass Basket 2 85
No. 2 size, Hinge burner, Brass Basket........................3.60
No. 2 size, Argand Burner, Brass Basket........................3.85

These Lamps are adapted for screwing upon any Chandeer or Gas Fixture which may already be in position.

Chandeliers of every style and finish from 2 lights to 18 lights each.

Brackets of all the best varieties and Reflectors.

Hall Lights and Pendants in every style.

Special attention given to supplying Hotels, Churches, Stores, Manufactories and Schools.

Our Porcelain Shades, plain and decorated, are very beautiful, and give a soft, mellow light.

Our Patent Shade Holder, invented specially for this Lamp, has no equal for convenience and durability.

Our Lanterns are the only *perfectly safe* Kerosene Lantern in existence.

Our Chandelier Lamps are supplied with Hinged Globe Holders, and Hinged Porcelain Shade Holders, by which the Lamps may be lighted without removing Shade or Chimney.

Lamps for Street Railroads, Steamboats, R. R. Passenger Coaches, and Car Brackets made to order.

Our Illustrated Catalogues give full illustrations of all the above styles—price 40 cents, Address

MONTGOMERY & CO.,
GENERAL AGENTS, FOR THE U. S.,
52 Public Square, Cleveland Ohio.
Branch Office, 42 Barclay St., New York.

Page from trade catalog, ca. 1870, with 18 pages plus covers filled with testimonials and "critical tests by the most eminent scientific men." Note that several lamps were offered with choice of "Argand Burner" or "Hinge Burner."

Cleveland Non-Explosive student lamp. Height 23½". Gallery marked "Cleveland Study Lamp, Pat'd. Nov. 18, 1871, Mar. 10, 1863, Re Issued Dec. 30, 1873." The company made a variety of single and double student lamps. $550.00.

Perkins & House Non-Explosive Hinge Burner Lamps

Hand lamp burner knob is marked "Pat. Dec. 10, 67, Apr. 7, 68." The handle is embossed. Height 6". Some founts revolve on the foot. $50.00.

Stand lamp burner is marked "Patented Dec. 11th 1866, June 19th 1867." The top of fount is marked "The Perkins & House Non-Explosive Lamp Patented Dec. 11th 1866." Height of lamp is 9¾". The company made a wide variety of these lamps varying in height, style of foot, and decorative figural bases, etc. $50.00.

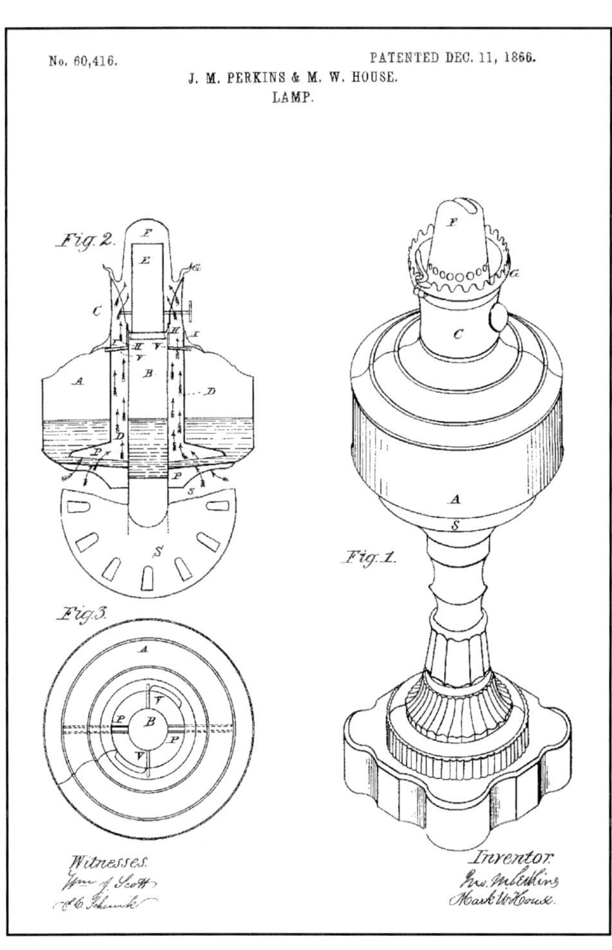

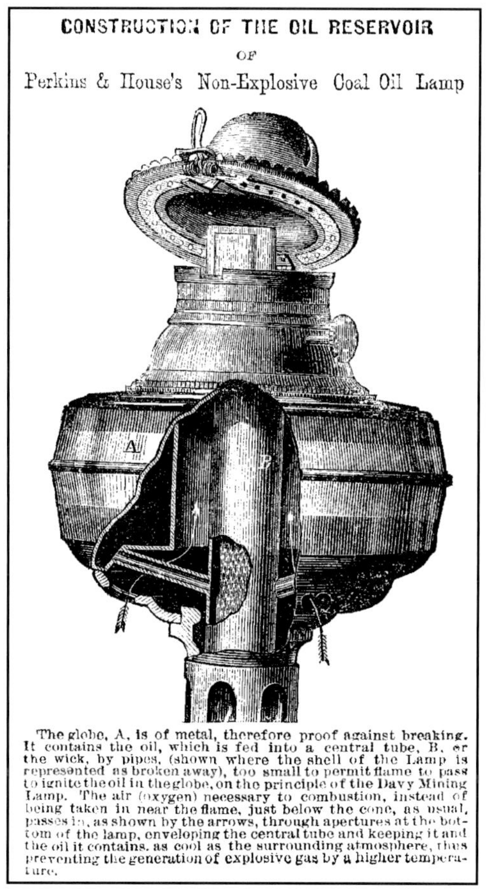

CONSTRUCTION OF THE OIL RESERVOIR

OF

Perkins & House's Non-Explosive Coal Oil Lamp

The globe, A, is of metal, therefore proof against breaking. It contains the oil, which is fed into a central tube, B, or the wick, by pipes, (shown where the shell of the Lamp is represented as broken away), too small to permit flame to pass to ignite the oil in the globe, on the principle of the Davy Mining Lamp. The air (oxygen) necessary to combustion, instead of being taken in near the flame, just below the cone, as usual, passes in, as shown by the arrows, through apertures at the bottom of the lamp, enveloping the central tube and keeping it and the oil it contains, as cool as the surrounding atmosphere, thus preventing the generation of explosive gas by a higher temperature.

Craighead & Kintz Company

1883 – 1898

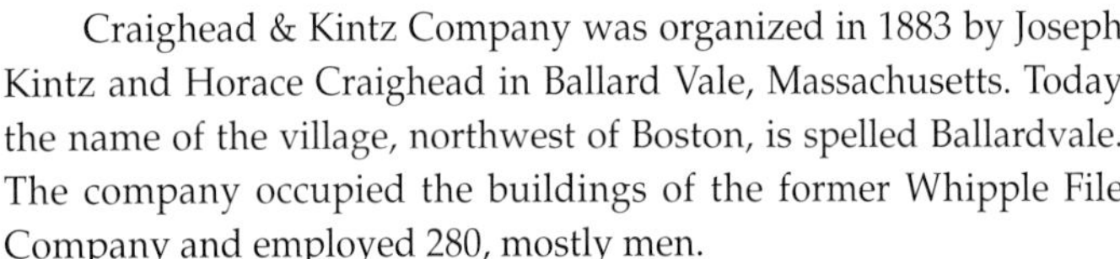

Craighead & Kintz Company was organized in 1883 by Joseph Kintz and Horace Craighead in Ballard Vale, Massachusetts. Today the name of the village, northwest of Boston, is spelled Ballardvale. The company occupied the buildings of the former Whipple File Company and employed 280, mostly men.

Craighead & Kintz bought the "assets and liabilities" of Craighead & Elwell Mfg. Co., of Bridgeport, Connecticut, according to announcements in *Crockery and Glass Journal*, March 1, 1883.

Horace Craighead was formerly associated with the Craighead & Elwell Mfg. Co., which reorganized as the Elwell & Kean Mfg. Co. Elwell & Kean were manufacturers of "library lamps, brackets, kerosene fixtures, decorated and bronze lamps" in Bridgeport, Connecticut. The company may have continued as a supplier for Craighead and Kintz.

Joseph Kintz came to America from Germany. He worked with P. J. Clark in Meriden, where Kintz held many patents from 1871 to 1880 (several of his early patents were for improvements in lanterns). Kintz was well known in the trade as an expert in metal working and electroplating. As a result, he consulted with several companies.

Kintz apparently brought a number of German workmen from Meriden to Ballard Vale (see MMI). Kintz left Craighead & Kintz in 1890 to become superintendent of the Pittsburgh Brass Company. He retired to Winsted, Connecticut, in 1899 and died there in 1901.

Craighead & Kintz made artistic brass and bronze articles and lamps. In 1884 the company sold standard composite lamps, library and hall lamps, and decorative items. All C & K lamps at that time were fitted with flat-wick burners.

A large 1892 catalog included piano and banquet lamps, decorated and elegant metal vase and figural lamps, library lamps, hall lamps, "lampadariums," candlesticks, ink stands, card receivers, figures, mirrors, onyx tables, cuspidors, photograph frames, and other specialties such as bronze plaques, bells, thermometers and decorative objects. The company manufactured fancy goods plated in gold, oxidized silver, and brass. The lamps were now fitted with center-draft Daylight burners.

Horace Craighead and Abner Wilcox were sales agents at 33 Barclay St., New York. The lamps were also advertised by the Daylight Lamp Co., 38 Park Place, New York. The elegant silk shades on many "C & K" lamps were made by Walter S. Berg.

The Daylight Burner Company sold a No. 2 flat-wick burner marked "Daylight" on the cone. I do not know if these companies are the same.

Craighead advised shareholders and creditors of court application for receivership on May 21, 1894, due to financial conditions.

A fire, reported as "half a million dollar blaze," put the company out of business on May 13, 1898.

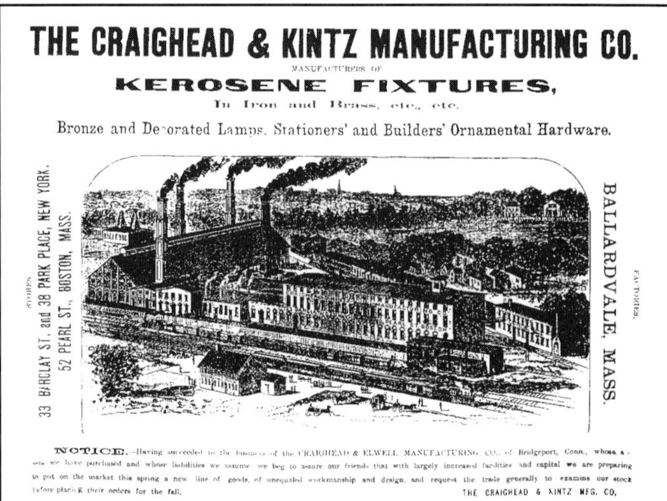

Advertisement in *Crockery and Glass Journal*, March 1, 1883, was a notice of change in business from Craighead & Elwell Mfg. Co., Bridgeport, Connecticut, to Craighead & Kintz Mfg. Co. The company was known as Craighead & Kintz Company in 1884. H. H. Elwell and Myles Kean (of Craighead & Elwell) organized the Elwell & Kean Mfg. Co. with Louis F. Dudley and moved back into the former Bridgeport factory.

Cover of undated catalog.
Courtesy Andover Historical Society.

Trade Names

The trademark "Daylight" was registered by K. E. Jacobsen and E. H. Fessenden on Sept. 3, 1889. They stated that the mark was used since February 1888.

Selected Patents, Center-draft Lamps

Joseph Kintz[1] one-half assigned to Craighead & Kintz

1888 389,577
1889 .... 400,854 unassigned

Horace Craighead assigned to Craighead & Kintz Co.

1892 471,507

Thomas Langston[2]

1887[3] .... 360,704 unassigned
1889[3] .... 404,848 assigned[4]
1898 .... 615,666 assigned Edw. Miller Co.

[1]Kintz held many other patents for improvements in lamp construction. He also held lantern patents. Also see Meriden Malleable Iron.

[2]Also many patents for lanterns.

[3]These patent dates marked on the gallery of most (not all) Daylight lamp burners. The date Sept. 3, 1889 is also on some galleries which is when the trademark was registered.

[4]Assigned to Edw. H. Fessenden and Kate E. Jacobsen, Brooklyn, NY.

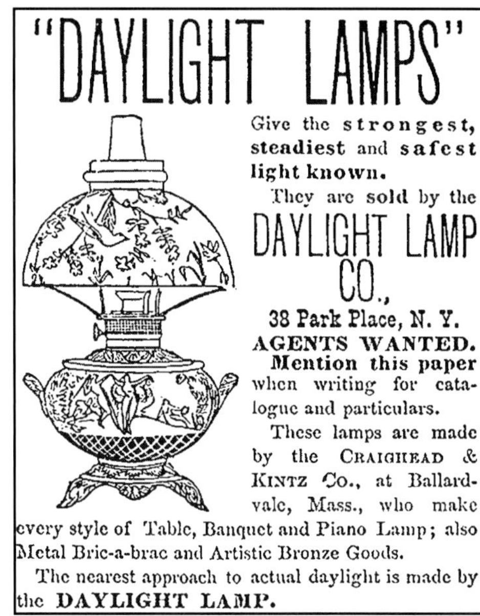

Advertisement, *National Farmer Magazine*, 1889.

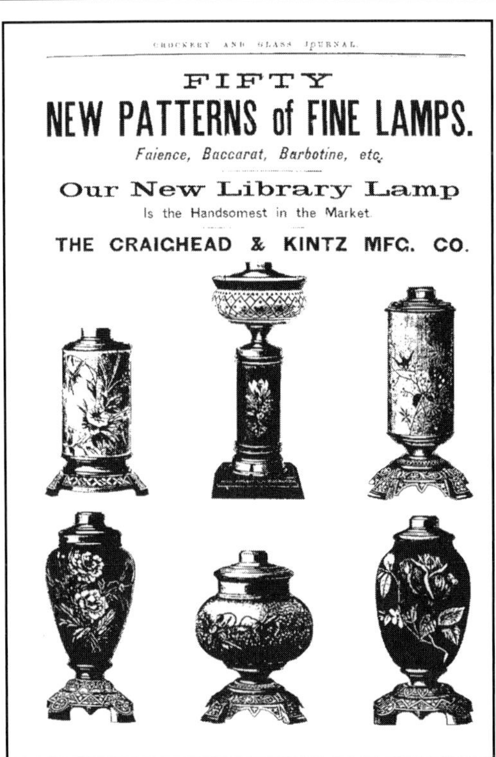

Advertisement, *Crockery and Glass Journal*, July 26, 1883. I believe Craighead & Kintz primarily made flat-wick burners, lamps, and accessories during the early 1880s.

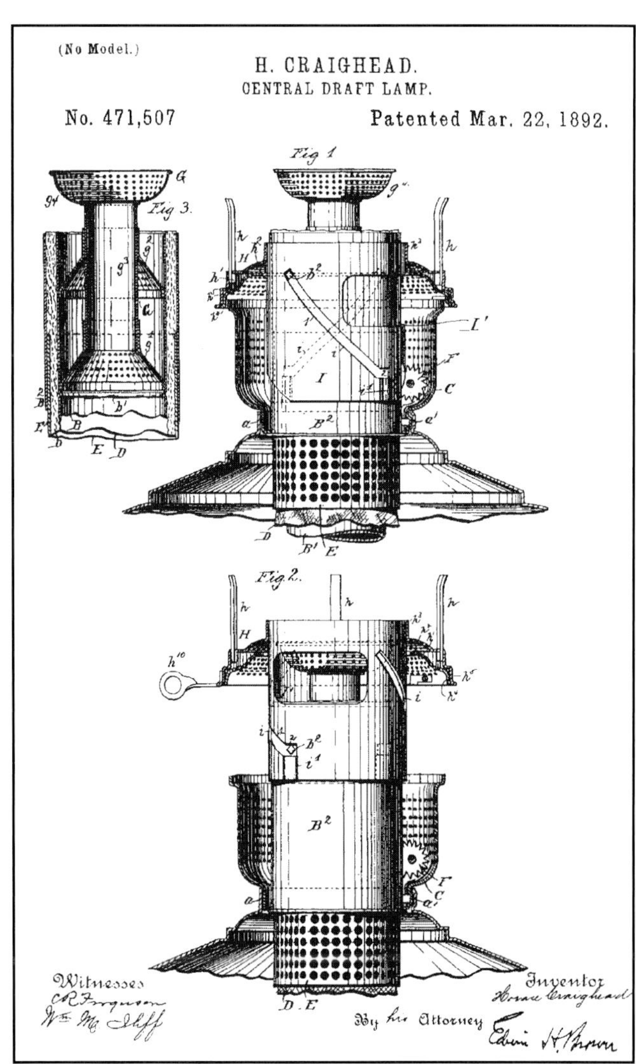

Daylight Burners

Galleries of most Daylight center-draft burners are marked with one, two, or three dates. The date of Sept. 3, 1889, found on some burners, is not a patent date but a notice of trademark number 16,975 for the words "DAY LIGHT" assigned to Jacobsen and Fessenden. I know not the relationship of these persons with Craighead and Kintz.

I believe burners sold circa 1887 were simply marked "Patented" or similar. There are at least three different Daylight burners plus burners without wick knobs.

Left to right: Daylight burner with "Patent Applied For" stamped on lift gallery. Daylight burner on right, non–lift gallery, is marked with one date: "Patent April 5, 1887." Daylight burners with lift galleries, for easy lighting (see right), are marked with three dates: "Patent April 5, 1887, Patent June 11, 1889, Patent Sept. 3, 1889." The last date is not a patent date but is the date of trademark registration.

The

Daylight

Not a flicker,
no smell,
no trouble.
Nothing but solid
comfort reading,
sewing or chatting
in its light.

Lamp.

Manufactured by Craighead & Kintz Co., 33 Barclay St., N. Y. Your Lamp Dealer will have it. Send to the Daylight Lamp Co., 38 Park Place, New York, for further information.

Advertisement, *Century Magazine*, 1891.

Craighead & Kintz burner with lift gallery. Gallery marked "Patented Mar. 22, 1892."

Daylight oil pot and burner with lift gallery and early flame spreader, "Always Rub Wick Even, Never Cut." Pot is 4¾" diameter and 3" to the rim. The gallery turns as it lifts. $100.00.

Craighead & Kintz oil pot and burner with lift gallery. Gallery marked "Patented Mar. 22, 1892." Wick adjustment is a push-pull rod. Pot is 5" diameter and 2" to the rim. The globe ring has been added. $100.00.

Daylight flame spreaders (Craighead patent 471,507). Left to right: Flame spreaders marked "Always Rub Wick Even, Never Cut" and "C K Ballardvale" were used before February 1888. The trademark "Daylight" was registered Sept. 3, 1889.

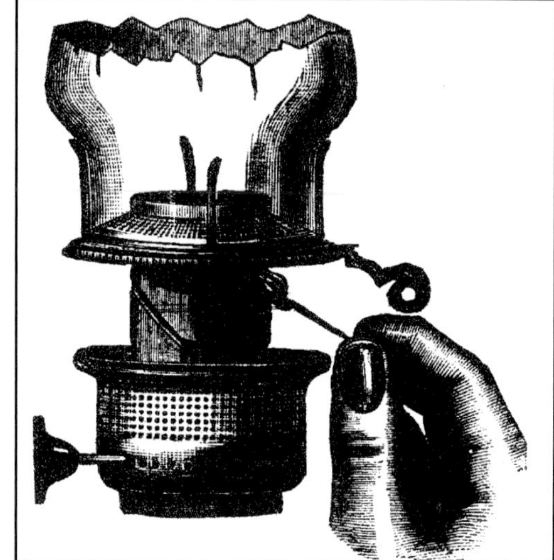

The Daylight's Easy Lighting Device

Its mechanism is as simple as A, B, C. You can understand it pretty well from the cut; the point is, as we have stated before to you, that you needn't take off or even touch shade or chimney in lighting the Daylight Lamp. Now, this is the only lamp so constructed...Banquet lamps seem to be the most popular at present...a cleaner lamp doesn't burn.

CGL, October 1891.

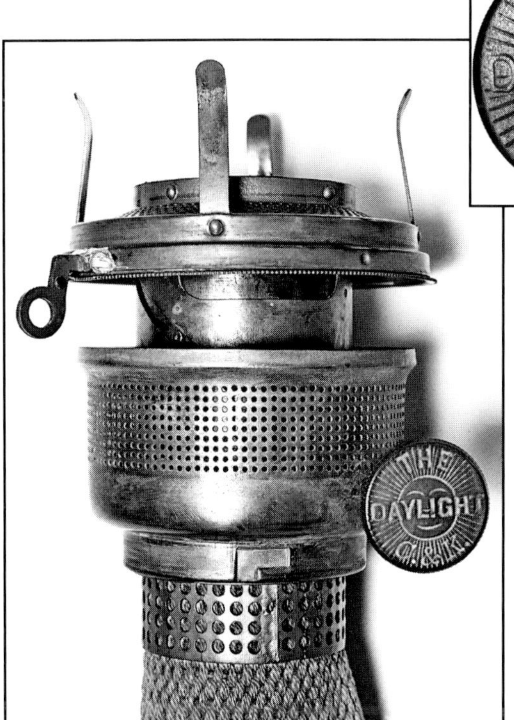

Daylight burner with lift gallery. The gallery is not dated. The first "Daylight" burners, made before Feb. 1888, may have unmarked wick knobs.

Wick knob.

"Daylight" flame spreaders. Left to right: Flame spreaders marked "Rub Wick, This End Up, Never Cut" and, right, slightly longer and silver plated, "Always Rub Wick Even, Never Cut."

Advertisement, *Pottery and Glass Reporter*, Oct. 10, 1889.

Advertisement, *Crockery and Glass Journal*, 1892.

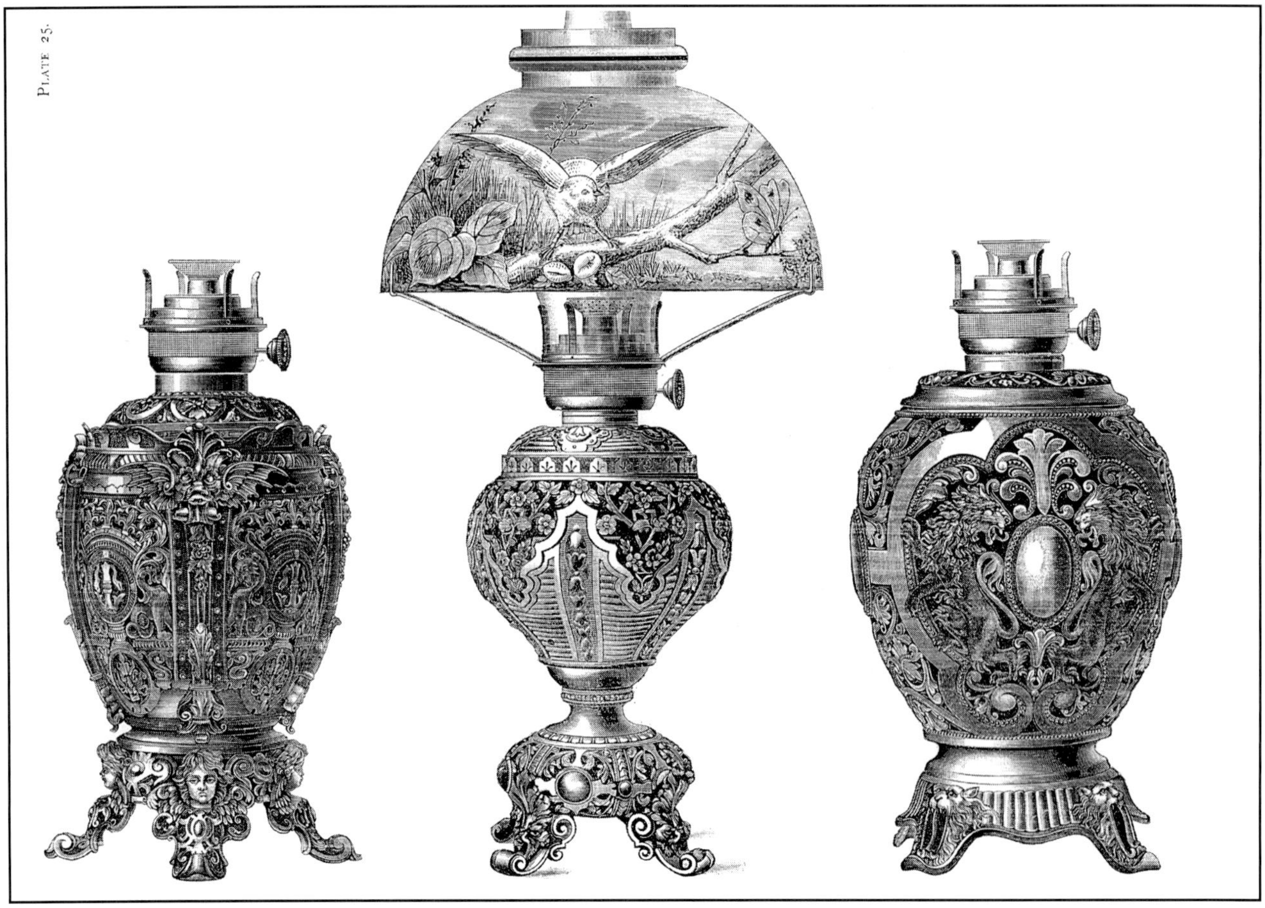

PLATE 25.

Daylight lamps, possibly silver plate.
Courtesy Allen Weathers and the Meriden Historical Society.

The

Daylight

There are lamps and lamps, and the question of amount of light is no longer the question; any of them give light enough. But the lamp that's easiest to light, easiest to take care of and keeps its oil fount coolest, that's the lamp of to-day and that's the Daylight.

Send for our A B C book on Lamps.

Craighead & Kintz Co., 33 Barclay St., N. Y.

Advertisement, *Century Magazine*, 1891.

THE

DAYLIGHT

Take off shade, take off chimney, apply the match, put on chimney, burn your fingers, put on shade, scorch it. No, no; nothing of the kind. Light your DAYLIGHT without removing shade or chimney, and do it as quick as a wink.

Send for our A B C book on lamps.
Craighead & Kintz Co., 33 Barclay St., N. Y.

Advertisement, *China, Glass and Lamps*, Oct. 28, 1891.

Love's Victory banquet lamp from advertisement by Craighead & Wilcox, *Crockery and Glass Journal*, Oct. 6, 1892.

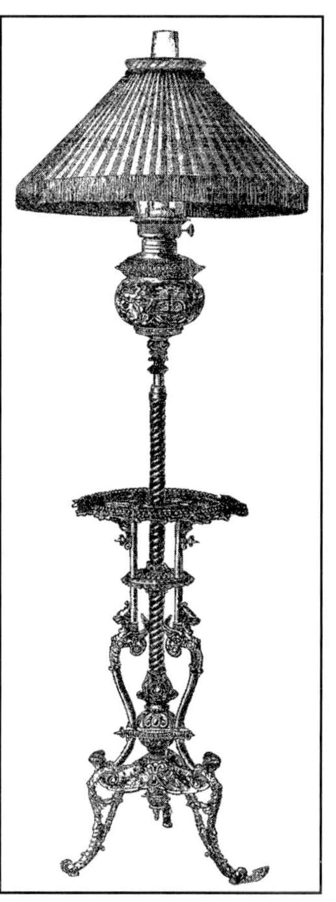

Daylight floor or piano lamp from advertisement by Craighead & Kintz Co., *Pottery and Glass Reporter*, Oct. 17, 1889.

Stork banquet lamp. This lamp was also sold by the Rochester Lamp Company, New York. Courtesy Doug and Judy Myers.

Daylite Company
1916 – 1920s

The Daylite Company was formed in Chicago by former employees of the Mantle Lamp Company of America, Chicago, Illinois. They were Harry G. Weaver, Theodore H. French, J. F. Novy, and Robert W. Buettner. Their intention was to sell Daylite mantle lamps in competition with the famous Aladdin brand. French held patents for incandescent mantle lamps.

Daylite lamps were sold as mantle lamps and as open-flame lamps. Daylite lamps sold as open-flame center-draft lamps are the ones illustrated here.

Edward Miller manufactured lamps for the Daylite Company. The Aladdin cap mantle, Aladdin chimney, and Aladdin Model 6 mounted wick can be used (Courter, 1997). Unmarked "Daylite" mantle lamps were sold by Montgomery Ward and possibly other mail-order catalog companies.

In 1917, the Mantle Lamp Company sued the Daylite Company (also incorrectly spelled Daylight) but lost the case.

I do not know whether the open-flame center-draft lamps were sold before, during, or as a result of the court case.

Daylite flame spreader for open flame burning. The top disc is steel. The flame spreader for the Daylite mantle lamp is a thimble marked "Model Daylite 8."

Daylite wick knob.

Daylite hanging lamp fount adapted for center-draft open flame. Height 9". $75.00.

Daylite stand lamp adapted for center-draft open flame. Height 12". $75.00.

Daylite Center-draft

The Daylite burner was made to burn a large flame or was modified for blue flame and a mantle. The French patent #1193134 for the Daylite incandescent mantle lamp was awarded Aug. 1, 1916. The patent illustrates a different wick raiser than shown here (see right). The Gregor and French patent #1312478 further modifies the incandescent lamp.

The Daylite gallery for open flame center-draft lamps was not designed for a mantle.

Daylite burner with wick raiser. The burner locks in place, whereas mantle burners usually have threads, a different gallery, and a different wick raiser (see right). Some wick raisers are marked "Pat. Aug. 1 – 1916."

The Daylite burner has a screen much like those found in Aladdin lamps.

Daylite Incandescent Burner

The Daylite mantle lamp flame spreader.

Daylite gallery for Kone Cap mantle.

Daylite burner with wick raiser and unmarked knob. The burner locks in place, and the wick raiser is marked "Pat. Aug. 1 – 1916." This is a mantle burner. Courtesy Doug and Judy Myers.

Dayton Manufacturing Co.

1883 – 1961

The Dayton Manufacturing Company, of Dayton, Ohio, produced railroad lamps, switch lights, conductors lanterns, and railway car furnishing goods. The company was a leader in railroad passenger car lighting.

The front one-half of the undated Dayton catalog No. 166 featured electric car lighting. The catalog also included kerosene, acetylene gas, and candle fixtures. Kerosene fixtures were offered with auxiliary electric lights. The catalog estimated to date 1915.

Center-draft fixtures for car lighting included car chandeliers with one to four burners and carside or bracket lamps. The company's lighting fixtures were substantial and elegant, typical of railroad lighting of the time. The company employed 169 in 1888.

Dayton purchased Post & Company in 1892.

Catalog No. 166 promoted the superior lighting provided by car chandeliers using the "student-lamp principle." Dayton center-draft car lamps were fitted with Moehring, Astral, and Improved Acme burners.

John Kirby Jr. assigned patents to Dayton Mfg. Co. beginning about 1883. In 1891 he was general manager. Kirby claimed credit for developing the Acme burner for Post & Co. in 1877 or 1878 (Wellington, 1892). Adams & Westlake sold lamps with a similar burner.

Many patents for car lamps were improvements in support, suspension, and brackets to operate the lamps while the train was in motion.

The heavy ornate lamps illustrated here were mostly used to light parlor cars, dining cars, private cars, office cars, sleeping cars, and some coaches. Some founts are stamped with the Dayton Mfg. logo underneath.

Dayton Manufacturing also operated a marine hardware and lighting division.

Trade Names

Center-draft burners — Acme.

Railroad fixtures — Acme Postal, Dayton, U.S. Standard Postal.

Selected Patents, Center-draft Lamps

J. Kirby, Jr., assigned to Dayton Mfg. Co.[1]

Year	Patent
1892	484,323
1894	520,265
1896	557,397
1896	567,833

[1]Kirby assigned earlier patents for coach and student lamps to Post & Co. Other patents held by Kirby (such as 480,412) illustrate the glass drip cup and flame spreader but did not specify center-draft. Also Kirby patent 643,141 for locomotive carbide headlight.

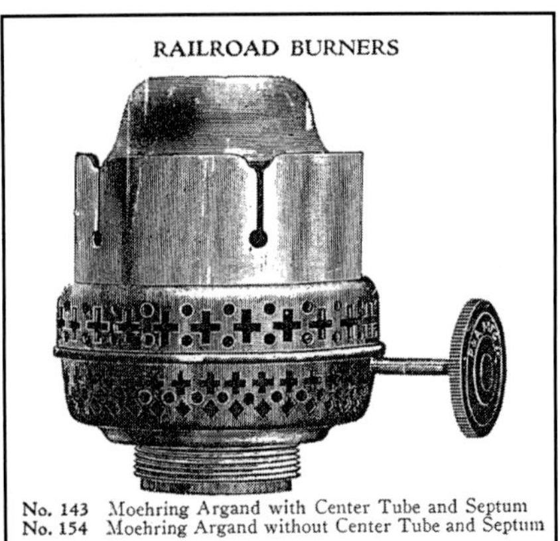
RAILROAD BURNERS

No. 143 Moehring Argand with Center Tube and Septum
No. 154 Moehring Argand without Center Tube and Septum

Moehring burner offered in undated Plume & Atwood catalog.

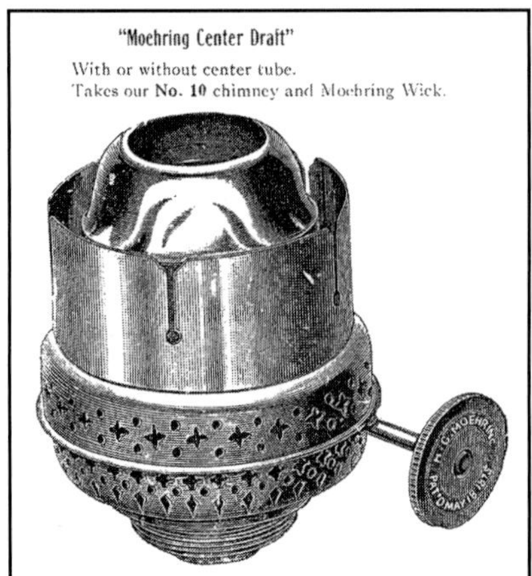
"Moehring Center Draft"
With or without center tube.
Takes our No. 10 chimney and Moehring Wick.

Moehring burner offered in Dayton catalog 166. This burner manufactured by Plume & Atwood.

Dayton Car Lamps

Dayton car chandelier No. 134 with No. 3 Dual burners. This lamp was also made for Moehring center-draft burners. A four-light version was also offered.

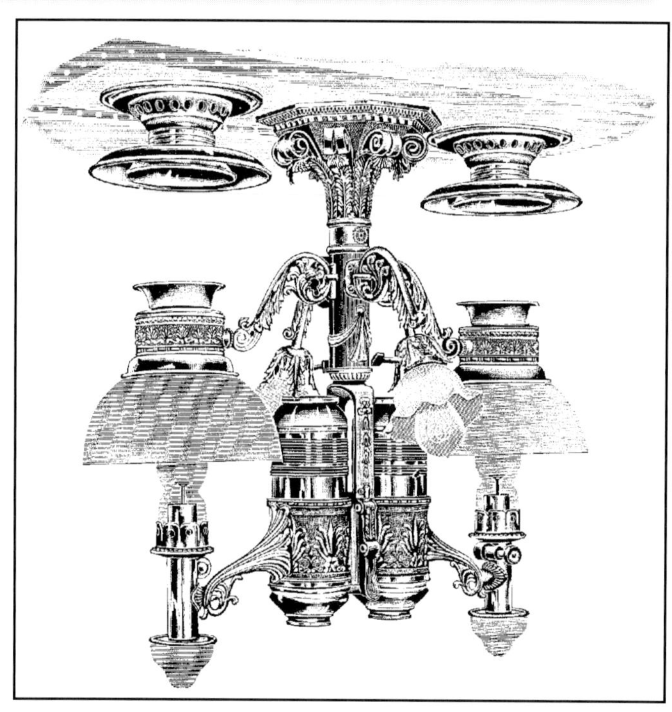

Dayton car chandelier No. 326 with improved Acme burners and supplementary electric lights.

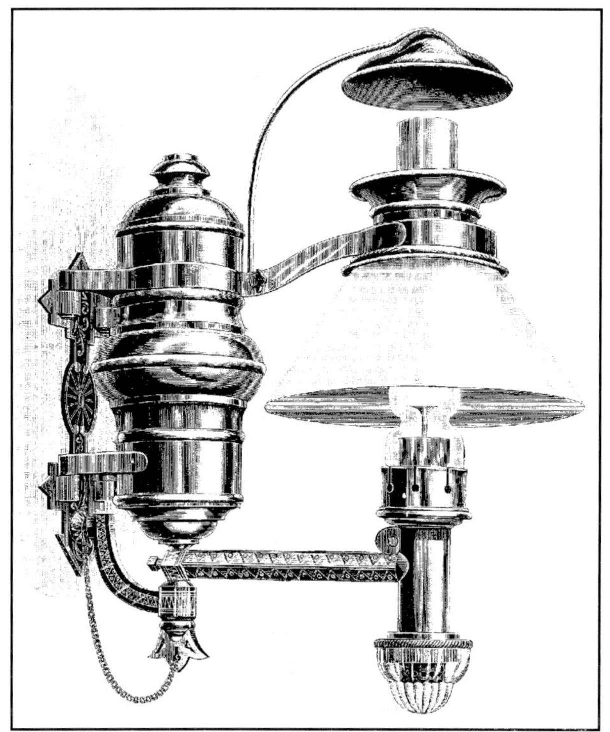

Dayton No. 74 carside lamp with improved Acme burner, glass drip cup, and flame spreader. This lamp appears identical to one made by Adams & Westlake.

Dayton car chandelier No. 18 with Moehring burners. A four-light version was also offered. This fixture appears to be fitted with lamps similar to those illustrated on the next page.

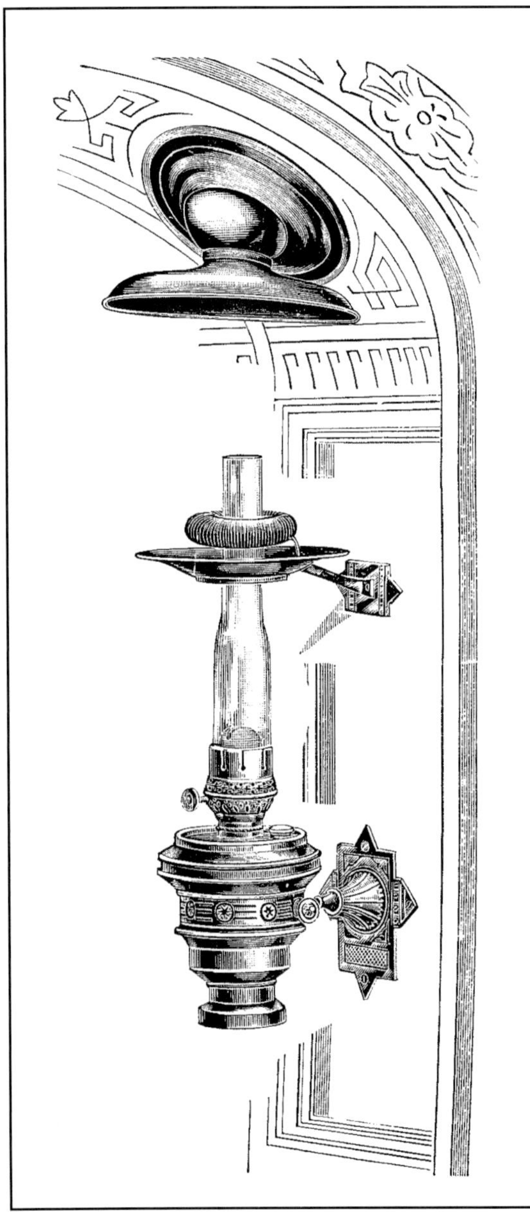

Dayton carside lamp No. 59 with Moehring burner. This lamp appears identical to one made by Handlan-Buck, of St. Louis (right). The ceiling canopy was adjustable and was furnished with smoke bell if desired.

Handlan-Buck Mfg. Company

Handlan-Buck Mfg. Company was a manufacturer of railroad lanterns in St. Louis, Missouri. Handlan-Buck was formed when Alexander H. Handlan became partner with M. M. Buck in 1901. The lamp illustrated here could be a rebranded Dayton product, or perhaps Dayton was a dealer or reseller of Handlan-Buck fixtures.

The lamp illustrated below is a center-draft fitted with Plume & Atwood's Moehring Argand railroad burner. This burner was made with or without a center tube and septum.

The burner knob is marked "The Plume & Atwood Mfg. Co., U. S. A."

The base and top of fount are marked "Handlan-Buck Mfg. Co., St. Louis."

Handlan-Buck railroad lamp made to use in side-car or ceiling wall brackets. Height of fount 8⅛". The removable base allows air to enter the center-draft tube. Dark bronze finish. The Dayton catalog offered 45 different finishes. $100.00.

Dithridge & Company

Fort Pitt Glass Works, ca. 1873 – 1902

The Fort Pitt Glass Works made a variety of decorated opal lamps and shades beginning in the late 1880s.

The Pittsburgh company, well known for its tableware and cup plates, dates to 1827. Edward Dithridge became owner in the 1860s and began making lamp glass and chimneys. His son George reorganized the company as Dithridge & Company in 1873 (Welker, 1985).

An undated catalog, ca. 1888 – 1889, included chimneys as Sun, Sun Electric, Moehring, Shaffer, and Rochester. Advertising during this time illustrated decorated vase lamps. Decorated shade, lamp, and chimney glass was the primary business at the time. The glassworks was moved to Jeanette, Pennsylvania, in 1890.

Vase lamps fitted with center-draft oil pots were advertised in 1891. The oil pots appear to have been supplied by Manhattan Brass and Plume & Atwood.

Dithridge & Company was purchased by the Pittsburgh Lamp and Brass Company in 1902, which reorganized as the Pittsburgh Lamp, Brass and Glass Company. I believe lamps with Fort Pitt and Dithridge flame spreaders date between 1891 and 1902.

Welker (1985) reported that Dithridge & Co. reorganized after Pittsburgh Brass went out of business in 1926.

Trade Names

Center-draft lamps — Fort Pitt, Dithridge, Young America.
Round-wick lamps — Princess lamps.
Flat-wick lamps — Baby Cleveland.

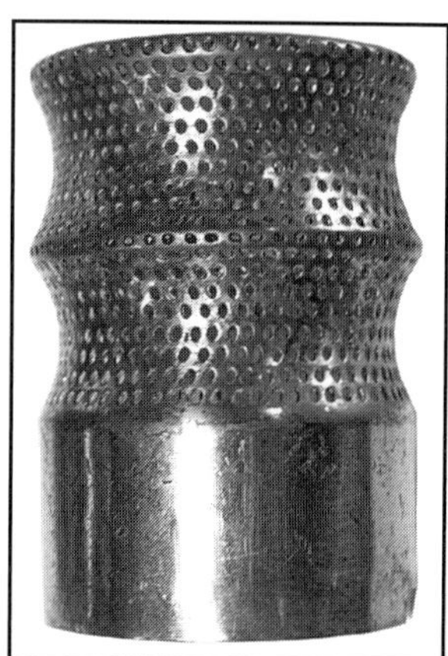

Flame spreaders found in center-draft lamps sold by Dithridge & Co. The Fort Pitt was made by Holmes, Booth & Haydens. The Dithridge was made by Hipwell Mfg. Co.

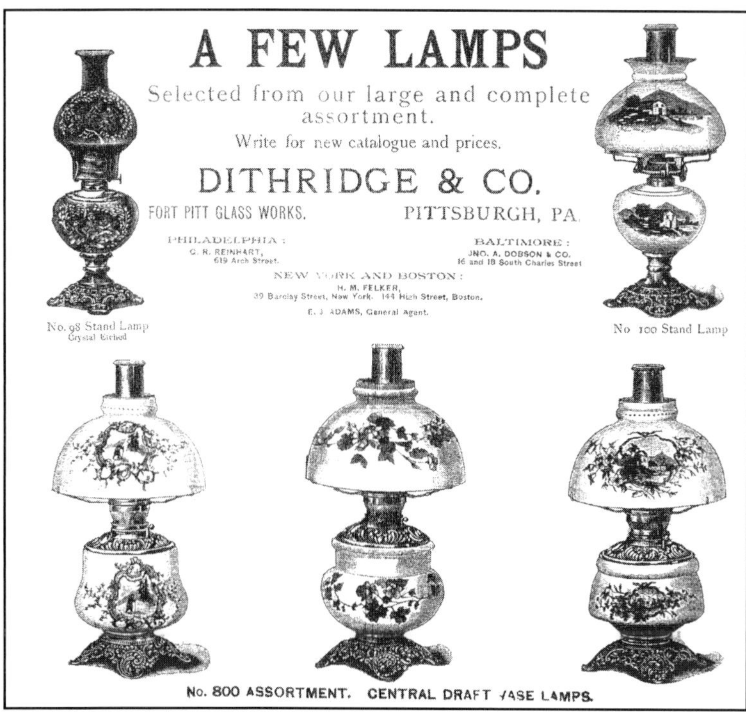

Advertisement, *Crockery and Glass Journal*, Sept. 15, 1892.

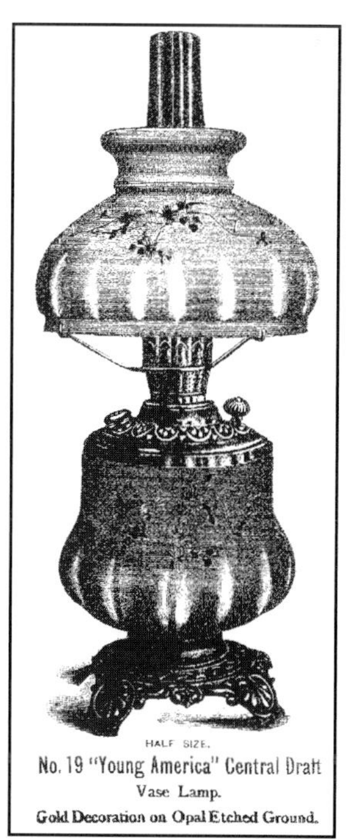

***CGJ*, Oct. 22, 1891.**

Fostoria Glass Company
1887 – 1986

Fostoria Glass, Moundsville. Fostoria moved to Moundsville in 1892.
Postcard image courtesy Robert and Donna Sperow.

Lamp Manufacture ca. 1888 – 1922

Fostoria Glass Company, of Fostoria, Ohio, is sometimes confused with Fostoria Shade and Lamp Company. The two companies both started with glasshouses in Fostoria, but they were totally separate companies.

The town of Fostoria was named for Charles W. Foster, father of the future Ohio governor and the first president of the Fostoria Shade and Lamp Company.

Fostoria Glass Company was incorporated in 1886 in Wheeling, West Virginia, and opened in 1887 in Fostoria, Ohio. Lucien B. Martin was president; William S. Brady, secretary; James B. Russell, plant manager; and Benjamin M. Hildreth, sales manager.

The company moved from Fostoria to Moundsville, West Virginia, in 1892 for "better supply of natural gas." The Seneca Glass Company moved into the glasshouse.

Collectors best know Fostoria Glass today for pressed glassware and novelties, candelabra, and pattern glass lamps using flat-wick burners. According to Welker (1985), Fostoria Glass became one of America's largest factories making handmade glass. Goding (2003) stated that 400 different glass patterns were made by Fostoria — with 340 different pressed items in the popular American pattern alone.

Fostoria made two center-draft vase lamps in clear pressed glass — Victoria and Virginia patterns — while in Fostoria, Ohio. The Virginia pattern was illustrated in *Pottery and Glassware Reporter*, July 18, 1889. Victoria is an early pattern glass and the lamp is rare. Each lamp was advertised as a "Central Draft Lamp or For Ordinary Burner."

The company became a major manufacturer of decorated center-draft vase lamps. According to Murray (1992), both decorated and colored glass vase lamps were made in Fostoria, Ohio, determined by glass shards found there. Much greater numbers of vase lamps, however, were produced after Fostoria moved to Moundsville.

Liebmann (1994) illustrates hundreds of decorated parlor vase and banquet lamps produced in Moundsville from 1897 to 1922. The opal vase lamps were fitted with matching decorated ball shades, Tam-o-Shanter shades, and half shades. Some were "equipped for electricity." Liebmann points out that Fostoria lamps were catalog differently than other wares. Nearly all Fostoria lamps were identified only by names, without corresponding catalog reference numbers.

A 1901 catalog illustrates a wide variety of center-draft vase lamps. The fancy decorated lamps were painted with scenes depicting flora, fauna, people, and scenes for every taste. The painting was permanently fired onto the glass. Collectors may study the variety of Fostoria lamps by visiting museums and reading other reference books about the company.

In 1902 Fostoria offered decorated vase lamps mounted in metal baskets with handles.

A 1906 – 1907 catalog is reprinted in *Lamps & Other Lighting Devices, 1859 – 1906* featuring etched crystal and etched blue crystal vase lamps.

The Rakow Library, Corning Museum of Glass, has several catalogs on microform for collectors to study.

Fostoria Glass Company lamps were mostly fitted with Plume & Atwood oil pots. The flame spreaders are easily identified as those made by Plume & Atwood. Fostoria did offer Success oil pots and burners in 1899 and 1900. Most catalogs, however, illustrate P & A oil pots.

Fostoria Glass also produced machine-made stand lamps, night lights, and pressed ware for flat wick burners. Several pattern lamps are illustrated by Liebmann both in clear glass and milk glass, some with matching shades.

The company produced electric portable table lamps in 1904 and 1909/1910 and gas "portable" table lamps from 1904 to 1912.

Kerosene and electric Fostoria lamps were sold through many mail-order catalogs.

The Fostoria Glass Company was "said to be assured" of merger into Pittsburgh Lamp, Brass and Glass Company (*CGJ*, Nov. 1901). However, the merger did not occur.

The Fostoria, Ohio, Glass Association operates the Glass Heritage Gallery in Fostoria, Ohio. The Gallery is a museum for the glass made in 12 glass plants in Fostoria.

You may contact the association at: www.fostoriaglass.com.

The Fostoria Glass Society operates the Fostoria Glass Museum in Moundsville, West Virginia. The museum is a good place for collectors to study Fostoria glass and Fostoria lamps. Website: www.fostoriaglass.org.

Trade Names

Center-draft lamps—Fostoria. Note that most Fostoria vase lamps were sold by name rather than by catalog number.

Fostoria Virginia vase lamp sold as "Connecticut Electric Lamp" by George F. Bassett in a 1889 catalog. This lamp was fitted with an oil pot made by Wallace & Sons. Courtesy David Broughton.

Fostoria Virginia vase lamp made in Fostoria, Ohio, circa 1888 or 1889. This lamp was fitted with a choice of oil pots — flat-wick burner or center-draft burner, $500.00. Courtesy Fostoria Museum, Fostoria, Ohio.

Fostoria vase lamp featured on the cover page of *China, Glass and Lamps,* Oct. 7, 1891.

Fostoria Lamps

The Fostoria Glass Co., Moundsville, W.Va., have sent out to the trade a circular bearing on the merits of their superb lines of decorated lamps, globes and shades and decorated novelties for season of 1899 and 1900, and which contains the following pertinent matter:

"Last season our record for shapes, decorations and low prices was a cause of consternation to our competitors and a source of satisfaction to the trade. Lamp styles and decorations that had heretofore been high in price as to be a luxury that could be enjoyed only by a few, we placed at such prices as brought them within the reach of the masses, and as a consequence dealers sales and profits were materially increased. Our success, in this manner of handling the goods has proven satisfactory to ourselves and our customers, that we will this season push our efforts in this direction much further than ever, and will offer to the trade a line of decorated lamps which for novel and desirable shapes, rich decorations and colorings, and low prices, have never been equaled.

We have in store some genuine surprises in special trimmings, viz.: New bases, gold platings, all at lower prices than ever before quoted."

China, Glass and Lamps, Sept. 28, 1899

Fostoria Flame Spreaders

These flame spreaders, made by Plume and Atwood, are found in burners used in Fostoria vase lamps.

The patents dated 1893 and 1895 are for wick raisers, which help date the lamps.

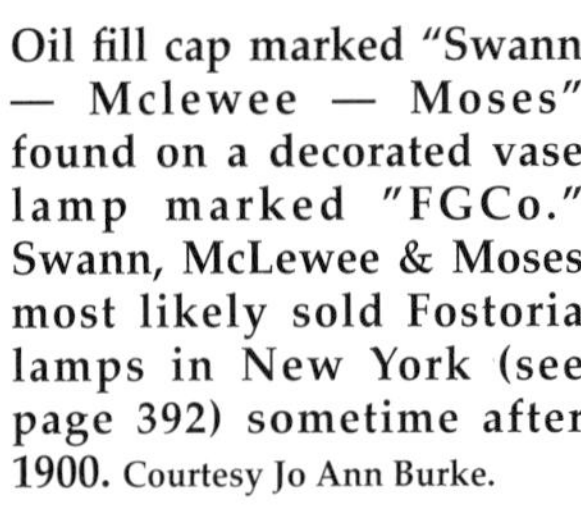

Oil fill cap marked "Swann — Mclewee — Moses" found on a decorated vase lamp marked "FGCo." Swann, McLewee & Moses most likely sold Fostoria lamps in New York (see page 392) sometime after 1900. Courtesy Jo Ann Burke.

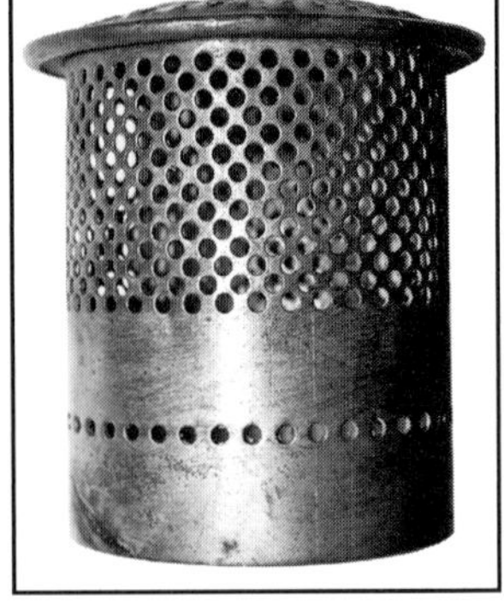

Dates on Above Flame Spreader	
Patent Dates	Patent Numbers
Sept 9 '90	436,093
Aug 26 '90	495,289
Apr 30 '95	538,476

Dates on Above Flame Spreaders	
Patent Dates	Patent Numbers
Aug 14 '88	387,756
Aug 26 '90	435,130
Sept 9 '90	436,093
Mch 24 '91	448,851
Jan 5 '92	466,551

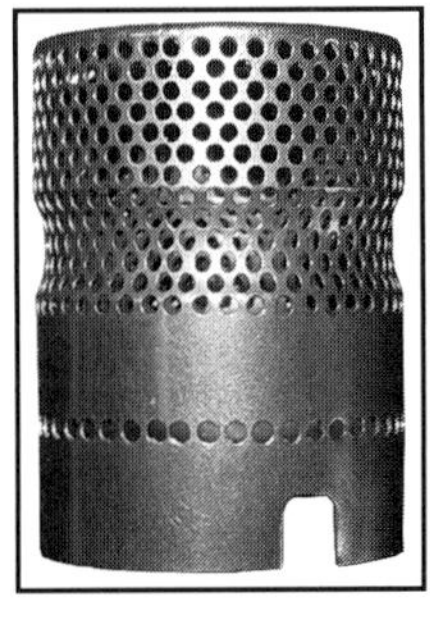

Fostoria #1 flame spreader with same dates as above. This flame spreader is identical in size and shape to the Plume & Atwood #1. Courtesy Kent Stratton.

"Three Beauties" including two Fostoria glass lamps, Moundsville. Postcard image. Courtesy Robert and Donna Sperow.

Fostoria Decorated Vase Lamps, Plume & Atwood Oil Pots

Fostoria vase lamp decorated with "Cupids." The cast-iron base is marked "FG Co." $500.00. Courtesy of Larry and Mary Arrojo.

Anna Bennett showing a typical Fostoria vase lamp, Fostoria Museum, Moundsville, WV. The museum is worth visiting to learn more about Fostoria Glass Company products and Fostoria lamps.

Fostoria Shade and Lamp Co.
(Consolidated Lamp and Glass Co.)

Fostoria Shade and Lamp Co., 1890 – 1893; Consolidated Lamp and Glass Company, 1893 – 1964

Fostoria Shade and Lamp and Consolidated Lamp and Glass have a common background and therefore are discussed together. Both companies manufactured large numbers of center-draft lamps.

Fostoria Shade and Lamp Company

The Fostoria Shade and Lamp Company was organized in Fostoria, Ohio, to manufacture decorative pressed and blown glass wares; Charles Foster was president; William S. Brady, vice-president; and James B. Graham, secretary-treasurer. Charles Foster became United States Secretary of the Treasury in 1893.

The company replaced the burned-out Buttler Art Glass Company in Fostoria.

The company operated one 10-pot furnace and one glass tank in 1891. Nicholas Kopp, Jr., was recruited from Hobbs, Brockunier and Company, Wheeling, West Virginia, as glass superintendent and factory manager. His father was employed by the Fostoria Glass Company and the young Kopp moved to Fostoria to work for the "new" company.

Kopp and the Fostoria Shade and Lamp Company gained national reputation for fine lamp glass and lamps. *China, Glass and Lamps* (July 27, 1892) reported these lamps being made that year: "center-draft lamps in rococo, gold-lined and gold bronze designs; banquet lamps in biscuit glaze and satin finish; vase lamps with removable brass founts; figured vase lamps; imitation vase lamps; stand lamps; sewing lamps; piano lamps; parlor lamps and several lines of night lamps in rose, orange, turquoise and pearl gray." The colorful glass vases with exquisite matching shades were trend setting in the day.

Collectors may study Fostoria and Consolidated glass at the Glass Heritage Gallery in Fostoria, Ohio. The museum includes many Consolidated lamps.

Consolidated Lamp and Glass Company

In 1893, the large glassware distributor of Wallace and McAfee Ltd., Pittsburgh, bought The Fostoria Shade and Lamp Company and renamed the new firm Consolidated Lamp and Glass Company. Officers were Frank G. Wallace, president; J. B. Graham, secretary; and Joseph G. Walter, treasurer. General offices and warehouses were in Pittsburgh.

At that time, Consolidated Lamp and Glass Company was said to be "the largest factory manufacturing lamps and shades in the United States" (*China, Glass and Lamps*, Dec. 13, 1893). A following report stated "Two thirds of the 14" shades and library lamp founts made in the country are sold here in Pittsburgh through the Consolidated Lamp and Glass Company..."(*China, Glass and Lamps*, July 4, 1894).

***CGL*, July 20, 1892. The oil pot and burner appear to be Royal by Plume and Atwood.**

The Consolidated Lamp & Glass Co.'s Purchase

The sale of the plant of the Fostoria Shade & Lamp Co., of Fostoria, Ohio, to the Consolidated Lamp & Glass Co., of Pittsburgh, was concluded on December 13. The price paid is not stated, but the plant is valued at $100,000. It is the largest factory manufacturing lamps and lamp shades in the United States. The principal stockholders are W. C. Brown and J. B. Graham, of Fostoria. The new company has a paid up capital of $200,000 and will largely increase the plant, which is already employing 250 people.

CGL, Dec. 20, 1893

Many early vase lamps were fitted with side-draft round-wick burners or single or double wick flat-wick burners. By 1895 center-draft oil pots were widely accepted and were prevalent in Consolidated lamps. Murray (1992) credits Plume & Atwood as the primary supplier of brass parts for lamps produced in Fostoria.

Consolidated built a new factory in Coraopolis, Pennsylvania, in 1895. The glasshouse in Fostoria operated until it burned in 1896. At that time all glass workers were transferred to the Coraopolis factory.

Consolidated produced many decorated vase lamps. An advertisement claimed "production of 400 dozen decorated lamps per day." See Wilson (1989) for information about Consolidated glass after 1926. The company continued in business until 1964 producing glass shades, replacement glass for Victorian lamps, and electric lamp glass.

Nicholas Kopp resigned as manager of Consolidated in 1900 to form Kopp Lamp and Glass Company in Swissvale, Pennsylvania. In 1902 Kopp Lamp and Glass became part of the Pittsburgh, Lamp, Brass and Glass Company.

Nicholas Kopp, Jr.

Nicholas Kopp was born in France into a family rich in glass-making experience. Kopp worked for Hobbs, Brockunier & Company as a glass chemist from 1888 to 1890. Murray states Kopp was

25 years old when he joined Fostoria; however, the Welkers (1985) gave his age as 35. Regardless of his age, he assumed major responsibility at Fostoria Shade and Lamp, rewarding Foster and the directors with his achievements in coming months.

Kopp developed new colors, finishes, and iridescent glass and cased glass for lamps. A 48-page catalog dated 1902 stated lamps that the company offered "fine colored glass in rose, canary and cerise or red.....we now have added Copper Ruby....heretofore manufactured only in Europe."

Arnold (1990) cites reference that Kopp was the "originator of the glass known as 'cased,' i.e., colored glass overlaid by clear glass."

Kopp was credited as "a prolific designer of new moulds" and lamp patterns for both Fostoria and Consolidated by Murray (1992). Murray (1992) listed glass patterns (including salt shakers) and illustrated many lamps. Kopp developed unique colored glass including cranberry, ruby, rubina, yellow cased glass and other opaque colors. He produced excellent selenium ruby glass.

When Pittsburgh Lamp & Brass ceased operation in 1926, Kopp organized Kopp Glass, Inc. This company continues today making special glass for traffic signal and railroad lenses, scientific glass and filters, airport and aerospace lighting, architectural and theatrical lighting, and automotive parts.

Patents

Kopp was granted many design patents including these, for shades on June 18, 1912: D42,631; D42,632; D42,633; and D42,634. Later, D47,334 and D47,335 were granted.

Glass

Kopp made similar, if not the same, glass in Fostoria and Swissvale when he worked for Fostoria Shade and Lamp, Consolidated Lamp and Glass, and Pittsburgh Lamp, Brass and Glass. Therefore, collectors must become familiar with patterns and other characteristics of the glass or lamp in order to attribute the lamp correctly. Pittsburgh lamps, for example, will invariably be fitted with Success oil pots and burners, while Consolidated lamps usually were fitted with Plume & Atwood oil pots and burners.

Original catalogs are extremely valuable; however, few are available to collectors. The Rakow Library at the Corning Museum of Glass has several catalogs on microform.

Kopp made glass in many colors and patterns. Colors of glass included opal, crystal, carnival, ruby, pink, amber or orange, blue, green, and yellow. The glass may be decorated, cased, or given a satin finish. Satin finish became popular over the clear crystal finish. Blue and orange satin lamps are rare.

Most lamps were listed by catalog number rather than by specific names. Names, however, have become known by collectors. The following names, courtesy of Ron Gibson, who owns and operates the 19th Century Lighting Company in Union City, Michigan, are patterns of vase lamps.

Fostoria Lamps

Lamp No. 1, Beaded Acanthus Leaf, Bull Elk, Gardenia, Melon Ribbed, Psyche, Tropical Orchid, Tulip, Vintage Grapes.

Consolidated Lamps

No. 24, Baby Face/Cherub Face, Cartouche, Chimney Globe, Clematis Swirl, Diamond Drape, Hanging Grapes, Lincoln Beaded Drape, Lion/Lion Safari, Lions Head, Oxford, Paisley, Pavillion, Plume, Primrose, Puritan, Sigma, Victoria.

Pittsburgh Lamps

Arabian Nights, Beaded Drape, Berry, 2nd Empire, Bullseye, Honeycomb/Medallion, Iris, Oakleaf, Nautical, Northwind Gargoyle, Peaches, Poppy, Regal Iris, Square Base Drape, Strawberry, Sunken Hollyhock/Button Tufted Drape, Vintage.

Lamps That Sell From the Consolidated Lamp & Glass Co., Coraopolis, Pa.

Lamps are not a side issue with us. They are our specialty; we center our attention upon them. We examine minutely every detail. The burners we use are the best that Yankee ingenuity and skill can construct. We have them made to our order and they reach us in car lots. So with our castings, for lamp feet and trimmings. They are designed by us and made to order, subject to our acceptance upon rigid inspection.

All the balance we make ourselves. The glass is made plain and in colors, in our 31-pot furnace department, 90 X 150 feet, where we turn out, every working day in the year, 800 dozen of lamps, or nearly 50,000 lamps per week, together with globes and shades to match, and pure lead chimneys, which do not crack from flame contact.

We employ the highest skilled artists in our decorating department, sixty in number, no novices or amateurs, but the graduates of the best technical schools extant, at home or abroad. We use original designs exclusively. Our decorating department covers a space of 40 X 220 feet, reinforced by our engraving, photographing and etching departments, covering a floor space of 80 X 100 feet.

We are fully equipped for business. Make lamps that are substantial and finely finished in every detail, and are beauties in color, design and decoration.

We shall make, during the current year, over 2,500,000 lamps, embracing night lights, banquet, parlor, sewing, hall and hanging lamps in the finest colors ever put on the market. Our terra cotta has not yet been imitated, and our rich yellow, pink, pearl and coral are acknowledged trade makers. No better goods made for holiday trade. Prices are right. Samples at Standard Building, 531 Wood Street, Pittsburgh, or 16 Murray Street, New York.

China, Glass & Lamp, Nov. 18, 1896

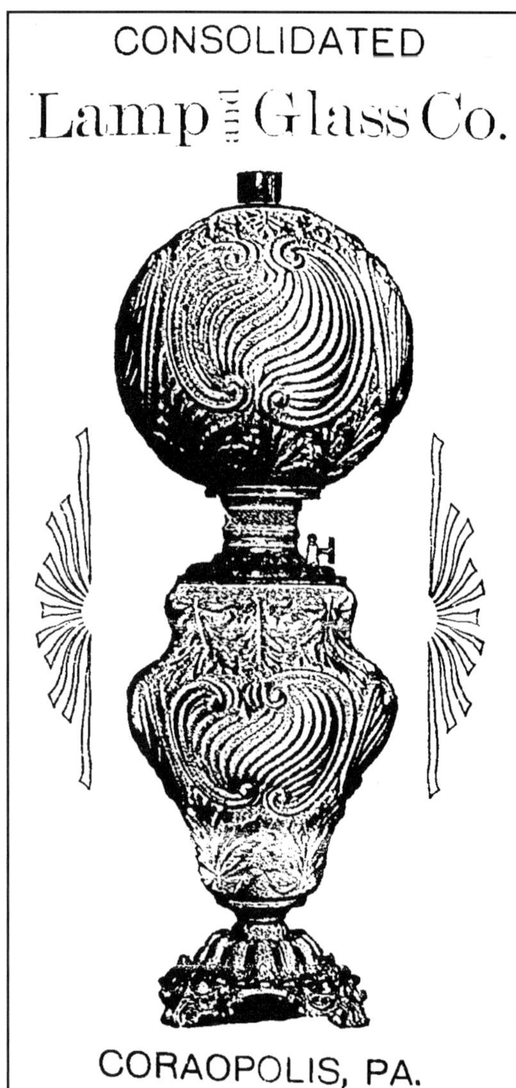

Cover of 1902 catalog.
Courtesy Catherine Thuro.

China, Glass and Lamps reported that "one car of decorated goods per day" was shipped by Fostoria Shade and Lamp Company in Fostoria, Ohio. The Little Jewel oil pots were made by Ansonia Brass and Copper Company. (Sept. 17, 1891).

The Lamp Season

The idea that lamps have their season, and close with the year to open again in July or later, is founded on business methods pursued twenty years ago....manufacture of lamps has become a special industry, carried on year around...Now, immense establishments, like Consolidated Lamp & Glass Co., Dithridge & Co., Washington Glass Mfg. Co., Gillinder & Sons, The Phoenix Glass Co.., etc make lamps, globes and shades all the year around, and keep shipping them as regularly as they are made.

Then there are the metal lamp manufacturers who are constantly turning out new patterns, and while they systemize their factory work and alternate between lamp making and art metal work, their growing export trade is gradually forcing them to work their lamp departments all year.

CGL, April 28, 1897

Advertisement, *Crockery and Glass Journal,* September 21, 1905. The company had salesrooms in New York, Buffalo, San Francisco, Pittsburg, Chicago, and Philadelphia.

Consolidated Flame Spreaders

Flame spreaders found in oil pots used in Consolidated vase and banquet lamps. The patents were assigned to Plume and Atwood. Catalogs prior to 1893 state "Royal Center Draft Burners" were used.

Patented, Sept. 9, 1890, Apr. 11, 1893, Apr. 30, 1895.

Patented, Sept. 9, 1890, Apr. 11, 1893, Apr. 30, 1895.

Patented, Aug. 14, 1888, Aug. 26, 1890, Sept. 9, 1890, March 24, 1891, Jan. 5, 1892.

Patented, Aug. 14, 1888, Aug. 26, 1890, Sept. 9, 1890, March 24, 1891, Jan. 5, 1892.

Patented, Aug. 14, 1888, Aug. 26, 1890, Sept. 9, 1890, March 24, 1891, Jan. 5, 1892.

Consolidated banquet lamp. *CGL*, October 16, 1895.

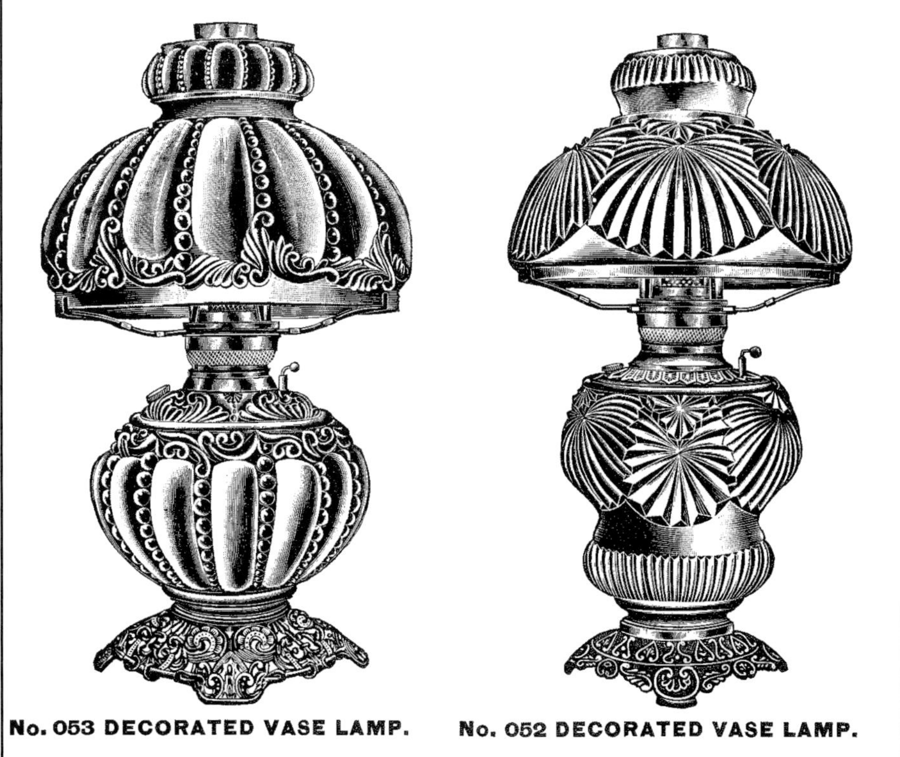

No. 053 DECORATED VASE LAMP. **No. 052 DECORATED VASE LAMP.**

Fostoria Shade and Lamp Co. vase lamps, Pitkin and Brooks catalog, 1892. These lamps are most likely some of Nicholas Kopp's early colored glass production. The catalog states that 052 was made in bright rose and turquoise, and 053 was made in yellow and rose satin. Courtesy David Broughton.

Gill & Company

Lamp Manufacture ca. 1905 – 1906

Gill & Company was a manfacturer of gas and electric globes and shades with salesrooms in New York, Boston, and Philadelphia. The company advertised decorated center-draft vase lamps for the 1906 season.

Gill & Company claimed glass and lamp factories; however, the company was most likely a reseller of Fostoria or Consolidated decorated vase lamps.

Have You Seen Stella?

Rather a pretty name with which to christen a lamp, but this one deserves it. Decoration consists of a snowball design in Limoges tints of brown and green. Possesses a white metal base with a gold-plated finish. Reference to accompanying illustration makes it unnecessary to dilate upon the gracefulness of its shape. It is lamps of this character that sell strictly on their own merits.

New York Office: **25 West Broadway.**

GLASS FACTORIES:
York and Thompson Sts.
Lehigh and Salmon Sts.
LAMP FACTORY:
Lehigh and Salmon Sts.

GILL & CO.,
Incorporated,
PHILADELPHIA, PA.

CGJ, September 28, 1905.

CGJ, holiday issue, December 5, 1905.

Here's Another

of the many lamps that help to make our line one of the most favorably talked of in the market. Printer's ink, of course, doesn't do justice to its attractiveness. To be properly appreciated must come under personal observation at our showrooms.

New York Office: **25 West Broadway.**

GLASS FACTORIES:
York and Thompson Sts.
Lehigh and Salmon Sts.
LAMP FACTORY:
Lehigh and Salmon Sts.

GILL & CO.,
Incorporated,
PHILADELPHIA, PA.

CGJ, September 7, 1905.

Lamp and Brass Works of W. J. Gordon

1885 – 1888

The Lamp and Brass Works of W. J. Gordon was successor to the Cleveland Non-Explosive Lamp Company. Gordon's Lamp and Brass Works was listed in the Cleveland City Directory from 1885 to 1888 at Main and SE corner of Center Streets.

William J. Gordon was one of Cleveland's leading citizens. He was a successful business man, civic leader, and public benefactor. Gordon formed the first woodenware works in the Cleveland area, and he helped establish the Cleveland Iron Mining Company, of which he served as president. He established a large wholesale grocery business in Ohio and, as a wealthy businessman, he was active in many civic projects.

According to the *Cleveland Plain Dealer* (Nov. 24, 1892) Gordon "was one of the organizers of the Commercial Mutual Insurance Company of Cleveland, which was an exceedingly prosperous concern until the great Chicago fire. Not discouraged by this disaster, he rendered great service in the establishment of the Mercantile Insurance Company, of which he was chosen president."

Gordon retired from business in 1871, with an obvious interest in nonexplosive lamps judging by his patents of 1872 and the Lamp and Brass Works bearing his name. Gordon held two unassigned patents, along with Mark W. House, for nonexplosive lamps. The patterns were granted in 1872 (see the Cleveland Non-Explosive Lamp Co.).

Gordon sold his Lamp and Brass Works business to the Lane Mfg. Company, which moved the operation to Kenosha, Wisconsin, in 1888. Gordon was apparently in declining health and died in 1892. His obituary omitted his involvement and interest in the lamp business.

The Cleveland lamp.

The Cleveland Lamp

This advertisement implies that the Cleveland lamp had a glass fount similar to the Harvey Electric Safety Lamp. The Harvey lamp was illustrated in the 1888 H. Leonard & Sons catalog with a similar burner and chimney.

The text copy, however, states the Cleveland lamp "is made in plain and embossed founts of pure bronze metal."

I have no information about the possible relationship of the Harvey lamp and the Cleveland lamp.

Trade Names

Center-draft lamps — Aurora, Improved Aurora, Improved Magnum, Cleveland, Harvey Electric Safety Lamp, Orient.

Advertisement, *Crockery and Glass Journal*, 1886.

Improved Aurora

Improved AURORA Lamps-1888

SIMPLE IN CONSTRUCTION.
HANDSOME IN DESIGN.
BEAUTIFULLY FINISHED.

WICK and CHIMNEY STAPLE IN THE MARKET.

ADAPTED FOR ALL PURPOSES.
IN VASES, PIANO & BANQUET LAMPS, PARLOR, DESK AND SHOP LAMPS, STEAMSHIP AND R. R. COACH LAMPS.

WICK MOVEMENT THE SIMPLEST.

No. 203 Chandelier Fount.
Height 8$\frac{3}{4}$ inches.
Brass, Rich Gold, or Nickel.

EASILY CONTROLLED AND REGULATED. NO BURNED FINGERS.

No. 200 Plain Vase Lamp.
Height 9$\frac{3}{4}$ inches.
Brass, Rich Gold, or Nickel.

WICK ADJUSTMENT ABSOLUTELY PERFECT.

No. 201 Embossed Vase Lamp.
Height 9$\frac{3}{4}$ inches.
Brass, Rich Gold, Nickel, Antique Brass, or Japanese.

No. 202 Stand Lamp.
Height 11$\frac{1}{2}$ inches.
Brass, Rich Gold, or Nickel.

OUR IMPROVED **AURORA** LAMPS are now arranged to ELEVATE the WICK FROM THE BOTTOM on the principle of our Improved Magnum Lamp. The Thumb Button is within easy reach and away from the Heat. The LIGHT produced is UNSURPASSED in VOLUME, WHITENESS and STEADINESS.

WICK ELEVATION POSITIVE and ACCURATE.
HEIGHT OF FLAME CAN BE ADJUSTED TO A NICETY.
EASILY RE-WICKED.

Send for Sample, Examine it, Try it, Test it thoroughly, and we know you will place your orders with us.

MANUFACTURED BY

Lamp and Brass Works of W. J. Gordon,
CLEVELAND, OHIO.

These lamps were apparently made for a short time before W. J. Gordon sold the Lamp and Brass Works to Lane Mfg. Co., formed in November 1888. Lane manufactured a variety of Aurora lamps with newly designed flame spreaders, mostly called New Aurora. Lane promoted its lamps to a wide variety of distributors. Advertisement courtesy Ohio Historical Society, Columbus, Ohio.

Haida Lamp and China Co.

ca. 1886 – 1898

China, Crockery and Fancy Goods

Haida Lamp and China Company was an importer and retailer with a store located at 53 – 55 Warren Street, New York City. The company appears at this address from 1891 through 1898 in the New York City directory.

Officers were Thomas Parish, president; Edward A. Unger, vice president; and Benjamin Unger, treasurer.

Advertisements by Haida Lamp Works suggests that Haida manufactured lamps. However, many Haida lamps are identical with the Improved Bristol lamps manufactured by the Bristol Brass and Clock Company. I suspect most of the brass lamps and accessories were purchased from Bristol Brass. See Bristol Brass for more details about Haida-brand lamps.

Haida also sold lamps made by other companies. The Royal Haida was made by Plume & Atwood. The P & A flame spreader was marked and patent dated. I have identified lamps made by Meriden Bronze and Rochester or Edward Miller in Haida catalog No. 7.

The 1893/1894 Haida catalog No. 7, in the Metropolitan Museum of Art Print Room, confirms that Haida was a major distributor of kerosene lamps. The catalog featured banquet and piano lamps, hanging lamps, and decorated parlor lamps.

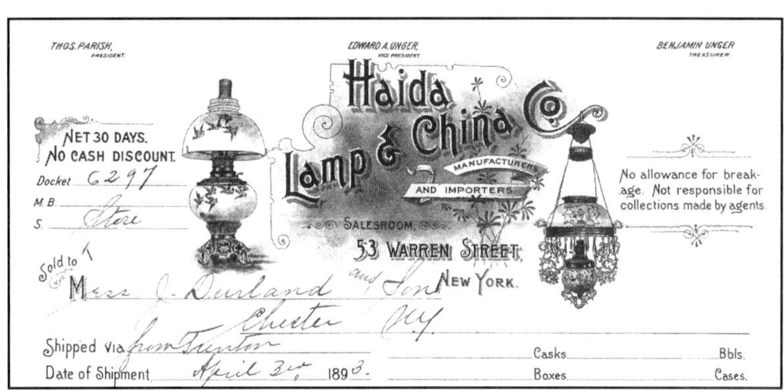

THOS. PARISH, PRESIDENT. EDWARD A. UNGER, VICE PRESIDENT. BENJAMIN UNGER, TREASURER.

Haida Lamp & China Co. MANUFACTURERS AND IMPORTERS. SALESROOM, 53 WARREN STREET, NEW YORK.

NET 30 DAYS. NO CASH DISCOUNT.
Docket 6297
M.B.
S. Store

No allowance for breakage. Not responsible for collections made by agents.

Sold to Mess. J. Durland and Son, Chester NY

Shipped via from Trenton
Date of Shipment April 3rd 1893.
Casks / Bbls. / Boxes / Cases.

Letterhead dated 1893.
Courtesy Dan Edminster.

Haida No. 2 stand lamp. Height 12". Haida lamps have a characteristic decorative band and are marked "The Haida" on the burner assembly. Made by Bristol Brass and Clock Co. $100.00.

HAIDA LAMP WORKS,

—— MANUFACTURERS OF ——

LAMPS.

— SALESROOM, —

53 WARREN ST., NEW YORK.

Advertisement, *CGJ*, May 29, 1890.

HAIDA LAMP.

EIGHTY CANDLE POWER

THE ONLY PERFECT WICKING DEVICE.

HAIDA LAMP AND CHINA CO.,

MANUFACTURERS.

53 WARREN STREET. NEW YORK.

Advertisement, *CGL*, 1890.

Haida Lamp and China Co.

Trade Names

Center-draft lamps — Haida, Royal Haida, Our Darling, New Darling, Princess Boudoir.

Royal Haida flame spreader was made by Plume and Atwood.

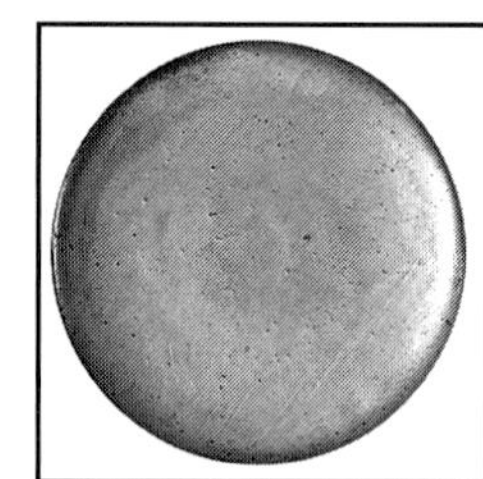

Haida flame spreaders are the exact size and shape as the Improved Bristol. Many unmarked.

Our Darling

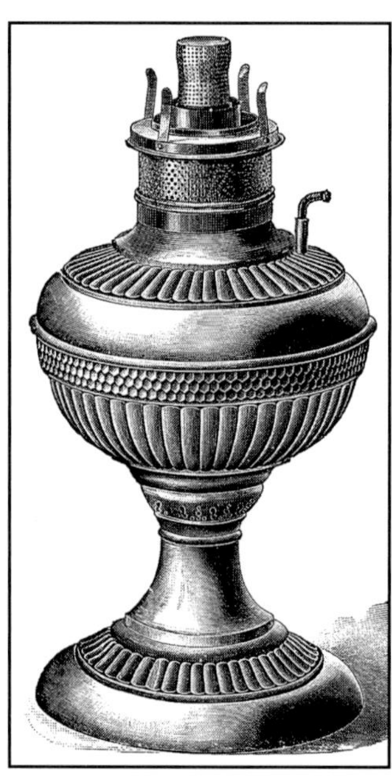

Our Darling No. 1 lamp made for Haida by Holmes, Booth and Haydens. Height 11". This design is similar to HBH Keystone No. 1 lamp.

Haida No. 2 oil pot used in decorated parlor lamps. $75.00.

The bars twist to hold and lock the ball shade in place.

R. Hollings & Co., Boston, made fine brass piano and organ lamps. This Haida fount is mounted on a Hollings brass extendable floor lamp. The fount is marked "The Haida, Pat'd July 15 '90." The Hollings stand is signed "R. Hollings & Co. USA, Pat. Nov. 20th 1888." This is patent No. 393,031 by John H. Rouse assigned to Hollings.

Haida No. 2 parlor lamps. Left: oil pot and burner made by Bristol Brass (see oil pot above) and right: oil pot by Plume & Atwood. Advertisement *CGL* Sept. 9, 1891.

Hektograph Manufacturing Co.

Lamp Manufacture 1883 – 1891

William S. McLewee was manager of the lamp department for the Hektograph Manufacturing Company. The factory was in Brooklyn, New York, with showrooms in New York City. This company manufactured Hectograph machines that made copies from a gelatin surface during the 1880s.

McLewee held several lighting patents as well as those for a cigar lighter and gas burners. Hektograph announced the addition of a lamp department under the direction of Mr. W. S. McLewee, "known to the lamp trade throughout the country," in October 1883. The company added a decorating department to produce decorated porcelain shades and a globe and chimney department to produce etched and patent sand-blasted goods.

I presume that William S. McLewee was also involved in or was owner of the McLewee Brass Manufacturing Company, of New York City, which merged into American Lamp and Brass Co. in 1892.

McLewee held two patents, granted in 1892, improving center-draft lamps. These were unassigned and may have had importance in the merger with American Lamp.

Of interest is McLewee's Non-Mechanical, No-Chimney Lamp. McLewee's patent (290,340) directed air to the flame in such a manner as to eliminate the need for chimney draft. I suspect the lamp met with limited success.

Hektograph claimed to be sole manufacturer of the Hickok Calcium Burner, patented by Edwin Hickok (357,599; 365,745; 386,822), in 1887 and 1888. The Hickok was a round-wick, side-draft burner.

Of further interest, I note that McLewee held two patents on mechanical lamps (320,080; 320,081), granted in 1885.

Selected Patents, Center-draft Lamps

William S. McLewee[1]

1883 .... 290,340 (no chimney)
1892 .... 471,822 (unassigned)
1892 .... 471,823 (unassigned)

W. F. Folmer

1887 .... 365,739 side draft burner

[1]Also see American Lamp & Brass Co. and Clark Brothers' Company.

H. H. Hipwell Manufacturing Co.

1887 – 1903

Hipwell Manufacturing Company, 1903 – Today; Lamp Manufacture 1892 – Early 1900s

H. H. Hipwell Manufacturing Company, a Delaware Corporation, was founded as Pittsburgh's first stamping plant by Harry H. Hipwell in 1887. The company manufactured sheet metal and wire goods, lamps, and electrical supplies.

Harry H. Hipwell (1865 – 1940) was the son of Thomas Hipwell (1840 – 1903), a founder of Pittsburgh Brass Company and assignor of many lamp patents (1881 – 1895) to Manhattan Brass Company. Thomas joined Harry in the business and was the force to help create Hipwell center-draft lamps.

During my visit we found a large portrait of Thomas Hipwell (see his portrait in the chapter on the Manhattan Brass Company). Thomas retired to Allegheny, Pennsylvania, where he died at his home, 2417 Osgood Street, in 1903.

H. H. Hipwell Mfg. Co. made hand lamps and "knock-down shades" in 1892 (*CGL*, Aug. 24, 1892). Harry's first and second initials were omitted in some advertising prior to 1903.

Hipwell Manufacturing Company was incorporated in New Jersey in 1903. The company bears this same name today (2007).

The city directory in 1929 listed Harry H. Hipwell, president; Harry T. Hipwell, vice-president; and Earl W. Hipwell, secretary-treasurer; and the company was at 825 North Avenue W, the same address I found the Hipwell offices at in 2003. H. H. Hipwell died shortly after being elected to the board of directors of North Side Deposit Bank in 1939. He was succeeded by Harry T. Hipwell (1891 – 1958), Harry H. Hipwell, Sr. (1914 – 1998), and finally, Harry H. Hipwell, Jr. (1940), who sold the company in 2001.

Advertisements in *China, Glass and Lamps* in 1894 and 1895 illustrate embossed stand lamps and banquet lamps. The founts of some lamps are stamped "H. H. Hipwell, Allegheny, Pa."

The company made a variety of products over the years — oil stoves, gas stoves, tin jar and bottle caps, gas mantles, games, fire extinguishers, electric lamps and floor lamp finials, Lionel train accessories, automobile accessories and hood ornaments, early camera flash synchronizers, and switchboards for small telephone exchanges.

Batteries and flashlights became major products under the Hipco brand. The company discontinued lamp production to concentrate on batteries for wireless radios as well as for a multitude of industrial, home, and work uses. Batteries led to flashlights and lanterns of many types and sizes. The company, sold to George C. Parks in 2001, continues to make flashlights — one million per year.

Harry H. Hipwell, Sr.
Courtesy Hipwell Mfg. Co.

Hipwell building ca. 1900.
Courtesy Hipwell Mfg. Co.

Selected Patents, Center-draft Lamps

Harry H. Hipwell[1]

1892 472,354

[1]Also patents for gas burners assigned to Hipwell Mfg. Co.

Trade Names

Center-draft lamps — The Hipwell, Star, Allegheny, Victor or The Victor.

Lantern — Star Campaign (oil and candle) lanterns.

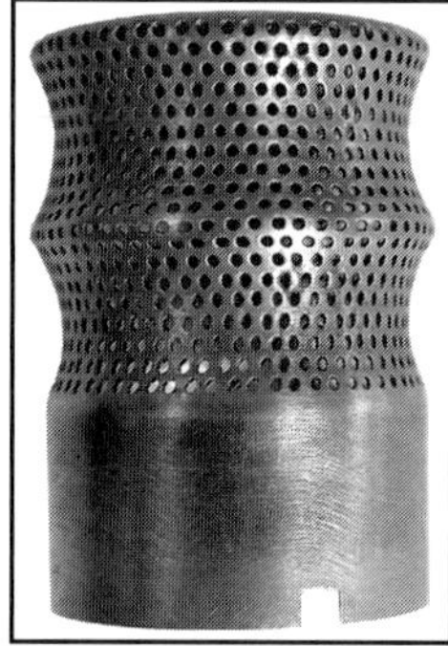

There are two different shapes of Hipwell flame spreaders. The one found in the Star lamp is unique to Hipwell (see next page). The "waisted" flame spreader (see above) was apparently sold (with burners and oil pots) to other distributors. The Hipwell Lamp waisted Hipwell flame spreader is identical in size and shape to those marked: "The M. E. Moore Bronze & Plate Co." (New York), "Dithridge & Co., Pittsburgh," and "Washington Glass Mfg. Co."

The Allegheny

Advertisement, *China, Glass and Lamps*, Nov. 16, 1892.

Hipwell Star

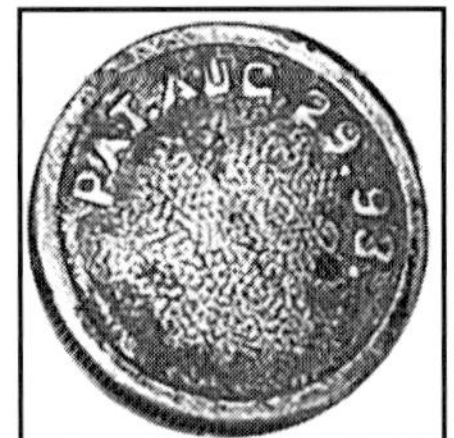

Oil fill cap in Star banquet lamp, marked "Pat. Aug. 29 '93." This is H. S. Chase patent 504,150 for "filling nipple and cap," assigned to Waterbury Mfg. Co.

Star banquet lamp. Height 15". Star banquet lamps were advertised on page 1 of Pitkin and Brooks catalog for 1897/1898. These lamps are found in several heights. $150.00. Courtesy Doug and Judy Myers.

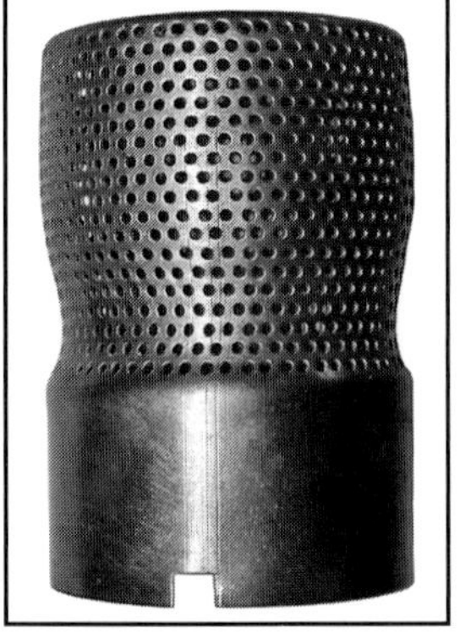

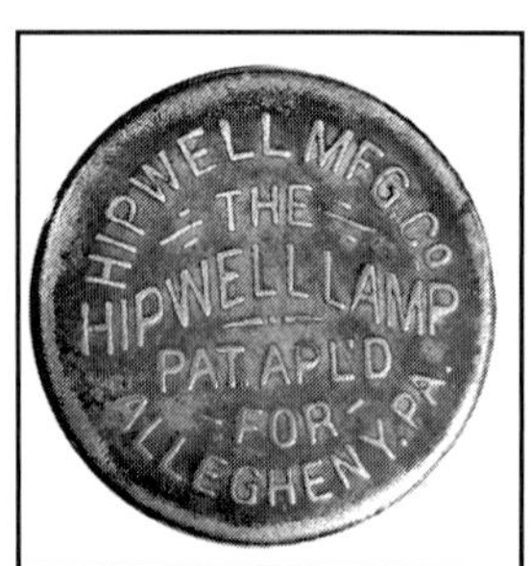

Hipwell flame spreader found in Star and other banquet lamps.

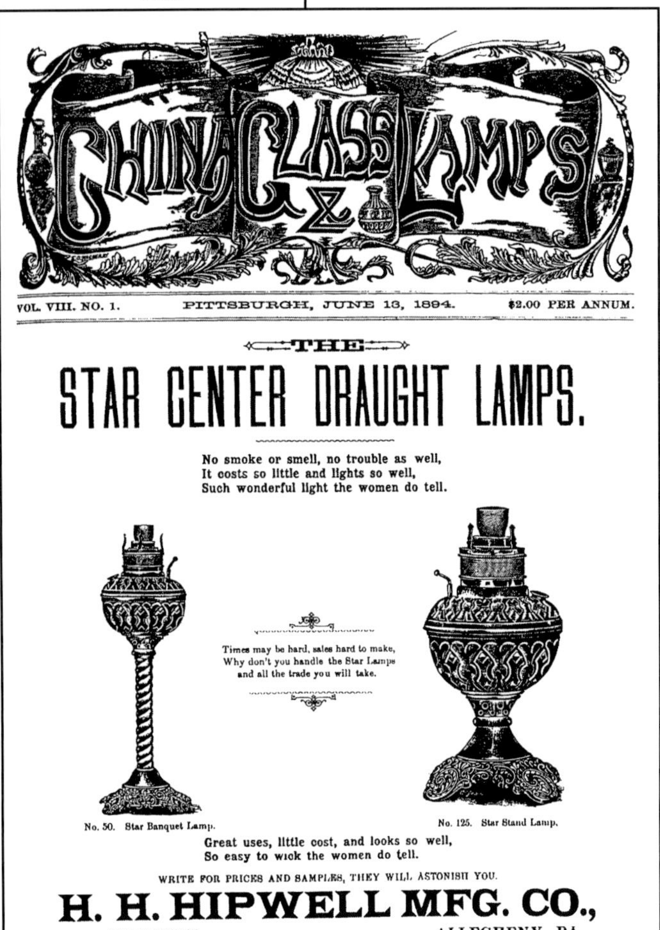

CHINA GLASS & LAMPS

VOL. VIII. NO. 1. PITTSBURGH, JUNE 13, 1894. $2.00 PER ANNUM.

THE

STAR CENTER DRAUGHT LAMPS.

No smoke or smell, no trouble as well,
It costs so little and lights so well,
Such wonderful light the women do tell.

Times may be hard, sales hard to make,
Why don't you handle the Star Lamps
and all the trade you will take.

No. 50. Star Banquet Lamp.

No. 125. Star Stand Lamp.

Great uses, little cost, and looks so well,
So easy to wick the women do tell.

WRITE FOR PRICES AND SAMPLES, THEY WILL ASTONISH YOU.

H. H. HIPWELL MFG. CO.,

CHICAGO SALESROOM,
5 Wabash Ave., D. O. Welty, Mgr.

ALLEGHENY, PA.

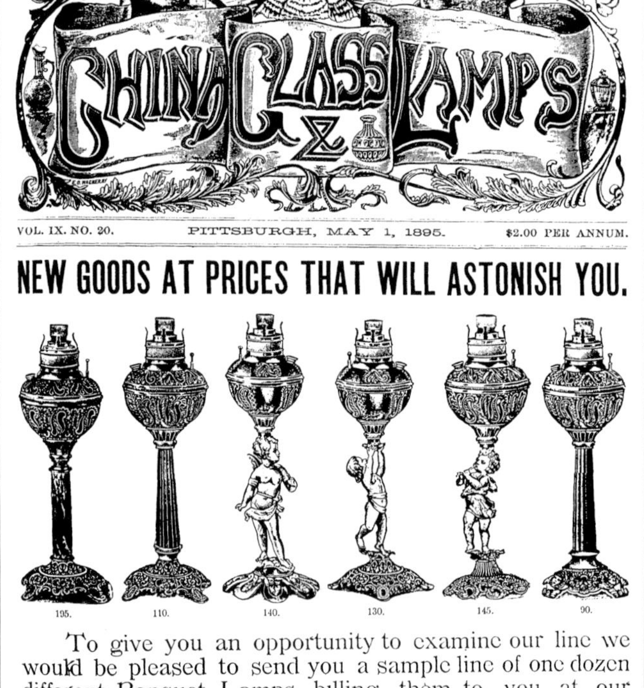

CHINA GLASS & LAMPS

VOL. IX. NO. 20. PITTSBURGH, MAY 1, 1895. $2.00 PER ANNUM.

NEW GOODS AT PRICES THAT WILL ASTONISH YOU.

195. 110. 140. 130. 145. 90.

To give you an opportunity to examine our line we would be pleased to send you a sample line of one dozen different Banquet Lamps, billing them to you at our quantity price, and if the prices and goods are not perfectly satisfactory you can return them at our expense.

HIPWELL MFG. CO.

ALLEGHENY, PA.

A PERFECT CENTER DRAUGHT LAMP.

BURNS A PURE WHITE STEADY LIGHT.

EQUAL TO ANY DUPLEX BURNER.

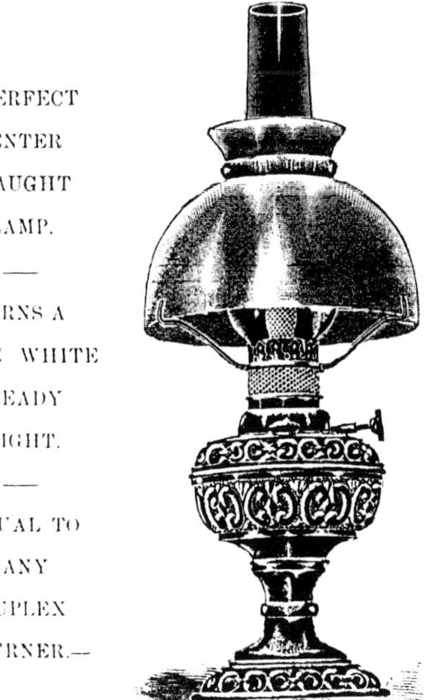

KEEPS —COOL— AND DRY.

A LITTLE BEAUTY.

THE MOST COMPLETE AND PERFECT WICK MOVEMENT.

H. H. HIPWELL MFG. CO., Allegheny, Pa.

New York Office, 16 Murray Street.

KNOCK DOWN!

Piano, Banquet and Vase Lamp Shade Holders.

12 DOZ. OF ANY SIZE IN A BARREL.

NOTHING LIKE IT.

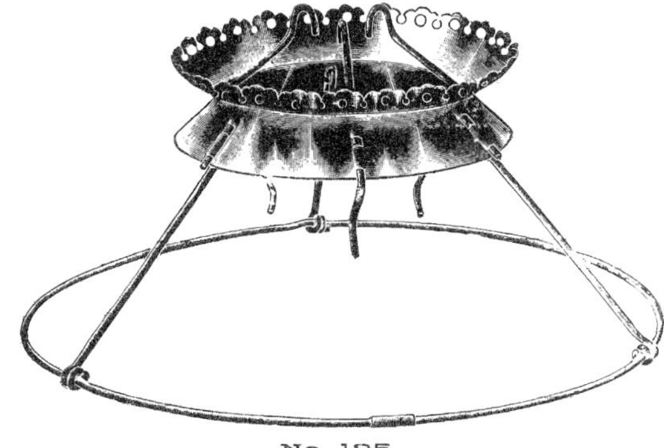

No. 125.

PRICES KNOCKED DOWN! COMPETITORS KNOCKED OUT!

MADE IN ALL SIZES. WRITE FOR PRICES,

—TO—

H. H. HIPWELL MFG. CO., Allegheny, Pa.

OR TO OUR

New York Office, 16 Murray Street.

Advertisement, *China, Glass and Lamps,* July 6, 1892.

The Victor

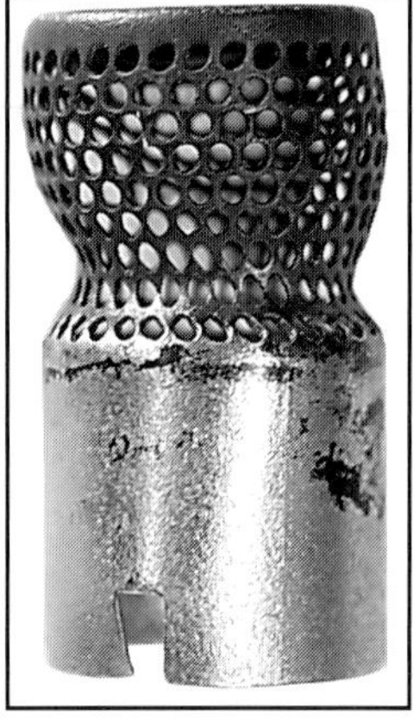

Victor No. 1 flame spreader. The top is plain, unmarked.

The Victor wick knob is marked "H. H. Hipwell Mfg. Co., Allegheny."

The Victor No. 1 junior lamp. Height 8". The top of the flame spreader is unmarked. The oil fill cap is plain. $225.00.

The Hipwell Lamp

Hipwell oil pot.

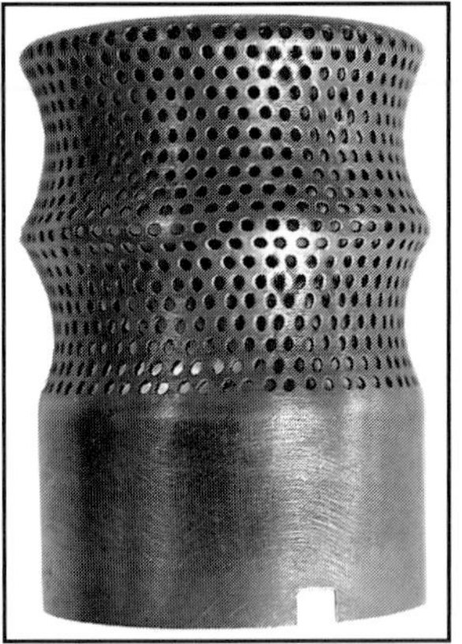

Hipwell waisted flame spreader found in Hipwell lamps. This shape and size is same as those from the M. E. Moore Bronze & Plate Co., Dithridge & Co., and the Washington Glass Mfg. Co. I assume Hipwell sold oil pots and burners to these companies.

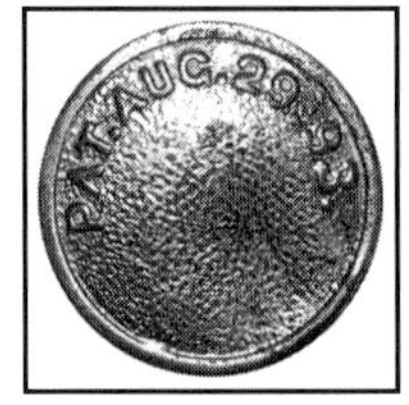

"Pat. Aug. 29 '93."

Oil fill caps found on Hipwell lamps.

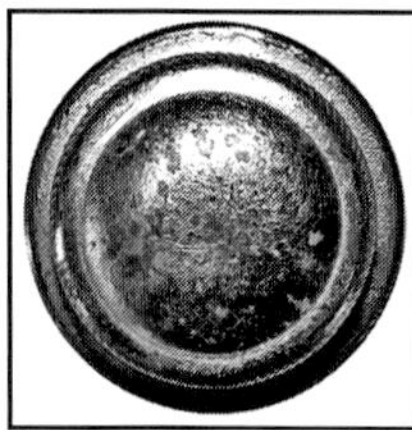

Vase lamp fitted with Hipwell oil pot. I do not know who made the glass or if Hipwell sold vase lamps. Height 20½". $275.00. Courtesy Hipwell Mfg. Co.

Hipwell stand lamp, fancy embossed fount. Height 11½". Two different cast-iron bases are found with this lamp. $250.00.

Other Products, Courtesy Hipwell Mfg. Co.

Hipwell gas mantle.

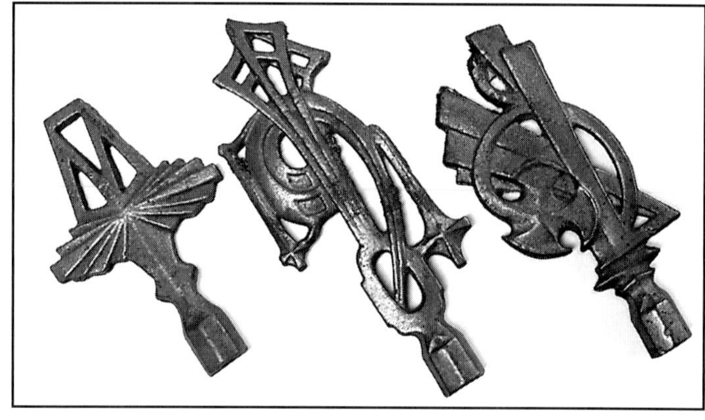

Cast-iron floor lamp finials.

Early Hipwell flashlight batteries, circa 1919.

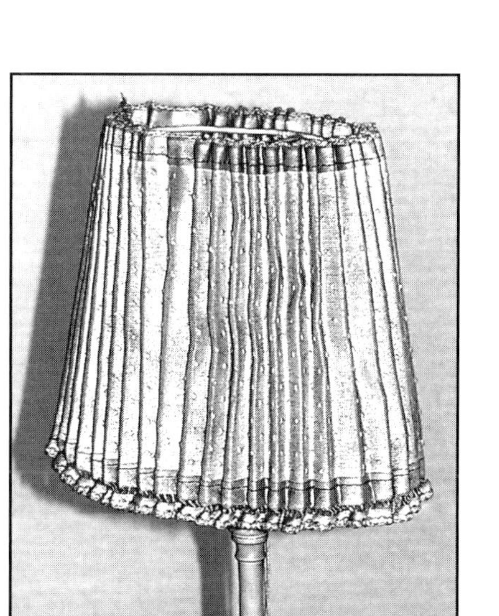

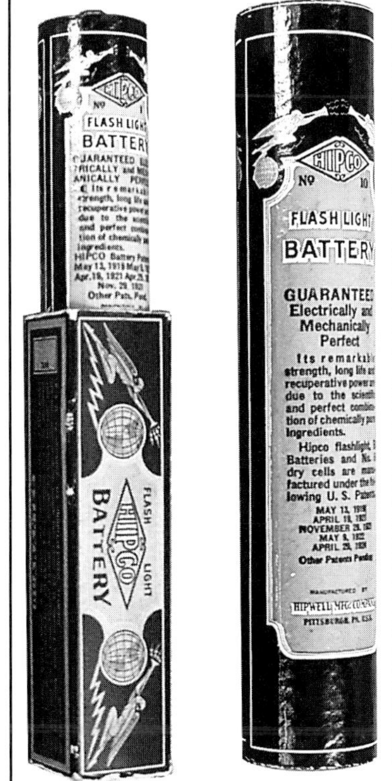

Hipwell batteries.

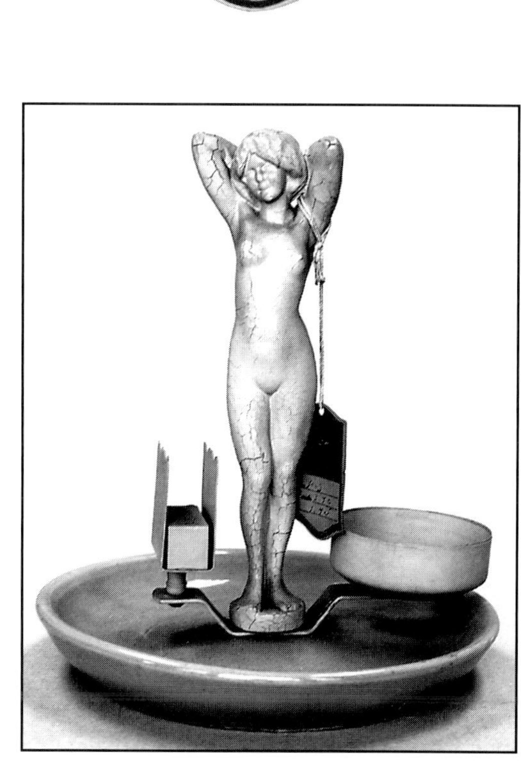

Cast white-metal Deco boudoir art lamp and smoking accessory.

Holmes, Booth & Haydens
1853 – 1912

Burner and Lamp Manufacture, 1860s – ca. 1912

Holmes, Booth & Haydens Company (HBH) was organized in Waterbury, Connecticut, by Israel Holmes in 1853 to roll and manufacture brass items on a large scale. Holmes was in charge of the rolling mill, Hiram W. Hayden was in charge of manufacturing, and H. H. Hayden in charge of marketing. John C. Booth was secretary. The company manufactured brass buttons for the military during the Civil War; knives, forks, and spoons; stoves; kettles; daguerreotype (photographic) plates; lamps; burners; and lanterns.

Hiram W. Hayden invented the brass spinning process in 1851 while he worked for Scovill Mfg. Company. Hayden's improvements in the spinning process gave the company an advantage in the manufacture of brass kettles and buckets.

Lewis J. Atwood worked for HBH, assigning patents for flat-wick burners to HBH, until Israel Holmes, Lewis Atwood, and John Booth left to form a new company named Holmes, Booth & Atwood in 1869. The latter was renamed Plume & Atwood in 1871.

The HBH nickel-silver business was bought by Rogers and Hamilton about 1886, which later became part of the International Silver Company.

Holmes, Booth & Haydens became part of American Brass Company in 1901, manufacturing kerosene lamps for some time after the consolidation.

Israel Holmes

Israel Holmes was born December 19, 1800. He became a teacher before entering the business world in 1830 to manufacture sheet metal and wire with Horace Hotchkiss and Philo Brown as the firm of Holmes and Hotchkiss. Two years later he was employed by J. M .L. and W. H. Scovill, who made metal buttons. The Scovills sent Holmes to Birmingham, England, to obtain technology and skilled workmen to improve their business. Holmes made three successful "raids" at extreme risk of fine or imprisonment under English law.

Lathrop (1926) stated: "It is no exaggeration to say that the (early) brass industry was imported from England in machinery, processes and labor."

Holmes left Scovill to help form the Wolcottville Brass Company to manufacture brass kettles in 1834. The kettles were hammered into shape from blanks. Holmes next organized and was president of the Waterbury Brass Company, formed in 1845. He bought Hiram W. Hayden's patent process for spinning, and as a result, Waterbury Brass soon controlled the manufacture of brass kettles, growing into the largest mill at that time.

In 1853 he formed the Holmes, Booth & Haydens company. According to Lathrop (1936), HBH was "the first company which, on a large scale, started out with a deliberate policy of manufacturing its own product." No doubt this success greatly influenced the destiny of Holmes, Booth & Atwood, which became Plume & Atwood.

Israel Holmes, 1800 – 1874.

The following account by Joseph Anderson (1896, pp. 325 – 326) describes the significant influence that Israel Holmes had in the brass rolling and manufacturing industry in Waterbury, Connecticut:

> In forming our estimate of the influence of Mr. Holmes's life upon the fortunes of his native town we are reminded of the saying of Augustus, that he "found Rome brick and left it marble." Of Israel Holmes, it is almost literally true that he found the manufactures of Waterbury wood and left them brass. It is due to him more than to any other man that the industrial activities of the place were directed into the prosperous course of brass manufacture. He was the original projector of the first "brass mill" proper that was ever established in the town; at his own risk and peril he brought over from England in three successive voyages the first skilled workmen for this and connected branches of industry (including the manufacture of German silver for spoons, forks, etc.), and of the five great brass mills now existing in the town, he was the first president of three. He devoted nearly thirty consecutive years to the development of Waterbury's brass industries. Among the industrial heroes — true knights of labor — who have won for the town its prosperity and given employment to its thousands of inhabitants, Israel Holmes should unquestionably be awarded a place in the first rank.

Holmes, Booth & Haydens was a major manufacturer of lamp burners, lanterns, kerosene lamps, and accessories. In 1883, the company claimed to have the "handsomest and most salable library lamps in the market." They introduced center-draft lamps by 1885, claimed the largest variety in the world by 1891, and offered 150 designs of lamps and lighting in 1899. Hiram W. Hayden was a prolific inventor, assigning many patents to the company. Lewis Atwood assigned at least six patents to the company before leaving in 1869.

The Star lamp was advertised before the patent was granted.

The HBH division of American Brass continued to produce lamps after the consolidation.

Trade Names

Center-draft lamps — Star, Star Electric, HB&H, Gladstone, Rival, Little Prince, Little Queen, Imperial Electric Lamp, Keystone, Prince, Gladstone, Perfect, Perfect Star, Search Light, Waterbury Electric.

Center-draft burners — Brighton, Brighton Electric, Victor Electric, Dual Electric.

Folded wick burners — Brilliant, New Brilliant, Waterbury Argand.

Flat wick burners — Sun, Sun Duplex, Standard Duplex, Star, Star Duplex, Waterbury Duplex, Aladdin (no chimney), Callender (no chimney), Windsor, Comet, Fireside, Unique, Richmond, and Pinafore.

Lanterns — HB&H.

Heaters — Tuxedo.

Selected Patents, Center-draft Lamps

Hiram W. Hayden[1] assigned to HBH

Year	Patent
1881	247,560
1881	247,561
1885	322,599
1888	390,079
1889	405,032
1894	513,638
1894	D23,809

Nicholas Jenkins assigned to HBH

Year	Patent
1885	320,476
1885	322,183

George W. McGill assigned to HBH

Year	Patent
1886	348,405

James F. Place

Year	Patent
1888	392,823 unassigned
1890	422,537 assigned to HBH
1893	509,324 unassigned

George C. Thomas

Year	Patent
1884	309,996 unassigned
1885	D16,078 unassigned

[1]Also many other patents.

Waterbury Electric

I believe the Waterbury Electric predates the Star Lamp, judging by patents on the burner base. The lamp used a flame spreader similar to the Star, with a wick extinguisher mechanism similar to the Perfect lamp (see next pages).

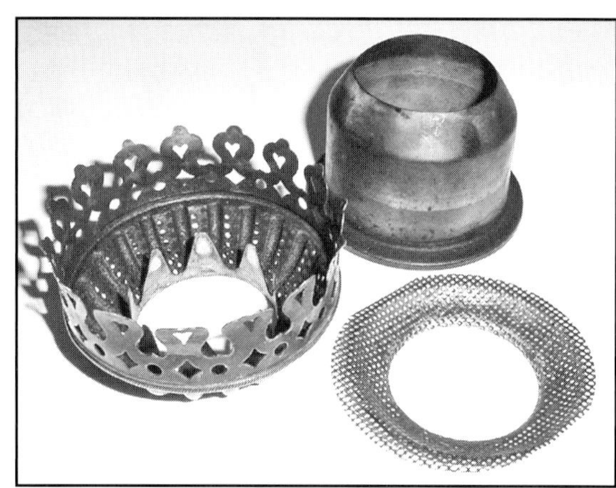

Burner gallery and parts.

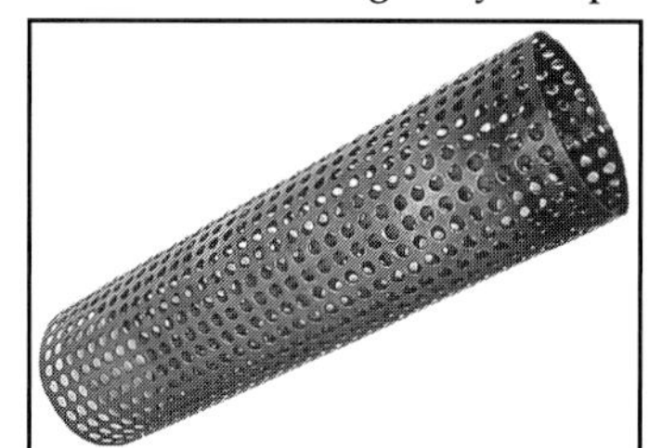

Wick carrier, 5" long.

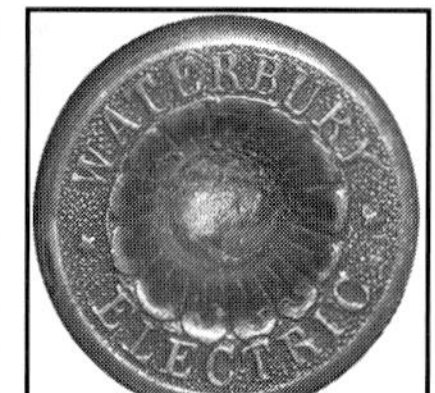

Wick knob.

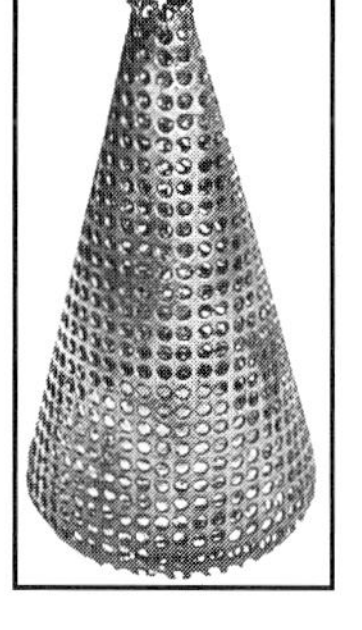

Screen found inside draft tube.

Waterbury Electric fount lamp. Height 8". Missing the flame spreader. The burner base is stamped: "Patented Aug. 16, 1870, June 13, 1871, Sept. 5, 1871, Sept. 27, 1881." $225.00. Courtesy Don Moore and Rick Valentine for photographs.

Star Lamp

A New Lamp

The newest thing in an oil-burning Argand lamp is Holmes, Booth & Hayden's "Star" lamp. Added to all the improvements of ordinary oil lamps, it possesses also a round wick, which is raised and lowered by a novel ratchet which never gets out of order. The flame deflector is a new contrivance which gives a cup-like form to the blaze, completely filling the largest size ordinary bulb chimney, forming a hollow flame 9" in circumference and equal to fifty candle power. Despite the fact of this immense light, almost electric in its glare, a chimney has never been known to break, and the flame will not smoke the chimney even though the wick is turned full up. Aside from this the lamp is absolutely non-explosive. In a word this "Star" lamp combines everything that is required in an oil burner. Several designs are shown, some in brass, others nickeled, and not a few to hang up and screw on gas chandeliers.

Pottery and Glassware Reporter, Jan. 29, 1885

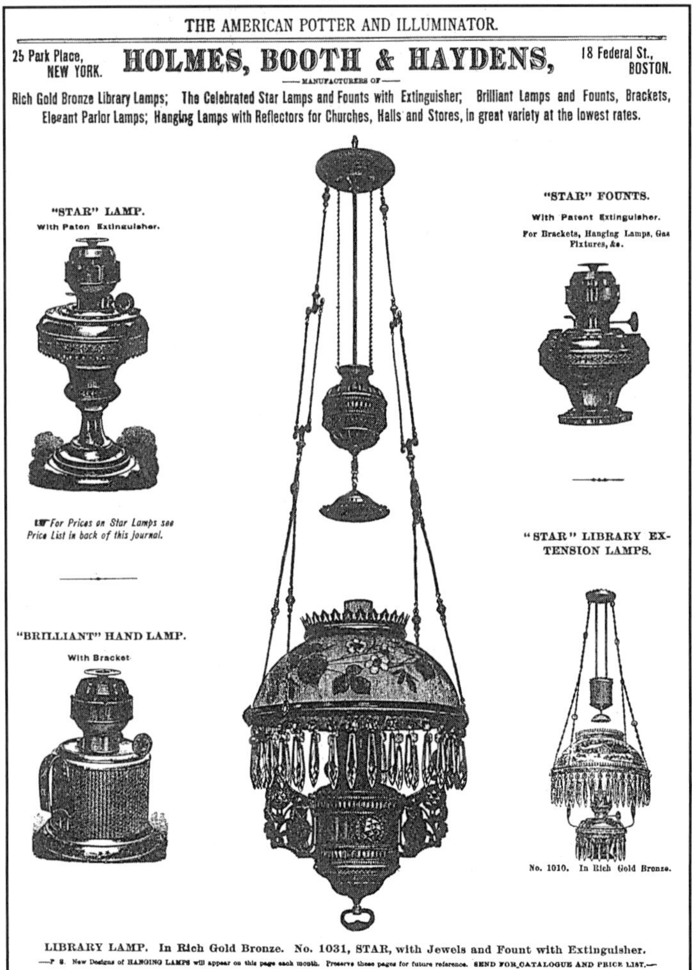

Advertisement, the *American Potter and Illuminator,* April 1886. These lamps were also sold by Henry and Nathan Russell in 1885.

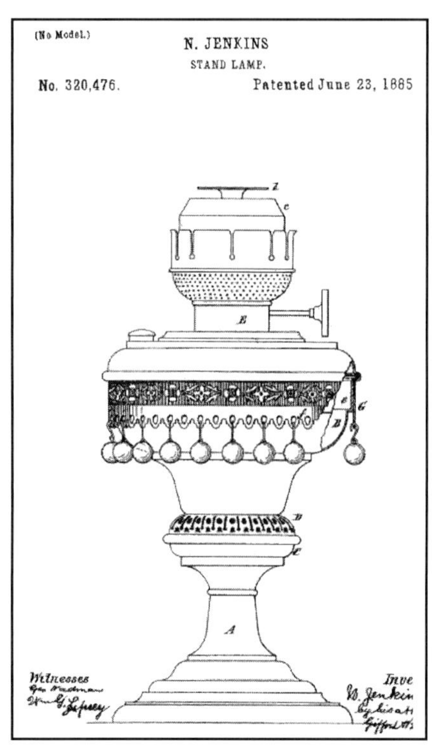

Star Lamp

Wick knob on Star lamps. The burner base is stamped "Patented Aug. 16, 1870, June 13, 1871, Sept. 5, 1871, Sept. 27, 1881, July 21, 1885."

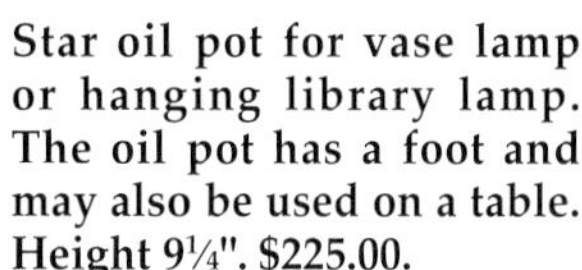

Star oil pot for vase lamp or hanging library lamp. The oil pot has a foot and may also be used on a table. Height 9¼". $225.00.

Star stand lamp. Height 12". The flame spreader is missing. There are two variations of burner screens of Star lamps. $250.00. Courtesy Fil Graff.

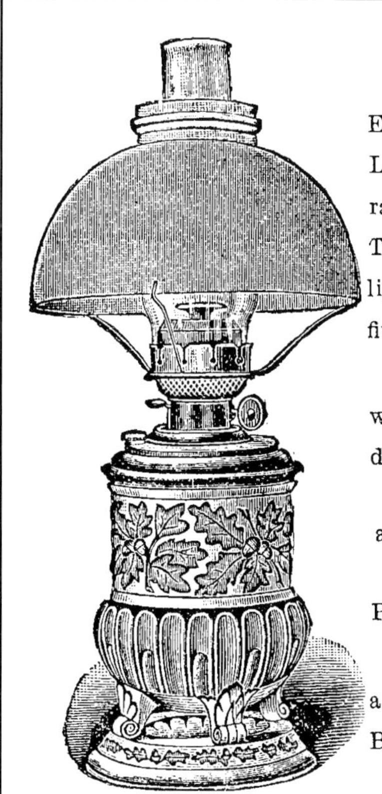

The No. 11 "STAR' ELECTRIC TABLE LAMP fitted to a decorated china stand. This lamp gives a light equal to sixty-five candles.

Fitted complete, with 10-inch plain dome shade.

An elegant bargain at our low price.

PRICE.

Per dozen.....

Packed ½ dozen in a barrel.

Barrels 35 cents each.

Star broadside advertisement. The pottery base is Avalon Faience by D. F. Haynes, Chesapeake Pottery, Baltimore. Courtesy Catherine Thuro.

The Perfect Lamp

This was an early center-draft lamp based on Hiram W. Hayden patents. The following patents are stamped in the neck portion of the burner: "PATENTED, Aug. 16, 1870 [106,363]"; "June 13, 1871 [115,955]"; "Sept. 5, 1871 [RE 4541]"; "Sept. 27, 1881 [247,560 and 247,561]"; "July 21, 1886 [error, should be July 21, 1885; 322,599]." The Perfect may predate the Star lamp.

Wick knob.

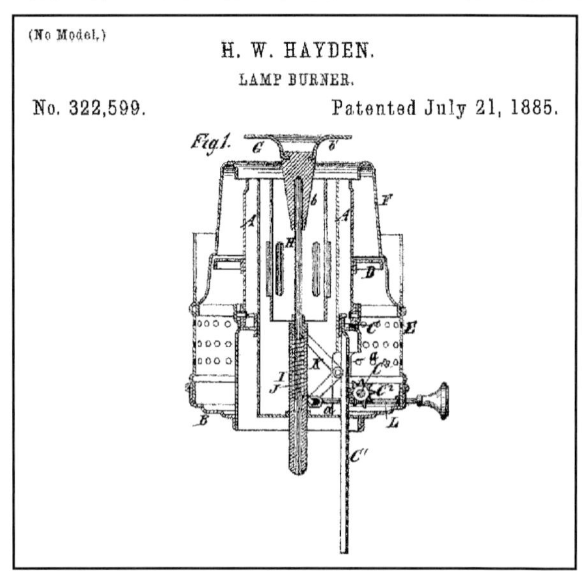

The Perfect stand lamp. Height 12½". Missing flame spreader and possibly part of burner. Lever raises and lowers the flame spreader. A mesh screen inside the gallery also raises and lowers with the flame spreader post. Lowering the flame spreader to extinguish the flame was safety feature of the time. $250.00. Courtesy Doug and Judy Myers.

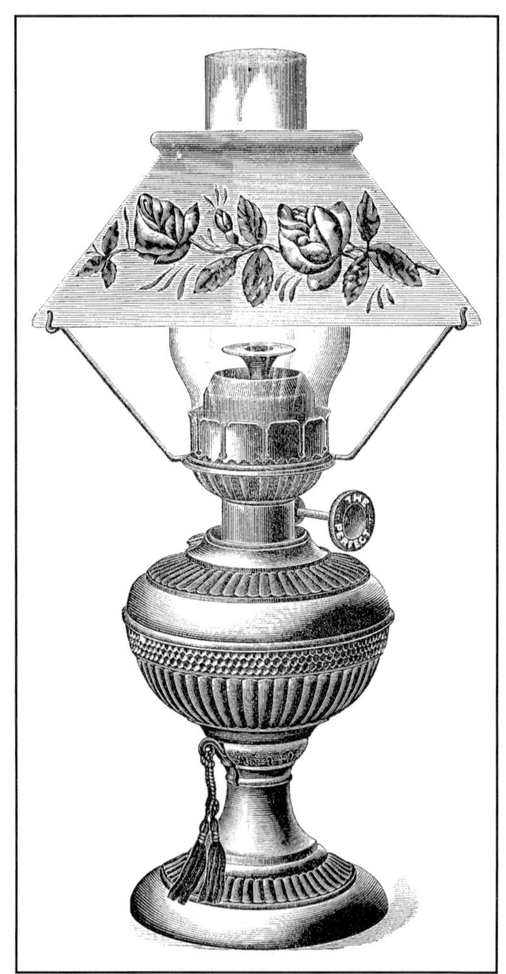
The Perfect stand lamp illustrated by Lovell Manufacturing Co. Limited, Erie, PA. Undated catalog advertised "Brilliant light, fifty candle power." I do not know any relationship with F. H. Lovell, NY. The embossed pattern is similar to one of the Keystone lamps.

The Gladstone Lamp, 1890 and Later

The Gladstone lamp was offered in many forms — stand, table, extension, and mammoth hanging. Holmes, Booth & Haydens advertised Gladstone lamps in 1890, claiming, "We manufacture the largest line and variety of Lamp Goods of any house in the world." The Gladstone was sold as the "Brass Electric Lamp" in the 1889 George F. Bassett catalog.

Gladstone flame spreader is marked on top "Pat. Applied For."

Extension Gladstone No. 2 stand lamp. *CGJ*, Dec. 11, 1890.

"The Gladstone" marked on top edge of fount.

Extension Gladstone, No. 2 stand lamp. Height 12½" unextended. The base is heavily weighted. $225.00. Courtesy Heinz and Ursula Baumann.

Broadside advertisement.
Courtesy David Broughton.

Gladstone lamps were exported in large numbers.

The Gladstone lamp may be signed on rim of the fount or along the base of the burner collar (see "sugar bowl" lamp below). Names on lamps helped the home owner to order the correct wick, flame spreader and chimney replacements.

The wick in Gladstone may be difficult to replace. It is easy to bend (push) the wick tube out of center in the process. The wick carrier is similar to Shaffer's patents and one in Lux-Dux lamps (see Shaffer Lamp Co.). A metal hook locks the wick carrier in place. There are two types of flame spreaders: long 2" versions and the short snap-on ones.

Flame spreader found in Gladstone and some Rival lamps.

The Gladstone wick carrier.

The Gladstone wick knob.

The Gladstone No. 2 table lamp ("Sugar Bowl"), 10" to top of wick tube. The snap-on flame spreader is missing. This flame spreader appears to be a smaller size than other HBH ones illustrated here. $250.00.

The Gladstone No. 2 fount lamp, 8½" tall. The top of the wick-raiser knob is marked "Gladstone, H. B. & H." $100.00.

The Rival, 1893 and Later

The Rival and Gladstone have common development features. Some flame spreaders found in both lamps snap into place on top of a specially formed wick tube.

I believe Rival lamps were sold over many years.

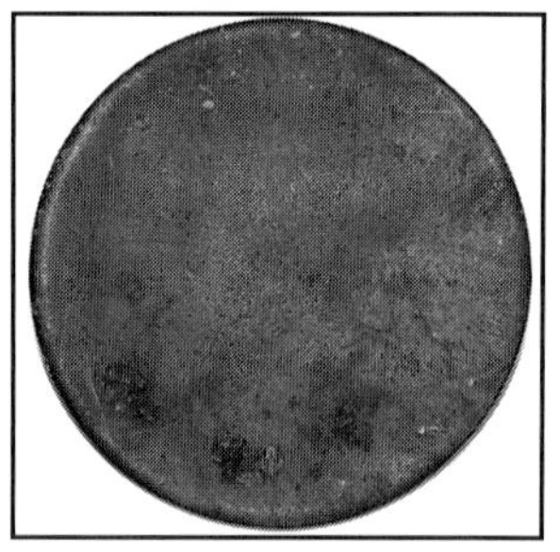

Flame spreader, 1" high, unmarked on top. This flame spreader plain or marked "Patent Appld For" on top.

"The Rival" in raised letters marked on top edge of fount.

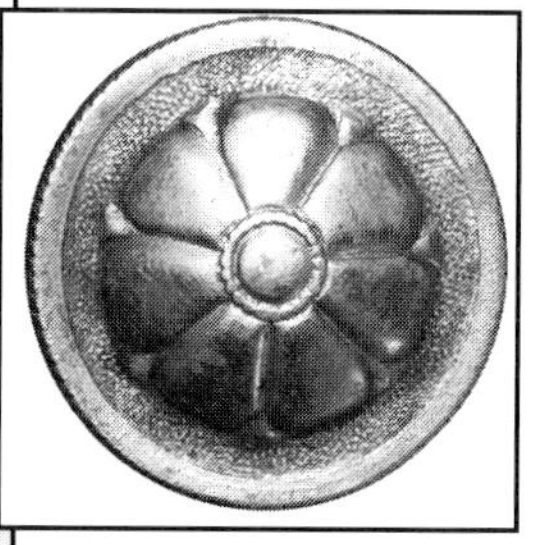

Oil fill.

"The Rival" No. 2 stand lamp. Height 12". Lift gallery. Note the screen on gallery top. This lamp has a flat loading weight. $175.00.

Flame spreader snapped into place.

Wick tube formed at the top to accept flame spreader.

Wick raiser bar and band. The band locks in place around the wick.

These Rival lamps were modified with a different wick tube, which accepts the more conventional flame spreader.

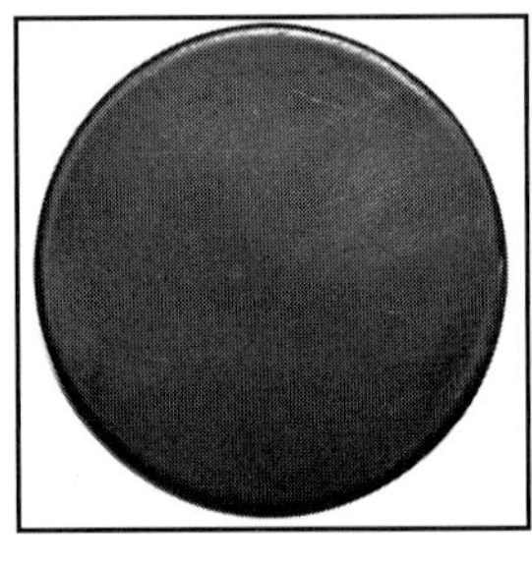

Flame spreader for Rival stand lamp. The top may be unmarked (above) or marked "Patent Appld For." Also see right.

"The Rival" logo is recessed in the top of the fount.

Rival No. 2 stand lamp. Height 11½". Lift gallery has no screen top. This lamp has a contoured loading weight and is also found with a cast-iron foot marked "HBH." $175.00.

An improved adjustable locking wick band for easier changing of wicks.

Flame spreader found in Rival hanging lamp fount. George Bohner was a wholesale jeweler in Chicago.

Oil fill found in Rival lamps.

Rival hanging lamp fount, marked "The Rival."

Rival Searchlight, George Bohner & Co. 1884 – 1920

GEORGE BOHNER & CO.
MANUFACTURERS & JOBBERS OF
GLASSWARE LAMPS CHANDELIERS
184 & 186 WABASH AV.
Chicago, Dec 7th 1891

Letterhead for George Bohner & Co., Chicago, 1891, claimed the company was "Manufacturers and Jobbers of Lamps and Glassware."

George Bohner & Company sold Rival Search Light lamps and apparently was a major reseller of lamps made by Holmes, Booth & Haydens in 1892.

George Bohner & Co. was listed in the *Lakeside Annual Directory of the City of Chicago* from 1884 to 1890. Bohner Manufacturing Company was listed in the *Chicago Business Directory* from 1905 to 1911.

George Bohner & Company was incorporated in June 1889 by Charles Morris, Joseph E. Bohner, and James F. Hogen. Mary A. Bohner and George Bohner were shareholders. The stated purpose of the company was to wholesale and retail lamp goods, gas and lamp fixtures, and electric lamps, and to manufacture these goods. The company also sold crockery, glassware, brass, bronze, and other metal goods.

Bill heads show the company doing business in 1886 at 55 and 57 Wabash Avenue, Chicago.

George Bohner held several patents for hanging and bracket lamps, including gas fixtures, from 1870 to 1885, and he most likely operated the lamp business as George Bohner & Co. before incorporation in 1889.

George Bohner held patent 732,334 for an incandescent vapor (gasoline) lamp in 1903 and was president of the Brilliant Gas Lamp Company in 1904.

I do not know the relationship between George and Joseph Bohner. I suspect they were father and son or brothers in the lamp business. Joseph moved to Ansonia to work for Wallace & Sons about 1891.

Selected Patents, Center-draft Lamps

Joseph E. Bohner[1] Chicago, Illinois

Year	Patent
1890	418,782
1890	439,718
1895	538,862

[1]Joseph Bohner held at least one patent (311,224) with George Bohner. By 1891 Joseph had moved to Ansonia, where he assigned patents to Wallace & Sons.

The Hayden

No doubt, the Hayden lamp was named for either H. H. or Hiram Hayden. The Hayden and the Perfect both used a mushroom-type flame spreader. They are interesting lamps that demand more study.

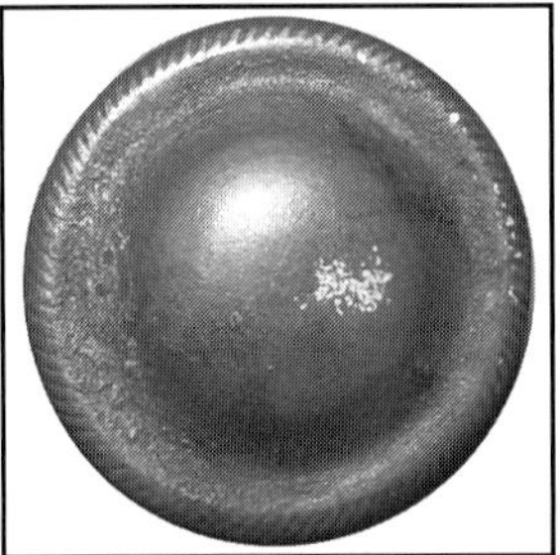

Oil fill cap.

The Hayden stand lamp. Height 12¾" to top of chimney clips. Missing flame spreader. Lever raises and lowers the flame spreader, supported by a central pin. Push-pull wick raiser. Redesigned burner basket, gallery, and chimney clips. Marked "The Hayden" on the top edge of the fount. $150.00.

Keystone 1891 – 1894 and Later

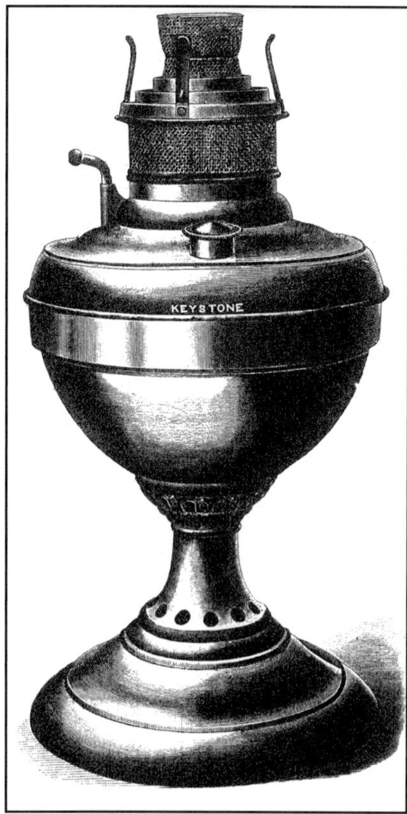

Oil fill cap.

No. 1 Keystone flame spreader.

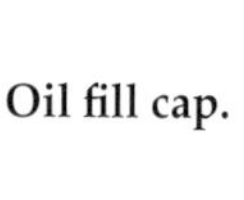

Oil fill cap.

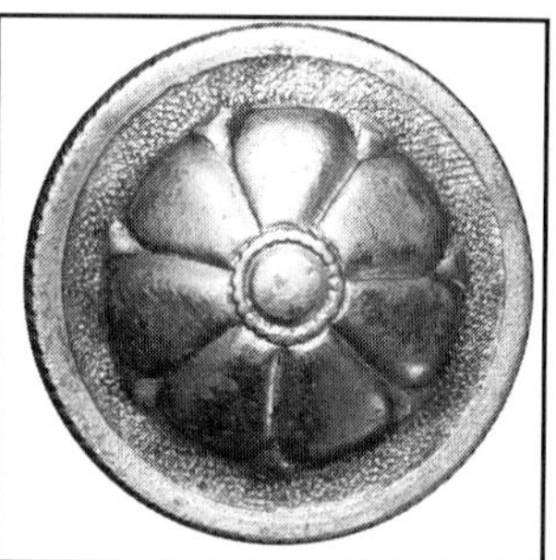

Keystone No. 2 stand lamp marked "Keystone" on top edge of fount. Otherwise same fount as illustrated above (*CGJ,* May 14, 1891) and similar to Hayden (on previous page). Non–lift gallery. Height 12". The top half of flame spreader missing. The diameter of flame spreader is 1⅛" to snap-on the wick tube.

Keystone No. 1 stand lamp (unmarked). Height 10". This lamp was advertised in *China, Glass and Lamps,* Oct. 26, 1892, and was possibly the same lamp sold as Our Darling by Haida. $150.00.

Keystone No. 2 oil pot marked "Keystone" below the burner collar. Lift gallery. Unmarked flame spreader.

Keystone wick raiser matches the patent below.

Keystone banquet lamp, marble base, illustrated with Gladstone oil pot in *CGJ*, Dec. 3, 1891. Height 18½". $275.00. Courtesy Kent Stratton.

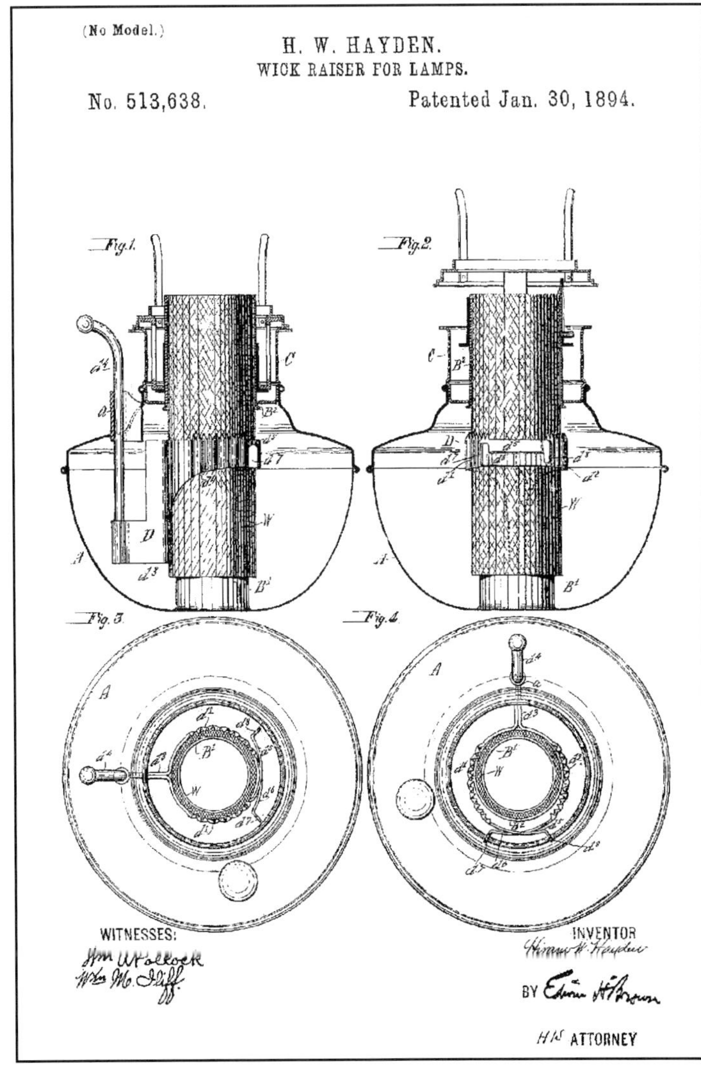

Little Prince and Little Queen

Plain (not embossed) Little Prince lamps were marked "Little Prince" on top of the fount.

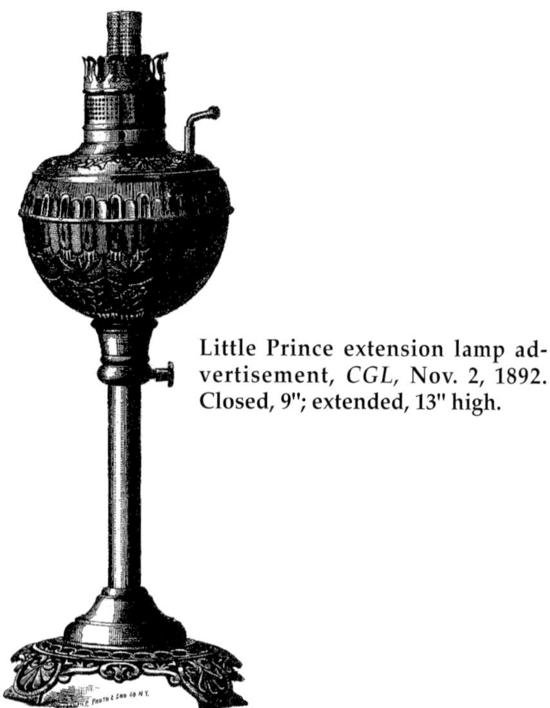

Little Prince extension lamp advertisement, *CGL*, Nov. 2, 1892. Closed, 9"; extended, 13" high.

Little Prince. Height 7½". $275.00.
Courtesy Mel Soderholm.

Little Prince. Height 8⅜". $175.00. Courtesy Kent Stratton.

Little Queen missing flame spreader. Height 5½". $150.00.
Courtesy Eileen White.

The Admiral

The quality of detail and finishing this lamp is suberb. I suspect Admiral lamps were made primarily as banquet or parlor lamps for higher-price markets. Much of the original gold finish is thin and worn on this lamp.

Burner with original shade ring attached.

The flame spreader for this lamp locks into place at the top of the specially formed wick tube. The Admiral flame spreader was also made in long form to slip into the wick tube of some lamps (see previous page).

This lamp also seen as an angel with wings.

The Admiral banquet lamp. Height 22½". The lamp is marked "Patent Appl'd For" in two places. $350.00.

The Admiral

I believe the Admiral lamps were made by Holmes, Booth & Haydens (HBH) based on design features and the wick tube construction. The flame spreader signed "The Admiral" also provides positive identification.

The lamp illustrated here was made after 1900, possibly after Holmes, Booth & Haydens became a division of American Brass Company.

I do not know if the Admiral was a branded product of HBH, a department store, or of an unknown distributor.

Other companies that sold the Admiral branded goods included Chicago Wheel Works, Chicago, Illinois, in 1896; Davis Cycle Co., Chicago, Illinois, in 1896 – 1898; and Admiral Bicycle Lamp Co., Columbus, Ohio, ca. 1908 – 1910.

The Admiral flame spreader found in the lamp below.

The Admiral wick raiser.

Admiral No. 2 stand lamp, cast-iron foot. Height 12½". $225.00. Courtesy Doug and Judy Myers.

Wick Carrier Lamps — American Brass Co.

I believe these lamps were sold after 1901 when Holmes, Booth & Haydens became an operating division of the newly formed American Brass Company. See list of distributors on next page.

Burner with wick carrier.

Wick knob.

J. D. Boyd & Co.

$100.00.

Unmarked No. 2 stand lamp. Burner base and gallery similar to The Admiral. The wick raiser, however, now uses a wick carrier which I believe was developed after 1900. Height 12½". $175.00.

Tuxedo

Tuxedo oil pot possibly sold by Simmons Hardware Co. This pot found with screen in bottom of wick tube (see above left). $75.00.

Lamps Sold to Other Distributors, Based on Flame Spreaders

H. W. Hayden's patent confirms origin of flame spreaders made by Holmes, Booth & Haydens. The early spreaders had smooth bases, as illustrated in the patent. I believe the ones without the notch and with an incised groove near the bottom were made after 1900.

Short Snap-on Flame Spreaders

Plain, unmarked top
Patent Appl'd For
The Admiral
Chautauqua

Long Flame Spreaders Companies and Dates Formed

Plain, unmarked top.................................. Patent Appl'd For
The Admiral
The George Bohner Rival Search Light, Chicago
J. D. Boyd & Co.
Byesville (Byesville Glass & Lamp Co. 1899)
Cox & Day Search Light, New York (courtesy Fil Graff)
Ellwood (Ellwood City Glass Co. 1905)
Fort Pitt (Combined Pittsburgh Brass Co. 1902)
Jefferson (Jefferson Glass Co. 1900)
NB&IW (National Brass & Iron Works 1891) (courtesy Fil Graff)
Tuxedo (Sold by Simmons Hardware 1908)

DESIGN.

No. 23,809. Patented Nov. 13, 1894.

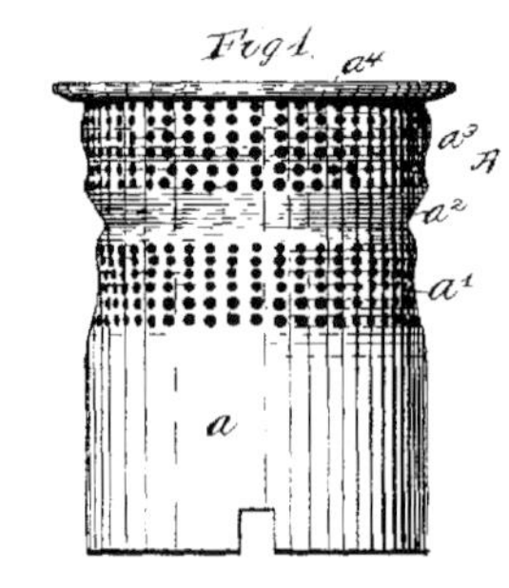

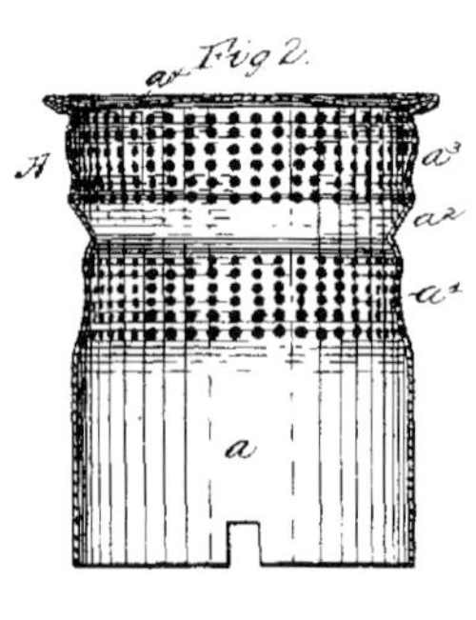

Left, snap-on; right, long with notch and long with groove.

The H.B.&H. Lamp — American Brass Co.

This H.B.&H. Lamp is marked with Joseph Gregory patents. Gregory did not assign most of his patents, collecting royalties from Manhattan Brass and Holmes, Booth & Haydens. An interesting note about this lamp is that three patents stamped in the flame spreader (653,449, 1900; 661,517, 1900; 693,006, 1902) all seem to refer to the Manhattan Smokeless lamp. However, Gregory's unassigned patent 594,007 (1897) seems to illustrate most features of the H.B.&H. Lamps photographed here.

H.B.&H. flame spreader, marked with three patents, for lamp lower left. This flame spreader is also found marked "H.B.&H., Made in U. S. A."

H.B.&H. flame spreader, marked with three patents, for lamp below.

The H.B.&H. Lamp. Height 12½". Wick knob of both lamps marked "Made in U. S. A." $175.00. Courtesy Fil Graff.

The H.B.&H. Lamp with self extinguishing flame spreader, Gregory patents. Height 12½". The tops of both flame spreaders are marked with the same patents. These lamps were sold after Holmes, Booth & Haydens became part of American Brass Company. I do not know how long American Brass continued to sell lamps and trimmings. Courtesy William Schreiber.

Judd Manufacturing Co.

Lamp Manufacture ca. 1893 – 1895

The Judd Mfg. Company, founded in 1869, moved to Wallingford, Connecticut, in 1877. Officers were Morton Judd, president; A. D. Judd, treasurer; F. T. Bristol, secretary; and E. M. Judd, superintendent.

The company manufactured upholstery and stationary hardware, brass and iron bedsteads, onyx and brass tables, cabinets and art metal furniture, and fancy goods.

I know very little about Wallingford lamps except information found in advertisements.

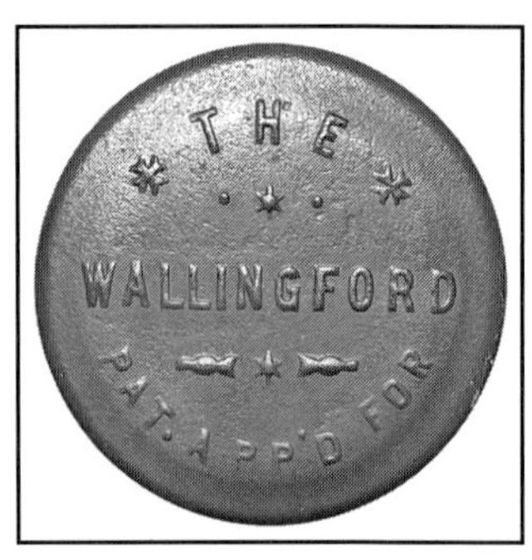

"The Wallingford flame spreader, Pat. App'd For," 1¼" diameter.

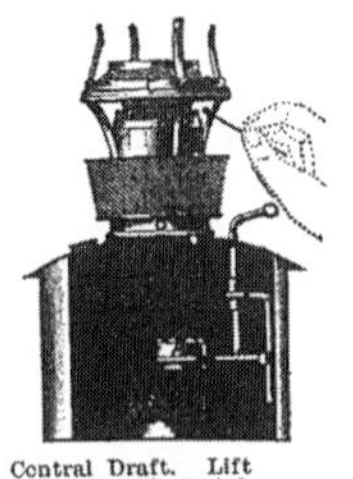

VASE LAMPS OF UNIQUE POTTERY,
BANQUET AND PIANO LAMPS
Fitted with our
NEW "WALLINGFORD" BURNER!

Advertisement, *Crockery and Glass Journal*, September 29, 1893.

H. L. JUDD & CO.,
87 and 89 Chambers St.,
NEW YORK.

Upholstery Hardware, Bedsteads, etc.

BANQUET LAMPS. PIANO LAMPS.

ENTIRELY NEW LINE.
ORIGINAL! ARTISTIC! NOVEL!

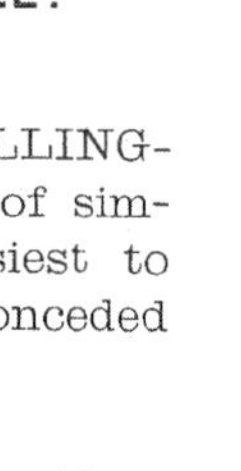

All fitted with our NEW "WALLINGFORD" BURNER, which is the acme of simplicity, and is the most efficient, easiest to light, quickest to wick, cleanest, and conceded to be the best burner on the market.

No. 9871.

FACTORIES:—Brooklyn, N. Y.; Wallingford, Conn.; Chattanooga, Tenn.

Advertisement, *Crockery and Glass Journal*, November 9, 1893.

Lane Manufacturing Company

1888 – 1905

Lamp Manufacture ca. 1889 – 1900

Opportunity knocks. The growing lamp market of the 1890s and the opportunity to buy W. J. Gordon Lamp Works and incentives from Chicago Brass Company to produce lamps in the midwest are possible reasons why Lane Manufacturing Company was organized in Kenosha, Wisconsin.

Lane Manufacturing Company was incorporated Nov. 13, 1888, to manufacture lamps and other brass and wood novelties. Incorporators were G. M. Simmons, W. W. Strong, and James Cavanaugh.

Investors purchased the equipment and tools of the W. J. Gordon Company. Lane Mfg. advertised a full line of fancy metal lamps in 1890 (Aug. 21, *CGJ*), stating that Lane "owned all of the patents," including those for Perkins & House Safety Lamps. Fred Keevan, previously in charge of the W. J. Gordon Lamp Works, moved from Cleveland to Kenosha as superintendent to organize the new plant.

Published records of company officers do not agree. My information primarily comes from Kenosha city directories. Gilbert Simmons was the first president, but he died Jan. 15, 1890. Other officers were F. W. Lane, vice president, and W. W. Strong, secretary and treasurer. E. D. Tuttle replaced Simmons as president and Frederick Robinson replaced Lane as vice president.

The Chicago Brass Company was organized in 1886 in Kenosha with skilled workers brought from the Naugatuck Valley in Connecticut (Lathrop, 1926). E. D. Tuttle, vice president and plant superintendent, moved from Waterbury, Connecticut. Chicago Brass furnished raw materials to Lane. The Chicago Brass Company was purchased by the Coe Brass Company in 1901 and, shortly thereafter, became part of the American Brass Company.

Advertisement, *Pottery and Glassware Reporter*, July 6, 1893.

Lane made a variety of kerosene lamps and apparently supplied F. H. Lovell with lamps for several years. Advertisements from 1892 to 1895 illustrate table lamps, hand lamps, hanging lamps, student lamps, banquet lamps, vase lamps, and piano lamps. Lovell sold Lane products under the Mogul brand name.

Lane Manufacturing was purchased by Sieg and Walpole Mfg. Co. about 1895 with financial backing of Frank S. Osborne, Chicago. Sieg and Walpole manufactured the Windsor bicycle. I suspect that Sieg and Walpole operated Lane Mfg. as a division for a number of years. The state of Wisconsin dissolved Lane Mfg. Co. in 1905.

The Solar bicycle lamp was made by the Badger Brass Mfg. Co., Kenosha. I do not know if this was also a division of Sieg and Walpole.

Lamp manufacturing continued after much of the Lane plant was destroyed by fire in 1893. The 1895 and 1898 Lovell catalogs included several lamps manufactured by Lane.

Trade Names

Center-draft lamps — Aurora, New Aurora, Gem, Volcano, Magnum, Improved Magnum ("best mammoth lamp made, 300 cp"), Cleveland Student Lamp, Perkins & House's Non-Explosive Lamps.

Lane Manufacturing Company

Lane Manufacturing Company was an aggressive marketer. The company made a variety of center-draft lamps and onyx tables for other distributors. Lane New Aurora lamps are commonly found today. The company competed by advertising low prices.

I have no information on Lane's "Fine Art Pottery Lamps," introduced in 1891. The company sold No. 1 lamps under the Volcano brand.

Lane continued to manufacture lamps, such as the Cleveland Student Lamp, previously made by W. J. Gordon and the Cleveland Non-Explosive Lamp Companies.

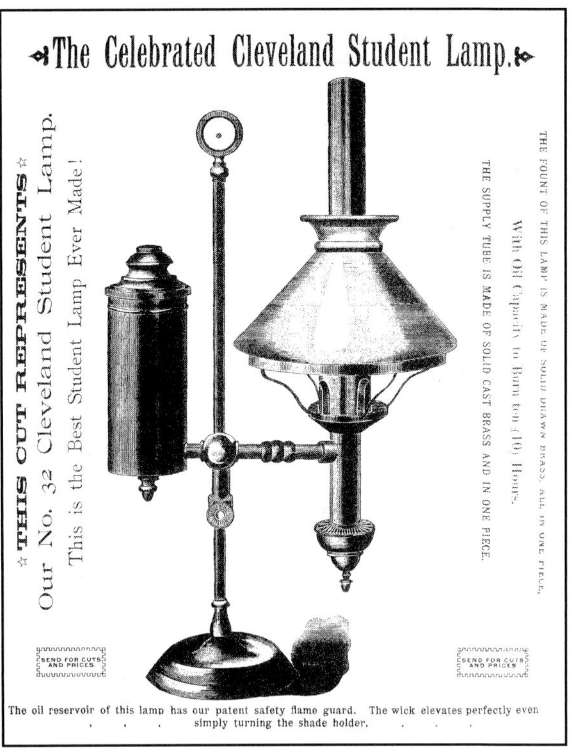

Lane advertisement, *CGL*, Sept. 2, 1891.

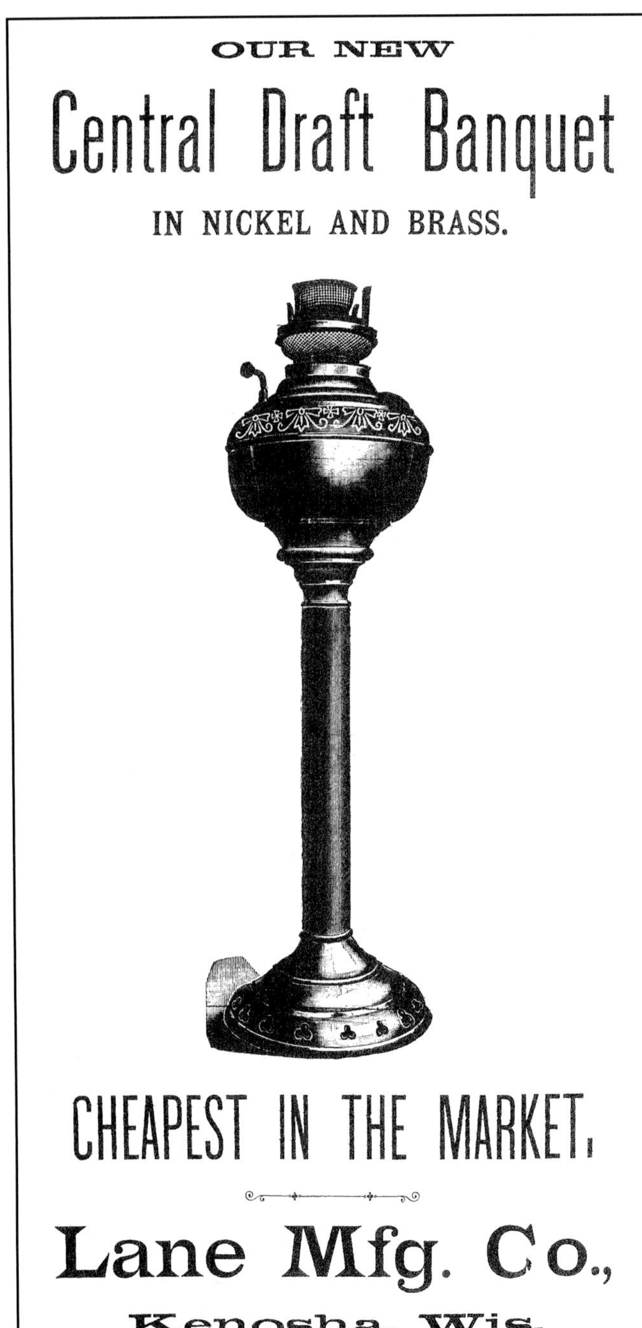

Advertisement, *CGL*, July 6, 1892.

New Aurora No. 2 stand lamp, embossed chime. Plain, non-embossed lamps are commonly found. This lamp is also found with No. 2 Gem flame spreader. Height 11½". $125.00.

New Aurora

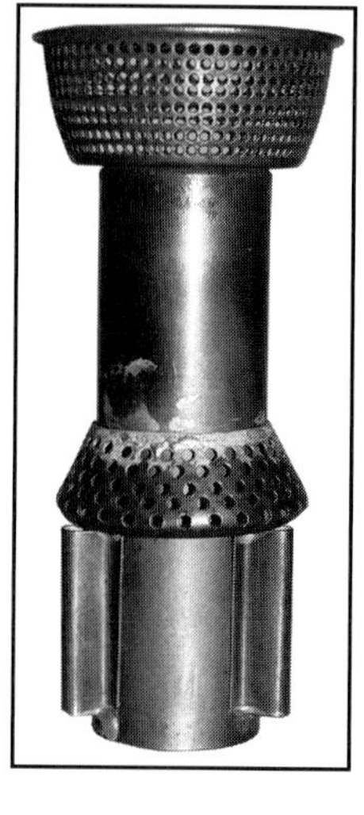

There are two versions of New Aurora flame spreaders that vary in length (3½" and 4⅝" long).

Oil fill cap, Lane lamps. Courtesy Doug and Judy Myers.

New Aurora oil pot with Aurora burner. Lane called its oil pot a "lift-out fount, fount lamp, or detachable fount." $75.00. Courtesy Doug and Judy Myers.

New Aurora No. 2 stand lamp with floral embossed fount. Height 11". $150.00.

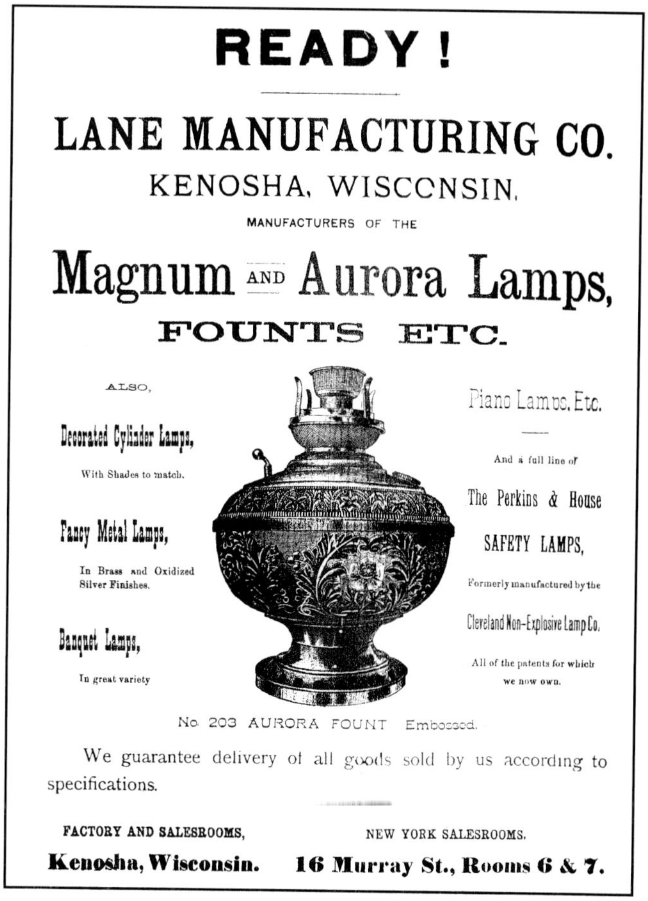

READY!

LANE MANUFACTURING CO.

KENOSHA, WISCONSIN.

MANUFACTURERS OF THE

Magnum AND Aurora Lamps,

FOUNTS ETC.

ALSO,

Decorated Cylinder Lamps,

With Shades to match.

Fancy Metal Lamps,

In Brass and Oxidized Silver Finishes.

Banquet Lamps,

In great variety

Piano Lamps, Etc.

And a full line of

The Perkins & House

SAFETY LAMPS,

Formerly manufactured by the

Cleveland Non-Explosive Lamp Co.

All of the patents for which we now own.

No. 203 AURORA FOUNT Embossed.

We guarantee delivery of all goods sold by us according to specifications.

FACTORY AND SALESROOMS, **Kenosha, Wisconsin.**

NEW YORK SALESROOMS. **16 Murray St., Rooms 6 & 7.**

Advertisement, *CGJ*, Aug. 21, 1890.

New Aurora

New Aurora No. 2 stand lamp, embossed fount. This lamp uses a short flame spreader. The little ball on the pull rod is missing. Height 11½". $150.00.

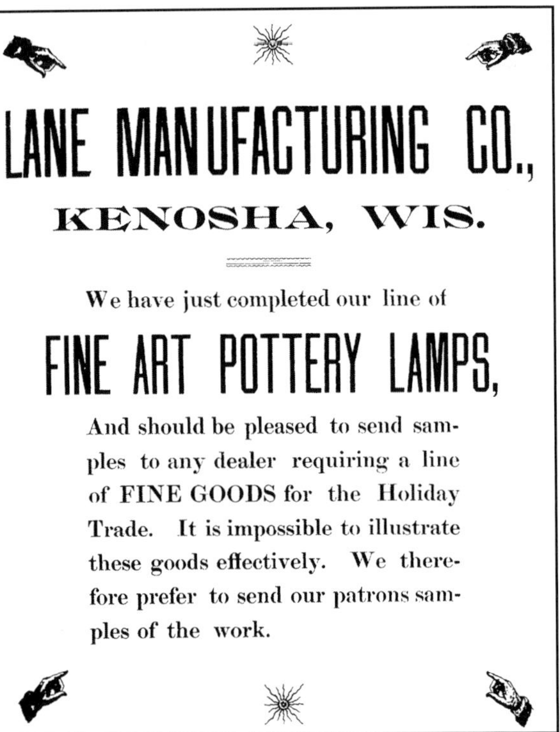

Advertisement, *Pottery & Glassware Reporter,* Aug. 13, 1891. Lane offered vase lamps beginning in 1890 fitted with flat-wick burners or with oil pots and center-draft Aurora burners.

INCORPORATED 1850.

Lane Manufacturing Company,

MANUFACTURERS OF

METAL BUTTONS

AND FANCY METAL GOODS.

SUSPENDER AND GARTER BUCKLES AND TRIMMINGS, ORNAMENTS, ETC.

Specialties from Brass and other Metals Made to Order.

FACTORY: 50 NORTH ELM STREET, WATERBURY, CONN.

1910 advertisement, *Waterbury City Directory.* I have no information on Lane Mfg. during this time period. It may be the same company that moved part of its operation to Kenosha in 1888.

Advertisement, *Pottery and Glassware Reporter,* May 4, 1892.

Lane Mfg. Flame Spreaders

Lane manufactured lamps that may be found with these brand flame spreaders. A company that bought enough lamps could justify having its names embossed on the top of the flame spreader. Lane flame spreaders vary in length from 4½" to 4⅝". Short 3½" flame spreaders are found in New Aurora and Gatch & Lauman lamps. The M. E. Moore flame spreader is 3¾" long. The long spreaders are interchangeable. The flame spreaders push into the center tube with some resistance. As a result, the top screens are easily bent or compressed, and the lamp will not burn properly. There is also a No. 3 Volcano flame spreader.

"No. 2 Gem."

"The Grand Rapids Lamp, H. L. & Sons." Courtesy Kent Stratton.

"Wemott, Howard & Co., St. Paul, Minn." Courtesy Doug Myers.

"M. E. Moore B. & P. Co, New York."

"No. 2 Volcano."

"Paragon, Peaslee Gaulbert Co., Louisville, KY." Courtesy Kent Stratton.

"C. L. Knapp & Co., Leavenworth, Kansas."

"Usher & Osborne, Boston, Mass."

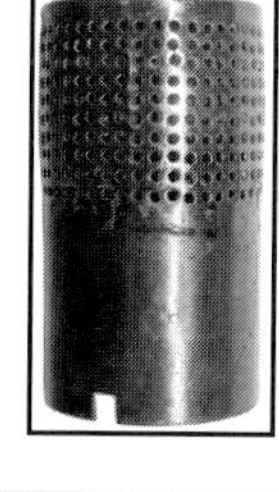

"No. 1 Volcano," 1¾" long, 15/16" diameter. Courtesy Kent Stratton.

"Gatch Lauman Lamp, Omaha."

"New Magnum, Kenosha, Wis."

Montgomery Ward & Co.'s Central Draft Metal Table and Hand Lamps.

We have selected this burner (after a careful comparison with all others) as being the very best; it will give more light according to the amount of oil consumed than any other lamp made. Try one and you will be more than pleased.

55634 Our World Beater Central Draft Table Lamp made of polished and embossed brass, good size, will hold more than enough oil for a long evening; trimmed complete with tripod, chimney, wick and 10-inch plain dome shade. Price....$1.75
55636 Same as 55634, Nickel plated. Price...2.00

Montgomery Ward catalog advertisement for lamp made by Lane Mfg. Co. The flame spreader is 4½" long and marked "Montgomery Ward & Co., Chicago."

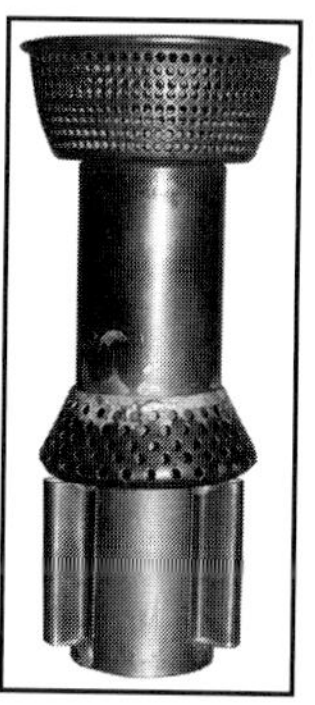

Gatch Lauman flame spreader, length 3½".

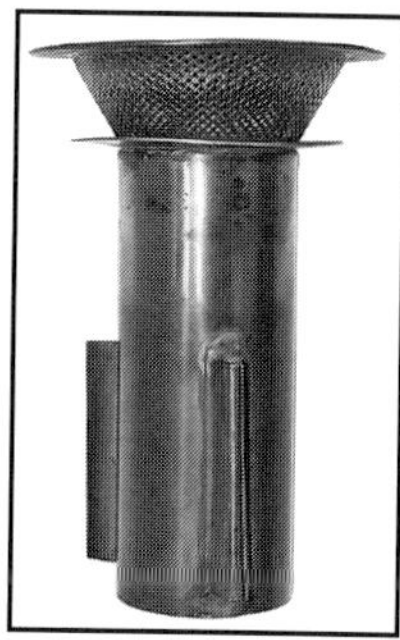

New Magnum for hanging lamp. Length 4¾". Courtesy Doug and Judy Myers.

F. H. Lovell & Co.
1864 – 1922

Lovell-Dressel Company, Inc., 1922 – 1968

F. H. Lovell & Company was a major importer and exporter of domestic, marine, and railroad lighting — a worldwide distributor of all types of lighting. Lovell sold lamps and burners made by Bristol Brass, Belgian, Rochester, Bradley & Hubbard, and most lamp companies over the years. Some lamps were branded for Lovell on flame spreaders, fill caps, and wick knobs.

Thuro (2001) stated that the "F. H. Lovell & Co. was the most important lamp merchant in America!" This conclusion stems from the number of catalogs and the vast inventory of lamps sold of numerous manufacturers. Read Thuro (2001) and Nelson (1989) for more information, history, and brands of lamps sold. Thuro (1989) has reproduced numerous pages of lamps in Lovell catalogs 1868/1869 and 1877/1878. The Rakow Library has numerous Lovell catalogs on microform.

F. H. Lovell & Co. was founded in New York as a wholesale distributor. The company moved to a new warehouse and factory in Arlington, New Jersey, in 1901. The company was bought by Adams and Westlake, Chicago, in 1970.

Many catalogs list Lovell as a manufacturer; however, Thuro and Nelson believe in-house manufacturing did not occur until after 1900. Prior to the move to New Jersey, Lovell had lamps custom made for it. I show some re-branded center-draft lamps here and identify the manufacturer.

F. H. Lovell & Co. exhibited kerosene lamps, burners, chimneys, and wicks in 1876 at the Centennial Exposition in Philadelphia.

Lovell bought rights to the Hitchcock mechanical lamp in 1898 and manufactured them for 20 years.

Lovell began selling lamps made by the Dressel Lamp and Railway Signal Company in 1887. Lovell bought the Dressel Railway Lamp Works in 1922. The Lovell-Dressel Company manufactured extensive railroad lighting and marine lighting for the Coast Guard and the U.S. Navy.

Trade Names

Center-draft lamps — Bristol Electric Lamps, Mogul, Improved Mogul, Fancy Mogul, Great Mogul. These lamps appear to have been made by Bristol Brass Clock Company and Lane Mfg. Company. In the 1898 catalog, Lovell sold Bradley & Hubbard lamps, Ansonia lamps, Belgian lamps, and Manhattan Brass lamps.

Flat-wick burner — Drummond.

Mechanical lamps — Hitchcock, Patent Mechanical lamp.

F. H. LOVELL & CO.,

MANUFACTURERS OF

Lamps, Lamp Trimmings, Wick,

CHIMEEYS, LANTERNS, ETC.

Patentees and Sole Manufacturers of the

Drummond Light Burner & Chimney,

Best In Use.

The merits of this Burner are:—That the body of the Burner being opened between the base-plate and the collar of the lamp, allows free circulation of air, and the brass gauze covering the whole surface of the burner, absolutely prevents explosion or heating, and any kind of oil can be used. The No. 1 Burner uses a 5-8 inch wick, and the No. 2 uses a ¾ inch wick, and owing to their peculiar construction, the No. 1 will give as much light as any No. 2 Burner; and the No. 2 will give more light than any No. 3 or Mammoth Burner now in use, and this without any peroeptible difference in the use of oil.

The Drummond Chimney is made from the best flint metal, and we guarantee it not to break from heat.

Patentees and Sole

Manufacturers of the Cyclops Sun Chimney,

Vulcan & Centaur Bulb Sun Chimneys and the Star Sun Chimneys.

The Cyclops Chimney will give ⅓ more light from an ordinary Sun Burner than any other Chimney in existence.

These Chimneys areall made from best Flint Glass and are warranted to give perfect satisfaction.

LECOUNT'S PATENT FELT WICK,

Manufactured under patent purchased by us of C. W. Lecount.

This Wick is coming into general use on account of its giving a brighter and steadier flame, never getting caught in the ratchet, exactly filling the tube, never getting discolored, and lasting much longer than cotton wick.

238 Pearl & 118 John St., NEW YORK.

Illustrated Catalogue and Price List sent on application

1875 advertisement. Lovell exhibited kerosene burners, lamps, and wicks at the 1876 Centennial Exposition in Philadelphia.

Improved Mogul Lamp

Improved Mogul No. 2 stand lamp made by the Bristol Brass and Clock Co. Height 12". Mogul lamps were sold by Lovell from 1895 to 1916 or later. Lovell may have bought the tooling from Bristol Brass. $150.00.

Flame spreader: "Improved Mogul, Pat. July 15 '90, U.S.A., F. H. Lovell & Co."

Dressel Belgian (Belgium)

Oil fill cap marked "The Dressel Railway Lamp Works, New York."

Wick knob marked "Belgium-Dressel, Arlington, N. J."

Heat deflector.

Dressell Belgian office wall lamp. The flame spreader is marked "The Dressel Railway, New York."$175.00.
Courtesy John Remackel.

Lovell Exported Hitchcock Lamps

An enterprising New York manufacturer is shipping lamps to Bagdad, home of Aladdin. He has made a lamp that seems to have captured the whole Orient, and princess and potentates are clamoring for his goods. Missionaries were responsible for the introduction of the lamps. Many of the buyers are exalted personages. The lamps go to the Emperor of Siam's palace at Bangkok, to the Sultan of Morocco's palace and to a number of caliphs at Damascus and viziers at Bagdad. These lamps burn kerosene oil, but they have no chimneys. By a mechanical device air is forced into the flame, which gives a clear white light, equal to twenty candle power.

CGL, June 1, 1900

Mogul Lamp

Great Mogul hanging lamp sold by Lovell in 1895. This identical image was advertised as the Improved New Magnum lamp by Lane Mfg. Co. in 1891 (*CGJ*, Jan. 1).

Mogul No. 2 stand lamp sold by Lovell in 1895. This is same lamp as the New Aurora manufactured by Lane Mfg. Co. I do not know how the flame spreader is marked.

F. H. Lovell Catalog 1898 – 1899

IMPROVED HITCHCOCK TABLE LAMPS.

H 1.

Lamp only, $3.00 each.

H 23.

Complete with 5 inch Opal Globe, $3.40 each.

H 3.

Complete with 5 in. Colored Globe, $3.50 each.

H 24.

Complete with 10 in. Decorated Shade, $3.75 each.

Lovell bought the Hitchcock lamps about 1898 and featured them on the cover of this undated catalog, which included 12 pages of Hitchcock lamps and accessories. Lovell noted on the back cover, "Special Notice: The National Lead Company have turned over to us their moulds for the production of artistic white metal work, including lamps, candle sticks, jardinieres, book holders, wall brackets, etc. A special pamphlet to be issued."

LITTLE JEWEL LAMPS IN ARTISTIC DESIGNS.

This little lamp is remarkably attractive for household use. Formerly it was only supplied in the nickel finish and had no ornamental features. These lamps combine both the useful features of the small lamp as previously sold, with the ornamental features of a parlor lamp

They are very attractive lamps to place on the bureau or on the chiffonier and the finish can be made to correspond to the decorations required. Finishes will be found on page 7.

X 189.

Price complete,.. $1.35 ea.
Price, Lamp only, 1.25 ea.

X 192.

Price complete,.. $1.90 ea.
Price, Lamp only, 1.75 ea.

All these may be had in the following finishes:
1. Verde Antique. 2. Old Dutch Silver. 3. Bright Gold. 4. Green and Ivory. 5. Old Brass.

X 190.

Price complete,.. $1.75 ea.
Price, Lamp only, 1.50 ea.

X 194.

Price complete,.. $2.75 ea.
Price, Lamp only, 2.15 ea.

Little Jewel lamps were manufactured by Ansonia Brass and Copper Company. Little Jewel continued to be sold by Lovell in 1916, long after Ansonia became part of American Brass Company. Lovell either purchased the tooling, or American Brass continued in the lamp business.

Manhattan Brass Company

1865 – 1926

Manhattan Brass Company was a major manufacturer of lamps and lighting, including center-draft lamps.

Manhattan Brass & Manufacturing Company was organized in 1865 as a fabricator of brass products, rather than as a brass mill. The company was established in the large and growing market centered in New York City, away from the traditional brass mills in Connecticut.

The company was listed in the *New York City Directory* from 1866 to 1925.

The company changed its name to Manhattan Brass Company in 1875 when it moved from 40 John and 469 1st Ave. to 83 Reade and 469 1st Ave. In 1918, Manhattan Brass was at 332 East 28th Street.

The officers in 1915 were Gilbert M. Smith, president and treasurer; Henry W. Hayden, vice president; and Emil F. Gennert, secretary. Manhattan Brass was liquidated in May 1926 due to low profit and high real estate values (Lathrop, 1926).

Thomas Hipwell (New Brunswick, NJ, Astoria and Long Island, NY) was a leading inventor for Manhattan Brass and a leader in the industry. He assigned many patents to Manhattan Brass from 1881 to 1895. Thomas was a founder of the Pittsburgh Brass Company, and the father of Harry H. Hipwell, who organized H. H. Hipwell Mfg. Co. in Allegheny, Pennsylvania, in 1887.

Manhattan Brass Co. was a major supplier of kerosene lamps, perhaps best known for Perfection student lamps and Spencer's Patent lamps. The company, however, manufactured several brands of center-draft lamps, and most likely made lamps on custom order for other companies and retail stores.

Manhattan Brass lamps were exported to countries around the world. They are found in many foreign catalogs.

Thomas Hipwell, 1840 – 1903.

Trade Names

Center-draft lamps — Perfection Student lamps, U.S. Electric, Home Argand, Yale, Princeton, New Manhattan, Sun, Sun Electric, Excelsior, Mammoth, Manhattan Smokeless, Young America.

Folded-wick burners — Diamond Light, Grand Central.

Flat-wick lamps — Home Parlor Lamp, Spencer's Patent lamp, Little Wonder.

Bicycle lamps — Dazzler, Cyclops, Frontlight, Unique.

Lanterns — Hero, Old Reliable, Hurricane, Storm, Woodward, IXL.

Flat-wick burners — Eureka, Grand, Gem. Many Manhattan burners were signed "M. B. Co. N.Y.," often with patent dates.

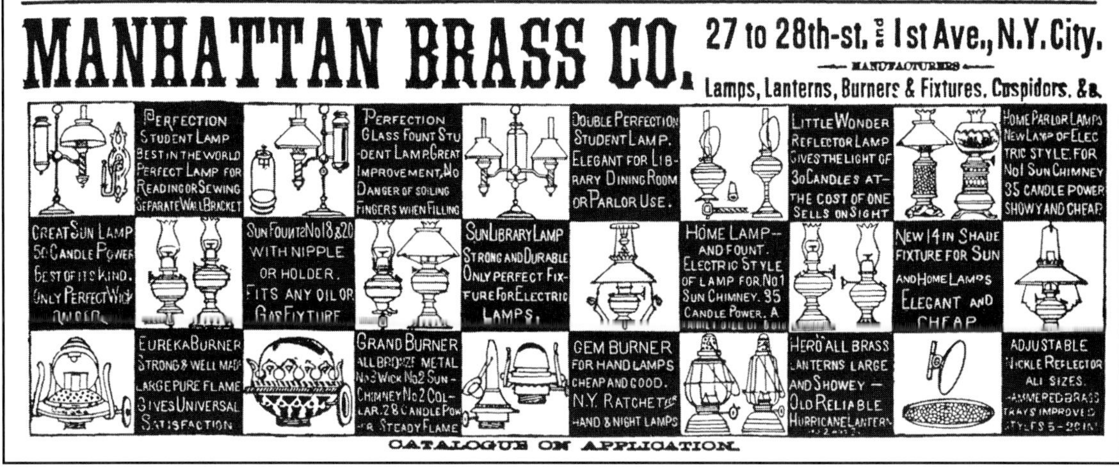

Advertisement, *American Potter and Illuminator,* April 1886.

Selected Patents, Center-draft Lamps

Thomas Hipwell assigned to Manhattan Brass

1881 239,383
1881 250,918
1882 256,216
1883 283,108
1884 302,658
1884 308,770
1885 314,178
1885 323,037
1891 457,587
1891 457,588
1892 471,791
1892 472,790
1892 477,366
1892 479,880
1892 480,404
1892 488,968
1893 499,386
1893 501,275
1895 534,103

Henry L. Coe[1] assigned to Manhattan Brass

1879 215,506

Joseph Funck[2] unassigned

1876 177,825
1877 198,600
1882 266,457
1895 534,100

August Gross[3] assigned to Manhattan Brass

1896 561,108

James H. White[4] assigned to Manhattan Brass

(with T. Hipwell) 1885 318,150
1891 444,867
1891 457,571

Joseph Gregory, unassigned

1897 594,007
1898 608,284
1900 653,449
1900 661,517
1902 693,006
1904 749,132
1904 752,901

[1]Also lantern patents.
[2]Also patents on MBCo. student lamps.
[3]Also other patents.
[4]Also bicycle lamps and lamp accessories.

Contrary to some reports, Manhattan Brass Co. was very good at marking its lamps — certainly its center-draft lamps. The company was diverse and a profilic manufacturer of brass lamps. They improved, innovated and changed as the times required. I will not be surprised to find "new" combinations of burners and fount styles in addition to those illustrated on these pages.

Sun Electric

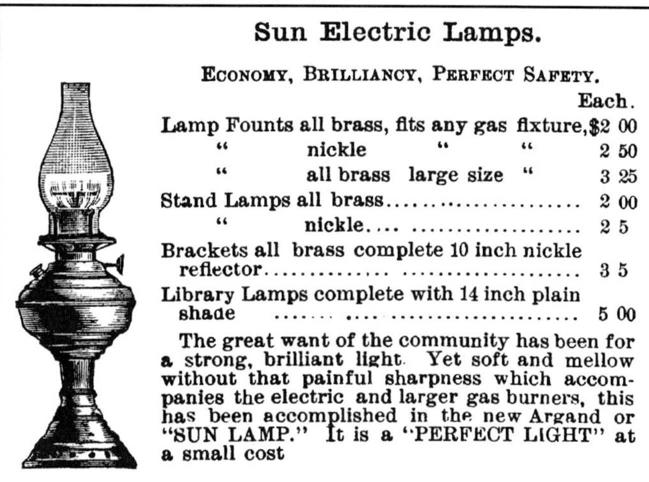

Advertisement, *American Potter and Illuminator,* April 1885.

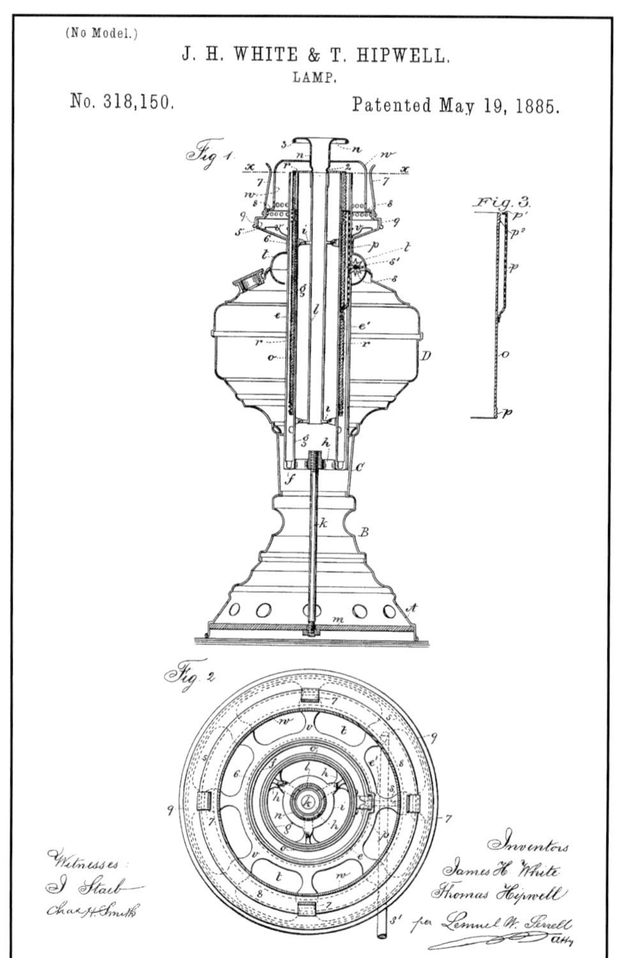

Patent, Sun and Home lamps.

Sun and Sun Electric

I believe the Sun Lamp and the Sun Electric Lamp to be the same lamps. However, there are two different flame spreaders for Sun lamps. The term *electric* became fashionable in 1885, and Manhattan Brass used the term to attract attention away from its competition. Bradley & Hubbard, for example, was not promoting center-draft lamps at the time.

The flame spreader for lamp below fits into a tube mounted inside the draft tube.

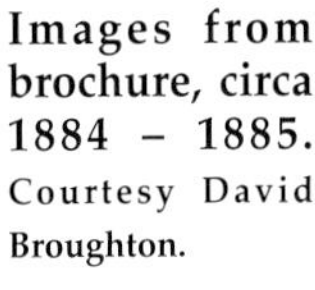

Images from brochure, circa 1884 – 1885. Courtesy David **Broughton.**

SUN LAMP

SUN REFLECTOR LAMP.

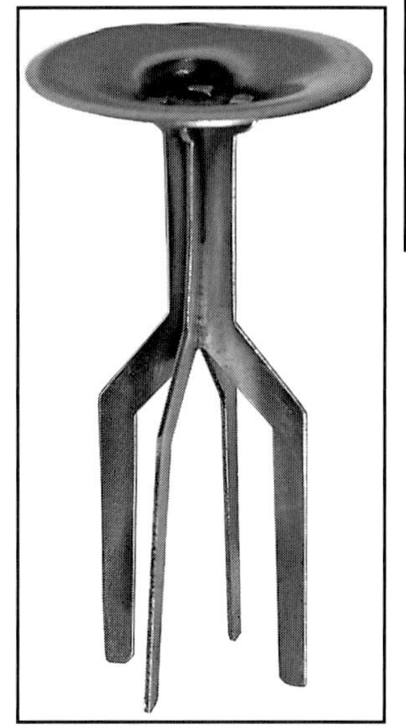

Sun flame spreader fits in draft tube of some lamps. Length 3½".

Sun No. 2 fount lamp. The flame spreader is missing, see patent 318,150. Height 9". $125.00.

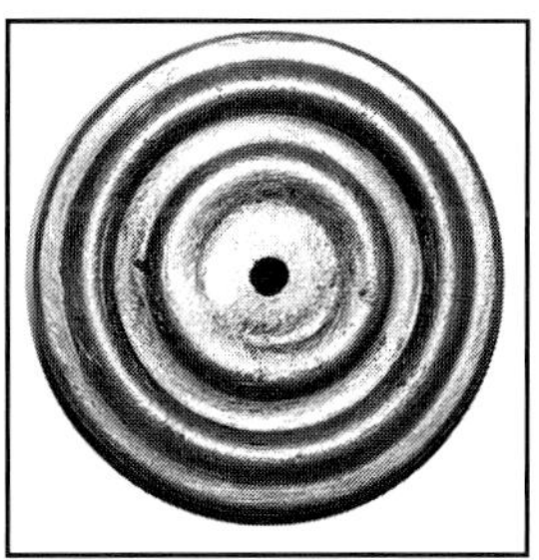

Oil fill cap.

Wick knob.

Sun No. 2 stand lamp missing flame spreader. Height 13¼". The wick (above) is a full ⅜" thick. $175.00.

Home Lamp or Home Argand Lamp

The Home Argand Lamp is a smaller version of the Sun Lamp. Manhattan Brass used the names Home Lamp and Home Argand Lamp in advertising. The oil cap below has been found on Sun Lamps as well.

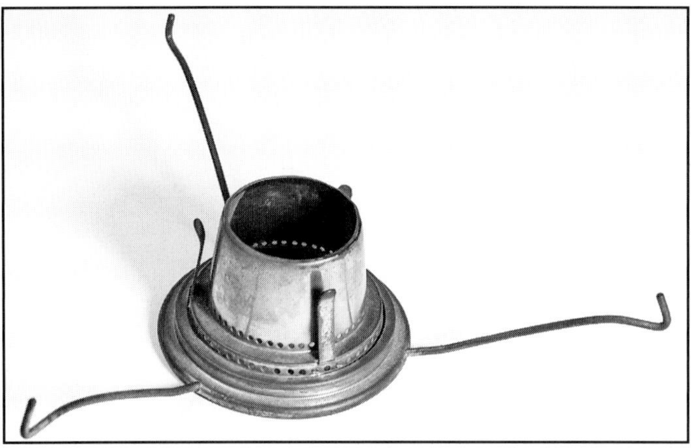

The gallery with two rows of vent holes was made with or without a tripod.

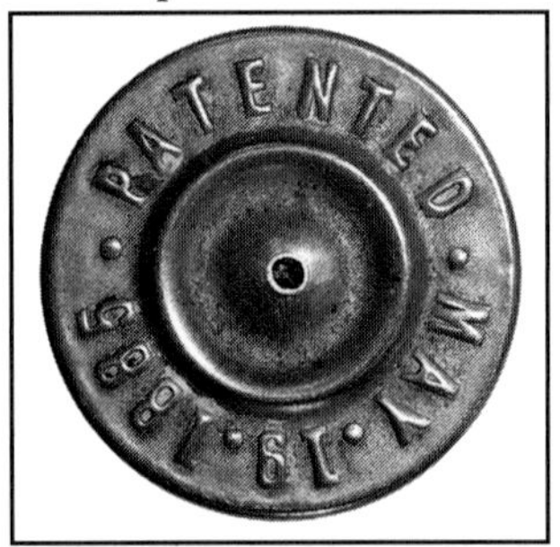

Oil fill cap. "Patented, May 19, 1885."

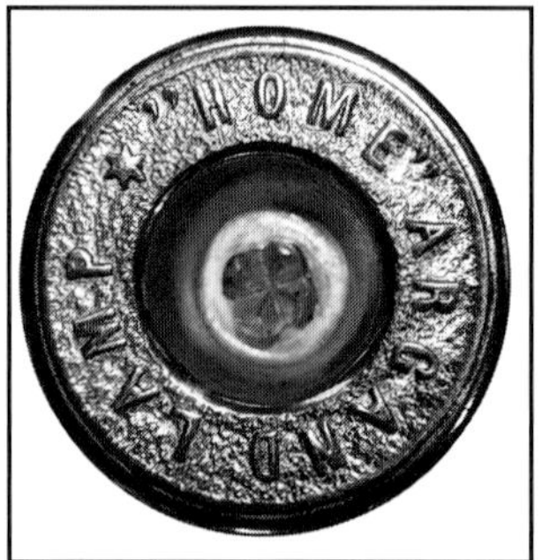

Wick knob marked "Home Argand Lamp."

Home Argand No. 2 fount lamp. Height 7½". $125.00.

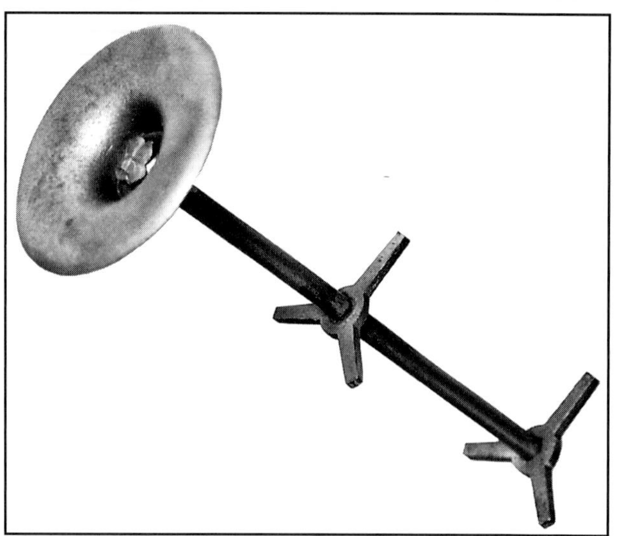

Flame spreader for 1" wick tube is 3½" long with top disc 1½" in diameter.

Home Argand No. 2 stand lamp. Height 12". $175.00.

U.S. Electric

The U.S. Electric was sold by H. Leonard & Sons, Grand Rapids, in 1888 and by Burley & Tyrrell, Chicago, in 1889. Plain lamps were listed as U.S. No. 2 or 20 in brass, nickel, or rich gold finish. Embossed lamps were called "Favorite."

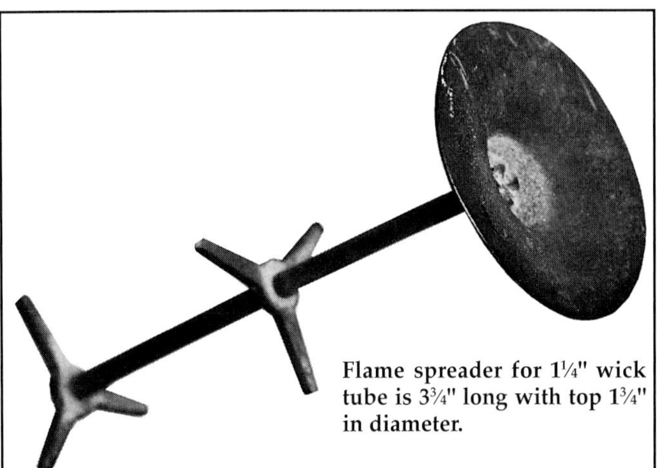

Flame spreader for 1¼" wick tube is 3¾" long with top 1¾" in diameter.

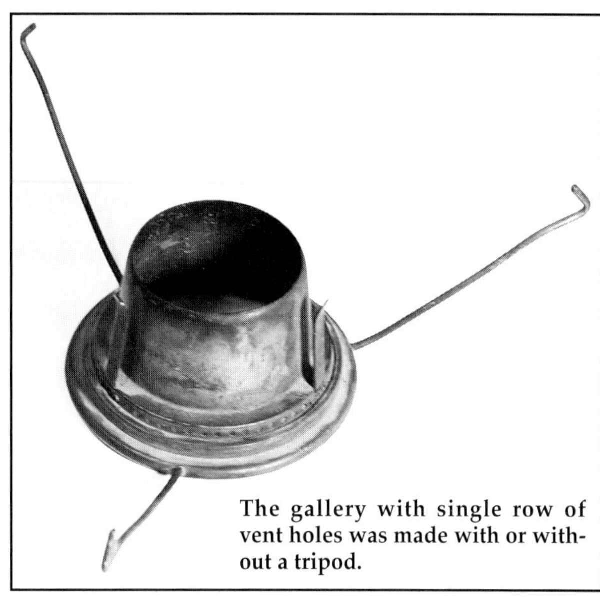

The gallery with single row of vent holes was made with or without a tripod.

Oil fill cap. "U.S. Electric Lamp."

U.S. Electric No. 2 stand lamp, missing flame spreader (see above). Height 12". $175.00. Courtesy Fil Graff.

U.S. Electric No. 2 fount lamp. Height 9". $125.00.

Princeton

Flame spreader stamped "Princeton Lamp Frink, New York, Pat. Jan'y 20 '91, Aug. 11 '91." I. P. Frink was a lamp dealer in New York City.

Flame spreader stamped "Princeton Lamp, Pat. Jan'y 20th '91, Aug. 11th '91."

MBCo. oil fill cap.

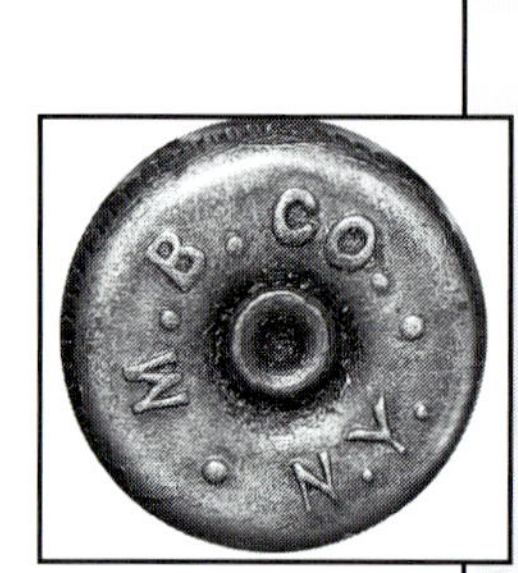

Wick knob above lamp.

Princeton No. 2 fount lamp found with flame spreader #1 (left). Lift gallery for lighting. The oil fill cap is the plain distinctive type found on many Manhattan Brass lamps. Both flame spreaders illustrated have been found in these lamps. $150.00.

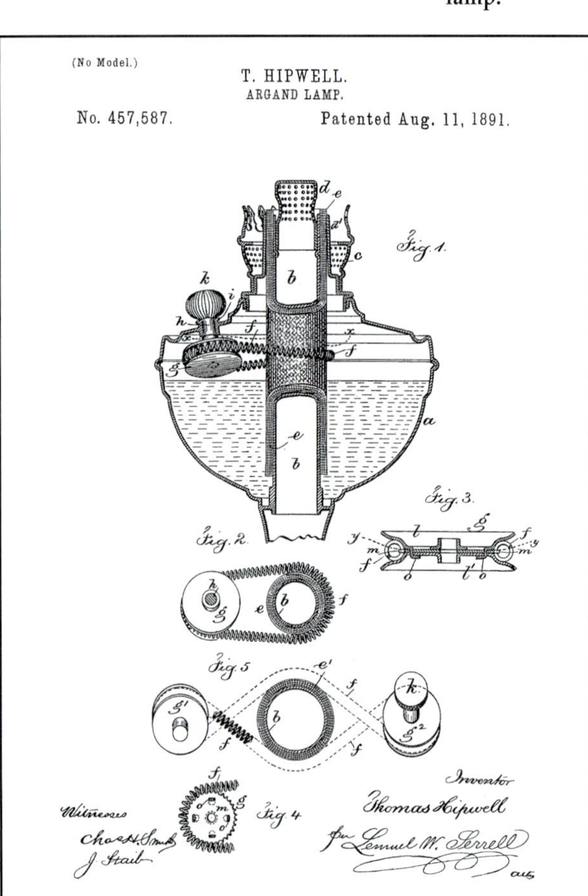
(No Model.)

T. HIPWELL.
ARGAND LAMP.

No. 457,587. Patented Aug. 11, 1891.

Note that there are two different Hipwell patents (457,587 and 457,588) for the wick raiser in this configuration. The difference is evident only by inspection of the inner mechanism.

Oil fill cap, lamp below.

Princeton with pull-rod wick raiser. Courtesy Kent Stratton.

Princeton No. 2 stand lamp found with flame spreader No. 2. The gallery does not lift. The oil fill cap is stamped "Princeton Lamp." $125.00.

Young America

Young America oil pots were advertised in vase lamps by Dithridge & Co. in 1891.

Young America stamped on top of fount "'Young America,' Pat Apl'd For" (see right). Missing flame spreader. Courtesy Doug and Judy Myers.

"'Young America' LAMP Pat. Apl'd For" stamped on top of fount. Also found with "Pat. Aug. 11 '91" stamped in the lower line.

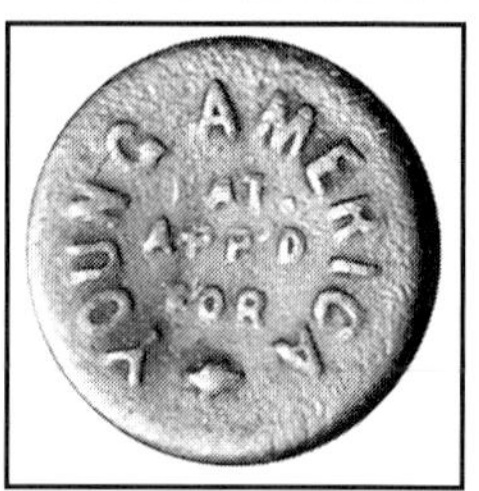

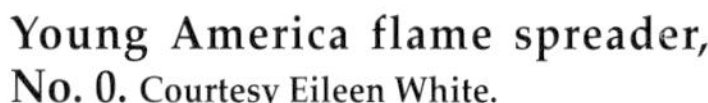

Young America flame spreader, No. 0. Courtesy Eileen White.

Young America stand lamp 7¾" high. Missing flame spreader. $200.00. Courtesy Doug and Judy Myers.

Young America stand lamp 8⅝" high. Cast-iron loading weight (right) is stamped "88 MAH B CO." $175.00. Courtesy Eileen White.

Yale

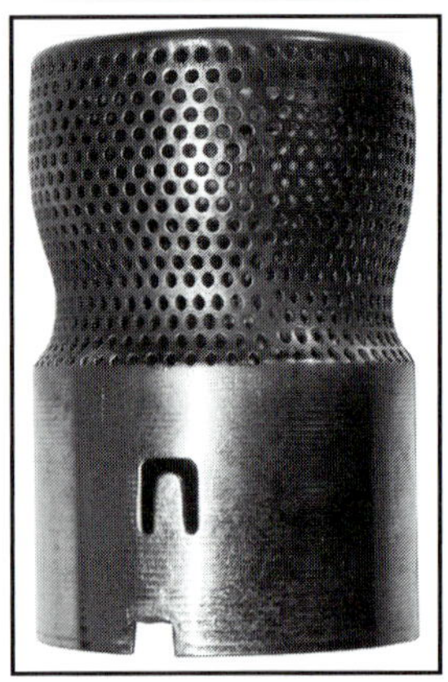

Unmarked Yale flame spreader.

Unmarked Yale flame spreader.

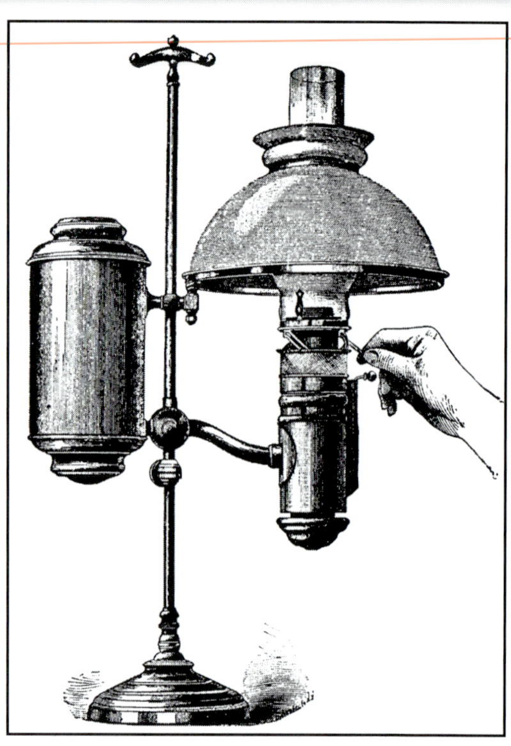

Yale student lamp No. 205, 75 candlepower; it cost $12.00 in 1896.

Oil fill cap.

Flame spreader marked "Yale Lamp, M. B. CO. N. Y., Pat. Jan'y 20th '91, Aug. 11th. '91, Dec. 27th '92."

Yale No. 2 stand lamp found with flame spreader #1 above. The gallery lifts for lighting. Height 11½". $100.00.

Wick knob, "Yale M. B. Co."

Yale No. 2 stand lamp found with flame spreader #2 above. Height 12". $175.00. Courtesy Heinz and Ursula Baumann.

Yale flame spreader.

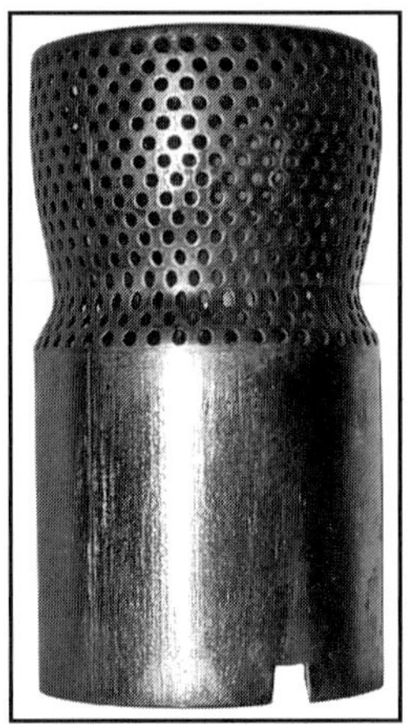

Both styles of Yale flame spreaders have been found in these lamps.

Yale "CODA" flame spreader.

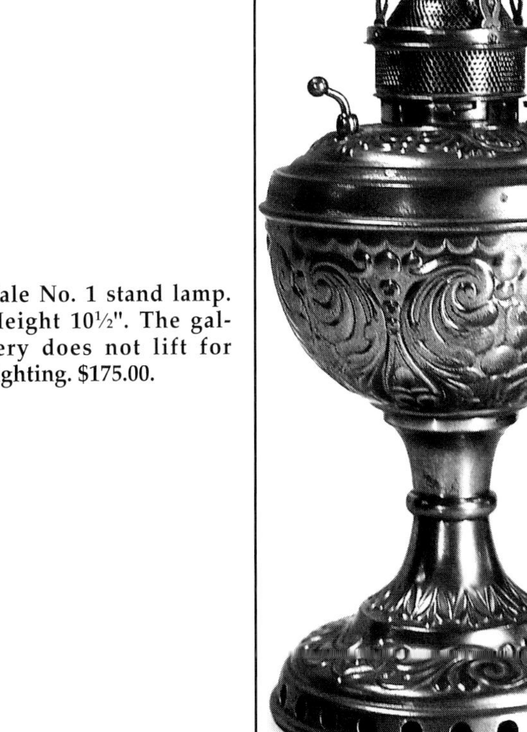

Yale No. 1 stand lamp. Height 10½". The gallery does not lift for lighting. $175.00.

Yale No. 1 convertible stand-wall lamp. Height 13". $225.00.

Manhattan Smokeless Incandescent

Oil fill cap unique to many Manhattan center-draft lamps.

Top of flame spreader is marked "Manhattan Smokeless Incandescent, MBCO N. Y., Pat. Nov. 27th 1897, Others Pending." The top is steel and is rusting.

Manhattan Smokeless No. 2 stand lamp. Height 13¼". The "gallery" lifts for lighting. $275.00. Courtesy Dick O'Connell.

Wick knob, unmarked.

Manhattan Smokeless No. 2 stand lamp. Height 12". The "gallery" lifts for lighting. $275.00.

Excelsior

Excelsior flame spreader, same as unmarked Yale flame spreader.

Wick knob marked "Excelsior, M.B. Co."

New Manhattan

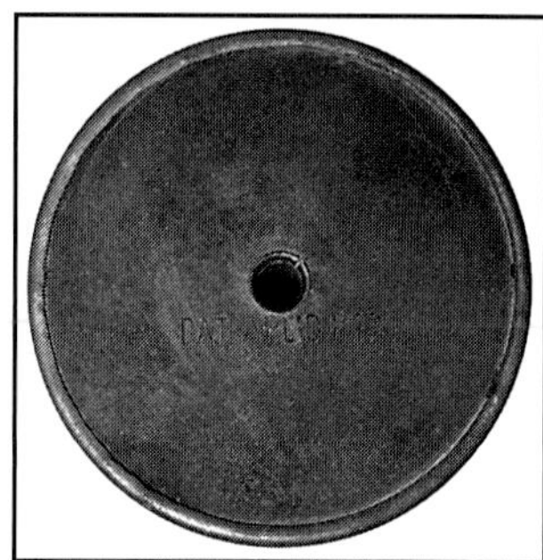

New Manhattan flame spreader. The top is marked "Pat. Apl'd For."

Excelsior No. 2 stand lamp with cast-iron foot. Height 12". The cast-iron foot is unmarked, but it is virtually identical with a Plume & Atwood foot, most of which are marked "P & A." $125.00.

Wick knob marked "Manhattan Brass Co. N. Y."

New Manhattan No. 2 stand lamp. Height 12¾". $250.00. Courtesy Heinz and Ursula Baumann.

Manhattan Hanging Lamp Fount

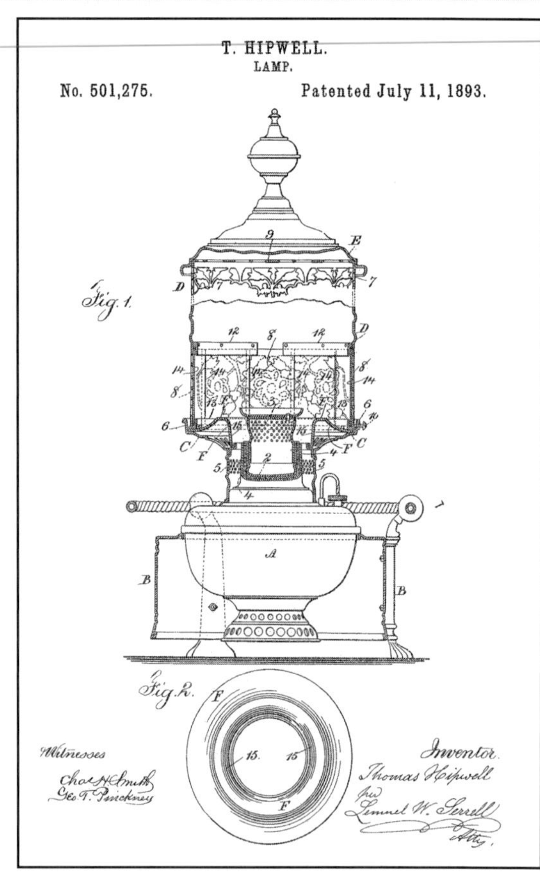

Manhattan Brass hanging lamp fount. $100.00.
Courtesy Bill Schreiber.

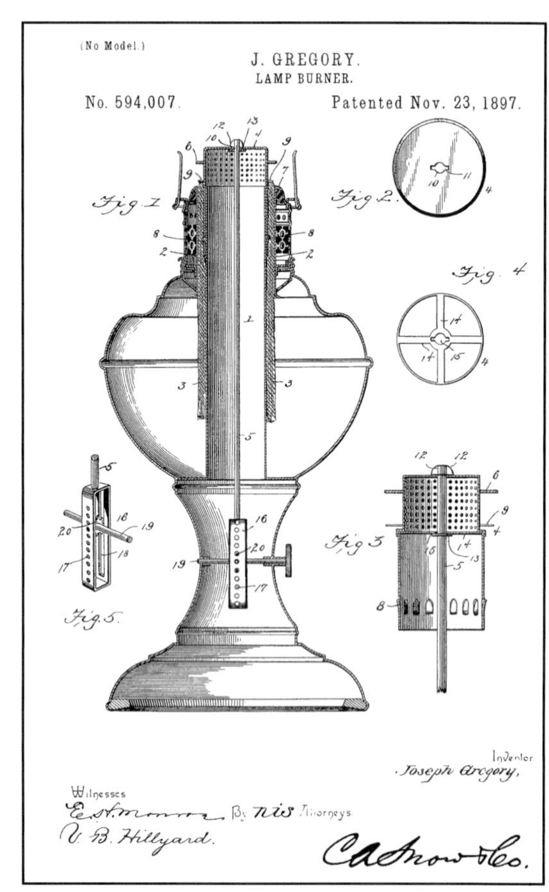

Perfection Student Lamps

Manhattan Brass Co. was quick to design, improve, and market student lamps in several sizes and forms. Manhattan Brass student lamps are frequently found today, although they are not marked as well as the stand lamps. The company sold student lamps for many years.

Perfection Study Lamps.

Recommended by the U. S. Government, who have over 10,000 in use in their various offices.

Each.

Perfection Standard complete nickle plated [see cut] .... $ 3 25

Perfection double, two burners, nickle plated complete 7 00

Warranted not to leak or get out of order.

Advertisement, *American Potter and Illuminator,* April 1886.

Advertisement, *The Delineator,* Nov. 1895.

Advertisement, *Crockery and Glass Journal,* June 21, 1883. The heavy-cast Perfection mammoth was called the Berlin lamp.

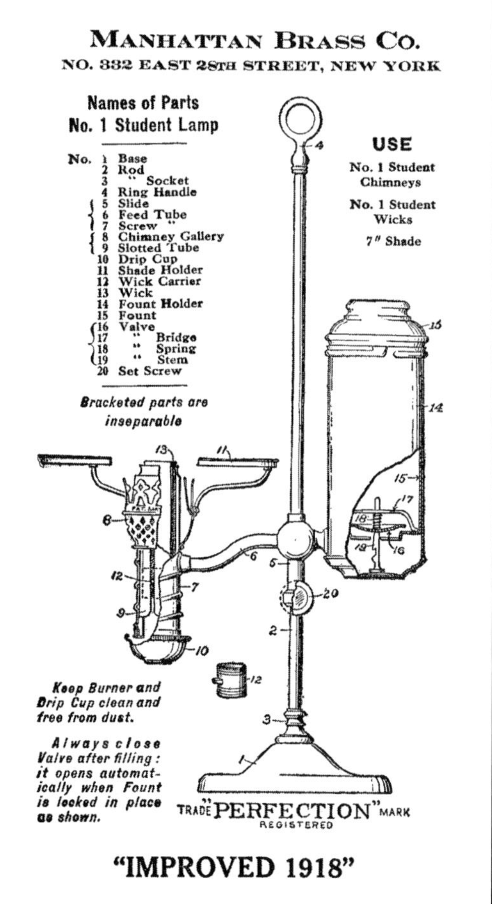

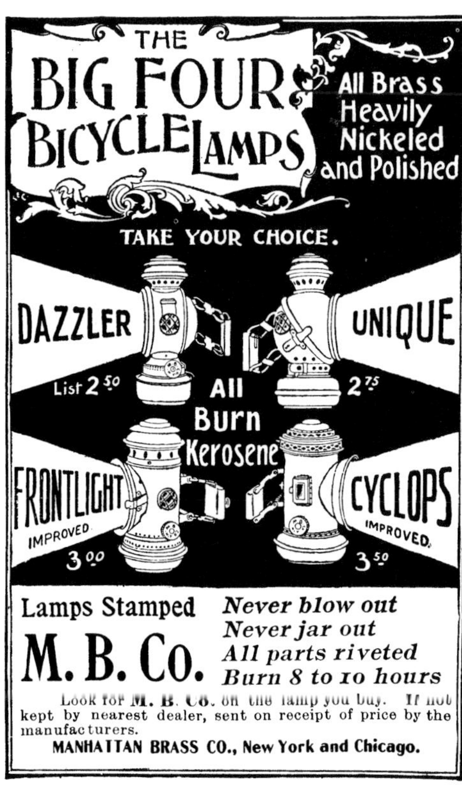

Advertisement, *McClure's,* 1897.

Master Lamp Company
(U. L. & B. Co.)

ca. 1909 – 1920

The Master Lamp was advertised and sold by Master Lamp Co., 90 West Broadway, New York City, United Lamp & Burner Co., 90 West Broadway, and Mountain Community, Inc., 176 Madison Ave., (Nr. 33rd. St.), New York City.

The Master Lamp was designed by Nelson Blount, New York, NY, and was invented by Blount and Stephen Burrough Morss (1858 – 1939), Rahway, New Jersey. Morss was the proprietor of a girls' seminary in his later years.

The Master Lamp Company was operated at 16 E 98th St. by Louis Folkman in July 1932. I do not know if this is the same company that sold the Master Lamp.

The Master Lamp was extensively advertised from 1913 to 1916 in the *New York Times* rotogravure picture section of its Sunday editions. The company claimed sales throughout the United States as well as foreign countries.

The company found a niche market, advertising through the *New York Times* to the wealthy with summer and winter homes. Small Master Lamp ads ran alongside ads for the Moon Motor Car, La Spirite Corsets, grand pianos, furs, and fancy clothing. Free booklets extolled the lamp's features.

Master lamps were offered in dull or brushed brass, bright or polished copper and jap bronze finishes. The shade was either white or yellow.

Morss was granted two patents (555,257; 569,795) in 1896 for non-combustible wicks. In 1900 he invented improvements relating to lamp flame spreaders which he assigned to Frederick W. Keasbey of Morristown, New Jersey. Keasbey was a well-connected prominent businessman and lawyer, former mayor, president of Morris County Savings Bank and president of Morristown Gas Light Company.

I suspect Keasbey financed the research of Morss and possibly the development of the Master lamp.

The Master Lamp was advertised as a "new process — no mantle" to boast its bright flame due to the unique flame spreader.

Morss invented an incandescent mantle lamp (1,173,842), but I do not know if it was produced for commercial sale.

Morss' last patent (1,546,938) in 1925 was for a gas generating oil burner. His obituary appeared in the *New York Times* on March 7, 1939.

Advertisement circa 1910.

Selected Patents, Center-draft Lamps

Stephen B. Morss assigned to F. W. Keasbey

Year	Patent
1900	641,217
1900	641,218

S. B. Morss

Year	Patent
1902	691,068
1902	701,919
1905	787,629
1909	941,163
1913	1,064,521
1913	1,068,601
1916	1,173,842

Nelson Blount assigned to United Lamp & Burner Co.

Year	Patent
1910	D41004
1911	1,008,777

The Master Light of Lights

For summer homes and summer camps,
commences where the sun leaves off.
Beautiful in form. Beautiful in performance.
Sweet, safe, sanitary and satisfactory.
The sunshine lamp produces its own gas as it
burns like a miniature sun.
Buy a perfect lamp, giving a perfect gift and
your eyes will thank you.

Selected lines from ads in the *New York Times*.

Master Lamp

There are variations in construction, but few have collected and studied the Master lamps, possibly made by Manhattan Brass Co. There are two flame spreaders, one with holes under the flange that covers the wick. I am informed that both burn very well.

I do not know if this lamp company or Stephen B. Morss is connected with A. S. Morss Marine Hardware in Boston, Massachusetts.

Top of flame spreader marked "U. L. and B. Co. New York, Master Lamp. Pat'd 1-9-1900, 11-23-1909, 11-29-1910, Made in U. S. A." The last date is a design patent. U. L. and B. Co. is United Lamp and Burner Company, New York, NY, a Delaware corporation.

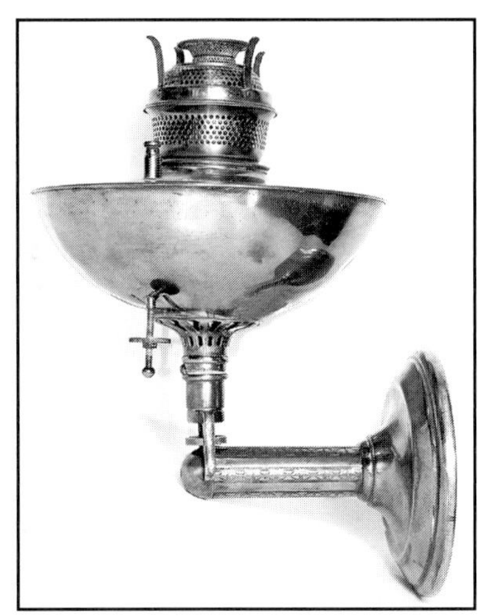
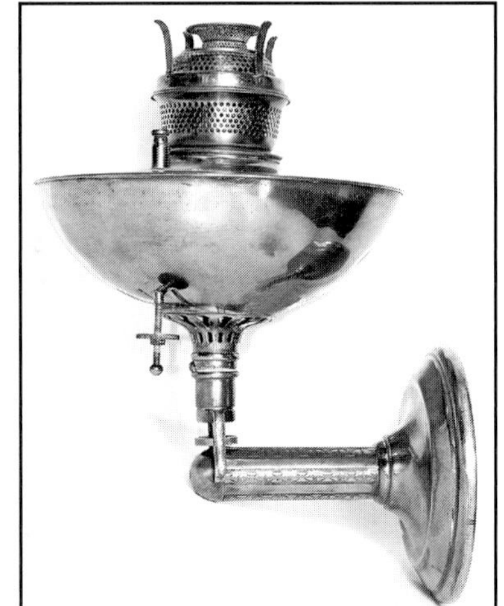

Master Lamp converted for wall or table use. The wall mounting is similar to others seen for Manhattan Brass Co. lamps. $225.00. Courtesy Kent Stratton.

Oil fill cap: "Master Lamp."

Master No. 2 stand lamp. Height 11". The gallery lifts for lighting. $200.00.

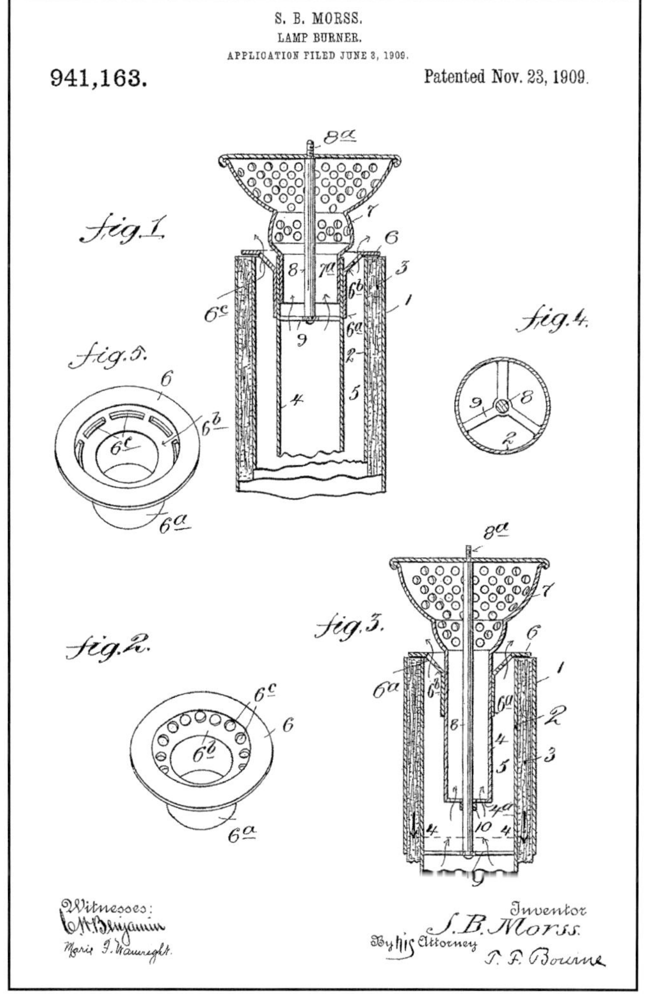

S. B. MORSS.
LAMP BURNER.
APPLICATION FILED JUNE 3, 1909.

941,163. Patented Nov. 23, 1909.

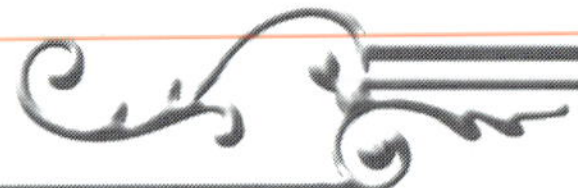

Matthews & Willard Mfg. Company

1890 – 1903

Matthews & Willard Manufacturing Company, Waterbury, was incorporated in 1890 with F.L. Curtis, president; C.P. Goss, treasurer; and George G. Blakeslee, manager. Matthews & Willard manufactured a general line of brassware products. Brooks (2004) wrote an excellent article on bicycle lamp makers of Waterbury stating that Matthews & Willard was in business at least since 1885 and 1886. The company first manufactured bicycle lamps as a specialty.

John C. Miller assigned several patents to Meriden Bronze Company, but left Meriden to work for Matthews and Willard about 1891 or 1892. Miller later assigned patents to the Miller Mfg. Co., Torrington, Connecticut, 1898 – 1899.

Matthews & Willard sued American Lamp & Brass Company and the Trenton Lamp Company for alleged patent infringements in late 1894. Four suits regarding fount holders and bases were filed against each company.

Wilcox & Matthews Company sold lamps with center-draft "Century" burners in 1890. I do not know the relationship of this company to Matthews & Willard Mfg. Co.

Matthews & Willard sold oil pots for use in hanging, banquet, and vase lamps. In 1898 Pitkin and Brooks offered a variety of M & W "lamps" which they suggested be replaced with Belgian burners.

Frederick M. Stevens assigned patent 730,981 to Matthews & Willard for a tubular lantern in 1903, the same year the company was bought by Scovill Mfg. Company. I suspect Scovill or the HBH division of American Brass Co. continued to manufacture M & W center-draft products for another five years or longer.

Trade Names

Center-draft lamps — M & W, Aladdin, Columbia. The Columbia was sold by the Trenton Lamp Company.

Bicycle lamps[1] — M & W 97, M & W 98, M & W 99. Acetylene — M & W Lancaster Gas Lamp, Star Lancaster Gas Lamp, M & W Duplex, M & W Rainbow.

[1]M & W furnished components for bicycle lamps made by the Noera Mfg. Co. in Waterbury.

M & W flame spreaders with and without year sold. Marked "The Improved Lamp, Patented Aug. 18, 1896."

Matthews & Willard conveniently dated their center-draft flame spreaders for the year lamps were sold — 1892, 1894, 1895, 1897, 1898, 1899, 1900.

The bottom of some hanging lamp founts are marked with patent dates of March 30, 1897, Nov. 23, 1897, and Dec. 14, 1897.

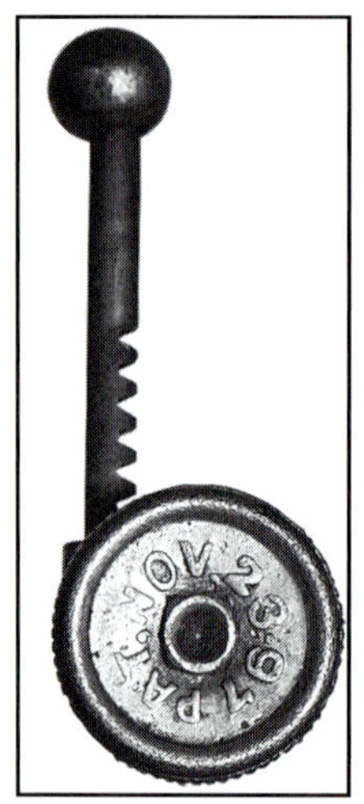

Wick knob marked: "Pat. Nov. 23 '97."

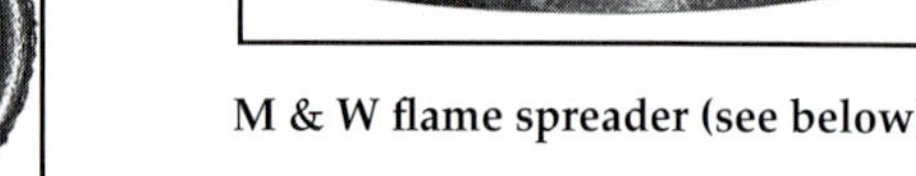

M & W flame spreader (see below).

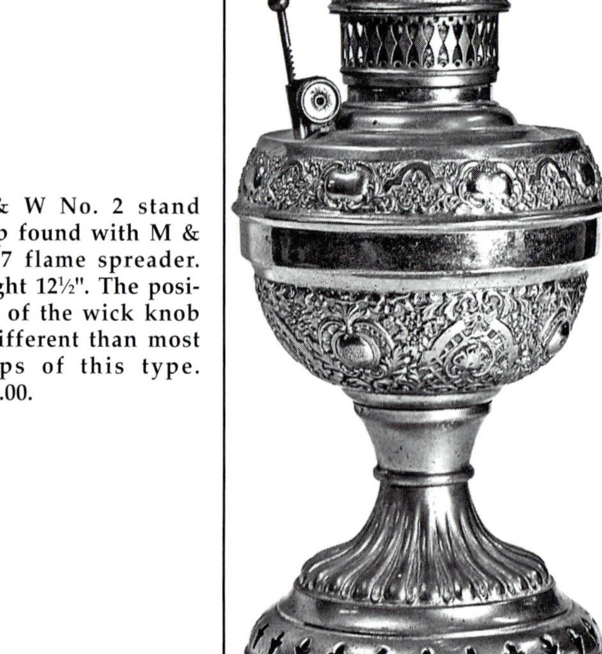

M & W No. 2 stand lamp found with M & W 97 flame spreader. Height 12½". The position of the wick knob is different than most lamps of this type. $175.00.

M & W Flame Spreaders

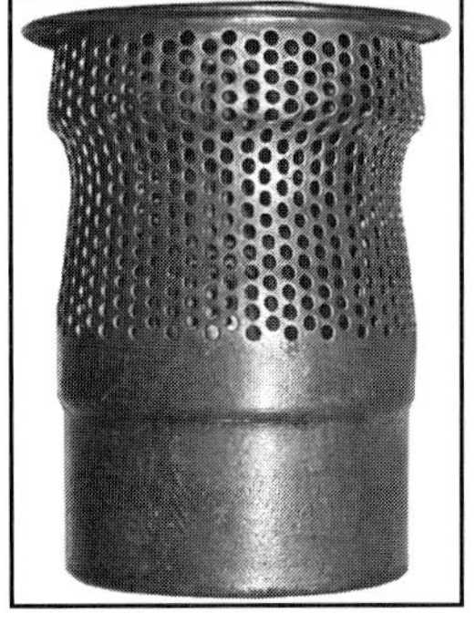

M & W flame spreader 95: "The Improved Lamp, M & W 95, Patent Applied For."

Note: M & W flame spreaders dated 1898, 1899, and 1900 are marked like M & W 97 on the preceding page.

D & W flame spreader made for an unknown company. It is shaped like M & W 95 above. Courtesy Kent Stratton.

Selected Patents, Center-draft Lamps

Year	Patent No.
John C. Miller unassigned	
1894	522,691
John C. Miller[1] assigned to M & W Co.	
1892	478,802
1892	483,850
1892	487,955
1895	532,981
1896	566,208
1896	566,209
1897	576,876

[1]Also patents on bicycle lamps (594,264 and 595,576), which appear on some center-draft lamps. Miller also has several design patents for cast vase lamps (22,422; 23,671; 23,672; 23,673; 23,674).

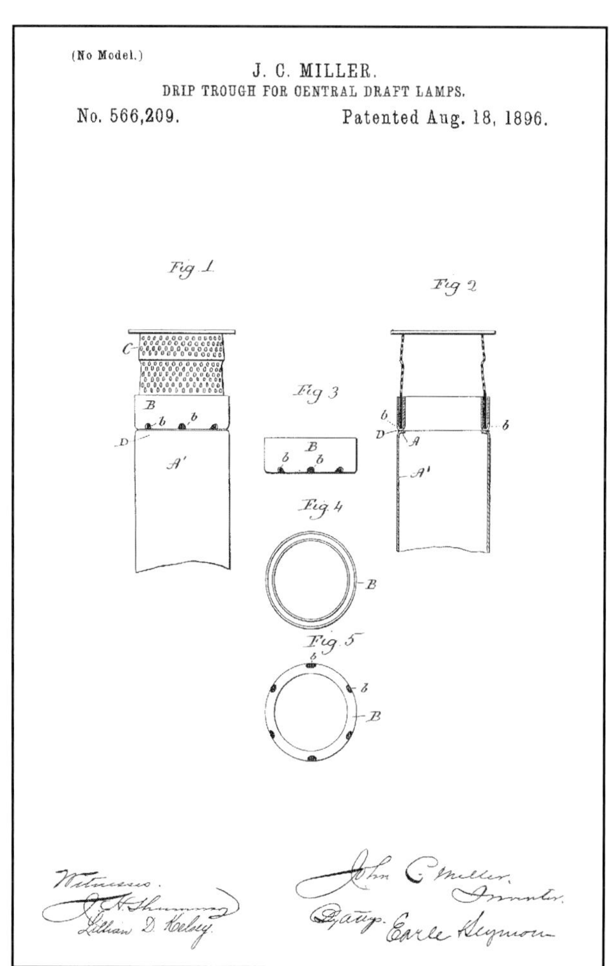

Miller patent 1896. M & W flame spreaders are often stuck in the wick tube due to the dried kerosene that failed to run out of the drainage holes.

M & W Banquet Lamps

Simmons Hardware Catalog 1906 – 1907.
Courtesy Dan Edminster.

M & W Oil Pots for Vase Lamps

Above: oil pots with M & W 95 flame spreaders. Height 7". Left: oil pot with M & W 94 flame spreader. There are at least three different types of wick raisers found in M & W burners, shown above and in lamps below. $75.00 each. Courtesy Dick O'Connell.

M & W Vase Lamps

Marshall Field & Co. Fall 1901.
Courtesy Heinz and Ursula Baumann.

The Aladdin Lamp

Based on the shape and design markings of flame spreaders, I believe Matthews & Willard manufactured The Aladdin, New Columbia, and Tuxedo center-draft lamps. They only differ in the flame spreaders used.

The New Columbia was sold by the Trenton Lamp Company, Trenton, NJ, in 1900 (*CGL*, June 1, 1900).

Flame spreader, "The Aladdin Lamp." Some of these flame spreaders are unmarked.

Wick knob for The Aladdin and New Columbia lamps.

Embossed Aladdin No. 2 stand lamp made by Matthews & Willard. Height 12½". $125.00.

Plain Aladdin No. 2 stand lamp made by Matthews & Willard. Height 12½". $75.00.

The New Columbia and Tuxedo Lamps

New Columbia oil pot. Height 7". The tank is suffering from metal fatigue stress cracks. $75.00.

Flame spreader, "The New Columbia Lamp, Pat. Pending." The shape and size are same as those of the Aladdin.

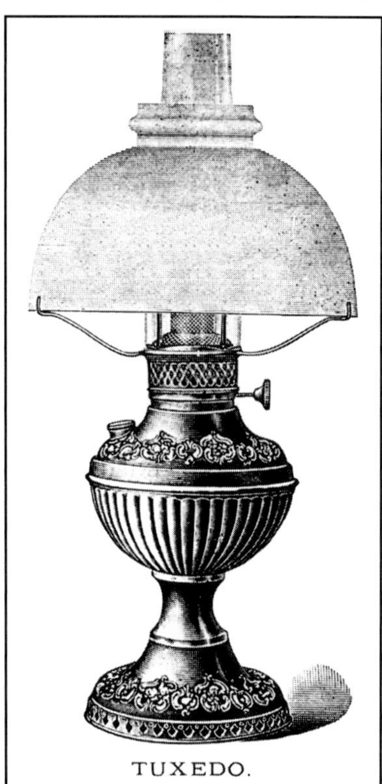

Tuxedo stand lamp illustrated in Simmons Hardware catalog in 1908. The lamp seems identical with the New Columbia made by Matthews & Willard. I do not know what flame spreader was used in this lamp, but assume it was the one illustrated in the chapter on Holmes, Booth & Haydens.

New Columbia No. 2 stand lamp. Height 12½". $125.00.

M & W Bicycle Lamp

The bottom of "M & W 98" bicycle lamp.

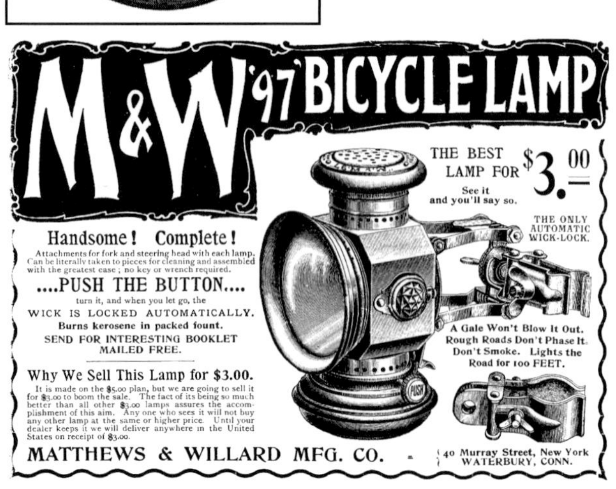

Advertisement, 1897.

S. Elwood May
1886 – 1888

In 1886 S. Elwood May, 11 Murray Street, New York, advertised May's New Ideal mechanical lamp along with the Bartholdi center-draft lamp in the *Crockery and Glass Journal*, (Sept. 30).

The Bartholdi lamp was advertised on a trade card by the Metropolitan Mfg. Co., 32 Cortland St., New York, as the "coolest and most durable lamp, cannot explode." Cost with white shade was $4.50.

S. Elwood May is best known for May's Ideal no-chimney lamps. He advertised as "sole proprietor and manufacturer" in 1884.

The Bartholdi lamp apparently did not meet with widespread success, as this lamp is not commonly found. The name was selected to correspond with the unveiling of the Statue of Liberty in New York Harbor on Oct. 28, 1886. At the time, many companies identified their products with the Bartholdi name to associate them with the famous statue and the renowned French designer and sculptor.

James G. Hallas's patent 381,009, assigned to S. Elwood May, was to control oil overflowing the wick and to prevent it dripping on the table. Hallas assigned many patents for improvements in flat-wick burners (1873 – 1884) to Benedict & Burnham Mfg. Company, Waterbury, Connecticut. I do not know, but I suspect that Benedict & Burnham manufactured the Bartholdi lamp for May.

Trade Names

Center-draft lamp — Bartholdi.
Mechanical lamps — May's Ideal, May's New Ideal.

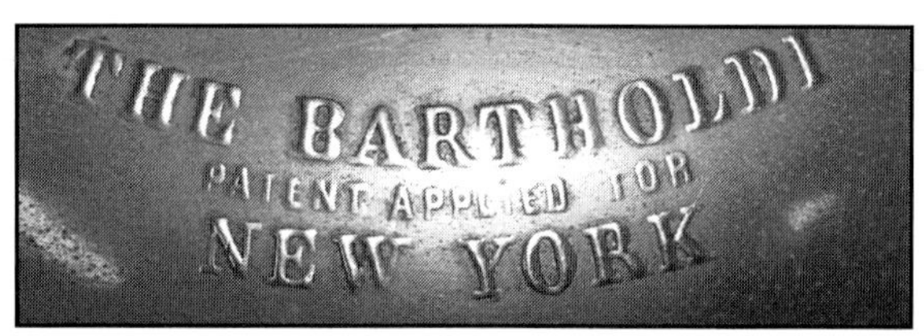

"The Bartholdi, New York, Patent Applied For."

Oil fill cap.

Wick knob, "S. Elwood May, N. Y."

Flame spreader.

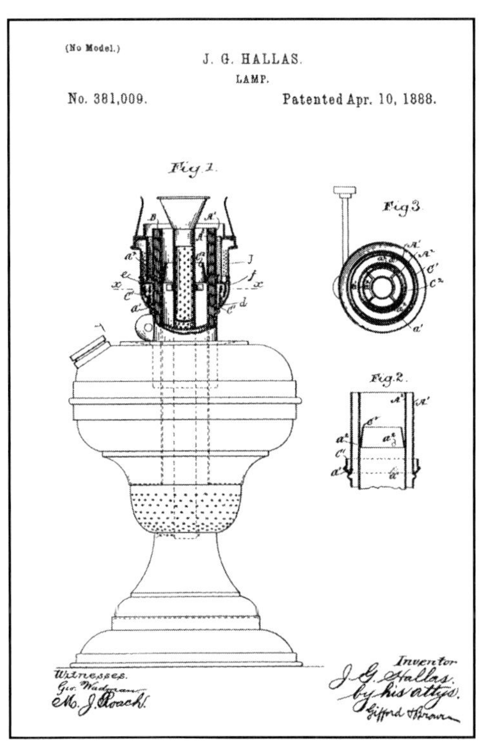

Bartholdi No. 2 hanging fount. Height 9½". $300.00.

The Bartholdi No. 2 stand lamp. Height 13". This burner is not the Hobart & Craig Bartholdi burner. $350.00.

Meriden Bronze Company

1884 – 1900

Letterhead, ca. 1899.
Courtesy Allen Weathers and the Meriden Historical Society.

Meriden Bronze Company, Meriden, Connecticut, succeeded Foster Hardware Company which produced ornamental gas fixtures. The officers in 1897 were Augustus H. Jones, president; William E. Gard (investor from Baltimore), secretary and treasurer; and Daniel A. Logan, superintendent. The directors were A. H. Jones, W. E. Gard, W. H. Lyon, John W. Coe, and H. Wales Lines.

Meriden Bronze manufactured "artistic gas and oil fixtures" as combination gas and electric fixtures, wrought iron architectural goods; and other goods — music easels, bells, and small brass tables. The company employed 250 in 1897.

The Meriden center-draft lamp, introduced in 1890, was made in piano lamps, banquet lamps, and parlor lamps, all bearing the Meriden name. Most of the Meriden center-draft lamps seen by the author have been vase or banquet lamps fitted with Meriden Bronze oil pots.

The Meriden Bronze salesroom was at 30 Park Place.

Augustus Jones started out as foreman in the brass foundry for Bradley & Hubbard (B & H). While there he assigned patent 246,316 (student lamp) to B & H. Jones also assigned patent 271,334 to the Charles Parker Company.

Franz Yokel and William Patzer assigned several patents for improvements in design and manufacture to Meriden Bronze.

John C. Miller left Meriden Bronze to work for Matthews and Willard in Waterbury after 1891. He assigned patents to Miller Manufacturing Co., Torrington, CT, in 1898 and 1899.

Meriden Bronze developed the Liberty stand and fount lamps, apparently selling few before the company went out of business. Financial depression forced the company to close in 1900.

After Meriden Bronze closed, Jones formed the A. H. Jones Company to manufacture white metal novelties.

I believe Meriden Bronze designed the Meteor lamp. The company may have first sold oil pots with the new burner design as "Meriden." The Meteor lamp first appeared in the 1895 Simmons Hardware Company catalog. Miller continued to make Meteor lamps after Meriden Bronze closed. I do not know if Meriden Bronze or Simmons originated the name Meteor. I believe either Edward Miller or Simmons Hardware Co. purchased the tooling and inventory of Liberty and Meteor lamps originally made by Meriden Bronze.

See Edward Miller & Co. for more about Liberty and Meteor lamps.

Trade Names

Center-draft lamps — Meriden, Princess, The Victor, Baby Meriden, Baby Victor, Liberty, probably Meteor.

Selected Patents, Center-draft Lamps

Year	Patent
John C. Miller assigned to Meriden Bronze	
1889	395,912
1889	396,946
1889	403,768
1889	407,100
1889	414,948
1890	430,871
1891	456,334
Eugene H. Peck assigned to Meriden Bronze	
1889	408,135
Augustus H. Jones[1] assigned to Meriden Bronze	
1892	476,541
1895	541,281
1896	554,935
1896	554,936
Augustus H. Jones unassigned	
1897	575,606
N. I. Johnson[2] assigned to Meriden Bronze	
1893	509,170
(w. Jones) 1896	564,017
(w. Jones) 1896	564,018
(w. Jones) 1896	573,223
Joseph C. Shull assigned to Meriden Bronze	
1896	554,038

[1] Also patents on hanging and piano lamps.
[2] Also patents on incandescent mantle lamps.

The Meriden Bronze Co.,

DESIGNERS AND MAKERS OF ARTISTIC

GAS, ELECTRIC AND COMBINATION

GAS FIXTURES,

Piano, Banquet, Reception and Table Lamps,

ONYX AND GOLD TABLES,
CABINETS, MUSIC RACKS, EASELS,
TEA AND CALL BELLS,
THE MERIDEN SILVER TONED CYCLE BELLS,
ART BENT GLASS SHADES AND GLOBES,

Our Designs are always desirable, with latest and finest finishes.

New York Salesroom, = 30 PARK PLACE.

SALESROOM, OFFICE AND FACTORY,

MERIDEN, CT.

Advertisement, 1899 *Meriden City Directory*.
Courtesy Allen Weathers.

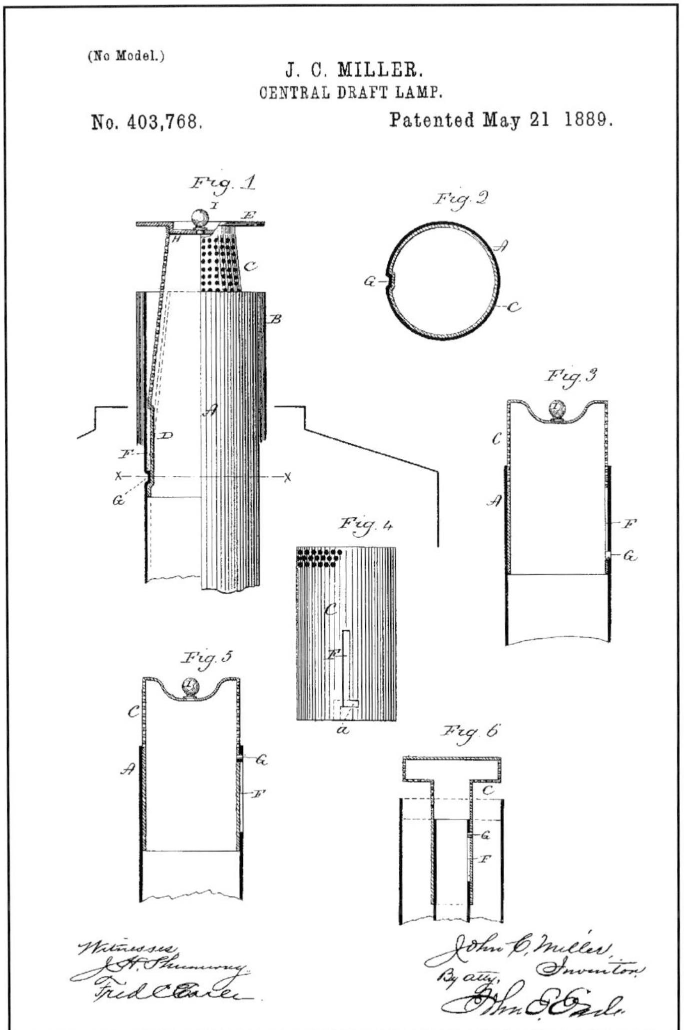

J. C. Miller Patent 403,768, Unique Air Distributor

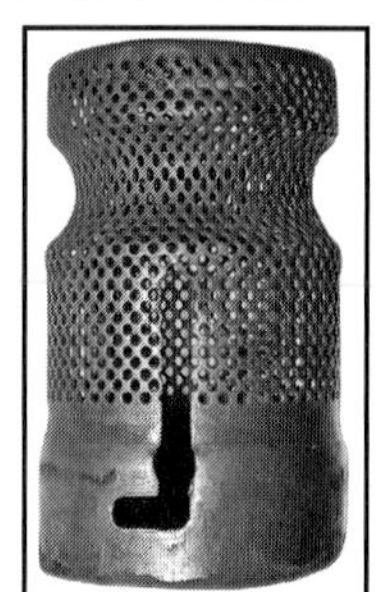

This unique lamp has a "permanent" flame spreader (air distributor) that cannot be removed for trimming the wick. J. C. Miller stated, "The object of my invention is to construct the distributor so that it may be disposed of to leave the wick free, but without removal from the tube." The flame spreader (right) has a groove allowing it to slide up or down and lock into place for burning. The top finger knob was removed from this example.

Meriden oil pot with burner basket removed. The air distributor was lowered into the wick tube, exposing the wick, which could then be raised or lowered for trimming.

Meriden oil pot fitted with J. C. Miller burner and air distributor based on patent 403,768. The burner base is stamped "The Meriden." Height 7", base diameter 5". $100.00.

The Victor — Embossed

The Victor stand lamp illustrated in Simmons Hardware catalog in 1899.

Oil fill cap found in the Victor .

Flame spreader for Meriden Bronze Victor stand lamp and fount lamps on this page. This flame spreader appears to conform to Jones 1892 patent No. 476,541.

Oil fill cap found in the Victor fount lamp below.

Meriden Bronze hanging lamp fount. Wick raiser is push-pull rod. $150.00. Courtesy Kent Stratton.

The Victor No. 2 stand lamp. The gallery does not lift. Height 12". This pattern found in hanging founts. $175.00.

Meriden Bronze fount lamp made to attach to floor lamp or piano lamp. Wick raiser is push-pull rod bent in 90-degree angle. $75.00.

The Victor

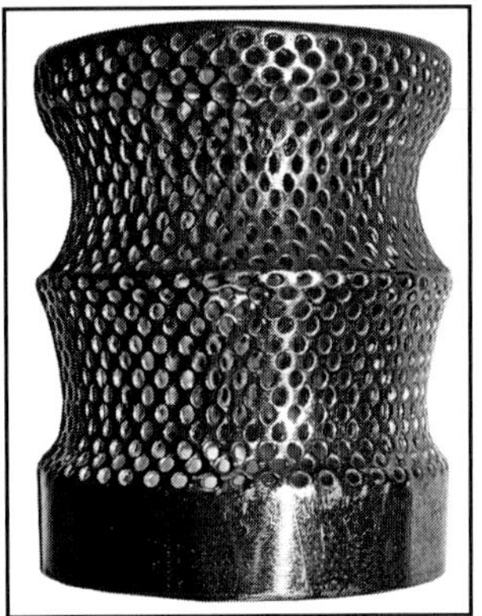

Flame spreader marked "Patented Jan'y 8, 1889; May 21, 1889; July 21, 1891; Nov. 9, 1891; June 7, 1892." I cannot locate a patent or trademark for the Nov. 9, 1891, date.

Oil fill cap.

"The Victor" is stamped in top of the fount.

The Victor No. 2 stand lamp. Height 12". This lamp has original deep gold plating finish. $75.00.

The Victor No. 2 stand lamp. Height 12". Some identical lamps are unmarked. $75.00.

Baby Victor

Baby Victor banquet lamp. The flame spreader is not marked. This lamp is found with identical fount but unsigned. Height 14¼". $250.00. Courtesy Alan Freeman.

Baby Victor night light signed "Baby Victor" on the fount, missing size 0 flame spreader. Height 7½". $150.00.

Meriden Lamp

Meriden oil pots are usually signed somewhere on top of the fount or around the base of the burner. Also found with "Pat. May 21, 1889" flame spreader.

Flame spreader marked "Patented June 7, 1892."

Oil fill caps found on Meriden oil pots.

Meriden oil pot with black finish to match lamp base. The flame spreader above is commonly found in Meriden oil pots. This pot also found with "The Meriden" oil fill cap. $75.00.

Meriden Bronze oil pot. Height 7½". The finish is a dark brown plating that matched the lamp vase. Meriden oil pots are commonly signed around the the base of the burner. This oil pot has been found with a Meteor-type burner (see right). $75.00.

Meriden banquet lamp with Meriden oil pot and Meteor burner base. $300.00. Courtesy Fil Graff.

Flame Spreaders

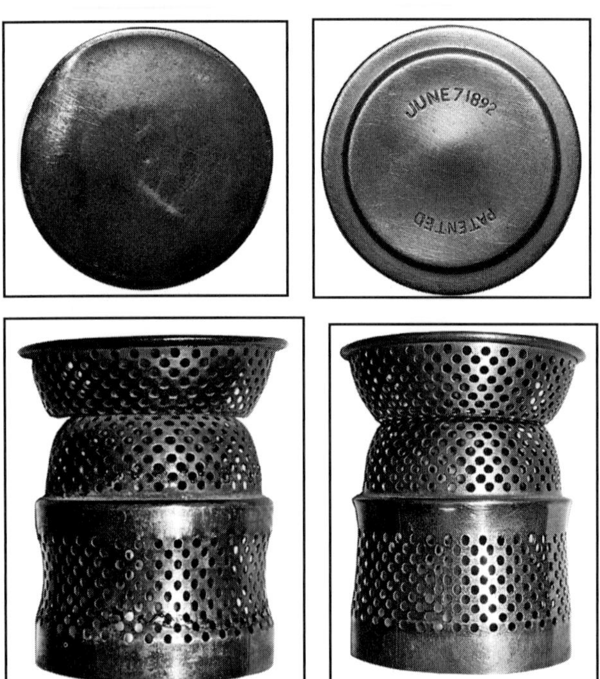

Meriden Bronze flame spreaders. Above left is unmarked and compressed. Above right marked "Patented June 7, 1892." These flame spreaders are easily misshaped when inserting or removing from lamps.

Meriden Bronze Banquet Lamps

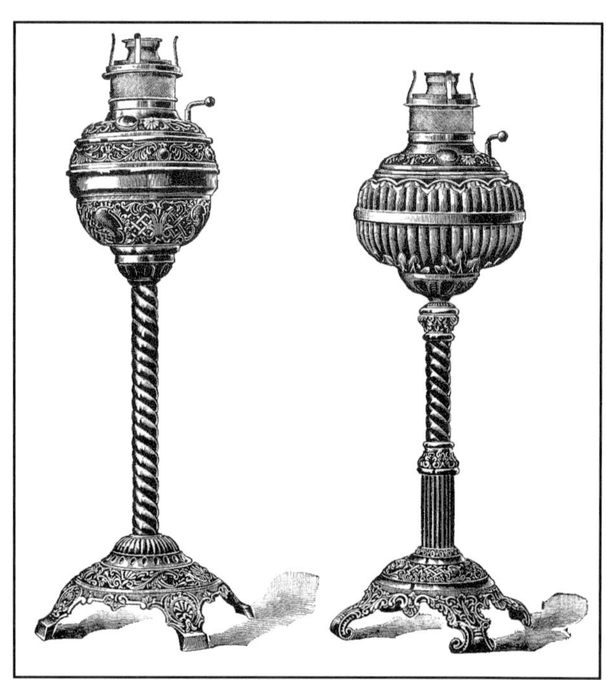

Meriden Bronze banquet lamps illustrated in Pitkin & Brooks catalog in 1892. Height 23". Courtesy David Broughton.

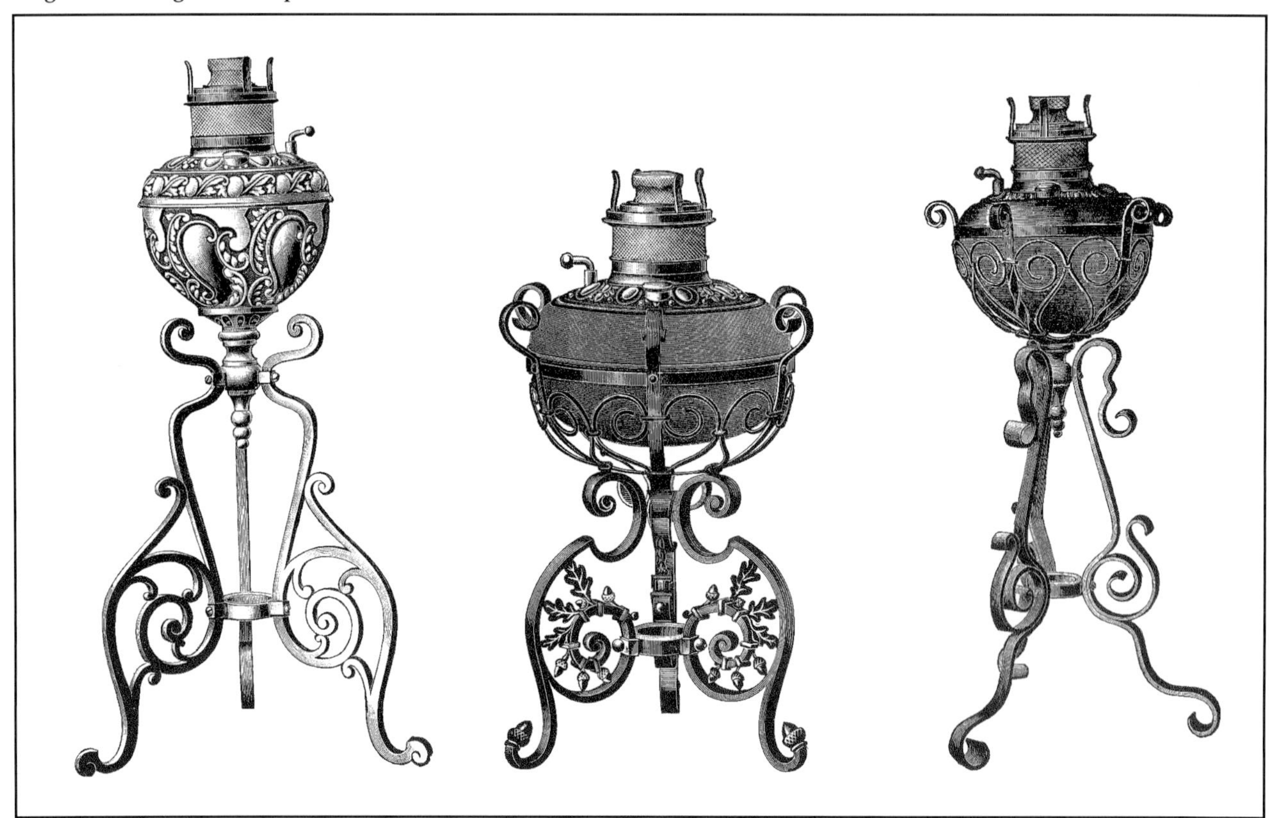

Meriden Bronze banquet lamps, black wrought-iron stands, illustrated in Pitkin & Brooks catalog in 1892. Height varies from 16" to 24". Courtesy David Broughton.

Meteor, 1895 – 1900

Meteor lamps were introduced in 1895 as "Absolutely without a Rival" by the Simmons Hardware Company, St. Louis. I believe Meriden Bronze developed the Meteor; however, Edward Miller & Company made Meteor-brand lamps after 1900. See Edward Miller & Co. for more information. These images are from the 1899 Simmons Hardware catalog.

The Meteor stand lamps are large and of heavy brass construction. The cast-iron loading weight on No. 2 stand lamps has four large feet to elevate the lamp and allow air flow into the central draft tube. Variations in design of the foot, other than shown here, have been seen. Meteor brand lamps were made in vase, banquet, No. 1 & No. 2 stand lamps, and No. 3 hanging lamp founts.

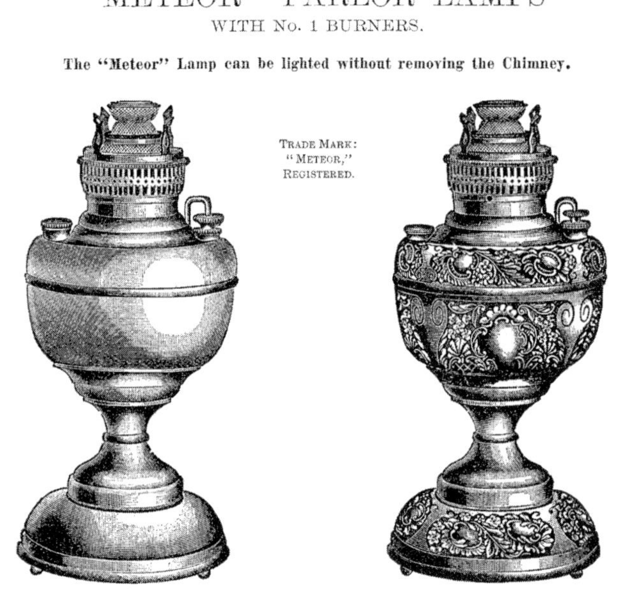

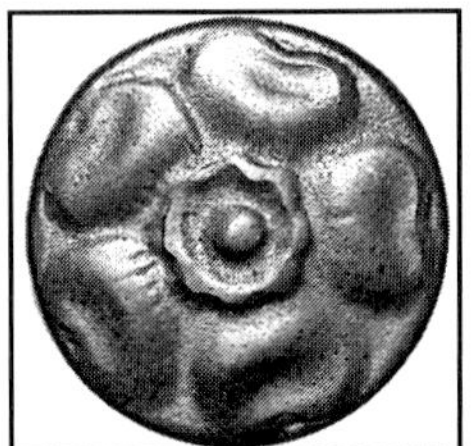

Oil fill cap.

No. 2 flame spreader.

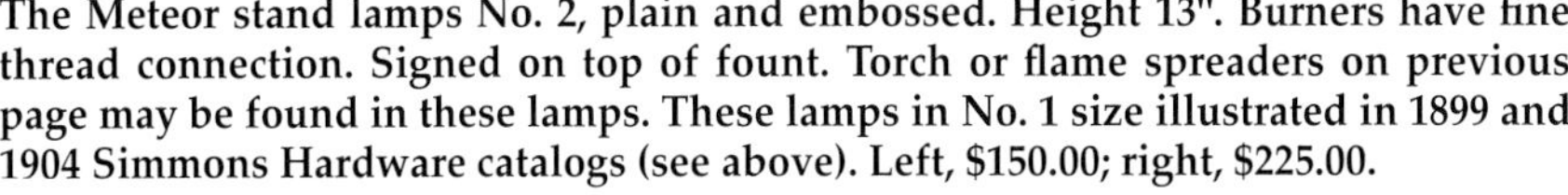

The Meteor stand lamps No. 2, plain and embossed. Height 13". Burners have fine thread connection. Signed on top of fount. Torch or flame spreaders on previous page may be found in these lamps. These lamps in No. 1 size illustrated in 1899 and 1904 Simmons Hardware catalogs (see above). Left, $150.00; right, $225.00.

Meteor banquet lamp. Undated Simmons Hardware Co. handbill.

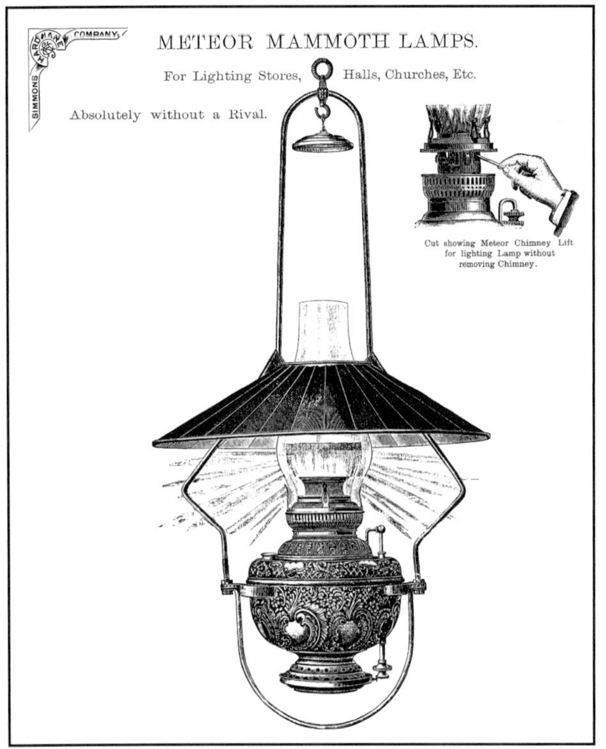

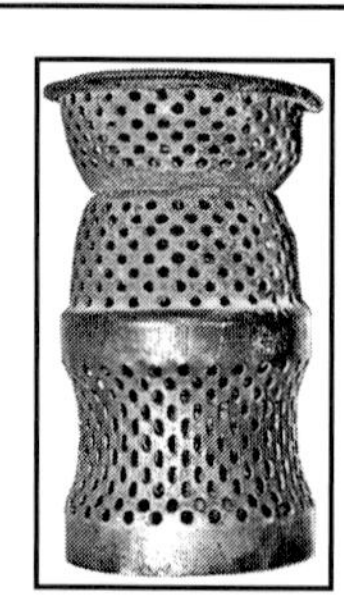

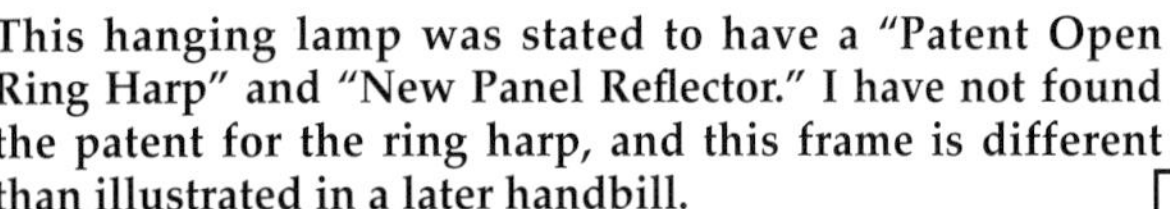

This hanging lamp was stated to have a "Patent Open Ring Harp" and "New Panel Reflector." I have not found the patent for the ring harp, and this frame is different than illustrated in a later handbill.

A. H. JONES.
WICK ADJUSTING DEVICE FOR CENTRAL DRAFT LAMPS.
No. 541,281. Patented June 18, 1895.

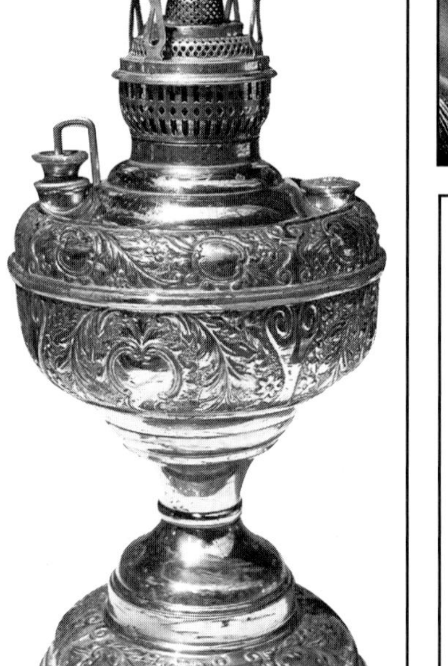

Left: No. 1 Meteor stand lamp signed "The Meteor Lamp." Height 10⅝". Right: No. 1 Meteor oil pot signed "Meteor," diameter 4", height to rim 2½". Both found with "June 7, 1892" dated Meriden Bronze flame spreaders and oil fill caps. Left, $175.00; right, $125.00. Courtesy Ted Hinsdale (left) and Jon Stratton (right).

Meriden Bronze Banquet Lamps 1893

Banquet lamps in Hibbard, Spencer and Bartlett catalog, 1893. Courtesy of Jeff Ebersole.

Liberty Lamp, 1898 – 1900

Liberty lamps were sold by Simmons Hardware beginning in 1899. Liberty was apparently designed by Meriden Bronze just before the company closed. I suspect Edward Miller or Simmons Hardware bought the tooling and inventory. The Meriden Liberty lamp differs from Liberty made by Edward Miller in the cast-iron foot and a larger post for the flame spreader.

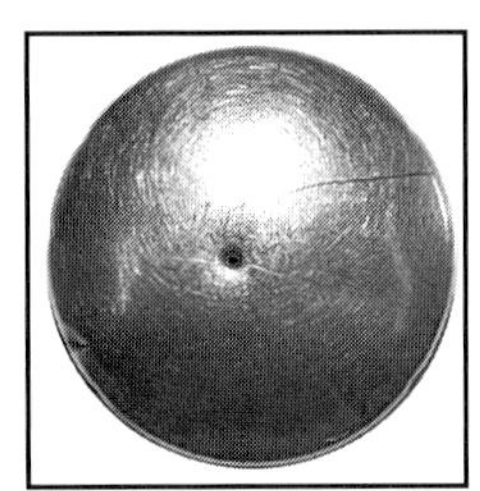

Oil fill cap.

Liberty stand lamp. Height 12". $175.00.

Wick knob.

Liberty burner and wick carrier.

Cast-iron loading weight and feet of lamps made by Edward Miller.

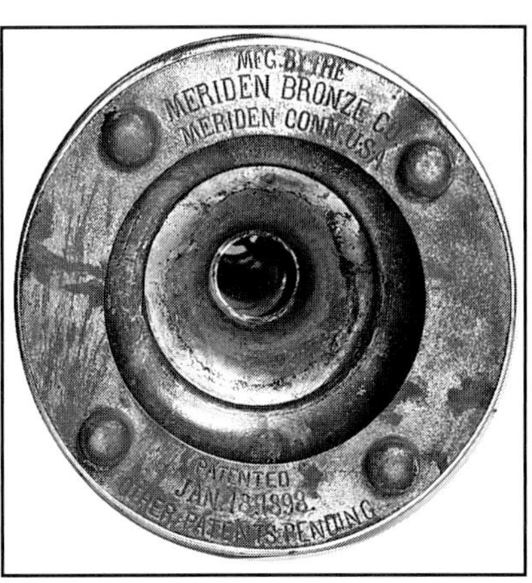

Cast-iron loading weight and feet. The iron is stamped "Mfg. by the Meriden Bronze Co., Meriden, Conn. USA. Patented Jan. 18, 1898, Other Patents Pending." These patents unknown.

Meriden Malleable Iron Company

1868 – 1901

Lamp Manufacture 1881 – 1892

Meriden Malleable Iron Company (MMI) was incorporated in 1868 in Meriden, Connecticut. The company manufactured cabinet hardware, drawer pulls, shelf brackets, ink stands, furniture casters, and brass and iron castings for plumbing.

MMI employed 150 in 1897. Officers at that time were George W. Lyon, president; Eli I. Merriman, secretary and treasurer; and Chas. L. Lyon, superintendent.

Joseph Kintz became superintendent of MMI in 1870. Kintz was associated with P. J. Clark as a tin worker in Meriden and held several unassigned patents for improvements in lanterns while he lived in Meriden and worked for MMI. Clark and Kintz also held unassigned patents for improvements in flat-wick hanging and bracket lamps.

Kintz left to organize Craighead and Kintz in Ballard Vale, Massachusetts in 1883. He was later employed as superintendent of the Pittsburgh Brass Company, 1890 – 1895.

The old MMI buildings were bought by the Meriden Fire Arms Company in 1905. Meriden Fire Arms was owned by Sears, Roebuck & Company, which sold the guns and pistols made there. Sears rebuilt and modernized the factory.

Trade Names

Meriden Malleable made outstanding hanging frames for library lamps. The company apparently distributed lamps and fixtures through department stores and distributors. No brands or trade names have been determined.

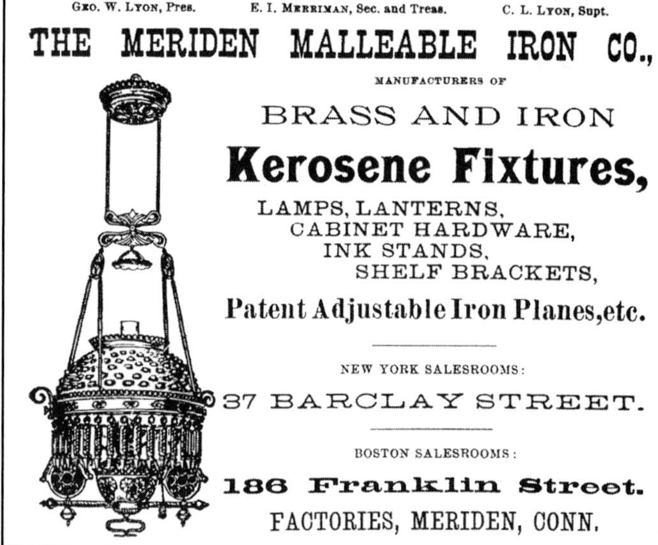

Advertisement, 1888 *Meriden City Directory*. Courtesy Allen Weathers.

Selected Patents, Center-draft Lamps

Lyman T. Lawton[1] assigned to Meriden Malleable Iron

1889 402,945

[1]Also patents on hanging lamps.

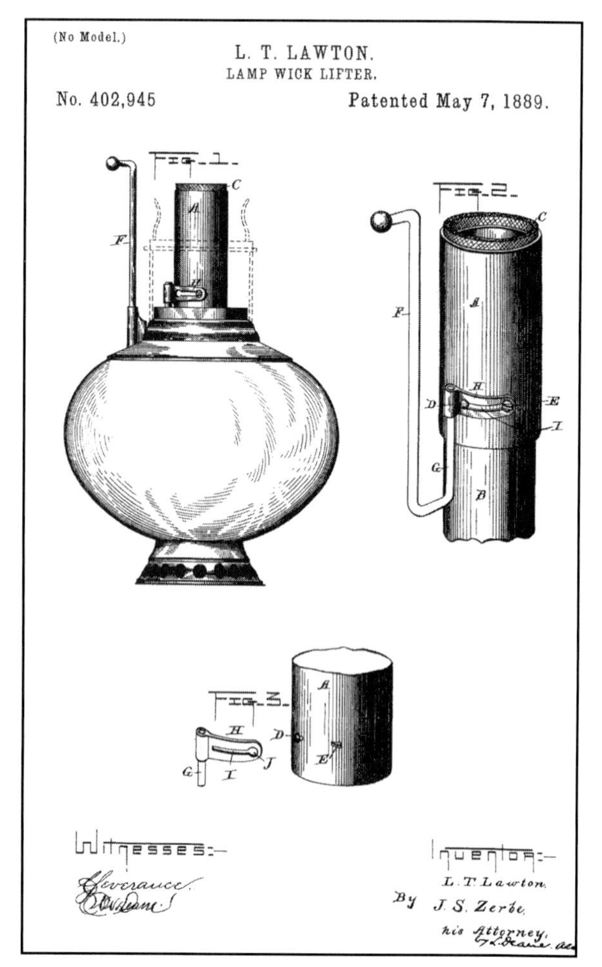

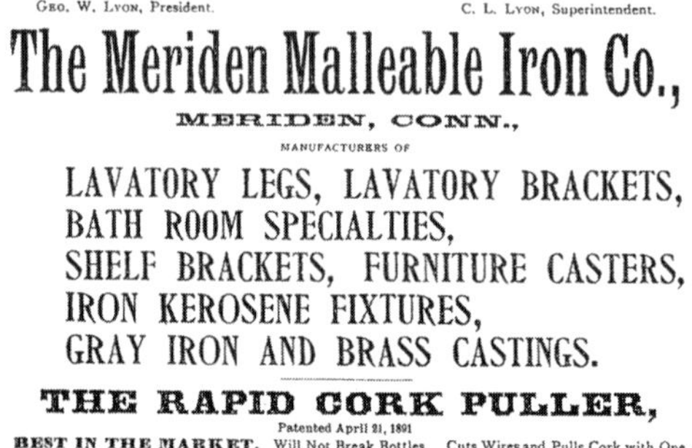

Advertisement, 1889 *Meriden City Directory*. Courtesy Allen Weathers.

F. Meyrose & Company

Western Railroad Lamp & Lantern Manufactory, F. Meyrose Lamp and Mfg. Co., ca. 1852 – 1907; Lamp Manufacture 1870 – 1901

Ferdinand Meyrose and his lamp companies in St. Louis, Missouri manufactured brass and tin lamps, student lamps, tubular station lamps, and railroad lanterns and street lamps.

The following listings are from the *St. Louis Business Directory*, courtesy of the St. Louis Public Library:

— In 1852, Ferdinand Meyrose was a worker of Britannia ware, Main & Second Streets. From 1857 to 1864, Bernard and Ferdinand Meyrose were manufacturers of candlemolds and Britannia ware at 192 S. 4th street.

— In 1870, F. Meyrose & Co. was listed as manufacturer of lamps and lanterns at 733 S. 4th street. Jacob Hiob was a lampmaker for F. Meyrose & Co.

— In 1890 Francis H. Meyrose was superintendent and in 1895 Alexander J. Meyrose was affiliated with Ferdinand, Bernard, and Francis in the business.

F. Meyrose Lamp and Manufacturing Company was incorporated in 1891 with capital of $100,000. Mr. Ferd Meyrose was president; Bernard H. Rust, vice president; and Louis Berry, secretary. The company employed 100 and also manufactured fire extinguishers endorsed by the St. Louis Board of Underwriters. Meyrose was said to be a native of Germany (Anon, 1895).

I suspect that Ferdinand was called "Ferd" in the trade and that Francis was a son or other relative.

An 1886 Western Raiload catalog illustrates a factory building at 731, 735 S. Fourth St., St. Louis, Missouri, with both F. Meyrose & Co. and Western RR at that address and established in 1852.

A letterhead dated 1890 listed F. Meyrose Lamp & Mfg. Co. as manufacturers of Mammoth Calcium hanging and stand lamps, Conductor's Favorite lanterns, street lamps, and kitchen lamps (courtesy Dave Broughton).

F. Meyrose Lamp & Mfg. Co. was not listed in the 1905 or 1910 city directories but was listed in the 1907 *Gould's Commercial Register*.

F. Meyrose's patents granted in 1888 (387,529 and 387,897) illustrated fount shapes which appear to be similar to those in the 1886 Western RR catalog. The 1886 lamps were advertised as "Diamond M Electric Lamps." I assume the *M* stands for Meyrose.

Meyrose employed the terms electric as well as calcium in advertising lamps. The term calcium was most likely a play on words referring to the bright incandescence created by heating calcium oxide. This was called limelight or Drummond light and used in Victorian theaters.

Meyrose entered the center-draft business early relative to the Connecticut lamp manufacturers and Meyrose lamps are relatively unknown by collectors. Barrett (1994) reports few Meyrose lanterns known. Black (1982, 1984), however, illustrated the Meyrose Little Boss cold blast lantern, patent No. 214,576, Apr. 22, 1879.

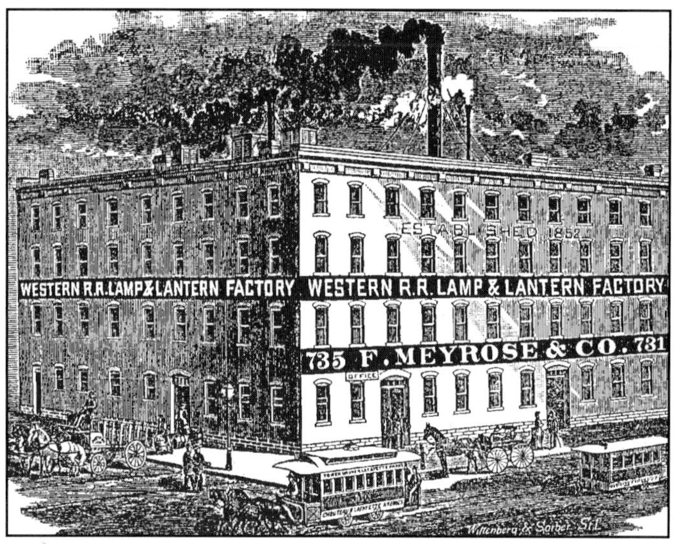

Factory of the Western Railroad Lamp & Lantern Manufactory, F. Meyrose & Co., St. Louis, Missouri.

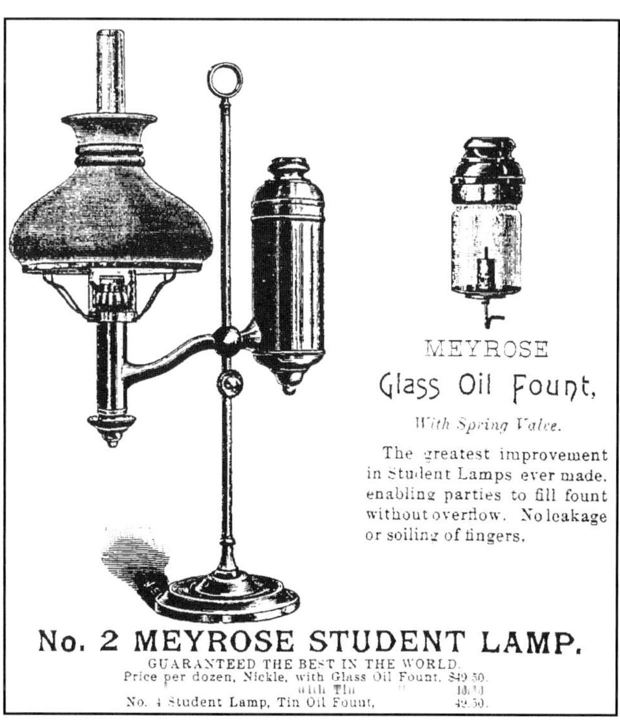

Meyrose student lamp illustrated in 1886 catalog of the Western Railroad Lamp & Lantern Manufactory.

Trade Names

Center-draft lamps — Meyrose, Meyrose Student Lamp, Diamond M Electric Lamp, Calcium, Mammoth Calcium.

Lanterns — Little Boss, Conductor's Favorite.

The Diamond M Electric lamps look suspiciously similar to the Marsh Electric lamps sold by the St. Louis Electric Lamp Co., J. W. Marsh, manager.

Selected Patents, Center-draft Lamps

Ferdinand Meyrose[1]

1886	355,194
1888	387,529
1888	387,897

[1]Also patents for lanterns, 1866 to 1901.

WESTERN RAILROAD LAMP AND LANTERN MANUF'RY,

F. MEYROSE & CO., Mfrs., 733 and 735 S. 4th St., St. Louis, Mo.

SEND FOR CATALOGUES.

56 Candle Power Electric Lamps and Founts.

No. 0 Lift Wire Tubular.

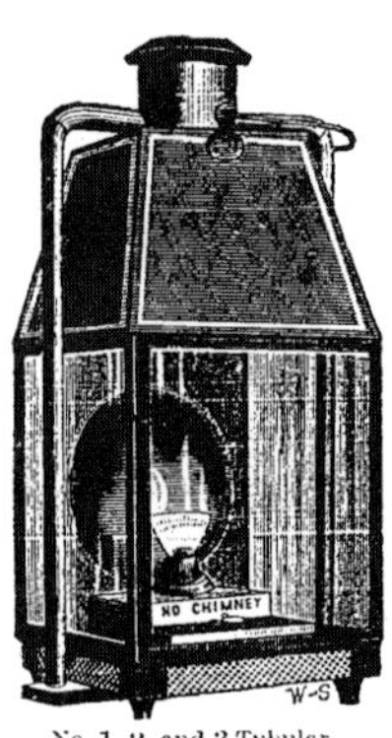

No. 1, 2, and 3 Tubular Station Lamps.

German Study Lamps with Glass and Tin Founts.

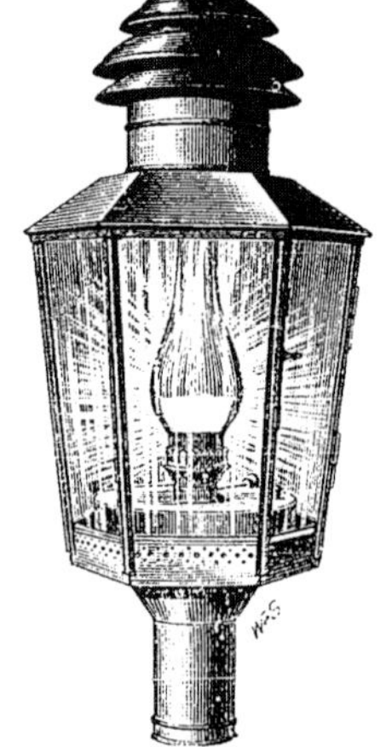

Electric Street Lamp and Electric Square Lamps.

Manufacture over 50 Varieties of Lamps and Lanterns. Send for Catalogues, Terms and Prices.

Advertisement *Pottery and Glassware Reporter* Dec. 5, 1885.

WESTERN RAILROAD LAMP AND LANTERN MANUF'RY,

ESTABLISHED 1852.

MANUFACTURERS OF THE

Celebrated ◇M◇ Electric Lamps AND Founts

THAT BEATS THEM ALL.

ALSO MANUFACTURERS OF

The Genuine Tubular Lamps and Lanterns,

Railroad and Vessel Lanterns. Student Lamps, etc.

Jobbing Trade Solicited.

Catalogues and Prices on Application.

F. MEYROSE, & CO., PROP'S

731, 733 & 735 S. 4th Street, ST. LOUIS, MO.

No. 5 Etlecric Drip Cup Stand Lamp.

No. 2 Electric Fount, finished in Brass, Gold, Bronze and Nickel.

Advertisement, *Pottery and Glassware Reporter,* Jan. 27, 1887.

Save Your Orders

FOR

The Meyrose M Electric Lamps AND Founts

IT WILL PAY YOU TO HANDLE THEM.

These lamps are not the wonders of the world, but they are the best Kerosene Electric Lamps in the market, and in conjunction with our Patented Diamond M Self Adjusting Wick Tube and Holder we defy the world to produce a better Lamp.

No. 5 Electric Drip Cup Hand Lamp.

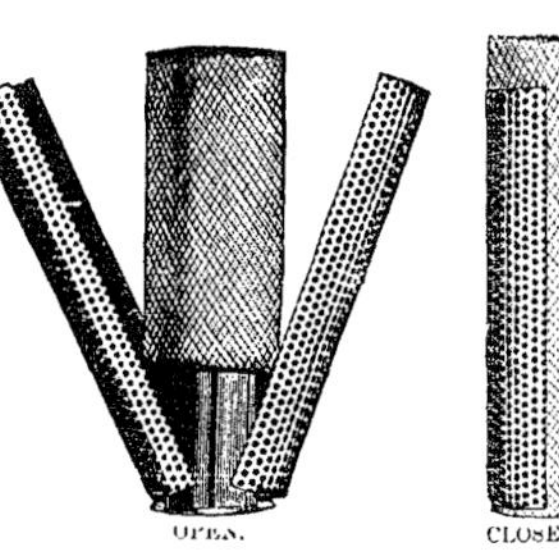

Diamond M Self Adjusting Wick Tube and Holder, the simplest and most valuable invention made, so simple that a child can wick the lamp in an instant. Requires no tying or spring fastenings.

No. 2 Electric Fount, finished in Brass, Gold, Bronze and Nickel.

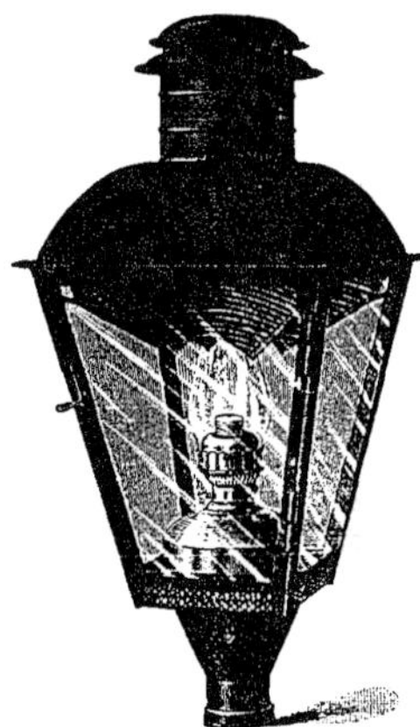

60 Candle Power Electric Street Lamp.

CARONDELET, SOUTH ST. LOUIS MO., April 8th, 1886.

TO WHOM IT MAY CONCERN:

We, the undersigned, appointed a committee by the citizens of Carondelet, in Mass Meeting assembled, to pass upon the merits of various Lamps brought before us, having carefully considered and tested the claims of the Marsh Lamps, made by the St. Louis Electric Lamp Co., the St. Louis Lamp, the Star, Fireside, Rochester, Caperson, Diamond, Hitchcock Lamp, Sun Electric Lamp and the Meyrose Diamond M Electric Lamp, we have unanimously decided in favor of the last above named Lamp, and do hereby cheerfully and conscientiously recommend the said Meyrose Diamond M Electric Lamps to all as the best of Lamps known to us, utility, economy and all other points taken into consideration.

Subscribed to by

John Kraus 8639 S. Broadway Chairman	President Klausman Brewing Co.
Francis [illegible] Jr Secty, 7329 Broadway	Clerk, S. St. Louis Police.
[illegible] Cummings 7401 S Broadway	Grocer.
Alexander Hecker 7221 S Broadway St Louis	Of Williamson & Hecker, Dry Goods.
[illegible] 8639 S Broadway	Proprietor Brewery Saloon.

SAMPLE ORDERS AND CORRESPONDENCE SOLICITED.

WESTERN RAILROAD LAMP AND LANTERN MANUF'RY,

ESTABLISHED 1852.

F. MEYROSE & CO.,

SOLE PROPRIETORS,

731, 733 and 735 S. 4th St., St. Louis, Mo.

Advertisement, *Pottery and Glassware Reporter*, Jan. 15, 1887.

Diamond M Electric Lamps

Diamond M stamped under the burner.

Diamond M Electric burner and flame spreader. Note the different burners and flame spreaders.

Diamond M Electric table lamp, with thimble flame spreader (see next page). Height 10". $175.00. Courtesy Kent Stratton.

Diamond M Electric parlor stand lamp, 1886 catalog.

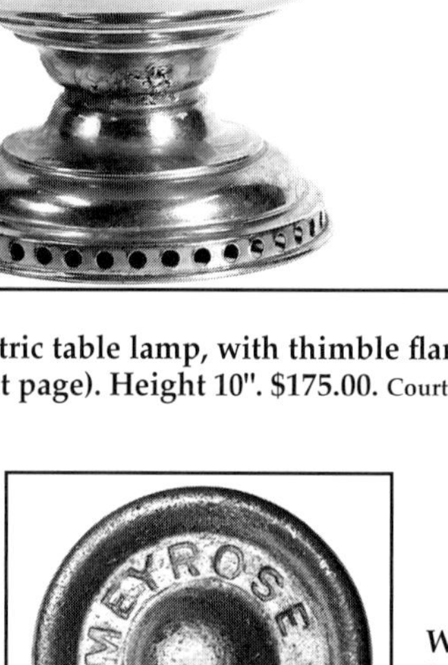

Wick knob.

Electric stand lamp with slate base, 1886 catalog.

Ivy Oak Electric lamp, 1886 catalog, with vase made by Avalon Faience Pottery, Baltimore. A similar vase was sold by Hitchcock; however, the vase shown here will not accept a Hitchcock lamp.

Diamond M Electric lamps illustrated in 1886 catalog of the Western Railroad Lamp & Lantern Manufactory. These lamps appear to use a flame spreader much like the one illustrated for Bristol Brass lamps.

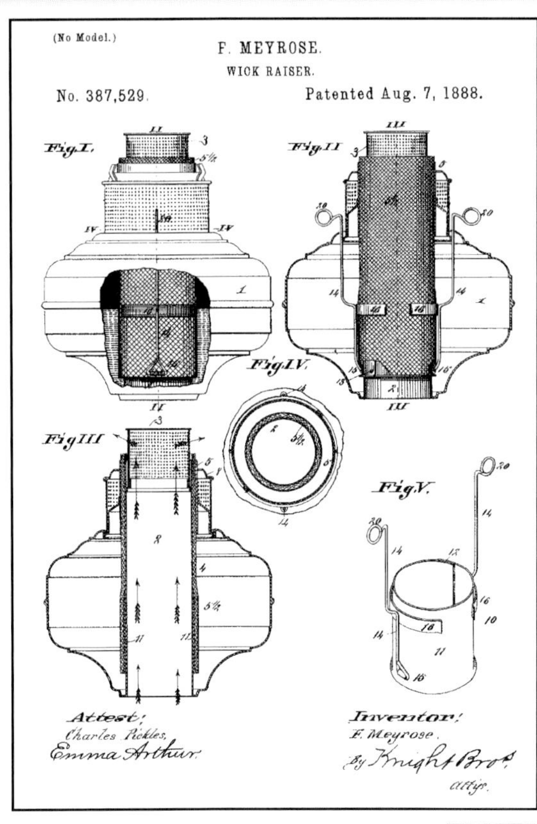

Meyrose

Flame spreader is unmarked. Length 2".

Meyrose stand lamp, height 12". $200.00.

Oil fill cap marked "F. Meyrose & Co. St. Louis."

Drip cup slips into wick tube.

Meyrose stand lamp, height 11½". $125.00.
Courtesy Glen Southard collection.

Meyrose

Meyrose "sugar bowl" table lamp, height 9¼". $150.00. Courtesy Heinz and Ursula Baumann.

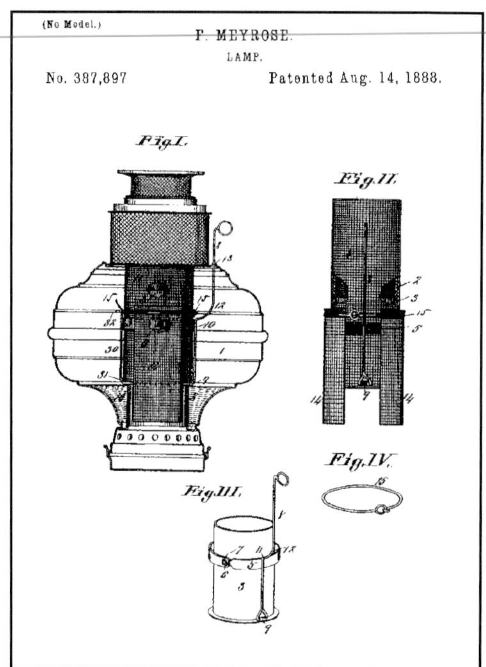

Meyrose stand lamp, height 12". The flame spreader is unmarked. The oil fill marked "F. Meyrose & Co. St. Louis." $125.00. Courtesy Heinz and Ursula Baumann.

Meyrose student lamp marked "F. Meyrose & Co., St. Louis, Mo." on top of the oil tank. Height 20½". This lamp was sold with a tin or a glass tank. $450.00.

Meyrose Calcium Lamp

The term "calcium lamp" implies brighter light and is a play on words as an appeal to the theatre crowd, which would translate it as "bright as limelight." Some chimneys of the period were also marked "Calcium."

Flame spreaders for Meyrose Calcium lamps.
Courtesy Heinz and Ursula Baumann.

Meyrose Calcium sugar bowl table lamp, height 9¼". I believe the oil fill cap is a replacement. $175.00. Courtesy Heinz and Ursula Baumann.

Calcium Parlor Lamp No. 141.

HOLD YOUR ORDERS

for Central Draught Lamps until you have seen our New Line of

CALCIUM LAMPS

65 CANDLE POWER.

MAMMOTH CALCIUM,

300 CANDLE POWER.

The most Brilliant of Lights and simplest in Lift Wick arrangements.

Also wait for the latest in TUBULAR LANTERNS

THE COMMON SENSE TILTING.

Catalogues and Prices on Application to Jobbers.

F. MEYROSE & CO., Mfrs.

731, 733 & 735 S. 4th Street, ST. LOUIS, MO.

SALESROOMS:	GENERAL SALESMEN:
W. R. DEMOREST & CO., 35 Murray St., New York. L. W. MARSTON & CO., Baltimore, Md. CERF SCHLOSS & CO., San Francisco, Cal. H. B. EDWARDS, New Orleans.	S. A. MILLER. O. A. STEMPLE.

ESTABLISHED 185[illegible]

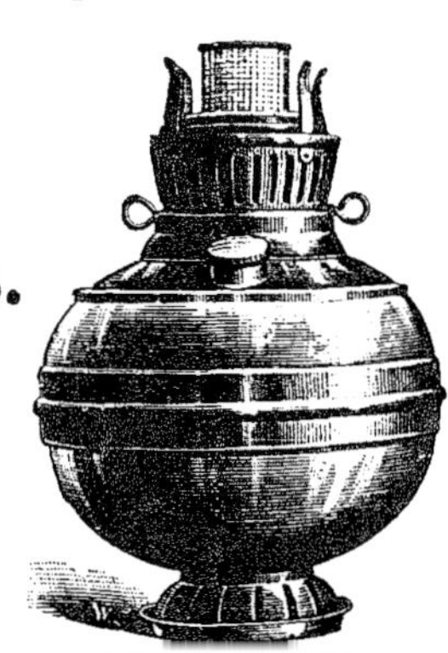

Calcium Fount, No. 110.

Advertisement, *Pottery and Glassware Reporter,* June 14, 1888.

Meyrose Hanging Lamps

> The Meyrose "Mammoth" 250-candle power lamp has the simplest and safest wick fastener in the world, burns 20 hours, and is a big lighter. It is simple, safe and durable, and uses No. 1 tubular globe. The Meyrose "Diamond M" mammoth chandelier, 500-candle power, is just the thing for hotels, churches, halls, etc. It is made on the student lamp principle and is one of the best illuminators in existence. These lamps and a great many other kinds are made by the Western Railroad Lamp and Lantern Manufactory, F. Meyrose & Co., proprietor, St. Louis, Mo.
>
> *Pottery and Glassware Reporter*, Oct. 27, 1887

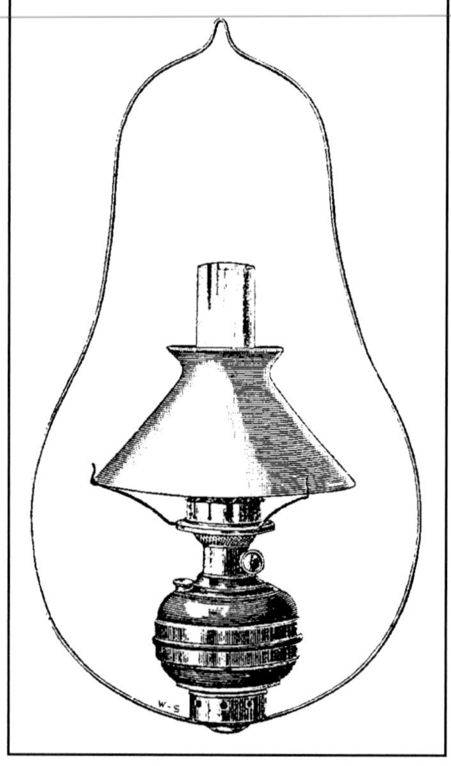

Electric Harp Lamp, 1886 catalog.

The Meyrose 300 Candle Power Lamp is not excelled by any.

Our Wick Movement is certainly the best in the world.

F. Meyrose & Co.,

731 to 735 S. Fourth St.,

ST. LOUIS, MO.

Advertisement for Meyrose Calcium hanging lamp, *Pottery and Glassware Reporter,* Jan. 1, 1891.

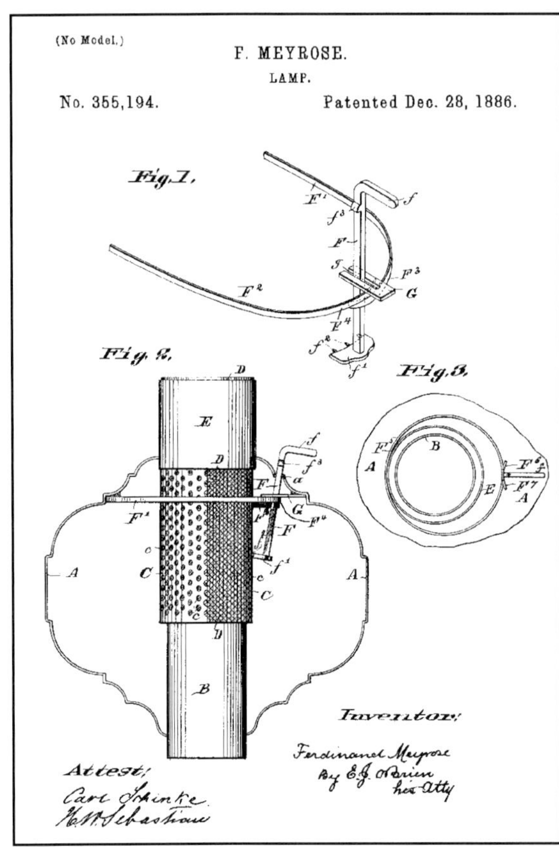

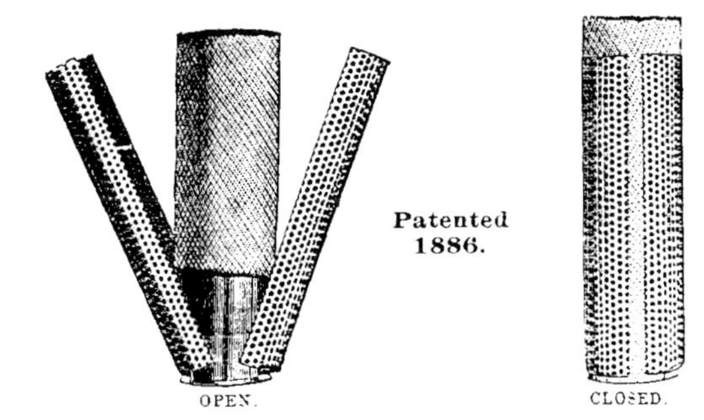

THE NEW IMPROVED DIAMOND M

Self-Adjusting Wick Tube and Holder.

For simplicity and convenience in re-wicking, and as an economiser in wick, it can not be excelled. A child can rewick or replace the wick in an instant, as it requires no *tying* or *spring* fastenings to hold it. It is simply slipped over the inner tube or wick holder and held tight in its place by the two outer perforated half shells. When closed together as shown in cut number 2, it is then ready for use in Lamp. It is well known that there is a great loss of wicks in Electric Lamps, which is done away with by the above improvement, as the wick can be built up by raising it as high as desired after being burned to the level of tube, then placing parts of the old or new wick underneath or on top of wick remaining on the tube, by this process the last drop of oil will be burned and no wick go to waste. The above improvement will only be used in Lamps of our manufacture, and no others.

Meyrose Conductor's Lantern

Meyrose Conductor's Favorite lantern. $300.00.

Oil pot and burner for Meyrose lantern. The burner is marked "E. Miller & Co., Meriden, Conn." Bottom of lantern marked "F. Meyrose & Co., St. Louis, MO."

Edward Miller & Company

1844 – 1924

The Miller Company, 1924 – Present; Burner and Lamp Manufacture 1860 – 1985

The Edward Miller & Company was one of America's premier lamp manufacturers during the late nineteenth century. Edward Miller managed the company with skill, always seeking innovation and competitive costs in manufacturing to improve his products. He became interested in kerosene burners and lamps early in company history.

In 1844, at age 17, Edward Miller, with help from his father, formed a partnership of Joel Miller and Son to make lamp screws, candlestick springs, and tinware in Meriden, Connecticut. Skills to manufacture these items were learned from his experience working for Horatio N. Howard and Stedman & Clark in previous years.

Telegraph Address: "APSA," NEW YORK. EDWARD MILLER, President. EDWARD MILLER, Jr., Sec'y and Treas. BENJ. C. KENNARD, Assistant Treas.

EDWARD MILLER & CO.
MANUFACTURERS OF
THE MILLER, THE JUNO AND THE ROCHESTER LAMPS

Lamp Burners and Trimmings, Brass and Bronze Tables, Lanterns, Machine Oilers. Brass Foundry and Rolling Mill, Bronze Die and Mould Castings a Specialty

ORGANIZED 1844. INCORPORATED 1866.

In all varieties for HANGING, FLOOR OR TABLE USE.

Salesrooms: ~~10 & 12 College Place, N. Y. City.~~ 63 Pearl St., Boston, Mass. 808 & 809 Masonic Temple, Chicago.

Remittance must be made in New York Funds and addressed to Meriden. No one is authorized to collect on our account without a written order. Prices Subject to Change Without Notice. *Not Responsible for Breakages.

NEW YORK STORE: 26 and 30 W. Broadway (formerly 10 and 12 College Place), and 66 Park Place.

Meriden, Conn. Oct 5. 1895

In 1848 Miller repaid his father's loan and renamed the business Edward Miller Company. He improved the facilities and continued to make brass screws, candle holders, and springs as specialities. Miller later began making lamp burners for camphene burning fluid, which gave better light than whale oil.

Miller recovered from a fire in 1856 only to face the country's financial panic in 1857. According to research by Allen Weathers (Scheips and Weathers, 1995), Miller saw the Vienna burner in New York City in 1858 as he was searching for new products to manufacture. He designed and made a similar burner for kerosene oil distilled from bituminous coal and was in good position for the popular demand that came with more economical fuel when petroleum wells were discovered in Pennsylvania.

From 1860 to 1876 the company held numerous patents for metal spinning lamps, lanterns, and burners, including the Marcy burner.

In 1866, a joint stock company was organized with capital of $500,000 under the name Edward Miller & Company to build a brass rolling mill and increase the capacity of the factory to accommodate the rapidly growing business for kerosene lamp burners.

Edward Miller, Jr., graduated from Brown University in 1874, about the time a creative engineering department was formed. The purpose was to study new developments in lighting and to develop patents for Edward Miller & Company. Edward Miller, Jr., assigned patents to the company, including patent 514,158 in 1894 for a wick raiser. Other men associated with creative engineering were R. B. Perkins, C. A. Holbrook, Frank Rhind, William C. Homan, and Frank T. Williams. Arthur Miller joined the company in 1884.

Edward Miller supported the American Lamp Burner Association, organized to "gain price stability" (see appendix and Scheips and Weathers, 1995).

Edward Miller & Company made fancy stand lamps, piano lamps, library lamps, bronze lamps, student lamps, decorated lamps, chandeliers, street lamps, and lanterns. By 1876, Miller was a major manufacturer of bronze ornaments, vases, mantle and desk ornaments, urns, cast brass items, statuettes, and art objects. The company exhibited bronze lamps and ornaments and tinners' hardware at the Centennial Exposition in 1876.

The company also made non-explosive hand lamps, night lamps, marine gimbal lamps, mill lamps, station lamps, and tubular lamps and lanterns. Smokeless oil heaters and Everlit (brand) bicycle lamps were also among their products.

By the 1890s, the company diversified into several new products — Miller 97 bicycle lamps, Majestic Bicycle (carbide) lamps, Miller Electrolite (acetylene) table lamps, Miller oil heaters (some 16 different styles of oil burners including one named Zenith), radiant incandescent gas burners, a mantle lantern named Ariel, marine lamps, and fancy table and hall lamps.

Edward Miller made kerosene mantle lamps for the Daylite Company in Chicago about 1915 to 1922. The same lamp was sold by Montgomery Ward in its catalog as the "Sunlight Kerosene Mantle Lamp." The open-flame, center-draft Daylite lamps are in a chapter so named in this book.

The company had stores in New York, Boston, and Chicago, as well as a large export trade. Sales rooms were opened in Philadelphia and San Francisco as the company prospered. Lamps made by Edward Miller were sold throughout the world.

Edward Miller manufactured Rochester lamps for Charles Upton beginning in 1884 and 1885 and, I believe, was the primary manufacturer of Rochester brand lamps until 1892, when the license

EDWARD MILLER & CO.,

MANUFACTURERS OF

Kerosene Burners,

Lamp and Lantern Trimmings,

Silvered Mica Reflectors, Machine-Oilers, Kettle-Ears,

AND A GENERAL ASSORTMENT OF

TINNERS' HARDWARE,

Center St., Head Miller St., Meriden, Conn.

(Store, 104 Chambers Street, New York City.)

Meriden Business Directory, 1870.
Courtesy Allen Weathers.

was granted to the Bridgeport Brass Company. Miller signed a licensing agreement with Upton to sell the Rochester Lamp, for which he paid a royalty of 35¢ per lamp to the Rochester Lamp Company, New York City, until 1906 (Scheips and Weathers, 1995).

In 1886 Miller hired Frank Rhind, who assigned 32 patents to the company during the next six years. Rhind was a prolific inventor, and his work resulted in development of the Miller lamp. Rhind left Miller to work for Bridgeport Brass (see obituary in the chapter about the Bridgeport Brass Company) in 1892, with encouragement by Charles Upton. William Homan and Frank Williams continued to improve Miller lamps after Rhind's departure.

Edward Miller sold patented gas fittings for table lamps in 1883. The gas attachment simply replaced the flat-wick burner in decorated and metal vase lamps. Miller also manufactured and sold acetylene and alcohol lamps.

Edward Miller purchased the Charles F. Monroe glass decorating factory in 1916, operating it until 1923.

Edward Miller died in 1909, and Edward Miller, Jr., became president. General Electric purchased the company in 1924, and the reorganized firm became known simply as the Miller Company. The Miller Company manufactured Vestal table and harp lamps (plain and embossed), burners, and lamp fittings well into the 1940s.

The Miller Company manufactured electric lamps of Early American design, tungsten filament lamps, mercury vapor lamps, and fluorescent lighting systems during the early twentieth century. The company was the first outside supplier for the General Electric Supply Company, beginning in 1926. The lighting portion of the company was sold to Harvey Hubbell, Inc., in 1985. The Miller Company continues in Meriden today as a specialty manufacturer of copper-based strip alloys for the electronic industry

Advertisement, *Crockery and Glass Journal*, Dec. 14, 1876.

Established 1844. Organized 1866.

EDWARD MILLER & CO.,

MANUFACTURERS OF

SHEET AND CAST BRASS,

Bronze Lamps,

BRONZE ORNAMENTS,

Kerosene and Fluid Burners,

LAMP AND LANTERN TRIMMINGS,

Brass Kettles, Machine Oilers,

TINNERS' HARDWARE, CAST BRASS, ETC.

Die Sinking and Forging done to order.

MERIDEN, CONN.

Store, 35 Warren Street, Cor. Church, New York.

EDWARD MILLER, Pres't. *W. H. PERKINS, Sec'y, and Treas.*
EDWARD MILLER, Jr., Ass't. Treas. *N. P. IVES, Agent, New York.*

Advertisement, ***Meriden Business Directory*, 1877.** Courtesy Allen Weathers.

Trade Names

Center-draft lamps — The Rochester, Rochester Jr., Juno, New Juno, Tiny Juno, Juno Factory Lamp, Miller (The Miller Lamp), Tiny Miller, Mammoth Store Lamp, Non Explosive Lamp, Vestal, New Vestal, Miller's Lumo, Miller's Vestal, Miller's Ideal, Dresden No. 1, Gem, Gaskell, Champion, Home Lamp, No.2 Empress, Liberty, Astral, Ideal, #3 Mammoth.

Mantle lamps — Daylite, Sundart, Sunlight.

Flat-wick lamps — Miller Duplex Study Lamp. Virtually all of the Miller center-draft founts were manufactured without a center-draft tube to be fitted with Miller side draft or similar flat-wick burners.

Folded-wick burners — Boudoir, Argand Burner, Sunbeam.

Lanterns — Tubular Lantern No. 16, Ariel.

Bicycle lamps — Everlit, Miller 97, Majestic, Leader, Beacon, Witch of the Night.

Flat-wick burners — Marcy's patent burner, E.M. Duplex, Improved Favorite, Victor, Luna, Apollo, Sun Hinge, Solar, Pilot, Venus, Stellar, Zenith (no chimney).

Round-wick burners — Boudoir and burners for alcohol, lard oil and heavy oil.

Alcohol — founts for Pyro alcohol lamps.

Acetylene — Electrolite.

Heaters — Juno, Miller, Miller Smokeless.

Selected Patents, Center-draft Lamps

Frank Rhind assigned to Edward Miller & Co.

1887 357,412
1887 .... 361,545 unassigned
1887 364,438
1887 372,639
1888 386,658
1888 388,445
1888 390,254
1889 395,757
1889 416,236-37
1890 429,743
1890 440,748
1890 443,868
1891 454,528
1892 478,288
1892 478,639
1892 481,674
1892 483,167
1892 485,429

Horace L. Clark unassigned patents

1889 414,753
1890 440,739
1890 441,642
1892 481,748

William C. Homan[1] assigned to Edward Miller & Co.

1889 408,306
1890 428,170
1890 434,029
1890 434,929
1892 471,083
1892 477,862-65
1892 .... D21,429
1892 .... D21,521
1892 .... D21534
1893 .... 491,965 unassigned
1893 494,862-63
1893 496,657
1895 537,890
1896 556,980
1896 564,309
1897 586,269
1898 614,471

Frank Theodore Williams[2] assigned to Edward Miller & Co.

1892 477,034-35
1893 499,273
1893 505,619
1895 539,761
1896 559,069
1896 571,631
1898 598,688
1900 644,786
1900 651,404
1900 659,333-34
1900 662,582
1900 662,583
1900 662,584
1901 671,464
1902 691,832
1917 1,235268

Russell B. Perkins[3] assigned to Edward Miller & Co.

1886 339,923

Roland L. Brewer assigned to Edward Miller & Co.

1890 428,882

Edward Miller, Jr., assigned to Edward Miller & Co.

1894 514,158

Louis Hornberger[4] assigned to Edward Miller & Co.

1894 .... D23,722

Frederick W. Ives assigned to Edward Miller & Co.

1895 535,499

Charles Maschmeyer[5] assigned to Edward Miller & Co.

1895 538,427
1897 578,251

Thomas Langston[6] assigned to Edward Miller & Co.

1898 615,666

[1]Also patents hanging, organ, bicycle lamps, inverted mantle burners.

[2]Also patents for bicycle lamps.

[3]Also patents on hanging lamps.

[4]Also design patents for fount holders for vase lamps.

[5]Also organ lamp patent assigned to Miller. In 1882 he worked for Craighead & Ewell Mfg. Co.

[6]He held patents relating to Craighead & Kintz Daylight lamps.

Trademarks for Oil-burning Lamps

The Juno trademark (below) was registered on May 9, 1893; the company stated that the mark had been used since January 1878.

The familiar "E M & Co." (see below right) and "Miller" (below left) trademarks were registered on May 9, 1893; they had been used since Jan. 4, 1893.

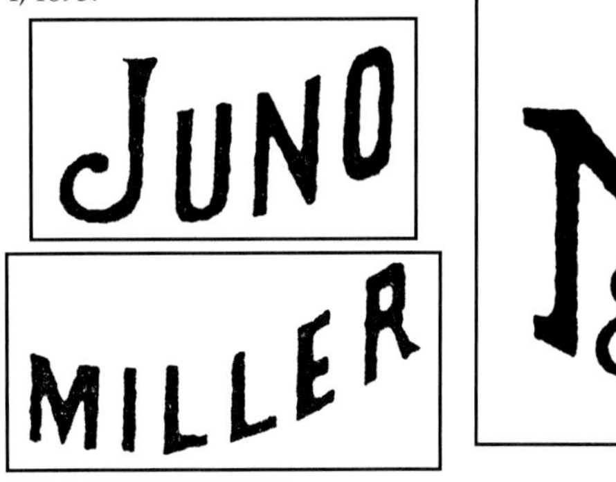

The Rochester Lamp Licenses and Agreements

Edward Miller gained enormous advantage in business when he agreed to manufacture Rochester lamps for Charles Upton and the Rochester Lamp Company. Miller agreed to fixed production costs each year (see agreement letter below, dated 1887), and in return, Edward Miller & Company was given rights to sell Rochester lamps. Miller agreed to pay a royalty for every Rochester lamp that he sold. Edward Miller & Company produced so many Rochester lamps that the company built a new factory addition in 1889 to supply the demand.

Licenses were later given to other manufacturers. In 1895 Upton licensed the Bridgeport Brass Company to manufacture and sell the New Rochester Lamp.

Michael Collins gave Edward Miller license to produce his burner for the royalty of 6¢ per dozen, the same as granted Wallace & Sons, on the condition of no more than four licenses in Connecticut (Weathers, 2003).

Competition among companies was intense as each worked to improve its share of the market. An improved wick raiser, better flame spreader and brighter light, better fuel economy, or a safer lamp could make a difference and promote sales. Patents were assigned to companies by their employees or bought outright from inventors. Other patentees (i.e., independent contractors) licensed their patents in return for royalties. People moved from company to company, by choice or by hire, to obtain their skills and knowledge.

Edward Miller & Co.
Manufacturers of
Fine Lamps, Bronze Ornaments, Burner Goods, Sheet Brass, Tinners' Hardware &c.

Stores:
New York Store. 51 & 53 Barclay St.
Boston Store. 38 Pearl Street.

Meriden, Conn. U.S.A. Jan. Ist, 1887

Rochester Lamp Co., N.Y. City.

We make you the following proposition. In consideration that you allow no one but ourselves to manufacture the Rochester Lamp Burner in the United States nor sell oil tanks with the Rochester Burner on to any one except as we may mutually agree, we will make you the following prices for the year 1887. No charge for packages del'd in New York or Boston as here-to-fore.

	Brass	R. Gold, Nickel or A. Brass
Founts NO. I	$ 9.50 Doz.	$10.50 Doz.
" NO.2	$ 10.50 "	$11.50 "
" NO.2 Emb.	$13.50 "	$14.50 "
Parlors NO.I	$12.00 "	$13.00 "
" NO.2	$13.00 "	$14.00 "
" NO.2 Emb.	$17.50	$18.50 "
Factory Fount	F.B. $ 9.00 "	
NO. 1724 Lamps	$24.00 "	
" 1730 "	$27.00	
" 1733	$24.00	

Very Truly
Edward Miller & Co

Agreed To
Rochester Lamp Co
Chas. S. Upton manager

Copy of letter.
Courtesy of Allen Weathers.

The Rochester Lamp

Edward Miller & Company advertised the Rochester Lamp extensively through 1890 with full-page advertisements in the May and June issues of *China, Glass and Lamps*. Apparently, Edward Miller primarily sold Rochester lamps at this time and had not developed the famous Juno or Miller center-draft brands. See Rochester Lamp Company.

An 1890 advertisement stating that Edward Miller & Co. manufactured "more than ONE MILLION (Rochester lamps) since 1885... and we show over ONE THOUSAND varieties (our store is an art room) of Library, Hall, Piano and Banquet Lamps, Chandeliers, Vase Lamps, etc."

Advertisement, *Harper's,* November 1888.

Advertisement, *Meriden City Directory,* 1890, the first year Miller advertised decorated glass lamps. Courtesy Allen Weathers.

Advertisement, *Meriden City Directory,* 1891. Miller did not advertise Rochester lamps in the directory after 1892. Courtesy Allen Weathers.

Edward Miller's catalog No. 43 (ca. 1894) offered both Rochester and Miller lamps. The catalog introduced the new "Miller Lamps" trademarked in 1893. Rochester chandeliers were illustrated with Rochester burners; however, Miller Founts were offered (see right). The fancy hanging lamps were fitted with embossed and frosted shades often used on gas fixtures.

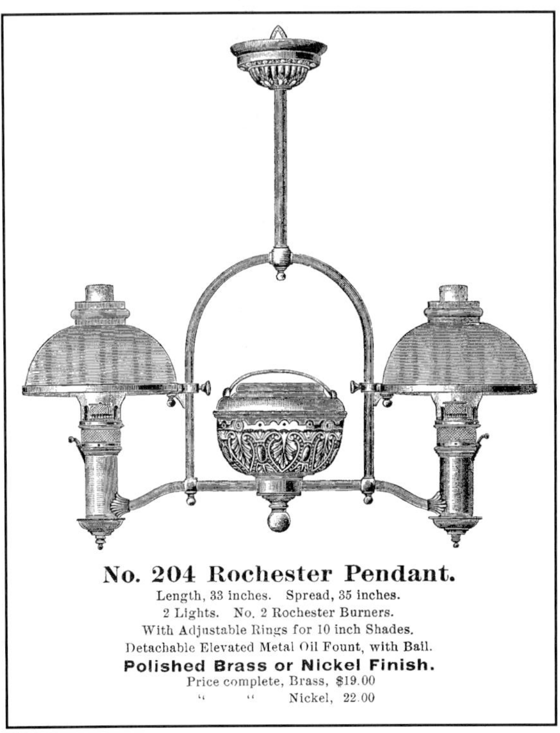

No. 204 Rochester Pendant.
Length, 33 inches. Spread, 35 inches.
2 Lights. No. 2 Rochester Burners.
With Adjustable Rings for 10 inch Shades.
Detachable Elevated Metal Oil Fount, with Bail.
Polished Brass or Nickel Finish.
Price complete, Brass, $19.00
" " Nickel, 22.00

No. 0775 Extension Chandelier.
For No. 02 Embossed Miller Founts, with No. 2 Burners.
Length, closed, 40 inches. Spread, 30 inches.
Band Pierced for 30 and Cusps for 20 and 12 Prisms.
Antique Brass Finish.

Price complete, with No. 02 Miller Founts,	2 Lights,	$13.50
" " " " " "	3 "	18.00
" " " " " "	4 "	22.50
" " " " " "	6 "	30.00

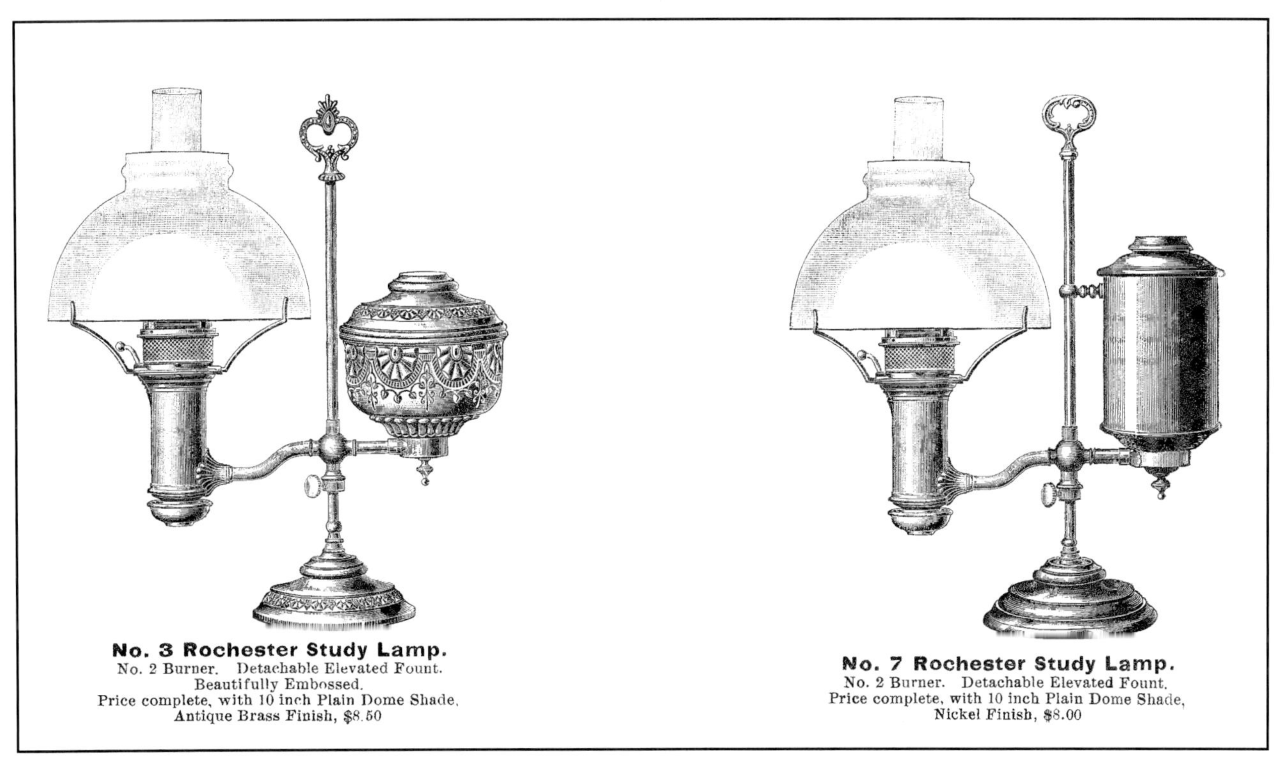

No. 3 Rochester Study Lamp.
No. 2 Burner. Detachable Elevated Fount.
Beautifully Embossed.
Price complete, with 10 inch Plain Dome Shade.
Antique Brass Finish, $8.50

No. 7 Rochester Study Lamp.
No. 2 Burner. Detachable Elevated Fount.
Price complete, with 10 inch Plain Dome Shade,
Nickel Finish, $8.00

The Juno Lamp

In mythology, Juno was the wife of Jupiter; she was the queen of the heavens and the goddess of light. Based on the trademark "Juno" registered in 1893, I presume the Juno center-draft lamp was introduced sometime in the 1892 – 1893 time period. The burners of Juno lamps lock with a bayonet connection and the wick raiser is a single round lift bar.

Miller No. 1 flame spreader.

Standard Miller No. 2 flame spreader with narrow rim found in burners of most No. 2 Juno lamps.

"Snowflake" oil fill cap found on Juno lamps.

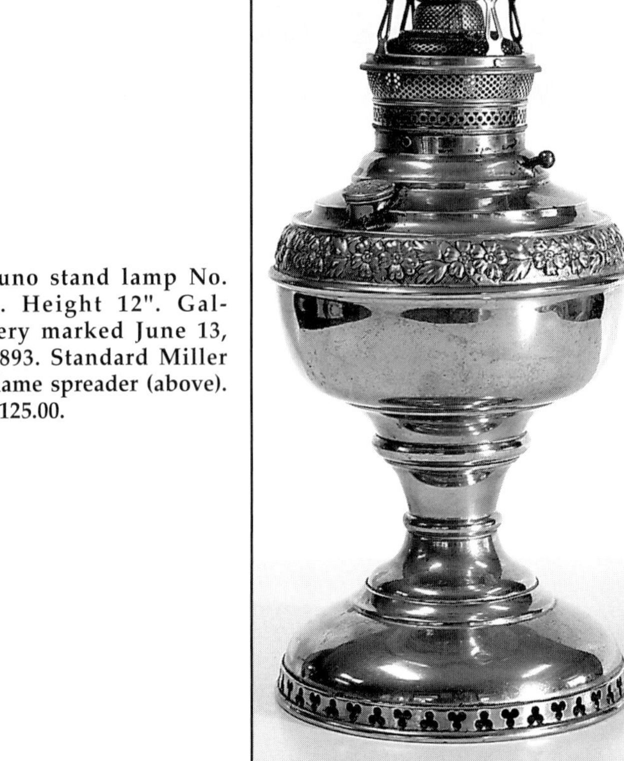

Juno stand lamp No. 2. Height 12". Gallery marked June 13, 1893. Standard Miller flame spreader (above). $125.00.

The Juno stand lamp No. 1. Height 10½". Lift gallery dated "Pat. June 13, 1893." Brass finish. Original shade holder. The 7" shade ring is marked "Pat. Apr. 13, 86." $150.00.

Miller Juno lamps were made over many years. We do not know how the earliest Juno lamps were marked — these examples may or may not represent the earliest lamps. Juno lamps were made in all sizes and a variety of embossed designs. The decorative cast foot and arms of Miller table lamps were made of white metal or brass — those on the lamp below were brass and nickel plated. The Falk, Stadelmann Company in England named one of its central-draft lamps Juno in an 1896/1897 catalog.

DIRECTIONS FOR

THE "MILLER" and "JUNO" LAMPS.

teeth in wick sleeve will disengage from wick, which may be easily removed. Empty oil from lamp, wash it out with hot water and *dry thoroughly*.

To Put in New Wick.

Have the teeth in wick sleeve rest in depressions in wick tube and push wick down over tube with the longer slot next to wick lift; press down wick lift to lowest point; if wick is set correctly, the top of wick will be just below top of tubes. Before replacing burner and thimble be sure that burner tube is securely locked. Refill lamp an hour or more before using.

The Dimensions of Chimneys for the MILLER AND JUNO LAMPS should be as follows:.

	No. 0.	No. 1.	No. 2.	No. 3.
Height,	7 in	8 in.	9 in.	12 in
Dia. of Bulb Outside,	2¼"	3 "	3¾"	5⅛"
Height of Slip,	⅞ "	1 "	1 "	1¼"
Top Opening Inside,	1¼"	1½"	1¾"	2⅛"

By using chimneys of above dimensions the best results will be obtained.

The Wicks and Chimneys to fit the Miller Lamp correspond in size to those used for the well known Rochester Lamp.

Use wicks stamped "MILLER."

Avoid Duplex or Sun chimneys. (OVER)

DIRECTIONS FOR

THE "MILLER" and "JUNO" LAMPS.

READ CAREFULLY AND SAVE THIS TAG.

To Put on Shade or Globe Holder.

Remove burner and burner tube, slip tripod ring over collar, with depression toward wire wick lift. Be sure that *burner tube* is securely *locked* in place before replacing burner.

Fill Lamp After Each Using.

See that thimble and chimney are pushed down to place.

To Light Lift Burner.

Lift the chimney holder and turn it to the left and it will remain locked; after applying the match, turn the chimney holder to the right and it will drop back into place.

To Extinguish.

Push wick lift down quickly and leave down when lamp is not in use.

To Trim.

Remove burner and thimble; rub off char with soft paper or cloth always in one direction.

Keep Burner Clean.

The perforations must not be allowed to fill up, wash both *burner* and *thimble* in hot soap suds or boil with borax or sal-soda.

To Remove Wick.

Remove burner, burner tube and thimble, raise wick lift to full height, when

(OVER)

Directions for use. Courtesy Kent Stratton.

The Juno stand lamp No. 2 with cast foot and decorative arms. Height 11". Standard Miller flame spreader and oil fill cap. $275.00.

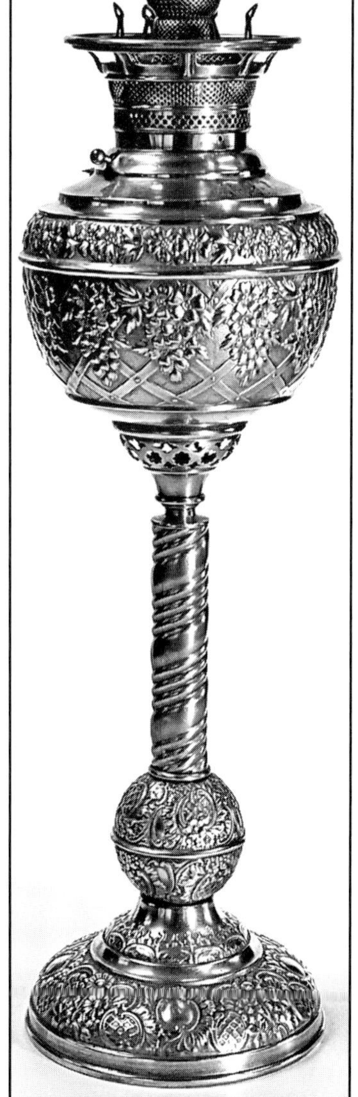

Juno banquet lamp No. 2 with fitter for ball shade. Height 20". Standard Miller flame spreader and oil fill cap. The fount is marked "The Juno Lamp" as above, right. $300.00. Courtesy Kent Stratton.

No. 30 Juno/The New Juno Lamp

About 1895 the Juno was improved with a thumb wheel wick raiser plus wick draw-bar (the draw bar provides rapid downward movement to extinguish the flame, Patent 539,761, see right). The new burners were listed as No. 30 Juno in catalogs. The early burners continued with bayonet connection. At some point the term New Juno was applied and may be found embossed on lamps. Unmarked lamps may have been sold to other stores. These are all grouped here as "New Juno" lamps even though some are embossed "The Juno Lamp." Flame spreaders with narrow or wide rim tops are found in this group of lamps.

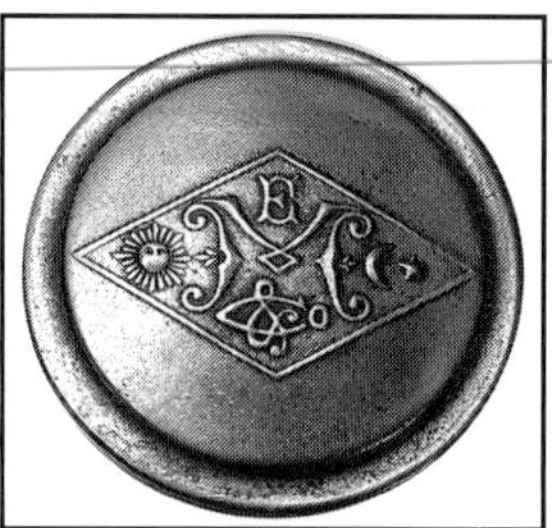

The snowflake oil fill cap is found on most New Juno lamps.

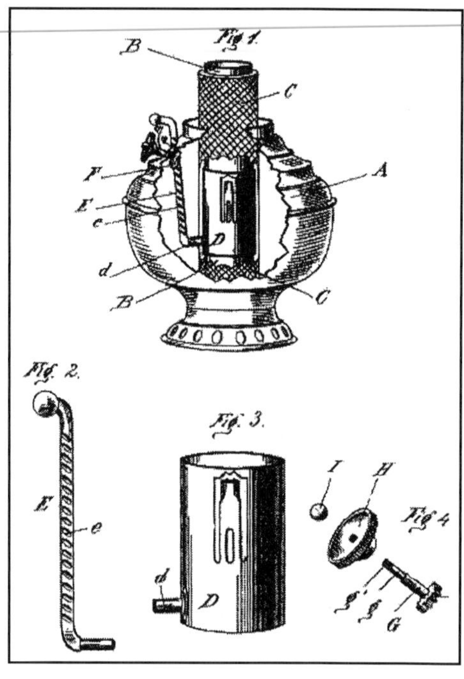

Drawing from Patent No. 539,761 by Frank T. Williams, 1895.

The Miller No. 2 flame spreader with narrow rim is found on many New Juno No. 2 lamps.

The New Juno No. 2 stand lamp. Height 12⅜". The burner is bayonet connection. The fount is marked (above). Patent marks: gallery — "June 13, 1893"; wick knob — "Pat May 21, 1895"; outer wick tube — "Pat'd, Nov 18, 90"; "Mar 29, 92"; "June 14, 92"; "Apr 4, 93"; "May 2, 93." $175.00.

The New Juno No. 2 stand lamp, cast-iron foot. Height 12¼". The burner has a bayonet connection, and the fount marked like the lamp on left. Patent marks are also the same, except the last two on the outer wick tube are missing: gallery — "June 13, 1893"; wick knob — "Pat May 21, 1895"; outer wick tube — "Pat'd, Nov 18, 90"; "Mar 29, 92"; "June 14, 92." $225.00.

No. 30 Juno/The New Juno Lamp

Miller No. 2 flame spreader with wide rim, missing the words "Made in." Some are plain and unmarked. All varieties of flame spreaders are found in New Juno lamps.

The New Juno No. 2 table lamp with cast-iron foot and cast arms. Height 10½". Early burner. Thumbwheel marked "Pat. May 21, 1895." Standard Miller flame spreader and oil fill cap. $200.00.

The New Juno stand lamp No. 2 marked "The New Juno, Made in U.S.A." on top of fount. Height 12". Standard oil fill cap and flame spreader. Thumbwheel dated May 21, 1895. $100.00.

Unsigned Juno stand lamp (No. 2). Height 12". Standard oil fill cap and flame spreader. Thumbwheel dated May 21, 1895. Some lamps are marked "The Gaskell Lamp" on top of the fount. $175.00.

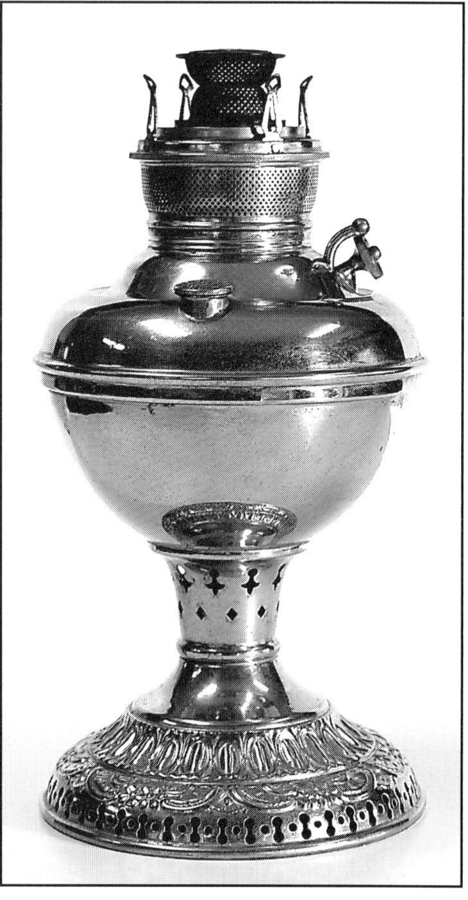

The Juno stand lamp No. 2. Height 12". Standard oil fill cap and flame spreader. Thumbwheel dated May 21, 1895. This lamp has a threaded burner base. $125.00.

The Gaskell Lamp

The Gaskell lamp is basically a New Juno with a slightly modified burner.

The Miller flame spreader found in Gaskell lamps has a standard Miller wide rim and is unmarked on the top.

I do not know the reason for naming the lamp Gaskell. Elizabeth Gaskell was a noted Victorian author in England during the mid-nineteenth century. Edward Miller & Company opened a salesroom in England, and the popularity of Gaskell's writings and of Miller center-draft lamps may be an explanation.

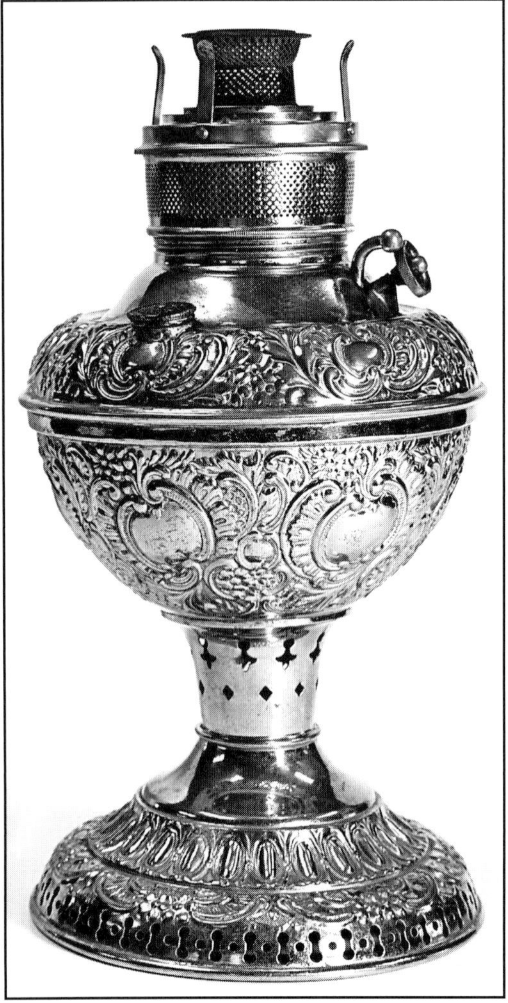

The Gaskell No. 2 stand lamp. Height 11½". Threaded burner base. $200.00.

The Louis Hornberger Burner

Louis Hornberger assigned design patent 23,722 to Edward Miller & Company for an embossed and pierced decorative burner. This premium burner is found in three configurations on a wide variety of lamps. Catalogs illustrate the burner on higher priced lamps, often gold plated.

The burners are dated "Oct. 23, 1894" around the bottom edge of the burner.

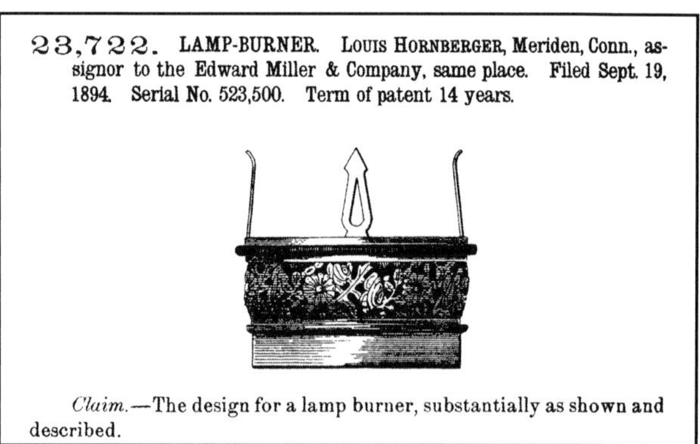

23,722. LAMP-BURNER. Louis Hornberger, Meriden, Conn., assignor to the Edward Miller & Company, same place. Filed Sept. 19, 1894. Serial No. 523,500. Term of patent 14 years.

Claim.—The design for a lamp burner, substantially as shown and described.

Notice in the *Official Gazette* of patent received Oct. 23, 1894.

Mt. Washington Colonial Ware kerosene banquet lamp with Miller Hornberger burner. Height 33½". $3,000.00. Courtesy Green Valley Auctions, Inc.; photographer William H. McGuffin.

Miller banquet lamp with Hornberger burner. These were advertised in 1896 as "Fine gold and onyx lamps," priced at $15.00 or more.

The Louis Hornberger Burner

Hornberger burner, non–lift gallery, fits directly into the fount.

Hornberger burners with lift galleries for easy lighting. The burner on right has added air ventilation in the gallery. These burners fit into the outer wick tube below. The burners with lift galleries are dated "June 13, 1893" on top of the gallery. These burners do not fit directly into a lamp fount, such as illustrated below left.

Outer wick tube and burner seat for Hornberger burners (above). The outer wick tube is marked "Pat'd, Nov, 18, 90, Mar. 29, 92, June 14, 92."

New Juno lamp with Hornberger burner. This lamp is unmarked. The burner is non-lift and fits lamp with bayonet connection. Height 11½". $175.00.

Miller oil pot with Hornberger burner, lift gallery. Height 7¼". This oil pot is signed "The Miller Lamp, Made in U.S.A." The pot is made to fit into a glass or metal vase. These oil pots are usually found in better quality vase lamps. $150.00.

The Miller Lamp

After success manufacturing and selling Rochester and Juno lamps, Edward Miller named the company's signature lamp "Miller" (or "The Miller Lamp") to take advantage of the company name and reputation. The Miller trademark was registered in 1893. The early Miller lamps use a bayonet burner connection; however, most found today have burner threads. The U-shaped wick-raising bar with knob was patented in 1892. Exceptions are the Tiny Miller and the Home lamps, which employ single "wire bar" wick raisers. Most Miller lamps are marked "The Miller Lamp."

Snowflake oil fill cap found on most Miller lamps.

Wick-raising thumbwheel marked: "2 Patents — June 28, 1892."

ESTABLISHED 1844. INCORPORATED 1866.

EDWARD MILLER & CO.,

MANUFACTURERS OF

"THE MILLER LAMP,"

LATEST AND BEST.

TRADE MARK

Chandeliers, Library Lamps, Bronze Lamps, Decorated Lamps, Bronze Ornaments, Student Lamps, Fine Sand Castings.

Sheet and Cast Brass, Kerosene Oil Burners, Lanterns, Brass Kettles, Machine Oilers, Tinners' Hardware.

MADE IN ALL STYLES AND SIZES.

The Only Perfect Center Draft Lamp.

FACTORIES:
MERIDEN, CONN.
STORES:
10 and 12 COLLEGE PLACE, NEW YORK.
63 PEARL ST., BOSTON, MASS.

Advertisement in the 1893 *Meriden Business Directory*, introducing the Miller Lamp. Courtesy of Allen Weathers.

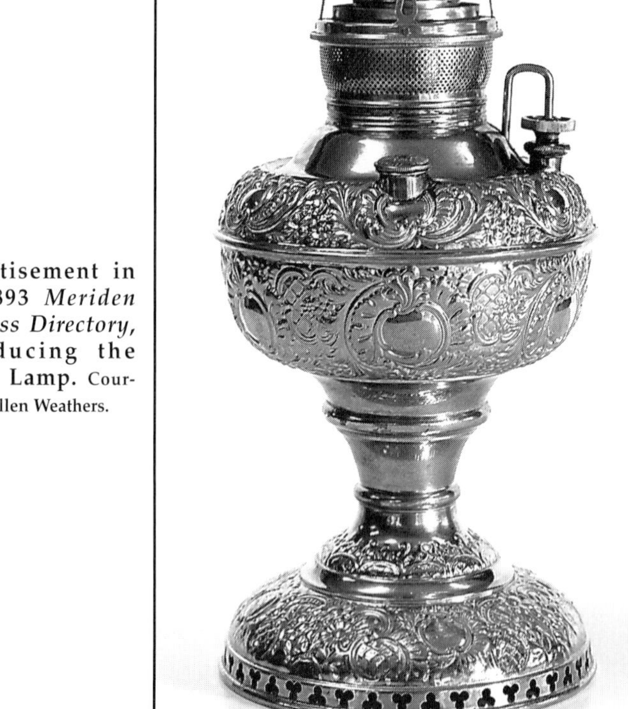

Unmarked Miller lamp No. 2. Height 11½". Snowflake oil fill cap and Miller No. 2 flame spreader. The flame spreader found in this lamp is unmarked on the top. $175.00.

The Miller lamp burner is found in all forms and varieties of lamps — hanging, floor or piano, vase, banquet, and stand. Some stand lamps were designed with extended stems for extra height. I have seen these advertised mostly in Australia. The embossed patterns are quite attractive and were not given names, as far as I know, by Edward Miller. The 1892 Homan patent for improved wick raiser was an advertised feature in Miller's 1894 catalog.

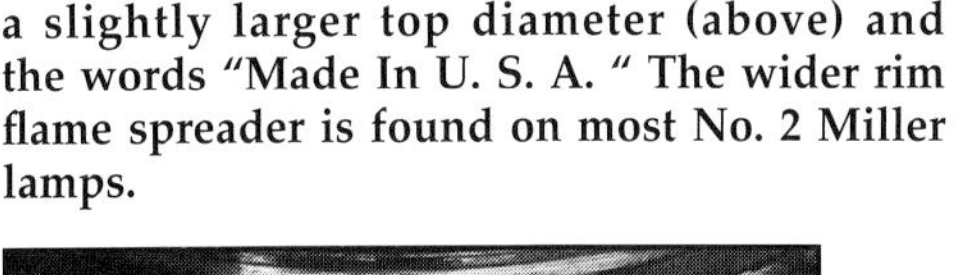

Flame spreaders found on Miller lamps have a slightly larger top diameter (above) and the words "Made In U. S. A. " The wider rim flame spreader is found on most No. 2 Miller lamps.

Flame spreader for Miller No. 1 stand lamp.

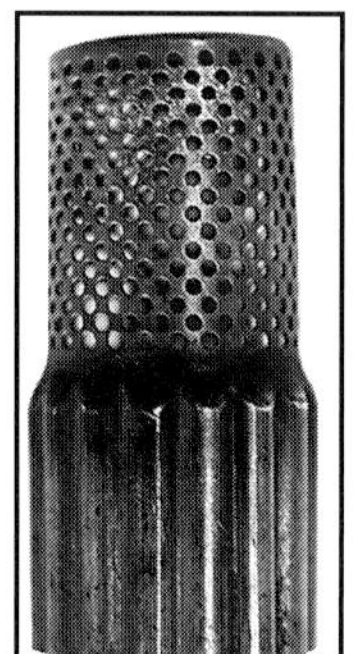

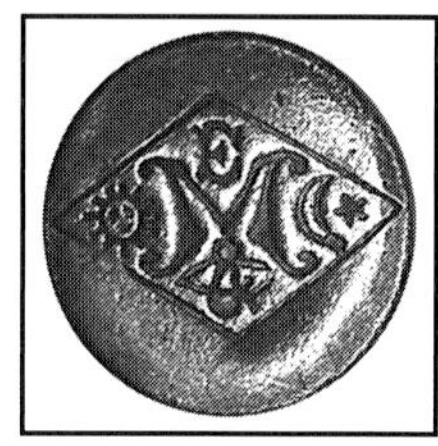

Flame spreader for Miller No. 0 lamp.

The Miller No. 2 stand lamp. Height 11½". Snowflake oil fill cap and Miller No. 2 flame spreader (see above). Thumbwheel marked as previous page. The embossed pattern is different than illustrated in the ad on previous page. $175.00.

The Miller stand lamp No. 1. Height 10½". Brass finish. Snowflake oil fill cap and Miller No. 1 flame spreader. $175.00.

The Miller stand lamp No. 0. Height 9½". Snowflake oil fill cap. The wick-raising thumb wheel is marked "2 Patents — June 28, 1892." A hand lamp matches this identical embossed pattern. $200.00.

The Tiny Juno and Home Lamps

The Tiny Juno lamps and the tiny Miller lamps are virtually identical in construction — they simply have different names — and perhaps they had different years of manufacture. The Tiny Juno is usually found with small snowflake oil fill cap. Home Lamps were inexpensive tin night lamps.

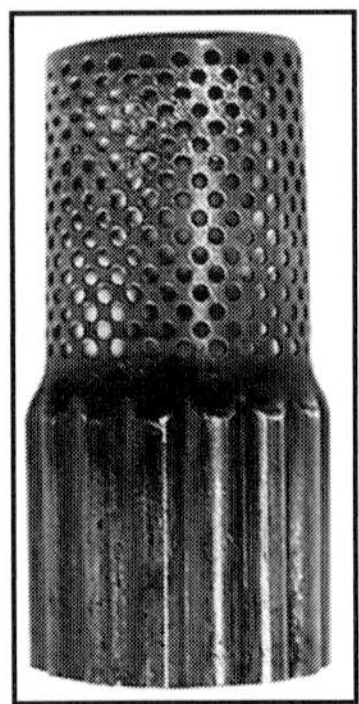

Flame spreader for Tiny Juno, Tiny Miller, and Home Lamp (No. 0) burners.

The Home Lamp (No. 0). Height 6¼". Miller oil fill cap. Tin with brass finish. Burner and oil fill cap are brass. The burner base is threaded. The Home Lamp is illustrated as Tiny Juno in 1904 catalog. $50.00.

Snowflake oil fill cap.

Tiny Juno stand lamp No. 0. Height 8⅛". $150.00.

The Tiny Juno hand lamp (No. 0). There are two sizes 7" and 6½" tall. $150.00.

The Tiny Juno fount lamp. Height 6⅜". $150.00. Courtesy Kent Stratton.

Tiny Miller Lamps

Tiny Miller lamps are found with either pull-bar wick raisers or the dated Miller raisers. The burners may be either bayonet or thread connection. The founts may be marked "The Tiny Miller" or simply "The Miller Lamp."

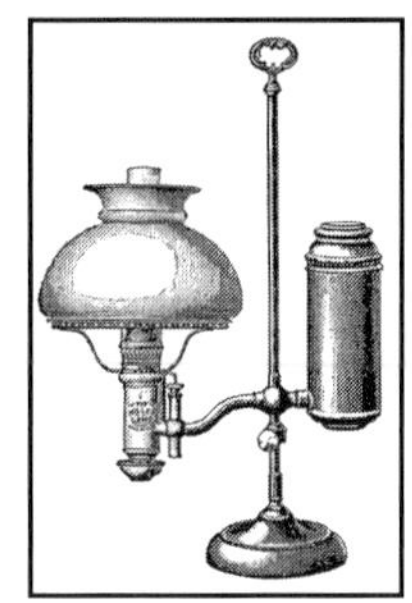

"The Miller Lamp" No. 0 study lamp, 1898. R — external wick raiser. Courtesy Kent Stratton.

The Tiny Miller (signed) banquet lamp with ball shade holder. Height 13". $350.00. Courtesy Richard and Barbara Dudley.

Tiny Miller oil pot with Miller dated wick raiser. The oil pot marked "The Tiny Miller, Made in U. S. A." The wall bracket is original Edward Miller & Co. $200.00.

Tiny Miller marked "The Miller Lamp." Height 9¼". Miller flame spreader. $300.00. Courtesy Kent Stratton.

Miller oil fill cap.

Tiny Miller hand lamp with Miller dated wick raiser. The fount is marked "The Miller Lamp, Made in U. S. A." Height 7½". $200.00. Courtesy Dick O'Connell.

Double wall bracket with Tiny Miller founts marked "The Miller Lamp." Shade holders 2½" fitter for ball shades. $400.00. Courtesy Jon Stratton.

Miller Non-Explosive Lamps

Edward Miller & Co. took advantage of consumers' fear of lamp explosions to promote the Miller "Non-Explosive" lamps — in both flat-wick and true center-draft (round wick) forms. The flat-wick lamps, illustrated in a 1904 catalog, are similar to the lamps manufactured by the Cleveland Non-Explosive Lamp Co. The non-explosive flat-wick lamps were sold as hand lamps, wall lamps, stand lamps, hanging lamps, and "Non-Explosive Factory Lamps."

Flame spreader with wide rim same as found on Miller and New Juno lamps.

Non-Explosive hand lamp with No. 1 Miller Sun Hinge skirt burner. Height 5⅜". Brass fount and foot. Burner marked "E. Miller & Company, Meriden, C.T., Made in U.S.A." Snowflake oil fill cap. $75.00.

Wick-raising knob functions with draw-bar as described for New Juno lamps.

Non-Explosive hand lamp with No. 1 Miller Sun Hinge skirt burner. Height 5⅜". Fount made of tin with brass finish. Burner marked "E. Miller & Co., Made in U.S.A." and most likely sold after 1921. $50.00.

Elegant Non-Explosive stand lamp No. 2 with cast-iron foot. Height 12". Standard Miller snowflake oil fill cap. Flame spreader same as found on Miller and New Juno lamps. $150.00.

The Dresden and Empress Lamps

The Dresden and Empress Lamps are large, fancy embossed lamps. Both have the wick-raising system found in New Juno lamps. The Empress flame spreader was a new design patented by Frank T. Williams and dated July 4, 1899. The Miller Dresden lamp was made with the same embossed body design as the Empress but with the standard flame spreader. The Dresden was illustrated in the 1904 catalog. The Empress, advertised until 1908, was also made as hanging lamp fount.

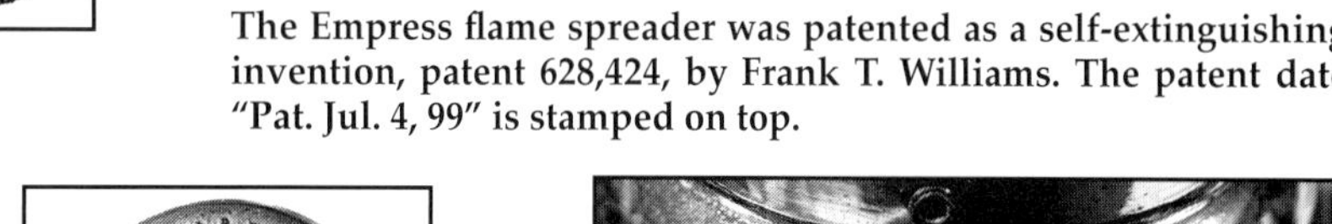
The Empress flame spreader was patented as a self-extinguishing invention, patent 628,424, by Frank T. Williams. The patent date "Pat. Jul. 4, 99" is stamped on top.

Oil fill cap.

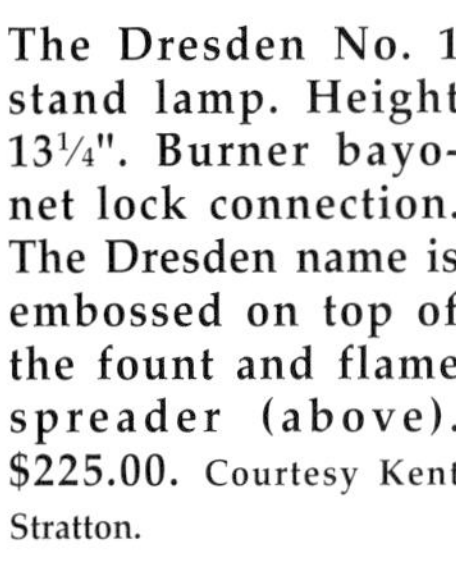
The Dresden No. 1 stand lamp. Height 13¼". Burner bayonet lock connection. The Dresden name is embossed on top of the fount and flame spreader (above). $225.00. Courtesy Kent Stratton.

The Empress No. 2 stand lamp. Height 13¼". Burner bayonet lock connection. The Empress name is embossed on top of the fount (above). Miller snowflake oil fill cap. $250.00.

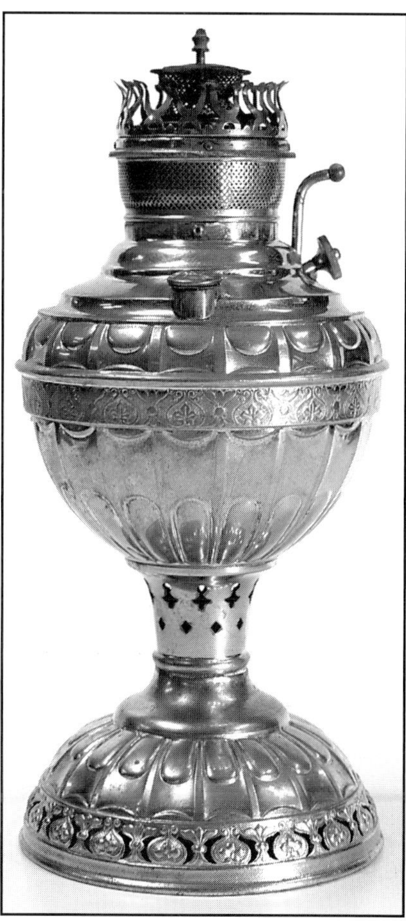

The Meteor Lamp, 1900 – 1910 or Later

Meteor lamps were featured by the Simmons Hardware Company, St. Louis, from 1895 to 1908. Simmons promoted the "cheerful, effulgent beams" of the Meteor.

I believe Meriden Bronze designed the original Meteor and that either Miller or Simmons Hardware bought the inventory when Meriden Bronze closed in 1900. Miller continued to make Meteor lamps for Simmons Hardware for a number of years. The Miller Meteor lamps are rebranded Miller lamps.

The wide-rim Miller flame spreaders are found in Miller Meteor lamp burners. Meriden oil fill caps are sometimes found on these lamps.

The No. 2 oil pot is 5" diameter. The No. 1 oil pot is 4" diameter.

The screen burner basket appears in the Simmons Hardware catalog in 1908.

Miller Meteor vase lamp No. 2 with removable oil fount and cast-iron foot. Burner has thread connection. Height 13⅛". Signed on top of fount. Miller oil fill cap and flame spreader. **$250.00.** Courtesy Glen Southard.

Left: Miller Meteor stand lamp No. 2. Burner has coarse thread connection. Height 12". Right: Meriden Meteor stand lamp No. 2. Height 13". Burner has fine thread connection. Both lamps are signed, but differently, on tops of founts. Left, $125.00; right, $150.00.

Meteor, 1900 – 1910 or Later, Simmons Hardware Co.

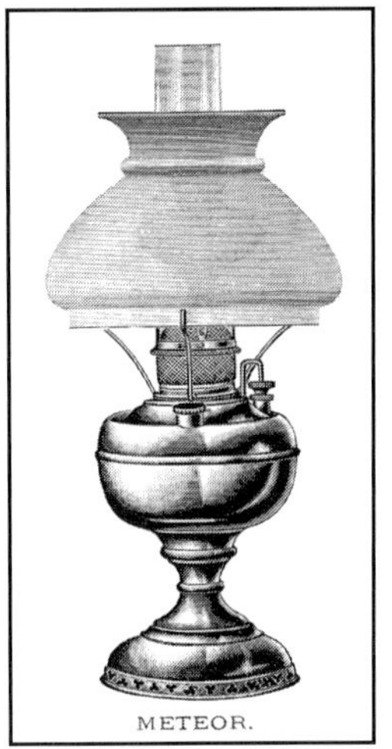

Meteor No. 3 hanging lamps. Left: Simmons Hardware catalog 1908. Right: Undated Simmons handbill. These images may be pre-1900 illustrations carried over from the Meriden Bronze Co.

Miller Meteor No. 1 stand lamp. Simmons Hardware catalog 1908.

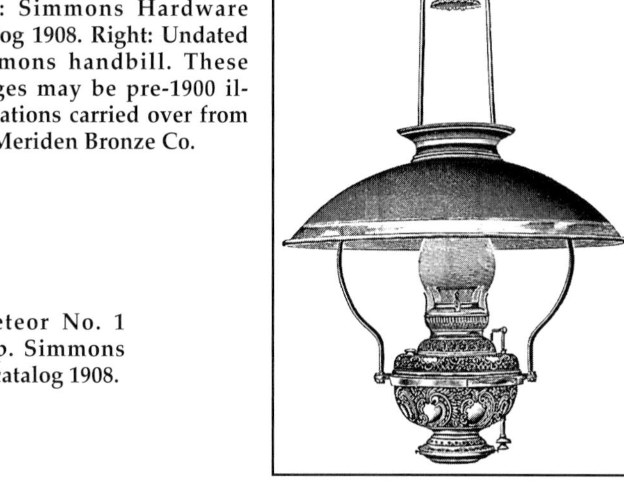

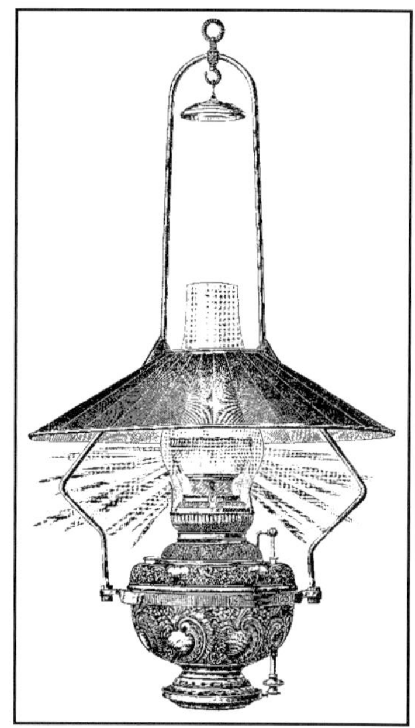

Meriden Meteor, 1895 – 1900

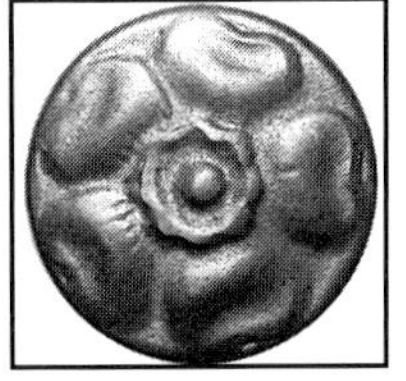

Meriden Bronze oil fill cap.

No. 1 Meriden Bronze flame spreader, "Patented June 7, 1892."

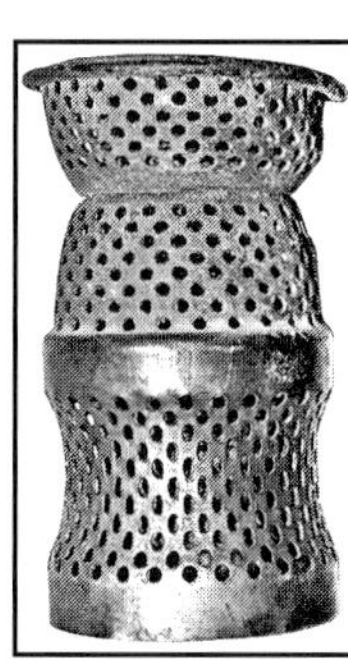

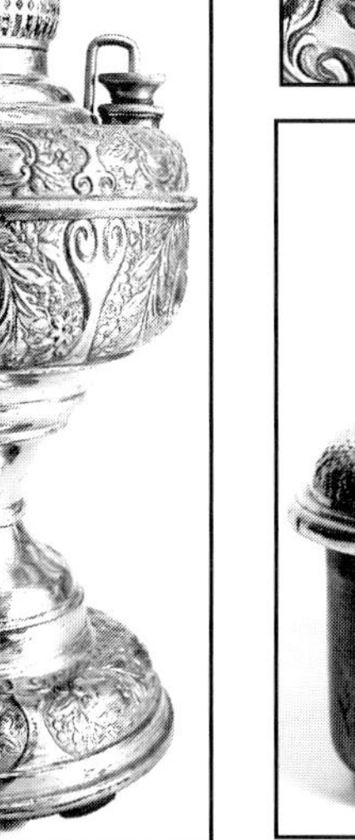

Left: No. 1 Meteor stand lamp signed "The Meteor Lamp." Height $10\frac{5}{8}$". Right: No. 1 Meteor oil pot signed "Meteor." Both fitted with Meriden Bronze flame spreaders and oil fill caps. Left, $175.00; right, $125.00. Courtesy Ted Hinsdale (left) and Jon Stratton (right).

Miller Meteor, 1900 – 1910 or later

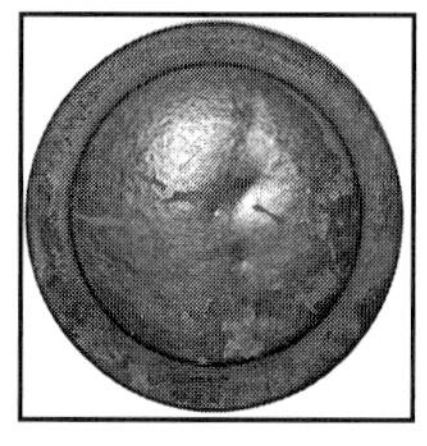

Miller wide rim flame spreaders found in Miller Meteor lamps. Left to right: plain or marked with or without "Made in U. S. A."

Left: No. 2 oil pot with Miller flame spreader and oil fill cap. Right: No. 1 stand lamp signed "The Meteor Lamp," with same pattern as the Miller stand lamp. Numerous patents on wick raiser, gallery, and outer wick tube. Left, $125.00; right, $175.00. Courtesy Ted Hinsdale.

Meteor Burners and Lamps

		Meriden Before 1900	Miller After 1900
Burner			
	Connection	Threads	Threads or bayonet
	Threads	Fine	Coarse
	Basket	Slots	Screen, holes
	OWT	Not dated	Patent dated (several patents)
	Wick raiser	Not dated	Patent dated (2 patents, June 28, 1892) tapered base
Flame spreader		Meriden dated June 7, 1892, or Torch in No. 2 lamps	Miller wide rim, with or without logo
Fount loading weight		Raised feet	Flat
Fount signed		"The Meteor Lamp" or "Meteor "(one line)	"The Meteor Lamp, Made in U.S.A." (three lines)

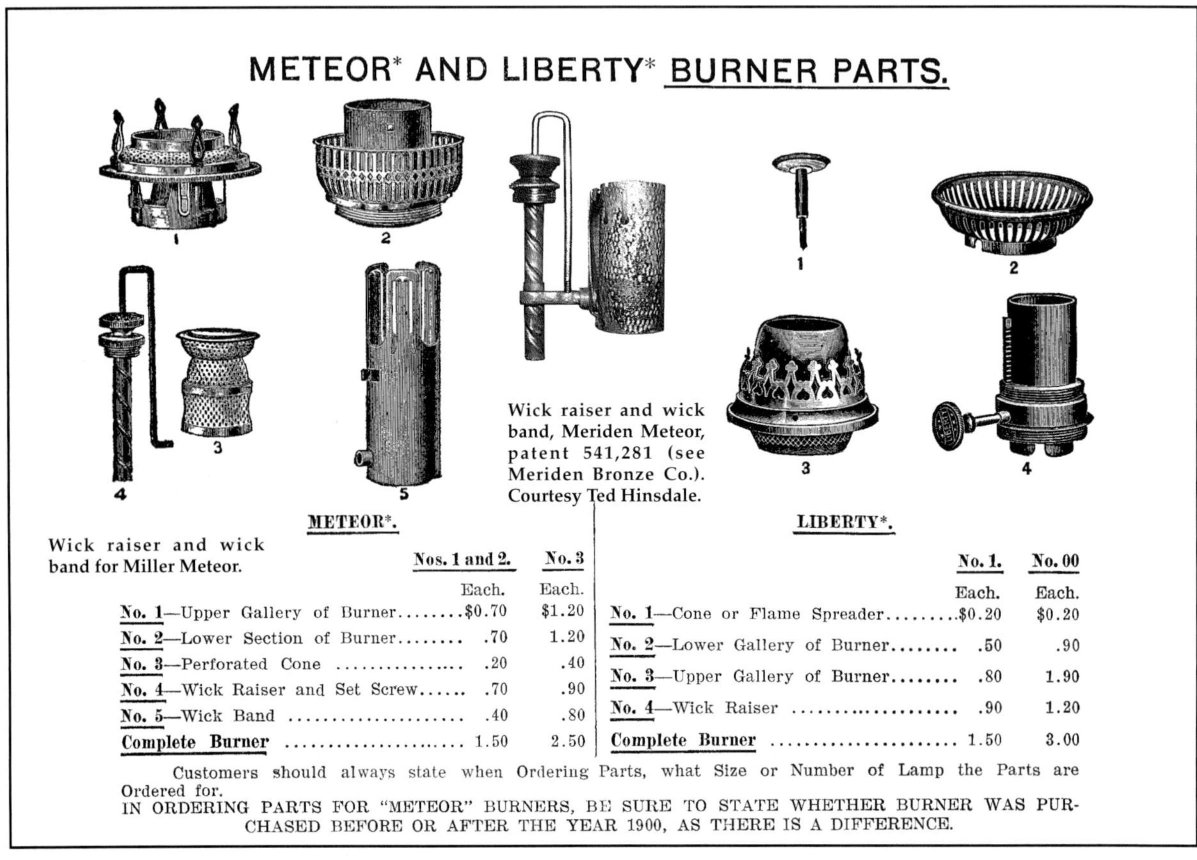

METEOR* AND LIBERTY* BURNER PARTS.

Wick raiser and wick band, Meriden Meteor, patent 541,281 (see Meriden Bronze Co.). Courtesy Ted Hinsdale.

Wick raiser and wick band for Miller Meteor.

METEOR*.

	Nos. 1 and 2. Each.	No. 3 Each.
No. 1—Upper Gallery of Burner	$0.70	$1.20
No. 2—Lower Section of Burner	.70	1.20
No. 3—Perforated Cone	.20	.40
No. 4—Wick Raiser and Set Screw	.70	.90
No. 5—Wick Band	.40	.80
Complete Burner	1.50	2.50

LIBERTY*.

	No. 1. Each.	No. 00 Each.
No. 1—Cone or Flame Spreader	$0.20	$0.20
No. 2—Lower Gallery of Burner	.50	.90
No. 3—Upper Gallery of Burner	.80	1.90
No. 4—Wick Raiser	.90	1.20
Complete Burner	1.50	3.00

Customers should always state when Ordering Parts, what Size or Number of Lamp the Parts are Ordered for.

IN ORDERING PARTS FOR "METEOR" BURNERS, BE SURE TO STATE WHETHER BURNER WAS PURCHASED BEFORE OR AFTER THE YEAR 1900, AS THERE IS A DIFFERENCE.

The above illustration was printed in the 1908 Simmons Hardware lamp catalog. Simmons Hardware must have purchased the old inventory when Meriden Bronze closed in 1900.

The Liberty Lamp

The Liberty lamp was sold in Simmons Hardware catalogs from 1899 to 1908. Liberty was a brand name featured by the St. Louis company. The Liberty burner is unique: "No. 1 Liberty Burner is smaller than No. 2 Rochester and larger than No. 1, but produces a greater volume of light than No. 2 Rochester."

Liberty assortment, Simmons Hardware, 1908.

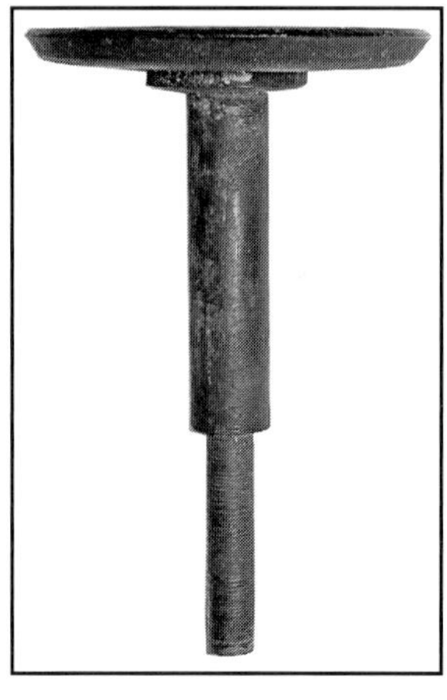

Liberty flame spreader is entirely made of steel.

Liberty No. 1 stand lamp, polished brass, probably not the original finish. The cast-iron loading weight has four large feet, similar to those on the Meteor stand lamp. Height 12". $125.00.

Liberty wick knob.

Liberty oil fill cap.

Liberty No. 1 stand lamp, embossed, nickel finish. Height 12". The wick found in this lamp is marked "Liberty." $175.00.

Liberty Hanging Lamps

Liberty hanging lamps were illustrated in Simmons Hardware catalogs and in Miller's 1904 catalog No. 116. The "No. 2/0 Liberty Burner is smaller than No. 3 Mammoth size and larger than No. 2, but produces a greater volume of light than the No. 3." The Miller frame bears the date "Apr. 1, 1890" which is for patent 424,712 (fount support ring) assigned to Edward Miller & Company by John I. Johnson.

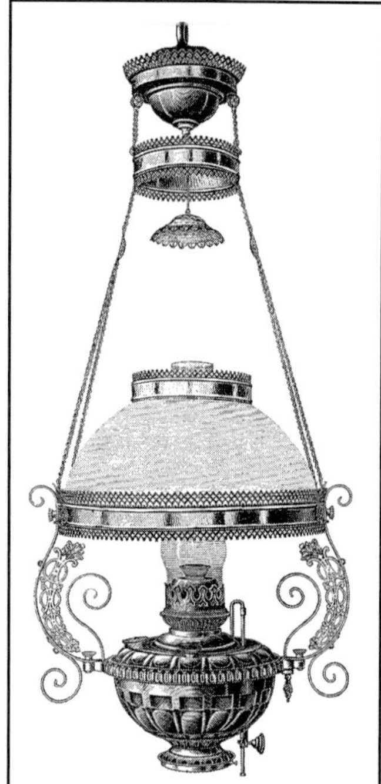

Oil fill cap 2/0 fount.

Wick knob 2/0 fount.

Liberty No. 1 fount lamp. Height 7¼". $100.00.
Courtesy Bill Schreiber.

Liberty No. 2/0 fount lamp. Height 9½". Flame spreader is common No. 2 Miller, wide rim. $125.00.

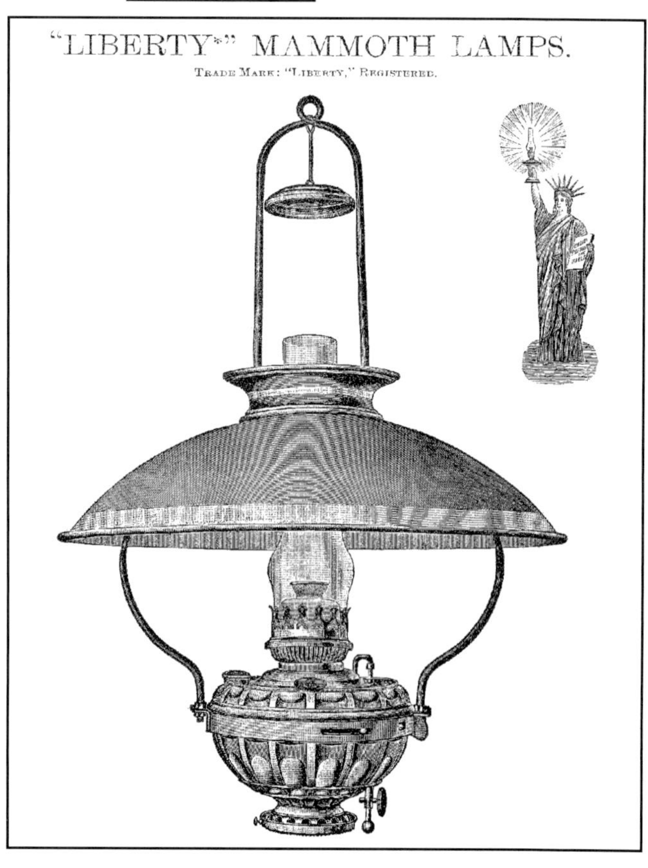

Liberty hanging lamps illustrated in Simmons Hardware catalogs.

Champion

Champion and New Vestal burners with "rack wick raiser and pinion" were introduced about 1904. The lamps were first named Champion, and later, Vestal. Champion burners are thread connection and marked "E. M. & Co., Made in U.S.A." $150.00.

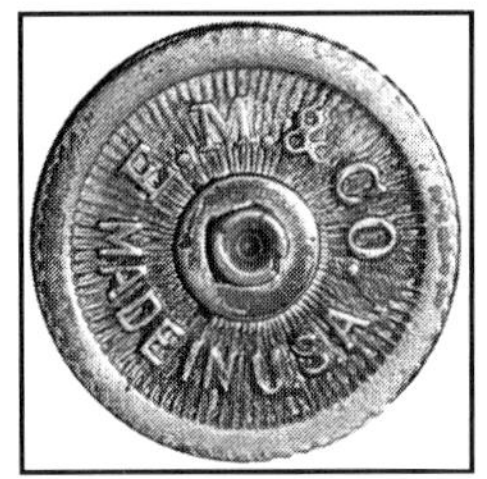

Champion embossed stand lamp No. 2. Height 11¼". Oil fill cap same as Vestal/ New Vestal.

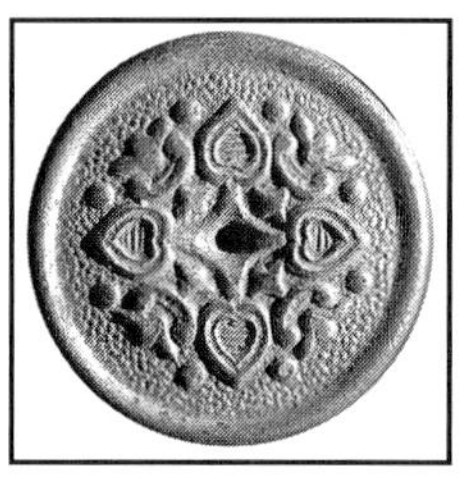

Champion/Vestal oil fill cap.

Wick knob for Vestal lamps marked "New Vestal, E. M. & Co."

Vestal/New Vestal

These lamps were advertised as Vestal lamps. The burners are marked "New Vestal," and the founts are marked "Miller's Vestal, Made in U. S. A." I have not found a burner simply marked "Vestal." Stand lamps, banquet lamps, and student lamps were sold into the 1940s, and catalogs identified them as No. 30 Vestal. The burners are thread connection. It is not surprising that many combinations of previous burners and founts are combined as the company used existing tooling and parts in a declining market to assemble kerosene lamps. The most expensive ($9.98) oil lamp in the 1917 Charles Williams catalog was a "Fancy Miller Vestal" with embossed base and stained glass shade.

Champion and Vestal flame spreaders. Four tabs hold the Vestal top disc in place.

New Vestal No. 2 stand lamp. Height 11¼". Lift gallery. Champion/Vestal oil fill cap and flame spreader. $75.00.

New Vestal No. 2 embossed stand lamp. Height 11¼". Vestal oil fill cap and flame spreader. $125.00.

New Vestal No. 2 embossed stand lamp. Height 11½". Miller snowflake oil fill cap and Vestal flame spreader. $150.00.

Miller's Vestal/New Vestal

Edward Miller apparently enjoyed mythology, as "Vestal" refered to a virgin dedicated to the Roman goddess Vesta and to the service of watching the sacred fire perpetually burning on her altar. Miller's Vestal study lamps were made in all sizes, including No. 0 in single and double student lamps. Catalogs illustrate the No. 0 lamps plain and embossed. Vestal lamps were sold from early 1900s until long after General Electric bought the company and the name changed to the Miller Company.

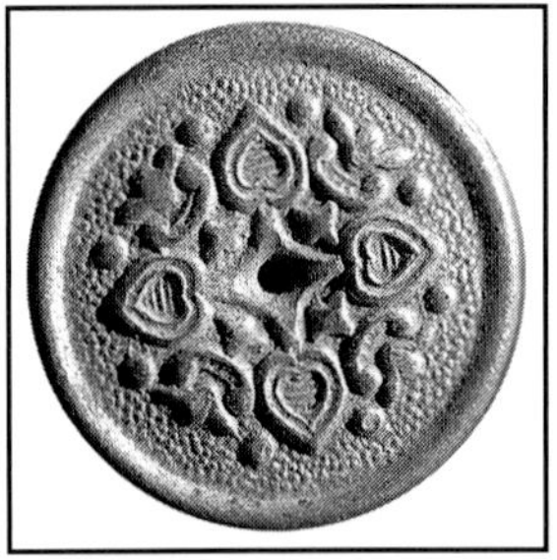

Vestal oil fill cap, called "feeder cap" in 1940 catalog.

Vestal/New Vestal founts are similarly marked.

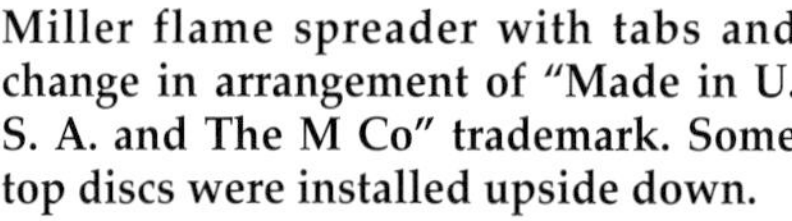

Miller flame spreader with tabs and change in arrangement of "Made in U. S. A. and The M Co" trademark. Some top discs were installed upside down.

Vestal lamp size 0 burner. The fount is marked "Miller's 0 Vestal, Made in USA." The wick knob is unmarked. Height 9½". $200.00. Courtesy Mark Mitchell.

New Vestal No. 2 stand lamp, name embossed on top of fount. Height 11¼". Wick knob marked "New Vestal, E. M. & Co." Champion/Vestal oil fill cap and flame spreader. $75.00.

New Vestal Made after 1924

Miller oil cap, found on this lamp.

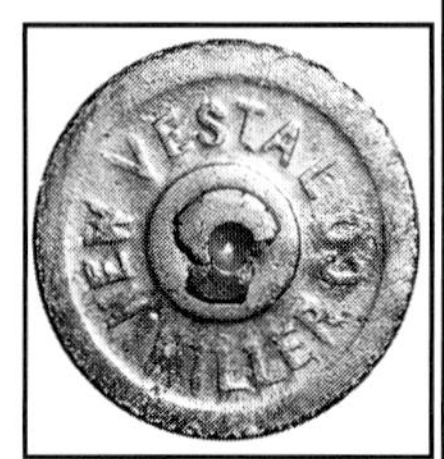

Wick knob "New Vestal, Miller Co."

New Vestal No. 2 stand lamp. "Miller's Vestal" embossed on top of fount. Height 12" due to larger and revised shape of the fount. Miller oil fill cap. The Miller trademark and word arrangement changed on the flame spreader. This lamp sold after 1924. $75.00.

Miller's Vestal

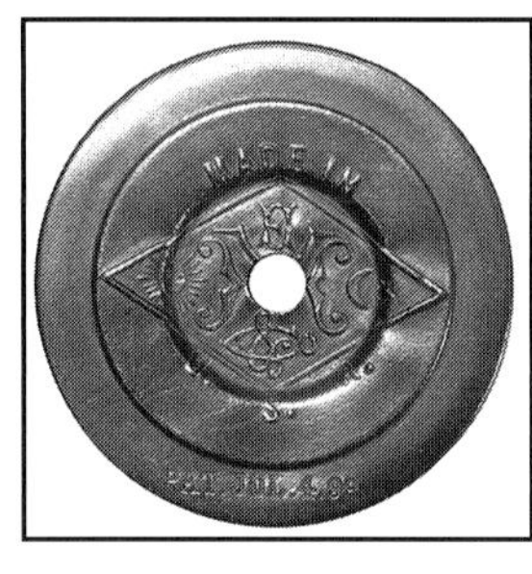

Flame spreader-self extinguishing patent, similar to the Empress lamp. Marked "Pat. Jul. 4, 99."

Oil fill cap.

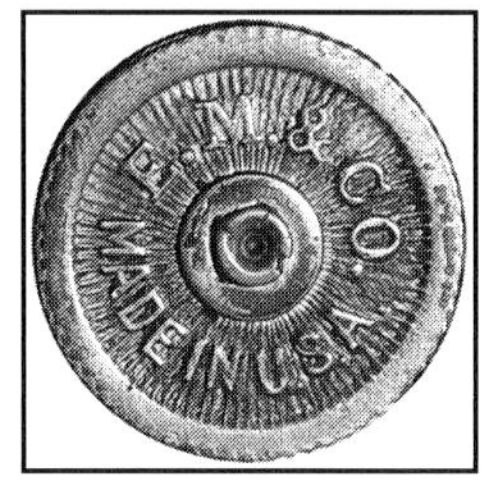

Wick knob "E. M. & Co., Made in U.S.A."

No. 2 stand lamp marked "Miller's Vestal, Made in U.S.A." Height 12". $175.00. Courtesy Kent Stratton.

Miller's Ideal Student Lamps

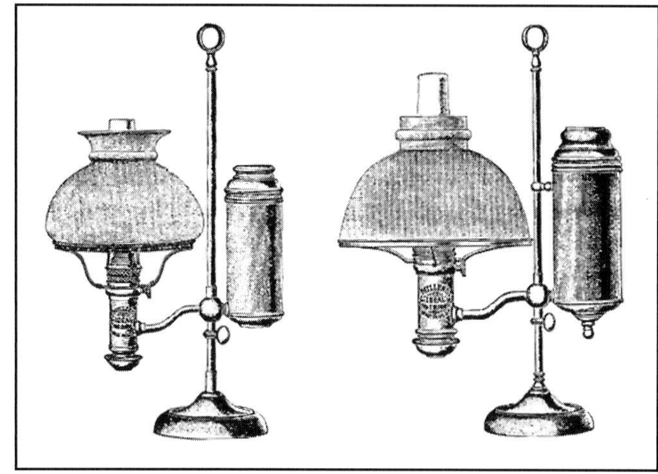

Miller's Ideal 1904 student lamps were made in burner sizes No. 0 and No. 1 (above), No. 2, and also double burners.

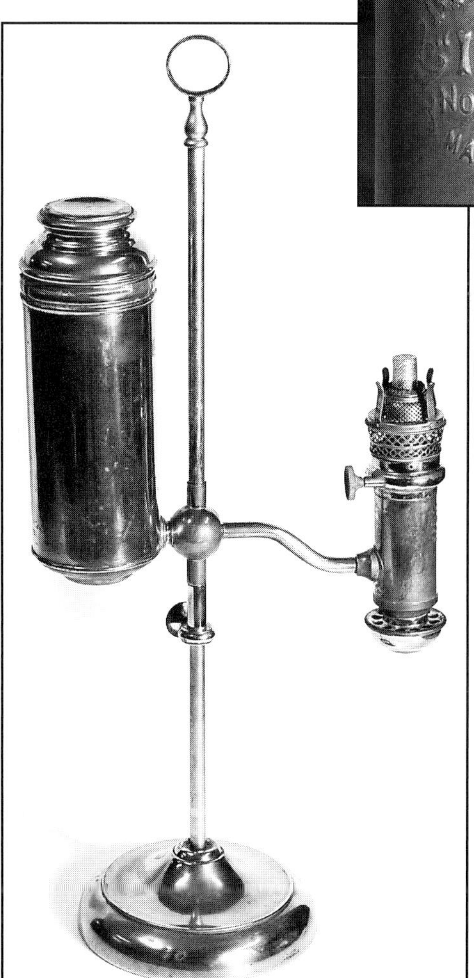

Miller's Ideal No. 0 student lamp. Height 20¼". Wick knob unmarked. $275.00. Courtesy Jon Stratton.

Lumo and Kyso Lamps

The Lumo and KYSO table lamps share similar lamp founts with different burners. Both burners, however, employ the Miller "rack wick raiser and pinion" introduced with Champion/Vestal lamps. Both have lift galleries for lighting the lamp.

I think the Lumo lamp was sold in hardware stores and gasoline stations, much like the Rayo in the 1920s. Other versions of lamps with the name Lumo were mantle lamps sold by the John S. Noel Company, of Grand Rapids, Michigan. The KYSO lamp was sold in Kentucky Standard Oil Stations during the 1920s. For more information see the Standard Oil chapter.

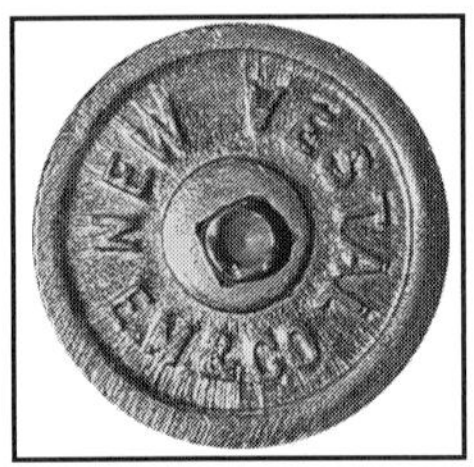

Lumo wick knob, "New Vestal, E. M. & Co."

KYSO flame spreader. Note that the top is fastened with four tabs.

The Lumo and KYSO oil fill caps are larger than caps found on other Miller lamps.

KYSO wick raising knob marked "Made in USA."

Miller's No. 2 Lumo center-draft stand lamp. Height 11". The wick knob is marked "New Vestal E.M. & Co." The burner is threaded connection. This lamp is found with a Miller No. 2 flame spreader. $75.00.

Wick carrier.

Miller's No. 2 KYSO center-draft stand lamp sold by Kentucky Standard Oil Company. Height 11¼". The wick knob is marked "Made in USA." The burner is threaded connection. $75.00.

The Electrolite Acetylene Lamp

The Electrolite won an award at the 1901 Pan-American Exposition but apparently never gained the widespread popularity of gas lighting.

THE ELECTROLITE WITH GLOBE FOR PARLOR AND RECEPTION ROOM.

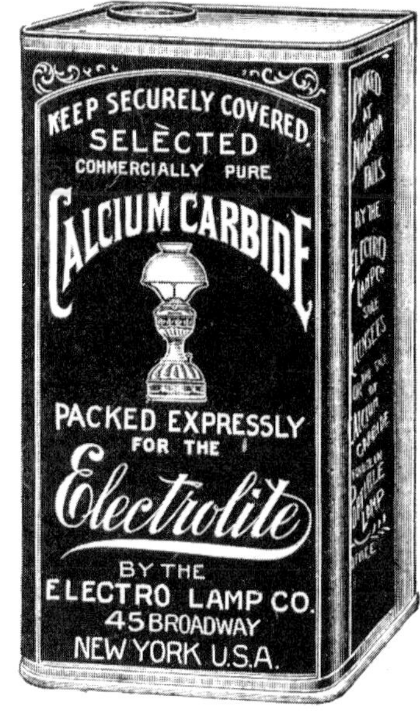

Electrolite Carbide sold by Edward Miller & Co. in 10 lb. cans; 75 cents F. O. B. Meriden.

Electrolite Acetylene lamp. Height 17½". Marked "Electrolite, Capacity 1½ lbs. carbide" on the fount. Also marked "Pat'd, Jan 10, 1899, Apr 10, 1900" on the burner base. The burner not shown. $400.00.

Advertisement, *Scribner's Magazine*, Feb. 1, 1901.

Ceiling Extension

Ceiling "Suspension Device," patent 481,157 assigned to Edward Miller Co. by George W. Baldwin. The extension was stamped "Aug. 23, 92" on the back. This basic design was illustrated as part of the suspension framework for Miller hanging and library lamps in 1893 and 1894. This unit was sold separately and was illustrated in Angle lamp catalogs.

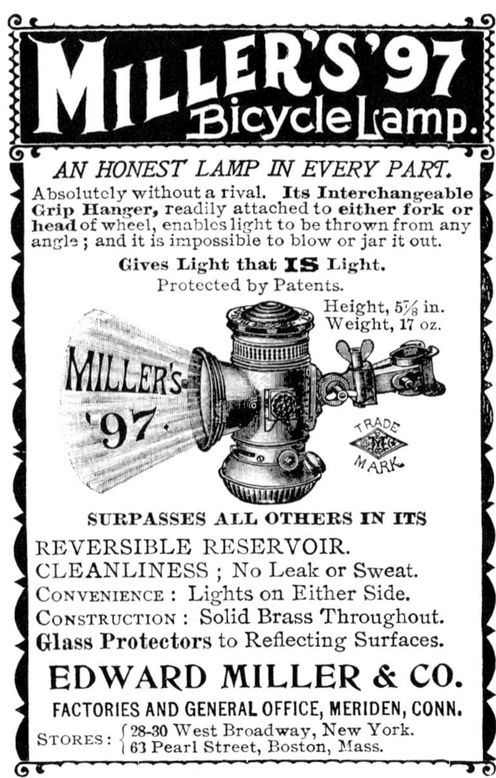

Advertisement, 1897 *Munsey's Magazine*.

Pyro Alcohol Lamps

Miller produced lamp founts for the U.S. Industrial Alcohol Company, New York. Denatured alcohol was touted as a new and perfect fuel for lamps, stoves, heaters, and flatirons after prohibitory taxes were removed in 1907. The tax made alcohol expensive to use for lighting and heating compared with kerosene. Pyro alcohol lamps are mantle burners. More information and illustrations are found in a 24-page, 1908 U.S. Industrial booklet, *Pyro Alcohol*.

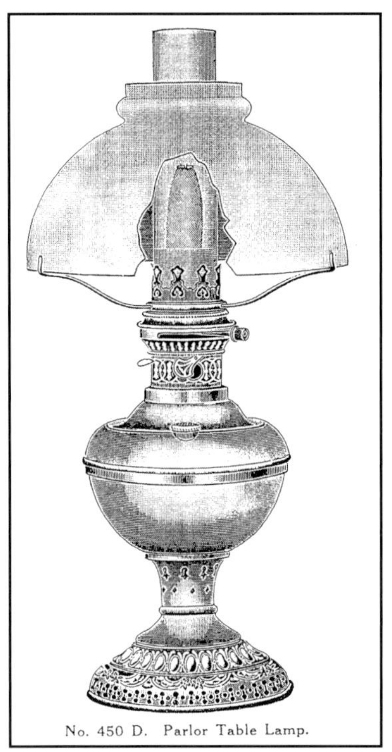

No. 450 D. Parlor Table Lamp.

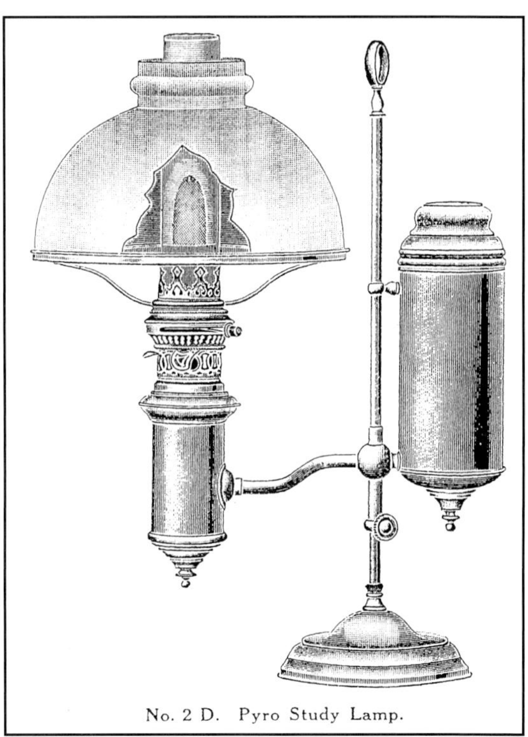

No. 2 D. Pyro Study Lamp.

Miller Oil Heaters

Edward Miller & Company was producing Juno and Miller oil heaters by 1893. The company created an oil burner division to supply demand for Miller's new heaters.

The heaters illustrated on the right side of this page use Miller No. 2 and No. 3 burners. Miller's 1894 catalog promoted the idea that the heater easily converted to "an elegant table lamp, by removing the frame." I suspect these same founts were used for stand lamps and hanging lamps as well as Miller heaters.

Miller Smokeless, and self-extinguishing, oil heaters were based on patents by Frank Williams (644,786, 1900, and 671,464, 1901), assigned to Edward Miller and Co. Williams had a related unassigned patent (628,424, 1899), which appeared on the flame spreader for the Empress stand lamp. These heaters were illustrated in catalog No. 116, ca. 1904.

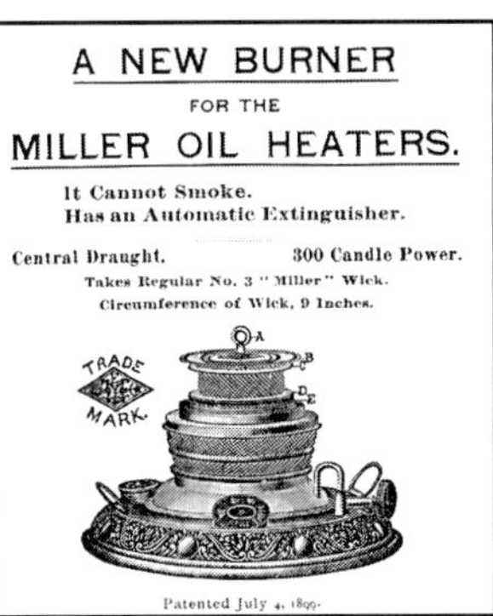

Undated brochure, ca. 1900.

Pages illustrating Miller oil heaters, catalog No. 43, ca. 1894.

Miller Gas & Electric Lamps

Edward Miller & Company was producing Electrolite acetylene lamps in 1901, gas portable lamps in 1901, electric fixtures in 1903, and many attractive electric table and hanging lamps by 1909.

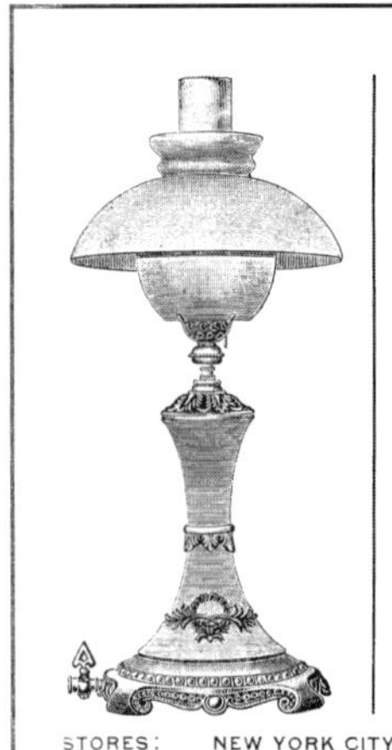

Edward Miller & Co.
FOUNDED, 1844
MERIDEN, CONN., U. S. A.
MANUFACTURERS OF
AN ELEGANT LINE OF
Portables for Acetylene, or Commercial Gas
OUR LINE OF KEROSENE GOODS IS UNEQUALLED.
We make the Famous....
MILLER AND JUNO LAMPS
IN FOUR SIZES OF BURNERS, AND IN ALL VARIETIES
FOR HANGING, FLOOR and TABLE USE.
STORES: NEW YORK CITY. 28 AND 30 W. BROADWAY.
BOSTON, MASS. 63 PEARL ST.
PHILADELPHIA, PA. 1113 MARKET ST.
(See Other Side)

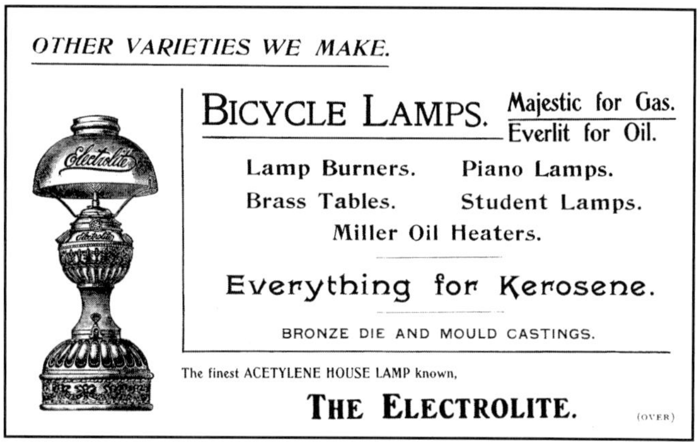

OTHER VARIETIES WE MAKE.
Electrolite
BICYCLE LAMPS.
Majestic for Gas.
Everlit for Oil.
Lamp Burners.
Piano Lamps.
Brass Tables.
Student Lamps.
Miller Oil Heaters.
Everything for Kerosene.
BRONZE DIE AND MOULD CASTINGS.
The finest ACETYLENE HOUSE LAMP known,
THE ELECTROLITE.
(OVER)

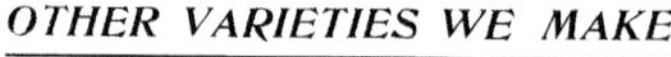

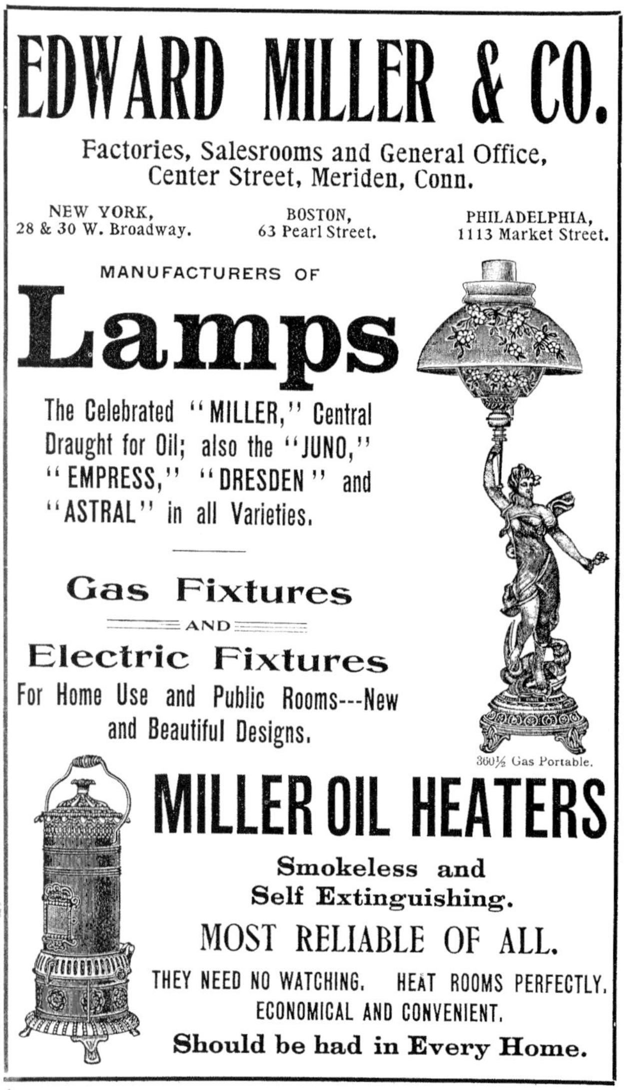

EDWARD MILLER & CO.
Factories, Salesrooms and General Office, Center Street, Meriden, Conn.
NEW YORK, 28 & 30 W. Broadway.
BOSTON, 63 Pearl Street.
PHILADELPHIA, 1113 Market Street.
MANUFACTURERS OF
Lamps
The Celebrated "MILLER," Central Draught for Oil; also the "JUNO," "EMPRESS," "DRESDEN" and "ASTRAL" in all Varieties.
Gas Fixtures
AND
Electric Fixtures
For Home Use and Public Rooms---New and Beautiful Designs.
360½ Gas Portable.
MILLER OIL HEATERS
Smokeless and Self Extinguishing.
MOST RELIABLE OF ALL.
THEY NEED NO WATCHING. HEAT ROOMS PERFECTLY. ECONOMICAL AND CONVENIENT.
Should be had in Every Home.

Advertisement, 1903 *Meriden City Directory*.
Courtesy Allen Weathers.

EDWARD MILLER & CO.
Salesroom, Office and Factories,
99 CENTER ST., MERIDEN, CONN.
STORES AND SALESROOMS:
New York City, 78 and 80 Warren Street.
Boston, Mass., 63 Pearl Street.
Philadelphia, Pa., 807 Chestnut Street.
Chicago, Ill., 90 Wabash Ave., Room 30.
MANUFACTURERS OF
ATTRACTIVE LAMPS AND FIXTURES.
ORIGINAL DESIGNS AND FINISHES
We invite you to call and see our Beautiful Furnishings.
Gas, Electric, Combinaton and Oil Fixtures.
Residences and Public Buildings equipped in an up-to-date manner.
SPECIAL DESIGNS MADE TO ORDER.
Large variety in stock for prompt shipment.
GAS AND ELECTRIC PORTABLES
ART GLASS SHADES, METAL OVERLAID.
Incandescent Gas Burners, all kinds of Lamps and Burners for Oil, Miller Oil Heaters, Etc.

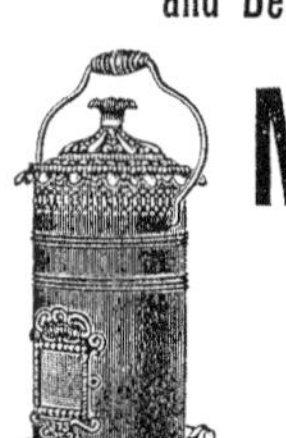

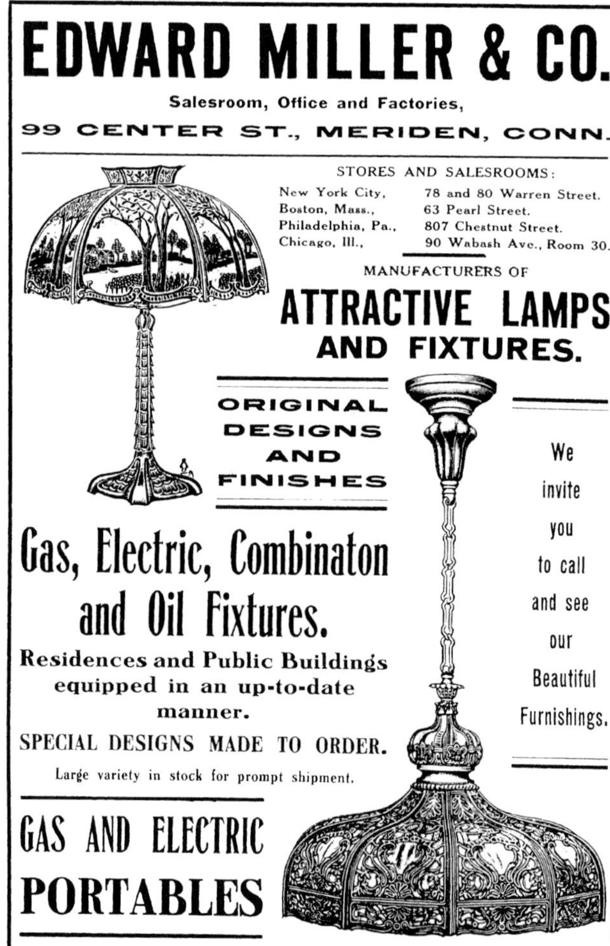

Advertisement, 1910 *Meriden City Directory*.
Courtesy Allen Weathers.

Miller Kerosene Lamps, 1893 – 1896

Miller library lamp 6847.

Advertisement illustrating the Hornberger burner, *Meriden City Directory*, 1896. Courtesy Allen Weathers.

Miller study lamp.

Miller banquet lamps, left 428, center 679, and right 680.

Miller Kerosene Lamps, 1893 – 1896

Miller table lamps, left 5035 and right 5025.

Miller non-extension chandelier 0728.

Miller piano lamp 634-203.

Miller wrought-iron banquet lamp 903.

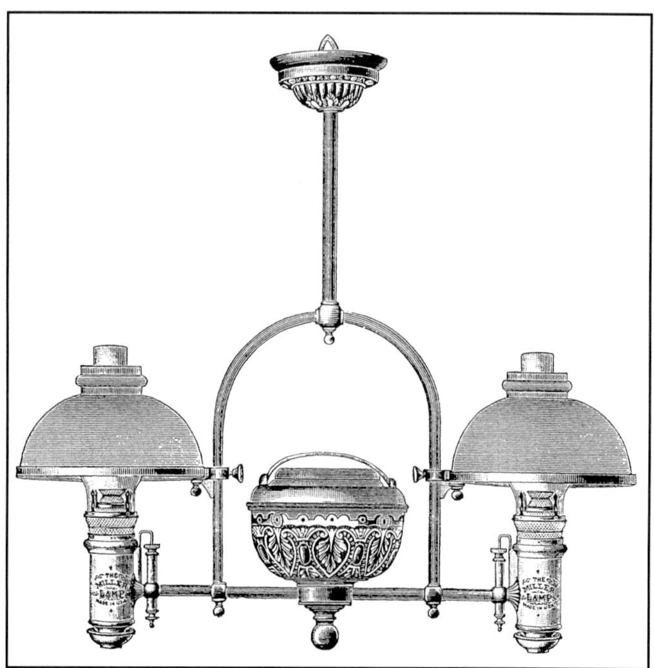

Miller pendant lamp 307.

Miller Kerosene Lamps, 1899 – 1905

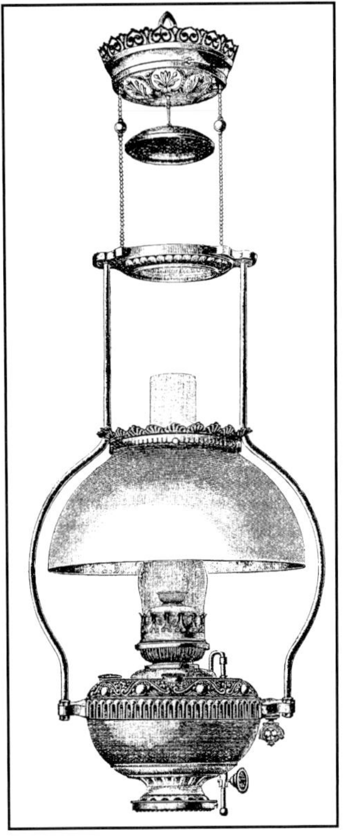

Mammoth Dresden with spring extension harp, brass or nickel finish.

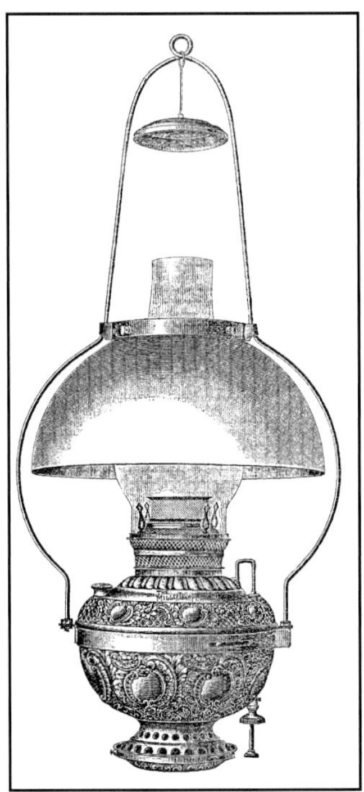

Mammoth Miller, brass or nickel finish.

Juno library lamp.

Juno factory harp lamp

Miller wall bracket lamp.

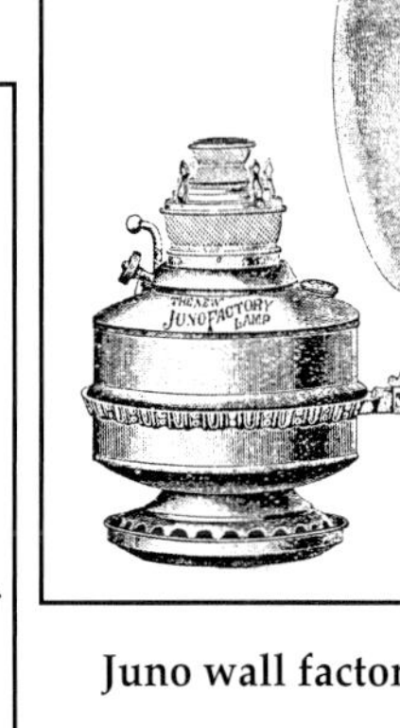

Juno wall factory lamp.

Miller vase table lamp, antique brass.

Miller vase or reception lamp. Also sold with Juno burner. Antique brass.

Miller Dresden stand lamp.

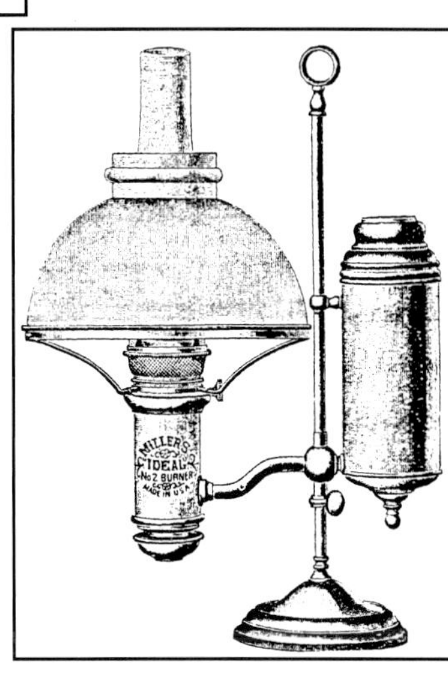

Miller Ideal Study Lamp, made in sizes Nos. 0, 1, and 2, and No. 1 double burners.

Miller Lamps, 1915 – 1924

Miller lamps in 1923 Sears-Roebuck catalog. Left: Miller hanging lamp fitted with New Juno oil pot sold as "The 'Homestead' Hanging Lamp." This style was also sold as a table lamp. Right: Miller No. 2 stand lamp sold as "The Old Reliable 'Rochester' Lamp." This lamp is most likely an unmarked Vestal.

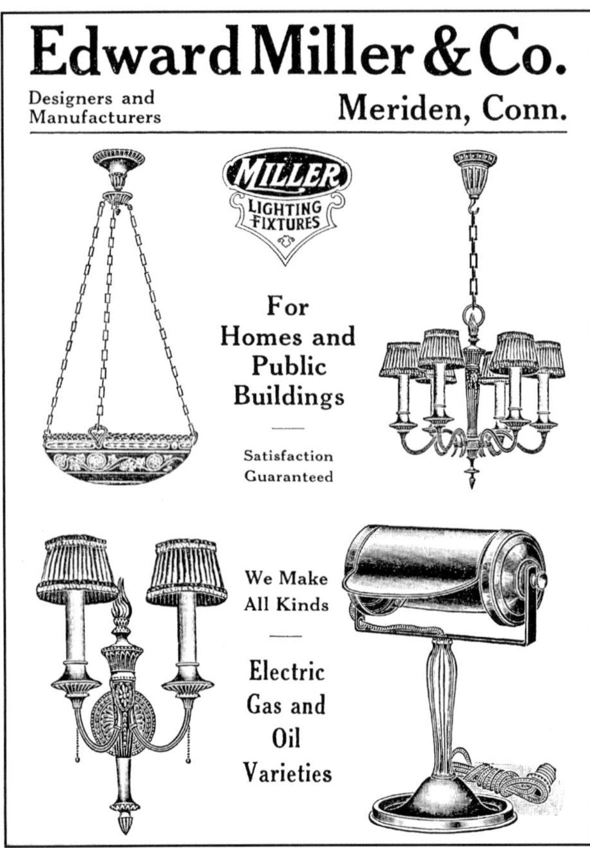

Advertisement, *Meriden City Directory,* 1915. The new Miller trademark first appeared for electric lamps in 1913.
Courtesy of Allen Weathers.

Miller Kerosene Lamps, 1924

Catalog X151 dated June 1, 1924 offered Miller and Vestal center-draft lamps in Nos. 0, 1, 2, and 3 burner sizes. Tiny Miller, Miller, and Vestal banquet lamps, Vestal study lamps, bracket lamps, harp lamps, and library lamps are illustrated. Juno burners were illustrated in No. 2 Miller founts. Miller Smokeless oil heaters were still being sold.

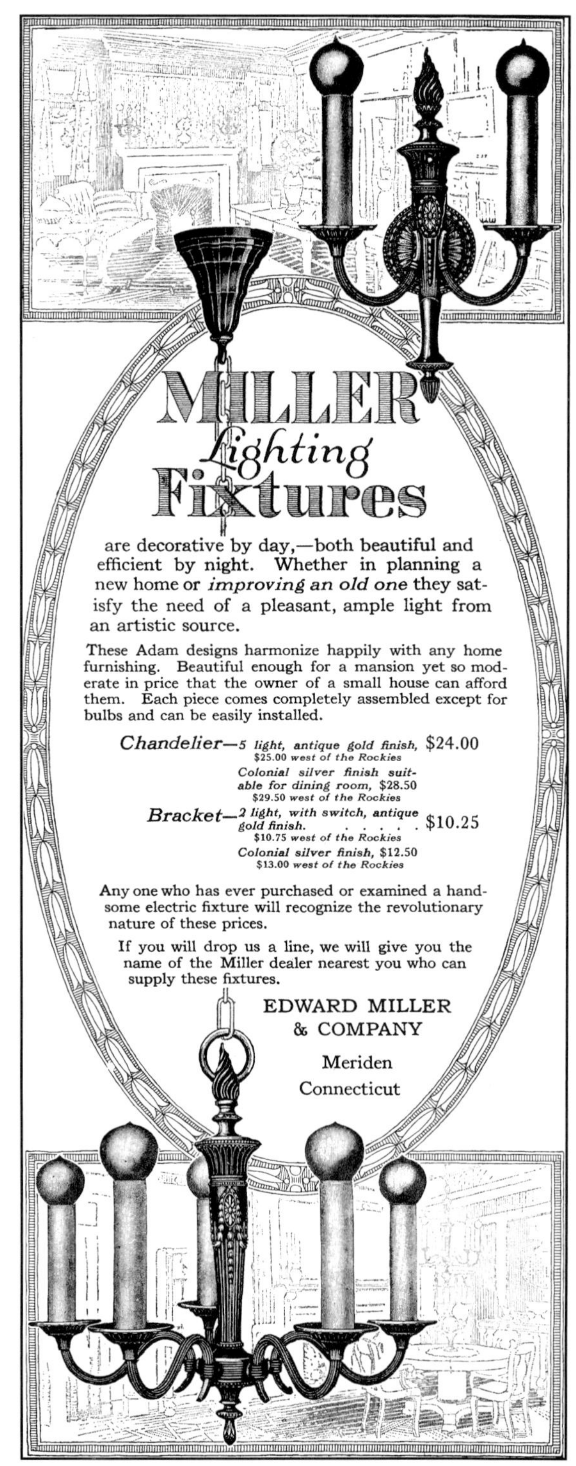

Advertisement, *Saturday Evening Post,* Aug. 30, 1919.

Nail City Stamping Company

1877 – 1897

Wheeling Lamp & Stamping Company and Nail City Lantern Co. also 1877 – 1897; Wheeling Stamping Company, 1897 – 1946; Lamp Manufacture 1891 – 1905

The Nail City Lantern Company was organized in 1877 to make Leader brand lanterns and lamp burners. The company also produced lithograph tinware and other metal specialties in Wheeling, West Virginia. A. W. Paull, Sr., was the first president and patent holder for the Leader lantern. The company was best known for lanterns.

The company advertised as the Wheeling Lamp & Stamping Co. in 1891 and as the Nail City Stamping Co. in 1892. The name "Nail City" originated because of the production of soft steel nails beginning in the 1830s.

The company reorganized in 1897. The officers were J. F. Paull, president; A. W. Paull, Jr., secretary and general manager; James S. Paull, assistant secretary; and Irwin Paull, treasurer. At the time, this specialty company was one of the largest factories in Wheeling making lanterns, lamp burners, and tops for fruit jars.

The Wheeling Lamp with Wellington Safety Burner[1] was introduced in 1892. The unique collar surrounds the burner to prevent siphoning of fuel. I suspect that Wheeling center-draft lamps were discontinued before the turn of the century.

Nail City Stamping Company advertised the Wellington Safety Burner as a feature of decorated glass vase lamps such as those sold by Bindley Hardware. I presume the glass was produced by the Eagle Glass & Manufacturing Company.

Eagle Glass & Mfg. Co.

In 1894 the Eagle Glass & Mfg. Co. was formed by four Paull brothers, of Wellsburg, West Virginia. The company made opal glass lamps, electric globes, nest eggs, and specialty items. Advertisements through 1901 illustrate night lights, vase lamps, and banquet lamps with flat-wick burners. An advertisement in *China, Glass and Lamps*, April 1901, announced "a complete new line of lamps and globes including Central Draft Lamps, Ready For 1901." A fire in 1902 destroyed much of the factory, and I do not know the extent of central-draft lamp production.

Hobson (1991) states that R. E. Dietz Co. purchased the lantern division in 1946; and the Wheeling Stamping Company continued in business until 1946, primarily making collapsible metal and plastic tubes (toothpaste, etc.).

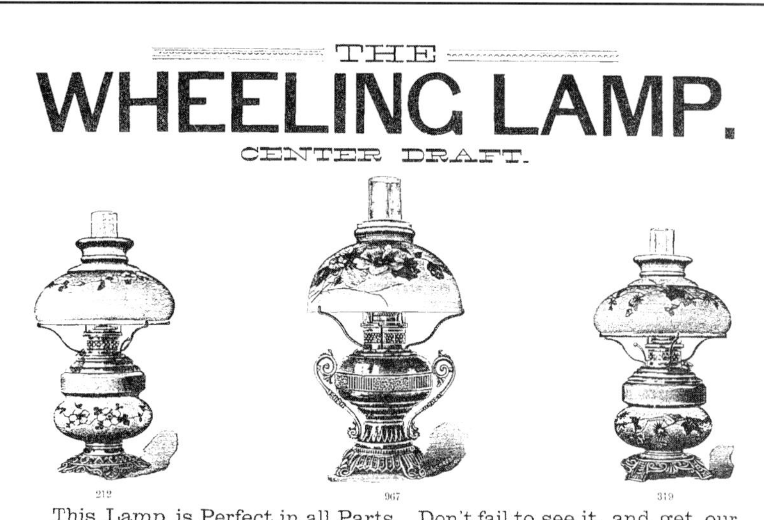

Advertisement, *Pottery and Glassware Reporter*, July 9, 1891. The lamps in this ad are not fitted with the Wellington Safety Burner.

NAIL CITY STAMPING CO.
Manufacturers of
MASON JARS AND TRIMMINGS,
"N. C. L. CO.'S" CRANK TUBULAR LANTERNS
Metal and decorated Center Draft and D. Collar Lamp.
Our designs and decorations are entirely new,
and are in the highest style of the art
Send for Catalogue, Lithographs and Prices.
WHEELING, W. VA.

Advertisement, *China, Glass and Lamps*, 1892.

[1]Henry Wellington, of New York City and Brooklyn, held several patents from 1877 to 1886 for street lights and oil chandeliers and a student lamp. He held patent 341,194 for a student lamp in the "vacuum-lamps" class. I do not know the relation between Henry Wellington and this company.

Trade Names

Center-draft lamps — Wheeling Lamp, Wellington Safety Burner.

Lanterns — Nail City, Leader, Paull's Leader, Ezy-Lit, Regal, Cold Blast.

The Wheeling Lamp

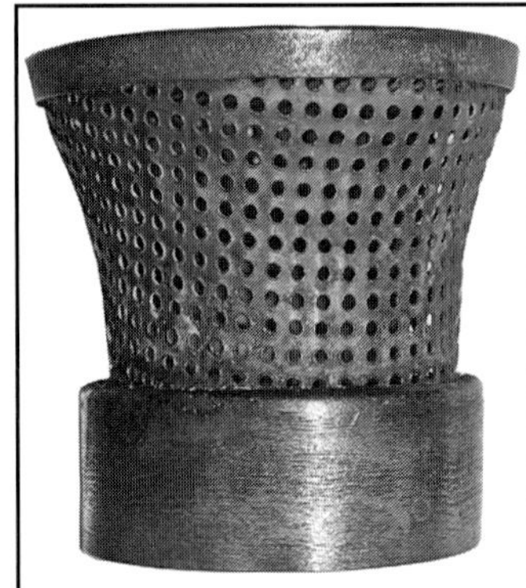

Wheeling Lamp flame spreaders. Tops marked "Wheeling Lamp," "Hollweg & Reese, Wheeling Lamp, Indianapolis," or "Wallace & McAfee" (not illustrated).

The Wheeling Lamp with Wellington Safety Burner. The lamps were finished in bronze, brass, or nickel. Height 11¼". $150.00. Courtesy Bill Schreiber.

Selected Patents Center-draft Lamps

Archibald W. Paull[1] unassigned	
1889	409,863
1890	420,093
1892	477,332
J. Reid assigned to Nail City Stamping Co.	
1894	513,059

[1]Also patents for lanterns.

Burner found in Wheeling Lamps. This burner seems to be adapted from earlier or different models of lamps.

Wheeling Lamp with bug screen installed.
Courtesy Fil Graff.

Wheeling vase lamps with Wellington Safety Burners sold by Bindley Hardware Co., Pittsburgh, 1893/1894. The fine art glass lamps were finished in gold, steel blue, and Damascus. Advertisements stated that lamps were made in styles ranging from bracket, stand, piano, and mammoth. Images on right courtesy Dan Edminster.

NAIL CITY STAMPING CO.

Manufacturers of

MASON JARS AND TRIMMINGS, ✣ ✣

"N. C. L. CO.'S" CRANK TUBULAR LANTERNS

Metal and decorated Center Draft and D. Collar Lamp.

Our designs and decorations are entirely new,

✣ ✣ ✣ and are in the highest style of the art

Send for Catalogue, Lithographs and Prices.

WHEELING, W. VA.

Advertisement, *Lamp Journal Supplement*, Sept. 22, 1892.

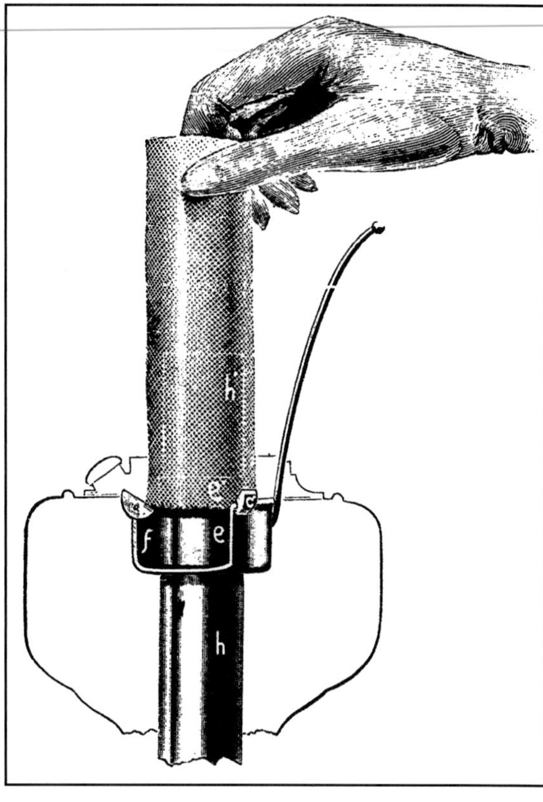

Advertisement for "The Wheeling Lamp, A New Ohio Valley Industry," *Pottery and Glassware Reporter*, June 18, 1891. The company promoted "their device for putting on the wick and raising or lowering the same as far ahead of any device ever before attached to a lamp."

The Safest & Cleanest Lamp Yet

No. 492 LAMP.

No. 492 LAMP, with Burner Removed.

THE "WHEELING" LAMP

With "Wellington" Safety Burner.

The "Wellington" Burner consists of a cylinder or jacket surrounding the removable burner and permanently attached to the Lamp Bowl. This effectually prevents the oil gathering on the outside of the Lamp, and at the same time enables the removable burner to be taken out and replaced with ease and safety, thus overcoming the difficulty that is experienced in removing and replacing the burner in other Centre Draft Lamps.

Besides the Metal Lamps, our line of DECORATED GLASS LAMPS is unexcelled for Beauty, Style and Finish. All of them have the "Wellington" Safety Burner.

NAIL CITY STAMPING CO.

WHEELING, W. VA.

Advertisement, *Crockery and Glass Journal*, Jan. 12, 1893.

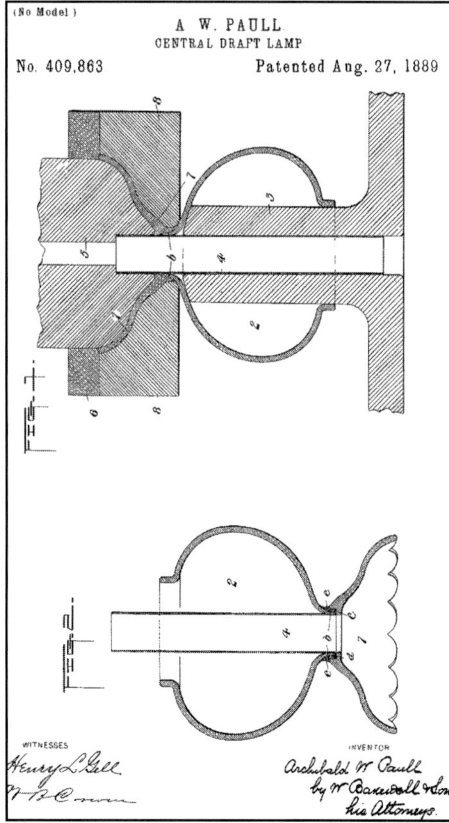

Patent 409,863 is for a glass fount with a metal center-draft tube.

Advertisement, *Crockery and Glass Journal*, Dec. 3, 1891.

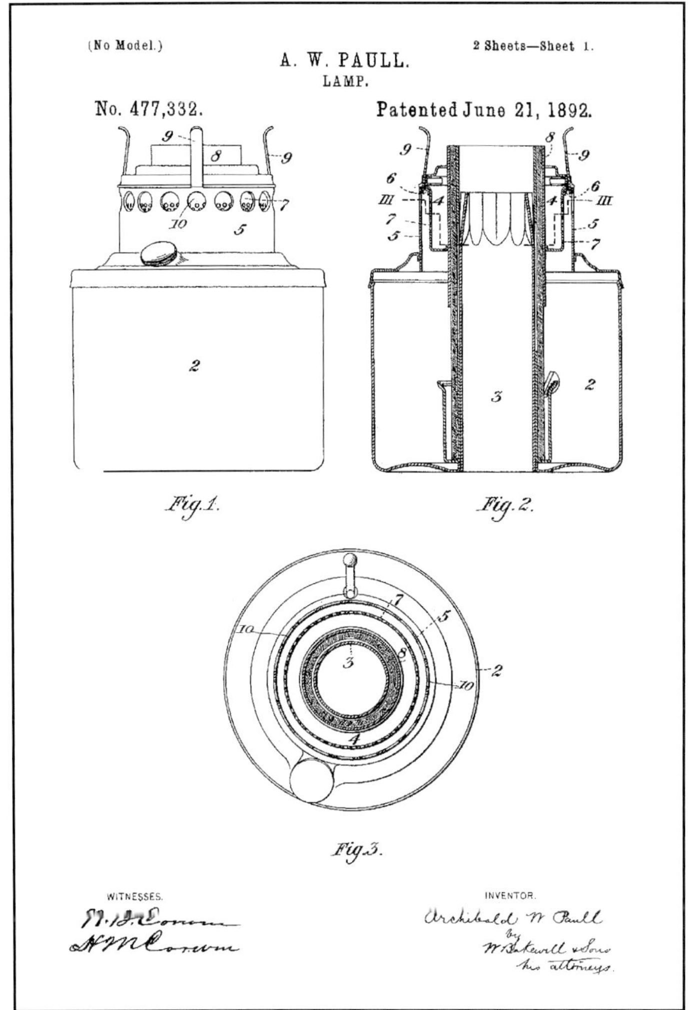

Undated trade card advertised the "refulgent rays" of light from this wonderful lamp.

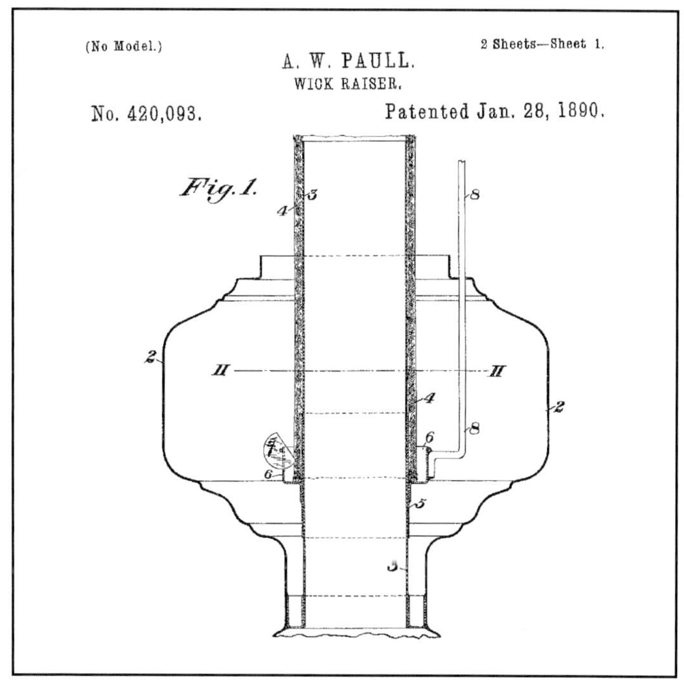

National Brass and Iron Works

1891 – 1911

Lamp Manufacture 1892 – ca. 1904

National Brass and Iron Works was incorporated in 1891 as a foundry in Reading, Pennsylvania, by Hiram K. Getz, Harvey H. Shomo, John G. Mohn, William H. Mohn, and W. W. Light. Officers were Hiram K. Getz, president; Howard E. Harbster, vice president and Charles G. Peocock, secretary-treasurer. The plant was located at Green and Tulpehocken Streets, adjoining the Lebanon Valley Railroad.

The company manufactured decorative and art metal goods — piano and banquet lamps, brass and onyx tables, cabinets, mirrors, frames, globes, and statuettes. Products included iron and brass castings with electroplate finishes of all types — gold, silver, nickel, brass, and bronze. Employment was reported as 150 in 1898.

National Brass and Iron was a major manufacturer of lamps, judging by the numbers of flame spreaders extant. National purchased oil pots and burners from several sources. The company primarily sold cast lamps to other distributors. I have not found a "National Glass Co." to which I can assign any known flame spreaders.

A fire destroyed portions of the plant in February 1904. At that time, the *Reading Eagle* newspaper reported 200 employees producing chandeliers, gas and electrical fixtures, vases, lamps, picture frames, and other novelties. I do not know if oil lamps were continued after the fire.

The last listing for National Brass in *Boyd's Directory of Reading* was in 1911.

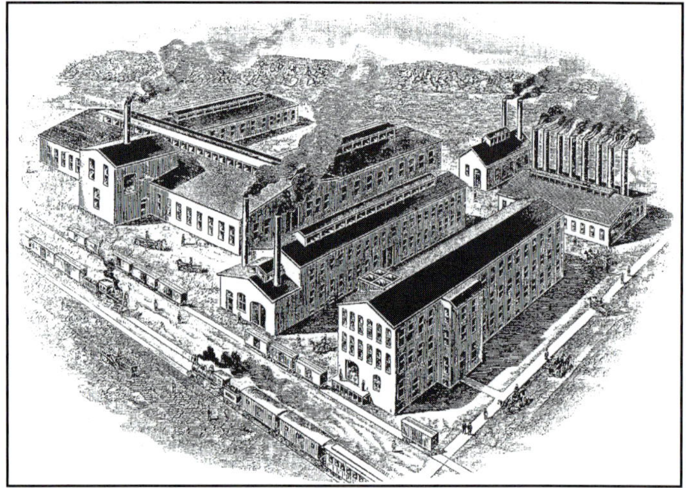

National Brass and Iron Works, ca. 1898.

Advertisement in *China and Glass Journal*, December 1892.

Trade Names

Center-draft lamps — Reading Lamp, National Lamp.

Flame spreaders left to right: "Reading Lamp" marked "Pat'd, Jan'y 20th 91, Aug, 11th 91" (Manhattan Brass); "The National Reading" marked "Pat July 15, 90, U. S. A." (Bristol Brass and Clock Co.); and "Reading" and "National" (Plume & Atwood patents). See Holmes, Booth & Haydens for an NB & IW flame spreader.

New Jersey Lamp and Bronze Works

1886 – 1922

Oil Lamp Manufacture until Mid-1890s

New Jersey Lamp and Bronze Works was located on the Raritan River in New Brunswick, New Jersey. Ralph W. Booth was manager. Nearby companies included Johnson & Johnson, a lumber yard, and a woolen mill.

New Jersey Lamp was a subsidiary of Consolidated Fruit Jar Company, established 1871, located on adjacent property. Consolidated Fruit Jar was among the first to make the Mason fruit jar. The two companies employed 500 in 1908. Officers of New Jersey Lamp and Bronze were Henry B. Kent, president; Theodore B. Booream, vice-president; and Thomas J. Buckley, secretary-treasurer. Sales offices were maintained in New York and Chicago.

The company advertised ornamental banquet and figural lamps including decorated lamps with center-draft oil pots. I believe the company purchased oil pots from the Manhattan Brass Company.

New Jersey Lamp advertised its oil lamps as safe to use because they employed the "Secor Lamp System." John Secor, of Brooklyn, New York, held patent 456,127 claiming an air-tight wick tube and a vented oil fount, thereby preventing danger of fire or explosion. E. H. Fessenden was agent for the Secor system.

New Jersey Lamp advertised electric bronze goods in 1893, when, I assume, it discontinued most of its oil lamps and concentrated on fancy electrical lights, fittings, and hardware for the New York City market.

Trade Names

Center-draft lamps — New Brunswick.

Advertisement, *China, Glass and Lamps*, July 13, 1892.

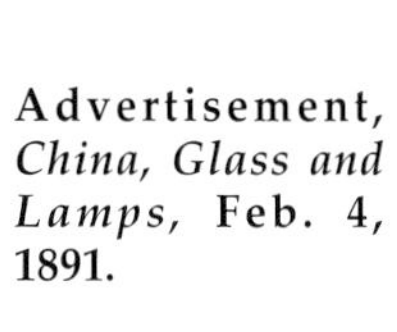

Advertisement, *China, Glass and Lamps*, Feb. 4, 1891.

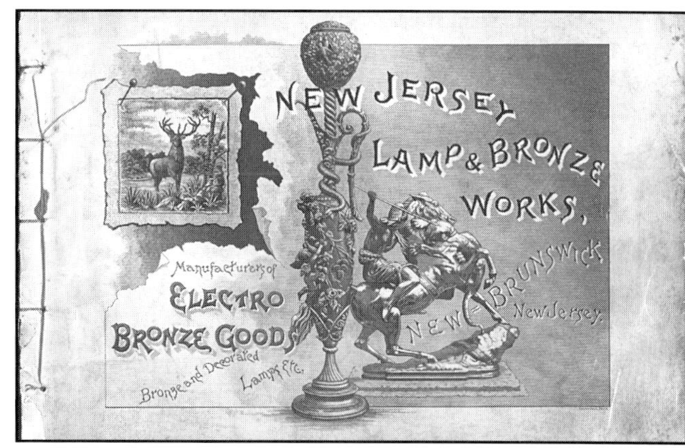

Cover of undated catalog, early 1900s. The 43 pages illustrate statuary (see below), clock figures, ewers, and vases in Japanese bronze, barbadienne, gold, silver, and gilt finishes.

Advertisement, *China, Glass and Lamps,* July 13, 1892. The large center lamp appears to be a Wallace & Sons burner. The other founts and burners appear to be same as those on the Princeton lamp.

Flame spreader, "The New Brunswick." Base $1^3/_8$" diameter. Also found unmarked. Courtesy Kent Stratton.

Below: broadside advertisement illustrating flat-wick lamps. Courtesy of Catherine Thuro.

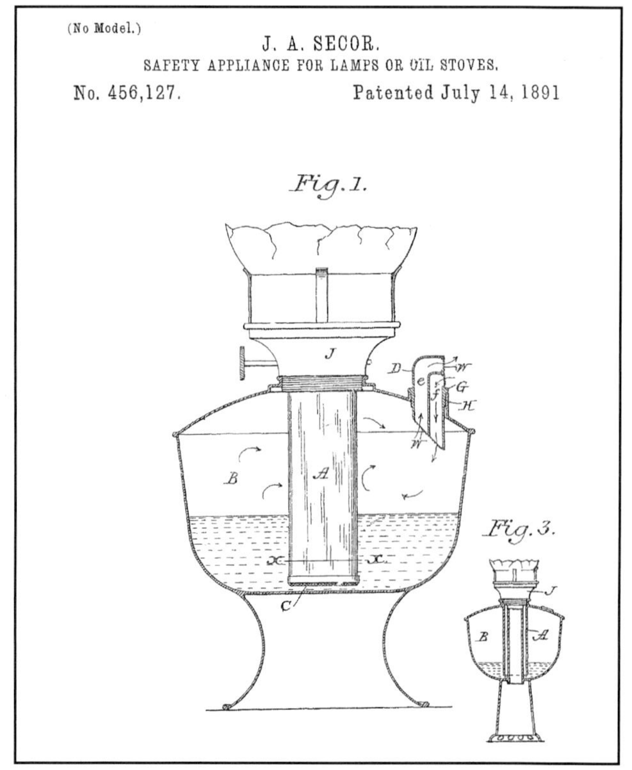

The Charles Parker Company

1876 – ca. 1957

Lamp Manufacture 1883 – 1950s

The Charles Parker Company, Meriden, Connecticut, was incorporated in 1876 by Charles Parker. He learned the hardware trade by working for several factories in Meriden and by operating his own business starting in 1829. Several members of the Parker family were involved in the businesses. Charles Parker was elected the first mayor of Meriden in 1867.

Charles E. Parker was presiden, his son Dexter Wright Parker, treasurer, and his son-in-law William H. Lyon, secretary. Charles Parker died in 1902 and Dexter became president.

Charles Parker was a pioneer in hardware manufacture. He was known throughout the world for the most popular goods. The company owned showrooms in New York and Boston selling wood screws, bench vises, 100 or more sizes and styles of coffee mills, machinist's tools, cabinet locks, hardware, piano stools, and shotguns.

Charles Parker lamps included chandeliers, library lamps, parlor lamps, piano lamps, banquet lamps, and hall lamps. Parker stand lamps are well-made, of heavy construction. Catalog No. 16, circa 1899, illustrates a variety of lamps, about one-half of which are flat-wick and one-half center-draft burners. Burley & Tyrell, Chicago, advertised Parker lamps as Peerless Electric lamps in 1889. The term *Peerless* indicated top-of-the-line, unmatched quality.

Parker designed and manufactured ornate, heavy cast-iron chandeliers beginning in the early 1880s. The ornate ones sold for more than $200. Center-draft lamps were incorporated into the Parker line within the decade.

Dexter W. Parker and Lewis Griswold held the majority of lamp patents assigned to Charles Parker Co. Many of their patents were improvements in hanging fixtures. Cast-iron frames were often signed "The Chas. Parker Co."

Subsidiaries included the Parker Clock Company, Union Works, the Meriden Curtain Fixture Company, and Parker Brothers. Parker Brothers manufactured lithographic presses and machinery but is best remembered for its breech-loading Parker shotguns. Parker Brothers supplied arms for the Union army during the Civil War. The Parker Clock Co. (1893 – ca. 1926) manufactured small clocks with alarms (the company was issued patents in 1897 and 1908). The companies operating under the Parker name employed about 1500 in 1906.

Parker produced lamps for the U.S. Army in 1899 and 1900. These lamps were marked "U.S. QM Dept., 1899 [or 1900], The Charles Parker Company."

In 1940, the Charles Parker Company purchased Bradley and Hubbard, also of Meriden, and continued manufacture of Rayo lamps in its Bradley and Hubbard division. The Parker Company manufactured both kerosene and electric versions of the famous Rayo table lamp and the Rayo student lamp during the late 1940s and early 1950s. The B & H factory buildings were demolished in 1973, along with the machinery, stamping dies, and most of the

company records. Richard Stamm (1993) reported that drawings and tooling for the Rayo were found when the Charles Parker Company buildings were razed in 1973.

Parker electric lamps were sold from 1909 throughout the 1920s and 1930s. Parker leaded art glass shades were overlaid with decorative pierced metal frames.

Collectors interested in the complete history of this company are advised to read *The Parker Story*, a two-volume history of Charles Parker companies.

Trade Names

Center-draft lamps — The Parker, Peerless Electric, the Peerless lamp — also marked "J. Wallis Cook, New York," Rayo.

Advertisement, *Crockery and Glass Journal*, June 21, 1883.

Selected Patents, Center-draft Lamps

Dexter W. Parker[1] assigned to Charles Parker Co.

1889 401,583

Lewis F. Griswold[2] assigned to Charles Parker Co.

1892 486,038

1897 586,028

[1]Also many patents on hanging and organ lamps.
[2]Also many patents on hanging lamps.

The Parker Lamp

Prior to Dexter Parker's patent (401,583), the Charles Parker Company concentrated on hanging lamps with flat-wick burners. Many were fancy library lamps designed for the finest homes. The tag (right) gives instructions to operate Parker's spring extension for hanging library lamps.

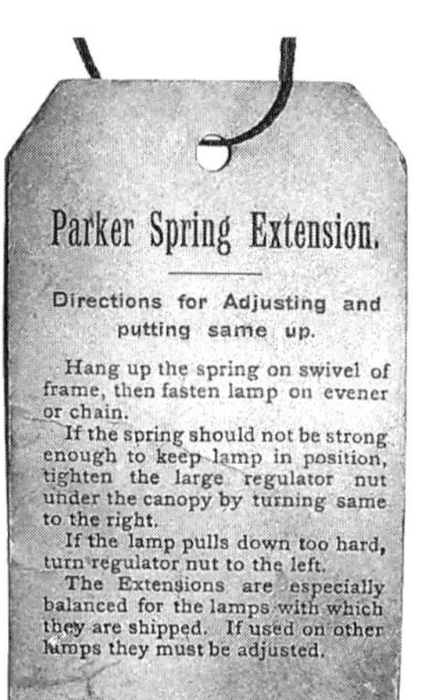

Parker Spring Extension.

Directions for Adjusting and putting same up.

Hang up the spring on swivel of frame, then fasten lamp on evener or chain.

If the spring should not be strong enough to keep lamp in position, tighten the large regulator nut under the canopy by turning same to the right.

If the lamp pulls down too hard, turn regulator nut to the left.

The Extensions are especially balanced for the lamps with which they are shipped. If used on other lamps they must be adjusted.

The Parker lamp, Parker's first center-draft stand lamp, was advertised in the 1889 *Meriden City Directory*.

Parker banquet lamps, catalog No. 16, ca. 1889. Courtesy Jack McNearney.

Parker library lamps, catalog No. 16, ca. 1889. These lamps illustrate two different wick raisers. Courtesy Jack McNearney.

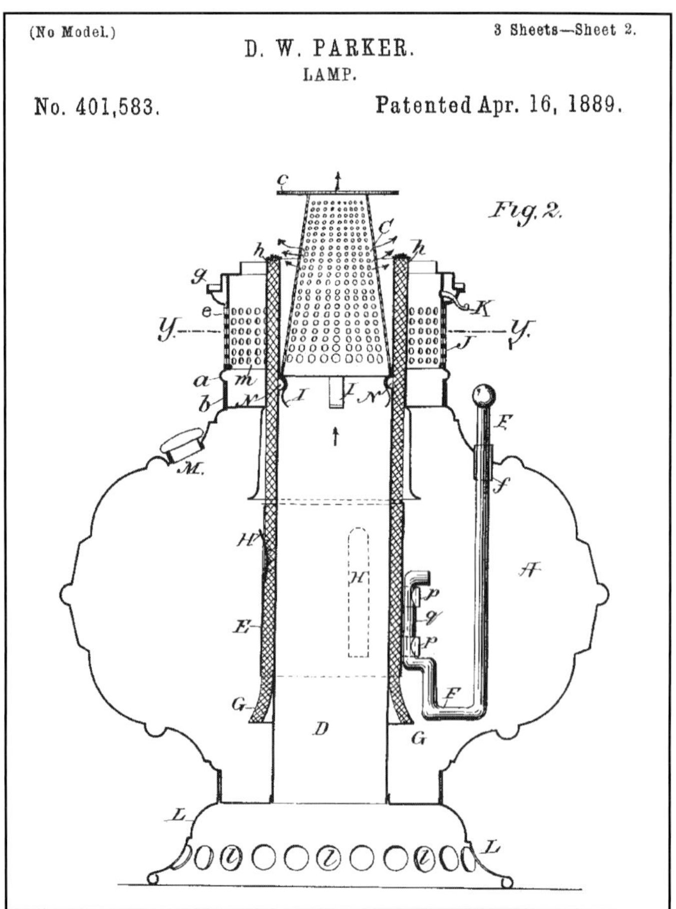

The Parker Lamp

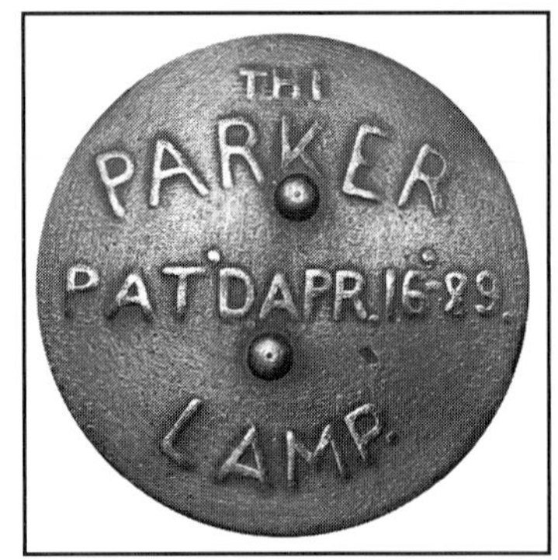

Flame spreader found in the Parker lamp below. The disc is steel.

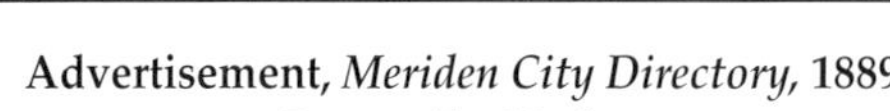

Advertisement, *Meriden City Directory,* 1889.
Courtesy Alan Weathers.

The Parker lamp, No. 2 stand lamp. The gallery lifts for lighting. Height 12". $175.00.

Oil fill cap.

The Parker lamp, No. 2 stand lamp. The fount is not marked. Same oil fill as above left. The gallery lifts for lighting. Height 12". The Parker flame spreader is shown on the next page. $175.00.

Flame spreader illustrated in Dexter Parker's patent 401,583. The disc is steel. This original design flame spreader is also found with a plain, unmarked top disc.

Flame spreader found in these Parker lamps (below) is marked "The Parker, Meriden, Conn."

Unmarked Parker No. 2 stand lamp with improved wick raising mechanism. The gallery lifts for lighting. Height 12". $175.00.

Wick knob.

Unmarked Parker No. 2 stand lamp. The gallery lifts for lighting. Height 12". $150.00.

The Peerless Lamp

The Peerless lamp (below), manufactured by the Charles Parker Company, was sold by J. Wallis Cook, a retailer in New York City. In late 1898 or early 1899, J. Wallis Cook and Vernon Cook organized the Mascot Mfg. Company in New York City to "manufacture lamps and novelties." Cook was possible distributor of Mascot lamp brackets made by Pease Mfg. Co., Philadelphia. Charles Parker shotguns were marked "Peerless" to indicate that they were the highest grade.

"The Peerless Lamp," also marked "J. Wallis Cook, New York" on the other side of the fount.

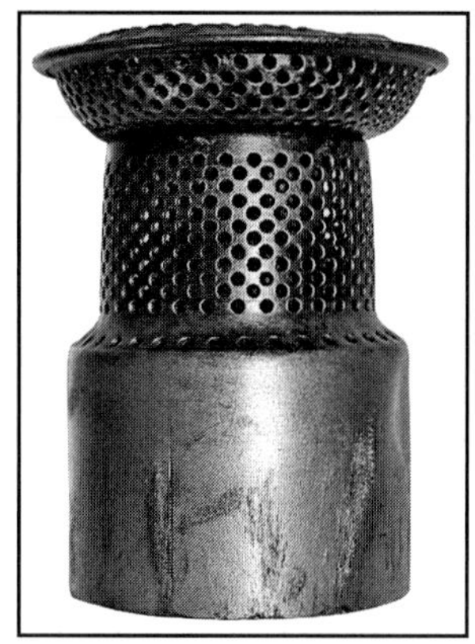

Flame spreader found in the Peerless lamp. This flame spreader is possibly found with a plain top.

Parker's Peerless No. 2 stand lamp. The gallery does not lift for lighting. Height 12". Lamp also found fully embossed. $175.00.

Undated broadside advertisement for the Peerless lamp.

Parker Military Lamps

Military barracks lamp dated 1899. The overall width is 34". Height 33". The support marked "Pat'd July 6, 1897." Plain white shades were used on Parker military lamps. $5,000.00. Courtesy Jack McNearney.

Military wall or bracket lamp dated 1899. The reflector is 10" diameter. The tank is 9½" long. The military lamps were fitted with white opal dome shades. $1,750.00. Courtesy Jack McNearney.

Officer's military desk lamp dated 1900. Height 20". Missing flame spreader. $1,750.00. Courtesy Jack McNearney.

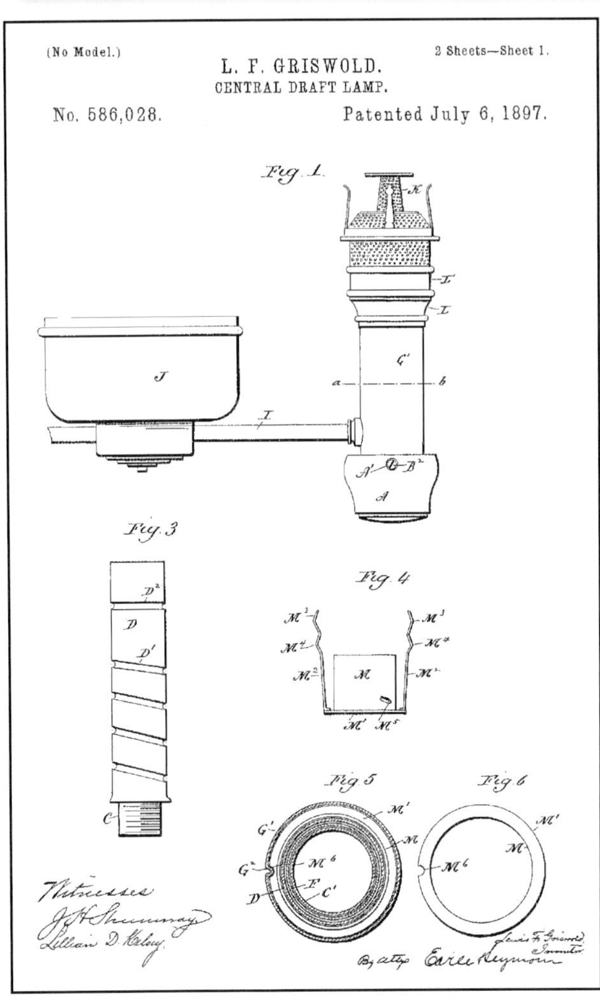

Griswold patent 586,028 for wick raising mechanism. Turning the drip cup raises and lowers the wick of the military lamps.

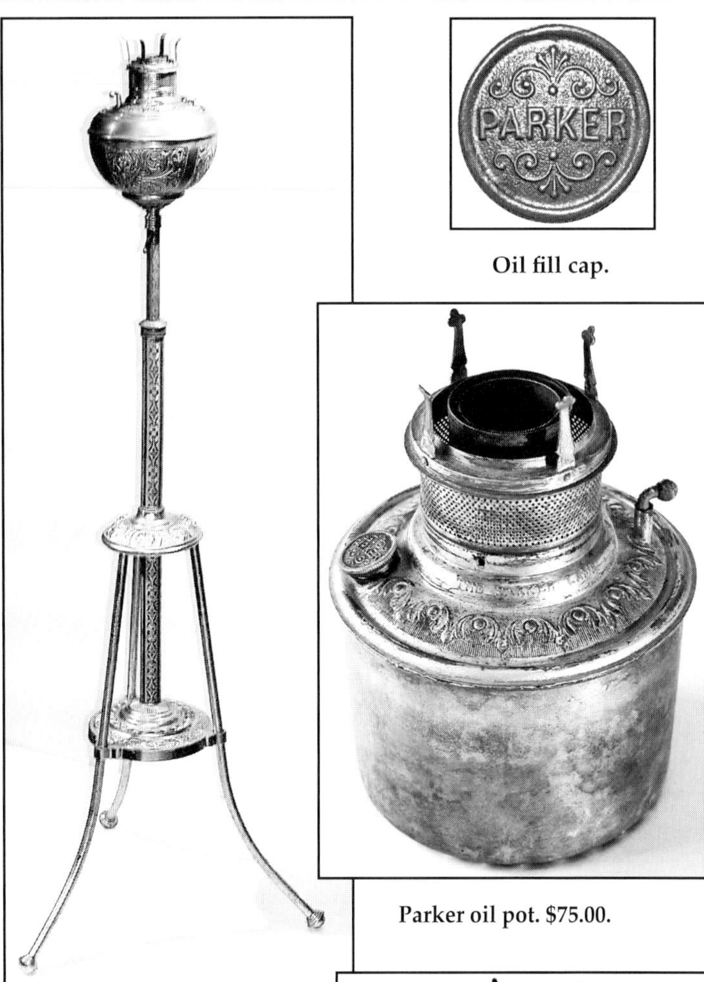

Oil fill cap.

Parker oil pot. $75.00.

Parker piano lamp finished in nickel silver missing flame spreader. Fount marked "The Parker Lamp." Height 50½". $500.00. Courtesy Jack McNearney.

The military lamps are marked "U.S. QM Dept., 1899 (or 1900), The Chas. Parker Co., The Parker Lamp." Courtesy Jack McNearney.

Parker oil pot with Parker flame spreader. Knob marked "Made in USA." $50.00. Courtesy Doug and Judy Myers.

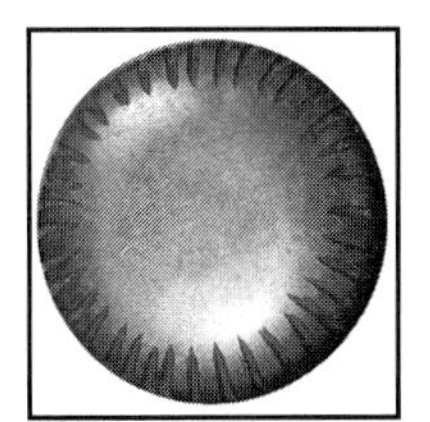

Oil fill cap.

Parker vase lamp missing flame spreader. Marked "The Parker Lamp" on the oil pot collar. Height 11¼". $175.00. Courtesy Jack McNearney.

Parker Library Lamps

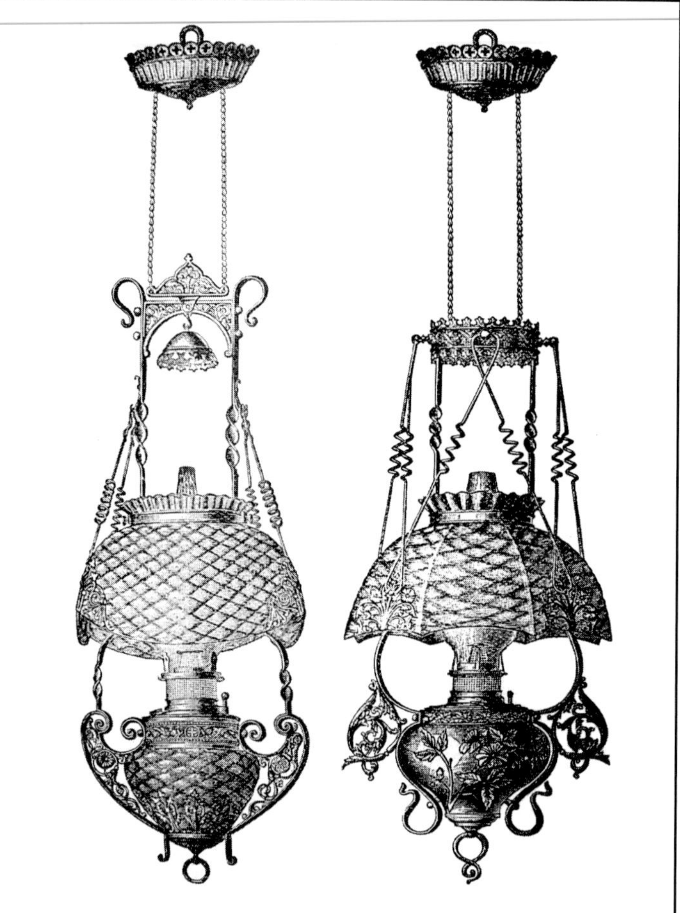

Parker *Peerless Electric Library Lamps, Center Draught*, sold by Burley & Tyrrell, Chicago, 1889. This little catalog offered outstanding lamps! These hanging lamps sold for $9.00 to $10.50 each. The ruby glass shades and glass fount holders were matching glass. The lamp far right had an etched metal fount holder. I suspect these lamps were sold with flat-wick burners before center-draft burners were introduced. Courtesy Rakow Library, Corning, NY.

Read the book *Victorian Library Lamps of the Nineteenth Century* to see outstanding Parker library lamps in color.

Parker library lamps, 1904 Pitkin and Brooks catalog. Courtesy Jim Hargis.

Parker clocks.
Courtesy Jack McNearney.

Pittsburgh Brass Company

1886 – 1898

Pittsburgh Lamp and Brass Company, 1898 – 1902; Pittsburgh Lamp, Brass and Glass Company, 1902 – 1926

Pittsburgh Brass Company was organized in Allegheny City, Pennsylvania, as a manufacturer of artistic brass and metal goods. The company made fireplace sets and fenders, andirons, cuspidors, umbrella stands, and lamps. The early lamps, until about 1890, were fancy piano lamps, table lamps, and hanging lamps with flat-wick burners.

Thomas Hipwell, one of the founders and the superintendent until 1890, assigned three patents for center-draft lamps to the company in 1890. Joseph Kintz was superintendent from 1890 to 1895 (also see Meriden Malleable Iron and Craighead & Kintz Co.).

Pittsburgh Brass advertised the Pittsburgh lamp extensively during the 1890s, claiming its share of the growing, and competitive, market for center-draft lamps. The company was said to be "the largest manufacturer of onyx tables in the country" (*CGL*, Nov. 14, 1894).

The company outgrew the factory on Sandusky Street and built new facilities on Locust Street in 1892. Lamps became an increasing portion of the business and the company name was changed to Pittsburgh Lamp and Brass Company in 1898; A. Ruben Miller was president and L. A. Lyman was secretary-treasurer.

The company reorganized again as Pittsburgh Lamp, Brass and Glass Company in 1902 by combining the Kopp Glass & Lamp Company of Swissvale, the Fort Pitt Glass Company of Pittsburgh, and Dithridge & Company of Jeannette. James H. Willock was president (he was also president of the Second National Bank); Frank G. Wallace, vice president; L. A. Lyman, secretary; and Frank S. Willock, treasurer. Nicholas Kopp became a director of the new company. George W. Blair, former president of Dithridge & Company and holder of many patents for glass lamps and lamp chimneys, was also a director.

Pittsburgh Lamp, Brass and Glass Company was incorporated in New Jersey with capital stock valued at $1,500,000. "The finest metal and glass lamps will be a feature of the new company," stated a 1901 press release (*CGL*, Dec. 14). "Brass goods will be made at the Allegheny factory, fancy opal novelties and glass specialties at the Dithridge Works and colored glass goods at the Kopp Works."

The success of the new company was evident in the fine lamps produced by Nicholas Kopp, who excelled in his craft. The Kopp works at Swissvale was operating at full capacity, the mold shop and shipping working overtime in 1903 (*CGL*, Dec. 5, 1903).

The Kopp works produced gas lighting fixtures, oil lamps, and a general line of clear, etched, opaque, colored, and decorated glassware. Colored signal glass was a specialty of Kopp Glass and Lamp Co. Oil lamps included stand lamps, banquet lamps, vase lamps, hanging lamps, and hall lamps. Chimneys were made in all sizes, along with a general line of flat-wick pattern glass lamps.

Fort Pitt Glass Works, 1905 postcard image.

The company became known as "Pilabrasgo" — an abbreviation of the longer name. The company advertised Success oil lamps, Pilabrasgo lamps, and Pilabrasgo decorated vases. In 1920 the company employed 1,200; W. L. Curry was president; Nicholas Kopp, vice president and general manager; W. F. McNaugher, secretary and assistant manager; and H. L. Brooks, treasurer.

As electric lamps became popular, Pittsburgh Lamp, Brass and Glass became known for its reading lamps of all kinds — electroliers, parlor, floor, boudoir, and desk lamps. Electroliers with reverse-painted scenes or stained glass were of excellent design and workmanship.

Pilabrasgo went out of business in 1926. Kopp Glass, Inc., reorganized and continues production of technical, commercial, and colored specialty glass today. Nicholas Kopp died in 1937.

Pittsburgh Brass Co. made lamps fitted with flat-wick burners from 1887 to 1890 (*PGR*, Nov. 17, 1887).

Pittsburgh Brass Company

Trade Names

Center-draft lamps — The Pittsburgh, The Mammoth, The Family, Aurora, Success.

Flat-wick pattern glass lamps — Baltimore, Bellevue (Coolidge Drape), Mission, Bead & Drape, more. See catalog No. 13 entitled *Pilabrasgo Success Oil Lamps and Decorated Vases*. Also see Dithridge & Company.

Selected Patents, Center-draft Lamps[1]

Thomas Hipwell assigned to Pittsburgh Brass Co.

1890 428,607
1890 439,593
1890 443,521

William M. Hoerle assigned to Pittsburgh Brass Co.

1890 432,311
1890 432,489
1890 435,357
1891 451,483
1892 466,919
1895 548,314
1896 557,270
1900 656,891

[1]Nicholas Kopp held many design patents. Also read the chapter on Fostoria Shade and Lamp Company (Consolidated Lamp and Glass Co.).

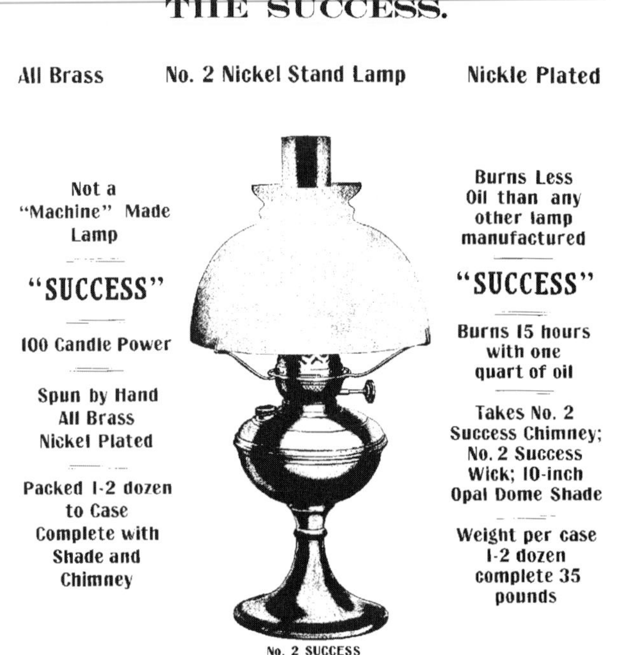

Success lamps were introduced in 1899 and sold for many years. This advertisement is from 1921.

Advertisement, *Crockery and Glass Journal*, 1886.

The Pittsburgh Lamp

Pittsburgh flame spreaders for No. 2 stand lamps and oil pots. The flame spreader on right is found in lamps below.

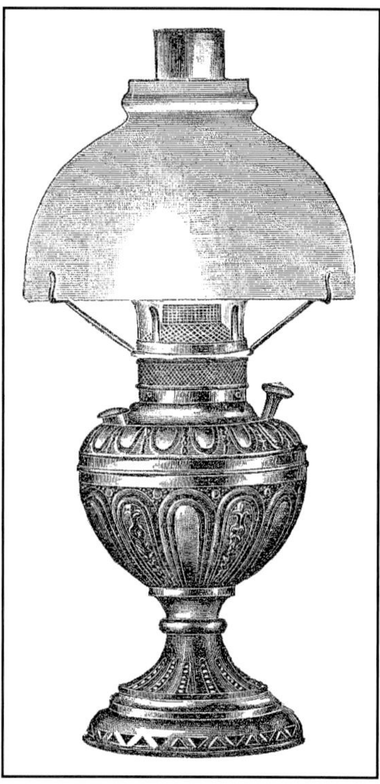

Pittsburgh No. 2 stand lamp sold by the Peaslee Gaulbert Company, Louisville, Kentucky, in 1897.

Pittsburgh No. 2 stand lamp, cast-iron foot. Height 11". $175.00.

Pittsburgh No. 2 stand lamp. $100.00.
Courtesy Fil Graff.

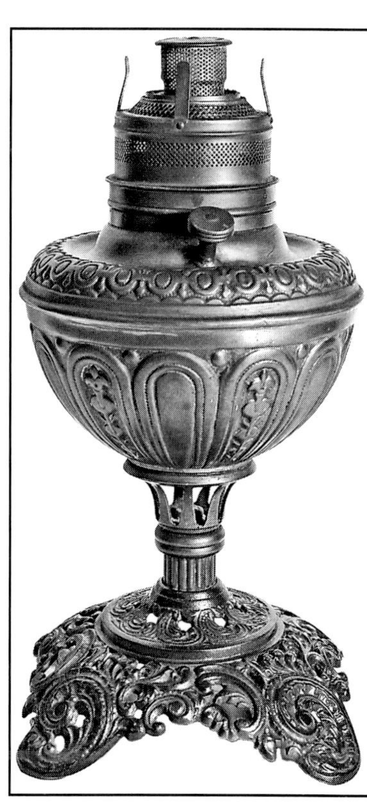

Pittsburgh No. 2 stand lamp, cast-iron foot. Height 12½". $175.00.

The Pittsburgh Lamp

Pittsburgh vase lamps, Marshall Field catalog, 1894.

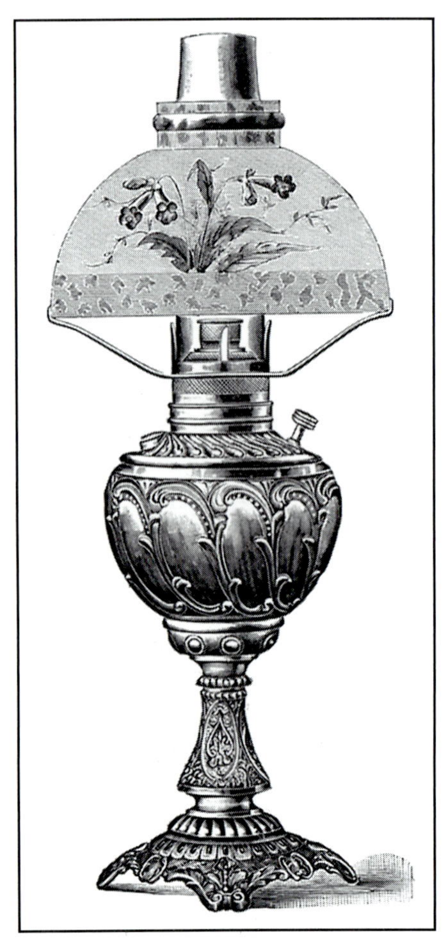

Pittsburgh banquet lamps, Marshall Field catalog, 1894.

The Pittsburgh Brass Company sold oil pots which are easily recognized in vase lamps, banquet lamps, and hanging lamps in trade catalogs. Pittsburgh stand lamps are less common today.

Oil pot with burner removed to show wick raising mechanism. The teeth grip the wick and rotate to raise and lower it.

Pottery and Glass Reporter, April 25, 1889.

Pittsburgh oil pot. Standard 5" diameter. $100.00.
Courtesy Kent Stratton.

The only reason why the Pittsburgh Lamp is not in every store in the country is: We can't make it fast enough—we can't make a tenth enough to go round.

There is another reason that has a certain weight: the wholesale price is higher.

There are a dozen or twenty makes of central-draught lamps. The Pittsburgh outranks the rest in the wholesale market.

No matter what price we might put on it, others would sell for less: they'd have to.

Send to us for a primer. Buy at home if you can.

PITTSBURGH BRASS COMPANY.
Pittsburgh, Pa.

Advertisement, *Harper's Magazine,* March 1892.

Pittsburgh hanging lamps, Marshall Field catalog, 1894.

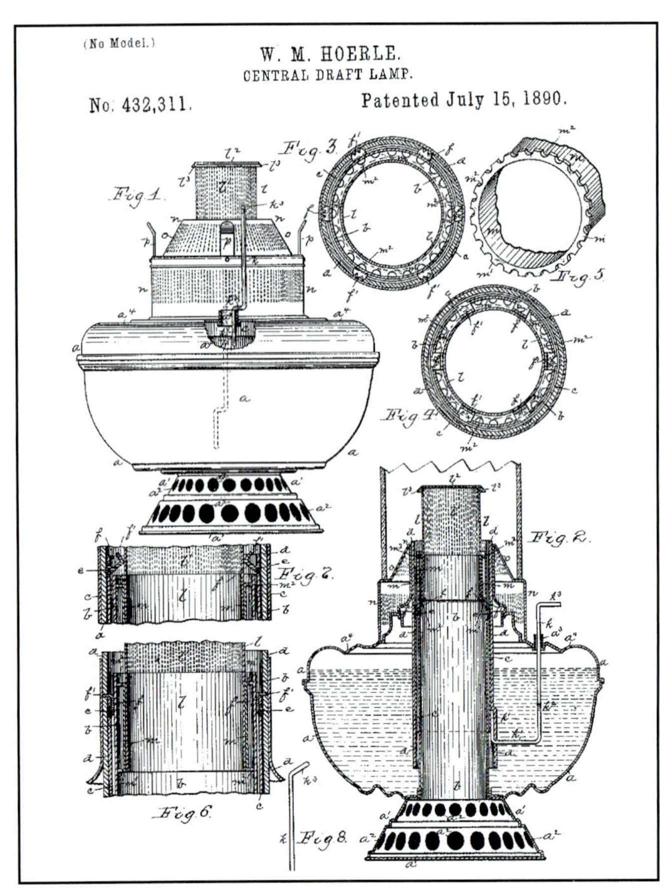

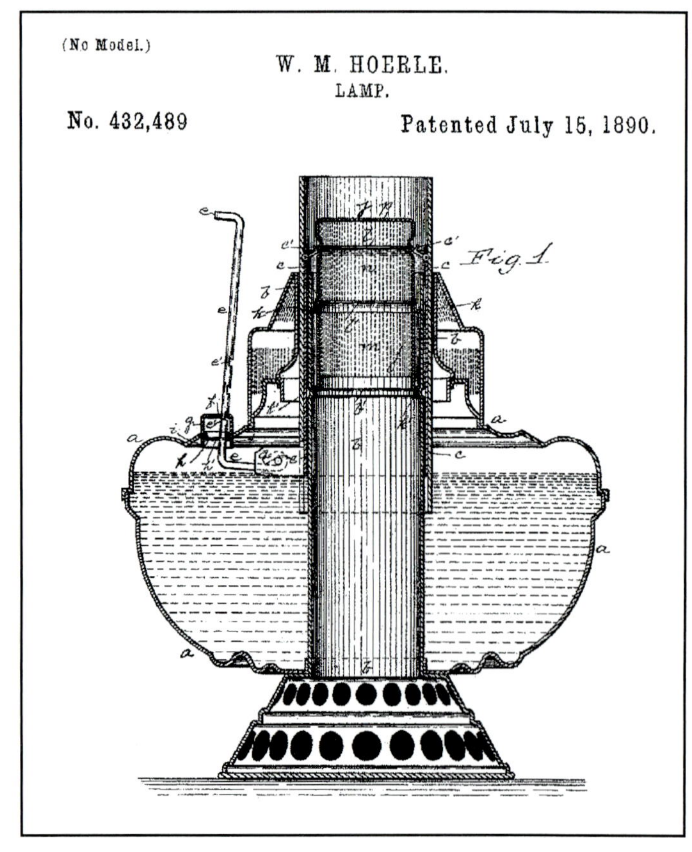

Retrospective.

We have won.

Returns are all in and conclusively show the unique originality and high art displayed in the line to be far in the lead. The Pittsburgh metal lamps have scored an unprecedented hit everywhere.

Our mammoth factory must operate day and night to the last minute in the year. And, then, the Pittsburgh lamps march onward, like conquering heroes, to win even greater popularity.

Prospective.

1899 —— January, February, March —— orders already booked and those coming in daily for Pittsburgh lamps, for delivery during these months, preclude the usual "shut-down" of our plant in January for repairs and alterations, heretofore an annual event. Not a wheel can stop.

All of which tells plainly enough which way the wind is blowing. Pittsburgh metal lamps have achieved success through sheer merit.

Pittsburgh Lamp & Brass Co.,

PITTSBURGH, PA.

ALLEGHENY, PA., Foot of Locust street. 82 West Broadway, NEW YORK CITY

China, Glass and Lamps, Dec. 8, 1898.

Advertisement, *Pottery and Glass Reporter,* June 4, 1891. Hanging lamps with this unique frame were sold by the Peaslee Gaulbert Company, Louisville, KY, in 1897. The harp and fount ring allow the fount to be removed from below.

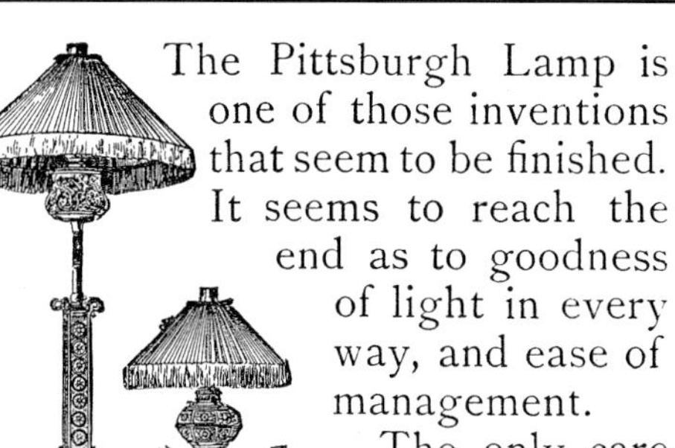

The Pittsburgh Lamp is one of those inventions that seem to be finished. It seems to reach the end as to goodness of light in every way, and ease of management.

The only care it requires is filling and wiping. Dirt falls out when the chimney is taken off, not into a pocket as in other central-draft lamps.

Putting in a new wick is a very easy matter indeed.

All this seems strange to one who knows how troublesome other good lamps are.

It is in all the good lamp-stores. Send for a primer.

Pittsburgh, Pa. PITTSBURGH BRASS CO.

Advertisement, *Munsey's Magazine,* 1894.

Success Lamp

The Success line of lamps was introduced in 1899 with the following editorial comment in *China, Glass and Lamps* (Feb. 23): "Surprise would be a more expressive name. If some metal lamp competitors do not fail of breath and fall down when the new Pittsburgh lamps are flashed forth, it will be a miracle indeed." Success lamps and lamps fitted with Success oil pots were sold for many years in virtually all major mail order catalogs. Original Success chimneys were 12" long and marked "PLB&GCo."

Early Success fount and common burner.

Early Success fount and common burner.

Common Success fount and burner.

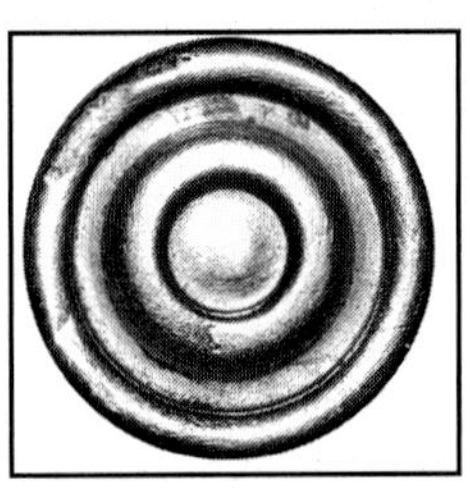

Early Success wick knob.

Early Success oil fill cap.

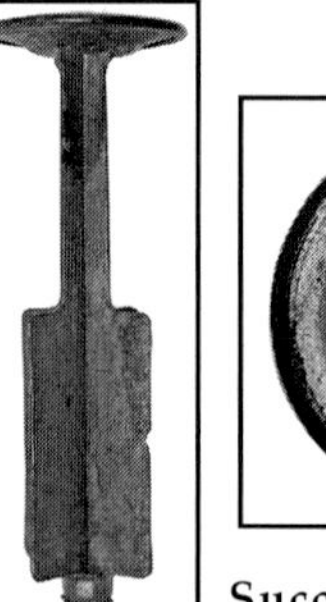

Success oil fill cap found on some early founts.

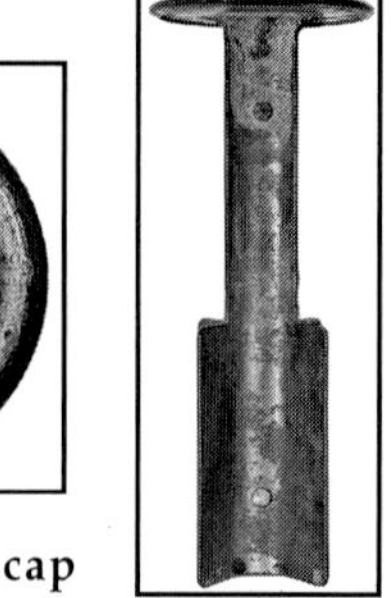

Common Success wick knob and oil fill cap.

Success No. 2 stand lamps. Left: early fount and early burner, $125.00; center: early fount and common burner, $75.00; right: common fount and common burner, $50.00. Height 12".

Early Success burner gallery.

Success cast-iron loading weight. The markings are often not distinct.

Early Success burner. The air deflector is stamped with the company name.

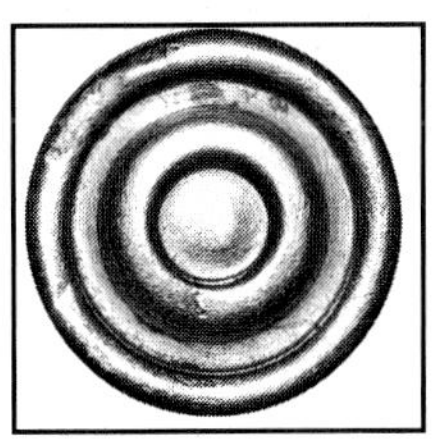

Early Success burner knob.

Common Success burner. The burner basket is now one piece and the gallery is assembled as one unit.

Common Success burner knob.

Earliest Success founts have recessed burner threads.

Some early and all common Success founts have a flat top of recessed burner threads.

Success wick knob and oil fill cap.

Success hanging lamp fount with pull-down base attachment. This lamp is finished in brushed brass. $75.00.

Success flame spreaders. Left, early; right, common.

Success wick knob and oil fill cap.

Success oil pots are found in numerous decorated vase lamps. They were extremely popular with many catalog companies. Height 8½". Standard 5" diameter. $50.00.

Success No. 2 parlor lamp. Height 12". These lamps, identified as S-3541 in the Pilabrasgo catalog, were fitted with "12" shades and 10" fitter." The lamps were finished in brushed brass, dark japan finish (above), and nickel plating. $150.00.

Aurora Lamp

The Aurora lamp is similar to the Success stand lamp. However, the Aurora burner gallery is steel rather than brass. Likewise the flame spreader is all steel. The Aurora was sold by Butler Brothers in 1916 catalog (see right).

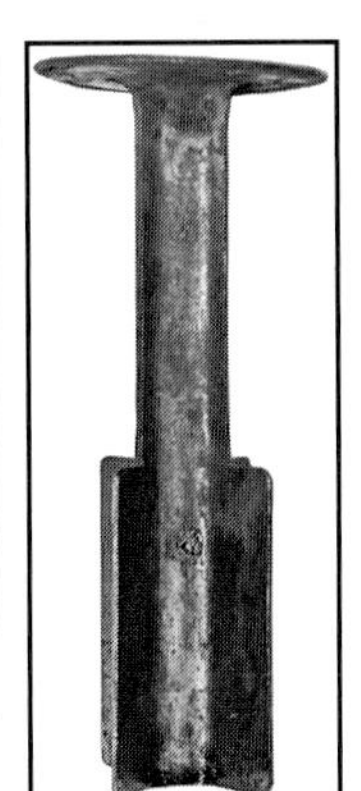

Aurora flame spreader, marked "Aurora" on top.

Aurora fill cap.

Aurora wick knob.

Aurora No. 2 stand lamp. Height 12". Shape of the foot is distinctly different compared with that of Success. $75.00.

Bottom view of Aurora cast-iron loading weight which has faint marks of "Pittsburgh Lamp and Brass Co., Pittsburgh" marking.

Success Lamp

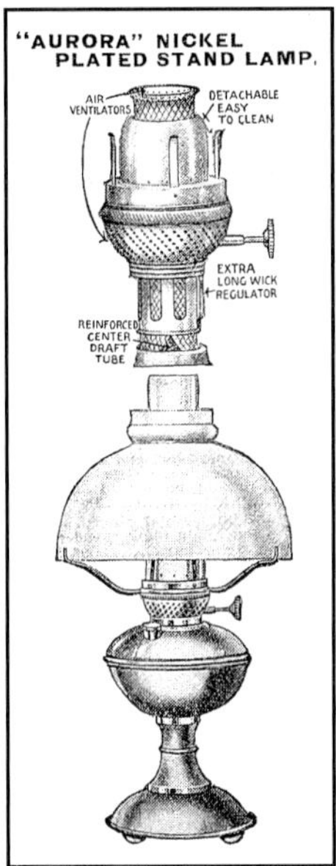

Success vase lamp. Pitkin and Brooks catalog No. 203, Chicago, 1904/1905. Courtesy Jim Hargis.

Success lamp with early burner, ca. 1900. Original shade ring for 10" ball shade. A similar lamp fitted with an oil pot was offered as a premium by Wm. Wrigley Jr. & Co. with the purchase of 10 cases of chewing gum. $175.00. Courtesy Kent Stratton.

Success Vase Lamps, Kopp's Cardinal Glass

This enterprising company have been able to get their full share of the fancy lamp trade and are among the leaders in their line. Nicholas Kopp, who is at the head of the plant, and who has become famous as a color maker, is again in evidence this season with a new color styled royal copper, which is expected to eclipse his famous cerise effect, which so many in the glass trade have attempted to duplicate.

Royal copper is a darker red than cerise, but the light effects upon it give a richer lustre, which will no doubt captivate trade and add to Mr. Kopp's fame as the creator of new color effects in glass. [At this time, Consolidated was making lamps in cerise glass developed there by Kopp.]

This company have also gone into the manufacture of signal lights for the railroad trade on a rather extensive scale. Previously the big factory at Corning, N. Y., was the almost exclusive producer of these lights and even excelled European glass manufacturers in producing some fine colors.

China, Glass and Lamps, Dec. 5, 1903

Crockery and Glass Journal, Nov. 16, 1905.

Pitkin and Brooks catalog No. 203, Chicago, 1904/1905.

Courtesy Jim Hargis.

Modern art lamps — pearl white etched glass decorated with gold-traced flowers in color. Pitkin and Brooks catalog No. 203, Chicago, 1904/1905. Courtesy Jim Hargis.

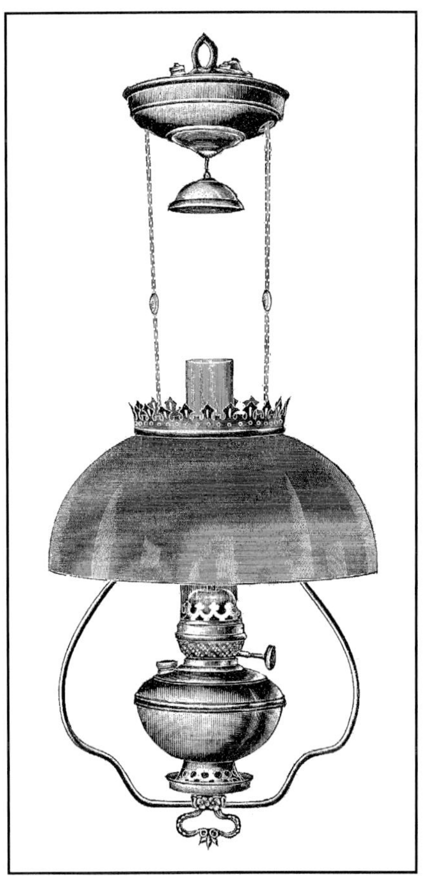

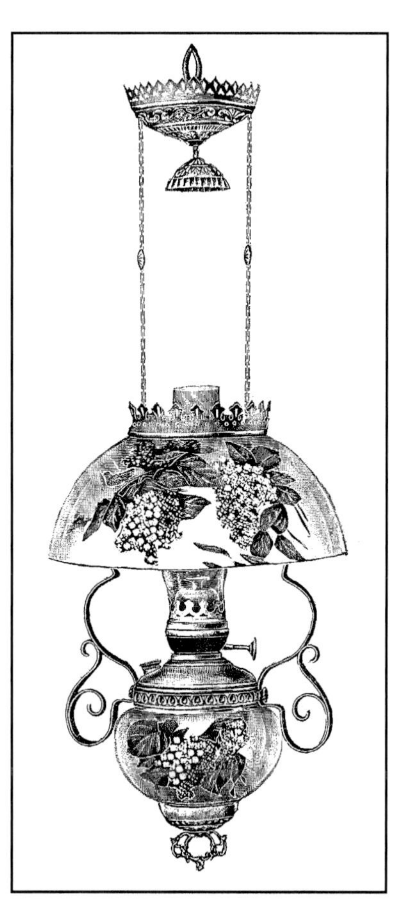

Success library lamps, Norvell-Shapleigh Hardware catalog, St. Louis, 1910.

Hand Decorated Success Vase Lamps

Butler Brothers catalog, 1909.

Norvell-Shapleigh Hardware catalog, St. Louis, 1910.

Plume & Atwood Mfg. Company

1869 – 1960s

On January 5, 1869, Holmes, Booth & Atwood Manufacturing Company was formed in Waterbury, Connecticut. Israel Holmes was president; David S. Plume, treasurer; and John C. Booth, secretary. Holmes, Booth & Atwood had left Holmes, Booth & Haydens to form the new company.

In 1871 the name was changed to Plume & Atwood Manufacturing Company (P & A) due to the similarity of the name with Holmes, Booth & Haydens. In the years that followed, "P & A" became the sign of quality in lamps.

Lewis J. Atwood

Lewis J. Atwood held numerous patents for improvements in burners, lamps, and manufacturing processes (beginning in 1862) when he was in charge of the "burner department" for Holmes, Booth & Haydens. In 1871, Atwood became a stockholder and officer in Plume & Atwood Mfg. Company where he continued to improve kerosene burners and lamps.

P & A operated two divisions — a brass mill in Thomaston, Connecticut, and a fabricating plant in Waterbury. The company had warehouses in Boston, Chicago, and New York.

When Israel Holmes died in 1874, Booth was elected president and Lewis J. Atwood became secretary. Atwood held 69 or more patents for improvements in coal-oil burners, lamps, and lamp fixtures. In 1880 the company was incorporated under Connecticut law. Atwood became president in 1890.

Lamps were made for every occasion — such as night lamps for the home, coach lamps, street lamps, automobile and bicycle lamps, and steamboat and railroad lamps. An early catalog of the company shows 57 types and sizes of burners.

Products made by P & A included burners for kerosene oil lamps; railroad oil lamps; oil heaters; chicken incubators and brooders; livestock water heaters; oil lighting lamps — household, street, automobile, and bicycle; lighting fixtures — household and bathroom; rivets and washers; lamp parts — clusters, vase plates, galleries, socket covers, reflectors, seating rings; straight pins; curtain rings; pen and pencil parts; and cosmetic products.

Plume & Atwood furnished burners and lamp parts to other companies, including Consolidated Lamp and Glass of Pittsburgh. P & A made the famous Aladdin lamp and incandescent coal oil

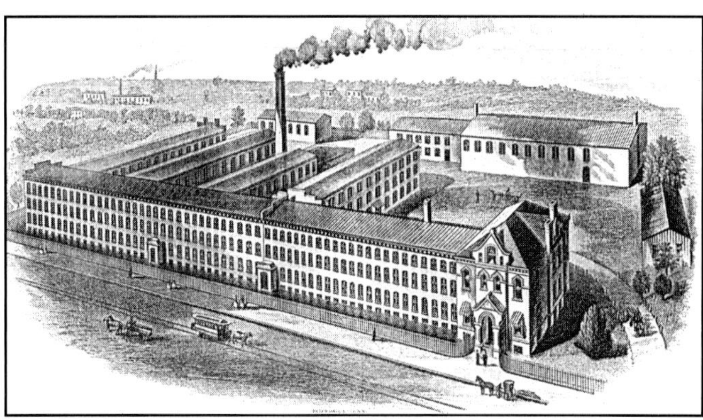

burners for the Mantle Lamp Company of America, Chicago and Nashville, from 1908 to 1955. A flood severely damaged the Waterbury plant in August 1955, destroying all the lamp-making machinery and stamping dies. After rebuilding, operations resumed October 1955 in Thomaston, Connecticut.

The company branched into a variety of metal working activities as the business grew and facilities expanded. P & A became Dorset Division, a subsidiary of the J. B. Williams Company, in the 1960s. Risdon Mfg. Company purchased Dorset in 1971. Risdon is still in business, although manufacture of Eagle burners was discontinued about 1983.

Trademarks

The Banner trademark was granted to P & A on Sept 25, 1906, for oil heaters, stoves, and lamps. The mark had been used since 1876.

Trade Names

Center-draft lamps — Fireside Electric, Banner Electric, Banner, Royal Electric, Royal, Little Royal, Little Royal Improved, Household Lamp, Colonial, Mammoth, Naugatuck, Plumwood, Sewing, Magnet, Jupiter, Paragon.

Round-wick, center-draft burners — Moehring.

Folded-wick, side-draft burners — Astral Argand, Electric Argand, Harvard, Moehring Argand, Victor Argand.

Flat-wick burners — Acorn, American Duplex, Banner, P&A Duplex, Climax, Dual, Duplex, Eagle, Fireside, Globe, Hornet, Model, New Calcium Light, Nutmeg, Oxford, Pioneer, Pet Ratchet, Sunlight, Sun Duplex, Sun Hinge, Unique.

Metal flat-wick lamps — Acorn, Climax, Collage, Dutchess, Fireside, Hornet, Little Brownie, Nutmeg, Pollyanna.

Bicycle lamps — Banner, Improved Banner, Jim Dandy, Climax, Banner Gas, and the Automatic acetylene bicycle lamps.

Lanterns — Ichabod, the Gipsy.

Lantern burners — Badger, Beacon, Callender, Dexter, Dudley.

Selected Patents, Center-draft Lamps

Lewis J. Atwood[1] assigned to P & A

(w. William F. Lewis)	1887	370,516
1888		386,953
1888		387,756
1888		388,105
1888		392,396
1889		400,819
(w. Tobey)	1889	405,388
(w. others)	1889	411,517
1890		435,130
1890		436,093
(w. Tobey)	1891	448,851
(w. Tobey)	1891	454,247
1892		466,551
1893		495,289
1895		538,476
Frederick W. Tobey assigned to P & A		
1890		430,258
C. E. Wirth[2] assigned to P & A		
1903		733,106

[1]Atwood held 69 or more patents.
[2]Also patents for incandescent burners.

Advertisement in the *Delineator Magazine,* 1895.

Advertisement, *Waterbury City Directory,* 1910. Courtesy Margaret J. Gibbs.

THE PLUME & ATWOOD MFG. CO.,
MANUFACTURERS OF
Brass, Copper and German Silver
IN THE ROLL, SHEET, WIRE AND ROD.
Copper and Brass Rivets and Burrs, Printers' Rule Strips and Galley Plates, Brass Door Rail, Brass Butt Hinges, Brass and Iron Jack Chain, Escutcheon Pins, Clock Bells, Etc.
"THE BANNER OIL LAMP STOVE."
"THE ROYAL LAMP."
KEROSENE OIL BURNERS AND LAMPS.
Lamp Trimmings in Great Variety.
Pins of Superior Quality.
Factories, 470 BANK STREET, WATERBURY, CONN.
Rolling and Wire Mills, THOMASTON, CONN.
SALES OFFICE, 279 BROADWAY, NEW YORK, N. Y.
BRANCH OFFICES, CHICAGO AND SAN FRANCISCO.
WALTER S. ATWOOD, Pres. JOHN B. BURRALL, Treas.
ROBERT C. SWAYZE, Vice-Pres. J. H. HURLBURT, Sec. and Ass't Treas.
JOHN L. SCOTT, Ass't Sec.

Plume & Atwood sold kerosene lamps, such as this one, well into the 1950s and 1960s. These included the Naugatuck, Magnet, and Colonial. Some lamps may not have been identified as P & A and may be constructed with older components. The flame spreaders may be unmarked or those marked "Waterbury," "Dorset," or with the patent dates of 1890 and 1893 (above). $50.00.

Fireside Electric

Plume & Atwood was quick to use "electric" to promote center-draft lamps that were new to the public during the 1880s.

Fireside Electric lamps were sold beginning in 1886 and sold by F. H. Lovell in 1887. They were replaced by the Banner Electric lamp.

Flame spreader for the Fireside Electric lamp.

Banner Electric — Post

Banner Electric lamps were sold from 1888 to 1893. The early Banner Electric lamps used a thimble flame spreader mounted on a post, similar to the Fireside lamp. The fount may be plain or embossed.

"Electric" was used in advertising until 1890. Banner Electric lamps were then sold simply as Banner lamps.

THE BANNER IS THE LAMP
STEADIEST, WHITEST, LARGEST.
THAT GIVES THE LIGHT
UNEQUALLED FOR SIMPLICITY AND EASE OF MANAGEMENT.
Made in graceful styles, but rather for use than ornament.
IT COSTS MUCH LESS
than other lamps, yet is equal to the most expensive for practical purposes. Do not be put off with any other. If you cannot get them from your dealer, write us.
THE PLUME & ATWOOD MFG. CO.,
NEW YORK. BOSTON. CHICAGO.

Advertisement in the *Delineator Magazine,* 1891.

Oil fill cap for Fireside Electric and Banner Electric.

Fireside Electric stand lamp No. 2. Height 12½". Also found in other forms. $150.00.

Fireside Electric stand lamp No. 2, redesigned fount. Height 12½". $150.00. Courtesy Heinz and Ursula Baumann.

Banner Electric stand lamp No. 2 with thimble-post flame spreader. Height 12". $175.00.

The "BANNER" Lamps and Founts.

The unqualified success of the Centre-draft "**Banner**" Lamps and Founts warrants our claiming them to be the best in the market. Having all the latest improved attachments—Drip Cup, Feeder Wick, Brass Tubes, and Wick movement, makes the "**Banner**" without an equal.

Owing to the increasing demand for a larger light, we have made a **No. 3** or **Mammoth** "Banner Fount, which has all the good qualities of the No. 2. WRITE FOR PRICES.

TAKE NO OTHER.

No. 2 "BANNER" FOUNT.

No. 2 "BANNER" LAMP.

Capacity, 3 to 4 Quarts.

BURNS ELEVEN HOURS.

300 CANDLE POWER.

10 inch "BANNER" TRIPOD.

No. 1 "BANNER" FOUNT.

No. 1 "BANNER" LAMP.

WERNER & LOEWE,

DETROIT, MICH.

Broadside advertisement for Banner lamps. The No. 1 Banner stand lamps have a different gallery than the No. 2 stand lamps.

Banner Electric — Thimble Flame Spreader

Top view of early Banner Electric embossed fount, also found smooth and plain. Note the screen inside the gallery.

Top view redesigned Banner Electric fount, ca. 1893. Note the raised rim on the top edge of the fount. This design was used extensively for Royal lamps.

Banner Electric stand lamp No. 2 with thimble flame spreader. Height 12". $125.00.

The P & A oil fill cap is found on Banner Electric lamps, ca. 1893, and Royal Electric lamps.

Banner Electric wick raising system.

Banner Electric stand lamp No. 2 with redesigned fount which is common to the early Royal lamps. Height 11½". $125.00.

Banner Electric Flame Spreaders

Thimble

Flame spreader for Banner Electric #2 stand lamp marked "Banner Electric Lamp, Patented, Aug. 14, 1888." Some have a screen baffle inside.

Redesigned flame spreader for Banner Electric stand lamp, ca. 1893, marked "Banner Electric Lamp, Patented, Aug. 14, 1888."

Flame spreader for Banner Electric #1 stand lamp marked "Banner Electric Lamp, Patented, Aug. 14, 1888." Courtesy Kent Stratton.

Flame spreader for Banner Electric No. 1 stand lamp, ca. 1893, marked "Banner Electric Lamp, Pat'd, Aug. 14, 88, Aug. 26, 90, Sept. 9, 90, Mar. 24, 91, June 16, 1891." Courtesy Kent Stratton.

Post-thimble

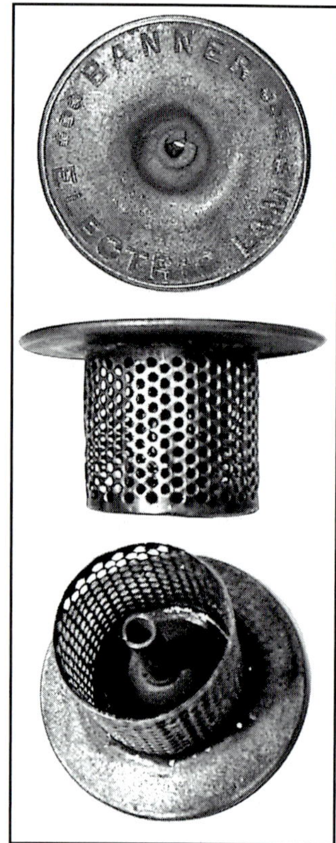

"Banner Electric Lamp."
Courtesy Heinz and Ursula Baumann.

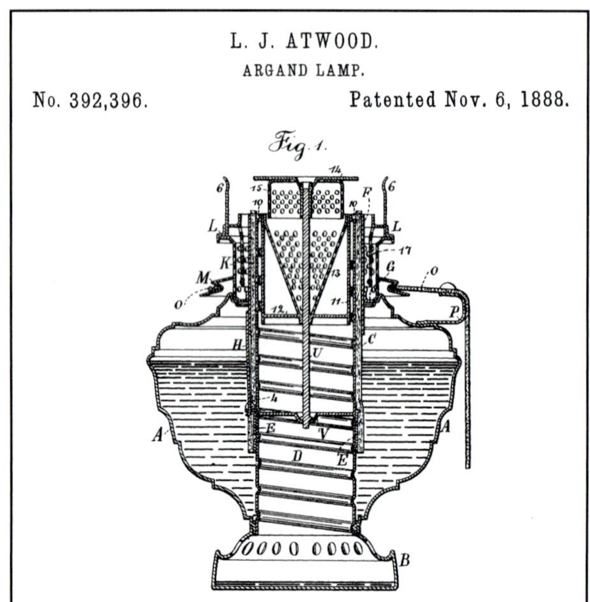

L. J. ATWOOD.
ARGAND LAMP.
No. 392,396. Patented Nov. 6, 1888.

Patent 392,396 illustrates the screw thread around the central air tube and the central post support of the flame spreader found in early Banner lamps. This patent actually was for the device to regulate the wick for a hanging lamp from below the lamp.

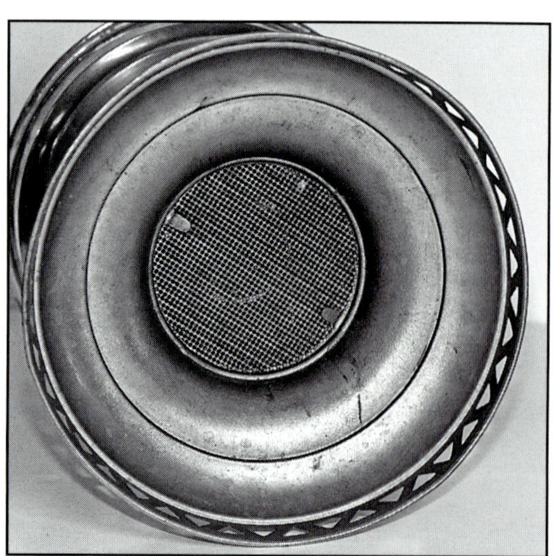

Insect screen in the bottom of the Banner Electric.

Banner Hanging Lamps

No. 3 Banner hanging lamps were sold for many years with a choice of glass or tin shades. In 1921, identical lamps were illustrated in the *Peaslee-Gaulbert Lamp and Glassware* Catalogue No. 198 as No. 3 Paragon. In contrast, Royal hanging lamps were available with No. 2 founts and burners.

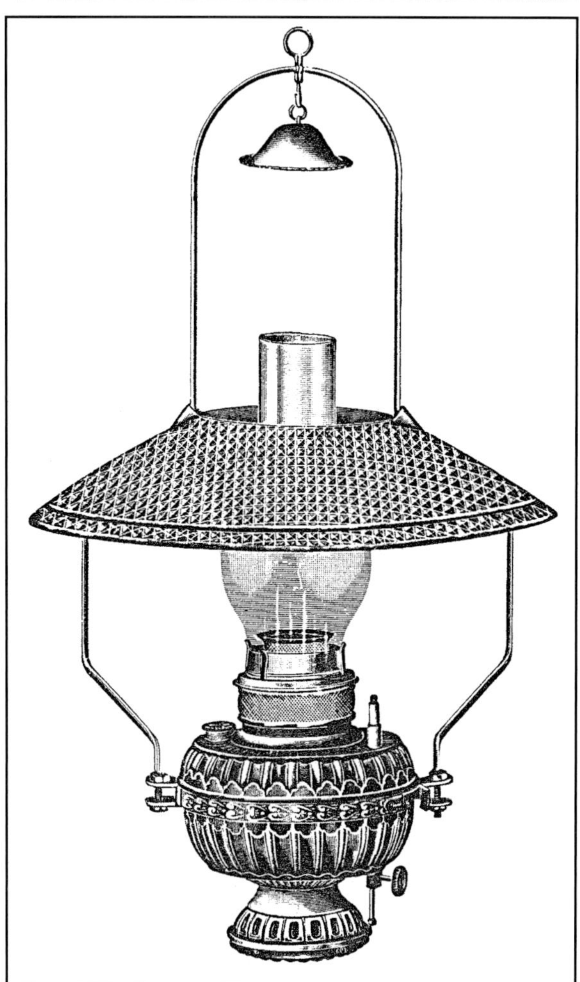

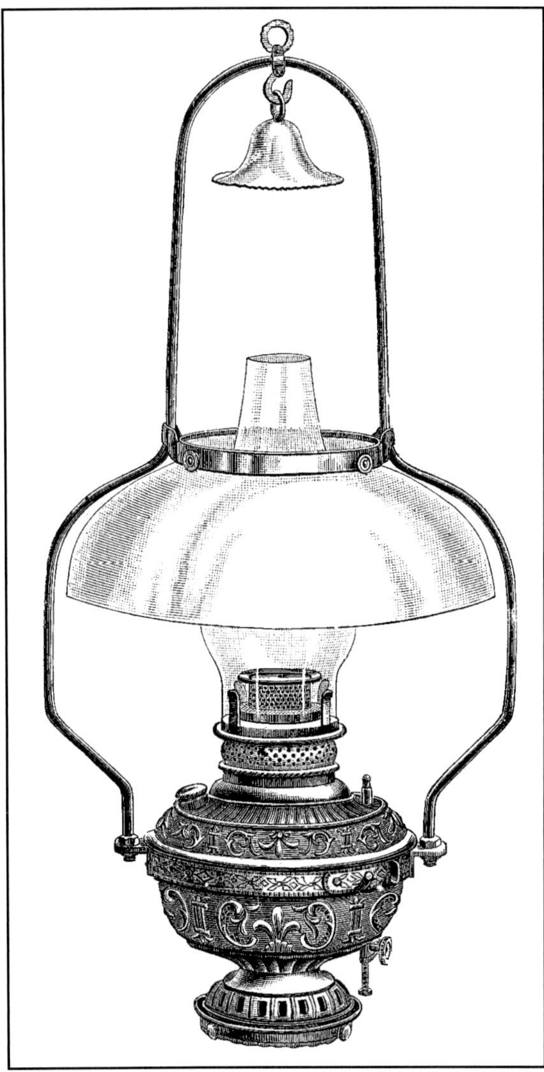

Top of flame spreader.
Courtesy Fil Graff.

Banner hanging lamp fount No. 3. $125.00.
Courtesy Fil Graff.

Royal

The Royal central-draft lamp became one of P & A's most popular "brands," introduced in 1890 and sold for many years. The first lamps were advertised as Royal Electric. Most Royal lamps were unmarked except for the flame spreader and a patent date on the wick raising mechanism. Burners used in Royal lamps evolved over time (below), and are found in all sizes and in lamp founts of many forms and embossed patterns. Early Royal lamps have a wire-rod-lift wick adjuster, while those made during and after 1893 have the improved ratchet adjustment to control the flame.

Early burner made in two forms: 1) The entire burner basket (non–lift gallery) slides off the wick tube of the earliest burner, and 2) others are made in one-piece with galleries fixed or lift. The lift gallery is dated "Pat. Apr. 11 '93."

Lift gallery marked "Pat. Apr. 11 '93." This burner was made for both bayonet and threaded connections.

Late burner, threaded connection, lift gallery.

Improved wick knob ratchet marked "Pat. Apr. 30 '95" on the left side.

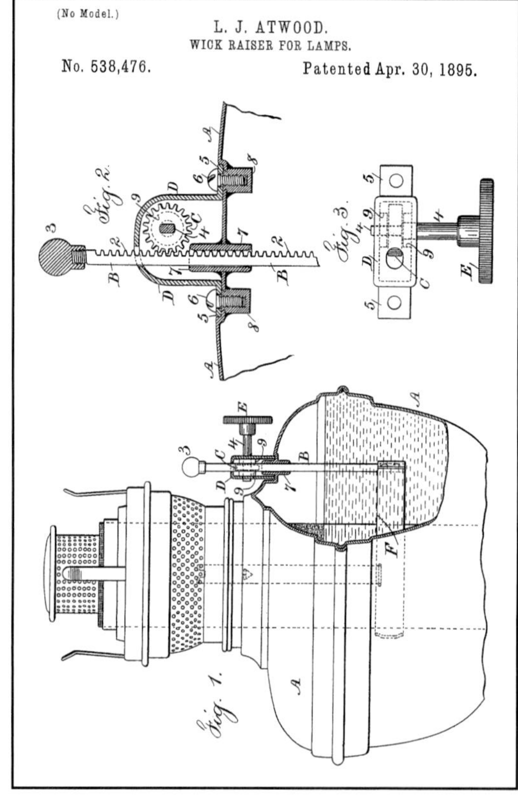

Advertisement in the *Delineator Magazine*, 1897.

Royal Flame Spreaders

The Royal, Pat. Aug. 14, 88.

"Royal, Pat'd Aug. 14, 88. Aug. 26, 90. Sep. 9, 90. March. 24, 91. Jan. 5, 92."

"Pat'd Aug. 14, 88. Aug. 26, 90. Sep. 9, 90. March. 24, 91. Jan. 5, 92."

"Pat. Apr. 11, 93. Sept. 9, 90. Apr. 30, 95."

"Patented, Sept. 9, 90. Apr. 11, 93."

"Royal, Pat'd Aug. 14, 88. Aug. 26, 90. Sep. 9, 90. March. 24, 91. Jan. 5, 92."

"Patented, Sept. 9, 90. Apr. 11, 93."

"P & A Royal, Pat'd Aug. 14, 1888, Dorset, Thomaston, Conn."

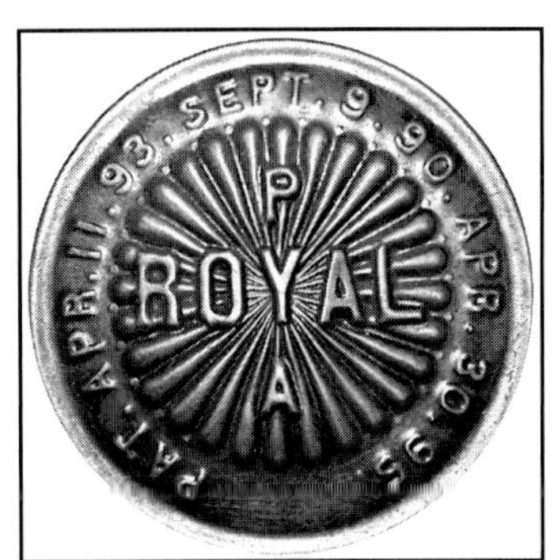

"P & A Royal, Pat. Apr. 11, 9. , Sept. 9, 90. Apr. 30, 95."

"P & A Royal, Pat. Apr. 11, 93. Sept. 9, 90. Apr. 30, 95."

Side-view of lower flame spreaders.

Royal Electric, 1890 – 1893

Royal lamps were introduced as Royal Electric lamps in 1890. "Electric" was dropped very soon, and the lamps were sold simply as "The Royal" or "Royal." The signed P & A oil fill cap was introduced with the Royal line. The early Royal (Electric) lamps have push-pull wick raiser rods — "the best LIFT wick movement," according to advertisements at the time.

Flame spreaders found in Royal Electric lamps.

Advertisement in *Crockery and Glass Journal*, Dec. 11, 1890, for "Banner and Royal Electric Lamps." Banner (left) and Royal Electric (right). The flame spreader has been redesigned for the Royal.

Oil fill cap.

Royal Electric stand lamp No. 2, non–lift gallery. Height 12". $150.00.

Royal Electric stand lamp No. 2, non–lift gallery. Height 12". $125.00.

Early Royal, 1893 – 1897

Early Royal burners are found in a variety of P & A founts. The patented wick raiser was introduced in late 1893 or early 1894, although the patent was not granted until 1895. The lamps illustrated have lift galleries.

Flame spreaders found in early Royal burners with improved wick raiser. The flame spreader not marked "Royal" may be a replacement or may have been on lamps sold to other retailers.

Royal stand lamp No. 2 with arms, lift gallery. Height 11". $175.00.

Wick knob.

Oil fill cap.

"The best goods are cheapest in the end. See that 'Royal' is stamped on Flame Spreader."
(Hibbard, Spencer, Bartlett & Co., 1893)

This lamp also sold by A. J. Weidener Company, of Philadelphia, as is marked on this oil fill cap.

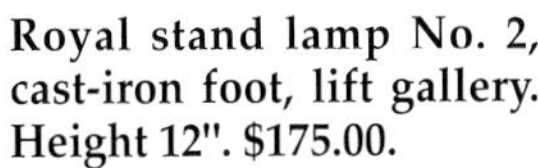

Royal stand lamp No. 2, cast-iron foot, lift gallery. Height 12". $175.00.

Royal stand lamp No. 2, cast-iron foot, lift gallery. Height 12". $175.00.

Royal stand lamp No. 2, cast-iron foot, lift gallery. Height 11". $150.00.

Most Royal lamps with this burner have threaded burner connection. The lamps illustrated have lift galleries.

Flame spreaders found in these lamps.

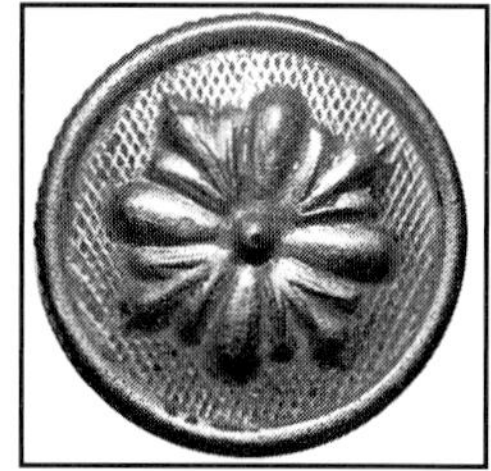

Oil fill caps found on these lamps.

Royal stand lamp No. 2, cast-iron foot, lift gallery. Height 12". $100.00.

Wick knob.

Royal stand lamp No. 2, lift gallery. This lamp is an exception as the burner has bayonet connection like the earler lamps. Height 12". $125.00.

Royal No. 1 Lamps

Flame spreaders for No. 1 Royal. Left: five patents; right: three patents. Some Royal No. 1 flame spreaders have straight sides. Courtesy Kent Stratton.

Royal No. 1 hand lamp. $250.00.
Courtesy Steve Gnan.

Oil fill cap.

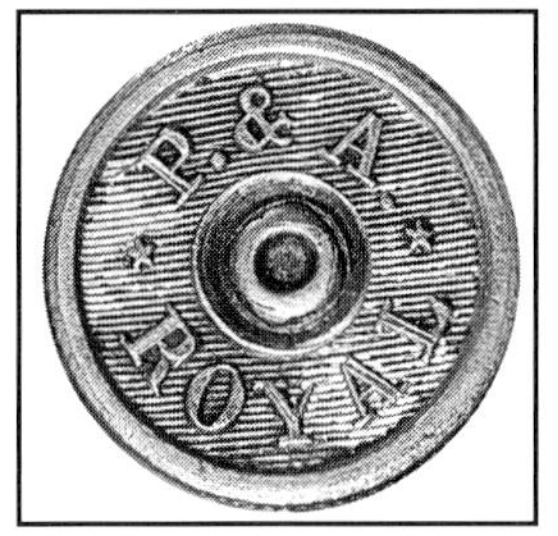

Wick knob.

Oil fill cap.

Wick knob.

Royal stand lamp No. 1, lift gallery marked "Pat. Apr. 11, 1893." Height 10½". $100.00.

Royal stand lamp No. 1, cast-iron foot, lift gallery marked "Pat. Apr. 11, 1893." Height 10½". $175.00.

P & A No. 2 Lamps 1905 and later

Royal

Flame spreader, "Patented Apr. 11, 93, Sept. 9, 90. Apr. 30, 95."

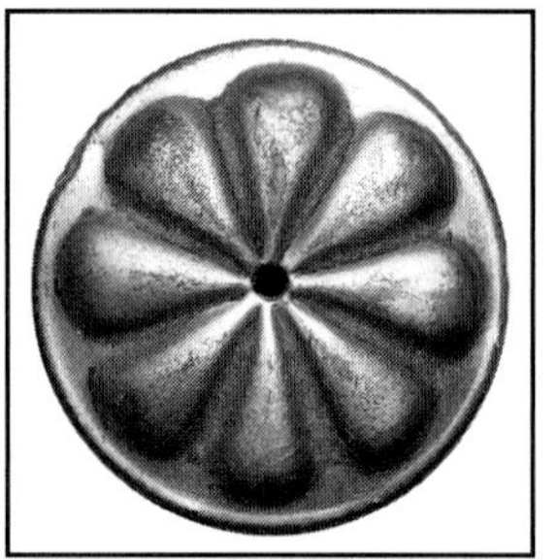

Oil fill cap.

Unmarked

Flame spreader often found in these lamps, "Patented Sep. 9, 90. Apr. 11, 93."

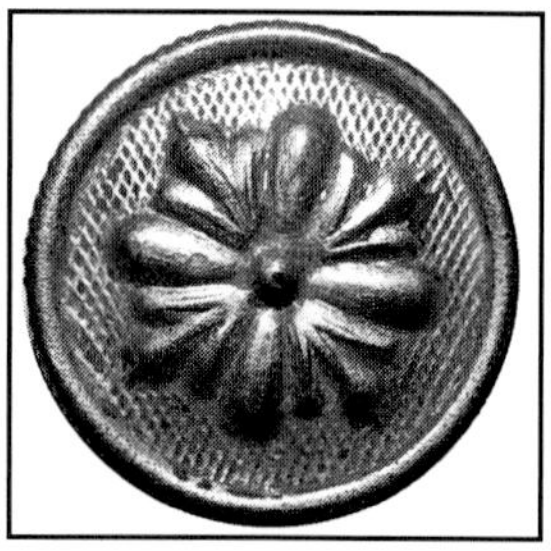

Oil fill cap.

Royal stand lamp, 1909 Butler Brothers catalog.

Later Royal stand lamp No. 2 lift gallery. Height 12". $125.00.

P & A stand lamp No. 2, cast-iron foot, lift gallery. Height 12". This lamp was possibly sold as Royal in later years, in which case the lamp would have been fitted with the Royal Waterbury flame spreader, illustrated on previous page. The wick knob is plain. These lamps are unmarked as P & A and were possibly "branded" by catalog sellers. $125.00.

Royal Lamps Branded for Other Sellers

Plume & Atwood sold oil pots and lamps with branded flame spreaders to many other lamp companies, hardware stores, and retail distributors. See Fostoria, Consolidated, Trenton Lamp, American Lamp and Brass, and Swann and Whitehead, among others. Much of our evidence is stamped on the flame spreader or on the oil fill cap. Many more examples will likely be found.

Flame spreader.

These flame spreaders are found in No. 2 lamps sold by other companies.

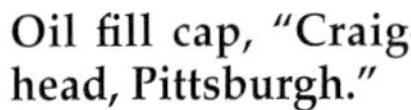

Oil fill cap, "Craighead, Pittsburgh."

S & W flame spreader, P & A patents.

S&W flame spreader with straight sides.

Royal Electric stand lamp No. 2, cast-iron foot, lift gallery. Height 12¼". $175.00. Courtesy Heinz and Ursula Baumann.

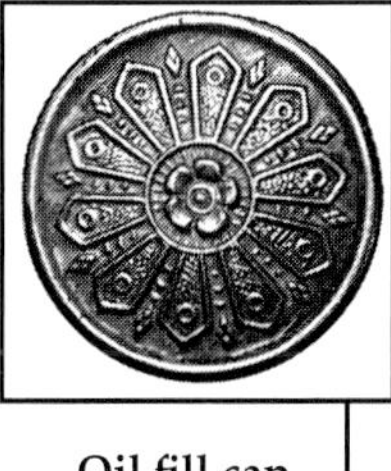

Oil fill cap.

"Royal" stand lamp No. 1, lift gallery, sold by Swann and Whitehead. Height 10½". $125.00.

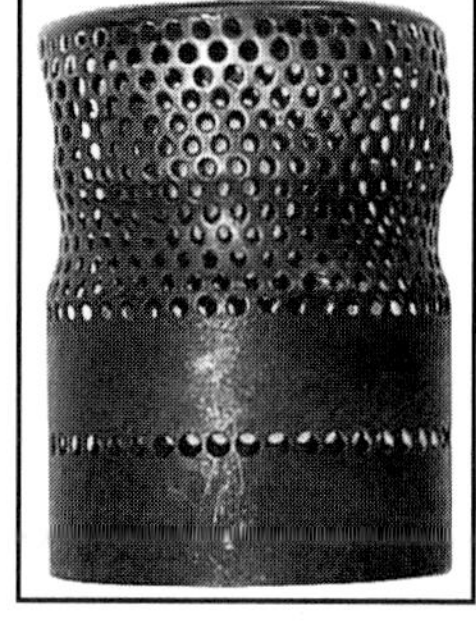

P & A flame spreader #1.

Little Royal 1892 – 1910

The Little Royal was advertised in 1892 as "Summer Lamps that burn one pint of oil in seven hours with twice the light of a No. 2 burner."

Advertisement from the Porter Company catalog for South America, 1894.

Little Royal burner.

Little Royal lamps may be plain or embossed. Height 8¼". Height of hand lamp is 6½". The oil fill caps are smooth and round; some are faintly marked "M'F'D in United States of America." The No. 0 size flame spreaders are unmarked with straight sides. Left, $175.00; center, $150.00; right, $175.00.

Little Royal

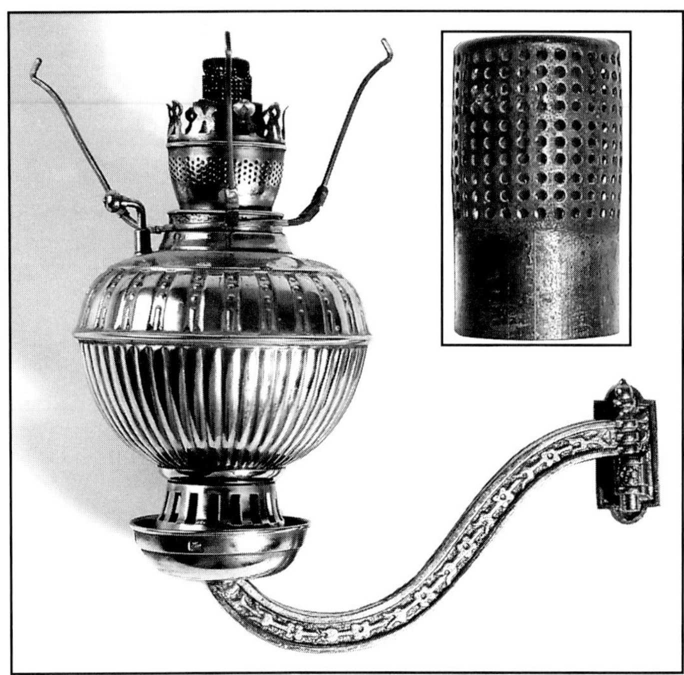

Little Royal wall lamp. $225.00.
Courtesy Eileen White.

Little Royal. Height 7½". $225.00.
Courtesy Eileen White.

Little Royal USA

Little Royal USA lamps are stamped "Manufactured in United States of America" on the tops of their founts. The burners are attached by threads. The flame spreaders are unmarked and found in two shapes — unmarked with straight sides (see left) or like those illustrated in the 1894 advertisement on previous page (and below right). The chimney gallery was modified as well.

Little Royal USA marked "Manufactured in United States of America" on top of the fount. Height 8". The gallery fence was redesigned as well. $100.00.

Improved Little Royal, 1905

Improved Little Royal with handles, cast-iron foot. Height 8¼". $275.00.

Little Royal Student Lamp

Wick knob, "The P&A Mfg. Co."

Flame spreader, burner, and wick carrier.

Little Royal student lamp, size 0 burner. Missing ring handle. Height 17¼". $400.00. Courtesy Joe MacDonald.

Improved Little Royal, marked "Made in USA" on the wick raiser. Height 6¼". $200.00. Courtesy Mel Soderholm.

Improved Little Royal, marked "Made in USA" on the wick raiser. Height 8¼". Found with early flame spreader. The Improved Little Royal has a thumb screw mechanism for raising and lowering the wick. Catalog pages illustrate the Improved Little Royal with the same burner found on Little Royal. Some Improved Little Royal burners are bayonet connection; others have threads. $250.00.

Plumwood, 1905

Plumwood lamps use the Royal wick mechanism. Plumwood lamps were made over several years, judging by the different flame spreaders. Catalogs illustrate No. 2 stand lamps and No. 2 and No. 3 hanging lamps.

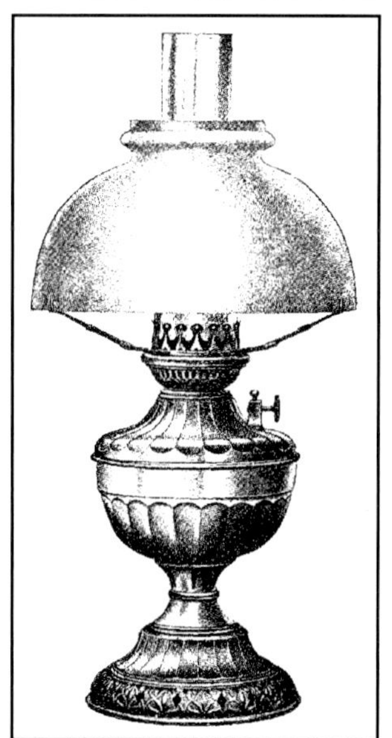

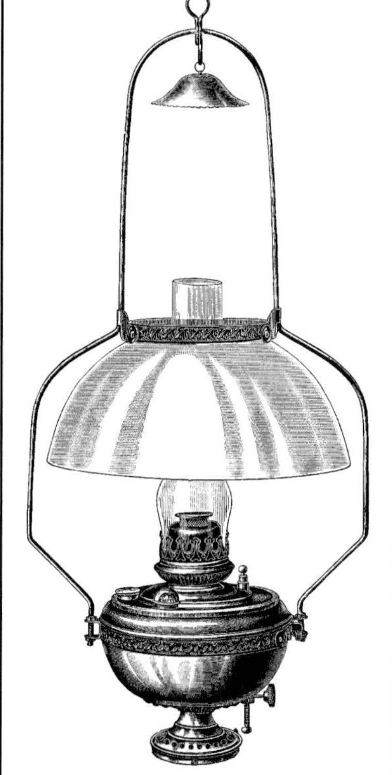

Wick knob.

Oil fill cap.

Plumwood Flame Spreaders

Plumwood stand lamp No. 2. Height $12\frac{3}{8}$". $125.00. Courtesy of Heinz and Ursula Baumann.

Magnet, 1905 – 1930s

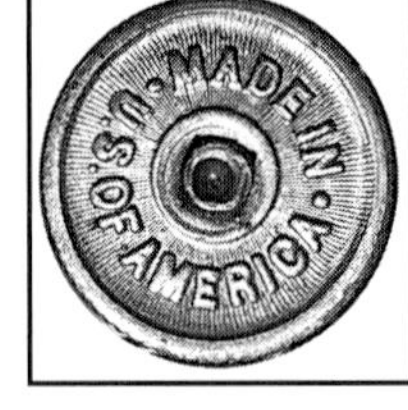

Wick knob.

Flame spreader.

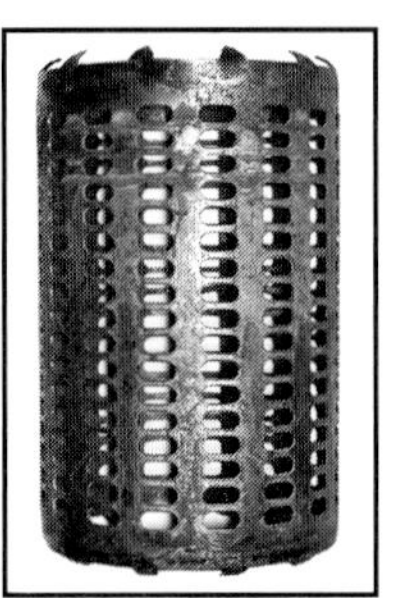

Wick carrier.

Magnet stand lamp No. 2. This is basically a large Naugatuck redesigned to hold 1½ quarts of kerosene. Lift gallery. Height 12". $50.00.

Colonial/Sewing Lamp, 1905 – 1930s

The Colonial or Sewing lamp was originally sold as the Colonial library lamp. The lamp was commonly finished in dark japanned bronze.

Wick knobs found on Colonial lamps.

Flame spreader.

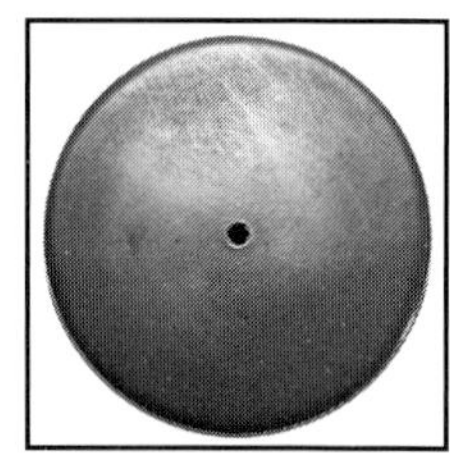

Oil fill cap. Some are vented, some are not.

Colonial or Sewing lamp No. 2 is found with one of two wick knobs (see above). Height 10¾". $125.00.

Naugatuck, 1905 – 1950s

Flame spreader usually found on later Naugatuck. This lamp is also found with the Plume & Atwood Waterbury flame spreader.

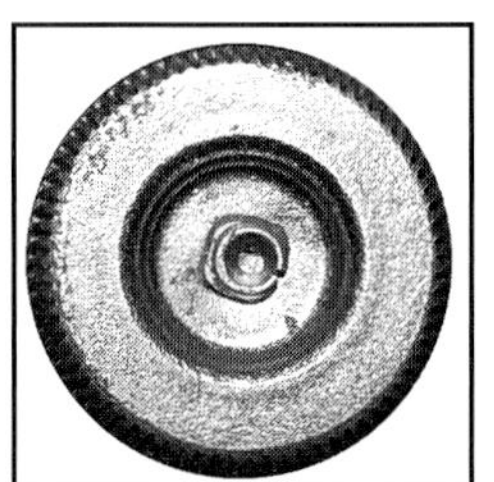

Wick knobs may be plain or marked "Made in U.S.A."

Flame spreader usually found on earlier Naugatuck.

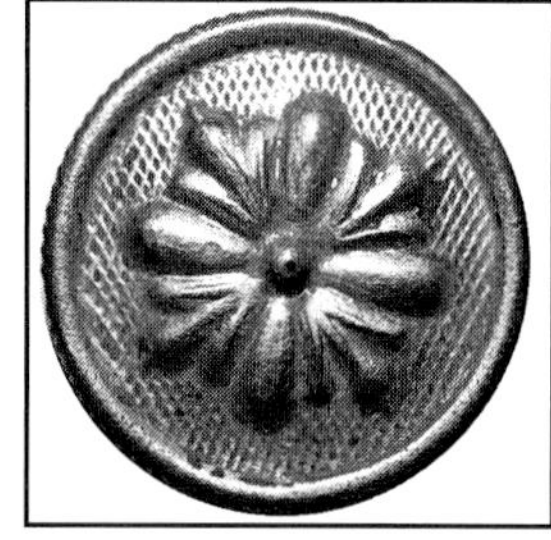

Oil fill cap.

Late Naugatuck stand lamp No. 2 found plain or embossed. Height 12". Lift gallery. Same oil fill as Magnet. This burner with large mesh holes is later than those with small mesh (see right). $50.00.

Wick carrier.

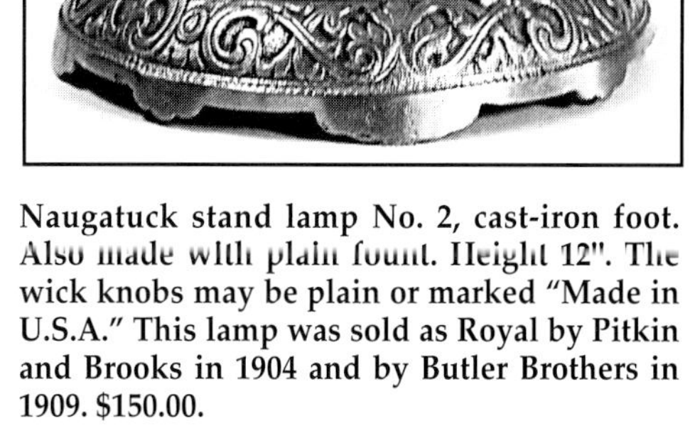

Naugatuck stand lamp No. 2, cast-iron foot. Also made with plain fount. Height 12". The wick knobs may be plain or marked "Made in U.S.A." This lamp was sold as Royal by Pitkin and Brooks in 1904 and by Butler Brothers in 1909. $150.00.

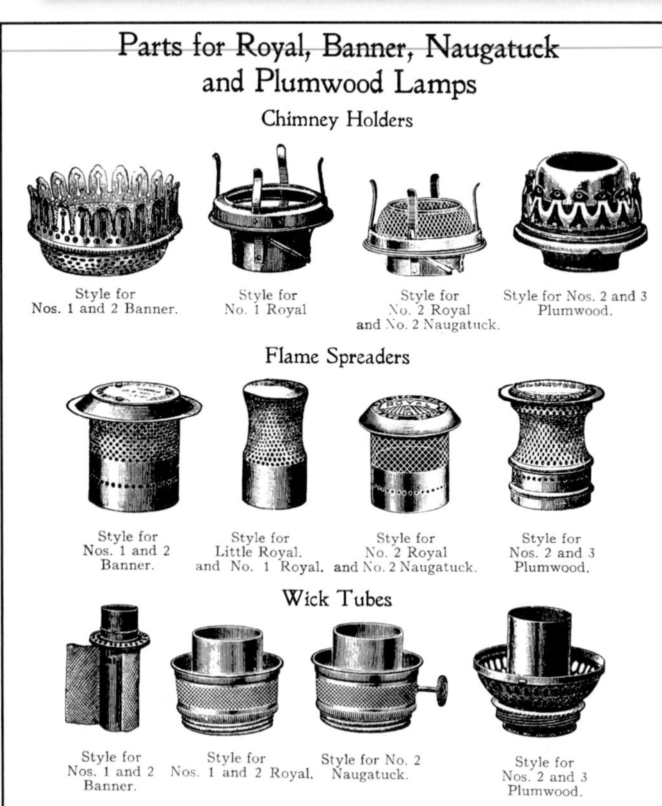
Parts for Royal, Banner, Naugatuck
and Plumwood Lamps
Chimney Holders
Style for Nos. 1 and 2 Banner.
Style for No. 1 Royal
Style for No. 2 Royal and No. 2 Naugatuck.
Style for Nos. 2 and 3 Plumwood.
Flame Spreaders
Style for Nos. 1 and 2 Banner.
Style for Little Royal. and No. 1 Royal.
Style for No. 2 Royal and No. 2 Naugatuck.
Style for Nos. 2 and 3 Plumwood.
Wick Tubes
Style for Nos. 1 and 2 Banner.
Style for Nos. 1 and 2 Royal.
Style for No. 2 Naugatuck.
Style for Nos. 2 and 3 Plumwood.

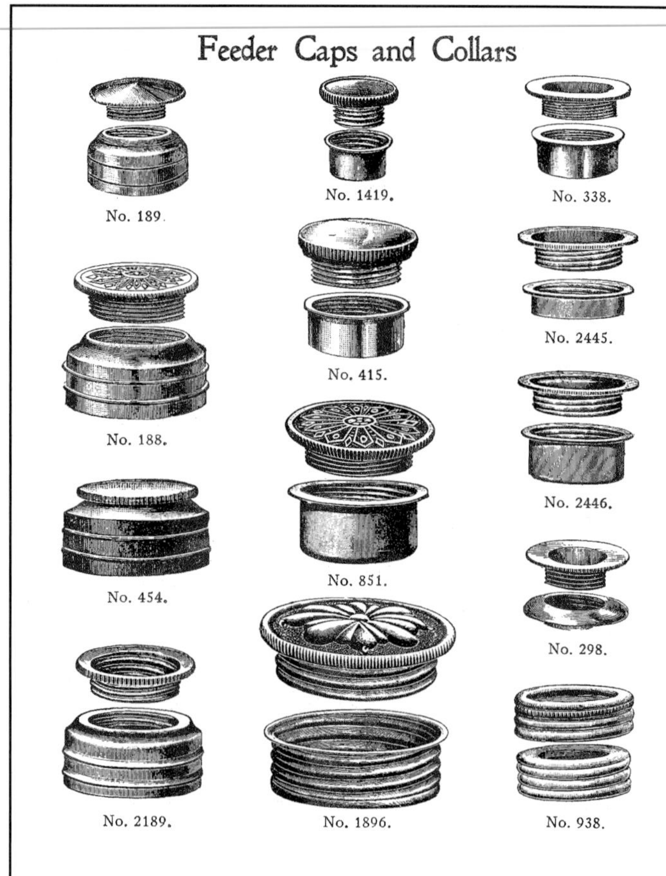
Feeder Caps and Collars
No. 189.
No. 1419.
No. 338.
No. 415.
No. 2445.
No. 188.
No. 2446.
No. 454.
No. 851.
No. 298.
No. 2189.
No. 1896.
No. 938.

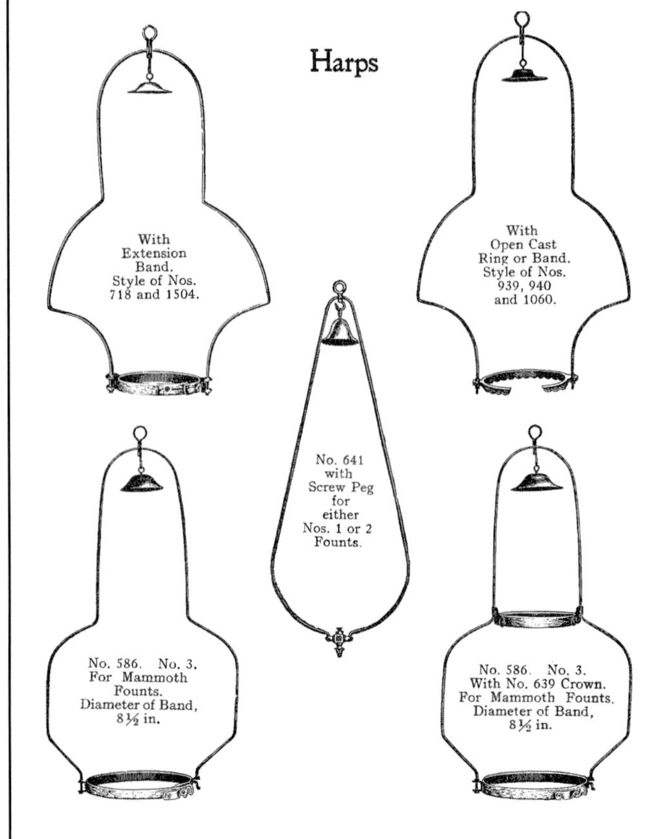
Harps
With Extension Band. Style of Nos. 718 and 1504.
With Open Cast Ring or Band. Style of Nos. 939, 940 and 1060.
No. 641 with Screw Peg for either Nos. 1 or 2 Founts.
No. 586. No. 3. For Mammoth Founts. Diameter of Band, 8½ in.
No. 586. No. 3. With No. 639 Crown. For Mammoth Founts. Diameter of Band, 8½ in.

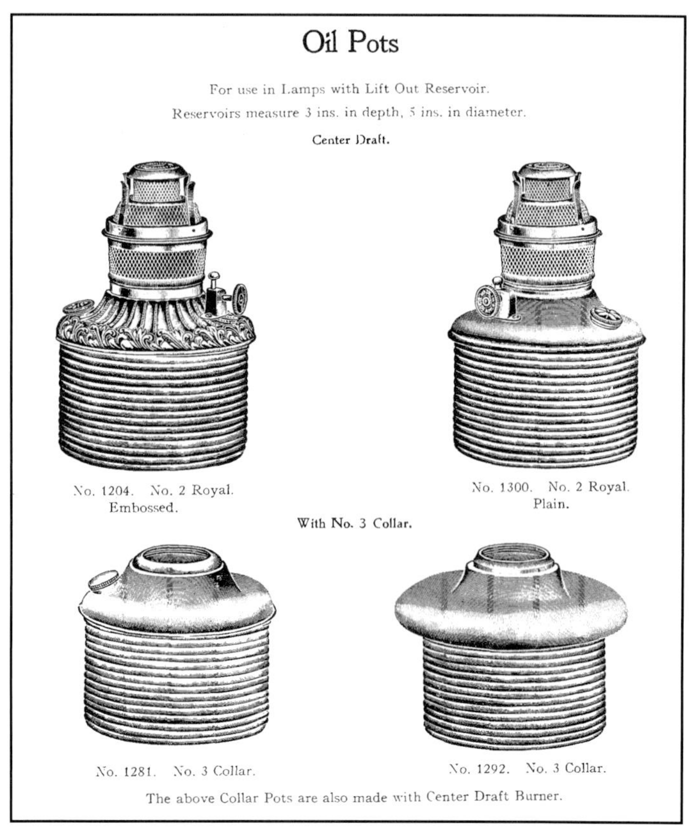
Oil Pots
For use in Lamps with Lift Out Reservoir.
Reservoirs measure 3 ins. in depth, 5 ins. in diameter.
Center Draft.
No. 1204. No. 2 Royal. Embossed.
No. 1300. No. 2 Royal. Plain.
With No. 3 Collar.
No. 1281. No. 3 Collar.
No. 1292. No. 3 Collar.
The above Collar Pots are also made with Center Draft Burner.

Other Kerosene Products

The Gregory Smokeless Device

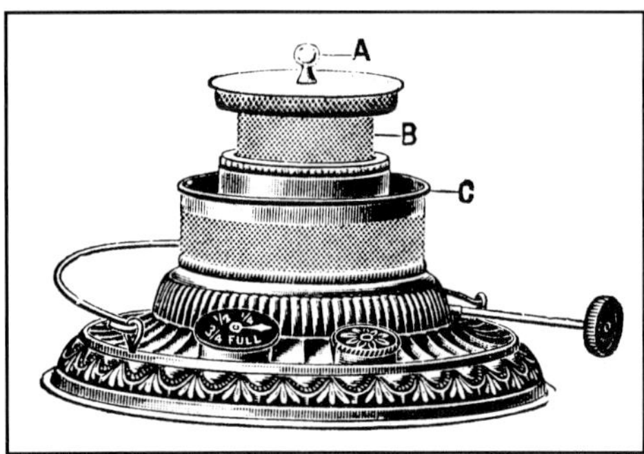

The oil heater cannot smoke because the stop nut, "A," limits the upward movement of the flame spreader, "B." And the flame spreader, "B," limits the upward movement of the wick.

Banner oil heater with "Gregory" Smokeless Device, ca. 1906. These heaters came in sizes of 6", 8", and 9" drums.

Advertisement, *Muncey's Magazine,* 1896.

Advertisement, *Muncey's Magazine,* 1896.

R. J. White, Twin Burner Lamp Co., Chicago, IL. White was the man who won the team and buggy for selling the most Banner Electric lamps in 1889. From a full page advertisement in *Crockery and Glass Journal,* Jan. 31, 1891.

Patent Lamp Extinguisher

This is a basic P & A lamp with unassigned patent No. 905, 543, Dec. 1, 1908, by Blasius Kovacic, East Pittsburgh, PA. When the burning lamp is tipped over, the flame spreader–extinguisher drops to cover the wick and smother the flame.

The top of the steel extinguisher cup is marked "Pat. Dec. 1, 08. 905, 543."

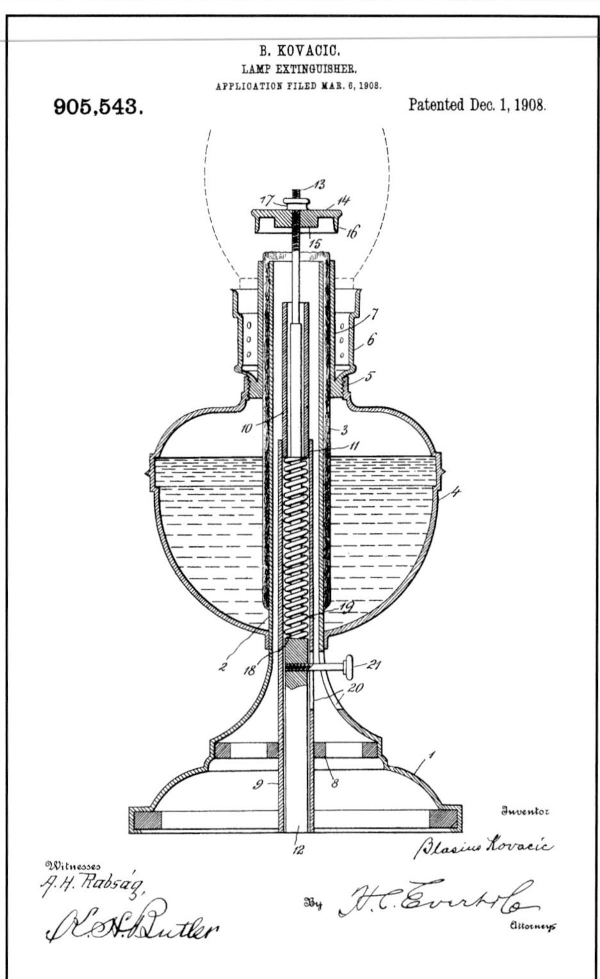

P & A stand lamp with 1908 extinguisher patent. Height 13" with extinguisher raised. Seems to be a production lamp; however, very few have been found. There is no flame spreader. $125.00.

A central rod supports the flame extinguisher, which puts out the flame when the lamp tips over. This mechanism differs from the patent (above).

Glass Household Lamp, 1889

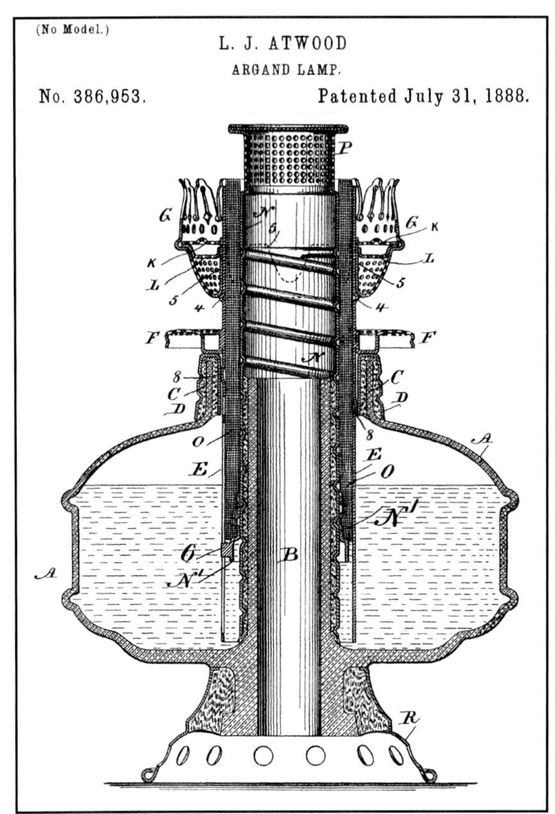

Advertisement in *Pottery and Glassware Reporter,* July 18, 1889.

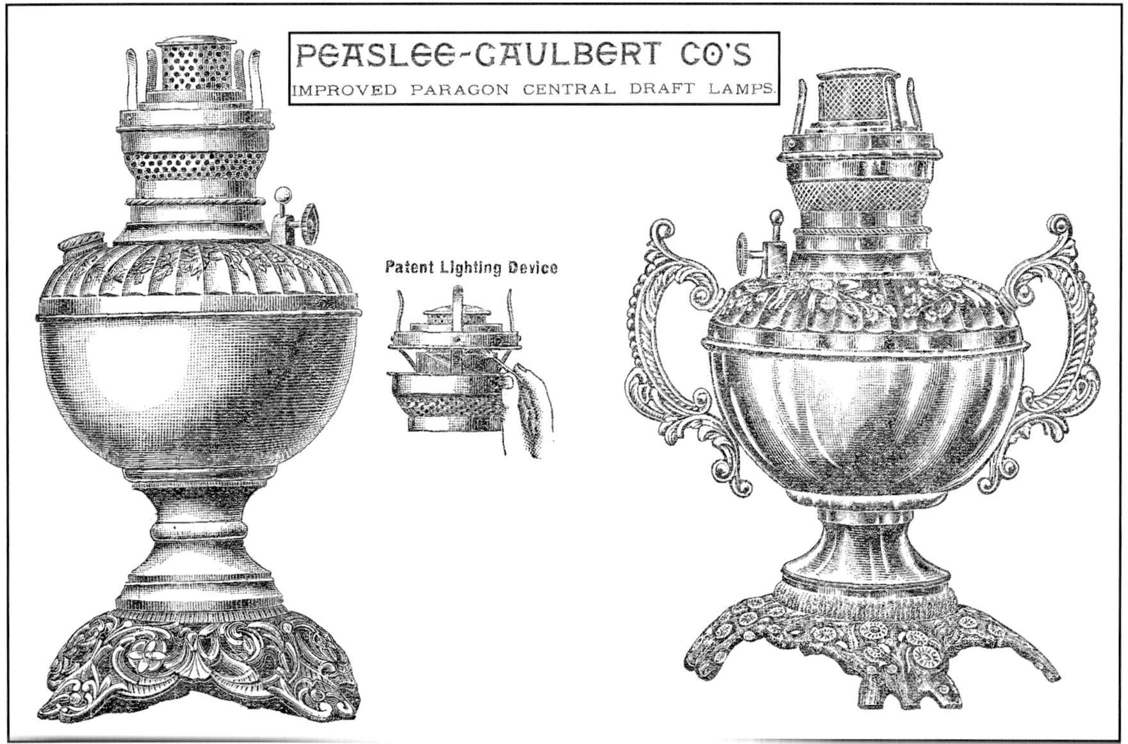

The Peaslee-Gaulbert Company, of Louisville, Kentucky, sold P & A lamps as Improved Paragon lamps in 1897. Paragon was also the name of the Paragon Safety Oil Company, Indianapolis. Paragon sold oil cans and illuminating oil, lubricating oil, and gasoline. The lamps illustrated are definitely of Plume & Atwood manufacture, appearing to be Royal burners. I have not found a Paragon flame spreader.

P & A Lamps 1904 – 1905

Lamps identified with Plume & Atwood Royal No. 2 burners in the Pitkin and Brooks catalog, 1904.
Courtesy James Hargis.

P & A Lamps 1909

Plume & Atwood lamps with No. 2 burners in the Butler Brothers catalog, 1909.

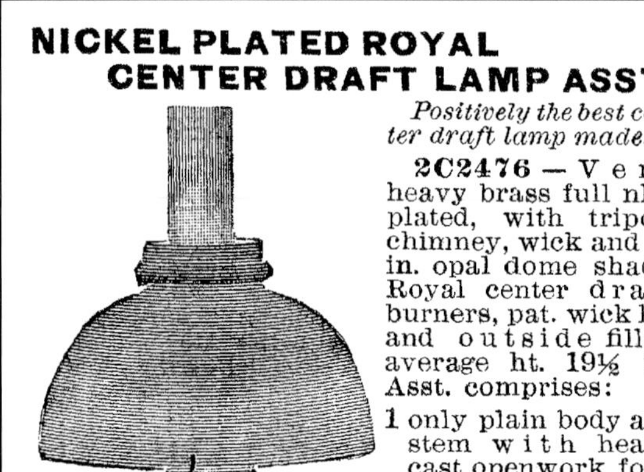

Plume & Atwood lamps with No. 2 burners in the Butler Brothers catalog, 1909.

P & A Lamps 1928 – 1931

Plume & Atwood lamps illustrated in Sears-Roebuck catalogs from 1928 to 1931. Note that the lamps were called Rochester at this time.

Post & Company
1869 – 1892

Post & Company was a manufacturer and supplier of railway supplies, machinists' tools, and equipment in Cincinnati, Ohio. The company sold locomotive headlights, rail car light fixtures, student lamps, conductors' lanterns, and office lamps. Post was an early developer of rail car lighting (White, 1978).

Officers were H. A. V. Post, president, and Alex Graydon, secretary. Joseph Kinsey was listed as president in the 1887 *Cincinnati City Directory*.

A fire destroyed the Cincinnati factory and office building in 1879. The company rebuilt in Ludlow, Kentucky, where it manufactured railroad supplies, hardware, and equipment.

Single and double "American Student Lamps" are illustrated in the 528 page catalog in the Cincinnati Historical Society Library. Offices were listed at 161 – 165 West Pearl Street, Cincinnati. A Cincinnati Post lamp is illustrated in 1888 H. Leonard & Sons Catalog, Grand Rapids, Michigan. The company was bought by Dayton Manufacturing Co. in 1892.

Trade Names

Student lamps — American Student Lamp, Home Lamp.

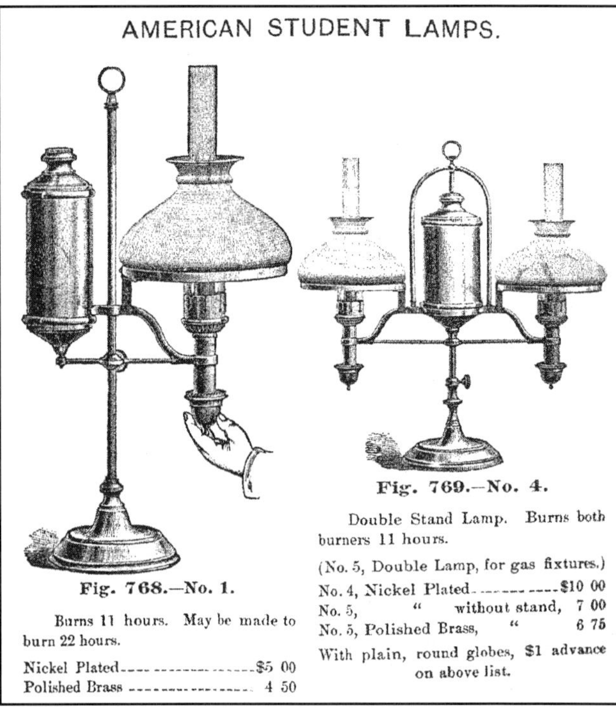

AMERICAN STUDENT LAMPS.

Fig. 768.—No. 1.

Burns 11 hours. May be made to burn 22 hours.

Nickel Plated $5 00
Polished Brass 4 50

Fig. 769.—No. 4.

Double Stand Lamp. Burns both burners 11 hours.

(No. 5, Double Lamp, for gas fixtures.)

No. 4, Nickel Plated $10 00
No. 5, " without stand, 7 00
No. 5, Polished Brass, " 6 75

With plain, round globes, $1 advance on above list.

Post & Company catalog No. 30, 1887.
Courtesy Ohio Historical Society.

Selected Patents, Center-draft Lamps

J. Kirby, Jr.[1] assigned to Post & Co.
1877 190,049
Otto Heller and William Donaldson assigned to Post & Co.
1884 302,251

[1]Also a patent for a flat-wick lamp and numerous patents for railroad lamps 1875 – 1900. Kirby assigned patents to Dayton Mfg. Co. in 1883.

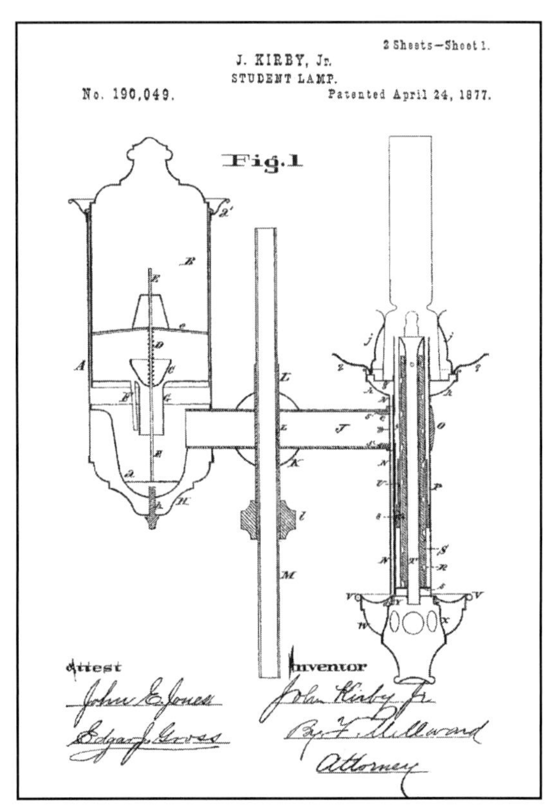

Post & Company American student lamp. Height 22". Oil fount marked on top (see above) "American Student Lamp, Pat. Apl. 24, 77, July 22, 84, Post & Co., Cincinnati, O." $325.00.

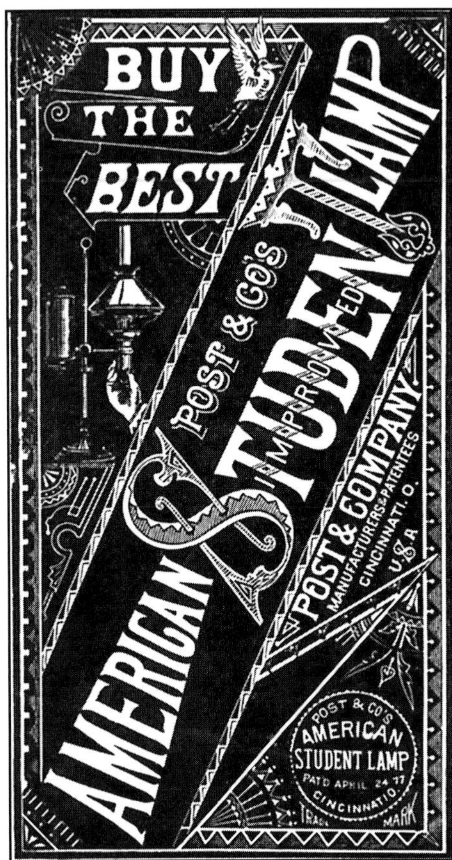

Post & Company American student lamp catalog, 1883.

AMERICAN STUDENT LAMP.

PRICE LIST

OF

American Student Lamp Trimmings.

Wicks, per doz., - - - - - -	$0.35
Chimneys, per doz., - - - - -	.90
Chimney and Shade (or Globe) Holders complete, plated, each, - - - -	.50
Chimney and Shade (or Globe) Holders complete, brass, each, - - - -	.45
Drip Cups, plated, each, - - -	.30
Drip Cups, Brass, each, - - -	.25
Wick Holders, each, - - - -	.10
Thumb Screws, brass or plated, each,-	.15
Oil Reservoirs, plated, each, - - -	.80
Oil Reservoirs, brass, each, - -	.75
"Top" Finger Rings, brass or plated each,	.25
Shades, 7-inch, Vienna, white, each, -	.20
Shades, 7-inch, Vienna, blue or green, each	1.00
Shades, 10-inch, Cone, white, each, -	.50

Ornamental Shades and Globes furnished to order.

We furnish numbers 2, 3, 5, 6, 9 and 10 in plain brass finish, with double-seamed reservoirs. These Lamps are specially designed to meet a want for cheap, durable lamps for *printing offices*, work-shops and other places where a fine finish is undesirable. Price, sixty cents reduction on the foregoing lists for polished brass.

(20)

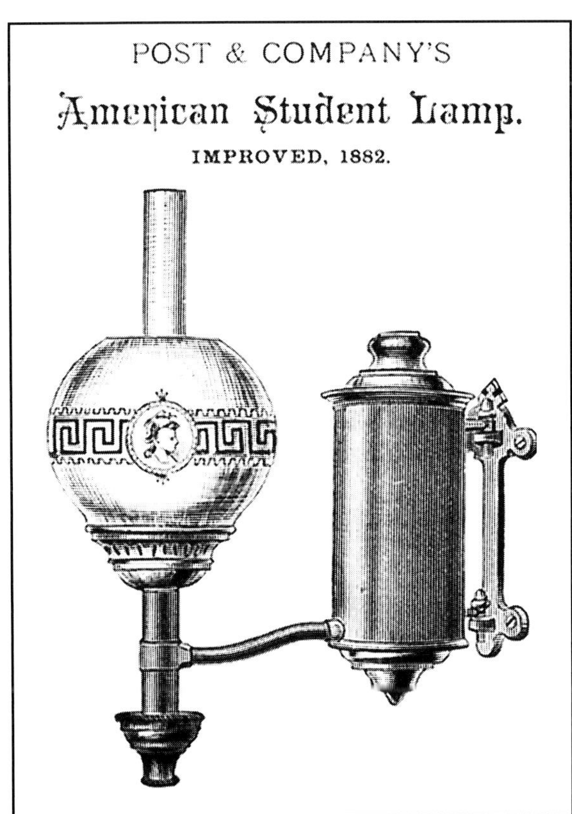

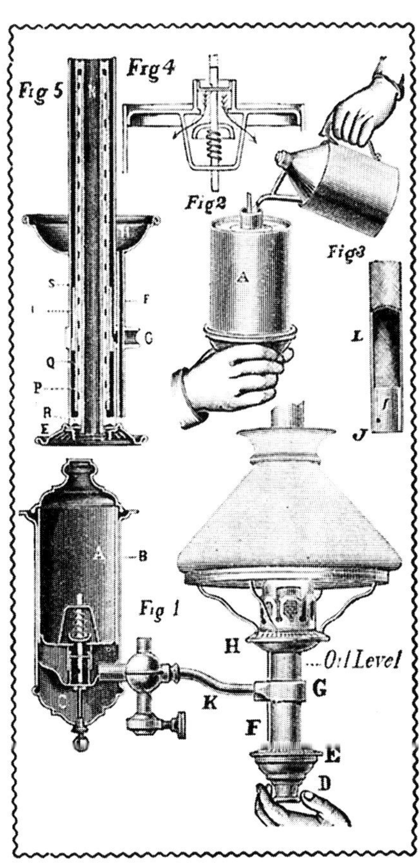

Rochester Lamp Company
1884 – 1905

The Rochester Lamp Company claimed to be "the largest lamp house in the world" in the early 1890s, with retail stores in New York, London, Paris, and Chicago. The company was not a manufacturer but rather a wholesale and retail seller of center-draft lamps made under patents controlled by Charles Sandford Upton (born Nov. 24, 1844, near Rochester).

Upton did not build or operate manufacturing plants. Instead, he contracted the manufacture of his lamps. Upton's marketing skills would make worthwhile study for budding entrepreneurs today.

Panel of trade card, 1893 Columbian Exposition.

Advertisement, *China and Glass Journal*, April 1889.

The story of the Rochester lamp has been written in some detail by Russell (1968) and Wenrich (1987) and is supported by documents in the Rochester (NY) Historical Society library. Credit for the development of an improved Argand burner with a "thimble" flame spreader to replace the Liverpool button has been given to Leonard Henkle, a machinist from Rochester, New York (Wenrich, 1987). His patent 292,114, granted January 15, 1884, gained the attention of Charles S. Upton, of Spencerport, New York. Henkle's improvements (patents 365,996, 1887, and 398,725, 1889) were assigned to Upton, who bought the rights to the patents from him. Upton obtained his own patent (379,836) in 1888, the first of several in following years.

Upton began his lamp trade in New York City selling lamps which he named Rochester in honor of the city in western New York. Several companies manufactured lamps, lanterns, and related lighting in Rochester but none were able, or willing, to manufacture Upton's new lamp (Wenrich, 1988).

Early Rochester lamps were made by Edward Miller and Company and, later, by other companies as the business grew. Miller was the primary manufacturer of Rochester lamps during the 1880s. Miller also advertised and sold Rochester lamps. Read the chapter on Edward Miller & Company for details of agreements between Miller and Upton.

Associated with Charles Upton in business were brothers Elijah Cobb Upton, Willard Upton, and George Albert Upton, and nephews Edward Hunt Upton, James Upton Pomeroy, and Charles Alexander Pomeroy (O'Brien, 1937). Charles Pomeroy was the sales manager and promoter of the Rochester brand world wide.

Upton was quick to protest and protect against infringement of his patents. He announced "Caution to the Trade" regarding the Ansonia Brass & Copper Company (see more under Ansonia) and the Bradley & Hubbard Manufacturing Company in 1888 and 1890.

The world came to know the Rochester lamp because Charles Upton advertised the lamp and its merits often and widely. He had spent nearly $200,000 in advertising by 1891, also stating that "two million [lamps] were in use and half a million sold yearly."

On May 1, 1890, the Rochester Lamp Company moved from 25 Warren Street and 1201 Broadway to a "new and commodious" location extending from 37 Barclay St. through 42 Park Place, New York City. The new company store became known as the "lamp palace"and claimed to exhibit over 3,000 lamps.

The company must have distributed thousands of numbered cards advertising the Rochester lamp as a drawing prize after the 1893 Columbian Exposition in Chicago. The cards turn up frequently today! The Rochester Lamp Pavilion featured a most unusual lamp — an ornate nine foot lamp with head of a bison. The head, mounted on Mexican onyx, was a bison killed by Buffalo Bill Cody. After a performance in 1898, Cody offered the lamp to French President Carnot, who refused the lamp, reported to be a "tasteless gift."

A photograph of the pavilion and showing the lamp is published in *The Book of the Fair* by Hubert Howe Bancroft.

O'Brien (1937) reported that Upton declined one million dollars to sell the company to a British syndicate.

The company sold a wide variety of piano lamps, banquet lamps, parlor and table lamps of all types, vase lamps, stand lamps, study (student) lamps, hanging and library lamps, hall lamps, and chandeliers. Railroad, steamboat, and street lamps were advertised in 1886. Rochester center-draft burners were used in Meriden Britannia Company gold- and silver-plated lamps in 1886 and 1887.

Charles S. Upton died Feb. 17, 1897. The company continued operation under Charles Pomeroy; however, the Rochester lamp no longer dominated the market by this time. The company was out of business by 1905, according to a letter from Bradley & Hubbard to a customer seeking a lamp with a "Rochester burner" (courtesy of Catherine Thuro).

Trademarks

Charles Upton received trademark registration for the name Rochester for lamps on December 22, 1885, and for lamp chimneys and wicks on April 24, 1888. He stated that the mark had been used since September 1, 1884. "The JR. Rochester" received trademark registration on May 12, 1891, and "Niagara" for lamps, lamp burners, and lamp chimneys on November 2, 1886. "Rochester Gas Burner" was published for use as a label on July 10, 1888, in the U.S. Patent Office's *Official Gazette*.

Brief History

The following information is reprinted from the Rochester Lamp Company catalog No. 36, 1891/1892:

> Then came the greatest improvement in lamps of the century, and so simple, it was a wonder it had not been thought of before. Leonard Henkle, an ingenious inventor, at Rochester, N.Y. conceived the idea of forming a cap or thimble, and putting it over the top of the central draft tube, and filling its sides all around with small holes like a pepper-box cover, and letting the air come up the tube and pass to the flame through all those small holes, as shown in the illustration [see above right].
>
> 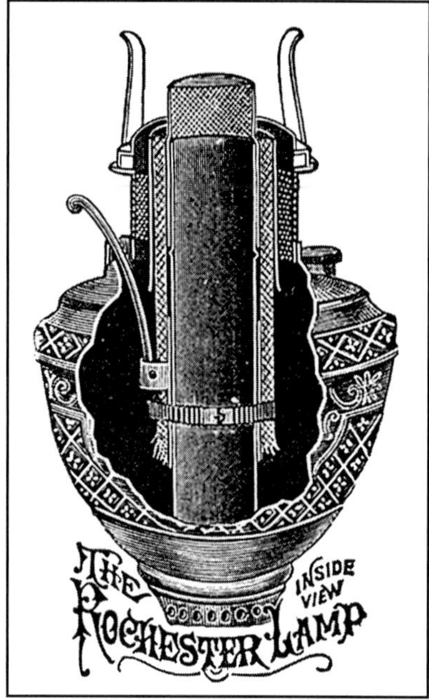
>
>
> The result was at once most wonderful; all parts of the flame all around its inside surface for over an inch high, were fed — peppered as it were, with nearly a thousand little jets of hot oxygen of the air. From a dull red, with the old button burner, the flame was instantly changed to one of dazzling white. High or low, there is no smoke, but a light really wonderful in its brilliant purity and volume. Steady, large, intensely white and beautiful, it was indeed a marvel to all to whom the inventor showed it.
>
> Several large lamp manufacturing companies heard of it, and sent experts to report on it. But they moved slowly, and while the investigation was going on, the lamp came under the notice of Charles S. Upton, a local capitalist. He saw at once the splendid possibilities open for the invention, and promptly bought the patent. Mr. Upton named the lamp "The Rochester," organized the present Rochester Lamp Co. (of which he is still president and manager), and put the lamp on the market. That was seven years ago. Dealers and large jobbing houses, were at first coy; they were averse to buying new goods when they had large stocks of the old style of lamps on hand. Their pecuniary interest was in selling what they had.
>
> Mr. Upton fell back on the merits of his invention; opened his own stores, and appealed to the people who bought and used lamps. The result confirmed his good opinion of the lamp. It was a most unbounded success. Wherever seen, or heard of even, they were wanted. He was overwhelmed with business. New designs, new styles, every conceivable demand for a lamp was met — all having the same incomparable burner.
>
> From one lamp seven years ago, we have now over 2,000 different designs and varieties, and there are upwards of two million in use. From one single idea, a little perforated cap or thimble, by a modest inventor, a vast business had grown up; thousands of men and women are kept employed, and many hundreds of families are being supported and educated.
>
> The number of Rochester Lamps now sold is over half-a-million a year; many of them most artistic, and some single ones, costing $1,000. This company now has

branch stores in Paris and London, another in Chicago, and our new and spacious quarters at 42 Park Place and 37 Barclay St., running through from street to street, is well known by the trade to be the **Largest Lamp Store in the World**. Such in brief is the history of the Rochester Lamp.

Here are some of the good points of The Rochester:

1. It is all metal — high-grade and hard-rolled and cannot break. **All accidents that have ever happened with kerosene, have been due to use of glass lamps, which break and scatter the oil if by chance they fall.**

2. The heat being circular, the expansion of the chimney is **equal all around**.

3. The air superheated in the thimble, thus causing a perfect combustion. Every part of the flame is supplied with these jets of hot air, and there is not a particle of **smoke nor odor**, every atom of carbon (smoke) is consumed and helps to make a light.

4. The perforated thimble slips **over** the outside of the tube — known as our **patent over-cone** — thus preventing all leakage, or siphoning out of oil.

5. The improved wire wick lift is perfect. No screws, ratchets, etc., to get out of order. The light can be **instantly extinguished**, which is not the case with the screw lift.

6. All parts are interchangeable. Every part or piece of one lamp, will fit any lamp.

7. The air flows up through the oil, and keeps it cool.

8. Burns any kind of oil — **such as sold by all stores**. The chimneys are made specially for us of **tough glass**, are tempered with oil, and will stand hard knocks without breaking.

9. The narrow wick band below the wick lift is corrugated or ribbed, as shown, so as not to bind the wick too tight, and the oil can rapidly pass up under it.

10. The wick band of the lift slides next to the tube, thus it never gets foul, and the wick is always free.

Some Lamps Are Tolerably Good.

But who wants a tolerably good egg?

And there is a heap of trouble with a tolerably good lamp.

There is one lamp that is GOOD (without the tolerable) and it has this stamp — "The Rochester."

There are three pieces only in a "Rochester," and over half a million sold yearly tells the story of its worth.

They don't like it — the "tolerably good" lamp makers — and yet we have concluded to drop the price on standard lines a few points.

The Rochester Lamp

China, Glass and Lamps, Aug. 5, 1891

A Light in the Business World

Reprinted from Rochester Lamp Co. catalog No. 36. Source: *New York Press*, Jan. 4th, 1891.

Story of Charles S. Upton of the Rochester Lamp Company. A country boy, with nothing but nerve and brain, becomes a wealthy man, respected and powerful — a typical American success of our own day.

Sometime in 1884 an industrious inventor from Rochester, N.Y., made his appearance among the brass manufacturing companies of Connecticut with a new model of a metal oil lamp. He did not meet with success in inducing any of them to adopt his novel invention, and returned to Rochester discouraged. Soon afterward the matter was bought to the attention of a gentleman in Rochester, who had speculated in a small way in patents and who had made some money in that way. The discouragements of the inventor had clouded his expectations somewhat, so that he was anxious to part with his patents for a moderate sum of ready money, and a trade was closed.

The purchaser found himself the owner of one patched up experimental lamp and several patents covering certain devices used in its construction. He tried at once to induce some manufacturer to make the lamps on royalty, but not one would touch them. His repeated discouragements finally exasperated him, and he rigged up a small shop in Rochester and commenced making a few lamps himself. He induced two young men to join him, and the three opened a small retail store in New York City. His partners became discouraged with the business and disgusted with his reckless expenditures for advertising, and one after the other left him. Still the plucky, persistent, pushing fellow, who had invested his money under, as he thought, good judgement, in this patent lamp, was determined he would not go back on that judgment. He mortgaged his homestead, bought out his partners' interest in the venture, brought his cot to his little store and kept right on making, advertising and selling that lamp. He fought it out on that line.

Today there is no corner in the civilized world so obscure that the light of that lamp is not seen and admired therein. Three millions of them have gone out to glad customers; instead of one, over two thousand different designs are now shown, and three-quarters of a million are now made yearly. From one man and a few boys in a single room, the force employed in manufacturing has grown to 2,500 mechanics and artisans, in four immense factories, whose weekly wages furnish support and comfortable homes to ten thousand people. Warehouses and salesrooms in Paris and Chicago are devoted to distributing these artistic goods, and another is being opened in London. While the wholesale house in Park Place, New York, is unquestionably the largest exclusively lamp store in the world.

To commence under such difficulties, with but a pittance of capital, and surmount all those obstacles, and establish in six years a prosperous and successful business, aggregating millions, and make for himself a royalty income from his patents besides of a handsome fortune yearly, is a record to be proud of. Such a man is entitled to rank among New York's most successful and honored merchants. If he has not joined the group of millionaires belonging to the metropolis, he will soon be there, and his achievements will command the respect of that exclusive circle.

The man who has accomplished this is Charles S. Upton, a modest, unassuming type of the self-made, live American. His name is indissolubly connected with the Rochester Lamp, for he it was who bought and still owns the patents, and who has expended a quarter of a million cold cash in advertising its merits. It must be a grim satisfaction to those men who could have bought these patents for a few hundred dollars and refused, to now note the fact that they pay the owner a royalty equivalent to a quarterly dividend on an investment of over a million and a half dollars worth of gilt edged securities.

Besides being president and treasurer of the Rochester Lamp Company, Mr. Upton is president of half a dozen other industrial enterprises in which he is financially interested, including the Magic Introduction Company, Billings Pipe Bender Manufacturing Company and others.

His success is another illustration of what may be done with an article of real merit by one who has the sagacity to make its virtues known to the public through newspaper advertising. It is said that for months after he opened his first retail store in upper Broadway it was his custom to pay every bill he owed on Saturday, and "blow" every dollar he had left into the Sunday newspaper columns. He followed this up tenaciously for over a year.

Mr. Upton is still comparatively a young man, being 46 years old. He is one of a family of seven boys and one girl, born near Rochester, N. Y. He inherits his nerve and commercial activity from his father, James Upton. He is a man of good education and a steam engine for business. The immense trade which he controls is due largely to his own personal energy and keen business sagacity. Understanding the popular wants, and knowing well that nothing can succeed unless it has real merit, he is quick to detect its prospective market and seize his opportunity; and having the nerve to back up his judgment by the most liberal outlay, where others might falter and fail, he forces the most signal success.

Advertisement in *Century Magazine*, 1892.

CHARLES S. UPTON.

Charles S. Upton Death of the President of the Rochester Lamp Company

Charles S. Upton, of New York city, son of the late James Upton, died yesterday morning at the residence of his nephew, Fred A. Upton, on the Charlotte Boulevard, about a mile north of the city line.

The deceased was born in the township of Greece in 1844, and was one of a family of eight children, of whom five are still living: Eli M., and Willard Upton of this city; James H. Upton of Charlotte; and Elizah C. and John Upton of Spencerport. In 1885, he married Ruby F. Price, who survives him. Mr. Upton was a very popular man and well liked by all who knew him. For a number of years he was connected with the Follett Lantern Works and later became the president of Rochester Lamp Company, with head offices in New York and branches in Chicago, Toronto, Paris and London.

About two years ago, Mr. Upton suffered a slight stroke of paralysis and since that time he has not actively engaged in business, but has spent his time in traveling. On Saturday last, he was in the city transacting business preparatory to an intended trip to Florida, when he received another stroke from which he never rallied.

The funeral will be held Friday afternoon at 3 o'clock from the home of John Upton at Spencerport. The interment will be made in Fairfield cemetery. Friends desiring to attend the funeral may take the 2:30 train from the Central Hudson station.

The Chronicle, Feb. 18, 1897

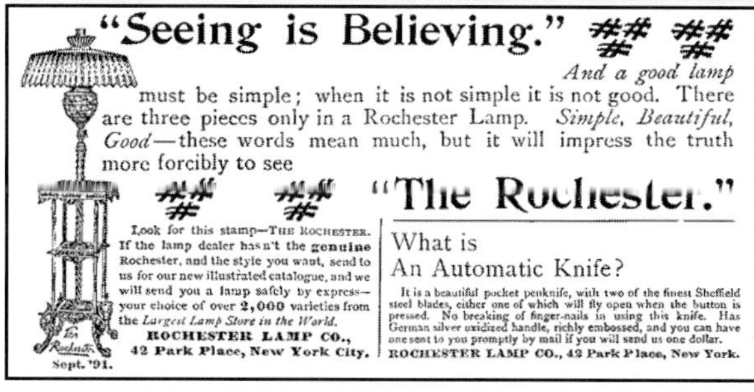

Advertisement in *Century Magazine*, 1892.

Trade Names

Center-draft lamps — Rochester, Rochester JR., the New Rochester, the New Rochester JR., Baby Rochester, Mammoth Library Lamp. "R. L. Co." marked on flame spreaders and cast bases.

Round-wick, side-draft burners — Niagara Central-Draft Burner.

Flat-wick burners — the Upton Burner, the Upton Duplex, Magic Pocket Lamp.

Street lights — Henkle Street Lamp, Rochester Standard (flat-wick) Tubular Street Lamp.

DESIGN.
L. HENKLE.
LAMP BURNER.
No. 17,090 Patented Feb. 8, 1887.

Selected Patents, Center-draft Lamps

Leonard Henkle[1] unassigned

Year	Patent
1884	292,114
1884	303,964
1886	348,969
1886	348,970
1887	D17090

Leonard Henkle assigned to Charles S. Upton

Year	Patent
1887	365,996
1889	398,725
1889	412,181
1889	415,108
1890	435,377
1891	459,400

Charles S. Upton unassigned

Year	Patent
1888	379,836
1888	381,042
1890	427,207
1892	474,979
1892	472,594 lamp stove

Frank Rhind[2] assigned to Charles S. Upton

Year	Patent
1885	333,338
1886	342,463
1888	382,270
1888	387,258
1889	407,492
1889	409,706
1890	440,608

Frank Rhind unassigned

Year	Patent
1885	312,762[3]
1885	322,321

Charles H. Broad, unassigned

Year	Patent
892	467,571

James U. Pomeroy[4] one-half assigned Charles S. Upton

Year	Patent
1894	517,361

[1]Also patents on lanterns, street lights, gas burner, and mantle.

[2]Charles Upton had a long relationship with Frank Rhind, before, during and after Rhind was employed by Edward Miller.

[3]E. H. Fessenden paid Rhind for rights to produce and sell this lamp.

[4]Center-draft lantern or street lamp using Rochester burner.

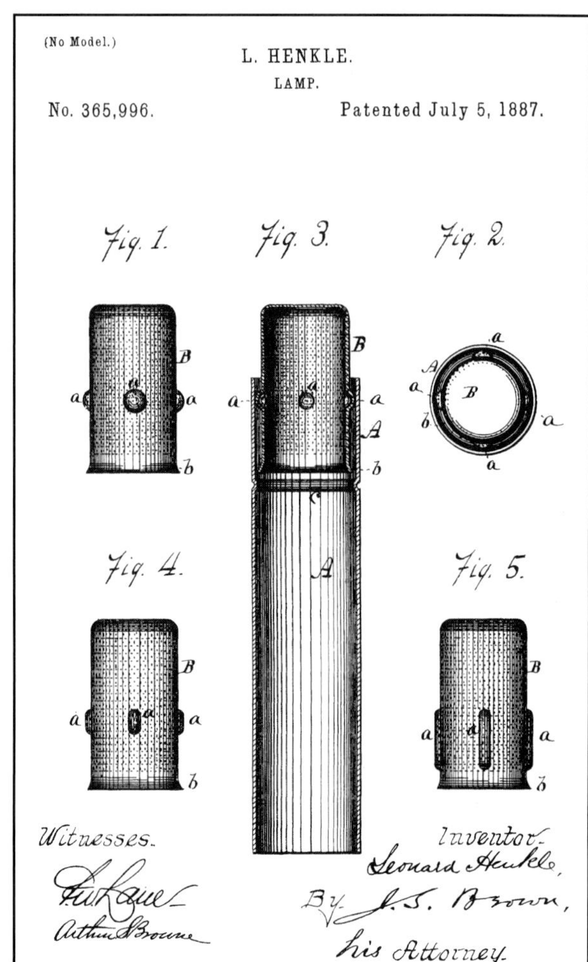

Rochester Lamps Made by Edward Miller and Co.

Edward Miller and Company manufactured Rochester burners, oil pots, and stand lamps under contract agreement with Upton. Miller also sold Rochester brand lamps. Upton extolled the variety of artistic designs stating that Rochester had 3,000 or more different lamps in its store. Fancy and cast lamp bases for large banquet lamps, floor lamps, and hanging lamps were supplied to Upton by several manufacturers. All were fitted with oil pots and burners made by Edward Miller and Co.

Charles Upton advertised Rochester lamps to the trade and to the public. This ad "cautions the trade" that he has full patent and trademark protection. Read more in the chapter on Ansonia.

POTTERY AND GLASSWARE REPORTER

ROCHESTER LAMP CO.,

MANUFACTURERS OF THE

Celebrated Rochester Lamp.

Artistic Designs in Decorated

LAMPS, CHANDELIERS, HANGERS, BRACKETS, SHADES and GLOBES.

WROUGHT IRON AND ANTIQUE BRASS

LANTERNS AND STANDING LAMPS, in Great Variety.

1201 Broadway,
Wholesale, 25 Warren St., } **NEW YORK.**

CHAS. S. UPTON, Pres. and Manager.

CAUTION TO THE TRADE.

Parties are passing through the country trying to sell Lamps and Burners with adjustable perforated cones and wick raisers that are direct infringements on our Rochester patents. Suits are and will be commenced against all parties dealing in such goods. This Celebrated Rochester Lamp and Burner enjoys Six Patents and is thoroughly protected, Trade Mark included.

ROCHESTER LAMP CO.

6437. Height 13 inches.

KO KO in Antique Bronze. Height 31 inches.

STORK PEDESTAL LAMP, Height 31 inches.

Advertisement, *PGR,* Feb. 24, 1887.

The Rochester 1884 – 1886

Leonard Henkle's patent for the thimble flame spreader was granted on Jan. 15, 1884. The Rochester trademark, granted in 1885, was used beginning Sept. 1, 1884. The earliest Rochester lamps found to date carry the Jan. 15, 1884, patent date embossed in the fount and gallery. The Rochester lamp was made in Nos. 1, 2, and 3 burner sizes. Henkle's design patent 17,090 for the Argand Burner, granted Feb. 8, 1887, was applied for on July 30, 1884. Heinz Baumann has reported a lamp bearing a March 6, 1884, patent date on the fount and gallery, plus a June 6, 1885, patent date on the wick-raiser band. These dates are unknown to the author.

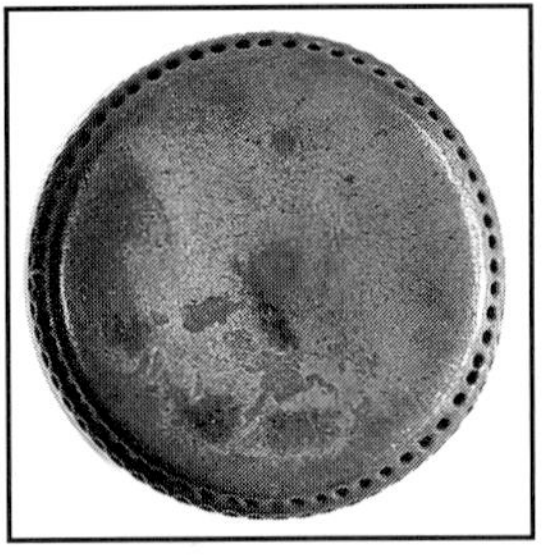

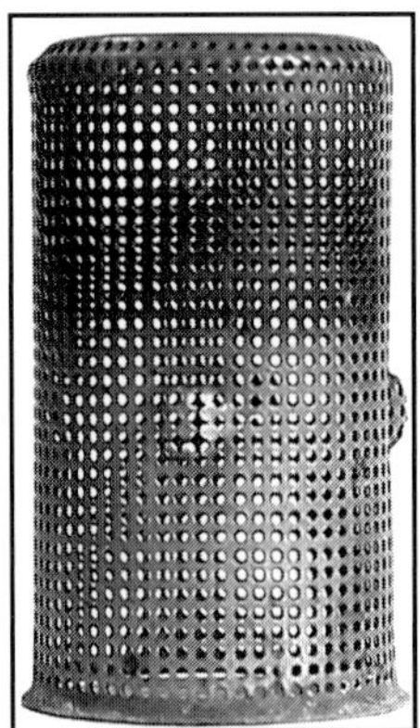

Flame spreader illustrated in patent 365,996. The flame spreader fits inside the wick tube. This example is not dated on top.

Flame spreader illustrated in patent 365,996, marked "This End Up."

Wick raiser.

Rochester stand lamp, height 11¼", marked with 1884 patent date on the fount (see above) and on top of the gallery. Slide-bar wick raiser. The flame spreader is unmarked (see above). I do not know the production period for this lamp; however, I believe the flame spreader and lamp are original and early. $75.00.

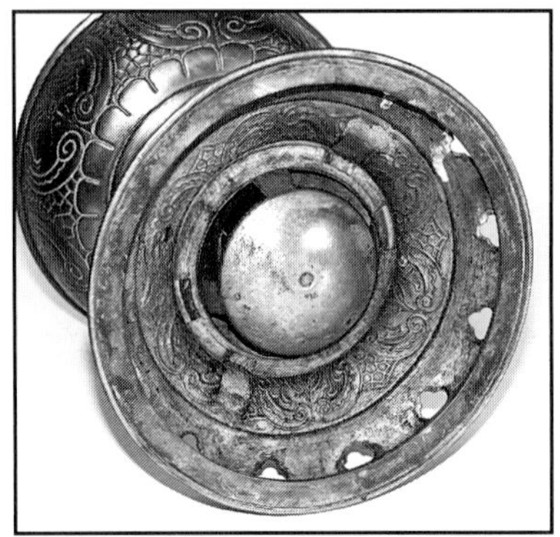

Drip cup inside foot.

Rochester stand lamp, height 11½", marked with 1884 patent date on the fount (see above) and on top of the gallery. Slide-bar wick raiser. The flame spreader is marked "This End Up" (see above). A drip cup is attached under the foot (left). $150.00.

Advertisement, *Pottery and Glassware Reporter*, May 20, 1886.

A Monster Lamp

The Rochester Lamp Co. have the designs ready and will finish this fall a monster lamp which it is proposed to mount on a tower at Niagara Falls. This lamp will measure nearly three feet across the top of the burner. The fount will hold seventy-two gallons of oil. It will be made circular in shape, with the burner in the center, and reflector above.

China and Glass Journal, June 25, 1891

Advertisement, *Pottery and Glassware Reporter*, July 22, 1886.

Advertisement, the *Tradesman*, 1887.

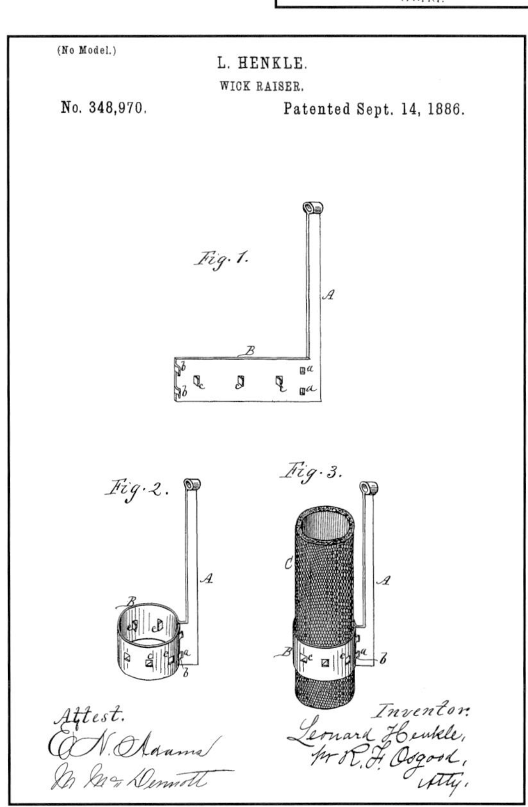

The Glass Rochester, 1886 – 1887

Frank Rhind assigned patent 342,463 for a glass center-draft lamp to Charles Upton. The Rochester glass fount lamp was advertised in the *Pottery and Glassware Reporter*, July 22, 1886. The stand lamp has been found in clear and colored glass, in the Daisy and Button glass pattern. In 1890, Upton advertised that Rochester lamps were all metal and would not break like glass lamps. I suspect that glass center-draft Rochester lamps were sold for a short time.

Rochester fount lamp with glass bowl. Height 9½". This pattern is Daisy and Button w/Cross Bars. $150.00. Courtesy Heinz and Ursula Baumann.

Advertisment *Pottery and Glassware Reporter*, July 22, 1886. No oil fill shown.

Rochester fount lamp with glass bowl, oil fill in metal cap. Height 9½". $150.00. Courtesy Paul Benkover.

Rochester stand lamp with glass fount and brass foot. The gallery is marked with 1884 and 1886 patent dates. There are clips under the foot for a drip cup. This clear glass lamp has also been seen in amber and vaseline glass. Foot may be embossed. Height 11½". $200.00.

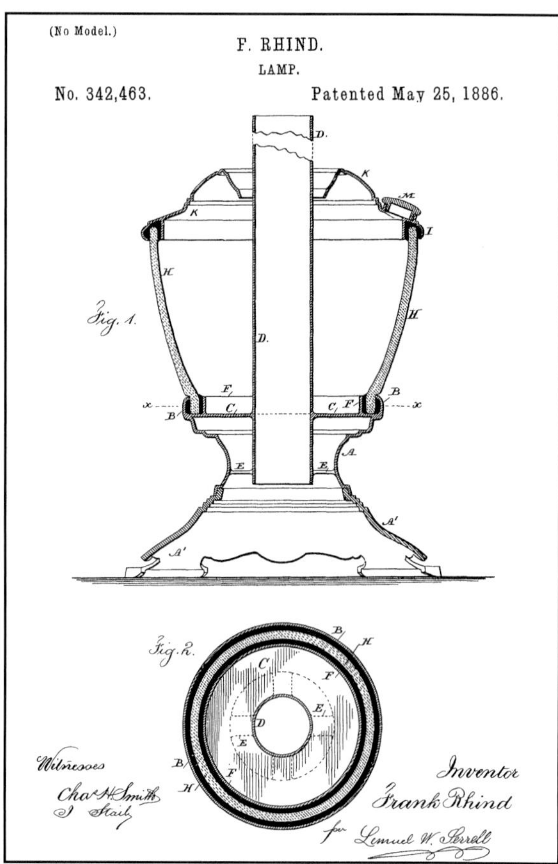

Advertisement, *Pottery and Glassware Reporter*, July 22, 1886. No oil fill shown.

The Rochester 1886 – 1888

The Rochester Lamp Company sold the same style of burners and stand lamps over many years. Sometime after 1886, the wick raiser was changed from a flat band to a rod. I believe both of these flame spreaders are correct for lamps dated 1886.

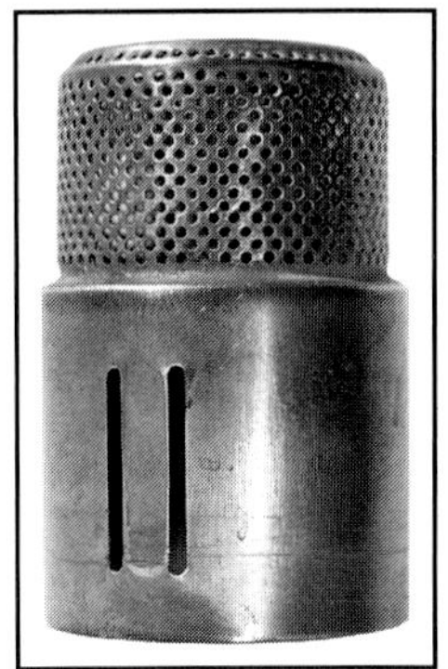

Flame spreader marked "PAT JUNE 7 87" on the top, no other markings.

Flame spreader marked "PAT AUG. 6, 89" on the side and "THE ROCHESTER, THIS END UP, Pat. June 7, 87" on top. The flame spreader fits outside the wick tube.

Rochester stand lamp, height 11¼", marked with 1884 and 1886 patent dates (see above). Slide bar wick raiser. The flame spreader is marked "June 7, 87" (see above). We do not know the production period for this lamp; however, I believe the flame spreader is original. Two clips under the foot held a drip cup or screen. Some wick raiser bars are marked "Sept. 14, 1886." $75.00.

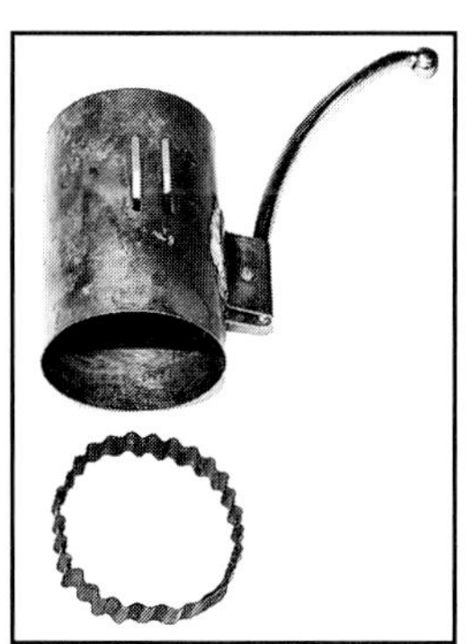

Wick raiser and band to secure wick.

Rochester No. 2 stand lamp marked "The Rochester, Pat. Sept. 14, 1886" on gallery and on top of the fount. Height 11½". Flame spreader marked "This End Up" and "June 7, 87." The wick raiser bar is dated Jan. 26, 1892. $75.00.

The Rochester 1887 – 1892

Charles Upton purposely marked every lamp "The Rochester." The company did such a good job advertising that most brass center-draft lamps were called Rochesters by collectors for many years into the twentieth century. Collectors today observe that many Rochester lamps and many Miller lamps share the very same founts, frames, and accessories. This is understandable, because Edward Miller and Company and the Rochester Lamp Company had a close working relationship during the late 1880s and early 1890s. I believe marking dates on the founts ceased about 1892 or 1893.

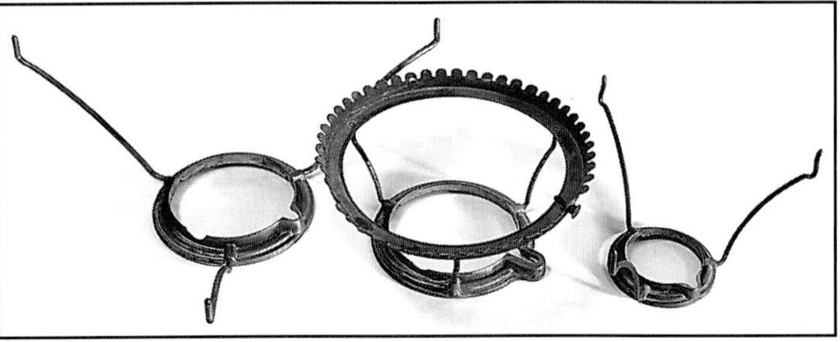

Rochester shade holders left to right: 10" tripod marked "Pat. Apr. 13, 86"; 5" shade holder marked "Pat. Apr. 13, 86"; 6" tripod for JR. Rochester marked "Pat. Apr. 13, 86."

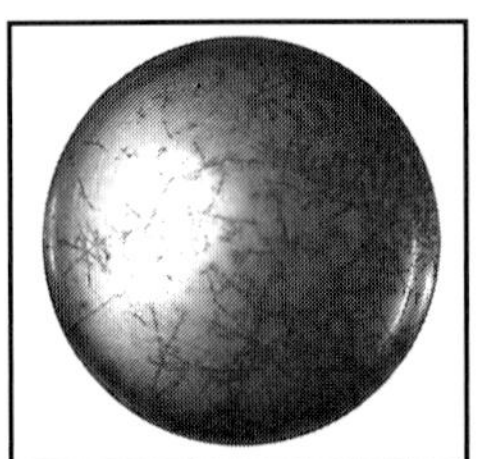

Rochester oil fill caps are plain and unmarked.

Rochester No. 1 stand lamp. Fount marked "Pat. Sept. 14, 1886." Gallery marked "Jan. 15, 1884, Sept. 14, 1886." Height 10½". Flame spreader marked "This End Up, July 5, 1887" (above). $75.00.

Rochester No. 2 table lamp stamped "THE ROCHESTER" and "Pat Sept 14 1886" on top of the fount. Height 10¾". Gallery marked "Pat Sept 14 1886." Flame spreader has the 1889/1890 mark. $150.00.

Rochester No. 2 table lamp stamped "THE ROCHESTER" in script on top of the fount. Height 10". Gallery marked "Pat Sept 14 1886." Flame spreader has "Aug. 6, 1889" mark. $225.00. Courtesy Bill Schreiber.

The Rochester 1890 – 1896

Rochester table lamp No. 2 with cast decorative arms and heavy cast foot. Height 9½". Shade holder in place. Fount marked "Sept 14, 1886." Flame spreader 1889/1890 mark (top right). $200.00.

Flame spreader for Rochester No. 2 table lamps sold after 1890. Top is marked "THE ROCHESTER, THIS END UP, PAT'D. Pat Oct 1 1889 & Aug 26 1890." On side, marked "Pat Aug. 6, 89." These flame spreaders have a small perforated thimble attached inside in the top (see right). The flame spreader fits outside the wick tube. Some flame spreaders are dated on top but *not* on the side and do not have the thimble inside.

Rochester vase lamp No. 2 with removable oil pot. Heavy brass lamp is silver plated. Sugar bowl–type with cast arms and cast-iron foot. Height 11". Stamped "THE ROCHESTER" on the burner collar. Gallery marked "PAT. SEPT 14, 1886." $225.00.

Rochester No. 2 stand lamp marked "The Rochester" in script on top of the fount. Height 12". Gallery marked "Pat. Sept 14, 1886." This model was originally sold in polished brass, rich gold, or nickel finishes. Flame spreader has 1889/1890 mark. $175.00.

The JR. Rochester

The JR. Rochester trademark for center-draft burners was granted May 12, 1891, stating the mark had been used since Jan. 1, 1891. These lamps are size 0.

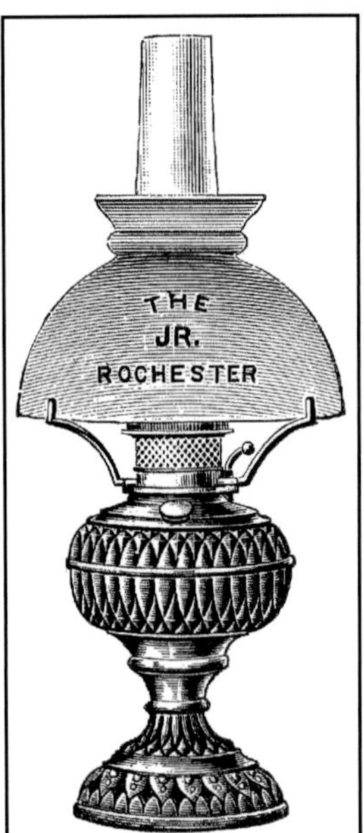

Junior Rochester stand lamp, Hibbard, Spencer, Bartlett & Co.

Flame spreaders for JR. Rochester hand lamps. Both marked "PAT Oct 7 1889 [and] Aug 26 1890" on top. The flame spreader fits outside the wick tube. I suspect these flame spreaders fit the Baby Rochester.

Some lamps were marked "The JR. Rochester, No. 4, Pat. Sep 14, 1886."

The Baby Rochester

Advertisement, *Pottery and Glassware Reporter,* March 8, 1888.

Junior Rochester hand lamp. Height 6½". Stamped "THE JR. ROCHESTER, Pat. Sep 14 1886" on top of fount (see above). $150.00.

Junior Rochester lamp designed for wall or hanging brackets. Height 6¼". $125.00.

Baby Rochester night lamp missing flame spreader. Height 5". $ 175.00. Courtesy Eileen White.

The New Rochester, 1895 – ca. Early 1900s

The New Rochester and New Rochester JR. lamps were made for Charles Upton and the Rochester Lamp Company. Read the chapter about the Bridgeport Brass Company for more details about these lamps and flame spreaders.

Advertisement, *Muncey's Magazine*, 1896.

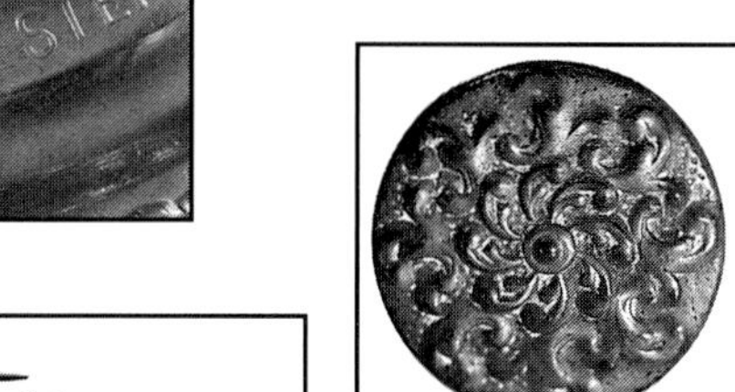

Oil fill cap on New Rochester and New Rochester JR. lamps.

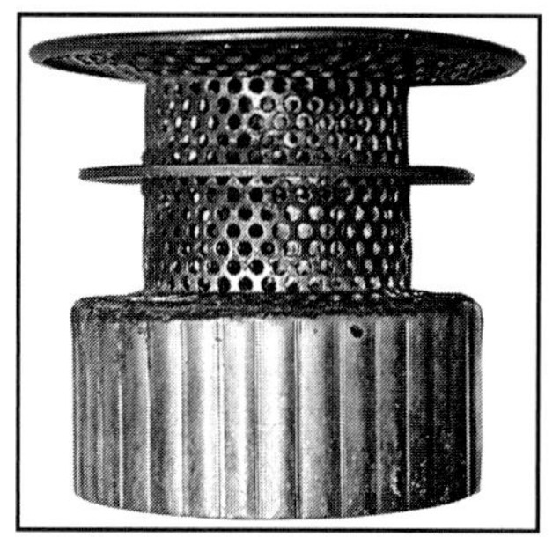

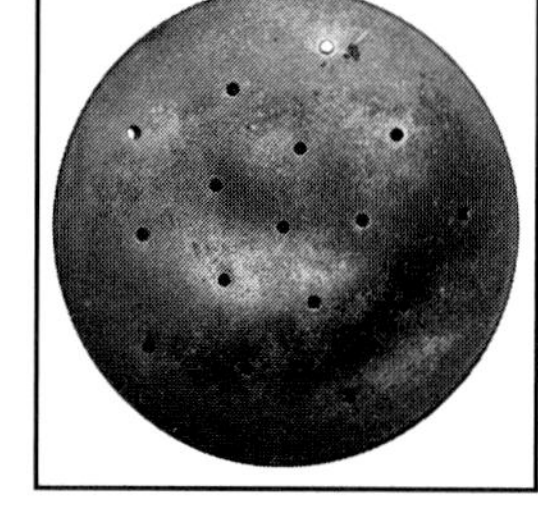

Flame spreader for New Rochester No. 2 stand lamp.

The New Rochester No. 2 stand lamp with gallery lift and push-pull wick-raiser rod. Height 13". Two styles of lift burners were sold between 1894 and 1897. $125.00.

Advertisement in *Munsey's Magazine*, 1896.

"The New Rochester"
Up to Date
As Perfect as a Watch.

Our various lines of goods including Lamps in

Metal, Onyx, Black Iron, etc,

SILK SHADES and MICA PROTECTORS of all kinds is complete and all orders can be promptly filled.

The Rochester Lamp Co.

MANUFACTURERS,

42 PARK PLACE, 37 BARCLAY ST., } New York.

C. S. UPTON, Prest.

CGL, November 20, 1895.

R. L. Co.

Rochester lamps are found with "R. L. Co." signatures on the flame spreader and cast into the underside of the base or foot. I believe these lamps were sold by the Rochester Lamp Company, Rochester, NY, sometime after the Rochester Lamp Co., New York, NY, closed about 1905.

The 1907 advertisement below offered "new" Rochester lamps in exchange for old Rochester lamps. I believe the new lamps were mostly inventory salvaged by the Upton and Pomeroy families who carried on the business, including interests in gas and electric lighting.

New Lamps for Old

should you have a **Rochester** that does not give satisfaction, return it to us, (if not injured) and we will give you a new one **FREE.**

The **Rochester** gives a soft, cheerful, mellow light of wonderful brilliancy, enabling weak eyes to read without straining. Made of brass throughout, any finish. Perfectly constructed, absolutely safe, *guaranteed*; millions in use.

We manufacture, import and deal in all sundries pertaining to light and heat—*oil, gas, alcohol, electricity.*

Agents wanted, men and women; experience unnecessary; permanent home employment, salary or commission. **Send stamp** for salesman's instructions and **Lamp Information,** the knowledge acquired through years of experience.

Rochester Lamp Co., Dept. P, Rochester, N.Y.

The American Magazine, October 1907.

Flame spreader marked "Made By The R. L. Co., New York, U.S.A., Patented Jan. 15, 1884, Dec. 29, 1885, Jul. 5, 1887." This flame spreader is identical to Edward Miller flame spreaders of the same period. The 1884 patent is 292,114 (Henkle), 1885 is 333,338 (Rhind), and 1887 is 365,996 (Henkle).

1888 Trade Card

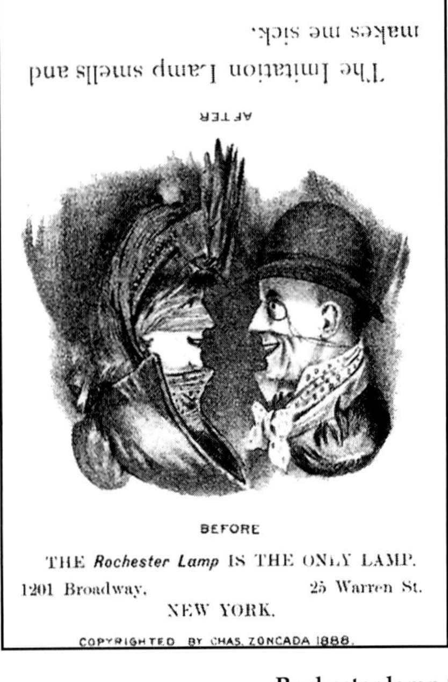

Rochester lamp trade card, 1888.

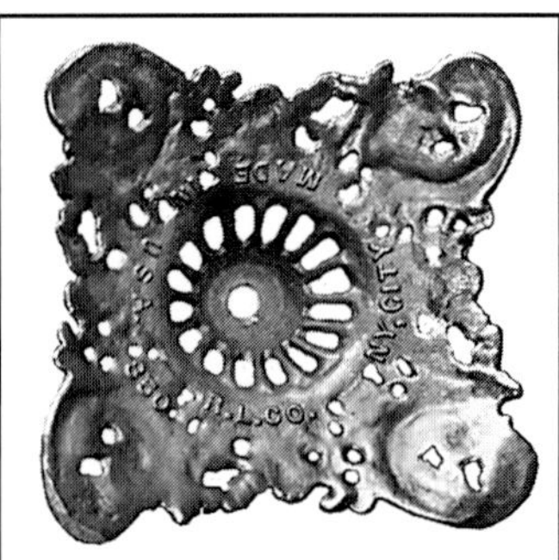

Cast-iron foot marked "Made in U. S. A., R. L. Co., N. Y. City." The cast bases of some large New Rochester vase lamps are marked the same way. These castings were used for many years.

Rochester Lamps 1895 – 1896; Hibbard, Spencer & Bartlett Co., Chicago

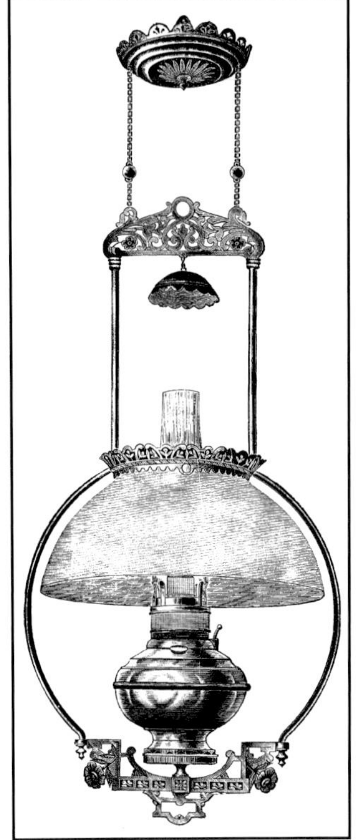

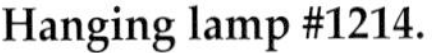
Hanging lamp #1214.

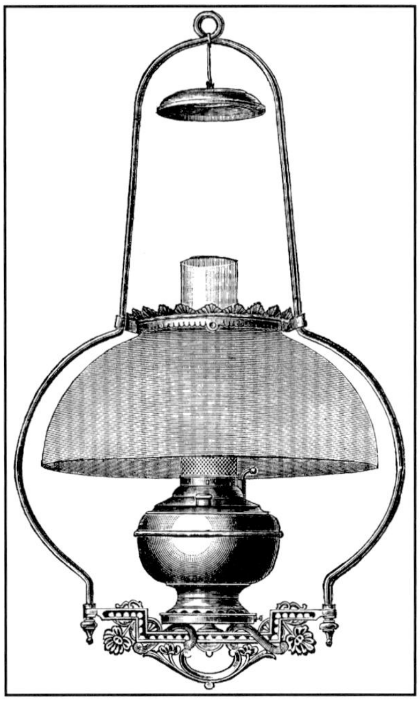

Store lamp #9173.

Chandelier #763.

Hall lamp #9186.

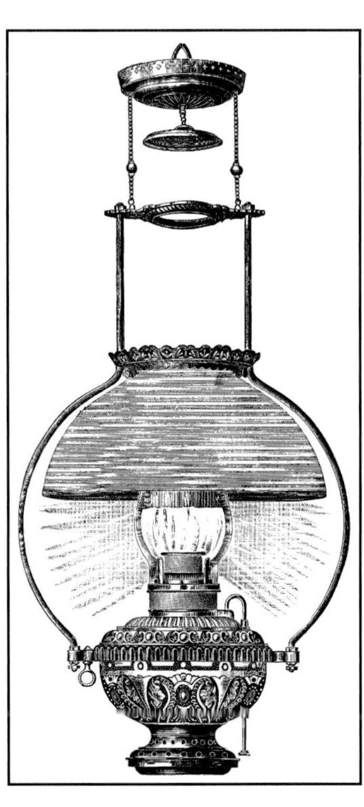

Mammoth hanging lamp #1014.

Library lamp #6905 with jewels.

Library lamp #695 with ruby vase and matching shade. Also sold in blue and pink glass.

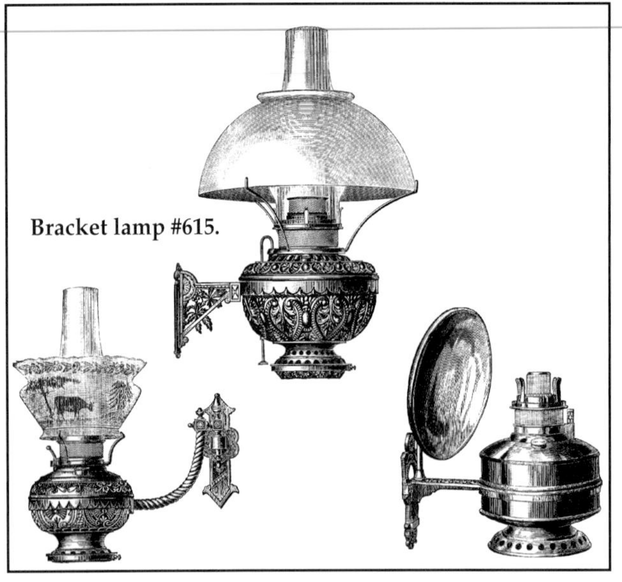
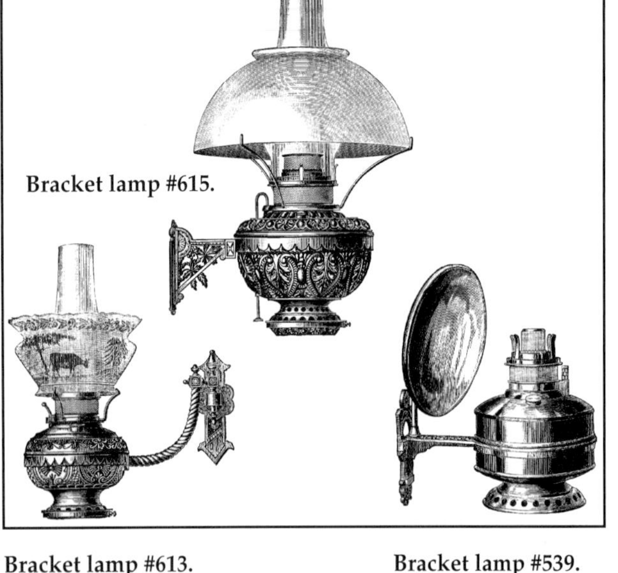

Bracket lamp #615.

Bracket lamp #613.

Bracket lamp #539.

Billiard chandelier.

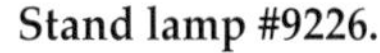

Stand lamp #9226.

Night lamp #666.

Student lamp #6891, gold inlaid shade.

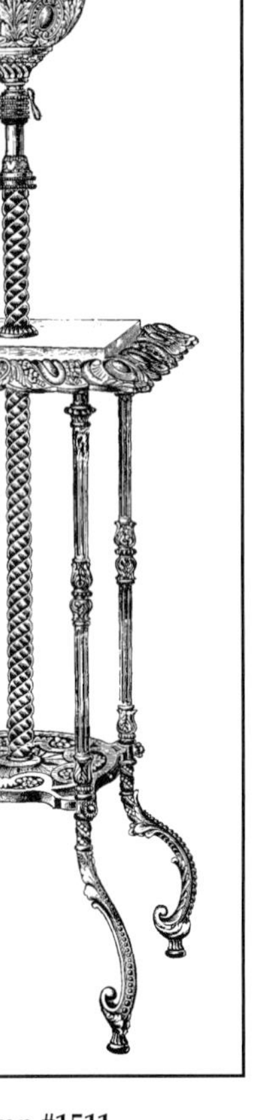

Piano lamp #1511.

Table (vase) lamps #9415, #9504, and #9404.

Interior view of THE ROCHESTER LAMP CO'S STORE,
42 Park Place and 37 Barclay Street, New York City.

THE LARGEST LAMP STORE IN THE WORLD.

The success of the Rochester Lamp has been one of the marvels of the great commercial and manufacturing enterprises of the country. The business was commenced in '84, the lamps being manufactured in Rochester, N. Y., and the output sold in a small uptown store in New York City — mostly at retail. Several times the company moved to larger quarters, until the present headquarters of the house, 42 Park Place and 37 Barclay Street, is unquestionably the largest exclusively lamp store in the world. The business of the house occupies four floors, running completely through the block, aggregating 24,000 square feet of floor space. To stand at either end of the principal salesroom, the view is like that of a public exposition of bric-a-brac, or a panorama of artistic lamps and chandeliers. In this one view over 2,000 different varieties attract the eye of the spectator.

Source: The photograph came from an unknown college yearbook, 1892. The text below it was copied from a similar advertisement in *China, Glass and Lamps,* Dec. 17, 1890.

Scovill Manufacturing Company

1850 – Present

Kerosene Burner Manufacture ca. 1860s – 1930s

Scovill Manufacturing Company, of Waterbury, Connecticut, was the largest brass-making company in the United States in 1920. The company began in 1802 as Abel & Porter Company making metal gilt buttons, and it was the only company in the United States to roll brass until the 1820s.

J. M. L. Scovill and William H. Scovill became owners of the company in 1827. The Scovills were the first to manufacture daguerreotype plates in this country. Scovill Manufacturing Company was incorporated in 1850 with J. M. L. Scovill, president (1850 – 1857), and W. H. Scovill, treasurer (1850 – 1854).

Scovill Mfg. Co. was a major manufacturer of brass, German silver, daguerreotype plates, ambrotype plates, cameras, munitions, buttons, medals, small brass goods, kerosene burners, student lamps, Welsbach gas burners, and coin blanks for the U.S. mint and for countries in South America.

Scovill registered the trademark for the famous Queen Anne flat wick burner in 1896, stating the name was used since 1880. The company manufactured German student lamps, according to its advertisements in Waterbury city directories. These lamps were likely made under license, since Miller and Solverson (1992) and Baumann and Wolfe (1994) do not list Scovill as a manufacturer of student lamps.

Scovill was assigned relatively few patents for lamp inventions. The Scovill brand, however, is well known among collectors, and Thuro (2001) lists 52 variations of Scovill flat-wick burners. Scovill burners were used by Standard Oil and other oil companies to promote sales of kerosene lamp fuels. I suspect Scovill manufactured the Mei Foo lamp as well as the House lamp which is commonly found with the Scovill No. 2 Queen Anne burner, marked "Rayo" on the burner cone. These burners were surely exported in large numbers. There has been no listing for Scovill or Queen Anne burner in *The Rushlight Index* since 1934.

Did Scovill manufacture center-draft lamps? I would not be surprised if the answer is yes, perhaps only under license. Sterne Russell assigned patents for student lamps and an Argand burner to Scovill, 1881 – 1885. A search of Scovill company archives may well reveal interesting results. For example, the Plume & Atwood Company made lamps and burners for the Mantle Lamp Company of America for many years; however, P & A never sold the Aladdin nor did it advertise its name as the manufacturer of the famous Aladdin lamp.

From 1890 to 1917, the number of employees increased from 1,200 to more than 13,500 (Pope, 1918). This period of rapid growth reflected the increase in use of copper for electricity, telephones, and trolley lines.

Scovill Mfg. Co. purchased the Matthews & Willard factory in 1903. I have no specific information on lamp or burner production from M & W tooling after that date. I suspect that Scovill continued to make the Tuxedo and possibly the New Columbia lamps. Another possibility is that Scovill sold the lamp tooling to another company.

SCOVILL MANUFACTURING CO.,
419 & 421 BROOME STREET,
NEW YORK,
MANUFACTURERS OF
KEROSENE LAMPS,
BURNERS,
--AND--
Lamp Trimmings.
FACTORY,
Waterbury, Conn.

Advertisement.
Courtesy Catherine Thuro.

Established 1802.
Cable Address: "SCOVILL."

SCOVILL MFG. CO.,
99 MILL STREET, WATERBURY, CONN.
THE LARGEST AND MOST FULLY EQUIPPED BRASS ROLLING MILLS AND METAL GOODS MANUFACTURING ESTABLISHMENT IN THE WORLD.

Brass and German Silver,
In Sheets, Rods, Tubing and Wire.

Butt Hinges,
Narrow, Middle, Broad, Desk, Ship, Stop, Spring and Pianoforte.

Coins and Coin Planchets,
Full Equipment for supplying Planchets or minting the same in any required alloys.

Buttons,
Military, Naval, Livery, Society, Railroad, School, Lasting, Silk and Dress.

Lamp Goods,
German Student Lamps, Kerosene Burners, etc.

Bicycle Goods,
Pumps, Oilers, Valves, etc.

Aluminum (pure),
In Ingots, Sheets, Rods and Wire.

Estimates for Specialties in Brass, German Silver and Aluminum Furnished on Application.

DEPOTS:
NEW YORK: No. 75 SPRING ST.
BOSTON: No. 170 SUMMER ST.
CHICAGO: No. 210 LAKE ST.

Advertisement, *Waterbury City Directory*, 1910.
Courtesy M. Gibbs.

Trade Names

Flat-wick lamps — Queen Anne, House Lamp.
Flat-wick burners — Queen Anne, Scovill.
Student lamps — unknown.

Selected Patents, Center-draft Lamps (Student lamps)

Sterne Russell assigned to Scovill Mfg. Co.

Year	Patent No.
1881	247,114
1884	297,015
1885	312,514

I believe Scovill made the House lamp (right) sold by Standard Oil and several catalog companies. The No. 2 House lamp is similar, if not identical, to the Queen Anne illustrated far right. I believe Scovill also made Mei Foo lamps for the Standard Oil Company.

No. 2 House Lamp with Queen Anne burner. $40.00.

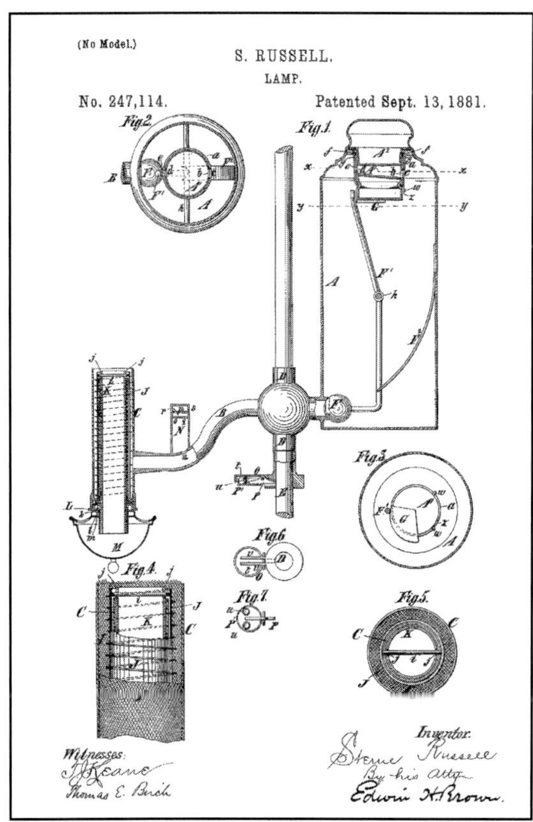

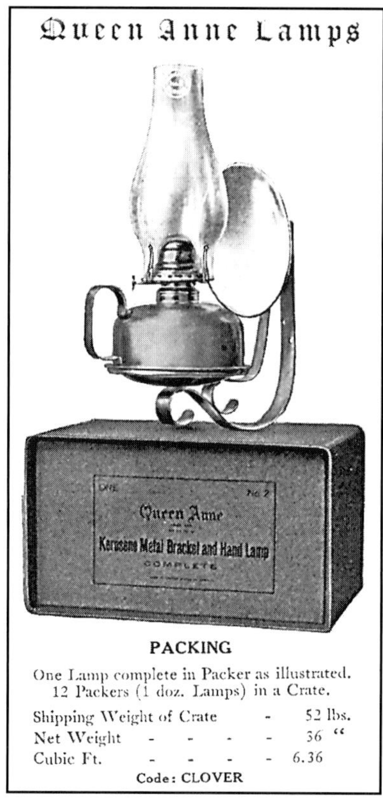

Queen Anne Lamps

PACKING

One Lamp complete in Packer as illustrated.
12 Packers (1 doz. Lamps) in a Crate.

Shipping Weight of Crate	52 lbs.
Net Weight	36 "
Cubic Ft.	6.36

Code: CLOVER

Queen Anne Lamps

PACKING

One Lamp complete in Packer as illustrated.
12 Packers (1 doz. Lamps) in a Crate.

Shipping Weight of Crate	36 lbs.
Net Weight	24½ "
Cubic Feet	3.02

Code: TIMOTHY

Pages from undated Scovill brochure advertising Queen Anne lamps, burners, and chimneys.

H. E. Shaffer & Companies

H. E. Shaffer & Co., 1869; Rochester Kerosene Burner Company, 1885; Rochester Burner Company, 1888; Shaffer Lamp Company, 1894 – ca. 1900

In 1868 Henry E. Shaffer moved to Rochester, New York from Rome, New York, where he had been a grocery store owner and wholesale grocery distributor (Kastner, 2003). In Rochester he was involved in manufacture of fruit jars, lamp burners and trimmings, and later, complete lamps.

Shaffer organized or was involved in several companies that manufactured burners and lamps. These companies were independent of the Rochester Lamp Company, of New York, New York.

In 1870 Shaffer lived at 304 Main Street, close to C. C. Goodale at 308 Main Street. Charles Goodale was proprietor of the Rochester Kerosene Lamp Manufactory, which also manufactured and sold fruit jars. The Rochester Kerosene Lamp Manufactory was operated by Goodale & Pells at 63 & 65 W. Main St. from 1877 to 1879. I am uncertain, but I suspect a business relationship between Goodale and Shaffer. Goodale was a "jobber and wholesale dealer of chandeliers, glass and fruit jars" and may have sold Shaffer's products.

H. E. Shaffer & Company was listed in Rochester city directories from 1869 to about 1873 as a manufacturer of fruit jars (O'Connell, 2003). In 1875, Shaffer was listed as importer and dealer in French china, earthenware, and porcelaine opaque goods. The company carried "a full line of cutlery, kerosene lamps, chandeliers, lamp chimneys, etc."

In 1871 Shaffer was a founder, treasurer, and business manager of the Consolidated Fruit Jar Company, New York City (O'Connell, 2005). I will not speculate on any connection that Shaffer may have had with the New Jersey Lamp and Bronze Works, New Brunswick, which was a subsidiary of Consolidated Fruit Jar Co.

Wenrich (1988) reported Shaffer's companies as the Rochester Kerosene Burner Company in 1885, the Shaffer, Miller & Huntington Burner Manufacturing Co. in 1887, and finally, the Rochester Burner Company in 1888. In 1888 Henry Shaffer was president, H. F. Peck, vice president, and E. A. Roworth, secretary-treasurer at 409 East Main Street, Rochester. Shaffer assigned patents to the Shaffer Lamp Company beginning in 1895.

From 1874 to 1880 patents for burners, lamp stands, and brackets were assigned to Henry Shaffer by Burbank (152,068), Spencer (218,406; 220,884; 223,254), and Barnard and Hanna (220,788).

The Rochester Adjustable Lamp Company appears in the *Rochester City Directory* for 1880, Henry E. Shaffer, treasurer. That year Shaffer was witness to Cartwright's patent (227,731), assigned to the company, for an adjustable stand or bracket lamp. At this time we know little more about Shaffer's connection with Charles Spencer and Shaffer's role, if any, in the Rochester Adjustable Lamp Company other than that he was company treasurer, secretary, and president at different times through 1884 (O'Connell, 2006). Manhattan

Advertisement, *Rochester City Directory*, 1871.
Courtesy Hyman Brenner.

Brass Company sold Spencer's patent lamps from 1876 to 1880. McDonald (2000) reported that Spencer's patent 171,537 was produced by Manhattan Brass as "Spencer's Patent Two Light Student Lamp."

Shaffer invented double and triple flat-wick burners sold by the trade name Perfection (patents 347,132 and 358,892). They were marked "S. P./Burner," which meant "Shaffer Perfection Burner."

The Lux-Dux center-draft lamp was introduced in 1888. At the time the company made or sold other lamp goods, including chimneys, shade holders, and collars. Lux-Dux lamps were made in table, piano, hanging, and banquet lamps, and few are found today. The Lux-Dux lamp was advertised heavily in the *Pottery and Glassware Reporter* in 1889.

In later years, Shaffer continued his work on lighting with improvements of gas and acetylene burners (patent 973,713). He died in Rochester on March 3, 1913.

Trade Names

Center-draft lamps — Lux-Dux, Lux-Dux No. 10, Mammoth, Shaffer Lamp.

Flat-wick burners — Shaffer Perfection, Shaffer Sun burner.

Thuro (*Oil Lamps 3*, p. 235) illustrates an advertisement suggesting that Shaffer also manufactured burners under the Lux-Dux name.

Shaffer Perfection burners are sought by collectors. These burners were made in Nos. 1, 2, and 3 collar sizes with variations in thumb wheels. They were made for both slip and lip chimneys. Shaffer chimneys with specially sized lips were required. Shaffer claimed the burners threw off a reflected light, each separate flame acting as a reflector to the other.

Refer to The Lampworks (www.thelampworks.com) for more information about Shaffer flat-wick burners and Charles Spencer's lamps.

Selected Patents, Center-draft Lamps

Henry E. Shaffer assigned Rochester Burner Co.

1888 386,758

Henry E. Shaffer[1] unassigned

1889 407,969
1889 407,970
1892 474,488
1892 .... 486,510[2]
1893 494,171
1893 503,007
1893 506,408

Henry E. Shaffer assigned to Shaffer Lamp Co.

1895 542,781
1895 546,435
1896 555,187

[1]Also patents for fruit jars and multiple wick burners.
[2]"Closed-fount lamp" could be glass.

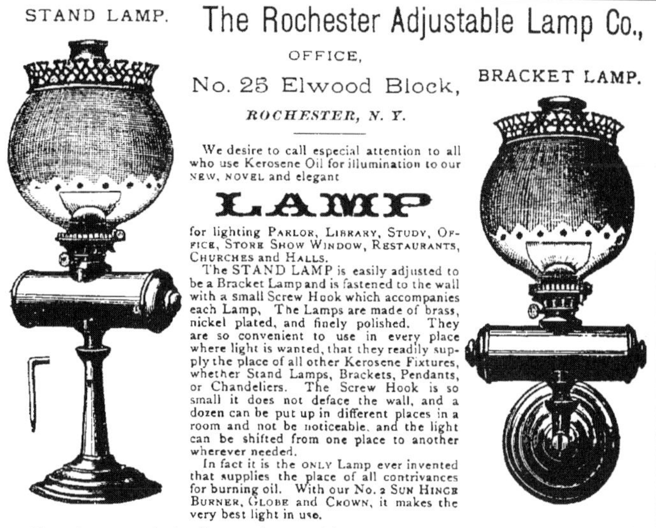

Advertisement, *Rochester City Directory*, 1880 – 1881. These lamps appear to be made under Spencer's patents assigned to Henry Shaffer. Courtesy Dick O'Connell.

H. E. SHAFFER,
IMPORTER OF AND DEALER IN
French China,
EARTHENWARE,
"Porcelaine Opaque" Goods,
FOREIGN AND DOMESTIC GLASS,
&c., &c.

A LARGE AND BEAUTIFUL ASSORTMENT OF
Plated Ware, Rich Bronzes,
BELGIAN AND BOHEMIAN GLASS,
Fine Vases and Fancy Goods,
Decorated Toilet Ware, Cuspadores, Novelties in Parian, Terra Cotta and Majolica Wares.

A FULL LINE OF
CUTLERY,
Kerosene Lamps, Chandeliers, Lamp Chimneys, &c.,
CONSTANTLY IN STOCK.
39 STATE STREET,
ROCHESTER, N. Y.

Rochester City Directory, 1875.
Courtesy of Dick O'Connell.

Advertisement, *Rochester City Directory*, 1886.
Courtesy Rochester Museum and Science Center.

The Lux-Dux

Lux-Dux means "leading light" in Latin.

I believe Lux-Dux lamps were advertised and sold until 1894 or 1895, possibly longer. After Henry Shaffer formed the Shaffer Lamp Company, the lamps and flame spreaders were no longer marked "Lux-Dux." I believe that Lux-Dux lamps were made by Holmes, Booth & Haydens and Shaffer lamps were made by Ansonia Brass & Copper Company.

The Macbeth Evans Glass Company listed chimneys for the Shaffer lamp in its 1901 catalog.

Lux-Dux No. 2 stand lamp, lift gallery. Height 12⅛". The fount is not marked. $150.00. Courtesy Heinz and Ursula Baumann.

The Lux Dux

In addition to their flat wick burners [Perfection] the company [will] add centre draft lamps to their business for the coming season. H. E. Shaffer, the inventor of the Shaffer "Perfection" burners, has succeeded in producing a centre draft, round wick lamp which takes the same wick and chimney as the "Rochester" lamp called the "Lux Dux" [light-leader]. It produces a very white light, and a steady light, in steadiness like the light of a German student lamp, and is of seventy candle power. Also a large centre draft lamp made on the same principle of the "Lux Dux," only very much larger in size, producing the same steady, white flame, of 275 candle power. This large-sized lamp is expressly for lighting stores, public halls, and, in fact, all business places where the best reliable lights are required. Those requiring a good light and using centre draft lamps should not fail to order the "Lux Dux."

The Industries of Rochester, 1888

"Lux-Dux, Rochester N. Y." is stamped into the top of most, but not all, Lux-Dux lamps.

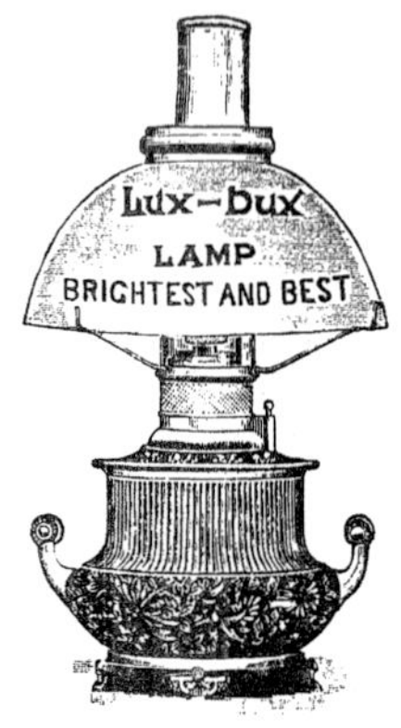

The Light of Other Days may perhaps be dim, but that of the

LUX-DUX LAMP

is the brightest and best of modern days.

ROCHESTER BURNER CO.,

ROCHESTER, NEW YORK.

New York Agency, LUX-DUX LAMP CO., 17 Warren Street.

Advertisement, *Pottery and Glassware Reporter*, Aug. 29, 1889.

Lux-Dux Flame Spreaders

"Patented, LUX-DUX, July 24th 1888" on large disc.

"Patented, LUX-DUX, July 24th 1888."

"Patented July 24th 1888."

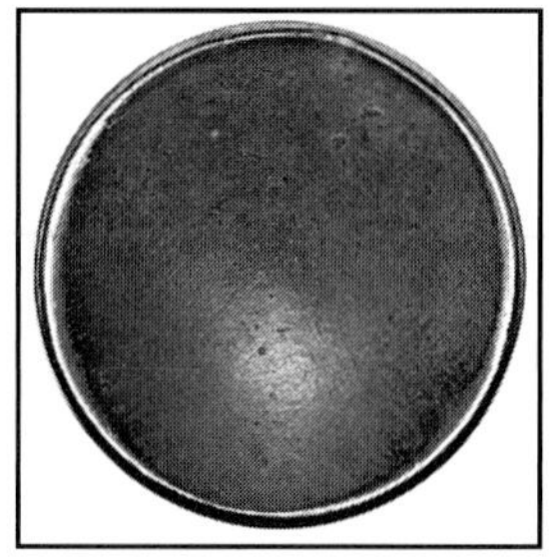

Unmarked, concave top and sides.

Length $2\frac{3}{4}$".

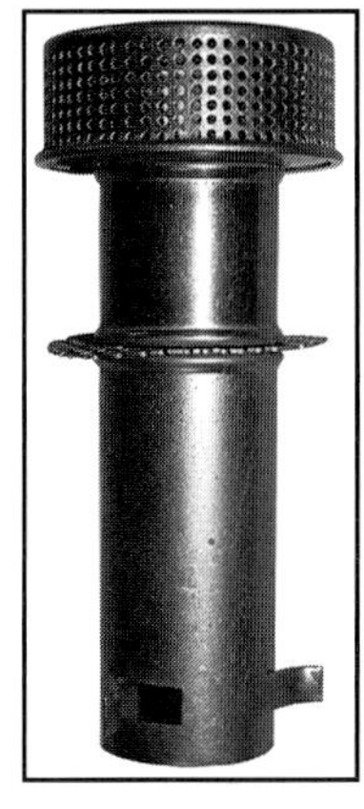

Length $3\frac{3}{8}$".

"Patented, LUX-DUX, July 24th 1888" under large disc (above).

"Patented July 24th 1888."

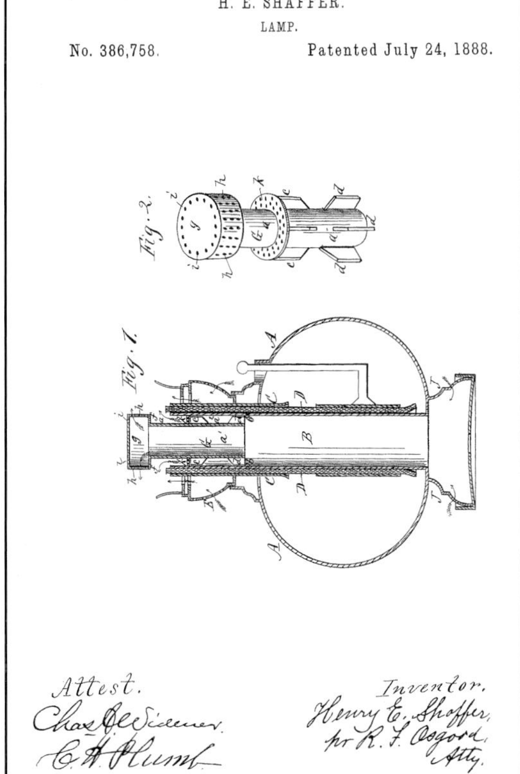

Lux-Dux burner.

More Lux-Dux

No. 2 stand lamp signed "Lux-Dux, Rochester, N. Y." on top of the fount. Height 12". $125.00.

Lux-Dux No. 2 hanging fount, lift gallery. Height 8½". This lamp fount is similar to that of the Gladstone. $100.00.

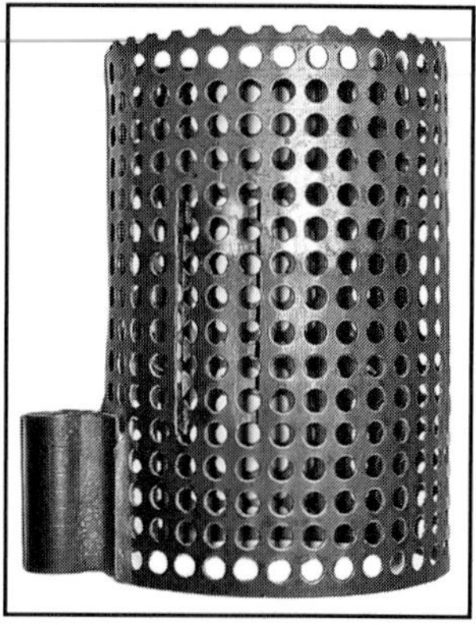

Wick carrier for Lux-Dux lamps. The wick raiser rod is shaped to insert and hook into the carrier, similar to that of the Gladstone (see HBH). A cross wire stop is fixed inside the wick tube to position the flame spreader at the correct height. Shaffer has several patents (407,970; 474,488; and 494,171). This is similar to Woodward 440,683 assigned to Ansonia.

Advertisement, *Pottery and Glassware Reporter,* July 18, 1889.

Lux-Dux No. 2 banquet lamp, lift gallery. Height 18". $175.00.

The Shaffer Lamp

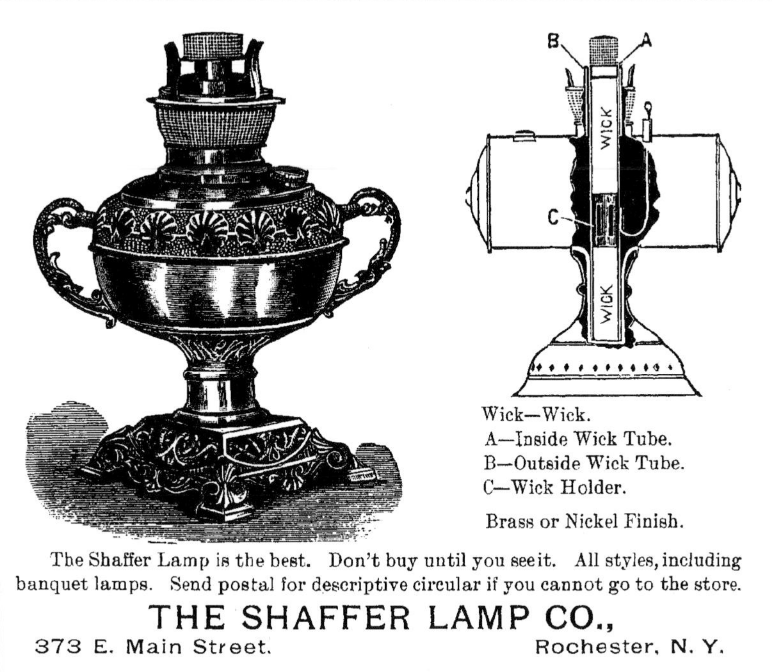

Advertisement, *Rochester Baptist Monthly,* Dec. 1894.
Courtesy Dick O'Connell.

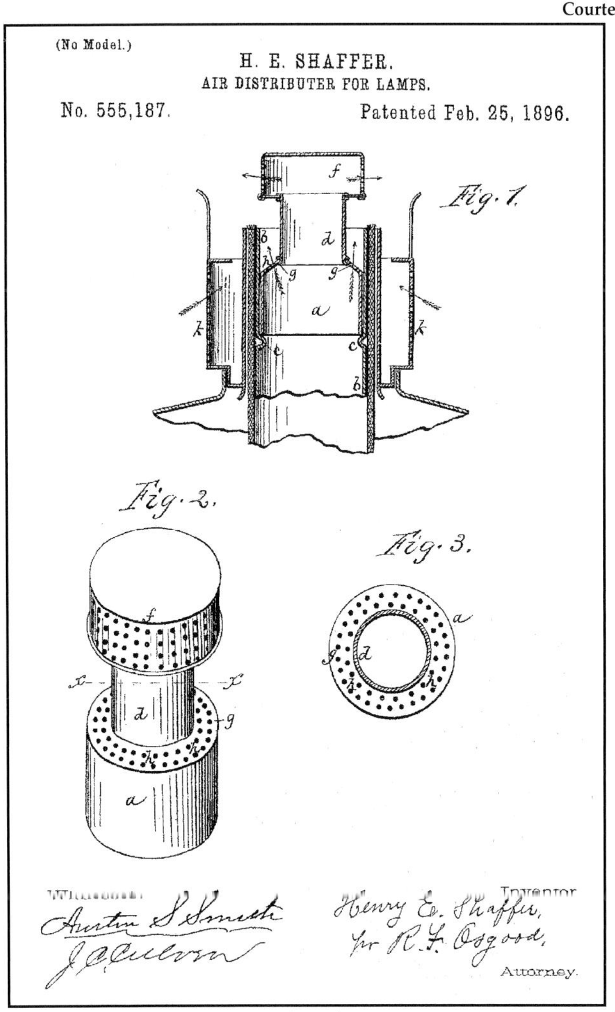

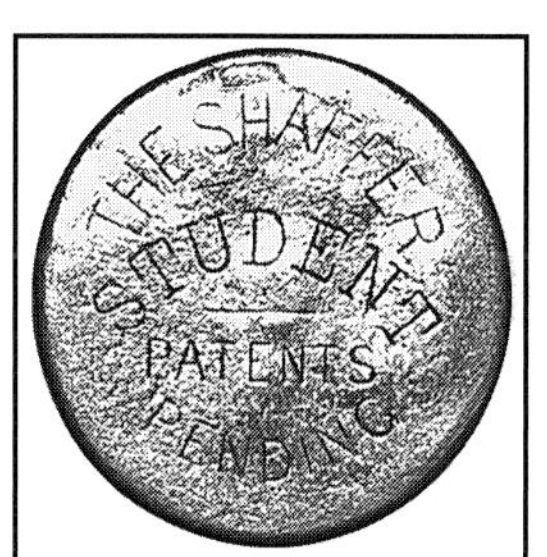

Flame spreader for Shaffer lamp marked "The Shaffer Student, Patents Pending." Length 2". Courtesy Kent Stratton.

St. Louis Electric Lamp Company

Casperson Electric Lamp, Marsh Electric Lamp, 1885 – 1892

The St. Louis Electric Lamp Company sold the Marsh Electric Lamp. This company is listed in the *1885 St. Louis City Directory* as "St. Louis Electric Lamp & Stove Co., 808 Pine St., St. Louis."

J. (John) W. Marsh is listed in the 1885 city directory as "mngr. St. Louis Electric Lamp Co., 808 Pine, r. 2307 Washington Avenue." In 1887 he is listed as "pres. Electric Lamp & Stove Co., 808 Pine, r. 3919 Washington Ave."

Marsh was associated with Robert H. David as principals of R. H. David & Co., Lamps, St. Louis, in 1889. There were no entries for either man in 1890 or 1891. The above information is courtesy of the St. Louis Public Library.

The (St. Louis) Electric Lamp and Stove Company was dissolved in 1892 according to records in the *Missouri Secretary of State's Business Entity Database*.

An 1890 letterhead for a Marsh Manufacturing Company, of Chicago, Illinois, listed goods as "fine cabinet ware and electric lamps." Cabinet ware included music stands and adjustable book stands. The Marsh letterhead illustrated the Meyrose Calcium (Electric) lamp, which suggests the Marsh Electric Lamp was not sold as late as 1890. The Illinois Secretary of State has no records for Marsh Mfg. Company.

The American Wick Mfg. Co. — "We make wicks for every style of burner in the market." American Wick listed Casperson Electric, but not Marsh Electric, in 1901.

I do not know how Casperson and Marsh were related other than these snippets which seem to bring them together selling "electric" oil lamps of the period.

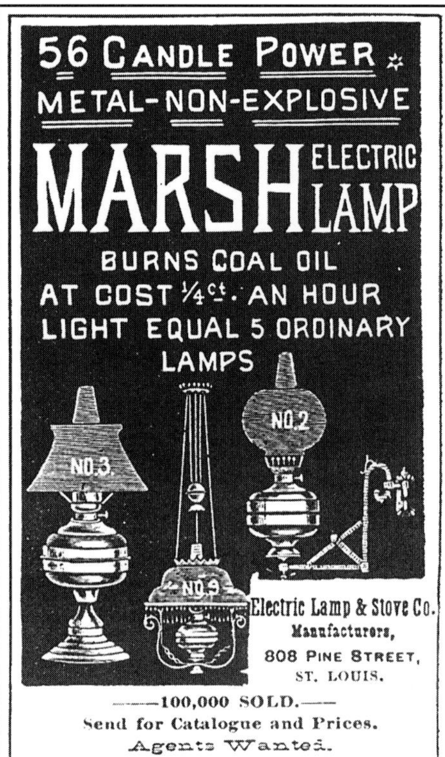

Marsh Electric Lamp trade card.
Courtesy David Broughton.

The Marsh Electric lamp is stamped "The St. Louis Electric Lamp Co., J. W. Marsh, Manager, St. Louis, MO."

Flame spreader.

Marsh Electric fount lamp. Height 9". $125.00.

Oil fill cap of Marsh Electric lamp.

Wick knob, Marsh Electric lamp.

Marsh Electric Lamp

Oil fill cap and name "Marsh" stamped on the neck of the burner.

Wick knob, Marsh lamp.

Marsh fount lamp. Height 8½". This lamp is found with "Marsh Electric" or stars wick knobs (above). I believe this fount was originally attached to a table stand. Some founts have three little feet. $75.00.

David J. Braun's Mason Electric

Logo stamped on the burner neck: "David J. Braun's Improved Mason-Electric."

Wick knob, Braun lamp.

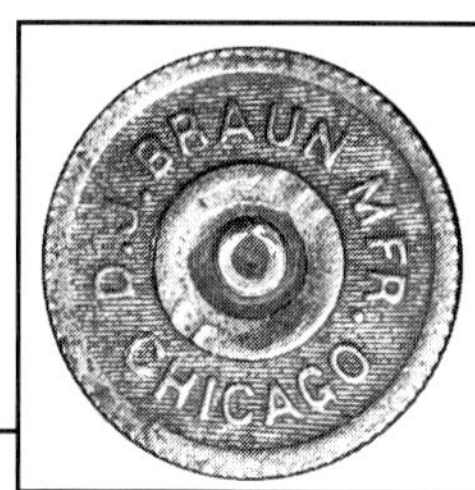

Braun Electric stand lamp. Height 12½". Part of the gallery and the flame spreader are missing. This lamp appears to be illustrated in the Casperson patent. $125.00.

THE IMPROVED 56 CANDLE POWER

ELECTRIC LAMP,

(Formerly the CASPERSON.)

1. Its 56 Candle Power considered, it is the cheapest light ever nvented.
2. By the laws of nature, it is non-explosive.
3. A chimney cannot be broken by it. It will melt first.
4. Even a child can wick it in one minute.
5. No smoke, no odor, no smoked chimneys.
6. Being made of Brass or Nickel, the Lamp will last a lifetime.
7. Should it accidentally fall, there is no danger, as it could not break. Many lives have been lost in similar cases with Glass Lamps.
8. The Fount can be attached to any Gas or Oil Fixture, such as Gas Burner, Oil Bracket or Chandelier, and used in lighting Stores, Factories, Offices, Railroad Cars, Churches, Parlors, Halls, Hotels, and Streets of Towns and Cities. We make two sizes large founts hold Five Pints, and small founts hold over one quart.
9. It costs less and gives more than double the light of the Student Lamp.

TOWNSHIP AND COUNTY AGENTS WANTED.

☞ Liberal discounts to the trade.

Electric Lamp and Stove Company,
808 Pine Street, St. Louis, Mo.

Advertisement, *Pottery and Glassware Reporter,* May 20, 1886.

The Electric Lamp and Stove Company, 808 Pine Street, St. Louis, advertised the Improved Electric Lamp in 1886. The ad indicates the lamp was fomerly the Casperson (Electric).

W. P. Casperson, of Chicago, Illinois, was granted patent No. 296,522, which seems to be identical with David J. Braun's Improved Mason-Electric Lamp. I do not know the relationship between David Braun and W. P. Casperson.

Trade Names

Center-draft lamps — Marsh Electric, Casperson Electric, Improved Electric, David J. Braun's Improved Mason-Electric.

Selected Patents, Center-draft Lamps

William P. Casperson

1883	282,958
1884	296,522

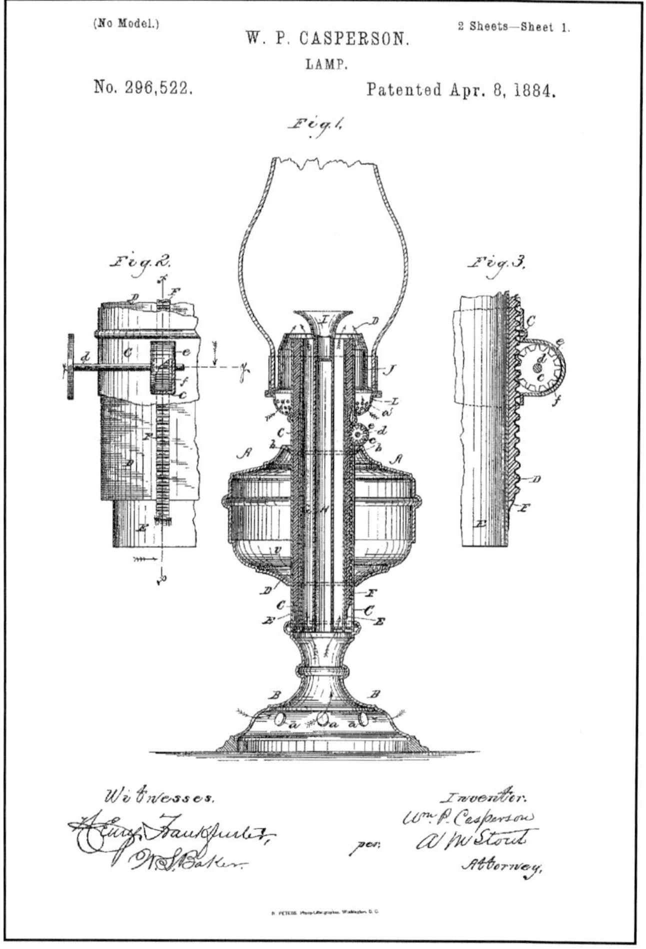

Standard Lighting Company

ca. 1884 – Early 1900s

The Standard Lighting Company, of Cleveland, Ohio, advertised No. 2 and No. 3 Globe-Incandescent lamps. The fount and burner were primarily sold for "New Process" heaters and a mammoth hanging lamp. However, the fount was also fitted into decorative cast-metal stands and sold for table use. Some stands to use lamps on the table were a modified heater base. The table and banquet lamps were large due to the sizes of the founts and burners.

The company advertised its Incandescent lamp as "the original large coal oil lamp," holding oil for eight hours of burning. Large catalogs, published from the mid-1880s to late 1890s, illustrated vapor street lights, wall torches, and an increasing number of New Process stoves and ranges. It seems the company first produced lamps and torches, branching into cooking ovens, heaters, and more elaborate stoves about 1897.

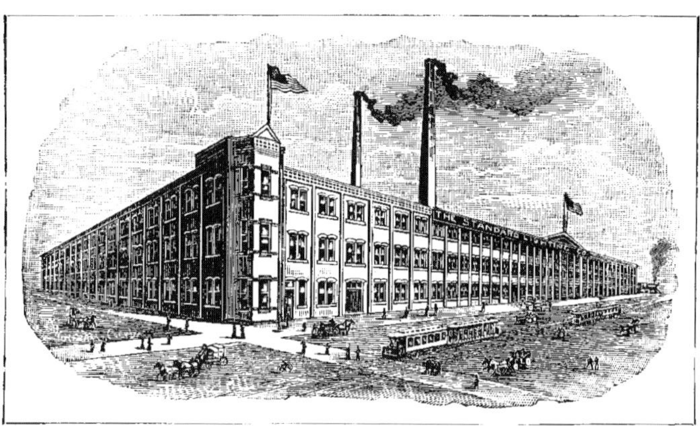

OFFICE AND WORKS, PERKINS AVENUE.

The covers of the 1896 and 1897 catalogs were titled *"New Process" Blue Flame Oil Stoves Manufactured by the Standard Lighting Co.* The company advertised its products as "Electric," "Blue Flame," and "Incandescent."

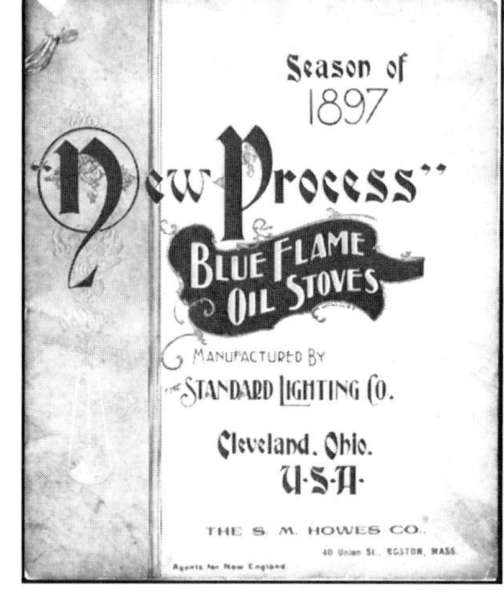

Advertisements claimed sales of 175,000 Globe Incandescent lamps by 1890.

The company changed its name from the Standard Lighting Company to New Process Lighting Co. about 1900. Thomas J. Little, Jr., assigned patents to the company for gas lighting improvements in 1902. Little went on to assign patents for city gas lamps to the Welsbach Light Company, Gloucester, New Jersey, after 1909.

The Luminous hanging lamp, advertised in 1892, is identical to the Globe Incandescent lamp. None of the founts seen by this author have carried patent dates.

Trademarks

"Globe Incandescent" was trademarked on Oct. 29, 1889, for coal oil lamps, lanterns, and chimneys.

Trade Names

Center-draft lamps — Mammoth Globe Incandescent, Globe Incandescent, Luminous, House lamp.

Heaters and stoves — New Process, Vigil, Blue Flame oil stoves.

No. 2 Globe-Incandescent Lamp.

320 CANDLE POWER!

The Cheapest and Best Coal Oil Lamp

FOR THE MONEY,

IN THE WORLD.

For Universal Lighting

Convertible, and Adapted to be used

EITHER AS A

Hanging or Stand Lamp.

NEEDED IN EVERY HOME!

The most agreeable and satisfactory **LIBRARY** and **DINING ROOM LAMP** made. Also especially intended for lighting

Stores, Offices, Halls, Churches, Factories, Billiard Rooms, Railroad Stations, Restaurants, and ALL

Large Areas where a

Powerful, Steady, Economical

Illumination is desired.

THE WICK, 9½ inches in circumference, is raised from **below, without Ratchets or Rollers.** A positive motion, and no **Sticking, Binding or Catching;** the best and most **reliable** wick movement ever used in a lamp; always in order and will last indefinitely; burns 3 inches of wick without re-wicking—so simple it can be done by a child.

WICK will last six months without attention; does not char and break. Lamp is **Absolutely** safe. **RESERVOIR does NOT GET HOT**—holds enough for eight hours burning, brilliantly illuminating an area of **Thirty-five Feet Square,** and costing **less than one penny an hour.**

CHIMNEYS are made of a special glass and **not liable to break nor melt with the heat.**

Fitted with our **Duplex Spreader Plate** this lamp makes a regenerative, **ODORLESS** flame—the whitest and handsomest ever produced.

Finished in polished brass, and is **Strong** and **Substantially** made

FOR THE MILLION

and the million **Will Take It,** as it is the cheapest Coal Oil Lamp ever offered and comes within the reach of all. Full Directions for Re-wicking, using and caring for it sent with each Lamp.

RETAIL PRICE.

Including Globe, 15 In. Tin Reflector, Harp, Wick and Smoke-Bell, ready for Use, – *$6.00*

Sent to any address, on receipt of price, or C. O. D.

INQUIRE FOR IT! INVESTIGATE IT!! BUY IT!!!

Price Lists, with full particulars, Cuts, Lithographs, etc., furnished on application.

Henry & Nathan Russell & Day, Agts., Importers & Exporters of GLASSWARE & LAMP FIXTURES, No. 42 Barclay St. New York.

Broadside advertisement.

Courtesy Catherine Thuro.

Selected Patents, Center-draft Lamps

Willoughby F. Kistler assigned to Standard Lighting

1887	372,626
1889	408,592 (unassigned)

Zebulon Davis unassigned

1886	342,584
1888	387,864-65
1889	408,591
1889	408,592
1889	415,502

Flame spreaders for No. 2 hanging lamp founts have steel tops. Left marked "Made by the Standard Lighting Co., Cleveland, O, U. S. A."

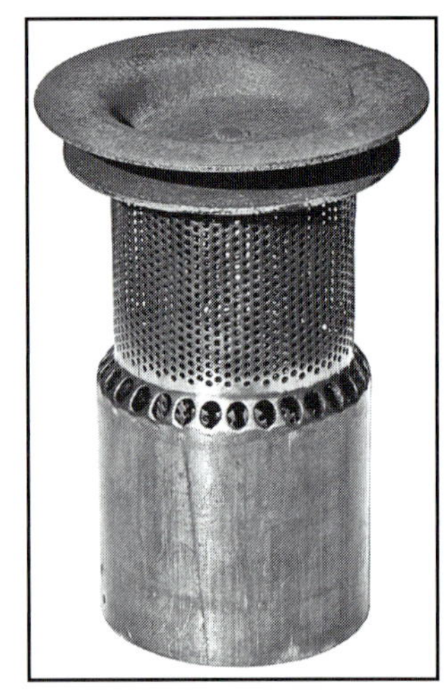

Flame spreader with "Duplex spreader plate."

Oil fill cap.

Globe Incandescent No. 2 hanging lamp fount. Height 12". Flame spreader marked on top. Oil fill cap unmarked. $100.00.

Globe Incandescent Lamp

Standard Lighting catalog, 1899.

Oil fill cap.

Globe Incandescent No. 2 hanging lamp fount. Height 13½". Long flame spreader unmarked. Oil fill cap marked (above). Bottom plate is signed. $100.00. Courtesy Bill Schreiber.

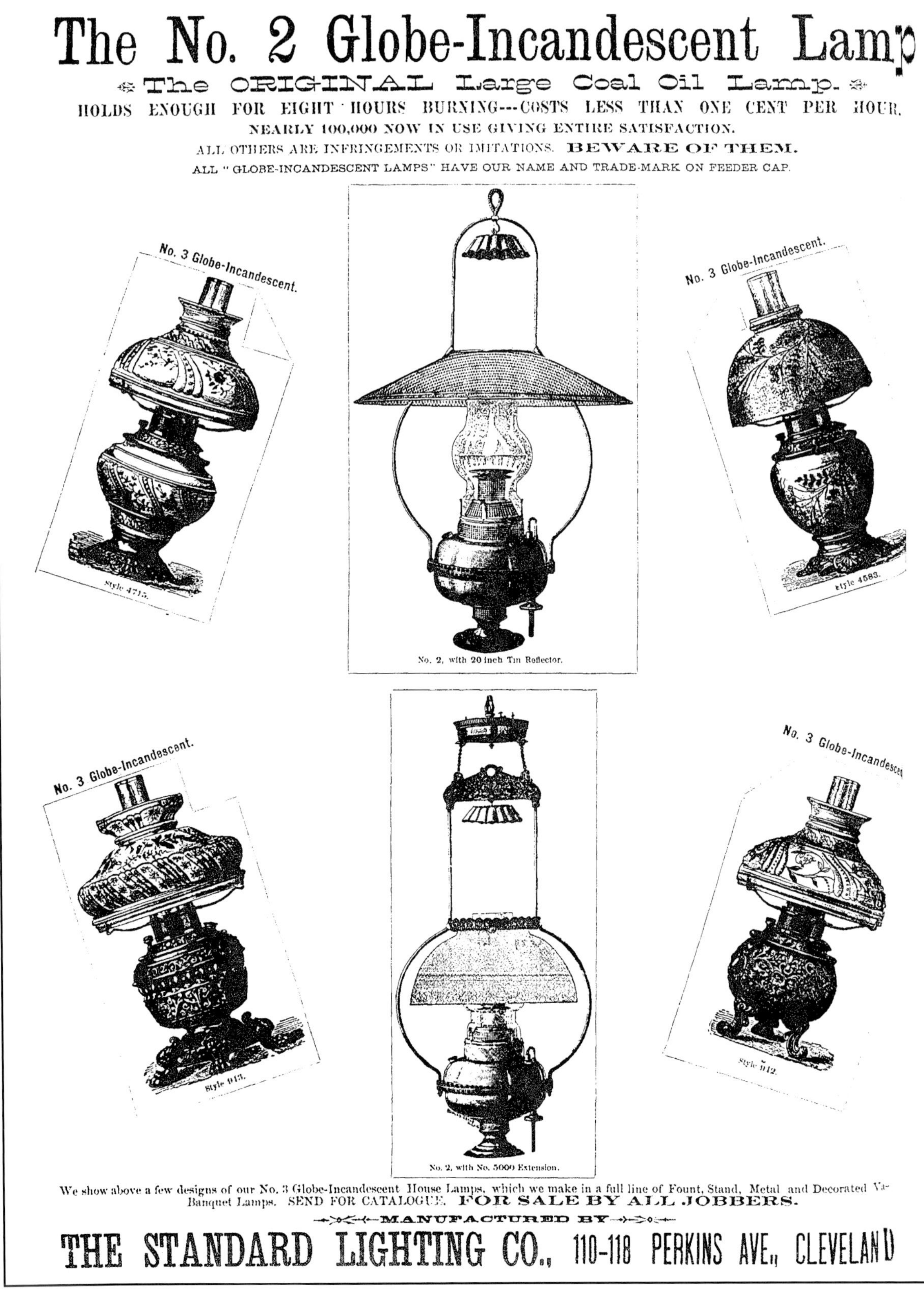

Advertisement, the *Pottery and Glassware Reporter,* Sept. 26, 1889. The vase lamps illustrated were fitted with "No. 3" Globe Incandescent burners and were called House lamps. Parlor lamps were also fitted with "No. 3" burners, which appear to be oil pots and burners made by the Pittsburgh Brass Company.

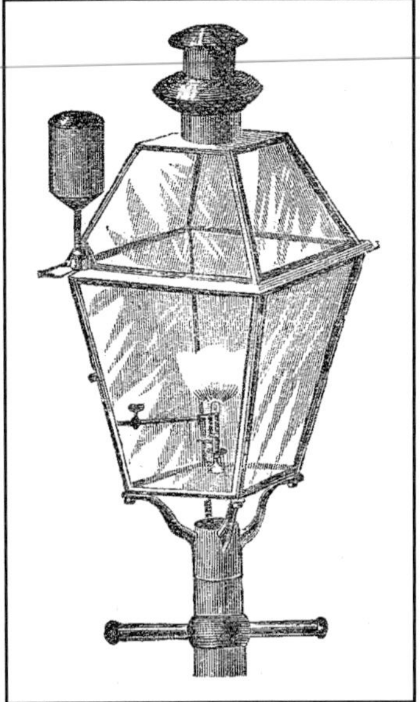

Globe Incandescent vapor street light.

"THE GLOBE-INCANDESCENT LAMP."

A LARGE ECONOMICAL LIGHT

FOR UNIVERSAL USE.

A Coal-Oil Burner Having 400 Candle Power.

PRODUCES A SOFT, STEADY, GOLDEN ILLUMINATION.

WITHOUT THE TRYING EFFECT OF THE ELECTRIC LIGHT.

The Wick is *TWELVE INCHES* in circumference, and is raised and lowered by a simple vertical movement—*WITHOUT RATCHET OR ROLLERS*—which insures a positive, even action, necessary to produce a bright, smokeless flame.

The Reservoir, which is made on the Student Lamp principle, holds six quarts of oil, and will supply the burner SIXTEEN HOURS, producing from common coal oil a light that will brilliantly illuminate a room *FIFTY FEET SQUARE.*

The flame can be extinguished as easily as gas, without removing the globe. It produces *LESS HEAT* than would the number of gas jets or small lamps necessary to furnish the same amount of illumination; offers the convenience of but *ONE RESERVOIR* to fill, and as it is provided with a large globe, dispenses with the *ANNOYANCE* of chimneys to clean.

It is intended for lighting ***Store Rooms, Halls, Churches, Hotel Offices and Dining Rooms, Restaurants, Saloons, Billiard Rooms, Factories,*** and all large inside rooms. Is *MUCH MORE* economical than electricity or gas, and produces a light *GREATLY SUPERIOR* to either.

Our Lamps are made of Brass, *HANDSOMELY FINISHED AND GUARANTEED* to operate *PERFECTLY.*

In ordering, always give height of ceiling.

ILLINOIS STREET-GAS CO.,
195 & 197 Michigan Street, Chicago.

Be Your Own Lighting Company.

ILLINOIS STREET-GAS CO., CHICAGO.

400 CANDLE POWER. 10 CENTS PER NIGHT.

THE GLOBE-INCANDESCENT LAMP.

Globe Incandescent lamp advertised by the Illinois Street-Gas Company 1895 – 1900 appears to be patent 342,584. Courtesy Leonard Gutekunst and Fil Graff.

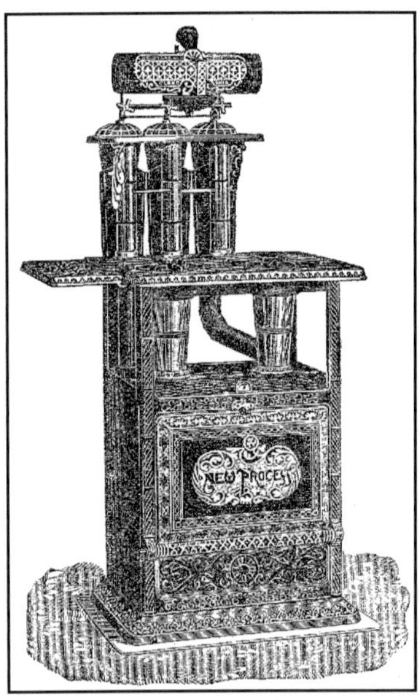

Globe Incandescent cabinet range with oven, 1894 catalog. In 1894, the company published a 250-page *New Process Catalog and Cook Book* which featured New Process kerosene and gas ranges. The cookbook included 20 catalog pages of stoves and lamps.

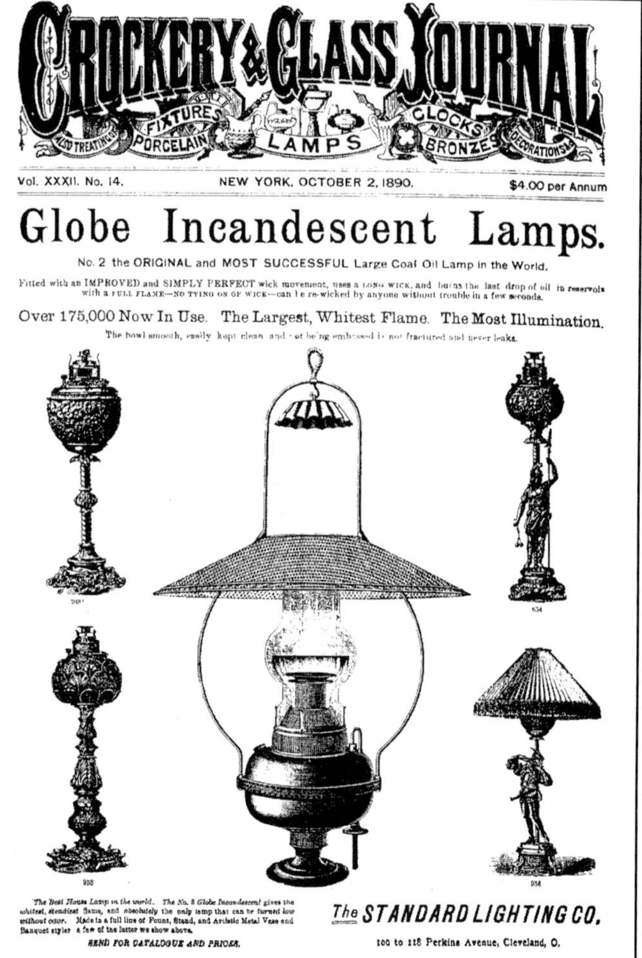

CROCKERY & GLASS JOURNAL

FIXTURES · PORCELAIN · LAMPS · CLOCKS · BRONZES

Vol. XXXII. No. 14. NEW YORK, OCTOBER 2, 1890. $4.00 per Annum

Globe Incandescent Lamps.

No. 2 the ORIGINAL and MOST SUCCESSFUL Large Coal Oil Lamp in the World.

Fitted with an IMPROVED and SIMPLY PERFECT wick movement, uses a LONG WICK, and burns the last drop of oil in reservoir with a FULL FLAME—NO TYING ON OF WICK—can be re-wicked by anyone without trouble in a few seconds.

Over 175,000 Now In Use. The Largest, Whitest Flame. The Most Illumination.

The bowl smooth, easily kept clean and not being embossed is not fractured and never leaks.

The Best House Lamp in the world. The No. 2 Globe Incandescent gives the *whitest, steadiest* flame, and *absolutely* the only lamp that can be turned *low without odor.* Made in a full line of Fount, Stand, and Artistic Metal Vase and Banquet styles a few of the latter we show above.

SEND FOR CATALOGUE AND PRICES.

The STANDARD LIGHTING CO.

100 to 118 Perkins Avenue, Cleveland, O.

Standard Lighting Company House lamp fitted with No. 3 Globe Incandescent center-draft burner and oil pot. These oil pots (also in the banquet lamps illustrated right) are standard 5" pots.

New Process Oil Heaters

NOVEMBER, 1894

THE WONDERFUL

"New Process" Oil Heater

$5.00

PLENTY OF HEAT AT A SMALL COST

Will heat a 20-ft. room comfortably in cold weather. Adapted for use in Bed-rooms, Bath-rooms, Dining-rooms, Offices, etc.

Convenient Economical Comfortable

The "New Process" Oil Heater makes a handsome furnishing for any room. Brass fount, nickel trimmed, Russia drum, with ornamental top which can be removed to use grate on top for cooking.

NO SOOT NO SMOKE NO ODOR

Simple Construction Easily Kept Clean

The "New Process" Oil Heater can be converted into our 300 candle power

Globe-Incandescent Lamp

The best in the world, by removing the drum, changing the spreader and placing the glass chimney in position.

Ask your dealer for the "New Process" Oil Heater. If he does not keep it get him to order it for you or send us your order direct. CIRCULAR SENT FREE.

THE STANDARD LIGHTING CO.
400 Perkins Ave., Cleveland, Ohio

Ladies' Home Journal, November 1894.

New Process Oil Heater, 1898.

Advertisements for Vigil lamp and stove (above) and torches (below) in flyer with 1899 catalog.

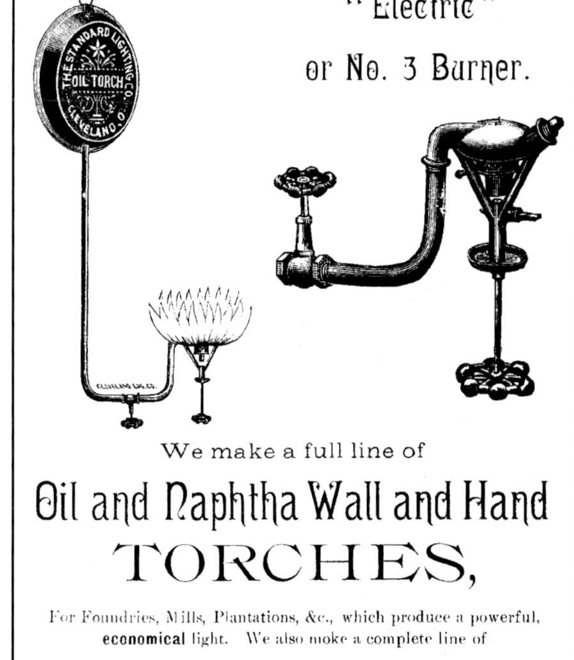

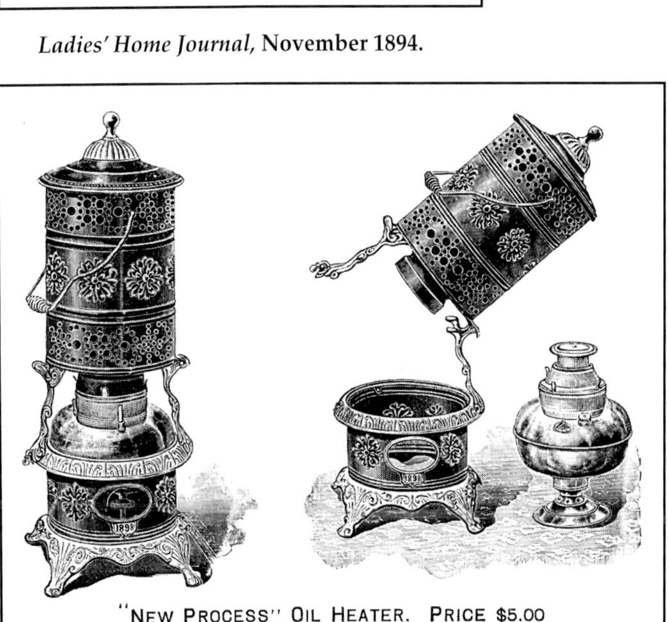

"NEW PROCESS" OIL HEATER. PRICE $5.00

New Process oil heater, 1899 catalog.

Standard Oil Company

Mei Foo, Perfection, and Rayo Lamps, ca. 1893 – 1950

Prior to 1911, Standard Oil Company was primarily in the kerosene fuel business. Selling lamps, heaters, and stoves promoted kerosene sales.

In 1859, John D. Rockefeller, age 19, entered business with Maurice Clark as Clark and Rockefeller, a trading company in Cleveland, Ohio. The company specialized in fish, meat, grain, farm implements, salt, and other commodities. Cleveland was an oil refining and shipping center with excellent railroad connections and shipping on the Great Lakes.

Andrews, Clark and Company was formed in 1863 with Samuel Andrews, an oil specialist. Rockefeller was the "Company." The business grew rapidly, and Rockefeller and his associates incorporated Standard Oil Company in 1870 with stock valued at $1 million. They bought refineries, pipelines, and other oil businesses around Cleveland.

In 1882 Standard Oil Trust was the largest company in the oil industry, controlling some 90 percent of U.S. refineries. The trust was dissolved by the Ohio Supreme Court in 1892. The companies were reorganized as Standard Oil of New Jersey (a holding company) in 1899, only to be declared in violation of the Sherman Antitrust Act by the U.S. Supreme Court in 1911.

During the early years, the primary business of Standard Oil was distillation of kerosene for light and heat. The company exported 85 percent of its kerosene in 1899. Sales of kerosene peaked in 1903. Naphtha and gasoline products did not surpass kerosene until 1911.

The company promoted its own brands; stressed uniformity, safety, and quality of product; and sold stoves, heaters, ovens, lamps, and lanterns. These items were sold at low prices to promote sales of kerosene.

Advertisement, *Munsey's Magazine,* March 1910. Standard Oil claimed 3,000,000 Rayo lamps were in use.

> **World's Fair**
>
> The Standard Oil Co. have a line of fancy lamps and silk shades in the upper gallery of the mines and mining department, and they help to show the effect of their principal product, kerosene oil.
>
> *China, Glass and Lamps*, Aug. 9, 1893

The name *Standard* in *Standard Oil* was selected by Rockefeller as an international brand to promote company standards in chimneys, wicks, and burners for flat-wick lamps.

The Pitkin and Brooks catalog, in 1898, stated that "Standard Oil buys Belgian lamps from us." This notice clearly established sales of center-draft lamps, by Standard Oil, eight years before the Rayo. I suspect that Standard Oil also bought lamps from Edward Miller & Co., Plume & Atwood, and Bradley & Hubbard for resale from 1893 to 1906. Standard Oil sold flat-wick lamps as well as center-draft lamps. We know that in 1902, Standard Oil sold 485,000 kerosene burning units, of which one-half were lamps and obviously not the Rayo brand.

Sales of Standard Oil kerosene averaged slightly over 10 million barrels (420 million gallons) each year from 1900 through 1911. During this period, naphtha and gasoline sales increased from 3.5 million barrels to surpass sales of kerosene. Refining in 1911 was described more as a skill than a science.

As sales of kerosene for use in lamps peaked, Standard Oil promoted domestic use for lanterns, stoves, and heaters. Bulk delivery wagons and railroad tank cars increased markets in rural states.

In addition to its primary use as fuel, Standard Oil encouraged "new ways" to use Perfection kerosene oil in the home — removing blood stains from clothing; cleaning bath tubs, sinks, and stoves; protecting screens from rust; cleaning windows; removing grass stains from delicate fabrics; and repelling wood insects and beetles. On the farm it could be used in a spray to kill chicken lice or used to destroy mosquito larva in stagnant pools, to remove grease and carbon, to polish windshields (mixed with six parts water), and to clean parts when overhauling motors.

Mei Foo

Socony (Standard Oil Company of New York) began selling kerosene in China in 1893, when the company was known as Vacuum Oil. The name Mei Foo was adopted for a small hand lamp, Chinese red in color with a broad base for stability. The name translated to "beautiful and trustworthy" or "beautiful companion."

Socony correctly envisioned the huge market of 400 million people in China. The Mei Foo lamp cost the equivalent of one day's wages and was at first given away to replace candles and poor homemade light sources.

Kerosene was shipped in five-gallon cans by clipper ship to China. Socony opened a glass factory in Shanghai in 1922 producing 1.5 million chimneys the first year, and 4 million in 1924.

The story of "big oil" and Mei Foo lamps was written by Alice Tisdale Hobart (1933) in her novel, *Oil for the Lamps of China*. She claimed her writing not to be history but rather "a composite of my experiences, observations and reflections during a life spent in China..." I believe much in her book to be based on factual experience.

According to Hobart, the Chinese did not completely trust the "Keepers of Light Company" — a company that could not have been more Western but looked Eastern. Socony was successful selling light to families on the edge of starvation as their first means of improving their existence.

Mei Foo lamp distributed in China in the 1890s. "If a person wishes to have luck, longevity, health and peace, he or she must live in a world of light." Howard Eastland said the little lamp translates as "beautiful and good." The lamp is 3¼" bottom diameter. $75.00. Photograph courtesy ExxonMobil Corporation, Irving, Texas.

Standard Oil played out similar marketing strategy in the United States, promoting the Perfection heaters and lamps and Rayo lamps and lanterns which provided light and heat to millions of families, all the while consuming gallons of kerosene in the process.

The Perfection

The Cleveland Foundry produced portable oil heaters beginning about 1894. It named its stoves and heaters "Perfection" in 1901 when Standard Oil began selling them. The Cleveland Foundry changed its name to Cleveland Metal Products in 1917 and again to Perfection Stove Company in 1925.

Standard Oil exhibited lamps, wicks, and heaters at the St. Louis World's Fair in 1904. At that time I believe, but have not confirmed, that Standard Oil introduced the Perfection lamp. These lamps were Bradley & Hubbard's newly introduced 1904 lamps. Until this time Standard Oil sold the B & H along with Belgian and other brands. Standard Oil decided to create its own brand for marketing purposes. The Perfection lamp was sold for a short time before the Rayo trademark was selected in 1906. Use of the name Perfection by the Cleveland Foundry for heaters and by the Manhattan Brass Company for Perfection student lamps may have been factors causing Standard Oil to change the brand name.

The Rayo

In 1906, the lamps purchased from Bradley & Hubbard were trademarked "Rayo" by Standard Oil. The Rayo lamp provided light for homes, farms, and stores for many years before electric lines came into rural areas. The lamp was said to "give a soft, clear, steady light — very restful to the eyes." The burner was "simple in construction and easy to re-wick and keep clean."

Standard Oil Company promoted sales of its petroleum products to expand its markets by investing in manufacturing companies and marketing stoves, heaters, lamps, and lanterns that used kerosene. Standard Oil trustees organized the American Wick Manufacturing Company in 1893 to make wicks for lamps and stoves. Existing wicks at the time were said to be of poor and variable quality.

Heaters and lamps were sold to low-income families at a low profit margin. Tank peddlers switched from five-gallon cans to one-gallon cans which were easier to refill and handle when filling lamps. According to SO historians (Hidy, 1955), tank-wagon drivers used tricks of the trade to sell Standard Oil kerosene, such as using an old lamp chimney to compare SO kerosene with a new chimney for the competitor's oil. New chimneys smoked up more quickly than old ones.

Rayo lamps were widely sold through hardware stores and mail-order catalogs from the 1920s into the 1950s.

Rayo branded lanterns, made by several manufacturers, were sold for railroad, marine, automobile, and hot-and-cold blast farm use. A Rayo barn lamp is scarce to find today.

Special mantle burners were imported in 1908 and 1909 to convert the Rayo to an incandescent mantle lamp. Montgomery Ward

How You Will Enjoy Reading by the Rayo Lamp

For Best Results Use Perfection Oil

No tired eyes or eye strain from its soft yet brilliant, steady glow, which floods the center table so that all the family has a *good light* by which to read, sew or study.

Experts everywhere agree that the light given by a kerosene lamp is best for the eyes.

3,000,000 middle western homes say there is no lamp like the RAYO—that it gives the most satisfactory light in either city or country homes. Ask your dealer for demonstration. Illustrated booklet on request. (245)

STANDARD OIL COMPANY (AN INDIANA CORPORATION) **Chicago, Illinois**

Advertisement, *20th Century Farmer Magazine*, 1915.

The elephant trademark was registered by Standard Oil of New York on Dec. 22, 1896.

STANDARD OIL COMPANY,
26 Broadway, NEW YORK.

HIGHEST AWARD FOR

LAMP, STOVE and TORCH WICKS,

AT COLUMBIAN EXPOSITION.

Advertisement, *China, Glass and Lamps*, Aug. 12, 1896.

sold a re-engineered "Rayo" mantle lamp from 1939 to 1941. The Ward lamps were not marked or otherwise identified as Rayo.

Trade Names

Center-draft lamps — Perfection, Rayo, KYSO (sold by Standard Oil of Kentucky, see Edward Miller & Company).

Flat-wick lamps — Mei Foo, House Lamp, Sterling.

Flat-wick burners — Queen Anne, Victor (these burners are marked "Rayo" or "Socony"), Sterling.

Lanterns — Rayo.

Heaters & stoves — Perfection, Perfection Junior, New Perfection, New Perfection Junior, Perfection Smokeless.

Standard Oil created many descriptive brand names for their heating and lighting fuels. These included Pratt's Astral Oil, Elaine, Eocene, Eupion, Radiant, Brilliant, Peerless, Silver Light, Tea Rose, Day-Light (Dec. 22, 1896; used since 1870), Gas-Light (Dec. 22, 1896; used since 1870), Family Safety Oil, Victoria (Jan. 19, 1897; used since 1881), Comet (Sept. 14, 1897; used since 1876), Aladdin Security Oil (ca. 1898), Aladdin Oil (Feb. 20, 1912, by West India Company; used since 1902), Perfection and Royal Daylight. Many of these names were in use since the early 1870s, even though official trademarks were not filed and granted until much later. Many foreign trade names were trademarked as well.

Household delivery of kerosene by wagon.

Trademarks

The familiar Rayo trademark was published in the *Official Gazette*, U.S. Patent Office, on October 2, 1906, by Standard Oil Company, Bayonne, New Jersey, "for use on oil lamps and heating, lighting, and ventilating apparatus." Many of the trade names for illuminating oils, listed above, were also trademarked. Many others, not listed here, were granted to various Standard Oil companies around the world.

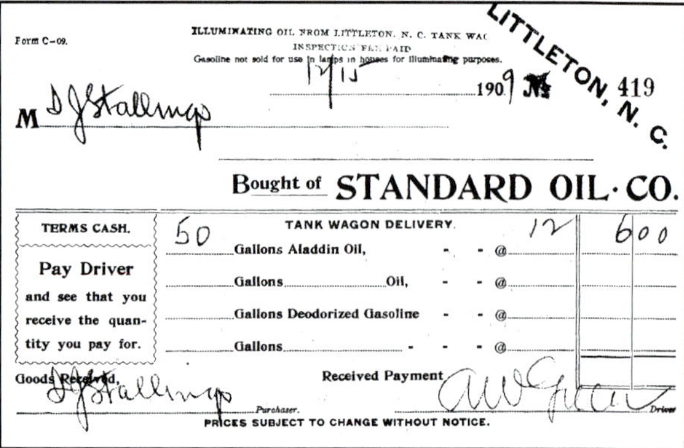

Form C-09.

ILLUMINATING OIL FROM LITTLETON, N. C. TANK WAGON

Gasoline not sold for use in lamps in houses for illuminating purposes.

LITTLETON, N. C.

1/1/1 1909 419

M D J Stallings

Bought of STANDARD OIL·CO.

TERMS CASH.	TANK WAGON DELIVERY		
Pay Driver and see that you receive the quantity you pay for.	50 Gallons Aladdin Oil, @	12	6 00
	Gallons ____ Oil, @		
	Gallons Deodorized Gasoline @		
	Gallons ____ @		

Goods Received, D J Stallings Purchaser. Received Payment A W Green Driver

PRICES SUBJECT TO CHANGE WITHOUT NOTICE.

Receipt for 50 gallons of Aladdin Oil, tank delivery. The cost from Standard Oil was 12¢ per gallon in 1909.

Perfection Lamps, 1904 and 1905

I believe Standard Oil introduced the Perfection lamp at the St. Louis Exposition in 1904. The Perfection Lamps are virtually the same as Bradley & Hubbard's 1904 and 1905 lamps. The wick carrier is patent 783,799 by William Penfield, applied for Dec. 30, 1904, and granted Feb. 28, 1905.

Perfection flame spreader dated 1904 and marked "Pat'd Nov. 20, 94. Mar 24, 96." Replacement flame spreaders with Feb. 28, 1905 patent date are also found in both 1904 and 1905 Perfection lamps.

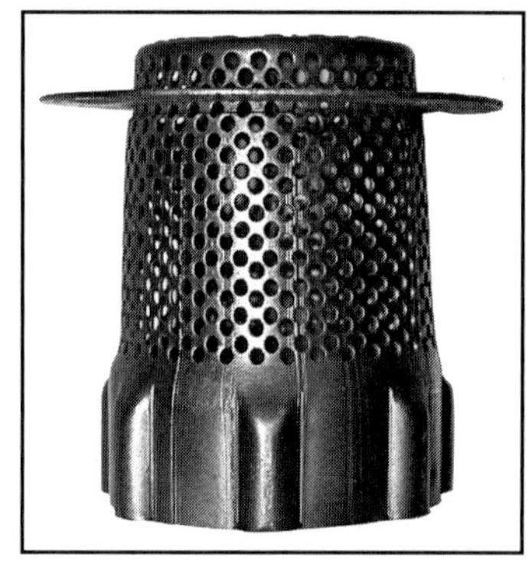

Perfection flame spreader dated 1905 and marked "Pat'd. Nov. 20, 94. Mar. 24, 96."

Perfection oil fill cap.

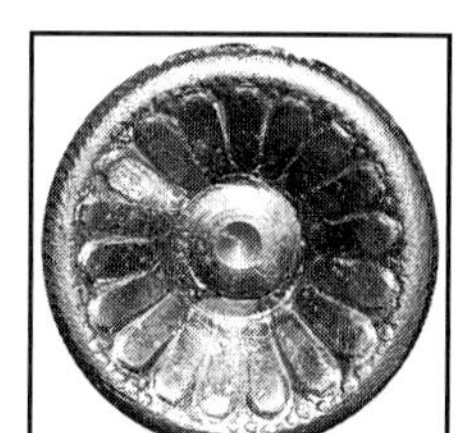

Perfection wick knob.

Perfection stand lamp, 1904. Height 12". The gallery does not lift. Some burners unscrew at the base of the burner basket (arrow). $50.00.

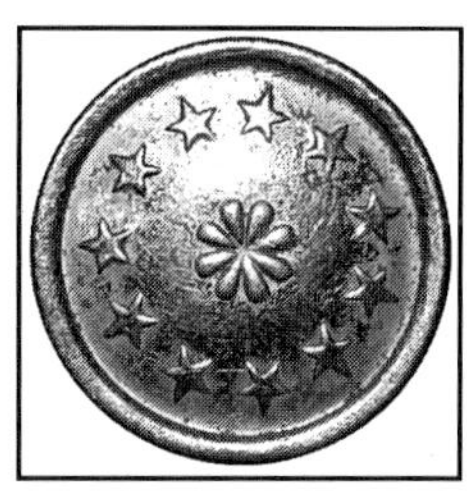

Oil fill cap often found on Perfection lamps.

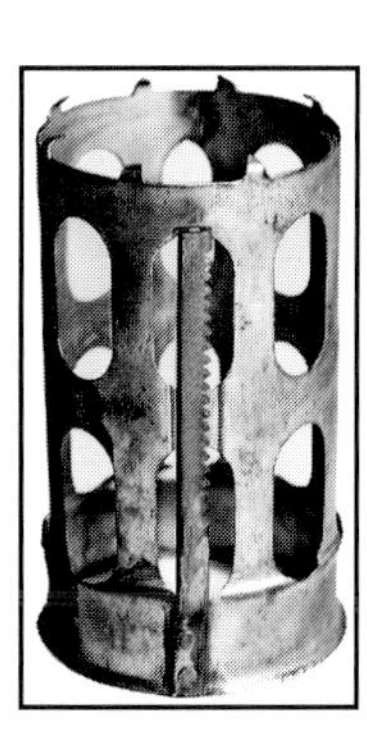

Wick carrier.

Perfection stand lamp, 1905, with B & H patent lift gallery for lighting. Height 12". $50.00.

Rayo Lamps 1906 – 1940 and Later

The Rayo trademark was approved Oct. 2, 1906. Read The Rayo Book by Fil Graff (2002) for more information and evolution of these burners. Standard Oil Company sold millions of lamps and made the Rayo famous worldwide.

Rayo flame spreader marked "Pat'd Nov. 20, 94, Mar. 24, 96, Feb. 28, 05."

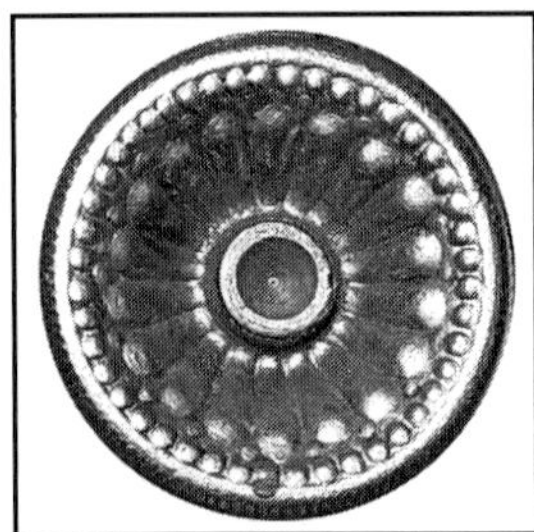

Rayo wick knob.

Rayo oil fill cap.

Rayo stand lamp with early burner and "spade" foot. Height 12". Some burners do not have lift gallery and unscrew at the base of the burner basket. $50.00.

Rayo stand lamp with spade foot. Height 12". Gallery marked "Patd Dec. 21, 1895." This burner was first made with a narrow gallery base that fit into the burner base (not shown here). $50.00 – 75.00.

Rayo stand lamp with slot foot. Height 12". Gallery marked "Patd Dec. 21, 1895." $50.00 – 75.00.

Socony Rayo

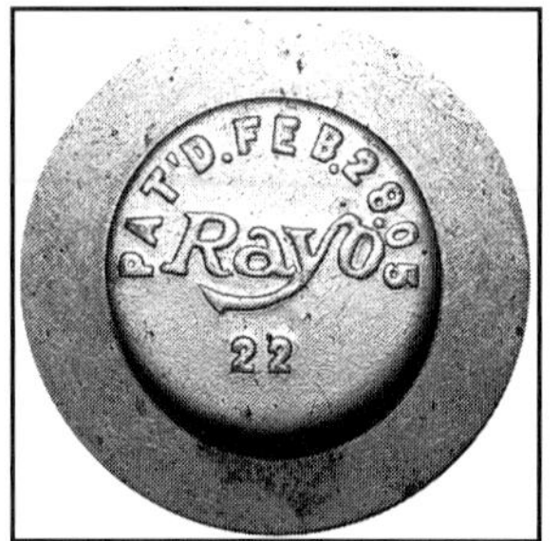

Socony Rayo flame spreaders.

Junior Rayo

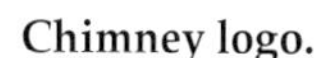

Chimney logo.

Junior Rayo flame spreader.

Socony Rayo oil fill cap.

Junior Rayo oil fill cap.

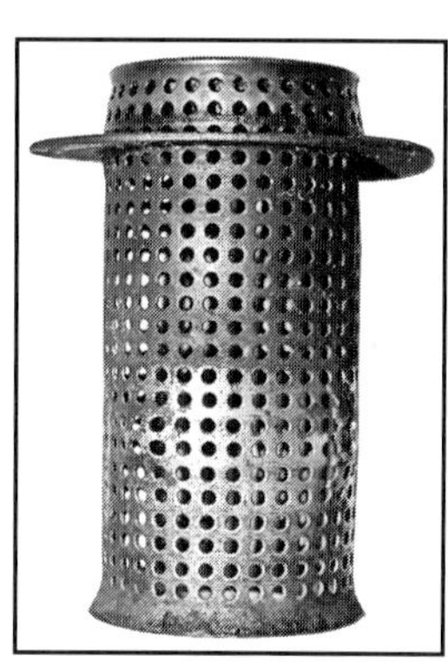

Socony Rayo stand lamp. Height 12". Gallery not dated. Tripod found on lamp marked "Patent Pending." $75.00.

Junior Rayo stand lamp. Gallery marked "Patd Nov. 20, 1894, Dec. 31, 1895, Feb. 28, 1895." Height 10½". $150.00.

Standard Illuminants and Trademarks

Standard Oil created descriptive brand names for its heating and lighting fuels. These included Pratt's Astral Oil, Elaine, Eocene, Eupion, Radiant, Brilliant, Peerless, Silver Light, Tea Rose, Day-Light (Dec. 22, 1896; used since 1870), Gas-Light (Dec. 22, 1896; used since 1870), Family Safety Oil, Victoria (Jan. 19, 1897; used since 1881), Comet (Sept. 14, 1897; used since 1876), Aladdin Security Oil (ca. 1898), Aladdin Oil (Feb. 20, 1912, by West India Company; used since 1902), Perfection, and Royal Daylight. Many of these names were in use since the early 1870s, even though official trademarks were not filed and granted until much later.

Cover of undated advertising brochure.

X-RAY BURNING OIL.

We do not make a business of selling burning oil, but if some of our customers want it, we will furnish them with a bright 150° Water White Pennsylvania Oil, 49° gravity. Guaranteed not to smoke or char the wick and not to give out the disagreeable odor so common to most of burning oils. This oil, while it retails for a few cents more than the ordinary grades, is nevertheless much more economical in actual use, as one lamp filled with it will give as much illumination as two similar lamps will give, filled with the cheap article. Besides, the light is whiter and softer, and does not injure the eyes. The wick never becomes clogged, and the lamp remains clean and free from gum or grease. A lamp filled with the ordinary oil will frequently go out when only half empty. Every drop of this oil will be consumed without affecting the quality of the light. To those wanting a high grade perfect illuminant, we especially recommend this oil.

The above catalog information explains a lamp fuel product made by the Commercial Oil Co., Cleveland, Ohio. The catalog is undated and estimated as early 1900s. I do not know if Standard Oil owned all or part of this company.

Brass tag bearing Victoria trademark granted Jan. 19, 1897; used since 1881. "Victoria Illuminating Oil Prepared Expressly for Use in the Australian Colonies."

Felt lamp pad to protect the table. These Aladdin branded products were not related to the Mantle Lamp Company of America and its famous Aladdin lamp. Courtesy Dave Ostblom.

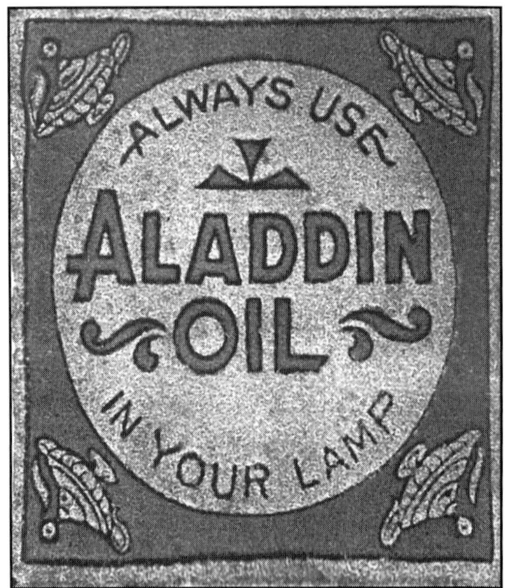

Felt pad to protect table. The Aladdin Oil trademark was granted to the West India Company on Feb. 20, 1912; it had been used since 1902. Photograph courtesy of Dave Ostblom.

Standardization of Wicks, American Wicks — 1907

Flat-lamp wicks and stove and heater wicks for 1907 were also included in this Standard Oil brochure.

IMPORTANT CHANGES

SPECIAL NET PRICES quoted on

AMERICAN WICKS

JULY 15th 1907

STANDARD OIL CO. OF N. Y.

ALBANY, = = N. Y.

MIDDLETOWN, N. Y. | UTICA, N. Y.
BINGHAMTON, " | SYRACUSE, "
POTSDAM, = = = N. Y.

WE DO NOT BREAK ORIGINAL PACKAGES

This list shows LIST PRICES and THE NET PRICES per Gross after deducting a discount of

60 & 10 %

WE INVOICE AT NET PRICES

WHEN SENDING ORDERS for Wicks of Unknown Name or Number, if possible, send sample

PRICES SUBJECT TO CHANGE WITHOUT NOTICE

CIRCULAR-LAMP WICKS

ALPHABETICALLY ARRANGED

NAME OF WICK	Quan. in Pakgs.	PER GROSS List Price	PER GROSS Net Price
Acme Circular,	1 Doz.	$5.25	**$1.89**
Banner No. 1,	"	3.75	**1.35**
" " 2,	"	6.00	**2.16**
" " 3,	"	14.85	**5.34½**
B. & H. " 0, Slitted	"	3.00	**1.08**
" " 1, "	"	4.50	**1.62**
" " 2, "	"	9.00	**3.24**
" " 96, Mam. Slitted,	"	22.25	**8.01**
Bristol " 1,	"	3.00	**1.08**
" " 2,	"	9.00	**3.24**
" " 3,	"	18.00	**6.48**

CIRCULAR-LAMP WICKS

ALPHABETICALLY ARRANGED

NAME OF WICK	Quan. in Pakgs.	PER GROSS List Price	PER GROSS Net Price
Belgian No. 1,	1 Doz.	$9.00	**$3.24**
" " 00,	"	13.50	**4.86**
Circular Moehring, 6 inch long	1 Gross	4.50	**1.62**
" " 8 " "	"	6.00	**2.16**
Cleveland Student,	"	3.00	**1.08**
Dresden No. 1,	1 Doz.	6.75	**2.43**
" " 3,	"	13.50	**4.86**
Eureka (R. R. Lamp),	"	4.50	**1.62**
Electric No. 2,	"	7.50	**2.70**
Globe Incandescent No. 2,	"	17.00	**6.12**
Nos. 1 and 2, German Student	1 Gross	1.10	**.39½**
Keystone No. 1,	1 Doz.	3.25	**1.17**
Little Prince,	1 Gross	3.00	**1.08**
Liberty No. 1,	1 Doz.	9.00	**3.24**
" " 3,	"	13.50	**4.86**
Miller No. 0, Slitted	"	3.00	**1.08**
" " 1, "	"	4.50	**1.62**
" " 2, "	"	9.00	**3.24**
" " 3, "	"	22.25	**8.01**
Niagara No. 1,	"	16.50	**5.94**
" " 2,	"	30.00	**10.80**
Pett Circular,	1 Gross	.60	**.21½**
Plumwood No. 2,	1 Doz.	5.25	**1.89**
" " 3,	"	13.50	**4.86**
Perfection Student,	1 Gross	3.00	**1.08**
" " Mam.	"	4.50	**1.62**
Parker No. 1,	1 Doz.	3.75	**1.35**
" " 2, Slitted,	"	9.00	**3.24**
" " 2, not Slitted,	"	4.75	**1.71**
" " 3,	"	18.00	**6.48**
Round Fluid, per dozen 60c.	"		**.21½**
Rochester, Jr.,	1 Gross	3.00	**1.08**
" No. 1,	1 Doz.	3.75	**1.35**
" " 2 (Reg.),	"	5.25	**1.89**

CIRCULAR-LAMP WICKS

ALPHABETICALLY ARRANGED

NAME OF WICK	Quan. in Pakgs.	PER GROSS List Price	PER GROSS Net Price
Rochester, No. 2, 8 in. long	1 Doz.	$6.50	**$2.34**
" " 3,	"	18.00	**6.48**
" " 1, Slitted,	"	4.50	**1.62**
" " 2, "	"	6.00	**2.16**
" (New) Jr. (A special lamp)	1 Gross	3.00	**1.08**
" " No. 1 (A special lamp)	1 Doz.	4.50	**1.62**
" " " 2 (A special lamp)	"	9.00	**3.24**
" " " 3 (A special lamp)	"	22.25	**8.01**
Royal (P & A) No. 1,	"	3.75	**1.35**
" " " 2,	"	7.50	**2.70**
" " " 2, Slitted,	"	9.00	**3.24**
Rayo,	"	9.00	**3.24**
Radiant No. 4,	"	6.75	**2.43**
" " 5,	"	13.50	**4.86**
Success " 2,	"	7.50	**2.70**
Victoria R. R. Lamps,	"	4.50	**1.62**
Tom Thumb, Round,	1 Gross	.30	**.10¾**

Wicks and Chimneys

Advertisement, *McClure's Magazine,* 1898. Charles L. Marshall, Newark, New Jersey, held patents 595,884 (1897) and 632,903 (assigned to N.J. Wick Co., 1899) for improvements in lamp wicks. He was primarily interested in incandescent mantle lamps; however, his ads stress that his "Brown Wick" is used in all lamps and burners.

Lamp wick made in Canada by the Hamilton Cotton Co.

SoCo was a trademark of Standard Oil of Indiana and was registered Jan. 13, 1925; it was used since Feb. 1922. This mark is found on several brands of chimneys. Courtesy Fil Graff.

Roll of Socony lamp wick.
Courtesy Lou Hopf.

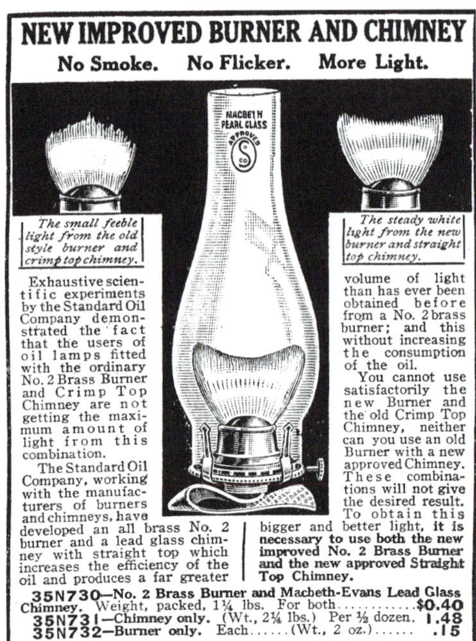

Sears-Roebuck catalog, 1923. See appendix for more information.

Familiar Rayo wick with box bearing NRA stamp.

PRESERVE THIS TAG.

In ordering Burners or Burner Parts for this lamp specify 1904.

DIRECTIONS FOR CARE.

For Best Results use Good Oil and "American" Wicks.

FILL EVERY DAY, being careful not to run the oil over.

KEEP ALL PARTS CLEAN. Empty Fount at least once a month.

TO LIGHT—Raise wick just above top of tube, remove chimney, apply the match, then replace chimney.

TO EXTINGUISH—Turn Wick down as far as it will go and light will flicker out.

KEEP WICK BELOW TOP OF TUBE when not lighted to prevent overflow of oil.

(OVER)

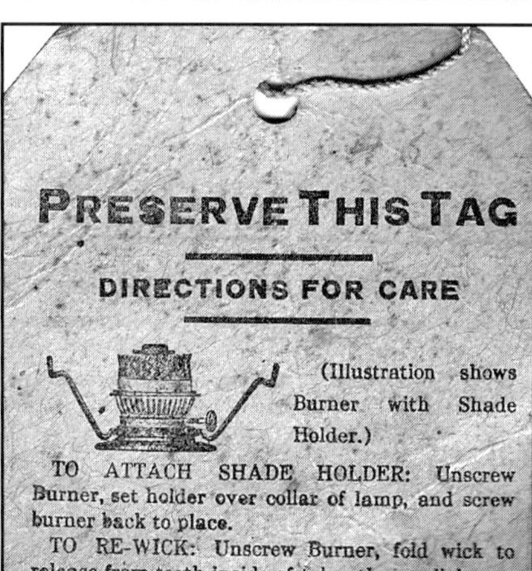

PRESERVE THIS TAG

DIRECTIONS FOR CARE

(Illustration shows Burner with Shade Holder.)

TO ATTACH SHADE HOLDER: Unscrew Burner, set holder over collar of lamp, and screw burner back to place.

TO RE-WICK: Unscrew Burner, fold wick to release from teeth inside of tube, then pull it out. Turn Wick Tube down far as it will go, fold new wick, put into burner tube from beneath evenly, having top about ⅝ of an inch below top of tube, fit smoothly to inside of tube so teeth will hold, slip it over lamp tube and screw on burner.

RE-WICK once in two months, if used every evening.

DO NOT CUT THE WICK, turn up so charred portion is exposed, rub off evenly from Left to Right.

(OVER)

PRESERVE THIS TAG

IN ORDERING BURNERS OR PARTS SPECIFY Rayo

DIRECTIONS FOR CARE

For Best Results use Good Oil and Rayo Wicks.

Fill every Day, being careful not to run the oil over.

Keep all Parts Clean. Empty Fount at least once a month.

To Light: Raise wick just above top of tube, Lift Chimney Holder, turn to the left, Light, and drop Holder back to place.

To Extinguish: Turn wick down as far as it will go.

Keep wick below top of tube when not lighted to prevent overflow of oil.

(OVER)

Tag, directions for care of the 1904 lamp.
Courtesy Doug and Judy Myers.

Tag, directions for care of the Rayo lamp.
Courtesy Jon Stratton.

Parts for Rayo Lamps

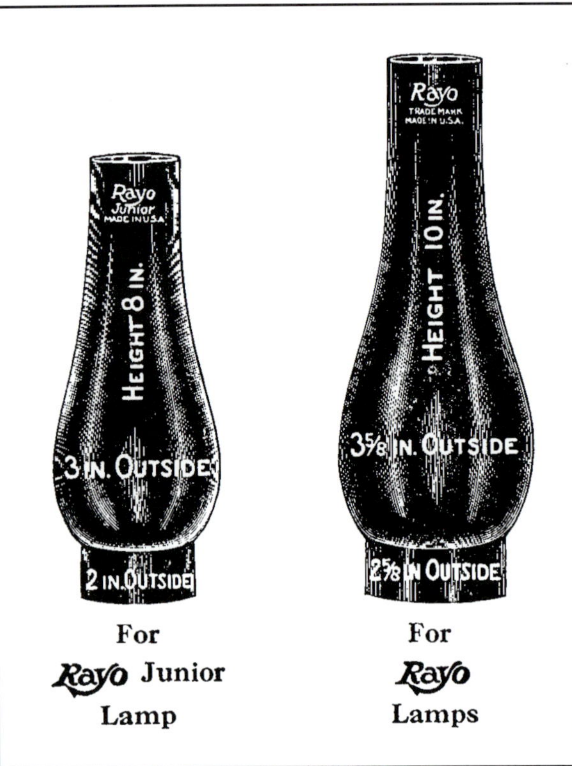

For Rayo Junior Lamp

For Rayo Lamps

Shades and Reflector for Rayo LAMPS

7-inch Opal Vienna Shade.

10-inch Opal Ring Top Dome Shade.

14-inch Opal Lip Top Dome Shade.

15-inch Tin Reflector.
Green outside, Bright inside.

Rayo LAMP BURNER.

Rayo
Is stamped on top of Flame Spreader.

Rayo JUNIOR LAMP BURNER.

Rayo JUNIOR
Is stamped on top of Flame Spreader.

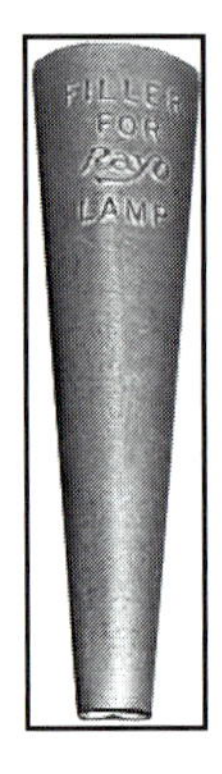

Filler for Rayo lamp.

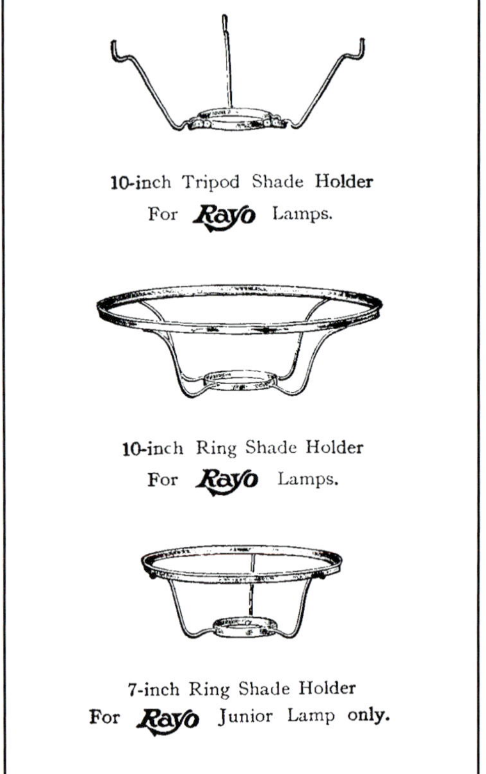

10-inch Tripod Shade Holder
For Rayo Lamps.

10-inch Ring Shade Holder
For Rayo Lamps.

7-inch Ring Shade Holder
For Rayo Junior Lamp only.

Oil Cans, Banquet Lamp

Can House, built of coal-oil cans, Tonopah, Nevada. Image from 1¢ domestic postcard.

"SOCONY" oil can. This trademark registered May 24, 1921; used since June 15, 1920. Courtesy C. Roger Paul.

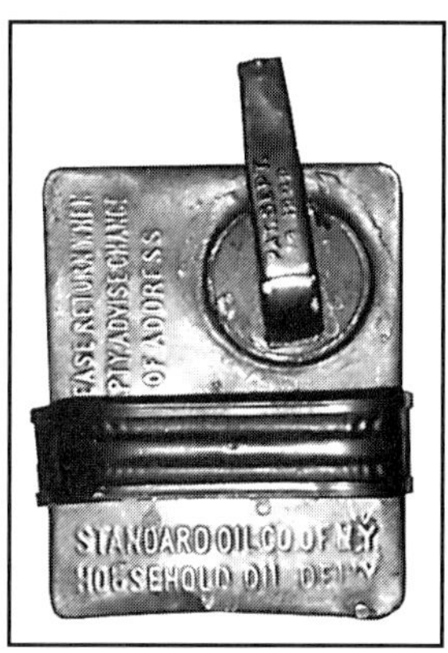

One gallon tin can for delivery of Household oil. Pat. Pending Sept. 1892. The trademark "SOCONY" was registered May 1, 1923; used since Feb. 26, 1908. Courtesy C. Roger Paul.

Advertisement, *20th Century Farmer Magazine*, 1915.

Rayo banquet lamp with decorative cast-iron base. The height 18" would help provide light promised in the ad (left). Found in nickel or brass plating. This lamp has worn brass plating. $125.00.

Heaters and Stoves

Aladdin Security Oil can, about 1898. Five gallons provided fuel for family use of stove, heater, and lamps. Courtesy John and Patricia Smith.

Fuel tank for Perfection heater with B & H lamp burner modified with Joseph Gregory patents 653,449 and 661,517 to limit smoke. The same patents were applied to Plume & Atwood "smokeless heaters." Courtesy Frank Wiedlocher.

Perfection junior cooking stove, marked "No. 3-2-1 Perfection, Made in U. S. A." B & H burner with F. T. Williams patent flame spreader. A larger, "New Perfection Junior Cooking Stove" was available in 1912. Courtesy Don Meily and Fil Graff.

Advertisement, *McCall's Magazine,* May 1908.

Advertisement, *McCall's Magazine,* January 1909.

Catalog Images of Rayo Lamps 1912 – 1921

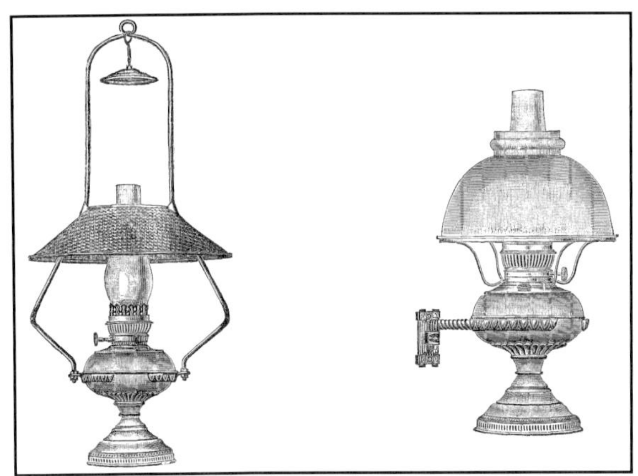

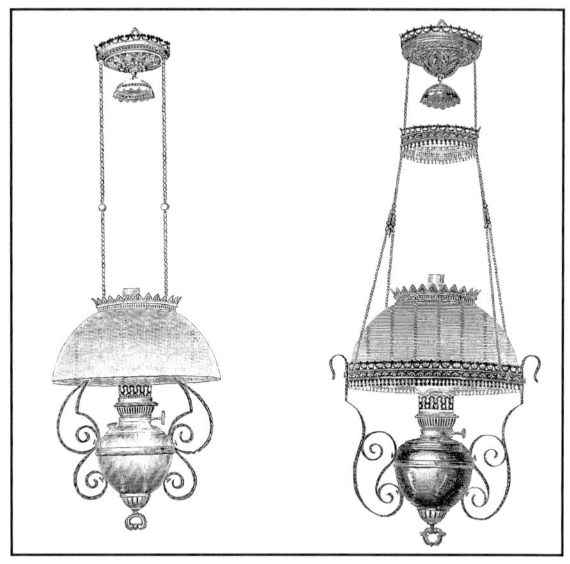

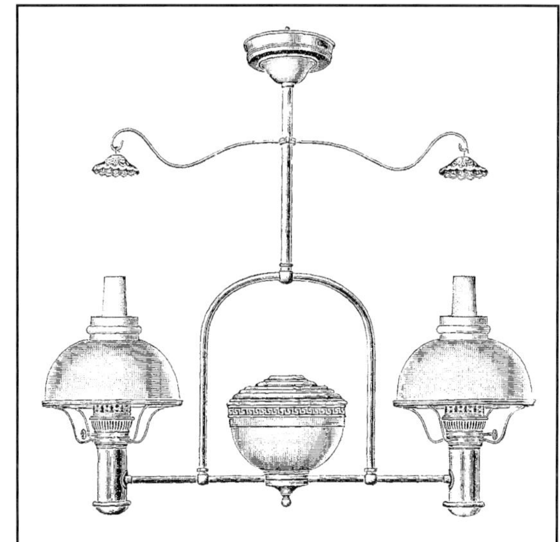

Swann and Whitehead
1880s – 1891

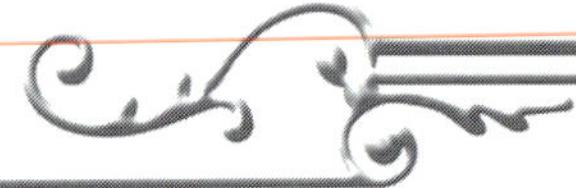

Swann, Whitehead & Clark, 1891 – 1893

The Swann brothers were decorators of lamps and shades. Edward Swann operated a decorating shop in Sandwich, Massachusetts, while Frederick Swann operated a similar business in Trenton, New Jersey, with William R. Whitehead. Their specialty was decorated opal lamps and shades.

Swann and Whitehead decorated shades and lamps for Clark Brothers', who became one of its best customers. Clark Brothers' converted one of its buildings into shade decorating for Swann and Whitehead after a fire destroyed their plant in 1887.

Another fire occurred in February 1891, after which Joseph Y. Clark sold his stock in Clark Brothers' and purchased one-third interest in Swann and Whitehead, which then became Swann, Whitehead & Clark.

Whitehead became president of American Lamp, Brass and Copper Company upon consolidation of Clark Brothers' Lamp, Brass and Copper Company, McLewee Brass Mfg. Co., and Swann, Whitehead & Clark in 1892 and 1893. William Russell Whitehead graduated as an engineer from Rutgers University in 1877. He started in business as a decorator of pottery goods and bought Mr. Tattler's interest in Swann, Tattler Company when Tattler retired.

Swann, Whitehead & Clark advertised the Banner lamp in *CGL* in 1891 (see right) and sold P & A oil pots in S & W vase and banquet lamps.

The company, however, was primarily a decorator and claimed its lamps were "interchangeable with all" in its advertisement on the next page. The oil pots and burners not identified in ads may be from American Brass, Ansonia, B & H, or Meriden Bronze.

Cover of catalog, circa 1891.

Best of Lamps
All metal
No smell
No smoke
Easy to wick
Ready to light

Least of care
Always ready
Many used
Price low
Sure to please

DECORATED

LAMP -:- SHADES.

We manufacture a complete line of ELEGANT DECORATED SHADES for HAND LAMPS, STAND LAMPS and GAS FIXTURES.

Novel Designs!

Low Prices!

Work Guaranteed!

For Sale by all Jobbers. Send for Illustrated Catalogue.

SWANN & WHITEHEAD,

TRENTON, NEW JERSEY.

Advertisement, *China, Glass and Lamps,* 1886.

Trade Names

Center-draft lamps — were given names; however, I doubt if the names appear on lamps. Some names — Adrian, Alaska, Barcelona, Bonheur, Columbia, Comet, Cordova, Devon, Dresden, Edna, Elsie, Fontleroy, Florence, Harvard, Ivanhoe, Jewel, Lafayette, Landseer, Majestic, Marguerite, Nina, Pavia, Plymouth, Puritan, Senator, Vassar, Verona, Victor, Vienna.

Center-draft burner — The Empire.

Selected Patents, Center-draft Lamps

Henry D'Arcus assigned to Swann and Whitehead
1890 438,101

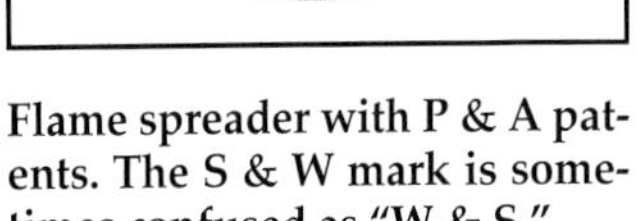

Flame spreader with P & A patents. The S & W mark is sometimes confused as "W & S."

The Harvard, 1891.

Oil fill cap.

No. 1 oil pot sold in Swann & Whitehead vase lamp. I suspect that S & W lamps also used similar oil pots from one of several manufacturers (see right). The flame spreader above is marked with Plume & Atwood patents. Some lamps have S & W oil fill caps; others have plain brass caps as found on this oil pot. Height 6½". Diameter of pot 4". $75.00.

THE
Centre Draft Lamp
Has Come to Stay
—AND—
Excellence is Properly
Claimed For Many Makes.
OUR LAMPS
Are Interchangeable With ALL.
—o—
The "Royal,"
The "Meriden,"
The B. & H.,"
The Ansonia Improved,
The "Belgian,"
The 'Gladstone."

Advertisement, *Pottery and Glassware Reporter*, Sept. 3, 1891.

Advertisement, *China and Glass Journal,* Aug. 13, 1891, promoting "the Celebrated Little Jewel in New Raiment." The Little Jewel burner and oil pot were made by the Ansonia Brass and Copper Co.

SWANN & WHITEHEAD

MANUFACTURERS OF

DECORATED VASE LAMPS

With greatly increased facilities, and all machinery for making Lamp Trimmings, we claim to be Headquarters for all styles of Table Lamps and Decorated Shades.

PROMPT SHIPMENT GUARANTEED.

OFFICE AND FACTORY,
Perrine Ave., Opp. OTT & BREWER.

NEW YORK SALESROOM,
12 Barclay St., A. J. BAILEY, Manager

TRENTON, N. J.,

Advertisement, *Pottery and Glassware Reporter,* July 25, 1889.

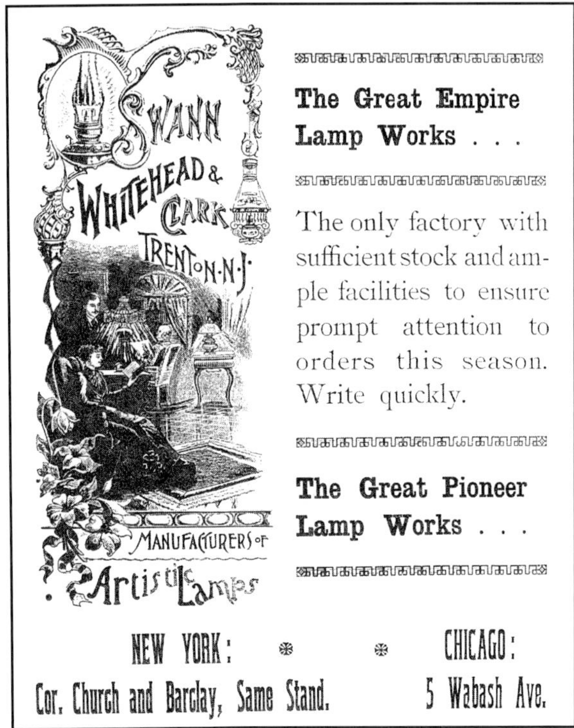

Advertisement, *Pottery and Glassware Reporter*, Dec. 17, 1892.

The Plymouth vase lamp with P & A oil pot, 1891.

Plymouth flame spreader made by Plume & Atwood.

Advertisement, *Pottery and Glassware Reporter*, Sept. 21, 1892.

Swann, Whitehead & Clark Vase and Banquet Lamps, ca. 1891

"With our King of center-draught burners — The Empire."

Adrian Assortment.

Banquet lamp, silk fringe shade.

Better banquet lamps, "China silk shades with flounce and silk lace."

Trenton Lamp Company

1892 – 1905

Trenton Lamp was primarily a retailer of lamps made by other manufacturers. The company exported Banner and Royal lamps to South America.

Trenton Lamp Company was listed in *Fitzgerald's Trenton and Mercer County Directory* in 1892 — Josiah Hellyer, president; A. L. Clark, secretary; and B. L. Stokes, treasurer. Hellyer was a dentist living in Carversville, Pennsylvania. F. W. Rockhill became secretary in 1894.

In 1890, Ricketts and Hellyer were listed as "lamp manufacturers" at 114 Dickinson, Trenton. I have no information on Ricketts and very little about lamps made or sold.

In 1896, Trenton Lamp had showrooms at 32 – 36 Park Place, New York (*CGL*, 1896). This was the same address as Dithridge Glass Co. and Ball, Dieters and Crowl, both sources of lamps in New York City.

Trenton Lamp "expanded" in 1900 to manufacture the Columbia lamp ("a new central-draft lamp") according to published notice (see right) indicating the lamp was newly patented. I have found no utility patents for this lamp.

The Columbia lamp was most likely manufactured by Matthews & Willard, which was already selling the Aladdin center-draft lamp. The Columbia and Aladdin lamps are identical except for the marking on the flame spreader.

Trenton Lamp Company was reported in financial receivership in 1901. The published notice said the company also made iron and brass beds (*CGL*, Oct. 26, 1901). The company was officially dissolved as a corporation by the state of New Jersey in 1905.

Wilson flame spreader marked "Manufactured by Trenton Lamp Co." found in glass vase lamp with oil pot believed to be made by the Ansonia Brass and Copper Company.

> The Trenton Lamp Co., after making one of the greatest uphill contests on record, close the season of 1892 well satisfied with the result. The arrangements for 1893 are nearing completion, the outcome of which will place them up among the leaders of lamp manufacturers.
>
> The metal department is under the immediate supervision of vice-president Bates, who in turn is ably assisted by that successful young machinist John W. Wilkes. Joseph Endler, the head of the department of design, has charge of the entire work in this branch, which alone assures success in the production of attractive decorations. The art department is under the direction of Thos. W. Obert, an artist of recognized ability.
>
> *China and Glass Journal*, Dec. 22, 1892

Letterhead.
Courtesy Wheaton Village Museum of Glass.

Trade Names

Center-draft lamps — Columbia and Wilson lamps.

The flame spreaders of these lamps are marked "The New Columbia Lamp" and "Pat. Pending." The Aladdin has no indication of Patent Pending or any patent date. The table founts for Columbia and Aladdin lamps are identical and unmarked. The Columbia lamp may have been named to promote trade in South America. See Wilson flame spreader on left.

Flame spreaders for Columbia and Aladdin lamps are identical in size, shape, and marking design to the M & W flame spreaders. Read the chapter on Matthews & Willard Mfg. Company for photographs and more information.

> The Trenton Lamp Co. have made such progress under the present management that their plant, although covering an area of five acres, is inadequate to permit them to meet the demands for their goods. A large addition to the plant has become necessary, so they contemplate erecting next month another building, 75 X 200 feet, four stories high. In this building will be manufactured what is known as the Columbia lamp, a new centre draft lamp which the company recently invented and patented, and which has already found favor among the lamp buyers and trade in general.
>
> *China, Glass and Lamps*, June 1, 1900

LÁMPARAS, ETC.

TRENTON LAMP COMPANY, TRENTON, N. J. E. U. DE A.

(LA CELEBRADA FÁBRICA DE LÁMPARAS.)

FABRICANTES DE

LÁMPARAS DE BANQUETE

LÁMPARAS DE METAL,

LÁMPARAS DE MESA DECORADAS.

TAMBIÉN

CAMAS DE LATÓN Y ESMALTADOS.

LOS PRODUCTOS DE ESTA FÁBRICA, SON LOS MÁS FINOS QUE SE CONOCEN, VENDIÉNDOSE SIEMPRE Á PRECIOS QUE DESAFÍAN COMPETENCIA.

Experiencia de Años en el Comercio de Exportacion.

TRENTON LAMP COMPANY, Trenton, N. J., E. U. de A.

Advertisement in Porter Company catalog in 1894. Royal lamps made by Plume & Atwood were illustrated.

Wallace & Sons
1848 – 1896

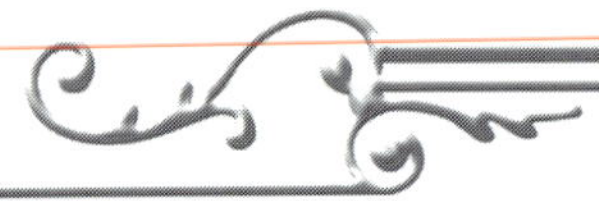

Lamp Manufacture ca. 1883 – 1896

The Wallace name is well rooted in Derby and Ansonia, Connecticut, history. Thomas Wallace (1797 – 1875) brought his wife and seven children from England in 1832 to work in America's developing brass industry. Wallace was expert in drawing wire, with an apprenticeship in England.

Thomas Wallace moved to Derby, where he started his own shop about 1848. He organized Wallace & Sons as a stock company in 1853 and taught the business to his sons — John, Thomas, and William. Wallace was active in civic affairs and represented Derby in the state legislature.

Wallace & Sons made brass and copper goods, wire, pin products, and lamp burners and lamps, and had a large warehouse and sales office in New York City.

Thomas DeForest assigned patents for lanterns (27,186; 27,666; 27,892) to Wallace & Sons in 1860; however, I have found no record of the company making lanterns.

Wallace & Sons produced several types of kerosene burners by 1876 and center-draft lamps by the late 1880s. I do not know who provided the incentive to manufacture burners and lamps in Wallace & Sons' highly successful brass fabricating business.

The company made center-draft hanging and stand lamps and the ones seen by the author are unmarked except for the flame spreader, which bears the "W & S" signature. An advertisement in 1891 included onyx tables, piano lamps, and banquet lamps; however, the company was struggling financially. The company may have produced silver-plated lamps.

The company employed 450 in 1880. At that time, William Wallace was president and Thomas Wallace was secretary and treasurer. Wallace & Sons met with financial troubles in the early 1890s, settling with creditors in 1894 (*CGL*, March 7, 1894). The Wallace & Sons factory was bought by Coe Brass Co. in 1896 (Coe became American Brass Co. in 1899, and later became Anaconda American Brass). At that time, Thomas Wallace, Jr., was managing director of the Waclark Company and was credited with many improvements in the technique of drawing wire.

William Wallace was a pioneer electrical inventor — he invented practical electric carbon arc lamps and lighted Ansonia's streets with them. Thomas Edison visited William Wallace's laboratory in 1878 to see his dynamos and arc lights. Edison purchased two generating devices called "telemachrons" from Wallace, calling him "a great brass manufacturer with a laboratory nearly perfect." In September 1878, Edison bragged that he could light "the entire lower part of New York City, using a 500 horsepower engine" (Quinn, 2005).

Ansonians credit Wallace with giving ideas to Edison for his incandescent electric lamp, which he announced in 1879 and patented in 1880.

William Wallace exhibited his experimental dynamos and electrical appliances at the Philadelphia Centennial Exhibition in 1876, the Mechanics Institute in 1879, and the Franklin Institute in 1884. He moved to Washington about 1893 and died in 1904.

Wallace & Sons.
Courtesy Derby Historical Society.

Trade Names

Center-draft lamps — Connecticut lamp, the Improved Connecticut lamp, which was advertised in 1891 as "now made with new wick raiser," W & S. A miniature piano lamp with an onyx table was advertised in 1892 as a boudoir lamp.

Folded-wick, side-draft burners — Challenge Argand, Columbus, Orient.

Flat-wick burners — Amazon, Derby, Sun, Sun-hinge, Orient, Little Giant, Challenge, and Surprise. Michael Collins licensed Wallace & Sons (and others including Edward Miller) to manufacture and sell his burner. In return W & S paid a royalty of six cents per dozen burners.

I believe the company possibly sold table lamps bearing the Derby name and with Derby burners.

WALLACE & SONS,

MANUFACTURERS OF

BRASS AND COPPER WIRE,

ROLLED, SHEET AND PLATERS' BRASS,

Copper Rivets and Burrs,

Brass and Iron Jack Chain, Escutcheon Pins,
Seamless Brass Ferrules,

COLLINS' PATENT SUN BURNERS.

ALSO,

Wallace & Sons' Eagle and Superior Pins.

MANUFACTORIES, ANSONIA, CONN.

Warehouses, 89 Chambers St. and 71 Reade St., New York.

Advertisement, *Ansonia Directory*, 1875. Wallace & Sons exhibited lamp burners, brass and copper wire, rivets, and brass pins at the Centennial Exposition in 1876. Courtesy Allen Weathers.

Selected Patents, Center-draft Lamps

Edson L. Bryant[1] assigned to Wallace & Sons

1886	338,137
1886	340,416
1888	380,858
1889	409,910
Joseph E. Bohner[2] assigned to Wallace & Sons	
1891	456,880
1891	456,881
Wolcott A. Hull[3] unassigned	
1887	D17,848

[1]Also patents on flat-wick burners, hanging lamps, cigar lighter.

[2]Also patents for hanging lamps and Globe fount for flat-wick burners. Related to George Bohner, president of Brillant Gas Lamp Co., Chicago.

[3] Hull assigned many patents to Ansonia Brass Company.

The Wallace Invention

Courtesy of Marian K. O'Keefe and the Derby Historical Society.

An Electrical Machine That Will Transmit Power By Wire

William Wallace, president, Wallace & Sons, received distinguished visitors to see his electrical invention during the Fall of 1878. They were Thomas Edison and his assistant Mr. Bacheller, and Professors Barker (University of Pennsylvania) and Chandler (Board of Health).

Wallace demonstrated his machines powered by a water-wheel from the nearby river to generate electricity to operate carbon arc lights installed in the Wallace foundry and the nearby Farrel foundry.

The power generated by the Wallace dynamo-electric machine was transmitted to Wallace's telemachon to light eight carbon arc lamps for the demonstration.

Edison was said to be "enraptured. He ran from the instrument to the lights and from the lights back to the instrument. He calculated the power of the instrument and of the lights, the probable loss of power in transmission, the amount of coal the instrument would save in a day, a week, a month, a year, and the result of such a saving on manufacturing."

The wonder and mystery of electricity was apparent to the Derby reporter as he described Wallace and his invention.

"If we were to attempt to characterize him...he (is) first master of himself, and then master of his own wit, until he himself had laid his own hand on one of the grandest successes of this age...the fact and the nature of this achievement of Mr. Wallace which casts the other inventions of the most boasted scientists entirely into the shade. If this invention or discovery of a new method of accumulating electrical force shall prove to be a real one, the name of our practical modest townsman will stand by the side of the first inventors of the age, or indeed, of any size."

The Derby Transcript, September 26, 1878

Editor's Note: Wallace apparently did not obtain patents on his inventions. Thomas Wallace became trustee of the Electro-Dynamic Co. organized by Abon Man and William Sawyer in 1879. Wallace & Sons was to manufacture and sell lamps under Sawyer-Man patents. Edison refused to consolidate with Electro-Dynamic. Sawyer died suddenly in 1883 and his patents ultimately were sold to Westinghouse Electric Co.

WALLACE & SONS,
MANUFACTURERS OF
Brass, Copper and German Silver in Sheets, Rolls, Wire Rods and Tubing. Rivets and Burrs, Soldering Coppers, Extension Lamps, Lamp Trimmings. and Kerosene Burners.
AGENTS FOR U. S. CARTRIDGE COMPANY.
WAREHOUSE,
89 Chambers and 71 Reade Sts., New York.
ANSONIA, CONN.

Advertisement, *Ansonia Directory*, 1888. Courtesy Derby Historical Society.

WALLACE & SONS,
MANUFACTURERS OF
Brass, Copper and German Silver
IN SHEETS AND ROLLS.
Brass, Copper and German Silver
WIRE and RODS.
TUBING,
Soldering Coppers.
Brass and Iron Jack Chain,
COPPER RIVETS AND BURS,
KEROSENE BURNERS
LAMPS AND KEROSENE LAMP GOODS
OF ALL KINDS.
ESCUTCHEON PINS, SEAMLESS FERRULES,
ELECTRIC COPPER WIRE,
Wrought Gongs, Door Rails, Stair Rods.
Copper Tacks and Nails, Brass Butts, Etc.
AGENTS FOR THE UNITED STATES CARTRIDGE COMPANY.
ROLLING MILLS AND FACTORIES:
ANSONIA, CONN.
WAREHOUSE:
89 Chambers St., and 71 Reade St., New York.

Advertisement, *Ansonia Directory*, 1883. An 1884 catalog of library lamps offered W & S lamps with lip burners or no burners at all. Courtesy Derby Historical Society.

Connecticut Electric Lamp

The Connecticut Lamp was illustrated and sold by George F. Bassett & Co. as the "Connecticut Electric Lamp" in 1889. These lamps illustrate the early straight flame spreader. These catalog images courtesy of David Broughton.

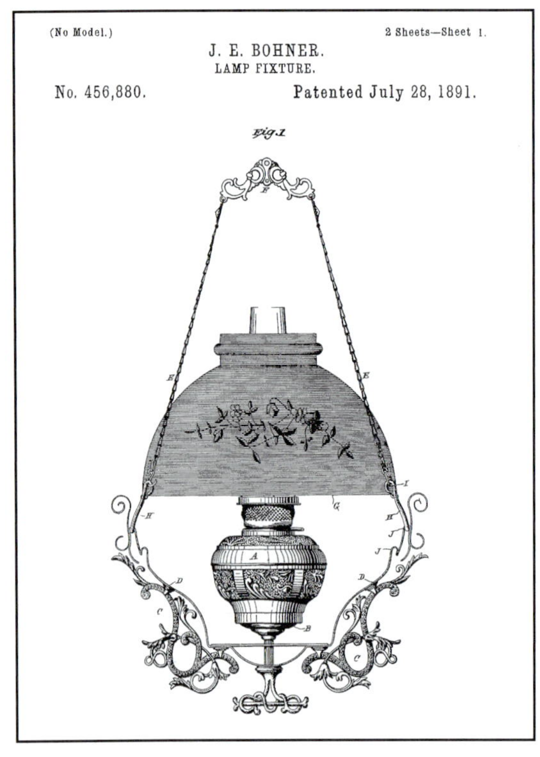

Flame spreader for the Connecticut lamp. The Mar. 15, 1887, patent is unknown. Courtesy Fil Graff.

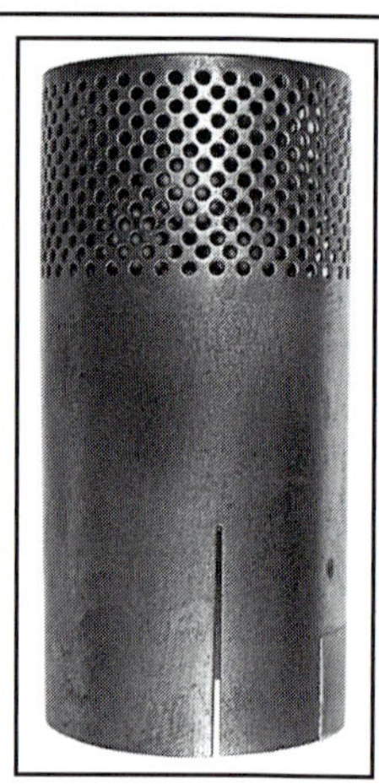

3" x 1½".

Connecticut Electric lamps sold by George F. Bassett & Company in 1889. Most were offered with either nickel or brass finishes. The lamp second from right has a glass fount. Courtesy David Broughton.

Improved Connecticut Lamp

WALLACE & SONS,

MANUFACTURERS OF—

Lamps, Lamp Goods, Tables,

Etc., Etc.,

29 Chambers St., New York.

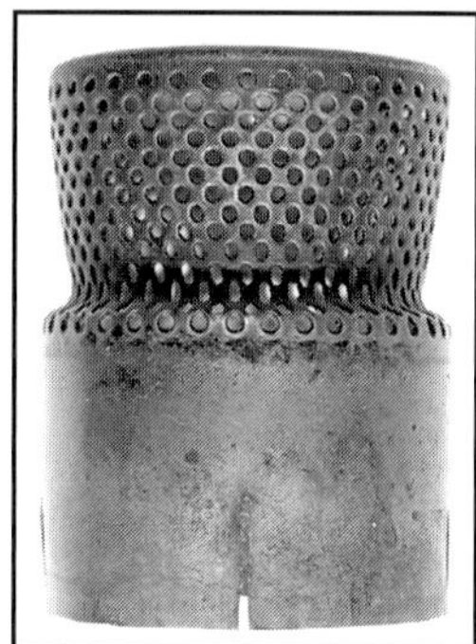

Flame spreader for the Improved Connecticut lamp.

WE are now ready to show our NEW SAMPLES for the jobbing trade, of Library Lamps, Banquet Lamps, Piano Lamps, &c. We think we have the "taking" line for this year. Such customers as have seen the goods are enthusiastic over them. We have largely increased our factory facilities and more than doubled the size of our showroom in New York. We were very successful with our goods last year and propose to be more so in 1892. Come and see what we have to offer.

Wallace & Sons,

The Improved Connecticut Lamp.

Improved Connecticut lamp illustrated in the 1891 Brides-McDowell Co. catalog, Louisville, KY.

Improved Connecticut No. 2 stand lamp. This lamp was fitted with the W & S flame spreader (above), which fits outside the wick tube. Height 12". The foot of this lamp appears to be flattened. The advertisement (left) for the Improved Connecticut lamp illustrates the earlier Connecticut lamp with different burner and flame spreader. $125.00.

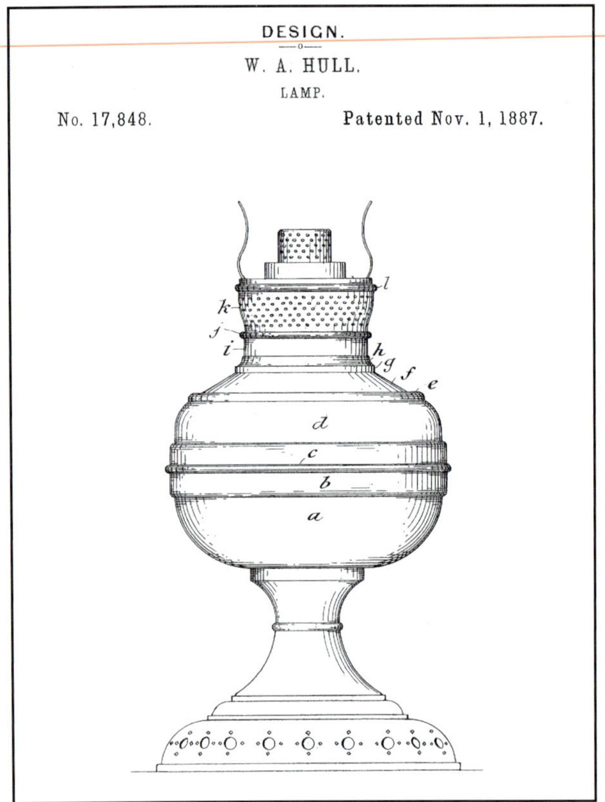

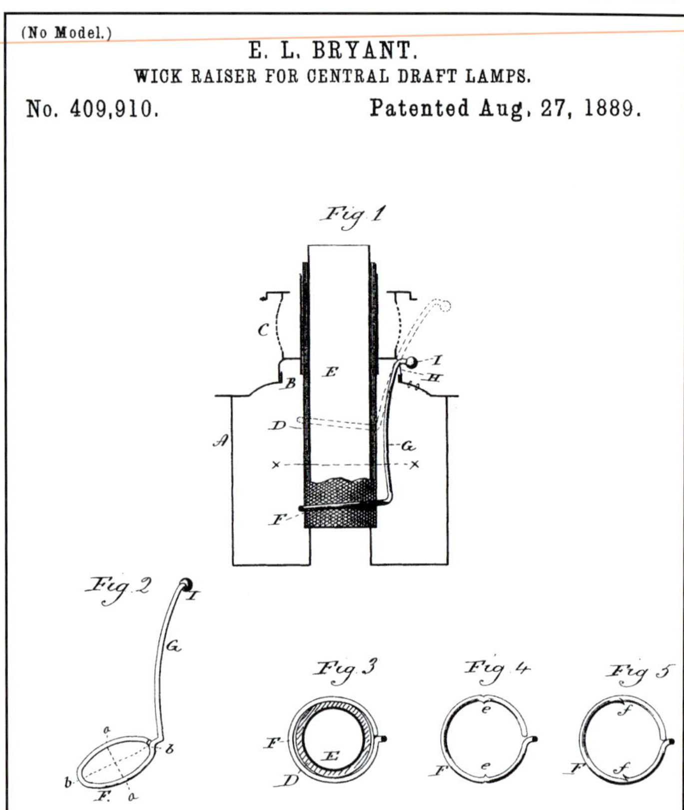

WALLACE & SONS,

MANUFACTURERS OF

THE "IMPROVED CONNECTICUT."

Library, Banquet and Stand Lamps, Chandeliers, Brackets, Kerosene Burners and Trimmings.

29 CHAMBERS and 5 READE STREETS, NEW YORK.

No. 224 "Improved Connecticut." No. 225 with No. 3 Collar.

We desire to call the attention of the trade to the "Improved Connecticut Lamp." Our *new method of raising and lowering the wick, also of re-wicking*, is so simple, it makes this lamp superior to all other central draft lamps in the market.

It is now made with a *Removable Thimble*, which overcomes the objection to the old style lamp of being difficult to wick

We have added to our line *Banquet and Bracket Lamps*, of which we have a variety of styles at popular prices.

We request that before you place your order for fall stock you will call and see us, or write for illustrations and prices.

The above cut shows our New Wick Raiser.

Advertisement, *China and Glass Journal,* May 8, 1890.

Improved Connecticut Lamp

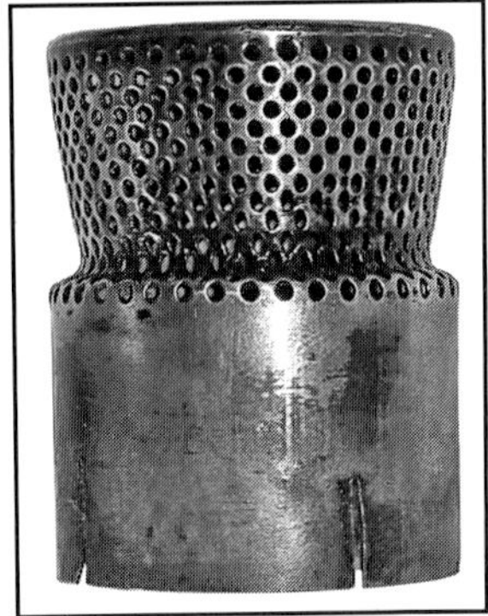

Flame spreader for Improved Connecticut No. 2 lamps. The flame spreader slips over the outside of the wick tube.

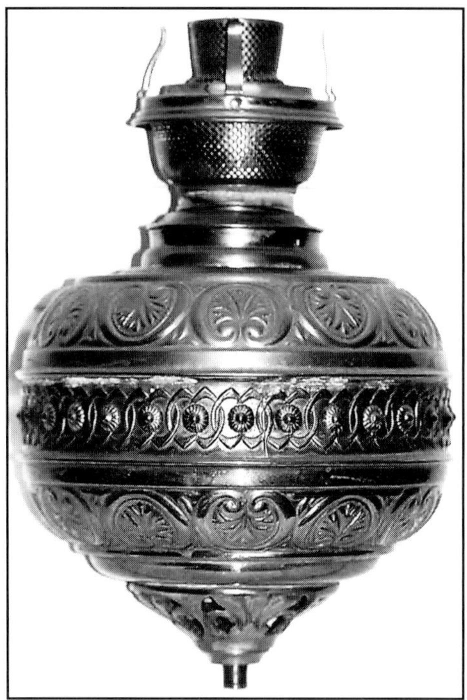

Wallace & Sons fount for mounting on a stand, such as the figure on the next page. The wick raiser bar is missing. The flame spreader is the same as the one at left. $75.00. Courtesy John Remackel.

Improved Connecticut No. 2 stand lamp with W & S flame spreader (above). Lift gallery. Height 13". $175.00.

Improved Connecticut fount for hanging or bracket lamp. The wick raiser bar is missing. The flame spreader is the same as the one top left. $100.00. Courtesy John Remackel.

Improved Connecticut Lamps, Hibbard, Spencer, Bartlett & Co. Catalog No. 204, 1893

All catalog images are courtesy of Jeff Ebersole.

Late W & S burner most likely used in these lamps (the images may be older ones). The wick raiser rod no longer penetrates the burner base.

Library lamp.

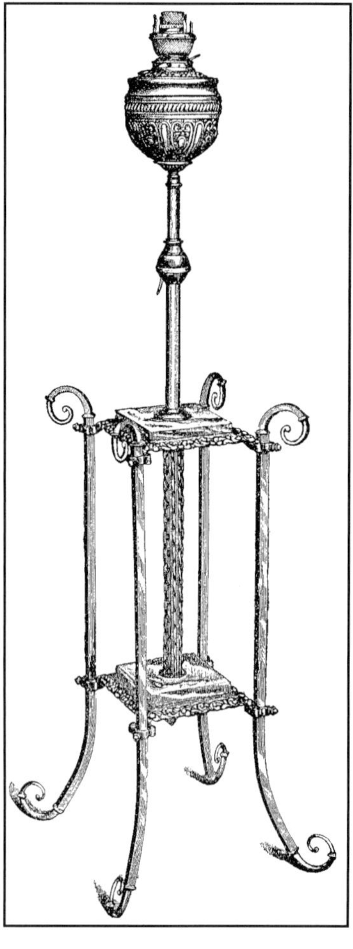

Banquet lamp.

Extension piano lamp.

W & S oil pot with new burner "improved" *after* the Improved version. Oil pot 3¼" tall; 5" wide. I am unsure that new flame spreaders were not designed. These oil pots are found in Wallace & Sons lamps. $75.00.

Appendices

New York Directory; Lamp, Glass, and Crockery Houses — 1896; from China, Glass and Lamps, *May 20, 1896*

Owing to recent changes and for the convenience of buyers visiting New York, we group the addresses of the following lamp, glass and crockery houses.

Brass Lamps

American Lamp & Brass Co., 44 Park Place
Bradley & Hubbard Mfg. Co., 26 Park Place
Bridgeport Brass Co. 19 Murray
Bristol Brass & Clock Co., 32 Warren
Edward Miller, 28 and 30 West Broadway
Hipwell Mfg. Co., 52 West Broadway
New Jersey Lamp & Bronze Works, 45 Maiden Lane
Plume & Atwood Mfg. Co., 29 Murray
Rochester Lamp Co., 42 Park Place and 37 Barclay
Swann & McLewee Mfg. Co., 44 West Broadway
Trenton Lamp Co., 32 and 36 Park Place
W. R. Noe, 33 Park Place
Wallace & Sons, 29 Chambers Street

Lamps and Glassware

Ball, Dieters & Crowl, 32 and 36 Park Place
Co-operative Flint Glass Co., 48 Murray
Consolidated Lamp & Glass Co., 16 Murray
Dithridge Glass Co., 32 Park Place
Geo. Duncan's Sons & Co., 52 West Broadway
Thos. Evans Co., 39 Barclay
Fostoria Glass Co., 64 West Broadway
Indiana Tumbler & Goblet Co., 63 and 65 Murray
McKee & Bros., 66 West Broadway
Miller & Co., 96 Church Street
Nail City Stamping Co., 48 Park Place
The Northwood Co., 46 West Broadway
Ohio Flint Glass Co., 231 Greenwich
Phoenix Glass Co., 42 Murray
Rochester Tumbler Co., 39 Barclay
Tarentum Glass Co., 24 Park Place
United States Glass Co., Church and Murray
Zihlmann Glass Co., 48 and 50 Park Place

Pottery Manufacturers

Art China Decorating Co., 9 Maiden Lane
Maddock Pottery Co., 18 Barclay
Owens, J. B. Pottery Co., 15 Park Place
Warwick China Co., 66 West Broadway
Wheeling Pottery Co., 66 W. Broadway

Importers

Charles Ahrenfeldt & Son, 50 to 54 Murray
Bassett, Geo. F.. & Co., 49 Barclay and 54 Park Place
Bawo & Dotter, 26 to 32 Barclay
Bishop & Stoner 96 Church Street
Edward Boote, 48 Park Place
Geo. Borgfeldt & Co. 18 to 24 Washington Place
Chas. L. Dwenger, 35 and 37 Park Place
Chas. Gericot, 42 West Broadway
Oscar Goerke Estate, 53 and 55 Barclay
Hamburger & Co., 20 W. Third Street
Haviland & Abbot, 29 Barclay
Haviland & Co., 45 Barclay
Hinrichs & Co., 29 to 33 Park Place
Hunt, Benj. F. & Sons 95 Pearl
Koscherak Bros, 47 Murray
Edward Rourke, 40 Barclay
L. Straus & Sons, 42 to 47 Warren
Lazarus, Rosenfeld & Lehmann, 62 Murray
Leonard, P. H. & Co., 76 and 78 Reade Street
Pouyat, J. 56 Murray
Vogt & Dose, 43 Barclay
Wolf & Gross, 47 Barclay
J. M. Young Importing Co., 37 and 39 Murray

W. R. Noe[1]

William R. Noe operated a lamp business at 33 Park Place in New York City in 1896. In 1887 Noe bought into the business of Botsford and Lacy, becoming full owner in 1893. Later W. R. Noe was located at 53 Murray Street.

W. R. Noe was an importer and manufacturer of lamp goods with a specialty of miniature night lights. The company also imported German Student lamps as well as other accessories, taking over the business from B. B. Schneider..

William R. Noe gained experience in the lamp business as a salesman for Holmes, Booth & Haydens during the 1870s and 1880s. He assigned two patents (D16,355, 348,291) to HBH in 1885 and 1886. Noe's sons later joined their father in W. R. Noe & Sons. William R. Noe, Sr. died in 1920. The business filed for bankruptcy in 1935.

[1]This information and the above letterhead are courtesy of Dan Edminster. His website (www.thelampworks.com) is an excellent source for more history of Noe and other companies and the lamps they sold.

The Large Brass Mills[1] Operating in 1895	
These mills manufactured most of the brass produced in the United States during the 1890s.	
Company and location	*Employees*
Scovill Manufacturing Company, Waterbury, Conn.	1,600
Ansonia Brass & Copper Company, Ansonia, Conn.	1,135
Holmes, Booth & Haydens, Waterbury, Conn.	1,012
Benedict & Burnham Mfg. Company, Waterbury, Conn.	967
Plume & Atwood Mfg. Company, Waterbury, Conn.	791
Bridgeport Brass Company, Bridgeport, Conn.	750
Wallace & Sons, Ansonia, Conn.	646
Coe Brass Company, Torrington, Conn.	650
Manhattan Brass Company, New York, NY	575
Randolph & Clowes, Waterbury, Conn.	550
Waterbury Brass Company, Waterbury, Conn.	525
Bristol Brass & Clock Company, Bristol, Conn.	455
Rome Brass Company, Rome, NY	397
Detroit Copper & Brass Mills, Detroit, Michigan	275
Seymour Mfg. Company, Seymour, Conn.	220
Birmingham Brass Company, Shelton, Conn.	206
Chicago Brass Company, Kenosha, Wisconsin	144

[1]Lathrop (1926) pointed out that 90 percent of the workers were employed in Connecticut with one-half in Waterbury.

American Association of Flint & Lime Glass Manufacturers

The American Association of Flint & Lime Glass Manufacturers (AAFLGM) was formed in 1874, and was composed of the principal manufacturers of pressed and blown tableware, bar goods, lamps and shades, chimneys, and other specialties in flint and opal glass in the United States. Its purpose was to encourage and represent members and protect the glass trade and commerce through exchange of information.

The glass industry over expanded as glasshouses were established in towns throughout Ohio, West Virginia and Indiana where new sources of natural gas were found. By 1900, however, the industry was consolidating as the "craze for glassworks founded on cheap natural gas" was over and many factories closed (Paquette, 2002). Paquette also documented many ventures in northwest Ohio during the gas boom of the 1880s.

In 1900 the AAFLGM represented 66 glasshouses operated by 43 companies. Of those 17 made assorted glass for gas and electric lighting, decorated lamps and lamp chimneys. Only six principally made lamp chimneys.

The Macbeth Evans Glass Company was formed in 1899 to purchase the automatic machine for blowing chimneys developed by the American Lamp Chimney Company, Toledo, Ohio. Macbeth Evans became the largest manufacturer of chimneys in the world.

Daily production of chimneys from 1880-1890 was estimated at 40,000 dozen or about 102 tons (Courter, 2003). This was the peak in chimney production which declined 10 percent by 1900.

Read Welker (1985) and Courter (2003) for more information about AAFLGM and other related glass industry organizations.

American Lamp Burner Association

Information courtesy of Allen Weathers.

Large manufacturers of brass lamps and burners signed "pooling agreements" that established prices for the stated purpose of "price stability." Such agreements, illegal today, were practiced widely during the last century. Agreements were also established for brass kettles and bicycle bells in addition to lamps (Scheips and Weathers 1995). I presume that fees collected by the association paid for management, compensation and enforcement. I assume such agreement was more or less a "gentlemen's handshake" and we have no way of knowing what "enforcement" really meant.

A document dated Feb. 29, 1892 outlined objectives of the association to stabilize prices and facilitate exchange of each other's patents with the purpose to exclude competition.

The following information is quoted from an agreement signed in February 1893:

> "We, the undersigned members of the American Lamp Burner Association namely,
> Plume & Atwood Manufacturing Company of Waterbury, Conn.
> Holmes, Booth & Haydens......................of Waterbury, Conn.
> Edward Miller & Company.......................of Meriden, Conn.
> Benedict & Burnham Mfg. Company........ of Waterbury, Conn.
> Bristol Brass & Clock Company ....of Forestville, Conn.
> Bridgeport Brass Company......................of Bridgeport, Conn.
> Manhattan Brass Company..................... of New York City.

"Do hereby agree each with the other, that from and after this date we will not sell Lamp Burners taking the Sun Chimney, to either export or domestic trade, at less than prices established this day, namely,

35 cents per dozen for No. 0
40 cents per dozen for No. 1
60 cents per dozen for No. 2

on Four Months time, or 5% discount for each payment within 30 days from the date of invoice, except for the purchase at one time and in one delivery, of not less than 5,000 dozen Sun Chimney Burners from any member of this Association, such purchase shall be entitled to a further discount of five (5) per cent.

"It being understood and agreed that the selling prices mentioned herein, and amount to be paid into the POOL as hereafter specified, may be changed from time to time by unanimous vote of the association."

A report in *China, Glass and Lamps*, February 16, 1899, indicated that the burner association was ongoing through the years, that Bradley & Hubbard joined the association and that price adjustments were needed:

> A reorganization of the American Lamp Burners Manufacturing Association was effected in Meriden, Conn., on Tuesday, which is intended to control prices on lamp goods. The meeting was held in the office of Bradley & Hubbard, and representatives of several leading lamp manufacturers of the country were present. The recent advance in the price of copper, it is said, necessitated a readjustment of prices on lamp burners and other parts of the lamp on which the metal is used.

The Management of Petroleum Lamps — 1889

In view of the numerous fatal and other accidents caused by petroleum lamps, the following suggestions as to the construction and management of such lamps have been made by Sir Frederick Abel and Mr. Boverton Redwood, chemist of the Petroleum Association, after investigating the causes of lamp accidents: 1. That portion of the wick which is in the oil reservoir should be inclosed in a tube of thin sheet metal, open at the bottom; or in a cylinder of fine wire gauze, such as is used in miners' safety lamps (28 meshes to an inch). 2. The oil reservoir should be of metal, rather than of china or glass. 3. The oil reservoir should have no feeding place nor opening other than the opening into which the upper part of the lamp is screwed. 4. Every lamp should have a proper extinguishing apparatus. 5. Every lamp should have a broad and heavy base. 6. Wicks should be soft and not tightly plaited. 7. Wicks should be dried at the fire before being put into lamps. 8. Wicks should be only just long enough to reach the bottom of the oil reservoir. 9. Wicks should be so wide that they quite fill the wick-holder without having to be squeezed into it. 10. Wicks should be soaked with oil before being lit. 11. The reservoir should be quite filled with oil every time before using the lamp. 12. The lamp should be kept thoroughly clean, all oil should be carefully wiped off, and all charred wick and dirt removed before lighting. 13. When the lamp is lit the wick should be at first turned down, and then slowly raised. 14. Lamps which have no extinguishing apparatus should be put out as follows: The wick should be turned down until there is only a small flickering flame, and a sharp puff of breath should be sent across the top of the chimney, but not down it. 15. Cans or bottles used for oil should be free from water and dirt, and should be kept thoroughly closed. These suggestions apply to ordinary mineral oil lamps such as are generally used, and not to benzoline or spirit lamps.

PGR, Oct. 31, 1889

The Care of an Oil Lamp — 1908

Few people understand the proper care of lamps and find them rather a tax to take care of, but if a lamp is properly looked after it will give a good clear light without odor if there is absolute cleanliness as to burner, wick and chimney. Do not leave the care of the lamps until they are needed at night, for this is dangerous, and never clean lamps on a table where food is prepared, but have a special place for the work. Spread several newspapers over the table or shelf and upon these set the various parts. Some housekeepers think it better to wipe off the burned portions of the wick instead of cutting it. The main thing is to remove it evenly. Any piece of wick dropped on the burner will cause an odor when the lamp is lighted. About once a month the wick should be removed and the burner boiled in hot soap-suds or a solution of washing soda. Wipe the inside of smoky chimneys with tissue paper before washing them. Care should be taken that they are thoroughly dry or they will break easily when heated. When first lighting a lamp keep the wick low to allow the chimney to heat gradually and do not leave it immediately after lighting it. Many a ceiling has been ruined by a smoky lamp.

Each day clean every portion of the burner with a piece of chamois. Lift the top of the burner and see that the small air holes in the burner are not stopped up with dust or charred wick. This is often the cause of a dim light and an ill-smelling lamp.

Do not allow a lamp to burn after the oil is exhausted nor temporize by turning it down. Both burner and wick will be saved by putting the lamp out. When cleaning the lamp rub off the charred portion of the wick with the finger or a match stick; never use scissors. In renewing the wick screw it up almost out of the socket and immerse for five minutes in oil; then lower the wick to proper height and screw the burner on firmly. If the lamp has been allowed to burn dry, a similar treatment is advisable.

If a lamp is constantly used, it should be filled every day, the wick trimmed and the burner wiped off; the chimney and shade also being looked after.

China, Glass & Lamps, January 4, 1908

Specifications for Petroleum Products,[1] September 1889; Pennsylvania Railroad Company, Motive Power Department

Five different grades of petroleum products will be used.

The materials desired under this specification are the products of the distillation and refining of petroleum unmixed with any other substances and conforming to the detail specifications below. Products having very offensive odor, or being mixed with other oils, will not be accepted. Shipments must be made as soon as possible after the order is received. All shipments received at any place on or after Oct. 1 must show the proper cold test, and all received on or after May 1 must show the proper flash point, and will be rejected if they fail, even though the order did not call for winter and summer oil, respectively, unless it can be shown that the shipments have been more than a week in transit. No preliminary examination of samples will be required, but a limited amount of special preliminary examination will be made on the request of the purchasing agent, for use of parties desiring the information. When a shipment is received, a single sample will be taken at random and subjected to test, and the shipment will be accepted or rejected on this sample. If rejected, it will be returned at the shippers' expense.

The following detail specifications will be enforced:

150° Fire-Test Oil[2]

This grade of oil will not be accepted if sample:

1. Is not "water white" in color.
2. Flashes below 130° Fahr.
3. Burns below 151° Fahr.
4. Is cloudy, or shipment has cloudy barrels when received, from the presence of glue or suspended matter.
5. Becomes opaque, or shows cloud when the sample has been 10 minutes at a temperature of 0° Fahr.

The flashing and burning points are determined by heating the oil in an open vessel, not less than 12° per minute, and applying the test flame every 7°, beginning at 123° Fahr. The cold test may be conveniently made by having an ounce of the oil in a 4-oz. Sample bottle, with a thermometer suspended in the oil, and exposing this to a freezing mixture of ice and salt. It is advisable to stir with the thermometer while the oil is cooling. The oil must remain transparent in the freezing mixture 10 minutes after it has cooled to zero.

300° Fire-Test Oil

This grade of oil will not be accepted if sample:

1. Is not "water white" in color.
2. Flashes below 249° Fahr.
3. Burns below 298° Fahr.
4. Is cloudy, or shipment has cloudy barrels when received, from the presence of glue or suspended matter.
5. Becomes opaque, or shows cloud when the sample has been 10 minutes at a temperature of 32° Fahr.

The flashing and burning points are determined the same as for 150° fire-test oil except that the oil is heated 15° per minute, test flame being applied first at 212° Fahr.

[1]The *Comparative Merits of Various Systems of Car Lighting*, Engineering News Publ. Co., NY. (see Wellington, Penniman and Baker, 1892).

[2]We reprint this paragraph simply because of its relation to the testing of the 300° oil, which is alone used in car lamps.

Suggestions for the Care of Lamps — ca. 1922

(From the brochure *More and Better Light*, right.)

IF YOUR LAMPS give a poor light, even with the new burners and chimneys, it is probably due to a poor wick or a wick that is clogged by having been in use too long. The following suggestions should be carried out to obtain utmost efficiency in your lamps and thus conserve the most priceless possession one has — their eyesight.

— Trim clean and fill daily and be sure to wipe all of the lamp.
— Trim the wick by cutting it very carefully with a sharp pair of scissors. An uneven wick is the main cause of a ragged flame.
— Be sure the holes in the burner are absolutely clear, so as to allow the air to enter.
— Don't fill the reservoir to the top, oil expends with heat and room should be allowed for this expansion.
— Empty the reservoir occasionally.
— Boil the burner a few minutes once a month in sal soda or lye-water.
— Keep oil and lamps clean. Dirt causes most of your lamp trouble.
— Have the wick turned low when you light it and turn it up gradually.

Editor's note: This brochure illustrates flat wick burners and chimneys and gives good hints for all lamps. Kerosene was an important product for Standard Oil into the 1920s and 1930s.

Standard Oil Co. brochure ca. 1922. The Perfection tag attached to the kerosene filler can with a wire.

CHANGES in the properties of kerosene which have taken place within the last five years have in no way impaired the light or heat giving qualities of the oil; in fact, a stronger and better light is obtained from Perfection Kerosene than was ever possible with the old grade of oils.

Nevertheless, many persons blame the kerosene for poor light, flickering flames, and smoking chimneys, when the trouble really is due to the burners

Note the improvement in the flame made by the new burner & chimney. Both lamps contain the same oil.

and chimneys used on the lamps. Up till now no change has been made in their design, to adapt them to the different burning conditions made necessary by the improved oil, which requires a large amount of oxygen to consume it properly.

Recognizing the fact that the users of Perfection Kerosene were unable to get a maximum service from the oil they burned, and realizing that the failure was due not to the oil, but to the devices for burning it, the Standard Oil Company (Indiana) set its experts to work to find a better burner and a more efficient chimney. After exhaustive research

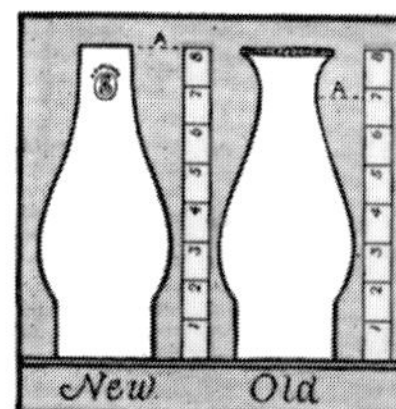

Draft is ended at line A. Note that 1¼" more draft is obtained with straight top chimney.

these men, working with the manufacturers of burners and chimneys, have approved a type of chimney and burner which scientifically regulates the draft, so that there is an even flow of air, without excess, on both sides of the flame. This entirely eliminates smoking chimneys and flickering flames and produces a volume of light far greater than has ever been possible before.

Note that the new type burner has a lower crown which brings the wick closer to the opening.

Every chimney having the approval of the Standard Oil Company (Indiana) has the mark shown below etched into it by the manufacturers. You can feel confident that a chimney bearing this mark will give complete satisfaction if used correctly; but you cannot use satisfactorily the new burner and the old crimp top chimney; neither can you use an old burner with a new approved chimney. To obtain the desired results, it is necessary to use both the improved burner and the new type chimney. Your dealer now has them for sale.

APPROVED
S O CO

Evaluating Your Lamp — Comments and Cautions

Names, Trademarks, and Patents

Some manufacturers named and marked their lamps which greatly helps identification. Marks embossed in the fount are usually easy to see and verify. Be cautious of similar marks on removable parts.

Inspect the lamp and burner carefully. Patent dates may be quite small and found in many locations.

Patent dates and other marks found on lamps illustrated in this book are noted in their captions.

Identification and Removable Parts

Flame spreaders and oil fill caps are often signed, dated or marked. Those found in old lamps may or may not be original to the lamp. Remember, some of these lamps are 75 to 100 years old! Use caution in your judgement of these items for correct identification.

There are many flame spreaders for center-draft lamps not included in this book. We simply do not know to which lamp they belong.

Obviously shades, shade holders and chimneys are accessories that are easily replaced and, although possibly old, may not be original to vase, hanging or floor lamps.

Most of the lamps illustrated in this book are table or stand lamps. The patents, patterns and other information will be helpful to identify hanging lamps, floor lamps and vase lamps. Remember, however, that removable oil founts may have been changed from the original lamp by the store, or by an owner years later.

Burners....

In our line of Banquet Lamps you are offered the choice of

Best Central Draft Burners

produced in the United States.

Chicago Chief, Royal, M. & W., Juno, Miller, B. & H.

All have the latest improvements, such as screw wick lift, chimney lift, etc.

They are all good, not a poor one in the lot.

Choice of burners, *Pitkin & Brooks* catalog 1897 – 1898.

Metal Finish and Plating

Nickel plating — many old lamps were made of brass and plated with a bright nickel finish. Nickel has proven over the years to be one of the best finishes for ease of cleaning the lamp during use.

Worn plating or finish will show signs of wear and age. Do not immediately regard such a lamp as a candidate for replating or stripping and polishing. Many collectors prefer to keep the original condition, assuming the wear is not a distraction. Evaluate years of patina carefully.

Other finishes include silver plating, gilt, polished brass, or other platings or decoration. Plating or finish other than nickel is stated in photo captions where thought to be original. Treasure your cast iron bases in original condition because they rust easily.

Condition and Metal Fatigue

Inspect carefully for repairs, rust and potential leaks.

Dents are removable by a person with tools and expert in restoration.

Stuck parts — do not force burners, galleries or wick raising devices as you can easily damage them.

Missing parts — may not be obvious. Inspect carefully for the flame spreader, internal wick raiser parts, and complete and intact gallery. Even the center-draft wick tube may be missing but not apparent upon casual inspection.

Old brass lamps often show signs of cracking due to metal fatigue. They may be acceptable shelf specimens but such lamps or oil pots are not suitable to fill with kerosene for burning.

Cleaning

Determine the best procedure for cleaning before you start. Use non-abrasive polish or mild detergent and a soft tooth brush for normal and light cleaning of grime and old oil. Avoid caustic and coarse cleaning agents. Be careful not to scratch or mar the finish or surface of the metal.

Size of Burners and Lamps

Burner size is usually an indication of lamp size. The larger the collar and burner — the larger the wick and chimney and taller the lamp. The size (No. 2 for example) is marked on some lamps. Lamps fitted with No. 0 burners may be quite tall.

Many old chimneys are also marked with name and size. The height of illustrated lamps is given in inches to the top of the burner with flame spreader in place. All sizes of lamps for each company or brand are not illustrated in this book. Some burners are interchangeable, many are not.

Sizes of Round-wick Burners and Chimneys

Burner Size[1]	Collar	Chimney Size[2] (varies)	Other Terms
No. 0	A	1½" to 1⅞"	Tiny (sometimes JR)
No. 1	B	2" to 2½"	Junior or JR
No. 2	C	2½" to 2⅞"	No. 2
No. 3	D	4" to 4½"	Mammoth

[1]Some foreign lamps reverse this designation. Night lights with Hornet burners may be designated size 00 with chimney bottom diameter of 1⅛".

[2]Diameter of base. Flat wick burners may be larger. Rochester chimneys were typically: No. 0 – 1$\frac{9}{16}$", No. 1 – 2", No. 2 – 2⅝", No. 3 – 4".

Tips for the Care and Feeding of Center-draft Lamps — Cleaning, Wicking, Fueling & Lighting, from Richard Dudley, the Lamp Doctor

You have just bought an old lamp, or better yet, a relative has given you an antique center-draft oil lamp. First, let's clean and evaluate the lamp as to condition and presence of essential parts. Take a little time in preparation and you will be ready to light and enjoy your lamp, which may be 70 to 100 years old.

Most folks who appreciate antiques want them to look like they have some age. So a little wear is OK, but not dents, damage, corrosion or rust. Following are conservative approaches to clean and restore your lamp.

Remove the Burner

Cleaning will be easier and more thorough when you remove the burner. Some burners are attached with thread connections; others lock with a bayonet connection. The bayonet type may turn to release in either direction. Many lift galleries can be removed in the same manner.

Most parts are usually easy to remove, but years of dried kerosene make good "cement." When you need to loosen the parts — burner, flame spreader and fill cap — never force them apart, even though you feel like beating them into submission. Brass is relatively soft and is easily bent or damaged by excess force from pliers or other tools.

Attack the burner and fill cap first. Spray with WD 40, rust-buster or other nostrums. Patience is the key. It took years to stick these parts and it may take a week of patient work to release them. Spray a little and try to remove, then repeat the drill. If this doesn't work, turn the lamp upside down and soak the stuck parts for a couple of days in K-1 kerosene. As a last resort, heat from a hair dryer often helps, especially on flame spreaders. The old dried wick may have to be carefully cut out in pieces.

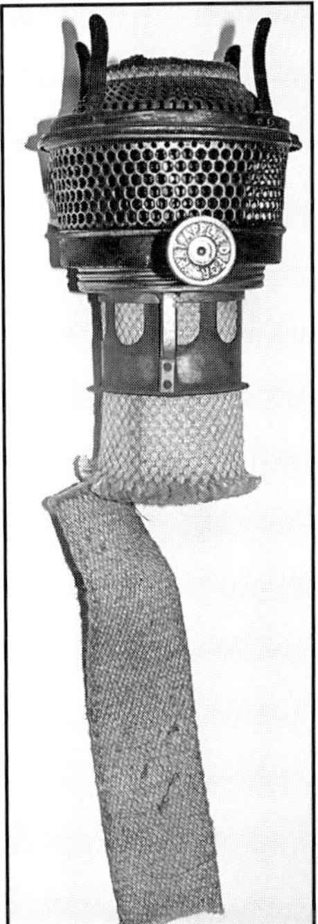

Center-draft burners before cleaning. Above: the old wick is dirty and clogged with residue, dirt and dried fuel.

Left: B & H burner before cleaning. The wick was short and the previous user sewed another wick to the bottom, a practice to conserve good burning wicks. Replace new wicks in these burners.

Cleaning

Wash a brass (finish) lamp in mild household detergent to clean off the attic dust or barn dirt. Use a soft brush to scrub the screens, designs and depressions. Rinse thoroughly and dry the lamp. If the metal has a nice dark uniform color (we call that patina if you are selling the lamp and dirt if buying), apply a coat of floor paste wax, and then buff with a clean (old) towel. This results in a warm rich patina that is highly regarded. Otherwise your choice is to buff the brass to a shiny surface and this is best done by a professional person who "strips and polishes" brass objects.

Wash dirty nickel plated lamps as above. If the finish is still dirty and tarnished (put on rubber gloves and work outside), spray oven cleaner on the outer surfaces. Allow the cleaner to work for about a minute, then use a soft brush to remove the build-up of dried oil and dirt. Wash immediately. Repeat the process to remove stubborn grime. It's almost like magic, the lamp may clean and "look new."

Use cleaning products with care and proper safe guards, eye protection and rubber gloves. Work in a well ventilated area and preferably outdoors.

I generally don't clean the inside of the font with anything other than a good washing with clean kerosene. Sometimes when doing repairs I use lacquer thinner to clean before soldering. Use a thin brush and rinse a couple of times followed by a good detergent/degreaser.

Clean burners with oven cleaner, carburetor cleaner, or a mixture of distilled water, tincture of green soap and ammonia. Some collectors soak parts in unsweetened Kool Aid mixture (very mildly acidic), which works fairly well, but sometimes turns the brass pink, in which case you need to recolor by polishing. Oven cleaner is easy to use and generally works very well. But caution is recommended. Apply after washing the lamp. Let it work for a minute, OR LESS, clean with soft brush and rinse immediately. An old tooth brush is handy to clean the burner screens and basket. I soak the parts again in clean water and repeat the process if needed.

Corrosion

In cases where the brass has spots of green corrosion, and if the damage is not too extensive, consider polishing with #0000 steel wool and brass polish or scrub pads (Scotch Brite or SOS sponge pads will not leave metal particles to later cause problems). Steel wool is mildly abrasive and removes the surface patina which is non reversible.

Polishing Lamps

After cleaning I use a good metal polish like Simichrome, applied per directions. Be careful not to scratch or wear off the delicate nickel plating, don't rub too hard on the sharp ridges, caps, knobs and seams.

This hanging fount has light corrosion a plus a hole that was repaired (arrow).

If a brass lamp is badly tarnished, use #0000 steel wool with the polish, and then follow up with polish and a soft cloth.

Regardless of the polishing method, you will need to remove any residue from the lamp recesses. I use lacquer thinner (this is what the polishing shops use) and a soft brush and plenty of soft rags. Flood the surface with the thinner and then wipe till it shines again. Gobs of residue will appear on the rag long after you think the brass is clean. There is another product, called PRE, available from the Eastwood Company (the car restoration people), which is good on embossed lamp surfaces.

Inspect the Brass for Cracks and Leaks

Now that the lamp is clean, inspect the metal for stress cracks (metal fatigue) and solder overflow from prior repairs The stress cracks will appear as faint lines in the metal or outright cracks. Stress cracks are due to improper annealing of the brass after it was spun into shape (see right).

It is a good policy to check for leaks, especially in the event stress cracks are found. Never use water (water is not as porous as kerosene) to leak check, use kerosene or lamp oil and set overnight with clean paper underneath. Make provisions (a pan) to catch the liquid in case the lamp does leak! If the lamp leaks and is a family piece, put it in a place to be admired, as a family heirloom.

Do You Have All the Parts?

Now, check for the proper parts. In the event of missing parts do not despair. There are dealers who specialize in the more common replacement parts. Fill caps come in different sizes depending on size of the fount or lamp.

Burners of the various brands are usually not interchangeable and replacements are often difficult to find. Therefore, check any lamp you are considering buying to make sure it has a complete burner. Check your burner to see if it has a gallery (chimney holder). These are made in two styles — one with four prongs and the other a full filigree chimney support ring. The burner may have a wick raising knob and mechanism (wick riser) or that mechanism may be located on the top of the font. If the burner has a knob, there should be a cylindrical "cage" (inside the fount) that will house the wick. All Rayo burners have this design. Since there were so many Rayo lamps made, these parts are often available from dealers, but many of the parts for other lamps are not. If the wick raising mechanism is located on the font, the parts often remain intact inside the fount. Check for a rod and usually a gear that meshed with the rod to elevate a "cage that fit directly on the inner draft tube," and had a wick attached by prongs or string.

Replace the Wick

From the above description it can be deduced that the wick installation is achieved by inserting the wick in the wick riser when it is attached to the burner and over the cage when it is on the wick tube. These center-draft wicks (often called Rayo wicks) fit most No. 2 size lamps, except the B&H No. 4 Radiant, Success and a few other lamps. The common universal wicks are available at lamp supply companies and some antique stores. Some dealers may have original, old wicks for your lamp. These wicks are usually stamped with the brand of the lamp.

Fueling

Now that your lamp is leak proof, clean and has a wick it is ready to fill with fuel. *Never* use gasoline, white gas or Coleman fuel in these lamps. There is considerable discussion by the experts on the best fuel. I suggest what the original manufacturers recomendeded — clean K-1 grade kerosene.

Allow me to present some other options. Water-clear lamp oil burns satisfactorily but avoid scented and colored lamp oils — over time they clog the wick with unburned residue. The same is true for red dyed K-1 kerosene sold at filling stations.

Fill the lamp with your preferred fuel and allow the wick to become fully saturated, by capillary action, at least 2 to 3 hours, preferably overnight before use.

Lighting the Lamp

Now, let's light the lamp. After the lamp has been filled and

Caution

Use fresh kerosene, always clear as water.
Do not over fill, especially in winter, as fuel will expand in warm room.
Install correct chimney for draft.
Use lamp on level surface.
Avoid breathing vapors.
Never leave the lamp unattended.
Keep lamp away from children.
Keep lamp away from flammable materials.
Extinguish lamp after use.

prepared, elevate the wick a minimum amount and light the wick on several places. Then place the chimney on the gallery and raise the wick to get the desired flame. *Never* leave a burning lamp unattended.

Since we did not discuss chimneys before, I'll touch on that briefly. The Rayo, the most common oil lamp, takes a 2⅝" x 10" chimney for proper draft. These are often found at hardware stores, antique shops and flea markets. This size fits a large number of No. 2 size lamps. See the lists of chimneys in the appendix for sizes that fit many brands of old lamps.

Shades

I am often asked if you can put a shade on your lamp. The answer is yes. Most companies offered shades for their lamps. Originally the Rayo had an under the burner tripod to mount a 10" shade. If the shade tripod or ring is missing, most No. 2 size lamps can easily be fitted with a replacement 2¹⁵⁄₁₆" inner diameter tripod (these must be modified slightly to fit the gallery). Choose plain white opal or a decorated shade that fits the decor. The Rayo lamp originally was marketed with either a plain white, no crown 10" student shade or a cased green 10" shade. Other makers added fancier and fancier shades to be more competitive.

A Final Thought

Many old lamps have been "wired" and converted to an electric lamp years ago. All is not lost if your lamp has been electrified with only a socket stuck into the inner draft tube and no holes drilled in the fount (vital fluid holding area). You are lucky if the draft tube has not been cut or damaged. Many times a flame spreader can be located and the lamp can be salvaged. If there is more extensive damage consult a lamp repairman with a good reputation.

Afterthoughts

See illustrations in this book to help identify the parts and construction of your lamp. The search for the proper original parts is worth your time and effort to restore and enjoy your old lamp and possibly a family heirloom.

Editor's Note: Richard and Barbara Dudley have published a book on restoring, repairing and lighting old lamps — *Restoration of Antique Oil and Electric Lighting Handbook*. Contact them at: http://www.lampdoctor.com.

Some Tools to Help

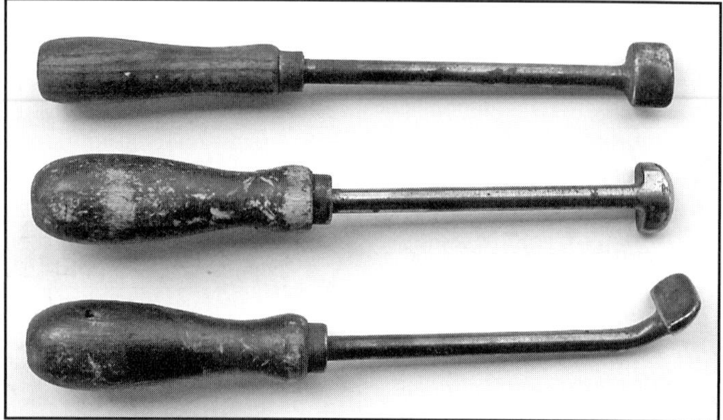

Tools for smoothing out dents in center-draft founts.

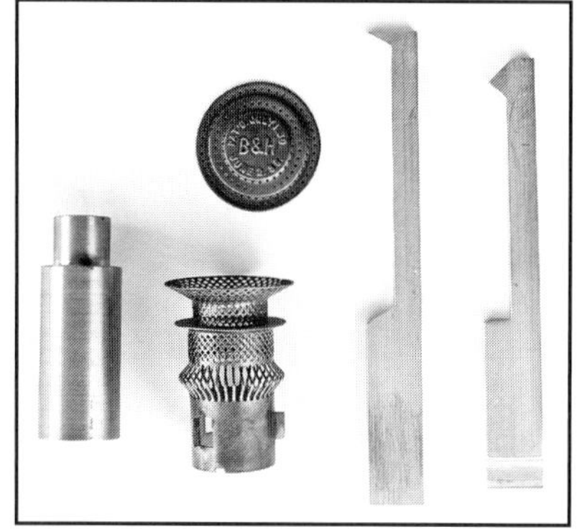

Tools for removing dents and reforming bent flame spreaders. These tools and dies are custom-made by machine shops for specialists in lamp repair. Courtesy George Bock and Kent Stratton.

Corrosion spots on the base of an old brass lamp. This lamp is best restored by chemical stripping and polishing to remove the damage.

A metal "baffle"may be found inside the draft tube of center-draft lamps. This acts as a heat-sink to help dissipate heat from the wick tube. At the same time, the metal baffle may act like a heating coil to preheat the draft air.

Shades and Accessories

The Meriden Flint Glass Company (1876-1888), West Meriden, Connecticut, supplied lamp glass for Meriden Britannia Company and chimneys and globes for brass lamp manufacturers in Meriden and elsewhere (Wilson, 1972 and Tobin, 2004).

The Meriden Britannia Company was a major stock holder as well as customer of Meriden Flint Glass. Tobin (2004) credits Horace C. Wilcox, president of Meriden Britannia, for the idea to establish a glass works in Meriden.

Meriden Flint Glass employed about 150 including decorators of note who went on to establish other well known glass companies.

Philip Handel was born in Meriden. His father was a foreman for the Charles Parker Company. Philip worked for Meriden Britannia Company and the Meriden Flint Glass Company before establishing a glass decorating business with Adolph Eydam in 1885 (Eydam & Handel Co.) and simply Handel & Co. in 1893 (DeFalco, et al., 1986, and Revi, 1968). Eydam became foreman of the C. F. Monroe company in 1892. Handel held patent 544,893 (1895) for conversion of an oil lamp to gas or electric. He established a foundry to manufacture his own lamp bases in 1902. The Handel Company (incorporated in 1903) opened a branch factory in New York City and Philip Handel died in 1914 (DeFalco, et al., 1986).

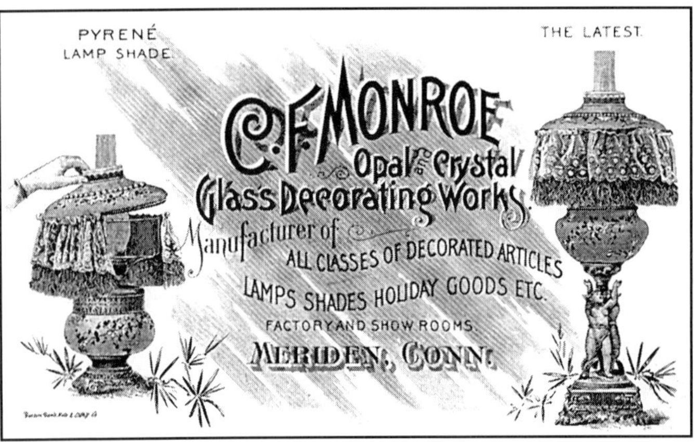

Advertisement.
Courtesy Allen Weathers.

Charles F. Monroe was a designer for Meriden Flint Glass before starting the C. F. Monroe Company in 1886; which he incorporated in 1892. He imported and decorated glass objects, including plating with fine Sterling silver. Monroe originated Wavecrest, a decorated opal glass, in 1898. He held patents 433,017 (1890) and 450,729 (1891) for lamp shades illustrated in the above advertisement.

Monroe Company shareholders included Edward Miller, Jr. (for Edward Miller & Company) and W. H. Lyon (for Charles Parker Company). Monroe furnished decorated glass shades for Miller and Parker lamps (Revi, 1968). By 1906 Monroe employed 200 artists, engravers and designers. Carl Helmschmied was designer for Monroe often painting landscapes. The Edward Miller Company purchased

MERIDEN FLINT GLASS CO.,

MERIDEN CONN.

Rich Cut Glassware,

AND

OPAL GOODS, PLAIN AND DECORATED.

Etched Globes & Shades.

Advertisement, *China and Glass Journal*, 1882.

the Monroe factory and equipment in 1916, operating it until 1923. C. F. Monroe remained as foreman until 1920 (Revi, 1968).

Carl V. Helmschmied joined C. F. Monroe in 1886 and left to form his own company in 1903. John H. Parker was a shareholder. The Helmschmied Manufacturing Company decorated vases, shades, globes and other elegant glass objects, often with nature scenes, birds and butterflies (Revi, 1968, and Gillespie, 1906). Some glass has C. V. H. molded in the base. He patented the "Illuminated Flower Pot" whereby a pipe for gas, oil, or electric was centered for a light fixture.

The Mount Washington Glass Works and Smith Brothers, New Bedford, Massachusetts, decorated opal glass lamp shades beginning in the 1870s.

Swann and Whitehead decorated shades for Clark Brothers and other manufacturers in New Jersey and New York.

The Fostoria Shade and Lamp Company, Fostoria, Ohio, supplied decorated shades and lamp glass for Edward Miller Co., Ansonia Brass, Holmes, Booth & Haydens and Bradley and Hubbard.

Thuro (2001) reported that Bradley and Hubbard bought shades from Dithridge & Co. and Washington Glass Mfg. Co. Other companies that made shades and globes include Buttler Art Glass Co., Gillinder & Sons and The Phoenix Glass Co. Many other companies furnished shades for lamp manufacturers and it is impossible to list them all.

I make no attempt to suggest original shades for lamps in this book other than illustration of lamps from original catalog pages. Lamp shades may be fancy or plain, glass or fabric and even paper. Most catalogs offered lamps with shades, however, many of the companies that manufactured brass lamps did not make glass. They purchased the shades and chimneys and resold them, sometimes as their own branded goods. Most hanging lamps and some vase lamps (certainly the decorated ones) were supplied with matching globes. Clark Bros., Fostoria Glass Company, Consolidated Lamp and Glass and Pittsburgh Lamp & Glass were exceptions as they designed and manufactured matching shades for their own lamps.

Variety of Shades

A wide variety of shades in shape, style, size, and materials were used on Victorian lamps. One cannot help but wonder about safety of the paper and fancy cloth shades advertised during the 1880s and 1890s. Collectors today generally prefer glass globes and shades decorated or styled to compliment the lamp and home decor.

Advertisement in the *Ladies' Home Journal,* November 1894.

Pitkin and Brooks offered numerous decorated shades for buyers who wanted a choice. In addition, the 1904/1905 catalog offered the identical hanging frame with a choice of three different brands of center-draft founts.

I suspect that most shades were selected by the woman of the house at the retail level. Even in catalogs such as Montgomery Ward, Marshall Field, and Pitkin and Brooks, the lamp and shade combinations were likely matched by the retail store for customer appeal and best profit margin, and not by the lamp manufacturer. Many glass houses made shades as their specialties. Even so, many people used lamps without shades, saving the extra expense.

PRICES OF SHADES.

SHADE No.		PRICE.
20103	for Piano and Tall Banquets,	$10.00
20820	" " " " "	7.50
18103	" Banquets about 24 inches high,	8.00
18822	" " " 24 " "	6.00
14902	" " " 20 " "	3.00

If you desire to *change Shade priced with any lamp* you can *add* or *deduct* according to above prices. Simply mention in ordering, the *Number of the Shade desired and Color.*

Shades Nos. 14902, 18822 and 20820 are made from good clear China Silk with colored lace to match Shade, and can be had in either Canary, Orange, Blue, Pink, Nile Green or Red.

Nos. 18103 and 20103 are made from Marceline Silk with wide Chiffon Trimmings to match color of Shade. These are beautiful Shades and can be had in either of the following delicate tints; Sunrise, Sunset, Peach, Tulip, Pink, Rose, Canary or Gold. All of the above Shades have Brass Hooks in the top, for hanging from top of Chimney, which is the best and most convenient way.

Shades by Edward Miller & Company, 1893 catalog.

Artistic vase lamp with Bristol oil pot and burner. Decorated dome shades, usually decorated by hand, were popular during the 1890s.

MONTHLY STATEMENT.

West Meriden, Ct., Aug 6th 1877

Mr. G. H. Clark Salisbury Ct.

In Acct. with The Meriden Flint Glass Co.

Terms, NET CASH. 30 days

July 2 Mdse 9 35

Paid Aug 11-77
Meriden Flint Glass Co

Should be pleased to recieve Check

Gents
Enclosed please find Check for $9 35/100
Yours Respect
G. H. Clark

Billhead.

Courtesy Gale Belliveau.

Consolidated Lamp & Glass Co., Coraoplis, PA.

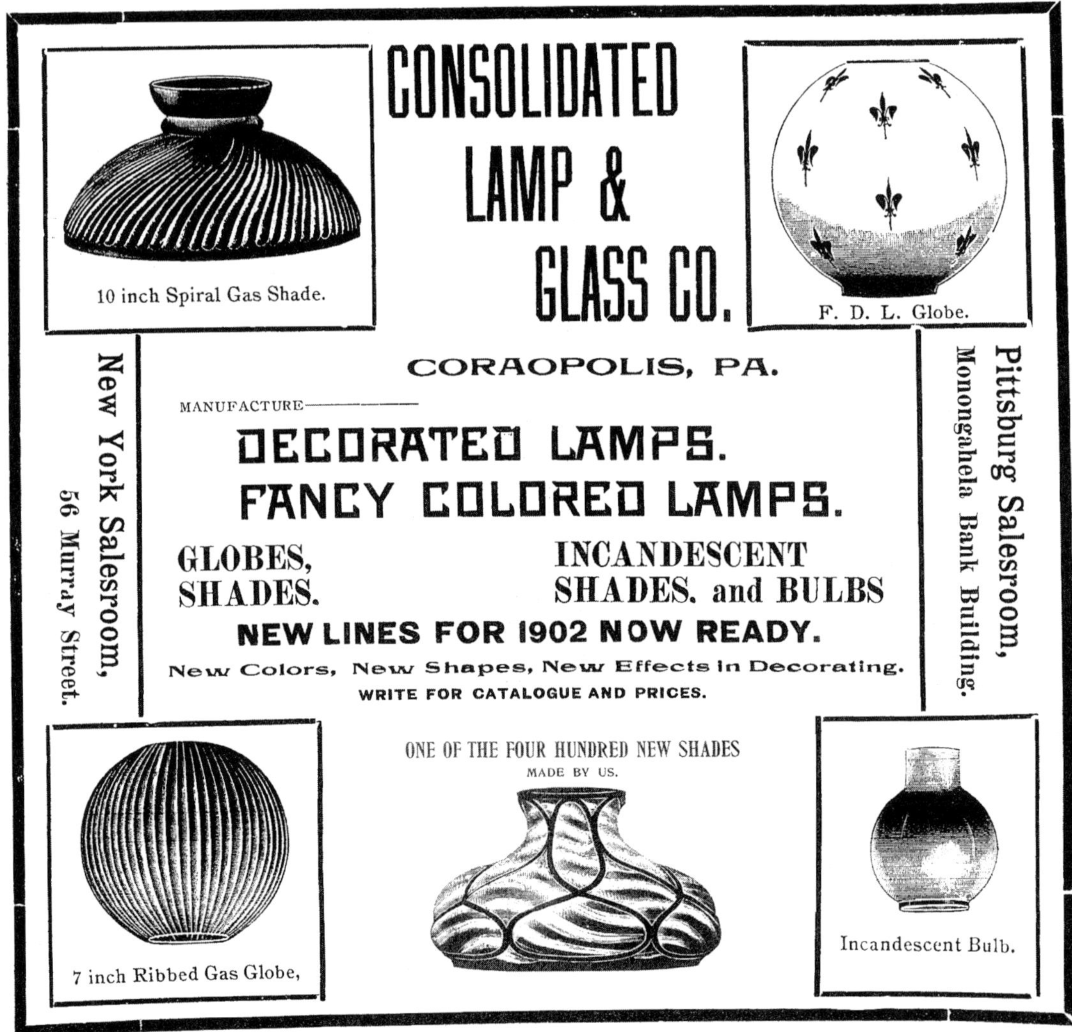

Advertisement, *CGL,* April 12, 1902.

Gillinder & Sons, Philadelphia

Advertisement, *CGL,* April 12, 1902.

Handel, Meriden

Signed Handel opal decorated shade.
Courtesy Doug and Judy Myers.

Signed Handel opal decorated shade.
Courtesy Patricia St. John.

Chief Library Lamp, Bristol Brass & Clock Co.

The Chief library lamp with Improved Bristol burner, 1892 Pitkins & Brooks catalog. The glass fount holder is decorated to match the shade. Courtesy David Broughton.

Macbeth-Evans Glass Company, Lamp Chimneys in 1901

Thomas Evans merged with George Macbeth in 1899 to form Macbeth Evans Glass Company, Pittsburgh. This company was the largest manufacturer of lamp chimneys in the world. They had factories in Pittsburgh and Charleroi, Pennsylvania, Marion and Elwood, Indiana and Toledo, Ohio.

The following copy is reprinted from a 1901 Macbeth catalog *How to Manage Lamps, Index to Lamps and Their Glasses, and Retail Catalogue*. The images of trademarks are courtesy of Hagley Museum and Library.

You can carry a lamp with no fear of the flame breaking the chimney if it's made of MACBETH Pearl Glass.

All chimneys so made have my name on them.

They never break from heat.

I have studied the requirements of every burner made, and no matter what burner you are using, I have the right chimney for it. It will secure most light, with no smudge or smoke.

My Lamp-Chimney Catalogue is full of practical suggestions about lamps and chimneys and wicks and oils, and how to keep them in order. It tells which chimney will give the best light on every kind of lamp. It saves a great deal of bother and money. I gladly mail it, free, to any one who writes for it. Address

MACBETH, Pittsburgh.

Advertisement, *McCall's Magazine*, March 1908.

Our Business

We make more than half the lamp-chimneys of the United States, and all the good ones.

Breaking of Chimneys

We say our good chimneys don't break in use.

They break from misuse. A wrong number may break or melt; if the burner is foul, the glass may break. A gust of cold air, on a hot chimneys, may break it.

Whenever the chimney is touched by the flame, it melts or breaks; it must not be touched by the flame. The shape of the chimney prevents, unless its working is thwarted by some misuse. In central-drafts, the flame is between two drafts, the central and outer drafts. When the burner is foul, this outer draft is partly stopped, and the flame gets pushed too near or against the chimney, and breaks or melts it.

Chimneys cannot be made to resist misuse or accidents.

More Light

Our good chimneys give more light than common ones; due to perfection of shape and proportion, right draft, right balance of drafts.

Try a common one. Turn the wick up till you get the most light it will give. Put on the good one. Now you can turn the wick higher and get more light, perhaps twice as much.

Common Chimneys

Our make or anybody elses, no great difference. Cheap metal, brittle, gets misty in use, and obscures the light; cheap make, the shape and proportions imperfect, the draft accidental.

Costs

Comparing common chimneys with good, the breakage is ten to one; the light is half, and the price is half.

To offer such goods is an insult to one's intelligence.

We make three grades: bad, middling and good.

We make the very cheapest we can, because half of the dealers won't buy any other. We are ashamed of them; and, of course, don't put our name on them.

We make the middling, because some dealers will buy them, who won't buy good ones. No name on them; we'd rather not sell them.

We make the good, and do our utmost to sell them: Macbeth pearl-top and pearl-glass; we are proud of them. Our low-grade lead glass we call flint.

A lamp chimney is a small thing, (however important) and it is strange a dealer will so belittle himself as to substitute an imitation for the genuine "Pearl-top" chimney, because it costs him a few cents per dozen less. Yet he does this—does it every day. We are blamed when these imitation things "don't work" and break. Every "Pearl-top" chimney bears a label for your protection. Look for it.

"Pearl-glass" (chimneys not pearled at top) are made of same quality of glass, and have etched near top MACBETH & CO., PEARL GLASS, in plain letters. These are for central draft and student lamps

Do yourself the justice to examine your next purchase and take no substitute for "Pearl-top" or Pearl-glass chimneys.

Pittsburgh, Pa. GEO. A. MACBETH & Co.

Advertisement, *Harper's Magazine*, March 1892.

Your Interest

You could better afford to pay a dollar apiece for our best than five or ten cents for bad or middling or even wrong number of good.

The Care of Lamps

Lamps smell and give poor light; (1) because they are not kept clean: or (2) the wick is poor or clogged by having been used too long; or (3) the chimney is wrong.

Trim, clean and fill daily, and wipe the whole lamp.

Trim by rubbing the char off the wick; this leaves it even. Don't cut it; you can't cut it even.

Keep the holes in the floor of the burner clear for draft.

Don't fill quite full; the oil expands with heat and runs over.

Boil the burner a few minutes once a month in sal soda or lye-water.

Empty the fount occasionally for sediment.

Don't open the lamp when hot; there is explosive vapor in it.

Light it with wick turned low, and turn up gradually; or you will get it too high and make smoke.

Move with care a lamp that has been burning long enough to get hot; or, better, don't move it.

Use the American Fletcher or Hyatt wick; and renew it once a month or two, no matter how fresh it looks; it gets clogged and don't feed freely.

Use oil of not less than 110° flash, for safety; the higher the flash, the safer the oil.

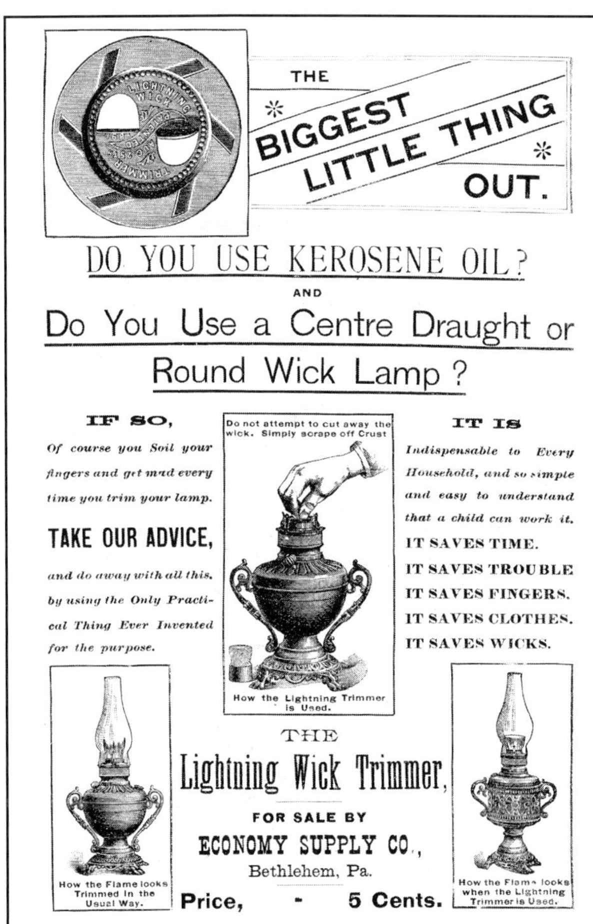

Macbethe-Evans Glass Company, Standard Brands and Trademarks in 1900

This copy is from the Macbeth-Evans Glass Company catalog *Lamp Chimneys, Lantern Globes and Silvered Glass Reflectors, Export Catalogue No. 103*, ca. 1900. The images of trademarks are courtesy of the Hagley Museum and Library.

The following brands are listed in order of quality. Each is distinguished by our trade-mark etched in the glass.

PEARL GLASS

Pearl Glass is a grade peculiar to us, and we hold it superior to all others. Pearl Glass is tough against heat, it is clear and stays clear, the shape is such to get full light from the lamps, and the accurancy and fineness of make secure full light. Pearl Top has a row of pearls around the top, the patent has now expired.

ZENITH

Zenith is a high-grade lead glass.

KEYSTONE

Keystone is a fine flint glass chimney.

IRON CLAD

Iron Clad is a fine flint glass chimney.

SUPERIOR

Superior is a fine flint glass chimney, same quality as Iron Clad.

CRESCENT

Crescent is a first quality lime glass chimney.

EMPIRE

Empire is a first quality lime glass chimney, same quality as Crescent.

Index to Lamps and Chimneys, Macbeth-Evans Glass Company — 1901

The following list is from MacBeth Lamp Glasses catalog No. 11 dated 1901 which states that the company provides chimney glasses for "most of the burners and lamps in use in the world." I have omitted flat wick burners and lamps.

Note: When more than one length is given, the taller chimney will work well, increasing draft, especially in higher elevations.

Lamp	Chimney Dia. x Length in inches
Acme Mail Car	2½ x 12
Admiral*	2⅝ x 12
Aladdin*	2⅝ x 9 or 10
American No. 1	2 x 8
American No. 2	2⅝ x 9
Aurora*	2½ x 10¾ or 12
B & H No. 0	1 9/16 x 7
B & H No. 1	2 x 8
B & H No. 2	2½ x 10 or 2⅝ x 10
B & H No. 89	4½ x 11
B & H No. 96	4 x 12
Baby Victor*	1 9/16 x 7
Banner No. 0	2 x 6½
Banner No. 1	2½ x 7½
Banner No. 2	2⅞ x 8½
Banner No. 3	4 x 12
Bartholdi,* Mays	2½ x 9 or 10
Bartholdi* No.2 burner	2⅜ x 9 or 10½
Bartholdi* No.3 burner	3 x 10½
Belgian No. 2	1⅞ x 9
Belgian No. 1	2½ x 10¼
Belgian No. 0	2⅝ x 11½
Belgian No. 00	3 x 9 or 12⅛
Belgian Mammoth	3 x 9 or 12⅛
Brighton No. 1	2 x 8 or 9
Brighton No. 2	2⅝ x 9 or 10
Brilliant Argand	1¾ x 10½
Brilliant Electric No. 2	3 x 10
Bristol Electric	2½ x 9
Bristol No. 1	2 x 8
Bristol No. 2	2⅝ x 9 or 10
Bristol No. 3	4 x 12
Bristol Mammoth	4 x 12
Challenge Argand	1¾ x 10½
Columbia*	2⅝ x 9 or 10
Connecticut	2⅝ x 9 or 12
Crystal Light	1¾ x 10½
Daylight	2⅝ x 9 or 10 or taller
Daylite*	2⅝ x 12
Dayton No. 11 Mail car	2½ x 12
Dresden No. 2	2½ x 10 or 12
Dresden No. 3	3 x 9 or 12
Dresden Mammoth	3 x 9 or 12
Drummond** No. 2	3 x 8¼
Duffield**	4 x 10
Electric Argand	2½ x 9
Electric No.1	2½ x 9
Electric No. 2	3 x 10
Empress No. 2	2⅝ x 12
Empress No. 3	4 x 12
Empress Mammoth	4 x 12
Eureka Central-draft No.2	2⅝ x 12
Excelsior*	2⅝ x 12
Fireside No. 0	2 x 6½
Fireside No. 1	2½ x 7½
Fireside No. 2	2⅞ x 8½
Gaskill*	2⅝ x 12
German-American Student	2 1/16 x 10½
Gladstone No. 2	2⅝ x 9
Gladstone No. 3	4 x 12
Gladstone Mammoth	4 x 12
Globe** Incandescent No.2	4½ x 11
Globe** Incand. Mammoth	4½ x 11
Haida No. 1	2 x 9
Haida No. 2	2⅝ x 9 or 12
Harvard	2 x 10½
Headlight,* standard	2½ x10
Headlight,* Ft. Wayne	2½ x 10
Hickok	2⅞ x 10
Hipwell,* Hipwell Star*	2⅝ x 12
Home Lamp*	1 9/16 x 7
Imperial**	2 7/16 x 12
Improved Ansonia*	2⅝ x 12
Improved M & W*	2⅝ x 12
Juno No.0	1 9/16 x 7
Juno No.1	2 x 8
Juno No.2	2⅝ x 12
Juno No.3	4 x 12
Juno* No. 30	2⅝ x 10
Juno Mammoth	4 x 12
Jupiter Mammoth* No.3	3 x 12
Kent	2 1/16 x 10
Keystone No. 1	2 x 8
Kleeman*	more than one size
Liberty No.1	2½ x 10¼
Liberty No.2	3 x 12⅛
Little B & H	1 9/16 x 7
Little Giant	3 x 10
Little Jewel	1⅜ x 7⅝
Little Prince	1⅜ x 7⅝
Little Royal	1⅜ x 7⅝
Little Wonder	4¾ x 10½
Lux-Dux*	2⅝ x 12
Magnet* No.2	2⅝ x 10
Magnum	4 x 10
Manhattan Student*	2⅜ x 12 & other sizes
Marsh*	3 x 12
Master*	2⅝ x 12
Meriden No. 2	2⅝ x 12
Meteor No. 1	2 x 8
Meteor No. 2	2⅝ x 12
Meteor No. 3	4 x 12
Meteor Mammoth	4 x 12
Meyrose No. 2	2⅝ x 12
Meyrose No. 3	4 x 9½ or 12

Miller Champion*	$2\frac{5}{8}$ x 10
Miller No. 0	$1\frac{9}{16}$ x 7
Miller No. 1	2 x 8
Miller No. 2	$2\frac{5}{8}$ x 12
Miller No. 3	4 x 12
Miller Mammoth	4 x 12
Miller Student	$1\frac{9}{16}$ x 7
Miller's Lumo*	$2\frac{1}{2}$ x 10
Moehring Argand	2 x $10\frac{1}{2}$
Monarch Central-draft	3 x 10
New Manhattan No.3	3 x 10 or 12
New Manhattan Mammoth	3 x 12
New Rival No.2	$2\frac{5}{8}$ x 12
New Vestal* No.2	$2\frac{1}{2}$ x 10
Niagra No.1	2 x 8
Niagra No.2	$2\frac{9}{16}$ x $9\frac{1}{4}$
Niagra* (marked Hero)	2 x 8
Paragon* No.2	$2\frac{5}{8}$ x 10
Paragon* Mammoth No.3	4 x 12
Parker No.2	$2\frac{5}{8}$ x 12
Parker No.3	$4\frac{1}{2}$ x 11
Parker Mammoth	$4\frac{1}{2}$ x 11
Perfection No.1	$1\frac{15}{16}$ x $9\frac{1}{2}$
Perfection No.2	$1\frac{15}{16}$ x $10\frac{1}{2}$
Perfection Mammoth	$2\frac{1}{4}$ x 11
Perfect Star Electric No.1	$2\frac{1}{2}$ x 9
Perfect Star Electric No.2	3 x 10
Pittsburgh No.2	$2\frac{1}{2}$ x 10 or 12
Pittsburgh No.3	$4\frac{1}{2}$ x 11
Pittsburgh Mammoth	$4\frac{1}{2}$ x 11
Plumwood No.2	$2\frac{1}{2}$ x 10 or 12
Plumwood No. 3	$4\frac{1}{2}$ x 11
Plumwood Mammoth	$4\frac{1}{2}$ x 11
Princeton*	$2\frac{5}{8}$ x 12
Radiant No. 4	$2\frac{1}{2}$ x 10 or 12
Radiant No. 5	$4\frac{1}{2}$ x 11
Radiant No. 98	$4\frac{1}{2}$ x 11
Radiant Mammoth	$4\frac{1}{2}$ x 11
Rayo*	$2\frac{5}{8}$ x 10 or 12
Rayo JR*	2 x 8
Rival	$2\frac{1}{2}$ x 10 or 12
Rival No. 2	$2\frac{5}{8}$ x 12
Rochester Jr or No. 0	$1\frac{9}{16}$ x 7
Rochester No.1	2 x 8
Rochester No.2	$2\frac{5}{8}$ x 9 to 12
Rochester No.3	4 x 12
Rochester Mammoth	4 x 12
Royal Argand	$2\frac{7}{8}$ x 10
Royal No.1	2 x 8
Royal No.2	$2\frac{5}{8}$ x 12
Royal No.3	4 x 12
Royal Mammoth	4 x 12
Shaffer	Made in two sizes.
Star No.0	2 x $6\frac{1}{2}$
Star No.1	$2\frac{1}{2}$ x $7\frac{1}{2}$
Star No. 2	$2\frac{7}{8}$ x $8\frac{1}{2}$
Star Electric No.2	3 x 10
Student German-American	$2\frac{1}{16}$ x $10\frac{1}{2}$
Student No.2	$4\frac{3}{4}$ x $10\frac{1}{2}$
Student No.1	$1\frac{5}{16}$ x $10\frac{1}{2}$
Student Mammoth	$2\frac{1}{4}$ x 11
Success	$2\frac{1}{2}$ x $10\frac{3}{4}$ or 12
Sun Electric No.1	$2\frac{1}{2}$ x $7\frac{1}{2}$
Sun Electric No.2	$2\frac{7}{8}$ x $8\frac{1}{2}$
Sunburst	$2\frac{1}{4}$ x 12
Tiny Juno	$1\frac{9}{16}$ x 7
Tiny Miller*	$1\frac{9}{16}$ x 7
Trenton No.1	2 x 8
Trenton No.2	$2\frac{5}{8}$ x 12
Tuxedo No. 1	2 x 8
Tuxedo No. 2	$2\frac{5}{8}$ x 12
U. S. Electric*	3 x 12
Vestal* No. 0	$1\frac{13}{16}$ x 7
Vestal* No. 1	$2\frac{1}{16}$ x 8
Vestal* No. 2	$2\frac{5}{8}$ x 10
Victor Size 0*	$1\frac{3}{8}$ x 7
Victor No. 1	$1\frac{5}{16}$ x $7\frac{1}{2}$
Victor No.2	$2\frac{5}{8}$ x 10
Victor No.3	4 x 12
Victor Mammoth	4 x 12
Waterbury Electric No.2	3 x 10
Waterbury Electric No.1	$2\frac{1}{2}$ x 9
Wilson Rochester	$2\frac{7}{16}$ x $9\frac{1}{2}$ or $2\frac{3}{8}$ x $10\frac{1}{4}$
Yale No.1	2 x 8
Yale No.2	$2\frac{5}{8}$ x 12
Yale No.3	4 x 12
Yale Mammoth	4 x 12
Young America*	$1\frac{3}{8}$ x $7\frac{5}{8}$

* From other sources to supplement MacBeth Evans list. These lamps may be earlier or later than the date this list was published.

** These are special-shape chimney glass.

Also see the 1898 *Illustrated Catalogue of the Chimney Department of the American Flint Glass Workers Union* (*Illuminator* Vol. 2, No. 2, 1988).

B & H chandelier with No. 2 fount lamps. The B & H chimneys are $2\frac{5}{8}$" x 10". Courtesy Kent Stratton.

Lamp Chimneys in 1908

— 4246 —

LAMP CHIMNEYS.

TO THE TRADE.—We offer the "Klear Krystal" Chimneys, believing that the great majority of dealers are alive to the value of handling strictly first-class goods. In the manufacture of "Klear Krystal" Chimneys none but the very best materials are used, and the greatest care is exercised in the proper annealing of the glass. Every Chimney, while undergoing this process, is subjected to a temperature of 800 degrees of heat, and every-one which passes safely through this test is ABSOLUTELY FIRE-PROOF. They are subjected to close inspection, and every one is perfect in size, shape and finish. They are UNDOUBTEDLY THE BEST Chimneys on the market, and dealers who wish to sell FIRST-CLASS GOODS should secure their sale. They cost no more than any other GOOD Chimneys, and really less than many INFERIOR brands. Beware of imitations. Every genuine "Klear Krystal" Chimney has the name "Klear Krystal" etched upon it, and is neatly wrapped in a printed white wrapper.

"Klear Krystal" Chimneys are made to fit all of the well known makes of Lamps on the market. We give below a comparative list of Miscellaneous Names of Chimneys and the corresponding name and number we carry in stock.

Miscellaneous Names.	No.	Our Name and Number.	No.
Acme Extra Heavy	1	Sun Ajax	1-AJ
Acme Extra Heavy	2	Sun Ajax	2-AJ
Acorn		Nutmeg	
Admiral	2	Rochester	2-R
Allnight		Gem	
American	2	Rochester	2-R
Ansonia	3	Rochester	3-R
Anvil Extra Heavy	1	Sun Ajax	1-AJ
Anvil Extra Heavy	2	Sun Ajax	2-AJ
Apollo		Welsbach	
Baby Meridan		Rochester	JR
Baby Victor		Rochester	JR
Banner	3	Rochester	3-R
Belgian	1	Liberty	1-L
Belgian	00	Liberty	00-L
Bijou		Little Jewel	LJ
B. & H.	1	Rochester	1-R
B. & H.	2	Regular Duplex	
B. & H.	3	Globe Incandescent	2-GE
B. & H. Radiant	4	Liberty	1-L
B. & H. Radiant	5	Liberty	00-L
B. & H. Radiant	89	Globe Incandescent	2-GI
B. & H. Radiant	92	Rochester	3-R
B. & H. Radiant	96	Rochester	3-R
Brilliant		German Student	2-G
Bristol	1	Rochester	1-R
Bristol	2	Rochester	2-R
Bristol	3	Rochester	3-R
Butter Cup		Nutmeg	
Cosmopolitan		Welsbach	
Daylight		Welsbach	
Dresden	1	Liberty	1-L
Dresden	3	Liberty	00-L
Electric for Globe	2	Globe Electric	2-GE
Empress	1	Rochester	1-R
Empress	2	Rochester	2-R
Empress	3	Rochester	3-R
Gladstone	2	Rochester	2-R
Gladstone	3	Rochester	3-R
Globe Etched	2	Etched Chimney	20
Haida	1	Rochester	1-R
Haida	2	Rochester	2-R
Haida	3	Rochester	3-R
Harvard		Moehring	
Hicks & Smith	3	Dual	3
Hornet		Gem	
Incandescent	2	Globe Incandescent	2-GI
International		Welsbach	
Ives	3	Dual	2
Juno	0	Rochester	JR
Juno	1	Rochester	1-R
Juno	2	Rochester	2-R
Juno	3	Rochester	3-R
Keystone	1	Rochester	1-R
Lip	3	Dual	2
Little Artic		Gem	
Little Artic B. & H.		Rochester	JR
Little Prince		Little Jewel	LJ
Little Royal		Little Jewel	LJ
Little Trenton		Little Jewel	LJ
Macbeth	4	Rochester	JR
Macbeth	6	Rochester	1-R
Macbeth	8	Rochester	2-R
Macbeth	9	Rochester 12-inch	2-R
Macbeth	10	Rochester	3-R
Macbeth	22	Regular Duplex	
Macbeth	26	Little Jewel	LJ
Macbeth	32	Liberty	1-L
Macbeth	36	Liberty	00-L
Macbeth	40	Electric	2-E

Miscellaneous Names.	No.	Our Name and Number.	No.
Macbeth	50	German Student	1-G
Macbeth	52	Mammoth Perfection Student	21-G
Macbeth	58	German Student	2-G
Macbeth	66	Globe Incandescent	2-GI
Macbeth	88	Moehring	
Macbeth	500	Sun	0-BT
Macbeth	502	Sun	1-BT
Macbeth	504	Sun	2-BT
Macbeth	514	Sun Hinge	2-HB
Mammoth Parker		Globe Incandescent	2-GI
Mammoth Perfection	9	Mammoth Perfection Student	21-G
Mammoth Pittsburg		Globe Incandescent	2-GI
Manhattan	2	Rochester	2-R
Meriden	1	Rochester	1-R
Meriden	2	Rochester	2-R
Meriden	3	Rochester	3-R
Meteor	1	Rochester	1-R
Meteor	2	Rochester	2-R
Meteor	3	Rochester	3-R
Midget		Little Jewel	LJ
Miller	0	Rochester	JR
Miller	1	Rochester	1-R
Miller	2	Rochester	2-R
Miller	3	Rochester	3-R
New Columbia	2	Rochester	2-R
New Manhattan	3	Liberty	00-L
Niagara	1	Rochester	1-R
Niagara	2	Rochester	2-R
Nobby		Nutmeg	
Oxford	3	Dual	3
Parker	2	Rochester	2-R
Perfection	1	German Student	1-G
Pittsburg	2	Rochester	2-R
Plumwood	2	Liberty	1-L
Plumwood	3	Liberty	00-L
Rex		Welsbach	
Richmond	2	Dual	2
Rival	2	Rochester	2-R
Royal	1	Rochester	1-R
Royal	2	Rochester	2-R
Slip	00	Nutmeg	
Star		Welsbach	
Stellar		Gem	
Student	1	German Student	1-G
Sun Beaded Top	0	Sun	0-BT
Sun Beaded Top	1	Sun	1-BT
Sun Beaded Top	2	Sun	2-BT
Sun Globe	2	Sun Globe	2-SG
Sunlight		Welsbach	
Sun Plain Top, Extra Heavy	1	Sun Ajax	1-AJ
Sun Plain Top, Extra Heavy	2	Sun Ajax	2-AJ
Sun Plain Top	1	Sun	1-PT
Sun Plain Top	2	Sun	2-PT
Trenton	1	Rochester	1-R
Trenton	2	Rochester	2-R
Tuxedo	1	Rochester	1-R
Tuxedo	2	Rochester	2-R
Twilight		Gem	
Victor Gas		Welsbach	
Victor Gas	1	Rochester	1-R
Victor Gas	2	Rochester	2-R
Victor Gas	3	Rochester	3-R
Wellington	2	Rochester	2-R
Wheeling	2	Rochester	2-R
Wide Awake		Nutmeg	
Young America		Little Jewel	LJ

Simmons Hardware catalog, GG, 1908.

Lamp Wicks in 1908

— 4259 —

LAMP WICKS.

FLAT WICK.

Per Gross

Nutmeg Night Lamp Wick; Length 8 in.; Width ⅜ in.; Weight per gross about 6 ozs........ $0.50
No. 0—(or E) Flat; Length 8 in.; Width ½ in... .60
No. 1—(or A) Flat; Length 8 in.; Width ⅝ in... .75
No. 2—(or B) Flat; Length 8 in.; Width 1 in... 1.10
No. 3—(or D) Flat; Length 8 in.; Width 1½ in.. 1.75
Weight per Gross about 1½ lbs.
Duplex; Length 10 in.; Width Flat, 1⅛ in....... 3.00
No. 3 Moehring; Length 7¼ in.; Width 2¾ in... 3.00
Weight per Gross about 3 lbs.

ROUND WICK.

Per Gross

Pet; Length 8 in.; Diameter ¼ in.............. $0.60
Weight per Gross about ½ lb.

CIRCULAR WICK.

Per Gross

No. 1G—or Large German Student; Length 3½ in.; Width when Folded Flat 1³⁄₁₆ in...... $1.10
No. 2G—or Small German Student; Length 3½ in.; Width when Folded Flat 1 in........ 1.10
No. 1P—or Perfection Student; Length 4½ in.; Width when Folded Flat 1¹⁵⁄₁₆ in......... 3.00
Mammoth Perfection; Length 4 in.; Width when Folded Flat 2 in.......................... 4.50
Cleveland Student; Length 4 in.; Width when Folded Flat 1⁷⁄₁₆ in......................... 3.00
Weight per Gross about 1½ lbs.
Acme or No. 11 Postal Student; Length 6 in.; Width when Folded Flat 2¹⁄₁₆ in........... 5.25
Weight per Gross about 4½ lbs.
Moehring Circular; Length 6½ in.; Width when Folded Flat 1⁷⁄₁₆ in........................ 4.50
Weight per Gross about 2¾ lbs.
One Gross in a Bundle.

CIRCULAR WICK.

Per Gross

No. 1—Belgian; Length 8 in.; Width when Folded Flat 2 in.............................. $9.00
No. 1—Liberty; Length 8 in.; Width when Folded Flat 2 in............................ 9.00
Weight per Gross about 6 lbs.
No. 00—Belgian; Length 8 in.; Width when Folded Flat 2⁹⁄₁₆ in........................... 13.50
No. 00—Liberty; Length 8 in.; Width when Folded Flat 2⁹⁄₁₆ in........................... 13.50
Weight per Gross about 9 lbs.
No. 1—Meteor; Length 6 in.; Width when Folded Flat 1⅞ in................................ 4.50
No. 2—Meteor; Length 7½ in.; Width when Folded Flat 2½ in........................ 9.00
Weight per Gross about 6 lbs.
No. 3—Meteor; Length 8½ in.; Width when Folded Flat 4⅜ in............................ 22.25
Weight per Gross about 15 lbs.
No. 1—Miller; Length 6 in.; Width when Folded Flat 1⅞ in................................ 4.50
Weight per Gross about 9 lbs.
No. 2—Miller; Length 7½ in.; Width when Folded Flat 2½ in............................. 9.00
Weight per Gross about 6 lbs.
No. 3—Miller; Length 8½ in.; Width when Folded Flat 4⅜ in............................ 22.25
Weight per Gross about 15 lbs.
No. 1—Niagara; Length 7½ in.; Width when Folded Flat 1¹⁵⁄₁₆ in.......................$16.50
Weight per Gross about 4½ lbs.
No. 2—Niagara; Length 7½ in.; Width when Folded Flat 2½ in.......................... 30.00
Weight per Gross about 12 lbs.
One-twelfth Gross in a Bundle.

CIRCULAR WICK.

Per Gross

No. 0C—Length 5½ inches; Width when Folded Flat 1⁵⁄₁₆ inches........... $3.00

For the Following Burners:

Jr. Rochester, Little Midget, No. 0 Miller, Baby Victor, Little Jewel, Trenton, Jr., Little Royal, Little Prince, Little Trenton, Young America

Weight per Gross about 1½ lbs.

Per Gross

No. 1C—Length 6½ inches; Width when Folded Flat 1⅞ inches............ $3.75

For the Following Burners:

No. 1 Rochester, No. 1 Trenton, No. 1 Bristol, No. 1 Yale, Haida, Jr.

Weight per Gross about 3½ lbs.

One-twelfth Gross in a Bundle.

Per Gross

No. 2HC—Extra Heavy; Length 6½ inches; Width when Folded Flat 2½ inches $7.50

For the Following Burners:

Banner, Tuxedo, No. 2 Royal

Weight per Gross about 6 lbs.

Per Gross

No. 2C—Length 6½ inches; Width when Folded Flat 2½ inches............ $5.25

For the Following Burners:

No. 2 Rochester, No. 2 Wheeling, No. 2 Gladstone, No. 2 Princeton, No. 2 Pittsburg, No. 2 Victor, No. 2 Ansonia, No. 2 Meyrose, No. 2 Aurora, U. S. Trenton, No. 2 Connecticut, No. 2 Yale, No. 2 Parker, No. 2 M. & W., No. 2 Day Light, No. 2 Rival, No. 2 Hipwell, No. 2 Bristol, No. 2 Keystone

Weight per Gross about 5 lbs.
One-twelfth Gross in a Bundle;

Per Gross

No. 3C—Length 8½ inches; Width when Folded Flat 4⅜ inches...........$18.00

For the Following Burners:

No. 3 Rochester, No. 3 Gladstone, No. 3 Pittsburg, No. 3 B. & H., No. 3 Bristol, No. 3 Princeton, No. 3 Meyrose, No. 3 Monarch, No. 3 Ansonia, No. 3 Wheeling, No. 3 Lux Dux, No. 3 Victor, No. 3 Parker, No. 3 Keystone

Weight per Gross about 16 lbs.

One-twelfth Gross in a Bundle.

WE MAKE NO CHARGE FOR PACKING.

Simmons Hardware catalog, GG, 1908.

MARSHALL PROCESS BROWN WICK

Prices Quoted Are Net

Group	Item	Per Gro.	Per Doz.
	Special o, ½-inch Bicycle	$0.40	
	*No. o or E, ⅜-inch wide	.30	
	*No. 1 or A, ⅝-inch wide	.38	
	*No. 2 or B, 1-inch wide	.52	
	*No. 3 or D, 1½-inch wide	.92	
	Searchlight, 5 inches long	.36	$0.05
	Brilliant Argand	1.20	.12
	Crystal Light Argand	1.20	.12
	Dietz, ¾-inch wide	.50	.05
	Pett Circular	.40	.05
	Duplex, 10 inches long	1.70	.20
	Oxford, 10 inches long	1.70	.20
	*Wide Awake	.26	
	*Nutmeg	.26	
	Gem, ½-inch	.50	.05
	No. 1 Student, German	.70	.10
	No. 2 Student, German	.70	.10
All the Same Wick	No. 2 Rochester	3.20	.35
	No. 2 Gladstone	3.20	.35
	No. 2 Pittsburg	3.20	.35
	No. 2 Bristol	3.20	.35
	No. 2 Aurora	3.20	.35
	No. 2 Connecticut	3.20	.35
	No. 2 Parker	3 20	.35
	No. 2 Day Light	3.20	.35
	No. 2 Keystone	3.20	.35
	No. 2 Wheeling	3.20	.35
	No. 2 Haida	3.20	.35
	No. 2 Princeton	3.20	.35
	No. 2 Victor	3.20	.35
	No. 2 Wellington	3.20	.35
	No. 2 U. S. Trenton	3.20	.35
	No. 2 Yale	3.20	.35
	No. 2 M. & W.	3.20	.35
	No. 2 Rival	3.20	.35
	No. 2 Banner, 6-inch	3.50	.35
	No. 2 Miller	3.50	.35
	No. 2 Juno	3.50	.35
	No. 2 .B & H	3.50	.35
Same Wick	No. 2 Electric	4.32	.45
	No. 2 Casperson	4.32	.45
	No. 2 Sun Electric	4.32	.45
	No. 2 P. & A. Royal	4.32	.45
	No. 3 Globe Incandescent	4.32	.45
	No. 2 Waterbury	4.32	.45
	No. 2 Plumwood	2.72	.30
	No. 2 Dresden	2.72	.30
	No. 3 Plumwood	6.40	.60
	No. 3 Dresden	6.40	.60
Same Wk	No. 1 Rochester	2.40	.25
	No. 1 Bristol	2.40	.25
	Haida Jr.	2.40	.25
	No. 1 Trenton	2.40	.25
	No. 1 Yale	2.40	.25

* Sold only in gross lots.

Group	Item	Per Gro.	Per Doz.
	Cleveland Student	1.92	.20
	Perfection Student	1.92	.20
Same Wick	O. Miller	1.92	.20
	Jr. Rochester	1.92	.20
	Little Jewel	1.92	.20
	Little Royal	1.92	.20
	Little Trenton	1.92	.20
	Little Midget	1.92	.20
	Baby Victor	1.92	.20
	Trenton Jr.	1.92	.20
	Little Prince	1.92	.20
	Young America	1.92	.20
	Sun Duplex	1.92	.20
Same	Princess	1.92	.20
	Victor Argand	1.92	.20
All the Same Wick	No. 3 Rochester	10.00	1.00
	No. 3 Pittsburg	10.00	1.00
	No. 3 Bristol	10.00	1.00
	No. 3 Haida	10.00	1.00
	No. 3 Ansonia	10.00	1.00
	No. 3 Lux Dux	10.00	1.00
	No. 3 Parker	10.00	1.00
	No. 3 Gladstone	10.00	1.00
	No. 3 B. & H	10.00	1.00
	No. 3 Princeton	10.00	1.00
	No. 3 Monarch	10.00	1.00
	No. 3 Wheeling	10.00	1.00
	No. 3 Victor	10.00	1.00
	Keystone	10.00	1.00
	No. 3 Miller	10.80	1.00
	No. 3 Banner, 7-inch	8.80	.90
	No. 2 Globe Incandescent	9.60	1.00

STANDARD OIL COMPANY OF N. Y.
26 BROADWAY,
NEW YORK, June 8, 1898.

The New Jersey Wick Co.,
Newark, N. J.

Gentlemen—We have made a number of careful and exhaustive tests of your "Marshall Process" Wick, and feel that we cannot speak too highly of its qualities.

Yours truly,
STANDARD OIL COMPANY.

PRODUCED last season, but not having an opportunity to TEST THOROUGHLY before our catalogue was issued a year ago, and wishing to feel POSITIVE this wick had MERIT, DID NOT QUOTE.

We have since tested SCIENTIFICALLY and now offer as the highest grade wick manufactured in the WORLD.

The "Marshall Process" Wick is scientifically perfect. It is the result of an exhaustive series of experiments, extending over a long period, for the purpose of producing a flexible fibrous wick of the **highest standard** for heating and lighting purposes, with **superior capillary power** and **perfect odorless combustion** of the oil; together with the quality of being a **non-conductor of heat** and slow combustibility of the materials of the wick, thus giving a light of the greatest illuminating power.

Pitkin and Brooks 1898 *Lamps Catalogue* advertisement.
Courtesy Jeff Ebersole.

Important Hardware Companies, Department Stores, and Catalog Sellers of Center-draft Lamps

Abrams & Co., Boston, MA
Abram French & Co., Boston, MA
R. J. Allen & Sons, Philadelphia, PA.
George F. Bassett Co., New York, NY
American-Belgian Lamp Company, NY
Bindley Hardware Co., Pittsburg, PA
Burley & Tyrrell, Chicago, IL
Butler Bros, Chicago & New York
Dodd, Glaescher & Werner, Cincinnati, OH
T. G. Evans & Co., Pittsburgh, PA
E. H. Fessenden, Brooklyn, NY
French, Potter & Wilson, Chicago, IL
Haida Lamp & China Co., New York, NY
Hibbard, Spencer & Bartlett, Chicago, IL
C. F. A. Hinrichs, New York, NY
R. Hollings & Co., Boston, MA
F. H. Lovell & Company, New York, NY
Macys, New York, NY
Marshall Field, Chicago, IL
McKenney & Waterbury Co., Boston, MA
Montgomery Ward, Chicago, IL
W. R. Noe, New York, NY
Ogden, Merrill & Greer, St. Paul, MN
Peaslee Gaulbert Co., Louisville, KY
Pitkin & Brooks, Chicago, IL
Rochester Lamp Company, New York, NY
Henry & Nathan Russell, New York, NY
Sears Roebuck, Chicago, IL
Standard Oil Company of New Jersey
Bennett Schneider, New York, NY
Shapleigh Hardware, St. Louis, MO
Simmons Hardware, St. Louis, MO
John Wanamaker, New York, NY
A. J. Weidener, Philadelphia, PA
Charles Williams Stores, New York, NY

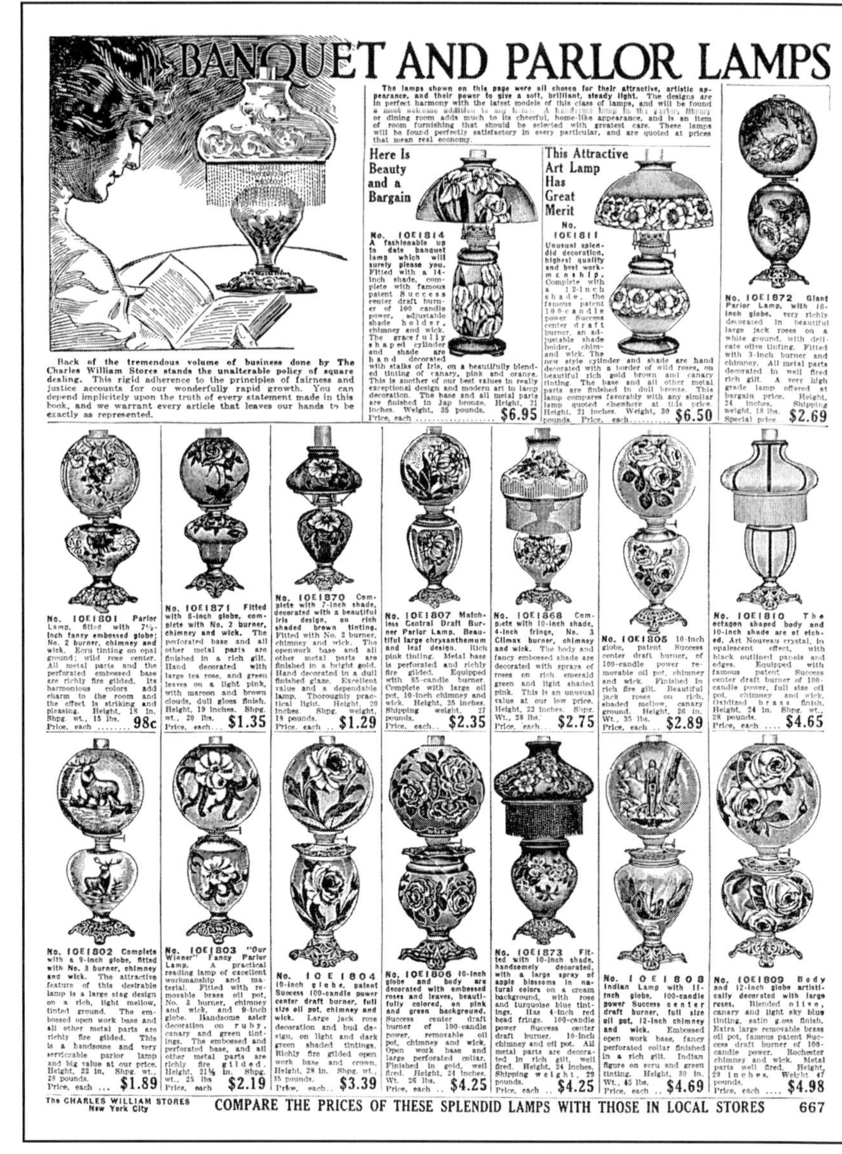

Charles Williams Stores. Above, 1914; this advertisement, 1917.

Side-draft, Folded-wick Burners

Side-draft burners were designed to provide air into a circular wick to improve light output. Most of these burners formed the round wick burning surface by folding one or two flat wicks into circular form. These are called folded wick burners by lamp researchers.

Some companies used the term "Argand" to describe their burners in comparison to the prevalent flat wick burners of the day. Side-draft burners were popular to retrofit flat wick lamps for better light.

Upon first inspection, some folded wick burners may be confused with true center-draft burners and lamps. The large burners used flame spreaders while the smaller ones did not. Original chimneys for many of these burners are difficult to find today.

Folded wick burners were developed as early as 1865 in Europe and imported into the United States; popular on student lamps. Read Kebapcioglu (1999) for illustrations of European burners and a wonderful history of Kosmos and Wild & Wessel burners. Read Bachler (1993) and Ursula and Heinz Baumann (1999) for more brands and in-depth discussion than can be presented here.

Advance, Ansonia Brass and Copper Co.

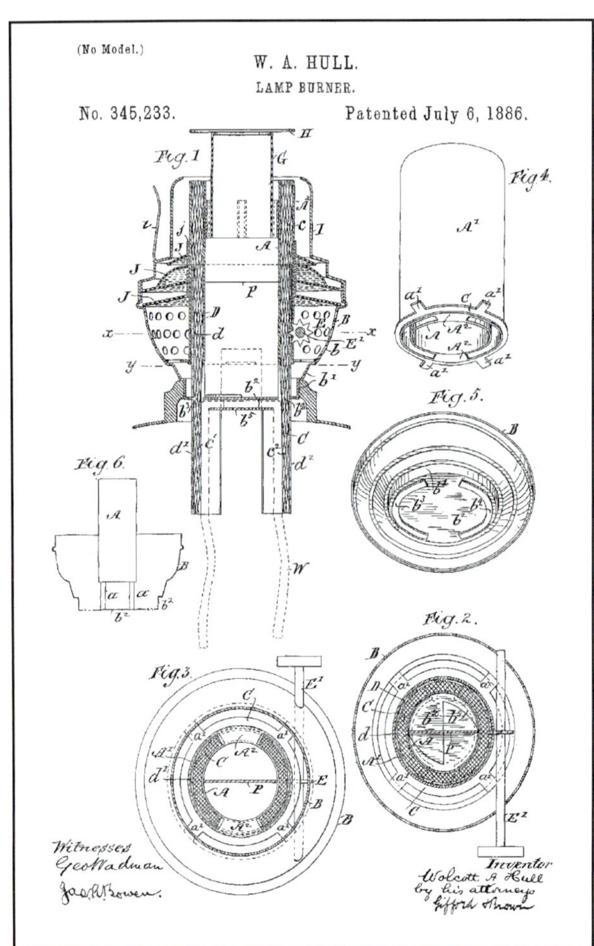

The Advance burner was advertised in *CGJ*, 1886.

Astral Argand Burner, Plume & Atwood

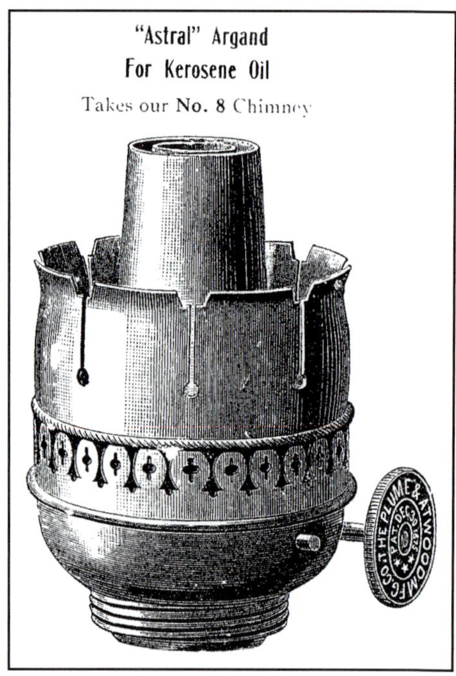

The wick knob is marked "Pat. Dec. 30, 1873." Ursula and Heinz Baumann (1999) illustrate an earlier version.

Bijou Burner, Wallace & Sons

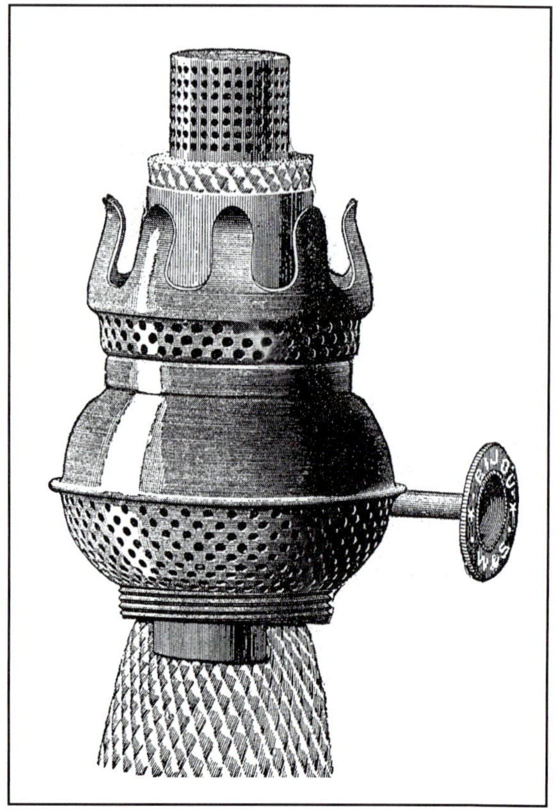

Bijou burner, Hibbard, Spencer, Bartlett & Co., 1893.

Bartholdi Burner, Hobart, Craig & Company

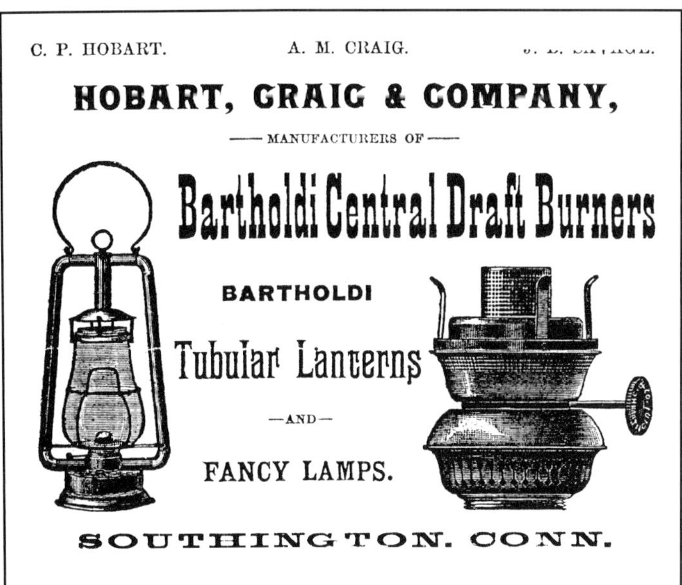

Advertisement, *Southington Directory,* 1887/1888.
Courtesy Southington Public Library.

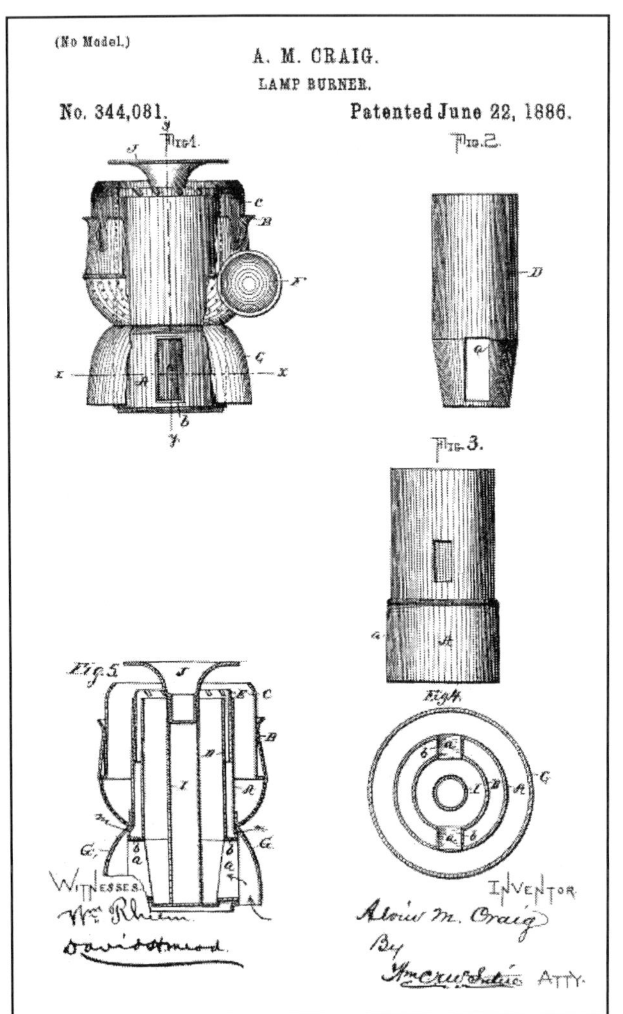

Bartholdi burner folds two flat wicks. The wick knob marked "H. C. & Co., Bartholdi." The gallery marked "Patd. Dec. 12, 82 – June 22, 86." There are several models of Bartholdi burners.

Columbus Burner, Wallace & Sons

Columbus burner missing flame spreader.
Courtesy Doug and Judy Myers.

Barton Burner, R. T. Barton Co., Standard Mfg. Co.

R. T. Barton's patent 499,499 (see right) was assigned to the R. T. Barton Company, possibly located in Bristol, Connecticut.

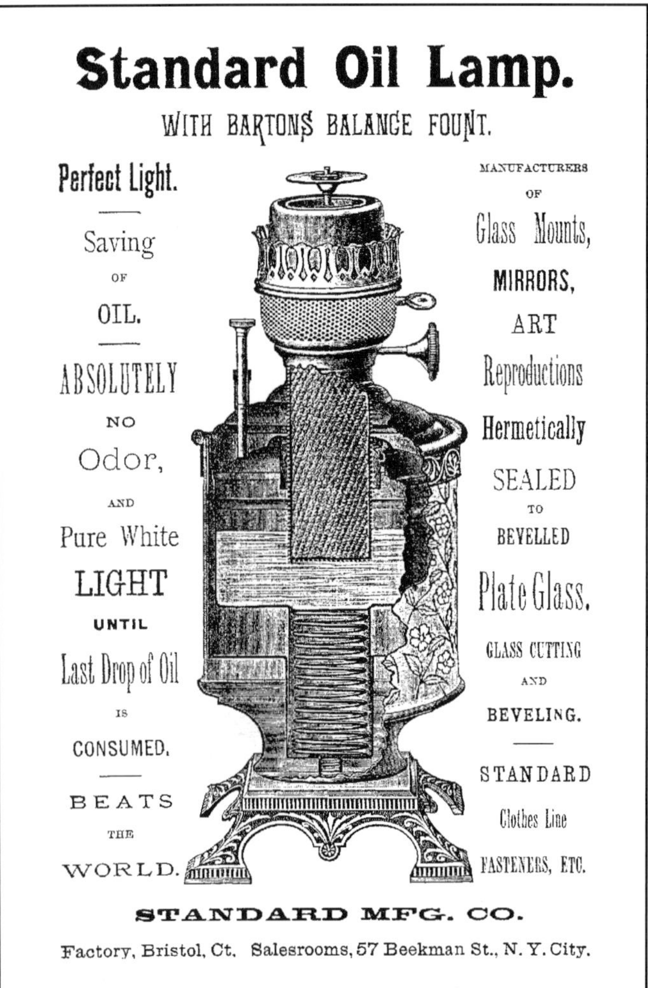

Advertisement, *Bristol City Directory*, 1891. This appears to be a round-wick, side-draft burner. Courtesy Allen Weathers.

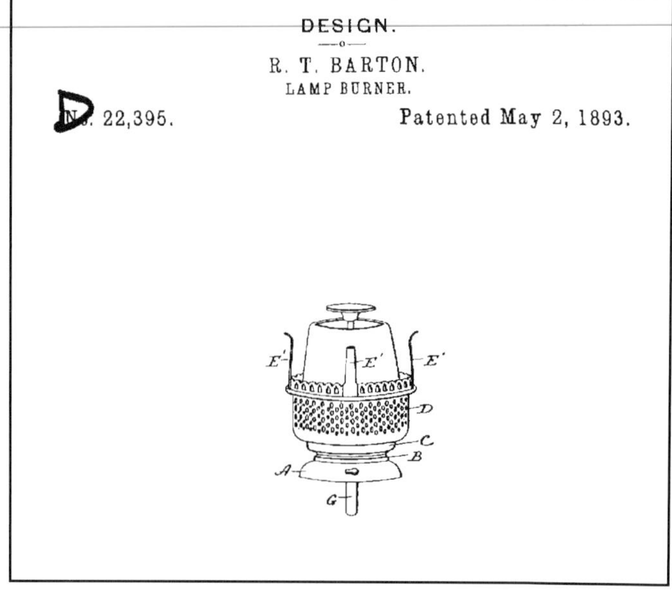

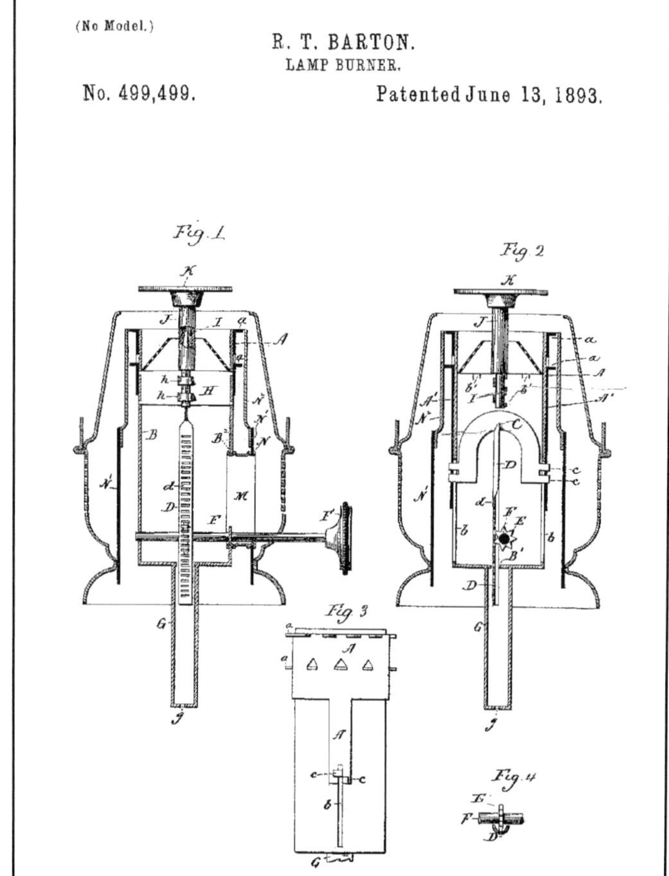

Bristol Electric Burner, Bristol Brass & Clock Co.

Flame spreader.

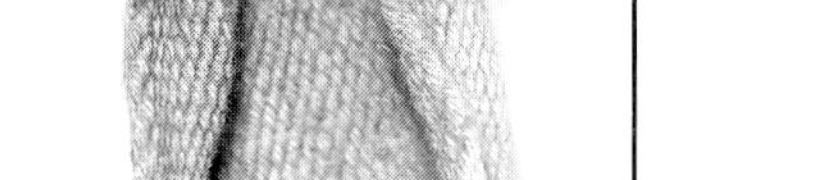

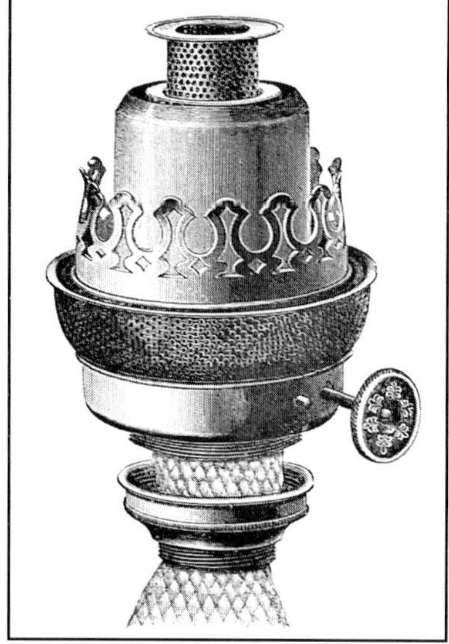

Electric Burner No. 126 sold by F. H. Lovell in 1887.

Wick knob.

Folded wick burner illustrated in Lovell Export catalog of 1887. Sold as "Electric Burner No. 126 to fit B or D collar." The burner illustrated (above right) was fitted with a thimble flame spreader (on a post?). There are no patent dates or other identification. The folded wick is illustrated as a V-shape form where air enters the circular-formed wick. Courtesy Mike Bradley.

Brighton Burner, Holmes, Booth & Haydens

Flame spreader marked "Pat. Appl'd For" on top.

Brighton burner. The wick knob is marked "Brighton" and "H. B. & H." Courtesy Heinz and Ursula Baumann.

Brilliant Burner, Holmes, Booth & Haydens

The Brilliant burner, marked with patent dates on bottom: Aug. 16, 1870, Jan. 13, 1871, March 30, 1871, April 18, 1871, Sep 5, 1871, Nov. 5, 1872. The saucer-shape holder for ball shade marked: "Pat. Applied For." The knob marked "The Brilliant."

Advertisement, *Crockery and Glass Journal*, 1881.

Kent Argand Burner, Bristol Brass

Kent burner, Bristol Brass catalog 1884.
Courtesy Jeff Ebersole.

Kent oil pot. The burner knob marked Pat. Sep. 19, 1871, Sep. 12, 1873. Courtesy Lou Hopf.

Niagara Burner, Rochester Lamp Co.

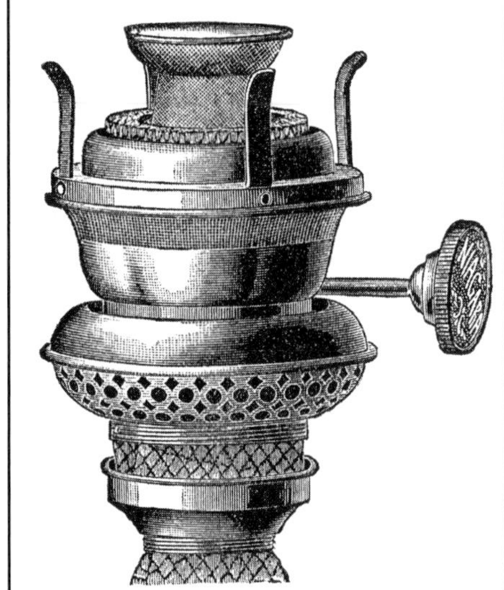

Niagara burner, Hibbard, Spencer, Bartlett & Co. 1893.

Niagara flame spreader is marked "Never cut wick but rub even." Length 2¾".

Niagara burner. The wick is thick and round, not folded. The wick knob marked "Niagara." Ursula & Heinz Baumann (1999) state that some burners are marked on the gallery: "Pat Jan. 15, 1884, Sept. 14, 1886" and others "Pat. Dec. 29 '85." The Columbus burner looks very similar.

Electric Argand Burner, Plume & Atwood

Trade card for P & A Electric Argand side-draft burner.

ELECTRIC ARGAND BURNER.

The Electric Argand Burner appears to be 1887 patent 370,516 held by Lewis J. Atwood and W. F. Lewis, assignors to Plume & Atwood Mfg. Co. Two flat wicks form the round-wick burning surface.

Gregory Patent, Plume & Atwood

Courtesy Heinz and Ursula Baumann.

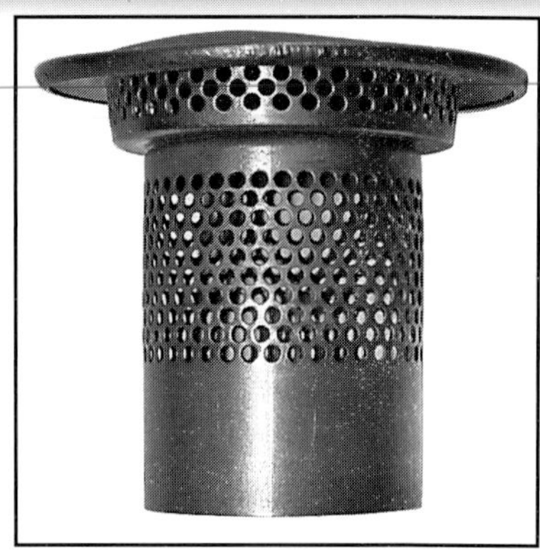

Flame spreader.

Wick knob.

Plume & Atwood stand lamp.
Courtesy Kent Stratton.

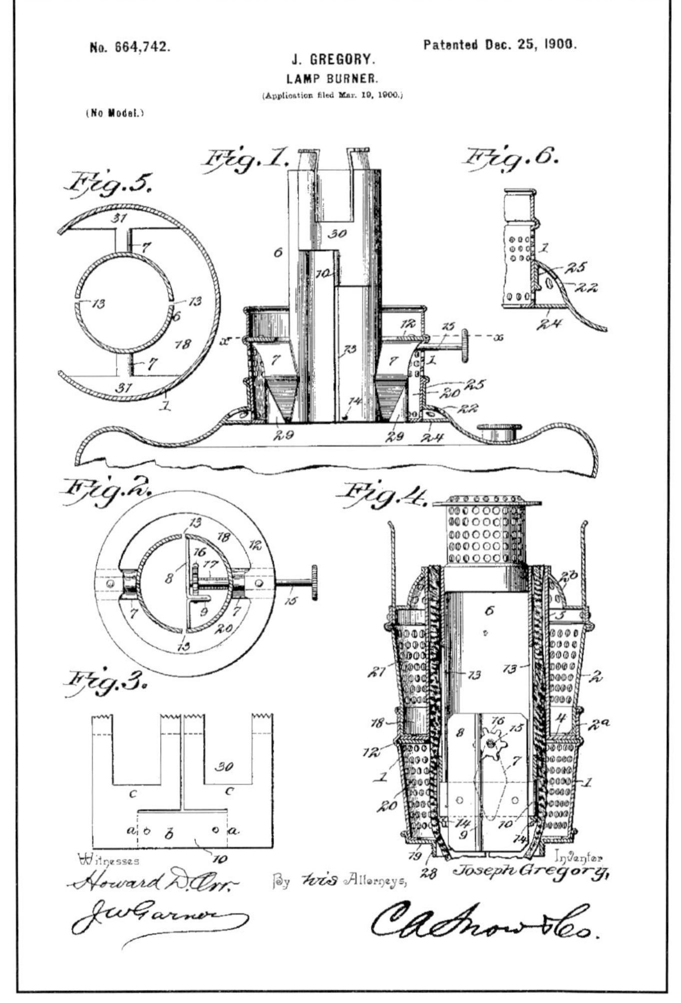

Hickok Calcium Burner, Hektograph Mfg. Co. (also see Royal Argand)

Hickok Calcium burner, missing top of flame spreader/extinguisher.

-- -- A WONDERFUL LIGHT. ------

THE

HICKOK CALCIUM BURNER

FOR KEROSENE OIL.

Burns a Seamless Round Wick. Gives a Light Equal to 60 Candles.

Of marvellous softness and brilliancy, and can be attached to any ordinary lamp. As a Reading Light it has no equal. The Duplex and other burners have had their day. THE HICKOK CALCIUM stands without a rival, and is one of the greatest inventions of this wonderful age It is absolutely safe; an explosion with it is simply impossible. Dealers having a stock of the ugly central-draught metal lamps or Duplex burners on hand, will tell you it is a failure. Do not believe them but see for yourself. 100,000 sold since November. You will not wonder at its great sale wnen you see its beautiful light. Central draft lamps have had their day. You can take the old burner off your lamp and put this one in its place. We have remedied several small defects which existed when we first put them on the market; they are now perfect and do not feed up more than any other burner.

In ordering ask for the NEW BURNERS.

SOLD BY ALL JOBBERS.

CHICAGO OFFICE:

110 Dearborn St.

HEKTOGRAPH MFG. CO.,

22 & 24 Church St., New York.

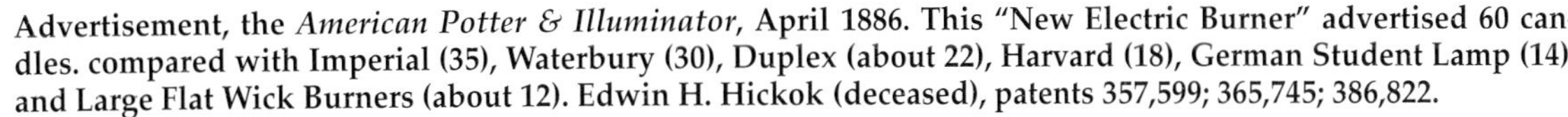

Advertisement, the *American Potter & Illuminator*, April 1886. This "New Electric Burner" advertised 60 candles. compared with Imperial (35), Waterbury (30), Duplex (about 22), Harvard (18), German Student Lamp (14), and Large Flat Wick Burners (about 12). Edwin H. Hickok (deceased), patents 357,599; 365,745; 386,822.

Royal Argand Burner, New York Brass Co.

Colorful trade card for Royal Argand Burner. The burner design and the advertised claims are virtually identical with the Hickok Calcium Burner. The wick knob on the card states "New York Brass Co."

ILLUMINATING POWER

OF THE

BEST BURNERS NOW IN USE.

THE ♦ ROYAL ♦ ARGAND.

THE ROYAL ARGAND	. . . .	65 Candles.
" Imperial, claims	. . . .	35 "
" Waterbury, "	. . . .	30 "
" Duplex, about	. . . .	22 "
" Harvard, "	. . . .	18 "
" German Student Lamp,	. . . .	14 "
" Large Flat Wick Burners, about	.	12 "
" Ordinary Flat Wick Burners,	. .	8 "

THE ROYAL ARGAND, therefore, has about twice the illuminating power of the best and largest burners now in use, and more than seven times that of the common burners, with the advantage of being about half the price of the largest of the burners named above, and it can be attached to any ordinary lamp.

We, therefore, unhesitatingly assert that THE ROYAL ARGAND is the best burner ever yet made, and the only one that uses a round wick successfully on a "B" collar.

—IT IS—

SIMPLE, HANDSOME and DURABLE.

The Sunbeam Burner

The Sunbeam "Central Draft Burner" was advertised in CGJ Dec. 3, 1891 by A. D. Giannini Co., 28 College Place, New York. Ursula & Heinz Baumann (1999) illustrate this burner as No. 3 size marked "Sunbeam Vera Pat. Dec. 3, '89." This is Frank Rhind's Patent 416,236 for an Argand Lamp, one-half assigned to Edward Miller & Co. The Sunbeam-Vera oil pot (right) found in a floor lamp by Doug & Judy Myers.

THE SUNBEAM.

Moehring and Harvard Burners, Plume & Atwood

No. 106. All Metal.

New Oxydized or Hammered Metal in dark bronze or silver, with movable brass oil founts. Height of lamp, complete, 21 in. Complete with round Wick, Moehring Burner and Etched Globe.

	Each.
With two handles, as shown in cut	$3 00
With one handle	2 50
Without handle	2 00

Moehring and Harvard burners require an air deflector (above) to burn properly. These drop out easily and are often missing.

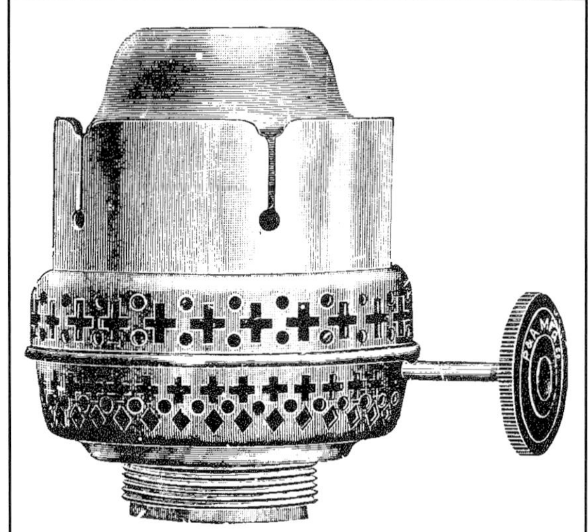

No. 143 Regular, with Inside Tube and Septum.
No. 154 Railroad, with Outside Tube only.

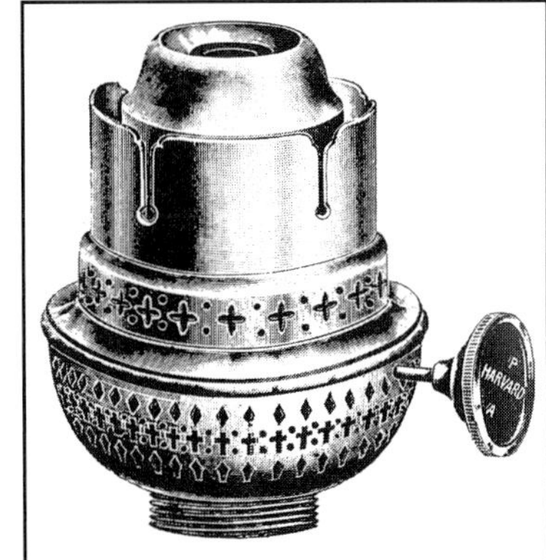

Harvard burner, Plume & Atwood.

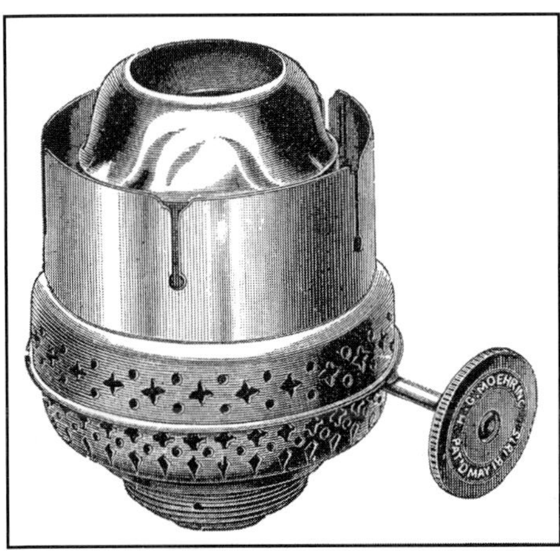
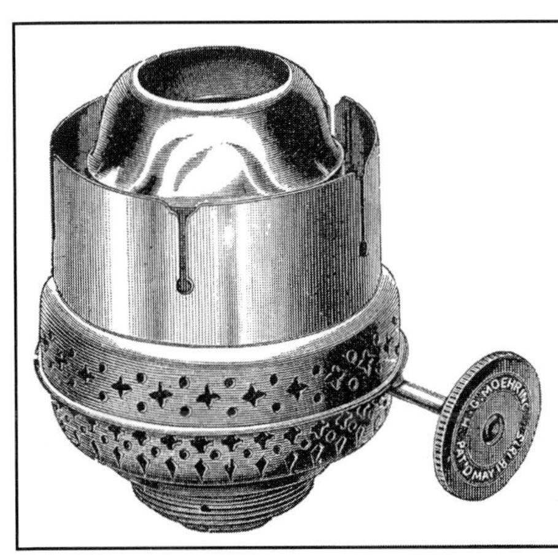

Moehring burner, Hibbard, Spencer, Bartlett & Co. 1893.

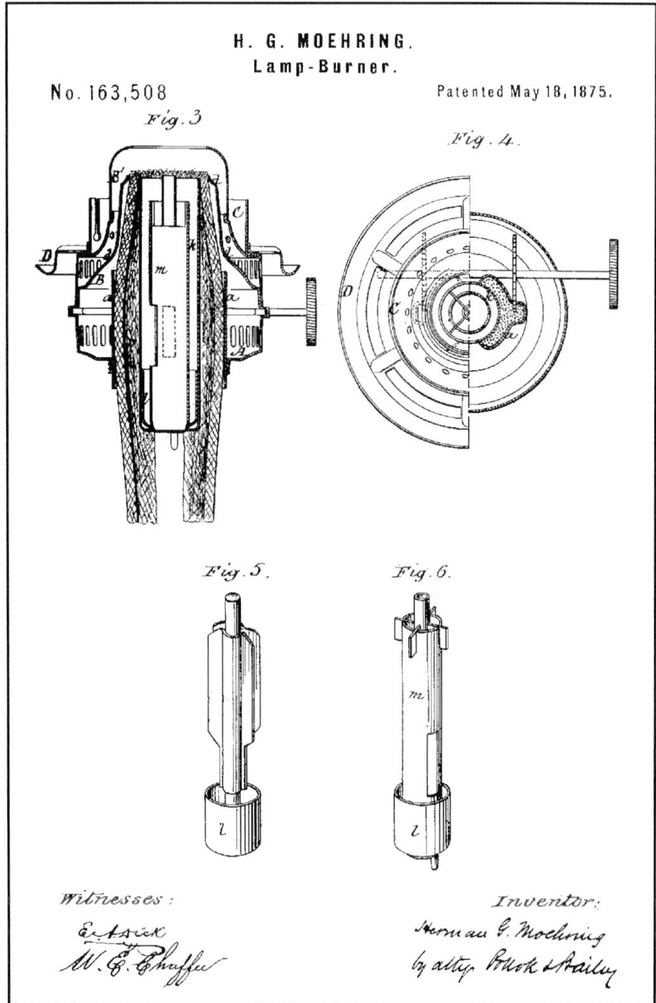

Kohler's Safety Argand Burner

Charles H. Kohler, Cleveland, Ohio, held two patents for this lamp burner: 239,964 and RE9859, both granted in 1881. The ball will fall off the support to extinguish the flame when the lamp is tilted or knocked over.

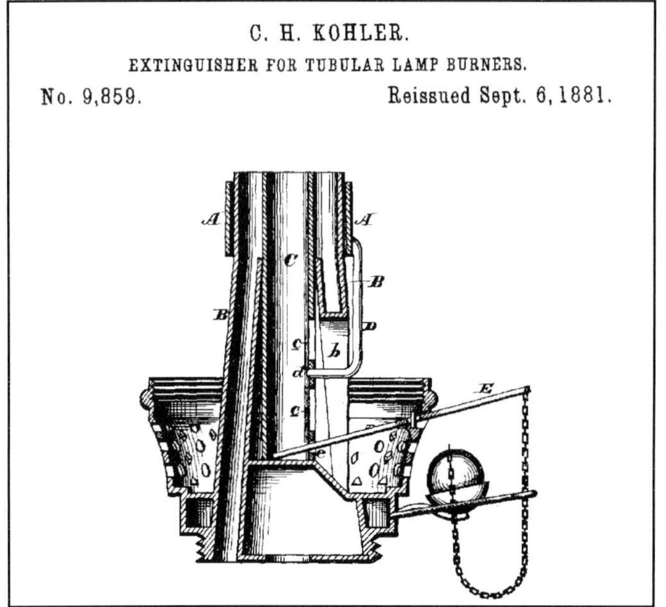

Leader Argand Burner, Bridgeport Brass

Advertisement, *Pottery and Glassware Reporter,* July 21, 1887. The Leader Argand apprears to be S. G. Stoddard's 1887 patent 356,968.

Grand Central Burner, Manhattan Brass Co.

Three wick burner marked on wick knobs "Grand Central, M. B. Co., N. Y." The three wicks form a round wick.

Imperial Burner, Bennett Schneider

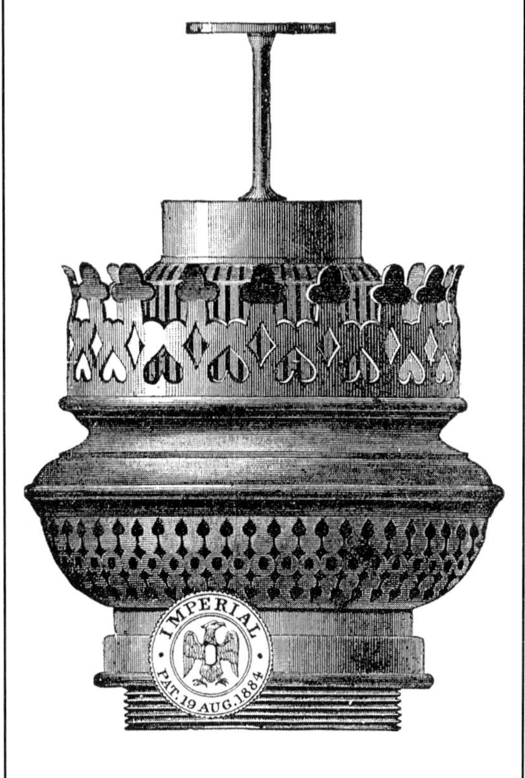

Imperial No. 3 burner, one of many German burners adapted for American threads. Hibbard, Spencer, Bartlett & Co. 1893.

The Reliable Burner

This burner is marked "The Reliable" on the larger wick knob. The smaller knob raises and lowers the flame spreader/extinguisher disc. I believe this burner to be patents 389,068, 1888 and 404,474, 1889 held by P. J. Foulon, assignor of one-half to George B. Constantine, Brooklyn, NY.

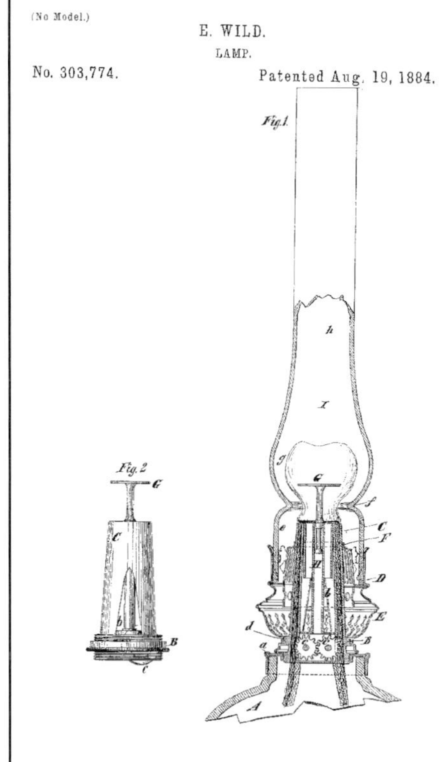

Emil Wild's patent 303,774 assigned to Bennett Schneider. Read Kebapcioglu (1999) for burner history and more about Emil Wild.

Other Folded Wick Burners

Read Ursula & Heinz Baumann (1999) for more information about these burners.

Bristol Argand (Bristol Brass)
Challenge Argand (Wallace & Sons)
Columbus (Wallace & Sons)
Crystal Light (Bristol Brass)
Diamond Light Argand (Manhattan Brass)
Daylight
Orient (Wallace & Sons)
Silver Light
The Atwood Argand (Plume & Atwood)
The Boudoir (Edward Miller Co.)
Victor Argand (Plume & Atwood)
Waterbury Argand Burner (HBH)

Wilson Burner, Wilson Mfg. Co.

George H. Wilson, St. Louis and New York, obtained patents 316,422 in 1885 and 451,718 in 1891 for improvements in folded wick burners.

Other flame spreaders marked "Wilson" have been found (see Trenton Lamp Company).

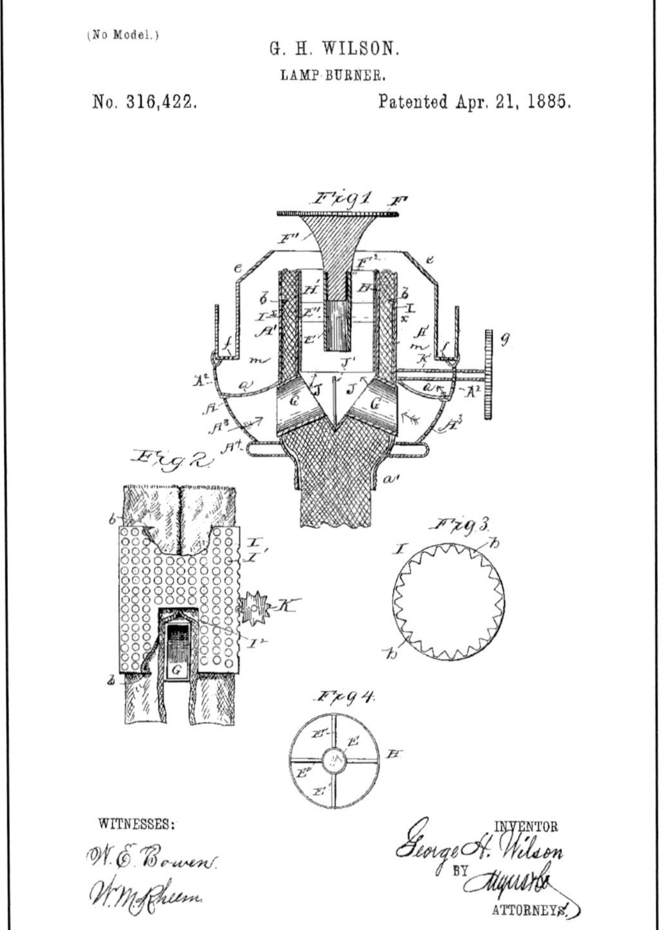

Flame spreader.

Wick knob marked "Wilson Manfg. Co., New York."

Wilson burner.
Courtesy Fil Graff.

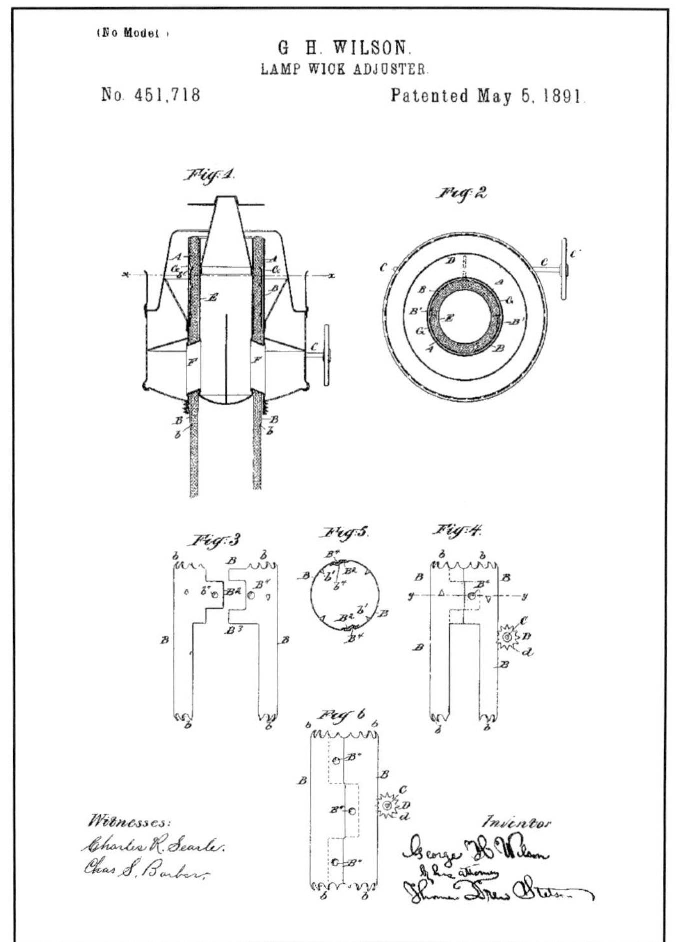

Lamps and Other Manufacturers

We know little about the following lamps and manufacturers. I appreciate help from anyone who can identify the companies and supply more information with advertising, catalogs or patents.

Cox & Day Searchlight Lamp

Flame spreader marked "Cox & Day Search Light New York." Courtesy Fil Graff.

Clark Brothers, Little Trenton? 1892 – 1893

The female burner threads are inside the burner basket, different than most lamps. This may be a signature for lamps made under McLewee's patent 471,822. See Clark Brothers for the Trenton Junior lamp.

Cox & Day fount lamp mounted on wall bracket. The flame spreader was made by Holmes, Booth & Haydens Division American Brass Co. We have no information on Cox & Day as a retail store. $175.00. Courtesy Fil Graff.

Small stand lamp, 7½" to top of wick tube. Flame spreader missing (0 size). Cast iron foot with open decoration. This lamp thought to be sold by Clark Brothers, Trenton, NJ. $125.00.

Duffield's Canadian Lamp, ca. 1885 – 1888

Duffield's Canadian lamp was patented by William Duffield, London, Ontario. The lamp was advertised as one of the largest hanging lamps at the time. The diameter of the wick tube is 2³⁄₁₆". The flame spreader is an adjustable wire coil said to heat the air more effectively than thin perforated metal.

I do not know if the stand lamp was ever made.

The fount is marked "Duffield's Canadian Lamp, Pat'd 1886." Courtesy Bob Duffield.

Selected patents, Center-draft Lamps

William Duffield, unassigned

1885	D16,398
1886	340,704
1886	342,826

Top of flame spreader and burner of Duffield's Canadian hanging lamp fount. The disc is steel.

The Duffield hanging lamp fount. Height 8½". The wick tube 2³⁄₁₆" diameter. The wick knob marked "Brilliant." $150.00. Courtesy Bob Duffield.

Duffield's Canadian hanging lamp fount. Wick raiser is pull rod. The flame spreader appears to be original. $150.00. Courtesy Tim and Debbie Breen.

Duffield Lamp Patents

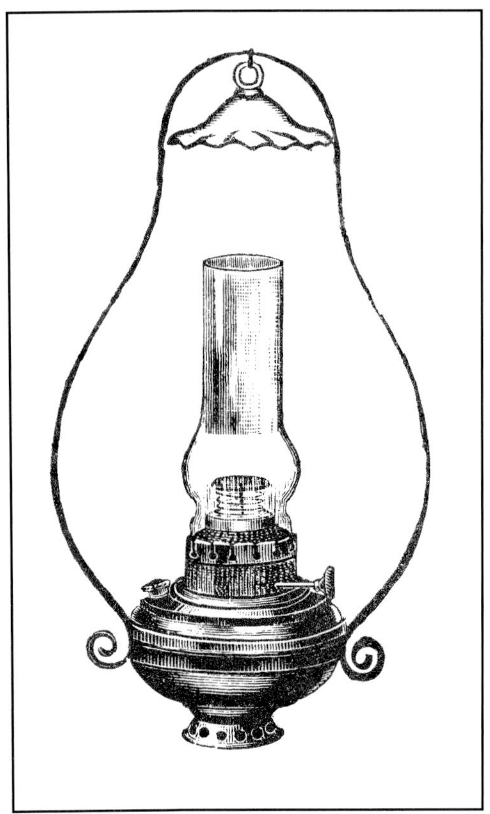

Duffield's Canadian lamp, H. Leonard & Sons, 1888.

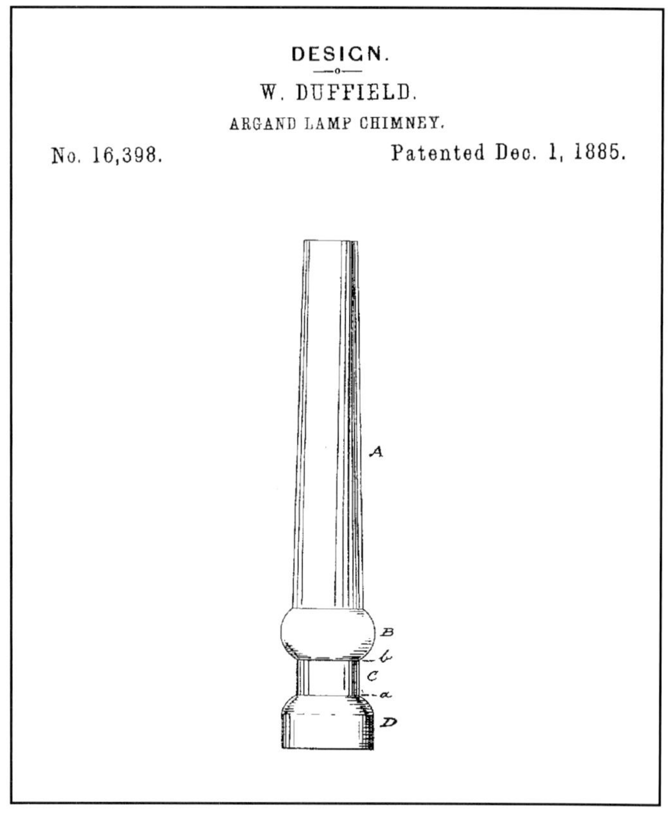

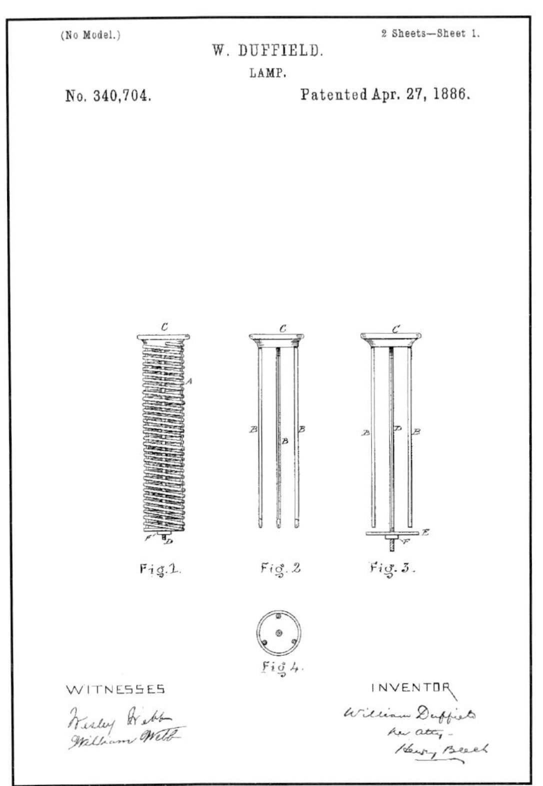

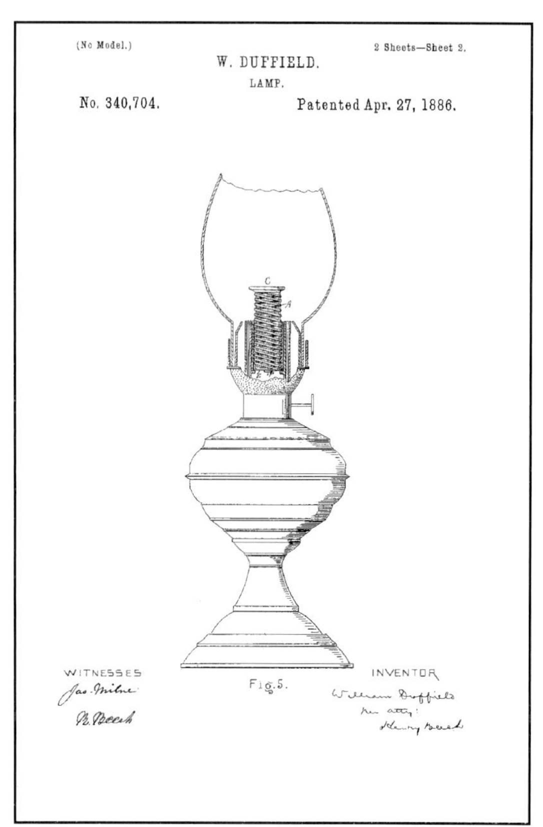

W & M Century Lamps

THE WILCOX & MATTHEWS CO.

42 Murray Street, New York,

OPEN THE BALL FOR 1890.

MANUFACTURERS OF THE

W&M Century Lamps

The Wilcox & Matthews Co., New York, introduced W & M Century Lamps with the "Century Centre Draft" burners in 1890. The advertisement in June 5 *CGJ* offered decorated bisque vase lamps and metal piano and banquet lamps.

The Young Canadian banquet lamp appears to be identical with the Apex produced by Ansonia Brass and Copper Company.

Dominion Tubular Lamp Company, Distributor of Lamps Made by Ansonia, ca. 1887 – 1891

Dominion Tubular Lamp Company, Montreal, Quebec, Canada, was primarily a manufacturer of lanterns and street lamps. They sold a variety of station, side lamps and hand lamps. I do not know if the company manufactured their goods in Canada. Dominion apparently was a distributor of center-draft lamps made by Ansonia Brass and Copper Company.

An 1887 catalog included the Royal Young Canadian banquet lamp and the Royal Improved Young Canadian stand lamp. Both of these lamps are identical to lamps produced by Ansonia Brass and Copper Company.

A disastrous fire destroyed the company premises on January 14, 1891 (*China, Glass and Lamps*, Jan. 21, 1891).

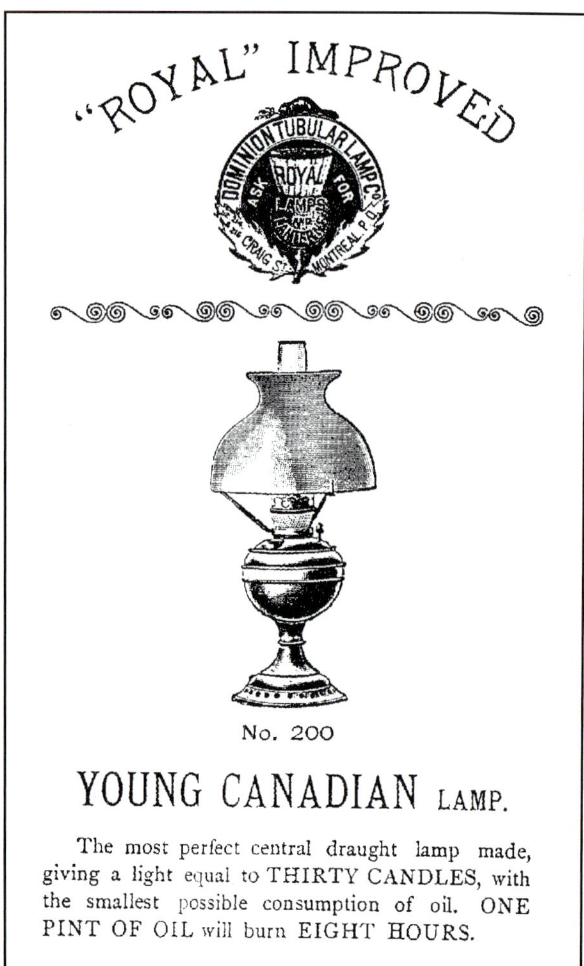

The Young Canadian stand lamp appears to be identical with Little Jewel produced by Ansonia Brass and Copper Company.

Edward H. Fessenden & Co.

Edward H. Fessenden and his company are mysteries to be solved. Edward Fessenden was an investor and retail merchant selling lamps at 38 Park Place, New York City. He lived in Brooklyn and appeared in Trows Directory from 1893 to 1896. In 1891, The Pottery and Glass Reporter described Edward Fessenden — "One of the quiet little men of whom little is heard, and yet who is playing an important part in the lamp business."

Fessenden employed Frank Rhind at salary of $25.00 per week, for one year, to develop and manufacture lamps under Rhind's patent 312,762. The contract with Rhind, dated March 1, 1885, was furnished courtesy of Allen Weathers.

Fessenden was in business with Frederick W. Kralert in the F. W. Kralert & Co., Brooklyn and Newark, NJ. The Newark firm decorated vase lamps and sold them with the Daylight burner and the Secor "Automatic Ventilator" safety system (CGJ Nov. 19, 1891).

The trademark "Daylight" was registered to E. H. Fessenden and Kate E. Jacobsen on Sept. 3, 1889. They apparently also registered the word with a smiley face in 1888 for use on glass chimneys (Peterson, 1968).

Selected Patents, Center-draft Lamps

Frank Rhind

1885 .... 312,762[1]

William Harper

1889 .... 400,208[2]

Thomas Langston

1889 .... 404,848[3]

[1]Contract with Edward H. Fessenden to manufacture.
[2]One-third assigned to Edw. H. Fessenden.
[3]Assigned Edw. H. Fessenden & Kate E. Jacobsen.

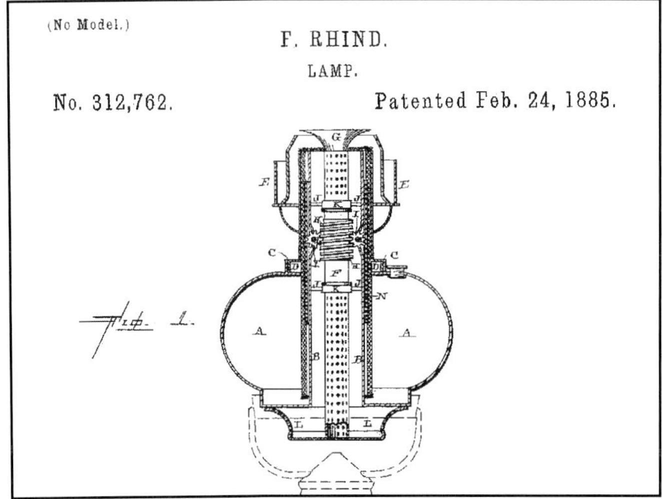

Rhind called part G a "spreading device." Fessenden called it a "sun disc and spreader."

P. M. & H. Lamp Company, P. M. & H. Rex Lamp Co., ca. 1899 – 1904

Weinrich (1988) reported the P. M. & H. Lamp Co. in Rochester, NY city directories from 1900 to 1902. The company name derives from initials of John M. Pfaudler, Wm. M. Mallett and Thos. P. Hill, all of Rochester.

The P. M. & H. Rex Lamp Co. was listed in *Rochester City Directories* at 409 Wilder Bldg. from 1900 to 1902 (O'Connell 2006). Officers were George Weldon, president, W. M. Mallett, secretary and George Wilder, treasurer.

I do not know if this company sold B & H Rex lamps.

Selected Patents, Center-draft Lamps

John M. Pfaudler

1892 478,815
1900 .... 645,005[1]
1900 .... 645,006[2]
1904 .... 773,980[3]

[1]Assigned 3/4 to William M. Mallet & Thomas P. Hill.
[2]Assigned part to William M. Mallet, Thomas P. Hill, Augustus H. Daniels & Bernard Feiock.
[3]Assigned 10/16 to Eugene M. Strouss, Isaac Stern & Herbert Wile.

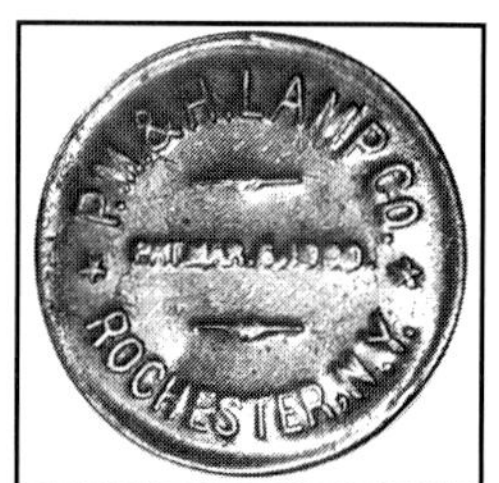

Flame spreader marked "P.M.&H. Lamp Co., Rochester, N.Y., Pat. Mar. 6, 1900." The bottom diameter is 1¼". Courtesy Kent Stratton.

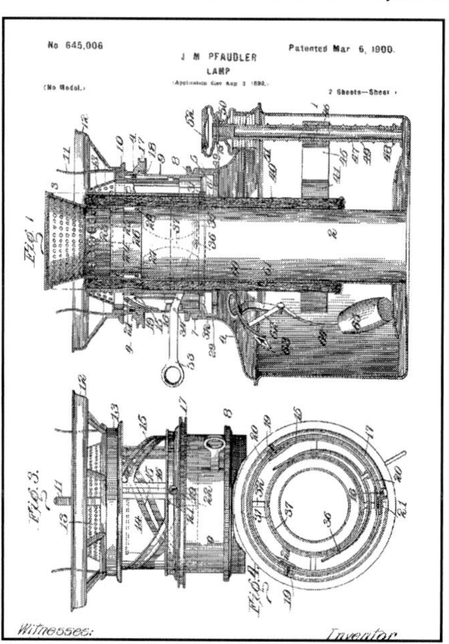

Imperial Lamp

ELECTRIC LAMPS.

IMPERIAL ELECTRIC LAMP with student movement. No ratchet to get out of order. The wick is raised and lowered same as on a student lamp. Lamp all made of solid brass and every lamp is warranted. The Imperial gives a soft and mellow light, but powerful enough to equal 65 candle power. A good lamp; recommended by the house.

Per doz.

IMPERIAL LAMP FOUNTS, brass, to attach to any chandelier or bracket...... $13 50

IMPERIAL TABLE LAMPS, BRASS. A splendid reading lamp 16 00

IMPERIAL TABLE LAMPS, NICKEL PLATED. An elegant lamp for the home, 17 50

Two sizes of Imperial lamps (large and small) were included in tests by the Lighthouse Board in 1888. I suspect Imperial to be either Manhattan Brass or Bristol Brass Company. An Imperial side draft burner lamp was sold by Bennett Schneider.

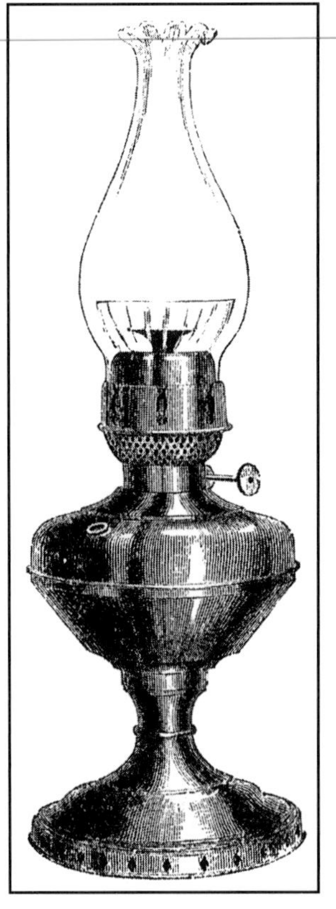

Electric Lamp No. 77 was advertised in the 1884 Lovell Export catalog as "The Wonder of The World! Light the entire parlor, fifty candles in one lamp." This fount appears identical to the Lightning Lamp below. The burner appears similar, if not identical, to Lamp No. 100 advertised by Lovell in 1887. I suspect this lamp made by Bristol Brass Co.

"Nickels" Lamp

John Nickels, Milwaukee, Wisconsin, assigned one-half of his patent (below) to several investors in Wisconsin. I do not know who made Nickels' lamps or how they were branded. The Nickels flame spreader looks very similar to a Veritas flame spreader from England.

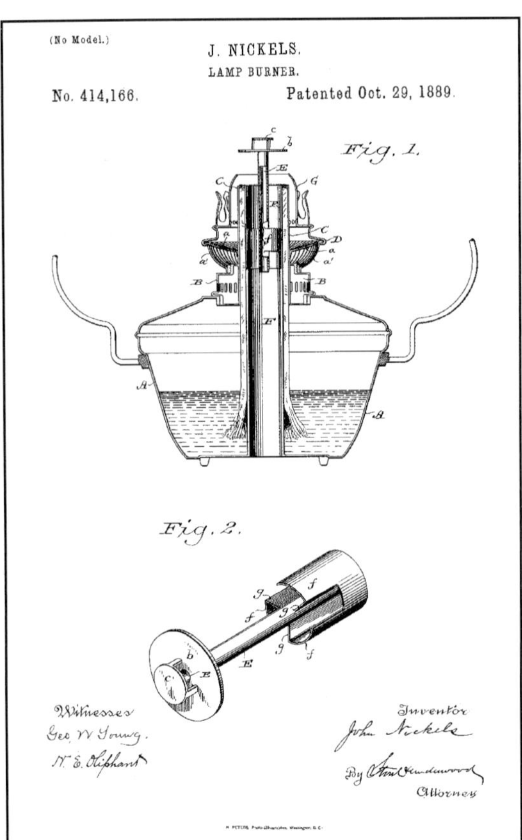

Improved Lightning Lamp

Illustration from a postal cover dated "New York, Feb. 12, 1886." This lamp reminds me of lamps made by Bristol Brass Company.

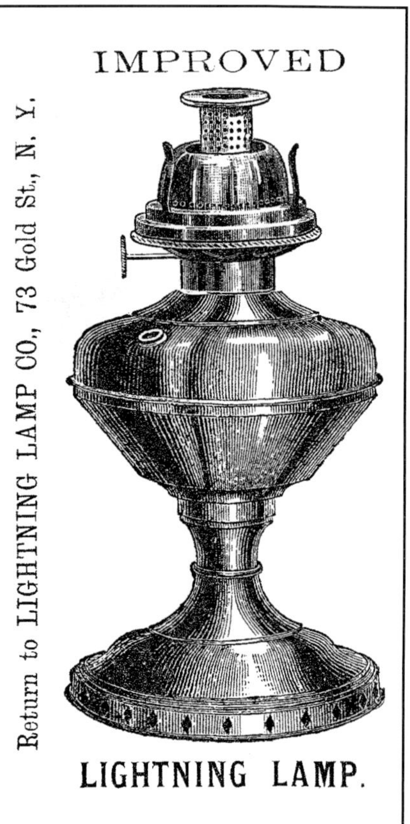

Meyrose Jumbo Lamp? F. Meyrose & Co.

I believe this lamp to be Meyrose No. 4 Jumbo Diamond M Electric Lamp. The Jumbo No. 4 fount was listed by Meyrose in an 1886 catalog. This lamp found by Cliff Youngstrom without burner. The original wick knob has been replaced with a Miller Solar disc.

The Meyrose burner and flame spreader fit perfectly (below right).

The neck is stamped "H. B. Mfg. Co." This mark and manufacturer are unknown at this time.

The base is weighted with a cast iron disc complete with holes for center draft.

"Jumbo" stand lamp, 15" tall. The lamp is nickel plated. The fount is large with capacity of five pints.

"Jumbo" stand lamp fitted with burner from a Meyrose lamp. The burner and flame spreader fit perfectly. Height 15½". $150.00. Lamp courtesy Cliff Youngstrom.

The Manchester Lamp, Daniel & Stewart, ca. 1886 – 1888

The Manchester lamp was advertised in1887 as a safety improvement in center-draft lamps to aid in filling the lamp. The entire burner and wick are removed to expose a funnel-like opening into the fount.

The patents were held by Alexander Stewart of Philadelphia. The Manchester was said to be owned and manufactured by Daniel and Stewart, Philadelphia, Pennsylvania. I have been unable to determine additional information about Mr. Daniel, origin of the Manchester name or who manufactured the lamp.

Selected Patents, Center-draft Lamps

Alexander Stewart, unassigned

1886 346,829
1887 358,230

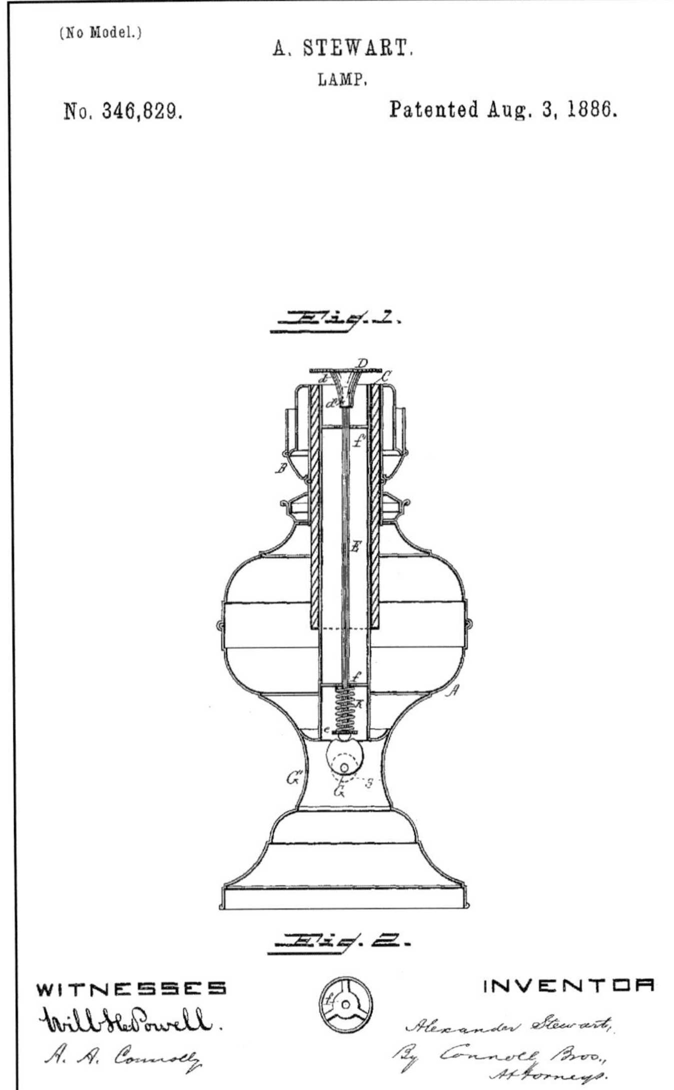

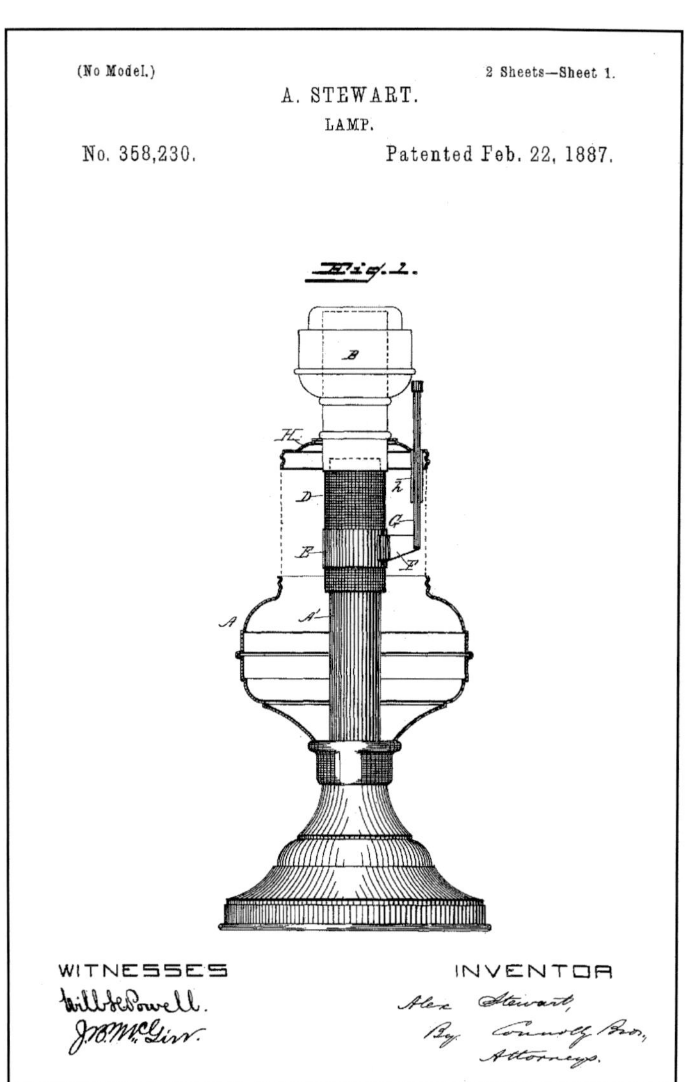

MANCHESTER.

65 CANDLE POWER.

PATENTED 1886 AND 1887 IN THE UNITED STATES AND EUROPE.

THE only Metal Lamp made in which the interior of the fount can be seen in filling. For simplicity, convenience, and illuminating power it has no equal. It is absolutely non-explosive. It cannot be filled while burning, thereby preventing accidents through carelessness in filling It is so constructed as to admit of being easily cleaned. It has a proper extinguisher. It is so simple that any mechanic can repair it if necessary. There is no chance for the oil to weep over and run down the sides of the lamp. It does not get dangerously hot.

The novel features of the MANCHESTER, not found in any other lamp, sell it on sight.

All lamps tested by atmospheric pressure to 10 pounds to square inch, and Warranted not to leak.

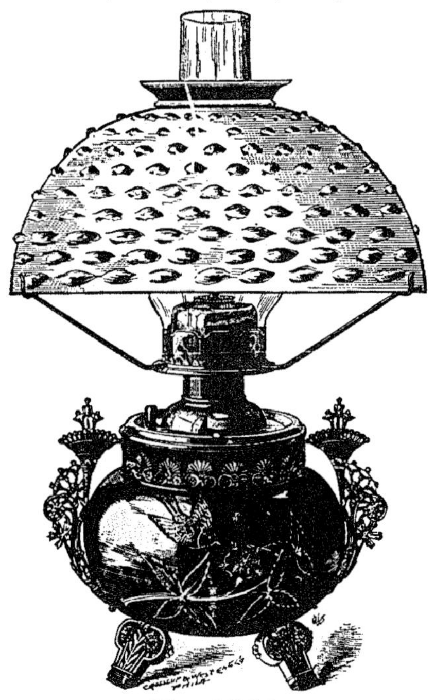

No. 1301.

STAND LAMP OPEN FOR FILLING.

We make it in all styles. Send for Catalogue of designs now ready. We are constantly adding new designs to our list,

AN AGENT WANTED IN EVERY TOWN.

DON'T GET CONFUSED.

Recollect the Name,

The Manchester Lamp.

The Whitest, Steadiest and Most Brilliant Light ever Obtained from Kerosene.

OWNED AND MANUFACTURED BY

DANIEL & STEWART,

819 & 821 Filbert St., Philadelphia, Pa., U. S A.

I. R. BURNS & CO., San Francisco, Cal., Agents for the Pacific Coast.

Advertisement, *Pottery and Glassware Reporter,* May 19, 1887.

Sunshine Lamp

Charles F. Monroe sold decorated shades to Edward Miller, Charles Parker and other lamp manufacturers. The pyrene shade has a glass top surrounded by a sliding silk curtain. Pyrene is an aromatic hydrocarbon in coal tar — the word originating from the Greek. Monroe received patents for his invention in 1890 and 1891. The glass shade and glass vase likely were made of the same glass and decoration by Monroe and sold for better lamps. I do not know if the Sunshine Lamp was center-draft.

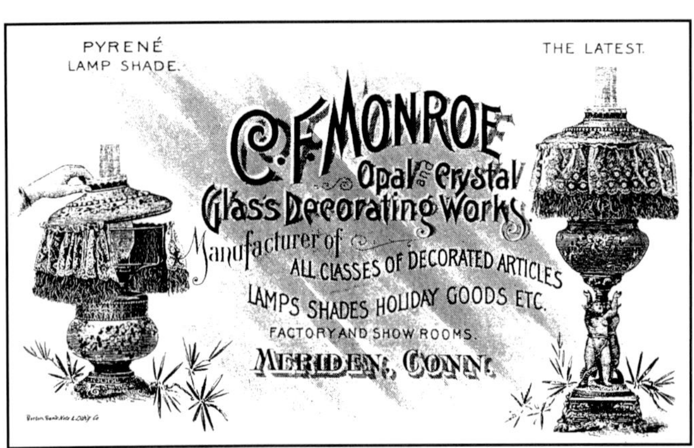

Courtesy Allen Weathers.

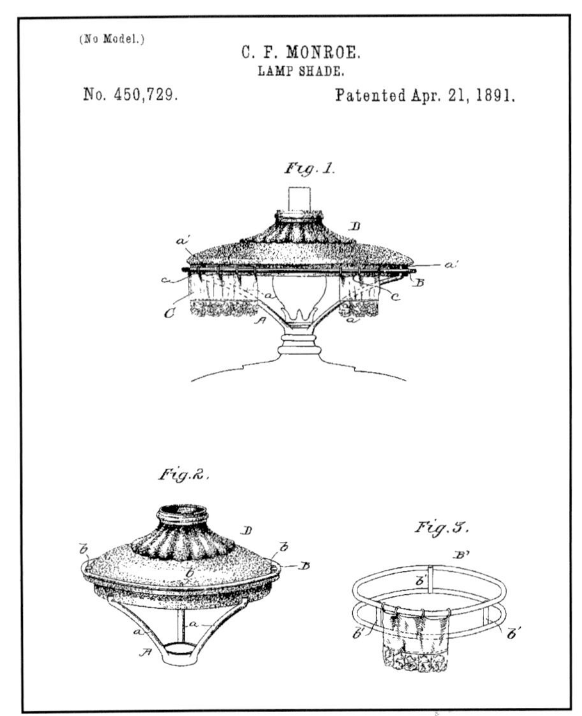

Unknown Oil Pot, Wallace & Sons, Pittsburgh Brass?

Flame spreaders that "fit": Left: unidentified flame spreader fits inside wick tube; right: Wallace & Sons fits nicely outside wick tube.

This appears to be a "plug" that was not removed (or installed) in top of the fount. It is marked with a star and the words "Full Out."

Wick knob. The lever arm turns to open "jaws" which grasp the wick. Top of wick tube is 15⁄16" diameter.

Unmarked oil pot, lift gallery burner, bayonet connection. Height 7" to top of gallery. Standard 5" pot. I believe the correct flame spreader fits outside the wick tube. Standard oil fill, cap missing. $75.00.
Courtesy Kent Stratton.

Unknown Flame Spreaders

P & A Royal

Well-made flame spreader marked "Royal" with patent dates: Aug. 14, 88; Aug. 26, 90; Sept. 9, 90; Mch. 24, 91; Jan. 5, 92. Length 2½", 1⅜" diameter. We do not know which lamp this fits. Courtesy Kent Stratton.

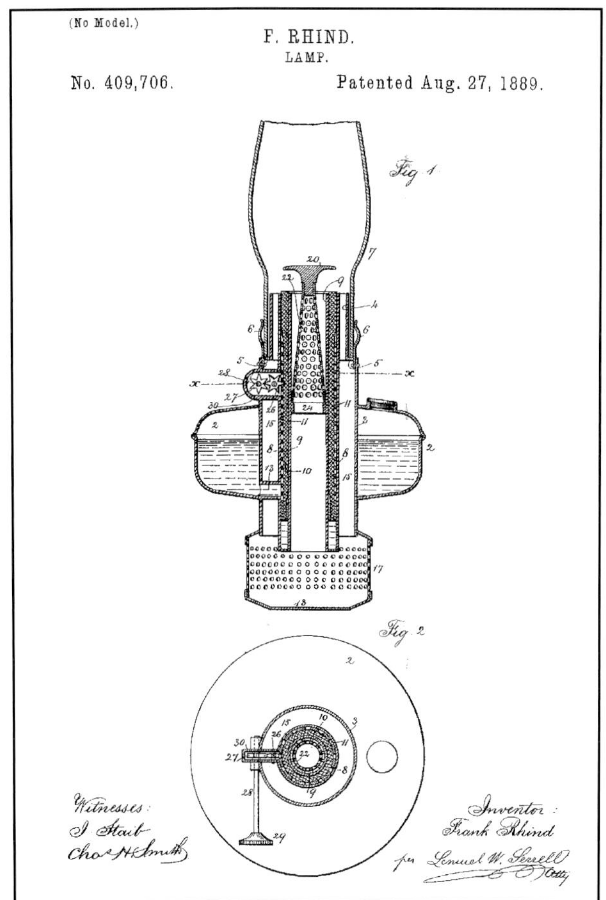

Frank Rhind was inventor extraodinaire! This unassigned patent specified a cone shape flame spreader inserted into the wick tube. I do not know if this lamp, or one similar, was produced. This type of flame spreader, however, has been found.

Bradley & Hubbard

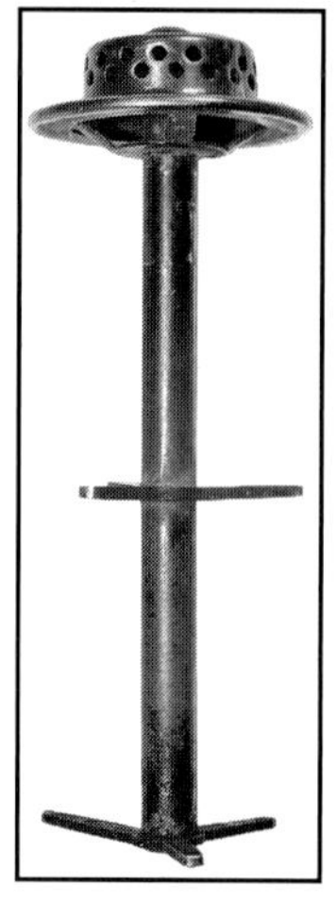

Flame spreader marked "Pat'd April 26, 1898." This is patent 603,105 assigned to Bradley & Hubbard. Which lamp does this fit?

Flame spreader marked "Mehlen, Pat'd. Nov. 20, 94, Mar. 24, 96, Feb. 28, 05." This is a B & H flame spreader that fits lamps for unknown distributor.

Rio Flame Spreader

Rio flame spreader fits unknown lamp or heater. This flame spreader is identical shape as the Angle (lamp) heater flame spreader and similar to a Parker flame spreader. I suspect the Rio could also be for a center-draft kerosene heater. Courtesy Jim Van Es.

Toronto Light King, Toronto Light King Lamp Co.

I know nothing about the Toronto Light King Lamp Company other than lamps are found with this name. I suspect these are branded by an American manufacturer.

Toronto Light King? Unmarked

Oil fill.

Wick knob.

Toronto Light King fount lamp. Height 9¼" to top of the gallery. This lamp has post for flame spreader which lowers to extinguish flame. Also found as stand lamps. $125.00.

Stand lamp same as or related to Toronto Light King. Unmarked fount slightly different shape. Same wick knob and oil fill cap as lamp on left. Height 12" to top of the gallery. This lamp has fixed post for flame spreader which does not lower to extinguish flame. $150.00. Courtesy Kent Stratton.

Scarlett Lamp, ca. 1870s

William Scarlett, Aurora, Illinois devised a lamp suggesting that ordinary metal lamps were inferior to glass bowls because the users could not see the oil levels. Therefore he suggested a "feed indicator" which determines the level of oil inside. The patent illustrates a flat wick burner and draft for what appears to be central-draft modification. I do not know if this lamp was ever produced.

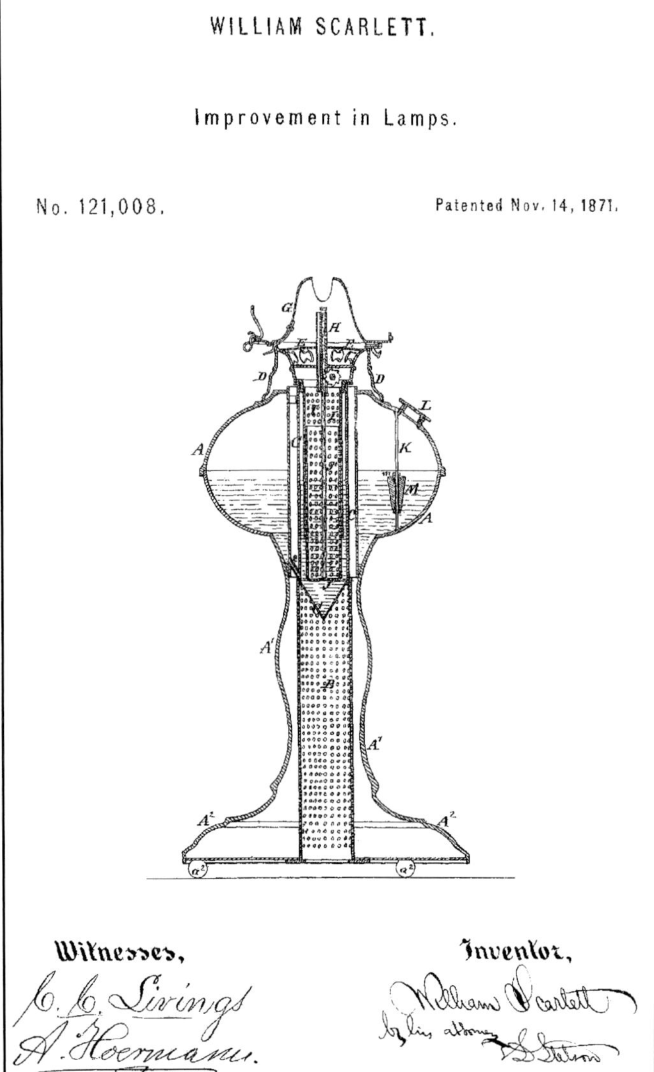
WILLIAM SCARLETT.

Improvement in Lamps.

No. 121,008. Patented Nov. 14, 1871.

Witnesses, Inventor,

C. C. Livings William Scarlett

A. Hoermann by his attorney

Unknown Oil Pot, Wallace & Sons?

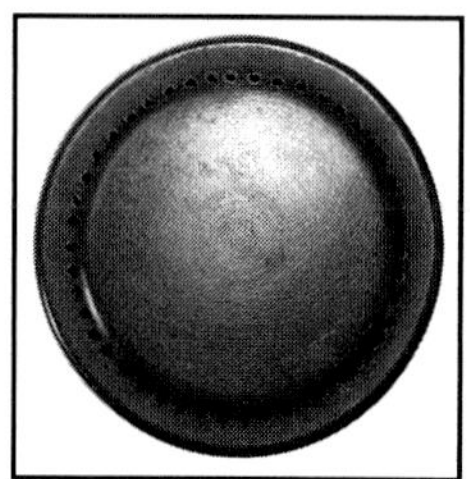

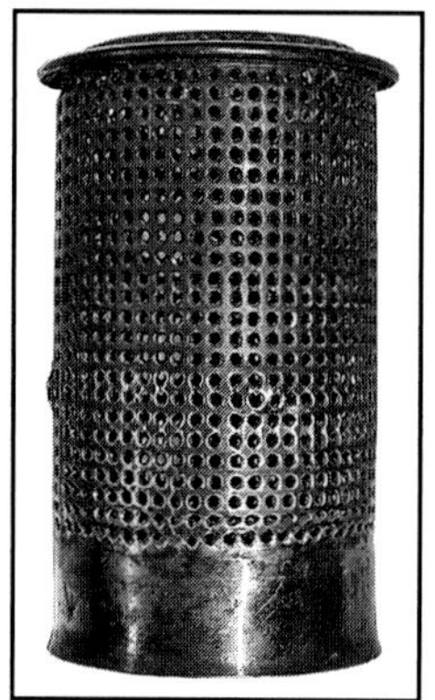

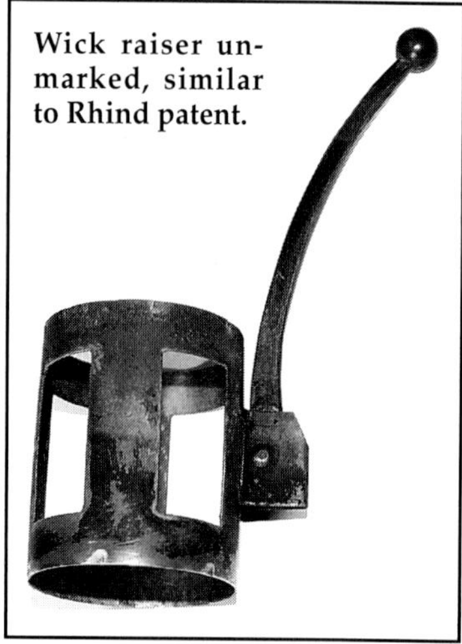

Wick raiser unmarked, similar to Rhind patent.

Flame spreader, 11/4 diameter and 2¼" long. Top unmarked.

Logo stamped into top of fount is winged anchor with key and "J T S."

Unknown oil pot. Tapered 5" pot. Height 8¼". Missing oil fill cap. The shape of the burner is similar to catalog images of Wallace & Sons lamps. $75.00.

American Automatic Lighting Co.

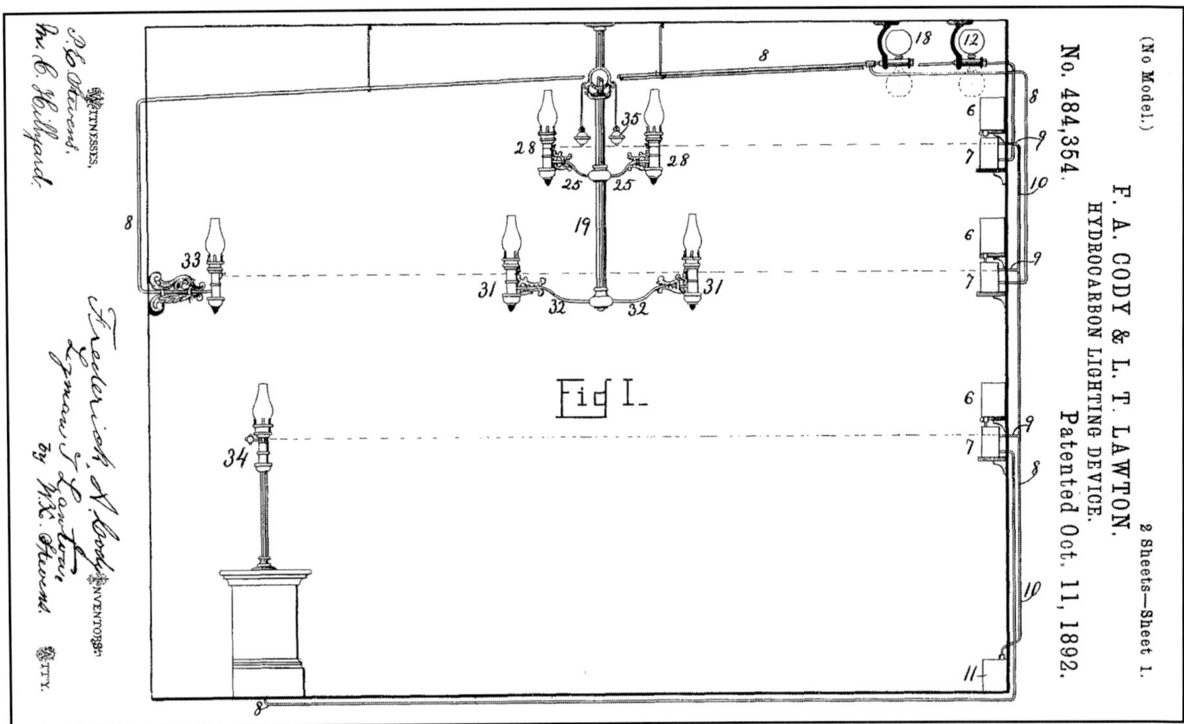

According to patent 484,354 this is a hydrocarbon lighting system for household hanging, wall and table lamps. The 1892 patent by F. A. Cody and L. T. Lawton was assigned to American Automatic Lighting Company in New Jersey.

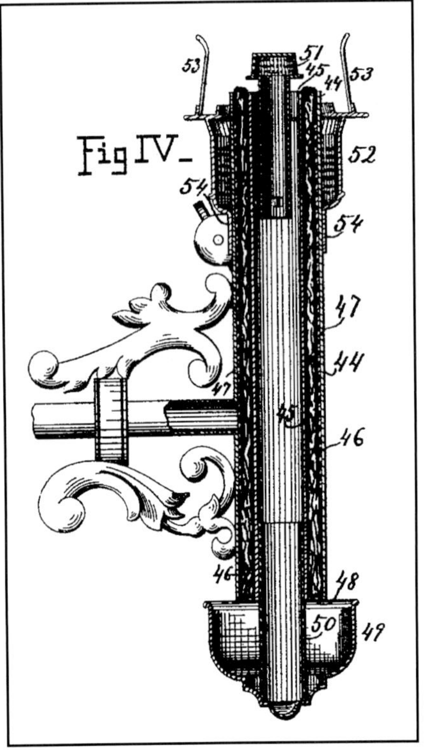

The burner for patent 484,354 employs a drip cup similar to railcar lamps. The flame spreader appears similar to those used in Lux Dux lamps.

Star Brass Mfg. Co.

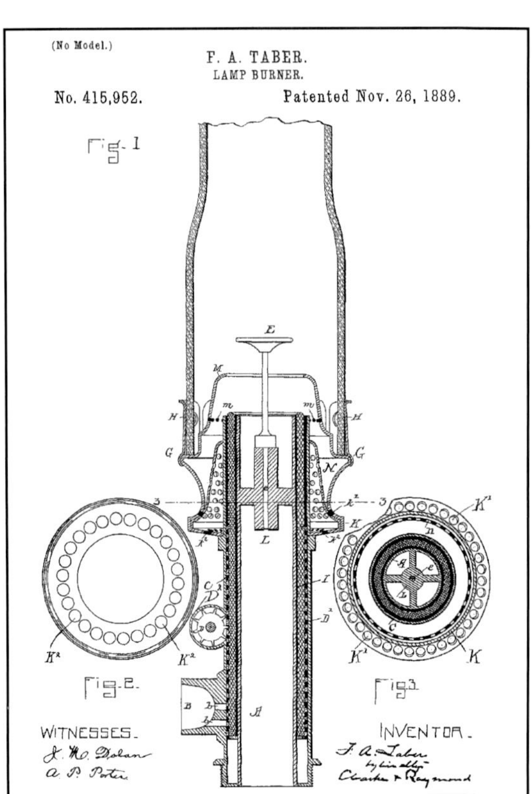

F. A. Tabor's 1889 patent 415,952 was assigned to the Star Brass Mfg. Co., Boston. The patent suggests the burner was developed for railcar lighting.

References

Adams, W. H. Davenport. 1875. *Lighthouses and Lightships*, Chapter III. The Illuminating Apparatus of Lighthouse. T. Nelson & Sons, London.

Anon. 1892. "Lighthouse Illumination." *Scientific American* 66(24):373.

Anon. 1895. *St. Louis Up To Date: The Great Industrial Hive of The ...... Mississippi Valley*. Consolidated Illustrating Co., St. Louis, Mo. Courtesy Jean E. Meeh Gosebrink, St. Louis Public Library.

Anon. 1901. "Death of Joseph Kintz." *Winsted Evening Citizen*, page 1, Oct. 22, 1901.

Anon. 1908. "The City of New Brunswick — Its History, Its Homes and Its Industries." *The New Brunswick Times*.

Anon. 1913. "Henry E. Shaffer, Business Man and Former Supervisor, Dies at Home, Was Resident of Rochester for 45 Years." *The Union and Advertiser*, March 4, 1913, Rochester, NY. Rochester Public Library, courtesy of Richard O'Connell.

Anon. 1920. *The Story of Pittsburgh Glass*, Vol. One, No. Five. First Nat'l Bank at Pittsburgh.

Anon. 1920. *Fifty Years of Glass Making, 1869 – 1919*. MacBeth-Evans Glass Company, Pittsburgh, PA.

Anon. Ca. 1922. *32 Tested Uses of Perfection Kerosene for the Home, Farm, Garage*. Standard Oil Company, 16 pp.

Anon. 1931. "He Showed Edison the Light." *The Sunday Republican Newspaper*, Nov. 8, 1931, Waterbury, CT.

Anon. 1950. *Bristol Fashion — The Bristol Brass Corporation, 1850 to 1950*. Published by Bristol Brass Corp.

Anon. 1957. *The Lamp*, 75th Anniversary of Jersey Standard.

Anon. 1972. *Lamps & Other Lighting Devices, 1850 – 1906*. The Pyne Press, Princeton.

Anon. 1984. "A History of Edward Miller & Company." *The Rushlight* 50(4):15 – 16.

Anon. 1985. "Bartholdi Central Draft Burner." *The Rushlight* 51 (2):11 – 12.

Anon. 1988. "1898 Illustrated Catalogue of the Chimney Department of the American Flint Glass Workers Union." *The Illuminator* 2(2): 4 – 16.

Anon. 1989. "Standard Oil's Mei Foo lamp." *The Rushlight* 55(1):12 – 13.

Anon. 1991. "The Passing of the Kerosene Lamp." *The Illuminating Engineer* (NY) 4 (1909):225. In: *The Rushlight* 57(2):17.

Anon. 1999. *Images of America Ansonia*. The Derby Historical Soc., Arcadia Press.

Anon. 1999. "One Hundred Years of Manufacturing Brass and Copper, The American Brass Company," reprint from *Connecticut Yesterday and Today*, The John Brett Co.

Anon. 2000. "Cleveland Non-Explosive Lamp Company's Works — Their Importance, Extent and Benefit to the Public." *Cleveland Leader*, Feb. 2, 1874, p. 4. In: The Rushlight 66(2):14 – 17.

Anderson, Joseph. 1896. *The Town and City of Waterbury, Connecticut, from the Aboriginal Period to the Year Eighteen Hundred and Ninety-Five*. Vol. II. Price & Lee Co., New Haven. Courtesy of Bruce Wood.

Arnold, Scott K. 1990. "Nicholas Kopp, Jr., Glassmaker Extraordinaire." *Glass Collector's Digest*, Oct./Nov. 1990: 43 – 47, 50 – 51.

Bachler, Kerry. 1993. "Folded Wick Burners." *HLSC Newsletter* 3(2): 6 – 10.

Bailey, Chris. 2005. "Ansonia Company Background." *NAWCC Bullentin* 47/4 (357):451.

Bancroft, Hubert Howe. 1894. *The Book of the Fair, Columbian Exposition at Chicago in 1893*. Bounty Books, NY.

Barlow, Raymond E. and Joan E. Kaiser. 1989. *The Glass Industry in Sandwich*, Volume 2, Schiffer Publishing Ltd., West Chester, PA.

Barrett, Richard C. 1994. *The Illustrated Encyclopedia of Railroad Lighting*. Vol. 1. The Railroad Lantern. Railroad Research Publications. Rochester, NY.

Bassett, Homer F. 1889. *Waterbury and Her Industries*. Lithotype Printing & Publishing Co., Gardner. Mass.

Baumann, Heinz, and John Wolfe. 1994. "Development of the Student Lamp Concept." Part I. *The Rushlight* 60(2): 2 – 13.

———. 1994. "Development of the Student Lamp Concept." Part II. *The Rushlight* 60(3): 3 – 14.

———. 1994. "Development of the Student Lamp Concept." Part III. *The Rushlight* 60(4): 2 – 13.

———. 1996. "Development of the Student Lamp Concept." Part 4. *The Rushlight* 61(1):2 – 9.

Baumann, Ursula and Heinz. 1999. "When Wild & Wessel Went West: the Folded Wick Kerosene Burner in America." *The Rushlight* 65(1):2 – 21.

Baumann, Heinz. 2003 – 2006. Personal communications.

Black, Linda. 1982, Rev. 1995. *Lantern Enlightenment*. Privately printed.

———. 1984. "Collecting Kerosene Lanterns." *The Rushlight* 50 (4): 2 – 8.

Blackaby, James. 1988. "The Course of Lighting Improvements." *The Rushlight* 54(2):2– 7. Contains an illustration of the Liverpool Button from Thomson and Redwood, "The Petroleum Lamp," London: C. Griffin, 1902.

Bluhm, Andreas, and Louise Lippincott. 2000. *Light! The Industrial Age 1750 – 1900*, Art & Science, Technology & Society. Van Gogh Museum, Amsterdam, Carnegie Museum of Art, Pittsburgh. Thames & Hudson.

Bredehoft, Neila and Tom. 1997. *Hobbs, Brockunier & Co., Glass Identification and Value Guide*. Collector Books, Paducah, KY.

Broughton, David. 1997. "Advertising Ephemera." *HLSC Newsletters* 7(1): 5-12 and 7(2):6-13.

———. 2003. Five *Early Victorian Kerosene Lighting Catalogs*. Vol. 2 (Tucker Mfg. Co., J. C. Ives Patent Lamp Co., Union Glass Co., Manhattan Brass Co.). Privately Printed. Vol. 3. 2005 (Adams & Co., George Bassett, Edward Miller, Pitkin & Brooks). David Broughton, Port Hope, Ontario.

———. 2005. "Chew, Sip and Clean Your Way to a Brighter Future! Lamps as Premiums in Late Victorian America." HLSC *Font & Flame* 6(2):3-16.

Brooks, C. J. 2004. "The Bicycle Lamp Makers of Waterbury (Part 1)." *The Rushlight* 70(2): 2-12.

References

Brooks, C. J. 2004. "The Bicycle Lamp Makers of Waterbury (Part 2)." *The Rushlight* 70(3): 12-18.

Caldwell, J. A. 1983. *History of Belmont and Jefferson Counties, Ohio.* (Reprint of 1880 edition.)

Calvin, Robert E. 1983. "Evolution of the Solar Lamp: Part IV, The American Contribution." *The Rushlight* 49(3):2-9.

Clark, F. B. 1941. *A Brief History of the Clark Brothers' Business Enterprises Starting in 1881*, typed copy courtesy of the Trenton Public Library, Trenton, N J.

Collins, George M. 1999. *Yaquina Head Light Station, Historical Odds and Ends.* Revised 2005. Privately published, Newport, OR.

Courter, J. W. 1997. *Aladdin — The Magic Name in Lamps*, revised. Privately Printed.

———. "Montgomery Ward's 1930 – 1940s Kerosene Mantle Lamps" and "The Mantle Lamp Company of America." *The Mystic Light* 30(1):1, 4-11.

———. 2003. "The U. S. Chimney Business, 1855 to 1900." *The Rushlight* 69(2):8-14.

———. 2003. "Glass Chimney Unions and Production: Reprints from the 19th Century Chimney Industry." *The Rushlight* 69(4):2-8.

———. 2004. "Chimney Makers' Wage and Move List (1896). *The Rushlight* 70(1):2-8.

Cuffley, Peter. 1982. *Oil & Kerosene Lamps in Australia.* Pioneer Design Studio, Pty. Ltd., Victoria, Australia.

Davis, William T., editor. 1897. *The New England States*, Vol. II. D.H. Hurd & Co., Boston.

DeFalco, Robert, Carole Goldman Hibel, and John Hibel. 1986. *Handel Lamps Painted Shades and Glassware.* H & D Press, NY.

Dolson, Hildegarde. 1959. *The Great Oildorado; The Gaudy and Turbulent Years of the First Oil Rush: Pennsylvania 1859 – 1880.* Random House, NY.

Dow, Harold B. 1945. Press release from the Director of Public Relations, Bridgeport Brass Company, Oct. 31, 1945 (From the Fox Collection), Bridgeport Public Library.

Ebersole, Jeffery. 2008. *Hanging Victorian Lamps of the 19th Century.* Collector Books, Paducah, KY.

Freeman, Alan. 2005 – 2006. Personal communication. Gibbs, Margaret J. 1989. Remembering Anson Greene Phelps. Editor, Ansonia Connecticut 100th Anniversary 1889 – 1989, p. 6.

Gillespie, C. B. 1896. *The Transcript Souvenir History of Ansonia, Conn.* Bacon Press, Derby, CT.

Gillespie, C. Bancroft and George Munson Curtis. 1906. *A Century of Meriden.* Journal Publ. Co., Meriden.

Gluck, Nancy. 2005. *Connecticut Silver Manufacturers*, undated list compiled for the Meriden Historical Society. Courtesy Allen Weathers.

Goding, Charles. 2003. The Fostoria Glass Company: Its History and Products. The Glass Club Bul. 195:5-10.

Goulding, Alan. 2002. "Holmes, Booth and Haydens." *HLSC Font & Flame* 3(2):10-22.

Graff, John F. Jr. 2002. *The Rayo Book*, Rev. Guild of Lamp Researchers Pub. #1. St. Thomas, PA. Website: www.lampguild.org.

———. 2004. *The Lamp Collector's Guide*, second edition. Privately printed, St. Thomas, PA.

Gruse, William A., and Donald R. Stevens. 1942. *The Chemical Technology of Petroleum.* Second Edition. McGraw-Hill, NY.

Guion, A. D. 1925. "The History and Development of the Bridgeport Brass Company." *The Metal Industry* Vol. 23 No. 8. In: *A Historical Sketch of Bridgeport Brass Company 1865 – 1925.*

Harrison, Tim, and Ray Jones. 2002. *The Golden Age of American Lighthouses.* The Globe Pequot Press, Guilford, CT.

Henderson, Wayne, and Scott Benjamin. 1996. *Standard Oil, The First 125 Years.* Motorbooks International, Osceola, WI.

Hidy, Ralph W., and Muriel E. Hidy. 1955. *Pioneering in Big Business: History of the Standard Oil Co. (New Jersey) 1882 – 1911.* Harper, New York.

Hobart, Alice Tisdale. 1933. *Oil for the Lamps of China.* Bobbs-Merrill, Indianapolis.

Hobson, Anthony. 1991. *Lanterns That Lit Our World.* Golden Hill Press, Spencertown, N.Y.

Hogan, E. P. 1969. "Victorian Silverplated Oil Lamps." *Spinning Wheel* 1969: 10 – 12.

Holland, Jr., Francis Ross. 1988. *America's Lighthouses, An Illustrated History.* Dover Publications, Inc., New York.

Hopkins, Albert A. 1913. *The Scientific American Cycopedia of Formulas.* Munn & Co., New York.

Hurd, D. Hamilton. 1888. *History of Essex County.*

Innes, Lowell. 1976. *Pittsburgh Glass 1797 – 1891.* Houghton Mifflin Co., Boston.

Kastner, Richard. 2003. Personal communication.

Kebapcioglu, Ara. 1999. "When We Were Wild" and "Wessel: Origins of the European Folded Flat Wick Kerosene Burner." *The Rushlight* 65(1):22 – 28.

Lathrop, William G. 1926. *The Brass Industry in the United States.* Mount Carmel, CT.

Lathrop, William Gilbert. 1936. *The Development of the Brass Industry in Connecticut.* Tercentenary Commission of the State of Connecticut, Committee on Historical Publications, Yale University Press.

Leflet, Herbert. 1997. *Index of Early U.S. Lighting Patents, 1836 to 1901.* The Rushlight Club. 140 pp.

Liebmann, Henry J. 1994. *A Compendium of the Fancy Painted Lamps & Accessories Glassware, Fostoria Glass Company, 1898 – 1922*, Vol. 8. Privately printed, available from the Fostoria Glass Museum, Moundsville, WV.

Lovell, Lane. Undated. *Analysis of Lovell-Dressel Co., Inc.* Unpublished 12-page review of railroad, marine, and Navy business from the 1950s and 1960s, courtesy of George Sherwood.

Madarasz, Anne. 1998. *Glass, Shattering Notions.* Historical Society of Western Pennsylvania, Pittsburgh.

Marvin, Charles. ca. 1887. *The Moloch of Paraffin.* R. Anderson Co., London. Reprinted copy courtesy of David Denny. 32 pp.

McDonald, Ann Gilbert. 2000. "The Lamp Patents of Charles F. Spencer." *Antique Trader*, July 19, 2000, 49 – 51.

Miller, Richard C., and John F. Solverson. 1992. *Student Lamps of the Victorian Era.* Antique Publications, Marietta, OH

Molloy, Leo. 1935. *Tercentenary Pictorial and History of the Lower Naugatuck Valley.* Emerson Bros. Press, Ansonia, CT.

Montgomery, Morton L. 1898. *History of Reading, Pennsylvania, Sesqui-Centennial, June 5 – 12, 1898.* Times Book Print, Reading, PA.

Morse, Sidney L. 1914. *Household Discoveries*, Rev. Ed. Success Company, Petersburg, NY. 1,205 pp.

Murray, Melvin L. 1972. *History of Fostoria, Ohio, Glass 1887 – 1920.* Privately printed.

———. 1992. Fostoria, Ohio, Glass II. Privately printed.

Nelson, Kirk J. 1989. "The F. H. Lovell & Co. Catalogue of 1877 – 1878." *The Illuminator* 3(2):3 – 15.

O'Brien, Emmet. 1937. "Rochester Lamps That Lit the World 50 Years Ago still burn." *Democrat Chronicle*, Rochester, NY, March 21, 1937.

O'Connell, Richard. 2003 – 2006. Personal communication.

Olmstead, Ronald. 1981. "The Solar Lamp and Its Relatives." *The Rushlight* 47(2):2 – 8.

Orcutt, Samuel, and Ambrose Beardsley. 1880. *History of the Old Town of Derby, Connecticut*. Springfield Printing Co., Springfield, MA.

Paquette, Jack K. 2002. *Blowpipes, Northwest Ohio Glassmaking in the Gas Boom of the 1880s*. Xlibris Corp.

Pearson, Dennis A. 1998. *Classic Lanterns*. Schiffer Publishing Co., Atglen, PA.

Peck, William F. 1907. *History of Rochester and Monroe County*, Vol. I. Rochester Public Library.

Peterson, Arthur G. 1968. *400 Trademarks on Glass*. Privately published. This booklet reprinted many times.

———. 1973. *Glass Patents and Patterns*. Privately published, Library of Congress Card No. 72-91628.

Pope, Wm. J., 1918. *History of Waterbury and The Naugatuck Valley, Connecticut*, Vol. 1. S.J. Clarke Publishing Co.

Quinn, Jim. 2005. "Edison's Light Turns 125, An Amazing Breakthrough — and Its Unintended Consequences." *Invention & Technology* 20 (3): 8 – 9.

Revi, Albert Christian. 1968. *American Art Nouveau Glass*. Thomas Nelson & Sons.

Roberts, Kenneth D., and Snowden Taylor. 1992. *Forestville Clockmakers*. Ken Roberts Publishing Co.

Roller, Richard. 1998. Roller Papers, personal files. Ball State University, Muncie, Indiana.

Russell, Loris S. 1968. *A Heritage of Light*. University Toronto Press.

———. 1984. "Abraham Gesner: Father of Kerosene Lighting." *The Rushlight* 50 (2):3 – 7.

Sabasino, Gregory. 1994. "Edward Miller: A Lifetime Dedication to Lighting." *The Rushlight* 60 (3):15 – 16.

Scheips, Marguerite T., and Allen L. Weathers. 1995. *The Miller Company, The First 150 Years*. Privately published by The Miller Company, Meriden, CT. 175 pp.

Seldon, A. 1963. *Some Rochester Inventions*. Rochester Hist. Soc. Pub. Fund Series XIV:192 – 211.

Serio, Anne Marie. 1984. "The Dietz Burner: The Earliest Known Flat-wick Coal Oil burner in America." *The Rushlight* 50 (2):8 – 13.

Shuman, John A. 1988. *American Art Glass*, Collector Books, Paducah, KY.

Smythe, J. Herbert, and F. Victor Christy. 1960. *Lamplighters All! A History of the Lamp Business*. Rosenthal & Smythe, Summit, NJ.

Sohn, Dan. 2002. "Notes on Gasoline (Petrol) as a Lamp Fuel." *Light International* 5(3): 2 – 4.

Spittler, Sonja L. & Thomas J., and Chris H. Bailey. 2000. *American Clockmakers & Watchmakers*. Arlington Books, VA.

Stamm, Richard. 1993. The Bradley & Hubbard Manufacturing Co. Castle Collection, Smithsonian Preservation Quarterly, Smithsonian, Washington, D.C.

Tag, Thomas. 2001. "Early American Lighthouse Illumination." *The Rushlight* 67 (1):2 – 14.

Tag, Thomas. 2002. "A Bit Unusual:the Search for Alternative Lighthouse Fuels." *The Rushlight* 68 (2):12 – 18.

———. 2002. *From Braziers and Bougies to Xenon*. Privately Printed.

Tarbell, Ida M. 1925. *The History of The Standard Oil Company*, Vol. I & II. Macmillan Co., NY.

Tobin, Dianne. 2004. "Meriden Flint Glass Company." *HLSC Font & Flame* 5 (1): 3– 8.

Thuro, Catherine M.V. 1976. *Oil Lamps, The Kerosene Era in North America*. Wallace Homestead, Des Moines, IA.

———. V. 2001. *Oil Lamps 3, Victorian Kerosene Lighting*. Collector Books, Paducah, KY.

Thuro, Catherine. 1987 – 1989. Editor, The Illuminator 1(4):4; Vol. 3:4 issues.

Warren, George F., and Frank A. Pearson. 1935. *Gold and Prices*. John Wiley & Sons, NY.

Weatherman, Hazel Marie. 1972. *Fostoria, Its First Fifty Years*. Privately published by the Weathermans, Springfield, MO.

Weathers, Allen. 2003 – 2005. Personal communications.

Webster, Thomas. 1856. *An Encyclopedia of Domestic Economy: Artificial Illumination Book IV*, pp. 119 – 206. J. C. Derby, New York.

Welker, John & Elizabeth. 1985. *Pressed Glass in America, Encyclopedia of the First Hundred Years, 1825 – 1925*. Antique Acres Press, PA.

Wellington, Arthur M., W. B. D. Penniman, and Charles W. Baker. 1892. *The Comparative Merits of Various Systems of Car Lighting*. Engineering News Publishing Co. 303 pp.

Wenrich, Jeanne. 1987. "The Rochester Lamp." *The Rushlight* 53(3):2 – 6.

———. 1988. "Lamp and Lantern Manufacturers in Rochester, N.Y." *The Rushlight* 54(1):2 – 7.

———. 1989. Bradley & Hubbard Manufacturing Company. *The Rushlight* 55(2):2 – 6.

White, John H. Jr. 1978. *The American Railroad Passenger Car*. Johns Hopkins Univ. Press. 699 pp.

Williamson, Harold F., and Arnold R. Daum. 1959. *The American Petroleum Industry, 1859 – 1899, The Age of Illuminants*. Northwestern Univ. Press., Evanston, IL.

Williamson, Harold F., Ralph L. Andreano, Arnold R. Daum and Gilbert C. Klose. 1963. *The American Petroleum Industry, 1899 – 1959, The Age of Energy*. Northwestern Univ. Press., Evanston, IL.

Wilson, Kenneth M. 1972. *New England Glass & Glassmaking*. Thomas Y. Crowell, New York.

Wilson, Jack D. 1989. *Phoenix & Consolidated Art Glass, 1926 – 1980*. Antique Publications, Marietta, OH.

Wingeetor, Charles A. 1912. *History of Greater Wheeling and Vicinity*. Two vols. The Lewis Publ. Co., Chicago & New York, pp. 833 – 834.

Wolfe, John J. 1999. *Brandy, Balloons, & Lamps, Ami Argand, 1750 – 1803*. Southern Illinois Univ. Press, Carbondale, Ill.

Wrege, Charles D., and Ronald G. Greenwood. 1984. *William E. Sawyer and the Rise and Fall of America's First Incandescent Electric Light Company, 1878 – 1881*. Business Economic History, 2nd Series 13:31 – 48.

Youmans, Edward L. 1858. *The Hand-Book of Household Science*. D. Appleton Co., New York & London.

List of Catalog References

Baker & Co. *Illustrated Catalogue Parlor and Library Lamps, Sun Electric and German Student Lamps*. 1884 – 1885. Buffalo, NY. Courtesy Buffalo & Erie County Library, Buffalo, NY. 11 pp.

Belgian lamps

The Celebrated Belgian Lamps, 1908 – 1909. Catalogue No. 3, American-Belgian Lamp Co., NY.

L. & B. Lampes Belges, Rechauds Belges, reprinted 2001 by Alex Marrick.

Belgian Lamps, 1898, 24 pp., Pitkin and Brooks, Chicago, IL, courtesy of Jeff Ebersole.

Belgian Lamps, ca. 1898 – 1899, Pitkin and Brooks, Chicago, IL, copy courtesy of Catherine Thuro.

Bindley Hardware Co., *House-Furnishing Goods*, Fall & Winter 1893 – 1894, Pittsburgh, PA.

Bradley & Hubbard Mfg. Co.

Illustrated Catalogue of Kerosene Fixtures & Stand Lamps, 1883, 1884, privately printed, David Broughton in Canada. ISBN-0-9689032-0-7. Website: www.sirlampsalot.com.

Decorated and Bronzed Metal Table Lamps. June 1988. No. 46 Catalogue, 34 pp. Reprinted 1995 by the Historical Lighting Society of Canada.

B & H Lamps. ca. 1890. Small undated catalog illustrating lamps and art metal goods.

Bristol Brass & Clock Co.

Price list of Kerosene Burners, Lamps, Lamp Trimmings, etc. 78 pp. 1874. Courtesy Jeff Ebersole.

Catalogue of Kerosene Burners, Lamps & Lamp Trimmings, 96 pp., May 1, 1889. Met. Museum of Art Print Study Room, NYC.

Burley & Tyrrell, Chicago, IL, 144 pp. 1889.

Consolidated Lamp & Glass Co. Numerous catalogs on microform, Rakow Library, Corning, NY.

Craighead & Kintz Co., ca. 1884 – 1885, undated copy, 50 pp., Andover Historical Society, Andover, MA.

Dithridge & Co., Fort Pitt Glass Works, Pittsburgh. Undated catalog, ca. 1888 – 1889. Reprint by West Virginia Museum of American Glass, Weston, WV.

Fostoria Glass Co.

Fostoria Glass Co. Numerous catalogs on microform, Rakow Library, Corning, NY.

Fostoria Glass Co. 1906. Reprinted, 1972, in: *Lamps & Other Lighting Devices*, 1850 – 1906. The Pyne Press, Princeton.

Haida Lamp & China Co., Catalog No. 7, *Lamps, Silk & Linen Shades*. 47 pp., 1893 – 1894. Met. Museum of Art Print Study Room, NYC.

Hibbard, Spencer, Bartlett and Co., Chicago, Illinois

Lamps, Chandeliers and Lamp Goods. 1891.

Lamps, Chandeliers and Lamp Goods. 1893. Copy courtesy Jeff Ebersole.

Lamps, Chandeliers and Lamp Goods, Rochester and B & H Lamps, privately printed in 1997, pages 1265– 1432 of 1895 – 1896. James Van Es, Herndon, VA.

Compact Catalogue. 1899.

H. Leonard & Sons. 1888. *The Illuminator*, 1(2):3 – 16, Published in 1987 by the Historical Lighting Society of Canada.

F. H. Lovell & Co.

Illustrated Catalog, 1895. Reprinted by Norman Jones.

Illustrated Catalog, 1898 – 1899.

Railroad Lighting Appliances and Fixtures, 1916. Reprinted by The Rushlight Club.

Numerous export catalogs on microform, Rakow Library, Corning, NY.

Macbeth-Evans Glass Co.

T. G. Evans & Co., China, Glassware, Lamps. Ca. 1895. Reprinted by The Rushlight Club, 1993.

Lamp Chimneys, Lantern Globes and Silvered Glass Reflectors, Export Catalog No. 103. ca. 1900.

Macbeth-Evans Glass Co., Reprinted, 1972, in Lamps & Other Lighting Devices, 1850 – 1906. The Pyne Press, Princeton.

Macbeth "Pearl Glass" and "Pearl Top" Lamp Glasses, No. 11 for 1901. Macbeth-Evans Glass Co., Pittsburgh, PA.

How to Manage Lamps, Index to Lamps and Their Glasses and Retail Catalogue, 1901. Macbeth-Evans Glass Co., Pittsburgh, PA. Reprint by The Rushlight Club, 1982.

Macbeth Index, Lamps and Lamp Chimneys, 1913. Macbeth-Evans Glass Co., Pittsburgh, PA.

Marshall Field & Co., Chicago, Illinois

Lamps, Dept. 9, 1901. Copy courtesy Heinz Baumann.

Illustrated Catalogue of Jewelry Department, 1894. 294 pp. Schroeder, Joseph J., Jr., 1970. Illustrated Catalogue Jewelry & Fashions. Reprint of 1896 catalogue. Gun Digest Publishing Co., Northfield, IL

McKenney & Waterbury Co., Boston. *We Light The World*. Courtesy Rakow Library.

The Meriden Britannia Silver-Plate Treasury, The Complete Catalog of 1886 – 1887. Dover Publications, 1982.

Edward Miller & Co.

Illustrated Catalogue of Lamps and Cigar Lighters, 1881, reprint Fairweather Antiques, 100 pp.

Catalogue No. 43, The Miller Lamp, ca. 1893, 49 pp.

Catalogue No. 116, Burners, Lamps and Trimmings, ca. 1904, reprint American Lamp Supply, 68 pp.

Catalog X151, *Miller Lamps, Burners, Accessories*, Oil Heaters, etc., 1924, 48 pp.

New Jersey Lamp & Bronze Works, New Brunswick, NJ. Undated, ca. 1900. 43 pages.

Ogden, Merrill & Greer, *Lamps and Lighting*. 1895. Copy from Cherry Hill Publications, St. Louisville, OH.

Peaslee Gaulbert Co., Louisville, Kentucky

Journal of Light No. 120, May 15, 1897. A price list of lamps and table glassware. Privately published.

Journal of Light No. 127, July 15, 1898. A price list of lamps and table glassware. Privately published.

Lamp and Glassware Catalogue No. 198. 1921. 174 pp.

Pilabrasgo Success Oil Lamps and Decorated Vases, Catalogue No. 13. Pittsburgh Lamp, Brass and Glass Company, Pittsburgh, PA. Reprinted by Antique and Colonial Lighting, Clarence, New York.

Pitkin and Brooks

Lamps Our Catalogue for 1897 – 1898. 96 pp. Courtesy Jeff Ebersole.

1898 Lamps. 98 pp. Courtesy Jeff Ebersole.

Lamps and Lamp Goods. Catalogue No. 203, 1904 – 1905. 105 pp. Pitkin and Brooks, Chicago, IL, copy courtesy of James Hargis.

Plume and Atwood

The Plume & Atwood Manufacturing Company. ca. 1906. Reprinted privately by J. W. Courter.

The Plume & Atwood Manufacturing Company. Copy used by Lane Lovell earlier than above. Courtesy George Sherwood.

Post & Co. American Student Lamp. 1883 – 1884. *A Manual of Practical Information and Household Recipes, Post & Company, Mfrs Railway, Telegraph and Telephone Instruments, and Celebrated American Student Lamp Improved 1882*. Cincinnati, Ohio. 12 pp.

Pyro Alcohol, U. S. Industrial Alcohol Company, New York, 1908, 24 pp.

Railroad Lamps

Dayton Car Lighting Fixtures, catalog number 166. The Dayton Manufacturing Co., Dayton, Ohio. Undated, 158 pages. Courtesy George Christy and William Schreiber.

Dreimiller. David. 1995. *The Dressel Railway Lamp & Signal Company*, 1926 Catalog of Railway Lighting Equipment. Hiram Press, Hiram, OH.

Railroad Marine Lighting Appliances and Fixtures. 1961. Catalog No. 500 reprinted by The Rushlight Club, 1983.

Railway Supplies, Machinery, Machinists' Tools and Supplies, Metals, Railway and Machine Shop Equipment. 1887. Post & Company Catalogue No. 30. Courtesy Ohio Historical Society.

Rochester Lamp Co.

The Largest Lamp Store in the World, 1891 – 1892, The Rochester Lamp Co., New York.

The New Rochester Lamp, Catalog No. 74, Season 1898 – 1899, 56 pp., printed for use in UK.

Robinson & Cary Company, St. Paul, MN. Catalog N0. 14, undated, ca. 1900 – 1910.

Henry & Nathan Russell & Day Illustrated Catalogue No. 15, Kerosene Fixtures. 1889. Courtesy Catherine Thuro.

Simmons Hardware Co., St. Louis, Missouri

Catalogue E, ca. 1899.

Catalogue F, copyright 1903.

Lamp Catalogue 468, 1905 – 1906. Courtesy Dan Edminster.

Catalogue G, Simmons Hardware Co. Encyclopedia, 1908.

Norvell-Shapleigh Hardware Co., St. Louis, M), catalog 1910.

Standard Lighting Co., Cleveland, Ohio

New Process Catalogue & Cook Book, 20 pages in front of the hardbound cook book. 1894.

New Process Blue Flame Vapor Stoves, Globe Incandescent Lamps, Oil Heaters, Torches. Season of 1895. Courtesy Strong Museum Library, Rochester, NY.

New Process Blue Flame Oil Stoves. Season of 1896.

New Process Blue Flame Oil Stoves. Season of 1897.

New Process and Standard Gasoline and Oil Stoves. 1899.

The Swann, Whitehead & Clark Illustrated Catalogue of Lamps, Branch of the American Lamp & Brass Co., Trenton, NJ. Ca. 1891. 40 pp.

R. E. Tongue & Bros., Philadelphia, PA. ca. 1915, 56 pp.

Veritas Lamp Works. 1896 – 1897. *Catalogue No. 53, Falk, Stadelmann & Co., Petroleum Lamps & Stoves*. Reprinted by the Historic Lighting Club, UK.

Victorian Catalog Reprints

Five Early Victorian Kerosene Lighting Catalogs, Vol. 2. Tucker Mfg. Co., J. C. Ives Patent Lamp Co., Union Glass Co., Manhattan Brass Co. Privately printed 2003 by David Broughton, Toronto, Ontario.

Four Victorian Kerosene Lighting Catalogs, Vol. 3, Historical Lighting Reprints. Adams & Co., George Bassett, Edward Miller, Pitkin and Brooks. Privately printed 2005 by David Broughton, Port Hope, Ontario, Canada.

Wallace & Sons, *Library Lamps*, July, 1884. Courtesy Jeff Ebersole. 16 pp. plus cover.

Index